FRONTIERS IN ECOLOGICAL ECONOMICS

Frontiers in Ecological Economics

Transdisciplinary Essays by Robert Costanza

Robert Costanza

Director, University of Maryland Institute for Ecological Economics and Professor, Center for Environmental and Estuarine Studies, University of Maryland, Solomons and Zoology Department, University of Maryland, College Park, US

Edward Elgar

Cheltenham, UK • Lyme, US

Published by
Edward Elgar Publishing Limited
8 Lansdown Place
Cheltenham
Glos GL50 2HU
UK

Edward Elgar Publishing, Inc.
1 Pinnacle Hill Road
Lyme
NH 03768
US

A catalogue record for this book
is available from the British Library

Library of Congress Cataloging-in-Publication Data

Costanza, Robert.
Frontiers in ecological economics : transdisciplinary essays by Robert Costanza / Robert Costanza.
Essays originally published in various journals from 1984 to 1995.
Includes bibliographical references and index.
1. Economic development—Environmental aspects. 2. Environmental economics. I. Title.
HD75.6.C694 1997
333.7—dc21 97–14366
CIP

ISBN 1 85898 503 X

Printed and bound in Great Britain by
Hartnolls Limited, Bodmin, Cornwall

Contents

Acknowledgements

The publishers wish to thank the following who have kindly given permission for the use of copyright material.

Academic Press for articles: 'Measures of Energy Costs and Value in Ecosystems' with Bruce Hannon and Robert A. Herendeen, *Journal of Environmental Economics and Management*, 1986, **13**, pp. 391–401 and 'Energy Intensities, Interdependence, and Value in Ecological Systems: A Linear Programming Approach' with Christopher Neill, *Journal of Theoretical Biology*, 1984, **106**(1), pp. 41–57.

Academic Publishing for the article: 'Resolution and Predictability: An Approach to the Scaling Problem', with Thomas Maxwell, *Landscape Ecology*, 1994, (**9**)1, pp. 47–57.

American Association for the Advancement of Science for the article: 'Embodied Energy and Economic Valuation', *Science*, December 1980, **210**, pp. 1219–24.

Ambio for articles: 'Predictability, Scale, and Biodiversity in Coastal and Estuarine Ecosystems: Implications for Management', with W. Michael Kemp and Walter R. Boynton, May 1993, (**22**)2-3, pp. 88–96 and 'A General Accounting Framework for Ecological Systems: A Functional Taxonomy for Connectivist Ecology', with Bruce Hannon and Robert Ulanowicz, *Theoretical Population Biology*, **40**(1), 1991, pp. 78–104.

BioScience for articles: 'Modeling Coastal Landscape Dynamics: Process-based Dynamic Spatial Ecosystem Simulation Can Examine Long-term Natural Changes and Human Impacts', with Fred H. Sklar and Mary L. White, February 1990, (**40**)2, pp. 91–107; 'Modeling Complex Ecological Economic Systems: Toward an Evolutionary, Dynamic Understanding of People and Nature', with L. Wainger, C. Folke and K-G Mäler, September 1993, (**43**)8, pp. 545–55 and 'Social Traps and Environmental Policy', June 1987, (**37**)6, pp. 407–12.

Blackwell Science for the article: 'Natural Capital and Sustainable Development' with Herman E. Daly, *Conservation Biology*, March 1992, (**6**)1, pp. 37–46.

Columbia University Press for articles: 'Goals, Agenda, and Policy Recommendations for Ecological Economics', with Herman E. Daly and Joy A. Bartholomew, in *Ecological Economics: The Science and Management of Sustainability*, R. Costanza (ed.), New York, 1991, pp. 1–15 and 'The Chesapeake Bay and Its Watershed: A Model for Sustainable Ecosystem Management?', with Jack Greer, in *Barriers and*

Bridges to the Renewal of Ecosystems and Institutions, Lance H. Gunderson, C.S. Holling and Stephen S. Light (eds), New York, 1995, pp. 169–213.

Elsevier Science for articles: 'Toward an Ecological Economics', with Herman E. Daly, *Ecological Modelling*, 1987, **38**, pp. 1–7; 'What Is Ecological Economics?', *Ecological Economics*, 1989, **1**, pp. 1–7; 'Valuation and Management of Wetland Ecosystems', *Ecological Economics*, 1989, **1**, pp. 335–61; 'Embodied Energy and Economic Value in the United States Economy: 1963, 1967 and 1972', with Robert A. Herendeen, *Resources and Energy*, **6**, 1984, pp. 129–63; 'Articulation, Accuracy and Effectiveness of Mathematical Models: A Review of Freshwater Wetland Applications', with Fred H. Sklar, *Ecological Modelling*, 1985, **27**, pp. 45–68; 'Model Goodness of Fit: A Multiple Resolution Procedure', *Ecological Modelling*, 47, 1989, pp. 199–215; 'A Flexible Assurance Bonding System for Improved Environmental Management', with Charles Perrings, *Ecological Economics*, April 1990, (**2**)1, 57–75 and 'Defining and Predicting Sustainability', with Bernard C. Patten, *Ecological Economics*, 1995, **15**, pp. 193–96.

Greenwood Publishing Group for the article: 'Integrated Ecological Economic Systems Modeling: Theoretical Issues and Practical Applications', with Lisa Wainger and Nancy Bockstael, in *Integrating Economic and Ecological Indicators: Practical Methods for Environmental Policy Analysis*, J. Walter Milon and Jason F, Shogren (eds), Westport, Praeger, 1995, pp. 45–66.

Heldref Publications for articles: 'The 4P Approach to Dealing with Scientific Uncertainty', with Laura Cornwell, *Environment*, November 1992, (**34**)9, 12–20 and p. 42 and 'Sustainable Trade: A New Paradigm for World Welfare', with Richard Borden, Paul Ekins, Carl Folke, Silvio O. Funtowicz, and Jonathan Harris, *Environment*, June 1995, (**37**)5, pp. 16–20 and 39–44.

Island Press for the article: 'Toward an Operational Definition of Ecosystem Health', *Ecosystem Health: New Goals for Environmental Management*, R. Costanza, B.G. Norton and B.D. Haskell (eds), Washington DC, 1992, pp. 239–56.

North Atlantic Books for the article: 'Ecological Economics: A New Approach to Understanding and Managing the Interactions of Humans and Nature', with Lisa Wainger, in *Mending the Earth: A World for our Grandchildren*, P. Rothkrug and R.L. Olson (eds), Berkeley, CA, 1991, pp. 50–58.

Sinauer Associates for the article: 'Valuation of Ecological Systems', in *Principles of Conservation Biology*, Gary K. Meffe, C. Ronald Carroll (eds), Sunderland, Massachusetts, 1994, pp. 449–50.

Springer-Verlag for articles: 'Dealing with the "Mixed Units" Problem in Ecosystem Network Analysis' with Bruce Hannon, in *Network Analysis of Marine Ecosystems: Methods and Applications*, F. Wulff, J.G. Field and K.H. Mann (eds), Heidelberg, 1989, pp. 90–105 and 'Assessing and Communicating Data Quality in

Policy-Relevant Research', with Silvio O. Funtowicz and Jerome R. Ravetz, *Environmental Management*, 1992, (**16**)1, pp. 121–31.

University of Texas Press for the article: 'The Effects of Taxation on Moderating the Conflict Escalation Process: An Experiment Using the Dollar Auction Game', with Wesley Shrum, *Social Science Quarterly*, 1988, **69**, pp. 416–32.

Every effort has been made to trace all the copyright holders, but if any have been inadvertently overlooked the publishers will be pleased to make the necessary arrangements at the first opportunity.

Introduction: Building Transdisciplinary Bridges at the Frontiers of Ecology and Economics.

Background and purposes of this book

This book collects together in one place a selection of essays on a variety of topics. They all relate in one way or another to understanding and modeling ecological and/or economic systems. The effort has been an explicit attempt to transcend disciplinary boundaries and construct an integrated picture of humans and the rest of nature. Most of the essays in this collection (83%) were co-authored with colleagues from a variety of disciplines (a list of these 28 co-authors is provided in the acknowledgments and the contents). It was an enormously fruitful and enjoyable way to work, allowing a constant and varying dialogue with a number of different disciplines contributing.

I came to this way of working from an academic background that was somewhat unusual. I started in Engineering, then earned an MA in Architecture and Urban Planning, and finished with a PhD in Systems Ecology with a minor in Economics at the University of Florida. I actually substituted economics for a foreign language requirement in my PhD program, so I like to tell people I took economics as a foreign language. Unfortunately, economics is still a foreign language to most natural scientists, as natural science is to most economists. And an even deeper language barrier exists between the arts and the sciences. But, I was able to enjoy the advantages of being multilingual and I recommend it highly. It not only made for a richer intellectual experience, but it allowed attacking some relatively untouched and important topics from a unique perspective. The combination of Architecture and Science was also rewarding (in hindsight). The arts focus on teaching people to *synthesize*, the sciences focus on teaching people to *analyze*. All human activities require a balance between synthesis and analysis and our educational system in segregating these functions has been giving people only half the training they need. Of course, most people pick up the 'other half' somewhere along the way, but our educational system could benefit, I believe, by a much more explicit attempt to teach both synthesis and analysis skills (along with communication skills) across the entire academic spectrum.

This collection of essays hopefully exhibits some of this balance between synthesis and analysis. It is divided into four sections: (1) creating an ecological economics; (2) material and energy flows in ecological and economic systems; (3) ecological and economic systems modeling and analysis; and (4) incentives and institutions. Within each section the papers are arranged in chronological order to give a sense of the development of ideas within that topic over time. Some background, perspectives, and a short synopsis of each of these sections is presented in turn.

Part I Creating an ecological economics

When Herman Daly and I were both on the faculty at Louisiana State University (he in the economics department, I in the Coastal Ecology Laboratory and the Department of Marine Sciences) we decided to do a special issue of the journal *Ecological Modeling* on the topic, ecological economics. Chapter 1 in this volume (Costanza and Daly 1987) was the introductory paper in the special issue, which also included contributions by David Pearce, Cutler Cleveland and many others. It laid out some of the main problems which we felt were not being adequately dealt with from the existing monodisciplinary perspectives and which required a new transdisciplinary treatment.

This enterprise was so enthusiastically received, both during the production phase and after the product was delivered, that we decided the next logical step was the creation of an entire new journal devoted to ecological economics. During the review process for this journal we discovered the amazing range and breadth of people already working on topics which could easily fit under the heading of ecological economics. But we needed a journal to pull these threads together and begin to weave them into a coherent cloth. Most potential publishers were not very sanguine about the prospects for *any* new journal, especially one with such a diffuse audience, but the reviews of our proposal were overwhelmingly favourable and in 1989 we published the first issue of Ecological Economics with Elsevier Science Publishers in the Netherlands. I became the chief editor, with Herman Daly, AnnMari Jansson, and David Pearce as associate editors and a star-studded editorial advisory board from both the social and natural sciences. Chapter 2 (Costanza 1989) was the lead article in the first issue of the journal, laying out the aims and scope of the new enterprise. We began with four issues per year. By 1995 the journal was publishing 12 issues per year. We also created the International Society for Ecological Economics (ISEE)[1] and began to hold biannual transdisciplinary conferences beginning in 1990 at the World Bank in Washington DC. ISEE now has several thousand members in over 60 countries and eight regional chapters.

This growing institutional infrastructure has allowed an expanding dialogue across several disciplines in the natural and social sciences. As pointed out in Costanza (1989), ecological economics is *not* intended to be a subdiscipline of either economics or ecology, nor is it a replacement for either of these disciplines. It is a different and complementary way of organizing our intellectual activities that is non-territorial, cooperative, collaborative, and focused on solving the many problems attendant on designing a sustainable and desirable way for humans to live on this planet and share it with other species. As one might imagine, it is sometimes difficult to get this message across in a non-threatening way to academics trained in the territorial, disciplinary model of intellectual organization. The transdisciplinary, cooperative, model is a decidedly different approach, but it has much to recommend it.

1 If you are interested in joining ISEE and/or subscribing to the journal *Ecological Economics*, contact: ISEE, Box 1589, Solomons, MD, USA Tel: (410) 326-7263, fax: (410) 326-7354, email: beckerman@cbl.cees.edu. You can also visit the following www home pages for more information about ISEE; http://kabir.edu/ISEE/ISEEhome.html, and the journal:http://www.elsevier.nl/catalogue/SA5/505/02700/02720/503305/503305.editors.html:http://kabir.cbl.cees.edu/ISEE/ISEEhome.html.

Chapters 4 and 5 (Costanza and Wainger, 1991, Costanza *et al.* 1991) are general overviews of the field of ecological economics. Chapter 4 offers a more popular version, while Chapter 5 is an overview consensus chapter from a book produced during a workshop following the first ISEE meeting in 1990. It represents a consensus of about 35 well-known ecologists, economists and others about the goals and research agenda for this emerging field.

Chapters 3 (Costanza *et al.* 1989) and 8 (Costanza 1994) address the complex and controversial issue of ecosystem valuation and management. Chapter 8 addresses some of the conceptual issues surrounding valuation, arguing for a broad approach that covers both social and natural sciences. Chapter 3 applies several different approaches to a case study in coastal Louisiana, ranging from more conventional Willingness-to-Pay (WTP)-based methods to less conventional energy analysis (EA)-based methods. One interesting result was the relative convergence of these methods, which are based on completely different assumptions. The links between energy and economic value are discussed in more detail in Part II.

Chapter 6 (Costanza and Daly 1992) expanded on the idea of natural capital and its links to sustainability, and put forward the idea of a natural capital depletion tax to help internalize the costs of environmental degradation (see also Chapters 25–29 in Part IV). Chapter 7 (Costanza 1992) develops an operational definition of the concept of ecosystem health as a goal for environmental management. Our default management goals for ecosystems tend to be tied up with trying to return them to some historical, more 'pristine' or 'untouched', condition. This approach is of only limited usefulness, since the choice of historical period is completely arbitrary, ecosystems are in a constant state of flux, and this approach considers all human interactions with ecosystems to be detrimental. A more sophisticated concept of ecosystem health is necessary, which allows for positive, sustainable interactions of humans as components of ecosystems, in ways that contribute to the sustainability of the whole system.

Chapter 9 (Costanza and Patten 1995) fills out this section by looking at the problem of defining (and predicting) sustainability. It argues that the *definition* of sustainability is quite easy. A sustainable system is one which persists or lasts. But we can only know which systems have persisted *after the fact*, so the real problem is predicting what systems or parts of systems will persist, under what quality conditions, for how long, and in what relationship to other parts of the system and other scales. We also need to explicitly state what systems or parts of systems or qualities of those systems we wish to sustain. This way of looking at sustainability clearly integrates the policy questions (what do we want to sustain?) with the scientific questions (how do we predict what will actually be sustained under a given set of conditions?) and separates them from the definition of sustainability itself.

Part II Material and energy flows in ecological and economic systems

The tracing of energy and material flows in economic and ecological systems has deep historical roots and has become an important way of integrating the study of these systems (Quesnay 1758, Podilinsky 1883, Soddy 1922, Lotka 1922, Cottrell 1955, Odum and Pinkerton 1955, Boulding 1966, Cumberland 1966, Ayres and Kneese 1969, Georgescu-Roegen 1971, 1973, Odum 1971, Ayres 1972, 1978,

Victor 1972, Lipnowski 1976, Cleveland *et al.* 1984, Cleveland 1987). But, despite the relative longevity and popularity of this approach, there is still an enormous amount of confusion about what energy, available energy, entropy and other related terms mean, and how they can be useful in studying integrated ecological and economic systems.

Energy is ubiquitous. It is property (the ability to do work), a characteristic, of all of the commodities produced in modern economies and in natural ecosystems.[2] However, it is often mistakenly treated as a commodity itself (i.e. oil, gas, biomass, electricity). This tends to confuse the issue, since it implies that other commodities can substitute for energy and that energy is not therefore an essential input. Other commodities can provide alternative sources for the energy required to drive systems, but one cannot substitute for the essential property of energy. Thus all productive factors have an available energy content which is essential for anything at all to happen. This distinction between energy as a property or characteristic of all things vs. energy as a commodity is essential and has some far-reaching implications, particularly as regards interpreting information about the relationship between energy and the economy. For example, one popular way to look at the relationship between energy and economic performance has been the ratio of fuel use to GNP or GDP over time. This ratio has declined by about 25% in the past decade in most OECD countries (although it has begun to rise again in some countries), and this has been interpreted as indicating an increase in the energy efficiency of the economic systems. While this *may be* the correct interpretation, it is certainly not the only possible one and it probably overstates the efficiency gains due to several conceptual and accounting problems in both the numerator and denominator of the ratio. Let us start with GNP.

GNP as presently defined has many acknowledged shortcomings as a measure of economic performance, including the fact that it ignores the contribution of nature to production, and does not adequately differentiate costs from benefits (Daly and Cobb 1989). Alternative indicators which do attempt to account for the loss of natural capital and to differentiate costs from benefits come to very different conclusions about the performance of the economy, especially in the last few decades. For example, Daly and Cobb's (1989) 'index of sustainable economic welfare' (ISEW, Figure 1) shows that when factors such as loss of soil and wetlands, costs of mitigating acid rain effects, and health costs caused by increased pollution are accounted for, the US economy is seen not to have improved at all since the 1970s.

Estimating total energy consumption for an economy is also not a straightforward matter because not all fuels are of the same quality (degree of organization, availability, or ability to do work). Electricity, for example, is more versatile and cleaner in end use than petroleum, and it also costs more energy to produce. In an oil-fired power plant it takes from 3–5 kcals of oil to produce each kcal of electric-

[2] The definition of energy is often confused by the necessity to state the *availability* of energy. For example, a substance can have a high energy content which is unavailable because it lacks organization in the form of a suitable gradient. Available or 'free' energy is necessary in order to do work and this requires an entropic gradient, like a temperature, chemical concentration, topographic, or other gradient. In the remainder of this paper, unless otherwise noted, available energy or low-entropy energy is implied.

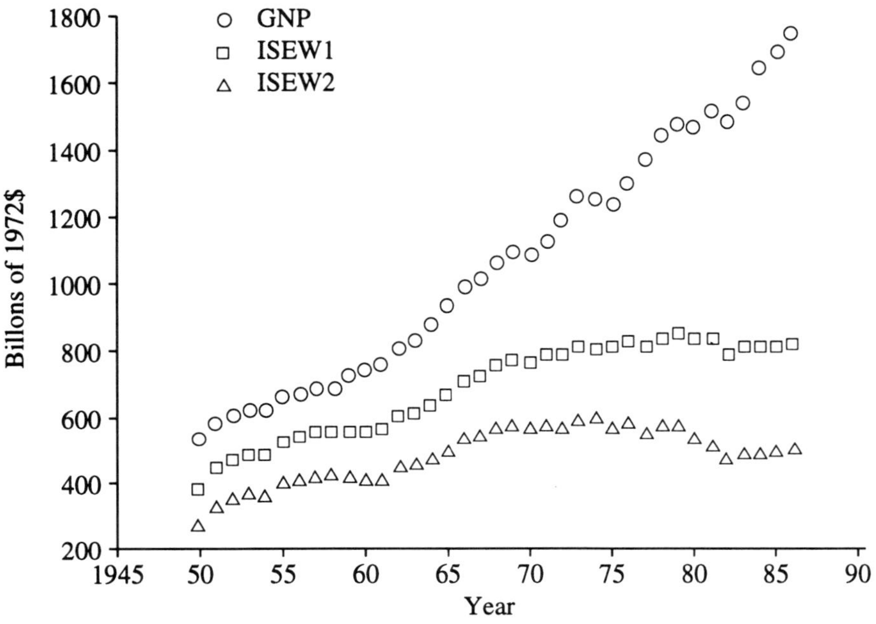

Figure 1 *US GNP compared to the Index of Sustainable Economic Welfare (ISEW, from Daly and Cobb 1989) for the interval 1950 to 1986. ISEW2 includes corrections for depletion of non-renewable resources and long-term environmental damage, ISEW1 does not.*

ity. Thus, adding up the raw heat equivalent kcals of the various forms of fuel consumed by an economy without accounting for fuel quality can radically distort the picture, especially if the mix of fuel types is changing over time.

Studies that have tried to adjust for fuel quality and distortions in GNP have painted a much less rosy picture of past energy efficiency gains and the potential for future gains. Cleveland *et al.* (1984) and more recently Kaufmann (1992) have shown that almost all of the changes in E/GNP (or E/GDP) ratios in the US and OECD countries can be explained by changes in fuel quality and the percent of personal consumption expenditures (PCE) spent directly on fuel. This latter effect is due to the fact that PCE is a component of GNP and spending more on fuel directly will raise GNP without changing real economic output. Figure 2 is an example of the explanatory power of this relationship for the US economy from 1932 to 1987. Much of the apparent gain in energy efficiency (decreasing E/GNP ratio) is due to shifts to higher quality fuels (like primary electricity) from lower quality ones (like coal). Renewable energy sources (like biomass and direct solar) are generally lower quality and major shifts to them may therefore cause significant increases in the E/GNP ratio.

Another way of looking at the relationship between energy and economic output uses cross-sectional rather than time series data. This avoids some of the problems

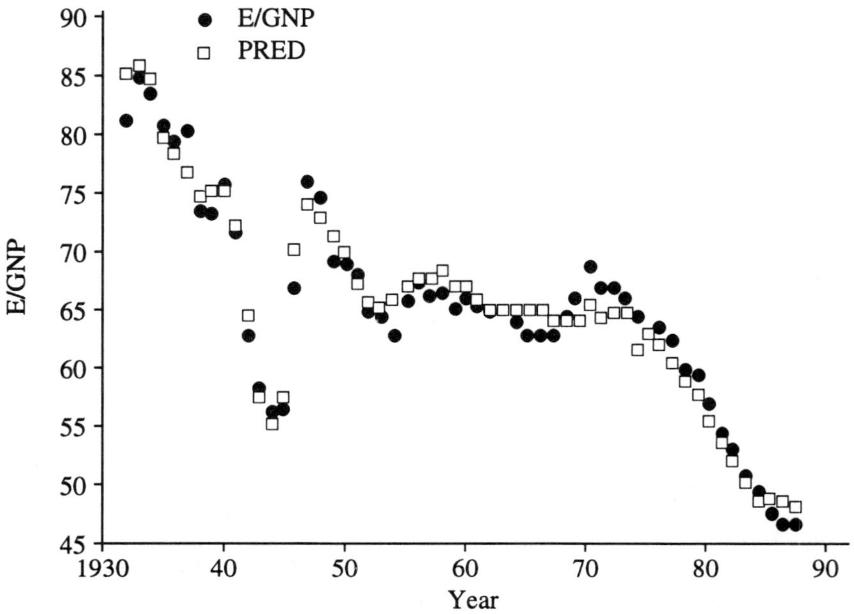

Figure 2 *The Energy/GNP ratio for the US economy from 1932 to 1987 and the predicted ratio (PRED) based on a regression model with percent of primary energy from petroleum (%PET) from electricity (%ELEC) and percent of Personal Consumption Expenditures spent on direct fuel (%PCE) as the independent variables (R^2 = .96). From Cleveland et al. (1984) and Kaufmann (1992).*

associated with changes in fuel mix and distortions in GNP. Chapter 10 (Costanza 1980) and Chapter 11 (Costanza and Herendeen 1984) use an 87-sector input-output model of the US economy for 1963, 1967, and 1973, modified to include households and government as endogenous sectors (so as to include labor and government energy costs) to investigate the relationship between direct and indirect energy consumption (embodied energy) and dollar value of output. It was found that dollar value of sector output was highly correlated (R^2 = .85 to .98) with embodied energy calculated in this way (though it was not correlated with direct energy consumption or with embodied energy calculated excluding labor and government energy costs). The significant outliers from this relationship are the natural resource extraction sectors: forestry, fisheries, agriculture, mining, etc. indicating where net energy was entering the system.

This finding was attacked on methodological grounds (Huettner 1982, Georgescu-Roegen 1979), but careful analysis showed these methodological objections to be unfounded (Costanza 1982, Costanza and Herendeen 1984). Yet, the results of both the time series and cross-sectional analyses have been more or less completely ignored by both conventional economists and environmentalists. The real objection, I believe, is a more fundamental reluctance to confront the implications of the results for conventional thinking about the energy/economy linkage and a strong desire for the linkage to be severed so that the politically more feasible option of efficiency gains could be pursued (see below). But if one makes some of the necessary adjustments to estimates of energy consumption, it appears that the link between these two is much stronger than the simple E/GNP ratio would indicate. While there is still plenty of room for debate, it appears wildly imprudent to conclude that western economies have been getting much more efficient at turning energy into economic activity, to say nothing of economic welfare. Much of the apparent gain in energy efficiency has come about by ignoring changes in the fuel quality mix and various GNP accounting problems, especially the failure to account for the destruction of natural capital, and the energy costs of labor and government services.

The policy implications of all this are important. Some believe that there are truly enormous possibilities for economic growth without corresponding growth in energy and material throughput. Energy efficiency, they argue, can be vastly increased (Lovins 1977, Lovins and Lovins 1987) as can the efficiency of water use and the use of other natural resources. Others (Costanza 1980 – Chapter 10, Cleveland *et al.* 1984, Hall *et al.* 1986, Gever *et al.* 1986) believe that the coupling between growth, development, and energy use is not so loose. This issue arises in the Brundtland Commission's Report (WCED 1987) where on the one hand the authors recognize that the scale of the human economy is already unsustainable in the sense that it requires the consumption of natural capital, and yet on the other hand they call for further economic expansion by a factor of 5 to 10 in order to improve the lot of the poor without having to appeal too much to the 'politically impossible' alternatives of serious population control and redistribution of wealth.

The big question is, how much of this called-for expansion can come from increased efficiency, and how much must come from throughput growth? This question is not addressed by the Commission. But statements from the leader of the WCED, Jim MacNeill (1990) that 'The link between growth and its impact on the environment has also been severed' (p. 13), and 'the maxim for sustainable development is not "limits to growth"; it is "the growth of limits"', indicate that WCED expects that most of the factor of 5 to 10 to come from efficiency increases, not growth of throughput. Is this really possible given the above analyses? No one is really sure, but it is irrational to *count on* these improvements in efficiency to save us from the tough decisions (see Chapter 2 – Costanza 1989).

An additional advantage of the input-output based approach to energy flow analysis is that it can be used with equal facility on both economic and ecological systems and can therefore be an important tool in their integration. Various aspects of this integration are explored in Chapters 12–15 (Costanza and Neill 1984, Hannon *et al.* 1986, Costanza and Hannon 1989, Hannon *et al.* 1991). Outputs from these models include detailed analysis of the structure and interdependencies in these systems, along with sets of energy-based 'shadow prices', calculable for any system where one knows the flow network in physical and/or monetary units. Costanza and Hannon (1989 – Chapter 14), for example, contains a 9-sector, global I-O model which includes both ecological and economic sectors and an analysis of their interrelationships. While this kind of static I-O analysis holds much promise for understanding the structure of linked ecological economic systems and for providing more objective approaches to valuation of natural capital, it is certainly not sufficient. It must be linked to more dynamic and spatially explicit approaches as described below.

Part III Ecological and economic systems modeling and analysis
Both ecological and economic systems are complex adaptive systems whose dynamic behavior can only be predicted within fairly broad bounds of uncertainty. This section covers a group of papers dealing with dynamic modeling of ecological and economic systems (Chapters 18, 21, and 23), the assessment of model performance (Chapters 16 and 17), scale and predictability (Chapters 20 and 22) and the assessment and communication of data quality in models and analysis in general (Chapter 19). A common thread running through all of these papers is a healthy respect for both the necessity and the limitations of modeling, and a broad view of what constitutes models and modeling. Chapter 21 (Costanza *et al.* 1993b) is a general overview of the problems of modeling systems in general and ecological economic systems in particular.

A model is any abstract representation of reality. A map, an architect's cardboard model of a building, a computer simulation, and a thought in our heads all constitute models. In this sense, we cannot think, talk, or dream at all without using models and every one of us is modeling constantly, day and night. Given this reliance on models, it is not surprising that we often confuse our perceptions and abstractions – our models – with reality. To avoid this 'fallacy of misplaced concreteness' (Daly and Cobb 1989) one must be constantly aware that we do *not* have direct access to the truth and all we can do is to imperfectly model reality.

But some models are better than others for specific purposes. Just as we would not do well to try to navigate an ocean liner using a street map of downtown Manhattan (even if it is a very good street map!) one must use models which are best suited to the problem at hand. But how to judge which models are best for what purposes? Chapter 16 (Costanza and Sklar 1985), Chapter 17 (Costanza 1989), and Chapter 22 (Costanza and Maxwell 1994) are approaches to this problem which try to assess the 'goodness of fit' of complex dynamic models over a range of model applications and resolutions, and to assess the overall effectiveness of models at meeting specific goals. Among other things, effectiveness is shown to be a function of the resolution (in space, time, and number of components) of the model, with intermediate resolutions probably offering the most effective models.

Many of the problems at the interface of ecology and economics are most observable and actionable at the regional or landscape scale. Many environmental management decisions are made at this scale and the necessity of transdisciplinary collaboration is more obvious at this scale. The complex problem of simulating large landscapes in both space and time is addressed in Chapters 18 (Costanza *et al.* 1990) and 23 (Costanza *et al.* 1995b). Chapter 18 is one of the first successful efforts to simulate spatially explicit ecosystem dynamics at the landscape scale. The Coastal Ecological Landscape Spatial Simulation (CELSS) model integrated spatially explicit hydrology, sedimentation, and nutrient dynamics, with plant ecology and succession to address the impacts of various human activities in coastal Louisiana. It was also an explicit attempt to use the model building process to help achieve a degree of consensus among stakeholders (in this case the US Corps of Engineers, the US Fish and Wildlife Service, and local landowners) by involving stakeholders in the process from the beginning. Chapter 23 takes CELSS one step further by integrating both the ecological and economic parts of the system in a dynamic, spatially explicit format, applied to the Patuxent River drainage basin in Maryland. Issues of the appropriate time and space scale to link the economic and ecological components of the model become important.

In building these complex models, and in doing any sort of transdisciplinary, policy relevant research, the issues of scale, resolution, predictability and data quality become very important. Chapter 19 (Costanza *et al.* 1992) addresses the issue of data quality and develops a system to 'grade' data according to its quality (NUSAP). Researchers generally understand the subtle issues of data quality as it relates to data they themselves collect. But we lose this information when using data collected by others (often for completely different purposes). In building complex models that involve data from many different sources we must somehow keep track of the relative quality of data. NUSAP is one example of a system designed to retain and communicate this largely subjective information about data quality. Without such a system to keep track of the many shades of gray in data quality, there is a tendency to revert to a simple black or white assessment that does not take full and honest advantage of the data available and tends to unnecessarily polarize and politicize quantitative issues.

The issues of scale, resolution, and predictability are covered in Chapter 20 (Costanza *et al.* 1993a) and Chapter 22 (Costanza and Maxwell 1994). A fundamental idea covered in these papers is that the predictability of systems is a function of the resolution at which we study them. This 'fractal like' relationship is thought to be essential to understanding complex systems, which cannot be adequately understood by studying them at only a single scale.

Part IV Incentives and institutions

Once we have determined the appropriate goals for our system, modeled the dynamics of its evolution, and agreed on policies for its management, there is still the problem of designing effective institutions to implement the policies. This depends on understanding and using the incentive systems that guide human behavior. The most effective way to change human behavior is to change the incentive structure to which individual humans respond. When this incentive structure is in conflict with the goals of the system one can be in a 'social trap' from which escape is very difficult. Chapter 24 (Costanza 1987) looks at this general problem of social traps as applied to environmental management. Once one starts looking, one can see social traps affecting many aspects of human behavior.

One of the more interesting experimental games that have been devised to study social traps is the 'dollar auction game' (Shubik 1971). The dollar auction is just like a normal auction except that both the highest and the second-highest bidder have to pay the auctioneer their bid at the end of the game, but only the highest bidder gets the prize. Players in the dollar auction game frequently bid much more than $1 for a $1 prize – an irrational result that is the product of a series of 'rational' decisions by the bidders. This happens because the structure of reinforcements in this game is a trap. If player A had bid $1 and player B had the second-highest bid at $0.95, player B reasons that if he drops out he loses $0.95 while if he raises to $1.05 he only loses $0.05 (assuming he wins the $1 prize). So he usually raises, and this pattern of 'rational' escalation (beyond the point where the overall outcome is rational) continues quite often to well beyond the $1 point.

The dollar auction trap can be converted to a trade-off by adding a 'bidding tax' large enough to make dropping out rational in both the short run and the long run. For example, if when player B was at $0.95 he was told that it would now cost $2 to enter a bid of $1.05 (a $0.95 bidding tax), he would reason that if he drops out he loses $0.95, but if he raises he loses $1 even if he wins the prize! So the chances that he would drop out and escape the trap are increased. Chapter 25 (Costanza and Shrum 1988) is an experimental analysis of this proposal. The experiments showed that in fact the bidding tax did tend to help people escape from the trap, but that its effectiveness depended more on the timing of the introduction of the tax, rather than the relative size of the tax. This could have significant implications for the design of revised tax systems aimed at using their incentive effects to modify behavior.

One of the most difficult aspects of designing effective institutions for managing environmental problems is the large amount of uncertainty associated with them. Chapter 26 (Costanza and Perrings 1990) and Chapter 27 (Costanza and Cornwell 1992) discuss this issue in the context of the precautionary principle and propose an 'environmental assurance bonding' system in order to deal with it. This system would change the burden of proof in environmental management so that the cost and risk of environmental impacts would be borne by the potential polluters, rather than the public. An assurance bond large enough to cover the worst-case damages would be assessed and held in escrow until the polluter could demonstrate that the damages were less than the worst case, at which point a full or partial refund would be issued. This system would completely reverse the incentives to pollute and lead to rapid development of new, more effective and environmentally friendly technologies.

The final two chapters in the collection address the issues of the management of the large regional ecosystem of the Chesapeake Bay (Chapter 28 – Costanza and Greer 1995), and of the environmental impacts of international trade (Chapter 29 – Costanza *et al.* 1995a). In both cases, the general principles learned from systems analysis, social traps, uncertainty analysis, and the precautionary principle are applied to practical environmental problems in a collaborative, multi-stakeholder framework.

Summary and conclusions

This collection of essays covers a range of theoretical and applied issues at the interface of ecology and economics. It makes use of collaborations that cross several disciplinary boundaries and develops policies that reflect this range of perspectives. It has been an explicit attempt to develop an 'ecological economics' which represents a new, transdisciplinary way of looking at the world which is essential if we are to achieve sustainability. Making sustainability operational requires the integration of three elements: (1) a practical, shared vision of both the way the world works and of the sustainable society we wish to achieve; (2) methods of analysis and modeling that are relevant to the new questions and problems this vision embodies; and (3) new institutions and instruments that can effectively use the analyses to adequately implement the vision. All three of these elements are covered in this collection to a greater or lesser degree. Hopefully, it will stimulate and encourage further work toward the goal of sustainability.

References

Ayres, R. U. (1972), 'A materials-process-product model', pp. 35–67 in A.V. Kneese and B.T. Bower (eds), *Environmental Quality Analysis*, Baltimore, Johns Hopkins Press.

Ayres, R. U. and A. V. Kneese (1969), 'Production, consumption, and externalities', *The American Economic Review*, **59**:282–297.

Boulding, K. E. (1966), 'The economics of the coming spaceship Earth', pp. 3–14 in H. Jarrett (ed.) *Environmental Quality in a Growing Economy:* Resources for the Future, Johns Hopkins University Press, Baltimore, MD.

Cleveland, C. J. (1987), 'Biophysical economics: historical perspective and current research trends', *Ecological Modeling*, **38**:47–74.

Cleveland, C. J., R. Costanza, C. A. S. Hall, and R. Kaufmann, (1984), 'Energy and the United States Economy: a biophysical perspective', *Science*, **225**:890–897.

Costanza, R. (1980), 'Embodied energy and economic valuation', *Science*, **210**:1219–24.

Costanza, R. (1982), 'Economic values and embodied energy: Reply to D. A. Huettner', *Science*, **216**:1141–3.

Costanza, R. (1987), 'Social traps and environmental policy', *BioScience*, **37**:407–412.

Costanza, R. (1989a), 'What is ecological economics?', *Ecological Economics*, **1**:1–7.

Costanza, R. (1989b), 'Model goodness of fit: a multiple resolution procedure', *Ecological Modelling*, **47**:199–215.

Costanza, R. (1992), 'Toward an operational definition of ecosystem health', pp. 239–56 in Costanza, R., B. Norton, and B. J. Haskell (eds), *Ecosystem Health: New Goals for Environmental Management*, Island Press, Washington DC, 269 pp.

Costanza, R. (1994), 'Valuation of ecological systems', pp. 449–50 in G. K. Meffe and C. R. Carroll (eds), *Principles of Conservation Biology*, Sinauer Associates, Sunderland, MA, 600 pp.

Costanza, R., J. Audley, R. Borden, P. Ekins, C. Folke, S. O. Funtowicz, and J. Harris (1995a), 'Sustainable trade: a new paradigm for world welfare', *Environment*, **37**:16–20, 39–44.

Costanza, R., H. E. Daly, and J. A. Bartholomew (1991), 'Goals, agenda, and policy recommendations for ecological economics', pp. 1–20 in R. Costanza (ed), *'Ecological Economics: The science and management of sustainability'*, Columbia University Press, New York, 525 pp.

Costanza, R., and L. Cornwell (1992), 'The 4P approach to dealing with scientific uncertainty', *Environment*, **34**:12–20.

Costanza, R., S. C. Farber, and J. Maxwell, (1989), 'The valuation and management of wetland ecosystems', *Ecological Economics*, **1**:335–61.

Costanza, R., and H. E. Daly (1987), 'Toward an ecological economics', *Ecological Modelling*, **38**:1–7.

Costanza, R., and H. E. Daly (1992), 'Natural capital and sustainable development', *Conservation Biology*, **6**:37–46.

Costanza, R., S. O. Funtowicz, and J. R. Ravetz (1992), 'Assessing and communicating data quality in policy relevant research', *Environmental Management*, **16**:121–31.

Costanza, R. and J. Greer (1995), 'The Chesapeake Bay and its watershed: a model for sustainable ecosystem management?', pp. 169–213 in L. H. Gunderson, C. S. Holling and S. Light (eds), *Barriers and Bridges to the Renewal of Ecosystems and Institutions*, Columbia University Press, New York, 593 pp.

Costanza, R. and B. M. Hannon (1989), 'Dealing with the "mixed units" problem in ecosystem network analysis', pp. 90–115 in F. Wulff, J. G. Field, and K. H. Mann (eds), *Network Analysis of Marine Ecosystems: Methods and Applications*, Coastal and Estuarine Studies Series, Springer-Verlag, Heidelberg, 284 pp.

Costanza, R. and R. A. Herendeen (1984), 'Embodied energy and economic value in the United States Economy; 1963, 1967, and 1972', *Resources and Energy*, **6**:129–64.

Costanza, R., M. Kemp, and W. Boynton (1993a) 'Predictability, scale, and biodiversity in coastal and estuarine ecosystems: implications for management', *Ambio*, **22**:88–96.

Costanza, R. and T. Maxwell (1994), 'Resolution and predictability: an approach to the scaling problem', *Landscape Ecology*, **9**:47–57.

Costanza, R., and C. Neill (1984), 'Energy intensities, interdependence, and value in ecological systems: a linear programming approach', *Journal of Theoretical Biology*, **106**:41–57.

Costanza, R. and B. C. Patten (1995), 'Defining and predicting sustainability', *Ecological Economics*, **15**:193–96.

Costanza, R. and C. Perrings (1990), 'A flexible assurance bonding system for improved environmental management', *Ecological Economics*, **2**:57–76.

Costanza, R. and W. Shrum (1988), 'The effects of taxation on moderating the conflict escalation process: an experiment using the dollar auction game', *Social Science Quarterly*, **69**:416–32.

Costanza, R., and F. H. Sklar (1985), 'Articulation, accuracy, and effectiveness of mathematical models: a review of freshwater wetland applications', *Ecological Modelling*, **27**:45–68.

Costanza, R., F. H. Sklar, and M. L. White (1990), 'Modeling coastal landscape dynamics', *BioScience*, **40**:91–107.

Costanza, R. and L. Wainger (1991), 'Ecological economics: a new approach to understanding and managing the interactions of humans and nature', pp. 50–60 in P. Rothkrug and R. L. Olson (eds), *Mending the Earth: a World for Our Grandchildren*, North Atlantic Books, Berkeley, CA.

Costanza, R., L. Wainger, C. Folke, and K-G Mäler (1993b), 'Modeling complex ecological economic systems: toward an evolutionary, dynamic understanding of people and nature', *BioScience*, **43**: 545–55.

Costanza, R., L. Wainger, and N. Bockstael (1995b), 'Integrated ecological economic systems modeling: theoretical issues and practical applications', pp. 45–66 in J. Walter Milon and J. Shogren (eds), *Integrating Economic and Ecological Indicators: Practical Methods for Environmental Policy Analysis*, Praeger Press, Westport, CN, 216 pp.

Cottrell, W. F. (1955), *Energy and Society*, McGraw-Hill, New York.

Cumberland, J.H. (1966), 'A Regional Inter-Industry model for Analysis of Development Objectives', Regional Science Association Papers 17: 65–94.

Daly, H. E. and J. B. Cobb. (1989), 'Misplaced concreteness: measuring economic success', pp. 62–84 in H. E. Daly and J. B. Cobb, *For the Common Good: Redirecting the Economy Toward Community, the Environment, and a Sustainable Future*, Beacon Press, Boston, 482 pp.

Georgescu-Roegen, N. (1971) *The Entropy Law and the Economic Process*, Cambridge, MA, Harvard University Press.

Georgescu-Roegen, N. (1979), 'Energy analysis and economic valuation', *Southern Economic Journal*, **45**:1023–1058.

Gever, J., R. Kaufmann, D. Skole, and C. Vörösmarty (1986), *Beyond Oil: the Threat to Food and Fuel in the Coming Decades*, Ballinger, Cambridge, MA, 304 pp.

Hall, C. A. S., C. J. Cleveland, and R. Kaufmann (1986) *Energy and Resource Quality: The Ecology of the Economic Process*, Wiley, New York, 577 pp.

Hannon, B., R. Costanza, and R. A. Herendeen (1986) 'Measures of energy cost and value in ecosystems', *The Journal of Environmental Economics and Management*, **13**:391–401.

Hannon, B., R. Costanza, and R. Ulanowicz (1991), 'A general accounting framework for ecological systems: a functional taxonomy for connectivist ecology', *Theoretical Population Biology*, **40**:78–104.

Huettner, D. A. (1982), 'Economic values and embodied energy', *Science*. **216**:1139–41.

Kaufmann, R. K. (1992), 'A biophysical analysis of the energy/real GDP ratio: implications for substitution and technical change', *Ecological Economics*, **6**:35–56.

Lipnowski, I.F. (1976), 'An input-output analysis of environmental preservation', *Journal of Environmental Economics and Management*, **3**:205–214.

Lovins, A. B. (1977), *Soft Energy Paths: Toward a Durable Peace*, Ballinger, Cambridge MA.

Lovins, A. B, and L. H. Lovins. (1987), 'Energy: the avoidable oil crisis', *The Atlantic*, Dec, pp. 22–30.

Lotka, A. J. (1922), 'Contribution to the energetics of evolution', *Proceedings of the National Academy of Science*, **8**:147–55.

MacNeil, Jim, (1990, January 23), 'Sustainable Development, Economics, and the Growth Imperative', Workshop on the Economics of Sustainable Development, Background Paper No. 3, Washington DC.

Odum, H. T. (1971), *Environment, Power and Society*, Wiley-Interscience, New York.

Odum, H. T. and R. C. Pinkerton (1955), 'Time's speed regulator: the optimum efficiency for maximum power output in physical and biological systems', *American Scientist*, **43**:331–43.

Podilinsky, S. (1883), 'Menschliche Arbeit und Einheit der Kraft', *Die Neue Zeit*, March-April.

Quesnay, F. (1758), 'Tableau Economique', in Kuczynski, M. and Meek, R. L. (eds), *Quesnay's Tableau Economique*, Macmillan, London.
Shubik, M. (1971), 'The dollar auction game: a paradox in noncooperative behavior and escalation', *Journal of Conflict Resolution*, **15**:109–111.
Soddy, F. (1922), *Cartesian Economics*, Hendersons, London.
Victor, P. (1972), *Pollution, Economy and Environment*, George Allen and Unwin, London.
WCED (1987) *Our Common Future: Report of the World Commission on Environment and Development*, Oxford University Press, Oxford, England.

References for Chapter 23

Alig, R. J. and R. G. Healy (1987), 'Urban and built-up land area changes in the United States: an empirical investigation of determinants', *Land Economics*, **63**:216–26.
Allen, T. and T. Starr (1982), *Hierarchy*, Chicago: University of Chicago Press.
Beaton, C. H. and W. R. Butcher (1989), 'The impact of regional land-use controls on property values: the case of the New Jersey pinelands', *Land Economics*, **67**:172–94.
Brown, G. M. and J. Roughgarden (1992), 'An ecological economy: notes on harvest and growth', Beijer Discussion Paper Series No. 12, Beijer International Institute of Ecological Economics, Stockholm, Sweden.
Brown, G. M. and J. Swierzbinski (1985), 'Endangered species, genetic capital and cost-reducing R&D', in D. O. Hall, N. Myers, and N. S. Margaris (eds), *Economics of Ecosystems Management*, Dordrecht, The Netherlands: Dr. W. Junk Publishers, pp. 111–27.
Clark, C. W. and G. R. Munro (1975), 'The economics of fishing and modern capital theory: a simplified approach', *Journal of Environmental Economics and Management*, **2**:92–106.
Costanza, R. and T. Maxwell (1993), 'Resolution and predictability: an approach to the scaling problem', *Landscape Ecology*, **9**:47–57.
Costanza, R. and F. H. Sklar (1985), 'Articulation, accuracy, and effectiveness of mathematical models: a review of freshwater wetland applications', *Ecological modeling*, **27**:45–68.
Costanza, R., B. Norton, and B. J. Haskell (eds) (1992), *Ecosystem Health: New Goals for Environmental Management*, Washington, D.C.: Island Press.
Costanza, R., F. H. Sklar, and M. L. White (1990), 'Modeling coastal landscape dynamics', *Bioscience*, **40**:91–106.
Debreu, G. (1974), 'Excess demand functions', *Journal of Mathematical Economics*, **1**:15–23.
Diamond, D. B. (1980), 'The relationship between amenities and urban land prices', *Land Economics*, **56**:21–32.
Duchin, F. (1985), 'Analyzing structural change in the economy', in M. Ciaschini, (ed.), *Input–Output Analysis: Current Developments*, London: Chapman and Hall, pp. 113–28.
—— (1992), 'Industrial input–output analysis: implications for industrial ecology', *Proceedings of the National Academy of Sciences*, **89**:851–5.
Ervin, C. A. and D. E. Ervin (1982), 'Factors affecting the use of soil conservation practices: hypotheses, evidence and implications', *Land Economics*, **58**:277–92.
Fitz, H. C., E. B. DeBellevue, R. Costanza, R. Boumann, T. Maxwell, and L. Wainger (in press), 'Development of a general ecosystem model (GEM) for a range of scales and ecosystems', *Ecological Modelling*.
Fitz, H. C., R. Costanza, and E. Reyes (1993), 'The Everglades Landscape Model (ELM): summary report of Task 2. Model Development', Report to the South Florida Water Management District, Everglades Research Division, West Palm Beach.
Hannon, B. and C. Joiris (1989), 'A seasonal analysis of the southern North Sea ecosystem', *Ecology*, **70**:1916–34.
Hofman, E. (1991), 'How do we generalize coastal models to global scale?' in R. F. C. Mantoura, J. M. Martin, and R. Wollast (eds), *Ocean Margin Processes in Global Change*, New York: John Wiley and Sons.
Holling, C. S. (1964), 'The analysis of complex population processes', *The Canadian Entomologist*, **96**:335–47.
—— (1987), 'Simplifying the complex: the paradigms of ecological function and structure', *European Journal of Operational Research*, **30**:139–46.
—— (1966), 'The functional response to invertebrate predators to prey density', Memoirs of the Entomological Society of Canada No. 48.
Kaitala, V. and M. Pohjola (1988), 'Optimal recovery of a shared resource stock: a differential game model with efficient memory equilibria', *Natural Resource Modeling*, **3**:91–119.
Keynes, J. M. (1936), *General Theory of Employment, Interest and Money*, London: Harcourt Brace.

Klein, L. R. (1971), 'Forecasting and policy evaluation using large-scale econometric models: the state of the art', in M. D. Intriligator (ed.), *Frontiers of Quantitative Economics*, Amsterdam: North-Holland.
Lee, L. K. and W. H. Stewart (1983), 'Landownership and the adoption of minimum tillage', *American Journal of Agricultural Economics*, **65**:256–64.
Levins, R. (1966), 'The strategy of model building in population biology', *American Scientist*, **54**:421–31.
Lines, M. (1989), 'Environmental noise and nonlinear models: a simple macroeconomic example', *Economic Notes*, **19**:376–94.
Lucas, R. E. (1975), 'An equilibrium model of the business cycle', *Journal of Political Economy*, **83**:1113–45.
Lynne, G. D., J. S. Shonkwiler, and L. R. Rola (1988), 'Attitudes and farmer conservation behavior', *American Journal of Agricultural Economics*, **70**:12–19.
Mäler, K.-G. (1991), 'National accounts and environmental resources', *Environmental and Resource Economics*, **1**:1–15.
Maxwell, T. and R. Costanza (in press), 'Distributed modular spatial ecosystem modeling', *International Journal of Computer Simulation*.
McMillan, D. P. (1989), 'An empirical model of urban fringe land use', *Land Economics*, **65**:138–45.
Nielsen, E. G., J. A. Miranowski, and M. J. Morehart (1989), 'Investments in soil conservation and land improvements: factors explaining farmers' decisions', Agricultural Economic Report No. 601, Economic Research Service, Washington, D.C.: U.S. Department of Agriculture.
Norris, P. E. and S. S. Batie (1987), 'Virginia farmers' soil conservation decisions: an application of Tobit analysis', *Southern Journal of Agricultural Economics*, **19**:79–90.
Norton, B. G. and R. E. Ulanowicz (1992), 'Scale and biodiversity policy: a hierarchical approach', *Ambio*, **21**:244–9.
O'Neill, R. V. and B. Rust (1979), 'Aggregation error in ecological models', *Ecological Modeling*, **7**:91–105.
O'Neill, R. V., A. R. Johnson, and A. W. King (1989), 'A hierarchical framework for the analysis of scale', *Landscape Ecology*, **3**:193–205.
O'Neill, R. V., D. L. DeAngelis, J. B. Waide, and T. F. H. Allen (1986), *A Hierarchical Concept of Ecosystems*, Princeton, NJ: Princeton University Press.
Rastetter, E. B., A. W. King, B. J. Cosby, G. M. Hornberger, R. V. O'Neill, and J. E. Hobbie (1992), 'Aggregating fine-scale ecological knowledge to model coarser-scale attributes of ecosystems', *Ecological Applications*, **2**:55–70.
Robinson, J. B. (1991), 'Modelling the interactions between human and natural systems', *International Social Science Journal*, **130**:629–47.
Robinson, J. B. (in press), 'Of maps and territories: the use and abuse of socio-economic modelling in support of decision-making', *Technological Forecast and Social Change*.
Saliba, C. and D. W. Bromley (1986), 'Soil management decisions – how they should be compared and what factors influence them', *North Central Journal of Agricultural Economics*, **8**:305–17.
Shortle, J. S. and J. A. Miranowski (1986), 'Effects of risk perception and other characteristics of farmers and farm operations on the adoption of conservation tillage', *Applied Agricultural Research*, **1**:85–90.
Shugart, H. H. (1989), 'The role of ecological models in long-term ecological studies', in G. E. Likens (ed.), *Long-Term Studies in Ecology: Approaches and Alternatives*, New York: Springer-Verlag, pp. 90–109.
Solow, R. (1956), 'A contribution to the theory of economic growth', *Quarterly Journal of Economics*, **70**:65–94.
Sonnenschein, H. (1974), 'Market excess demand functions', *Econometrica*, **40**:549–63.
Taub, F. B. (1987), 'Indicators of change in natural and human impacted ecosystems: status', in S. Draggan, J. J. Cohrssen, and R. E. Morrison (eds), *Preserving Ecological Systems: The Agenda for Long-Term Research and Development*, New York: Praeger, pp. 115–44.
—— (1989), 'Standardized aquatic microcosm-development and testing', in A. Boudou and F. Ribeyre (eds), *Aquatic Ecotoxicology: Fundamental Concepts and Methodologies*, vol. II, Boca Raton, FL: CRC Press, pp. 47–92.
Wroblewski, J. S. and E. E. Hofmann (1989), 'U.S. interdisciplinary modeling studies of coastal-offshore exchange processes: past and future', *Progress in Oceanography*, **23**:65–99.
Wulff, F. and R. E. Ulanowicz (1989), 'A comparative anatomy of the Baltic Sea and Chesapeake Bay ecosystems', in F. Wulff, J. G. Field, and K. H. Mann (eds), *Network Analysis of Marine Ecology: Methods and Applications*, Coastal and Estuarine Studies Series, Heidelberg, Germany: Springer-Verlag, pp. 232–56.

PART I

CREATING AN ECOLOGICAL ECONOMICS

Ecological Modelling, 38 (1987) 1–7 1
Elsevier Science Publishers B.V., Amsterdam – Printed in The Netherlands

TOWARD AN ECOLOGICAL ECONOMICS

ROBERT COSTANZA

Coastal Ecology Institute, Center for Wetland Resources, Louisiana State University, Baton Rouge, LA 70803 (U.S.A.)

and HERMAN E. DALY

Economics Department, Louisiana State University, Baton Rouge, LA 70803 (U.S.A.)

ABSTRACT

Costanza, R. and Daly, H.E., 1987. Toward an ecological economics. *Ecol. Modelling*, 38: 1–7.

Integrating ecology and economics is increasingly important as humanity's impact on the natural world increases. Current paradigms in both fields are too narrow (and seem to be getting narrower). This paper introduces and summarizes this special issue of *Ecological Modeling* devoted to ecological economics. There are eleven papers (including this one) that cover most of the important theoretical issues involved (applied papers are left for a future volume). These issues are: (1) sustainability; (2) inter- and intra-species distribution of wealth; (3) discounting and intergenerational justice; and (4) dealing with non-monetized values, imprecision, and uncertainty. This collection is seen as a hopeful first step toward a true synthesis of ecology and economics that could lead to better management of renewable and non-renewable natural resources and a sustainable future.

NEED FOR AN ECOLOGICAL ECONOMICS

The main impetus for this special issue is the hypothesis (some would say observation) that current economic paradigms have some serious shortcomings when it comes to dealing with natural resources. The relevant word here is serious. No economic system or body of ideas to analyze and control it can be perfect. But many economists believe that the remaining imperfections need not be cause for concern. Free marketeers believe that externalities are unimportant and that the system can be improved by giving the market an even more free (but still invisible) hand. Hard-line Marxists contend that better planning and political education will solve any remaining (minor) problems.

A second impetus is the observation that ecological paradigms tend to ignore human cultural behavior as an object of direct study. Ecologists are generally concerned with predicting the impacts of human activity *on* natural ecosystems, but not with understanding and predicting human behavior in the context of natural ecosystems.

The authors in this volume share the view that the remaining problems are *very* serious, and that fairly elaborate modifications to existing paradigms are necessary to address them. They cover a wide spectrum as to exactly what the major issues and problems are, however, and how we might go about rectifying them.

In this introduction we summarize the common threads running through the papers and put them in a larger context. We also mention a few additional topics that do not appear in any of the papers. We title this chapter: 'Toward an ecological economics' because the strongest thread linking these wide-ranging papers is the idea that a certain broadening of boundaries and perspectives needs to occur. Ultimately, we think this means that ecology and economics must be more fully integrated if either is to deal adequately with man's use of natural resources. This special issue is a hopeful step toward that synthesis.

MAJOR ISSUES, PROBLEMS, AND SOLUTIONS

Concern about natural resources has a long history in economics, but it has gotten short shrift in the 20th century as economists turned their attention to other topics. The classical economists of the 18th century were much more concerned with man's dependence on and interaction with nature than their contemporary counterparts. In this special issue of *Ecological Modelling*, CLEVELAND gives an historical account of ecological/biophysical models from the classical economists to the present. There is much here that is useful to remember and reiterate, and modern energy analysts can be seen as proposing a more technically sophisticated revival of many of these early ideas. CHRISTENSEN concentrates on the parallels and contrasts between the classical economists, modern Marxist economists and modern energy analysts.

The problems that result from ignoring man's interdependence with the natural world can be defined in many ways. The sections below summarize the major themes of the papers and provide some additional perspectives.

Sustainability: maintaining our life support system

The most obvious danger of ignoring nature in economics is that nature is the economy's life support system, and by ignoring it we may inadvertently damage it beyond repair. Several authors stress the fact that current economic systems do not inherently incorporate any concern about the sustainability of our natural life support system and the economies which depend on it. PEARCE discusses the reasons for the inability of existing forms of economic organization (free market, mixed, planned) to guarantee sustainability. He then lays out what he views as the necessary conditions for a sustainable, "ecologically bounded" economy. In his view the issue of sustainability is intimately connected with the issue of justice (both within species, between species, and between present and future generations) since justice in this context ultimately implies sustainability. HUETING attempts to apply some of these principles in order to quantify their economic implications. He concludes that saving the environment is not only economically possible, but also necessary for ensuring sustainability.

Intra- and inter-species distribution of wealth

Wealth is ultimately the capacity to support life and the enjoyment thereof. Therefore it is not really fanciful to think of sharing wealth in this sense with other species or with future beings. In animal populations all members have roughly the same 'standard of living' or level of per-capita resource use. Nor does that use rate change over time. Of course there exists territoriality and dominance hierarchies, so animal populations are not totally egalitarian. But they are not divided into social classes in which some have vastly more access to resources than others. For animals, respecting carrying capacity is mainly a matter of limiting population, with per-capita resource consumption levels remaining relatively constant and uniform. Of course for humans per-capita resource use varies greatly among social classes and is not constant over time. Consequently the issue of sustainability is not simply a matter of controlling numbers (although that cannot be omitted), but also includes the issues of sufficiency and equity of distribution. Staying within carrying capacity for humans involves not only population control, but also consumption control and distribution control. None of these are 'automatically' handled by free markets, nor are they popular topics. Modern economics has little to say about justice and even less about sufficiency, as PEARCE points out. HUETING considers the implications of scenarios that give explicit priority to the environment and to long-term considerations and shows them to be both practical and necessary. In general, however, our authors only scratch the surface of these important issues.

Turning from intra- to inter-species distribution of 'wealth' or carrying capacity, it is clear that modern economics has declared that our species should get an ever increasing share. This presumption leads to problems in that it ignores the instrumental value of other species to us in maintaining life support systems, and it ignores the intrinsic value of other species. The issue of instrumental value of other species arises frequently in these papers. Energy analysts calculate a form of intrinsic value based on the 'degree of organization' or embodied energy of things (including living things). There are practical and theoretical problems with this sort of calculation but the idea that things can have some value *independent of human perception* of that value is foreign to modern economics. To the average economist if a tree falls in the forest, it not only makes no sound, but it has no value unless there's a market in which consumers can reveal their preferences for timber. While the market can be a powerful and useful tool for allocating resources, one can think of many examples where humans have misperceived the value of natural resources (i.e. wetlands) until it was almost too late. Some notion of intrinsic value must therefore be introduced as a check on human perceptions and to allow us to study the economies of nature which do not include humans.

Discounting, intergenerational justice, and the time delay trap

Intergenerational justice is a strong motivating force in many of the papers. Its close connection to sustainability has already been noted. Often the present vs. future issue is thought to be objectively decided by discounting. But discounting at best only reflects the value of the future (all species in the future) to the presently existing members of one species, ours. The value of future life to the future beings themselves does not enter the calculation at all. GOODLAND and LEDEC, and PEARCE, examine some of the anomalies associated with discounting. It is worth emphasizing here that discounting is simply a numerical way to operationalize the value judgment that: (a) the near future is worth more than the distant future, and (b) beyond some point the worth of the future is negligible.

Most economists tend to treat discounting as rational, optimizing behavior based on people's inherent preferences for current over future consumption. However, there is evidence that discounting behavior may be symptomatic of a kind of semi-rational, suboptimizing behavior known as a 'social trap'. A social trap is any situation in which the short-run, local reinforcements guiding individual behavior are inconsistent with the long-run, global best interest of the individual and society (Platt, 1973; Cross and Guyer, 1980; Costanza, 1987). We go through life making decisions about which path to take based largely on the 'road signs', the short-run, local, reinforcements that we perceive most directly. These short-run reinforcements can include monetary incentives, social acceptance or admonishment, and physical pleasure or pain. Problems arise, however, when the road signs are inaccurate or misleading. In these cases we can be trapped into following a path that is ultimately detrimental because of our reliance on the road signs. Discounting allows us to give too little weight to the future (or other species, other groups or classes of humans, etc.) and thus helps to set the trap. Both economists and ecologists tend to fall into the trap of assuming that individuals are optimizing and then interpreting *all* observed behavior as optimal (since it is exhibited by optimizing individuals). By this reasoning discounting the future must be optimal because humans do it and they are optimizing individuals. The psychological evidence indicates, however, that humans have problems responding to reinforcements that are not immediate (in time and space), and can be led into disastrous situations *because* they discount too much.

Discounting future value by the rate of interest also provides an extremely tight link between ecological destruction and macroeconomic policy. Any exploited species whose natural rate of population growth is less than the rate of interest is under threat of extinction, even in the absence of common property problems. It is a bit far-fetched to imagine Paul Volker and the FED worrying about the effect of U.S. interest rate policy on deforestation in the Amazon, but that is simply evidence of the unwarranted isolation of economics from ecology, because such links really do exist.

Non-monetized values and the partial quantification trap

There is a limit to what we can do with numbers, just as there is a limit to what we can do without them. Not all values can be quantified in monetary terms at the same level of precision. Comparing non-monetized values with each other and with monetized values is difficult but obviously not impossible since we do it all the time. In an age of number crunchers, however, there is a danger that the more precisely expressible values will dominate the less precisely expressible values simply because their numerical character makes them easier to fit into models. Against this 'unfair' advantage of precise numbers, however, must be balanced an 'unfair' advantage of the poorly-measurable. If something can be precisely measured it is hard to exaggerate its magnitude. It is what it is. But imprecise values can be exaggerated, and exposing the exaggeration is not always easy.

One approach is to try to quantify all values in a common metric, on the grounds that any decision trade-off between the priced and the non-priced implies some shadow price implicitly given to what was not priced. That may be true, but it is the order of causation that is crucial. The fact that *after the fact* such a decision implies some shadow price does not mean that *before the fact* we have any means of calculating that price independently in order to use it as the basis of the decision.

The only solution to the partial quantification trap is to recognize and deal with the range of imprecision inherent in any decision. This means looking at the full range of possible outcomes, given the level of precision of our models and data, and making decisions in that context. It is seductive to try to obtain a precise, decisive, answer by using as input to precise mathematical models *only* that which we can measure precisely. But it is extremely dangerous to do so. As Albert Einstein once said; "the laws of mathematics, as far as they refer to reality, are not certain, and as far as they are certain, do not refer to reality."

Integration vs. cross fertilization

Some writers aim at full integration of economics and ecology. Others, more modestly, seek only cross fertilization by borrowing constructs from one discipline and applying them in the other. In this volume several strategies of integration are attempted. VAN DER PLOEG et al. summarize a broader range of attempts at various forms of integration and cross fertilization (what they call "stretching") that have thus far been made. VERTINSKY uses the concepts of diversity, stability and resilience from ecology to illuminate the functioning of the Japanese style of management and economic decision-making. Many ecologists have imported the economic model of input–output economics into ecology. Perhaps this particular borrowing is really the repayment of an old debt that economics owes to the life sciences, since the input–output model derives from Quesney's 'tableau economique' which was suggested to Quesney (a physician) by the analogy of the circulation of blood in the body to the circulation of income among social classes in the body politic.

Extending classical, neoclassical, and marxist analysis

The papers that do aim at a new integrative synthesis take several different starting points. GOODLAND and LEDEC, and PEARCE, attempt to expand the boundaries and concepts of neoclassical economics so as to embrace the important economic development issues of sustainability and carrying capacity, yet within an overall neoclassical framework of comparing costs and benefits at the margin.

CHRISTENSEN offers the notion that the extension of classical economics may offer greater possibilities of integrating ecology and economics than does neoclassical economics, and casts modern energy analysis as a form of classical revival. Similarly, KAUFMANN wonders if Marxist economics might not offer the best starting point for the development of integration, which he also sees as being exhibited in its early stages by modern energy analysts.

Systems ecology and energy analysis

The systems ecology approach exhibited by CLEVELAND and by NORGAARD seeks to envelop economics in an overall ecological framework: NORGAARD takes coevolution as the key concept, while CLEVELAND and other energy analysts take energy flows as the dominant integrating principle.

Both disciplines have been cross-fertilized, and indeed to a degree integrated, by borrowing from a third discipline, thermodynamics. The laws of thermodynamics set the basic conditions of usefulness of matter–energy, whether for metabolism or production, and define the way in which both economies and organisms live off the environment by "sucking low entropy from it" as Erwin Schroedinger put it, and as was seen by Frederick Soddy even earlier. Several of the papers incorporate this fundamental tenet in various forms. LAITNER looks explicitly at the implications of considering resource constraints (particularly energy) in constructing economic development strategies.

TOWARD A TRUE SYNTHESIS

To effect a true synthesis of economics and ecology is the second most important task of our generation, next to avoiding nuclear war. Without such an integration we will gradually despoil the capacity of the earth to support life. Gradual despoilation is certainly preferable to destroying it all at once in a nuclear war, but is still an unhappy prospect. The importance of the topic is more than sufficient justification for this special issue. It would be pleasant to report that the integration of economics and ecology has reached its full perfection in this volume. The truth, however, it that we are just a few steps beyond the beginning. We know this problem will increasingly attract the efforts of scientists and scholars in the future, and hope that this collection may in some way encourage and facilitate that important work.

REFERENCES

Costanza, R., 1987. Social traps and environment policy. BioScience, 37: 407–412.

Cross, J.G. and Guyer, M.J., 1980. Social traps. University of Michigan Press, Ann Arbor, MI.

Platt, J., 1973. Social traps. Am. Psychol., 28: 642–651.

Ecological Economics, 1 (1989) 1–7
Elsevier Science Publishers B.V., Amsterdam – Printed in The Netherlands

WHAT IS ECOLOGICAL ECONOMICS?

ROBERT COSTANZA

Coastal and Environmental Policy Program, Center for Environmental and Estuarine Studies, University of Maryland, Solomons, MD 20688-0038 (U.S.A.)

INTRODUCTION

Ecological Economics addresses the relationships between ecosystems and economic systems in the broadest sense. These relationships are the locus of many of our most pressing current problems (i.e. sustainability, acid rain, global warming, species extinction, wealth distribution) but they are not well covered by any existing discipline. Environmental and resource economics, as it is currently practiced, covers only the application of neoclassical economics to environmental and resource problems. Ecology, as it is currently practiced, sometimes deals with human impacts on ecosystems, but the more common tendency is to stick to "natural" systems. *Ecological Economics* aims to extend these modest areas of overlap. It will include neoclassical environmental economics and ecological impact studies as subsets, but will also encourage new ways of thinking about the linkages between ecological and economic systems.

We have chosen the name *Ecological Economics* for this area of study because it implies a broad, *ecological*, interdisciplinary, and holistic view of the problem of studying and managing our world. The "earth from space" cover of the journal reflects this global, holistic perspective. We did *not* intend to imply with the ordering of the two words in the title that the journal is mainly an economics journal: it is intended to be a new approach to *both* ecology and economics that recognizes the need to make economics more cognizant of ecological impacts and dependencies; the need to make ecology more sensitive to economic forces, incentives, and constraints; and the need to treat integrated economic-ecologic systems with a common (but diverse) set of conceptual and analytical tools.

There was much discussion of other possible names, such as "Economic Ecology" or "Ecology and Economics" or some conjoining of the two words that to me end up being confusing tongue twisters like "Ecolnomics" or "Econology." But *Ecological Economics* seemed to get closest to the meaning we desired while still being evocative to the uninitiated.

0921-8009/89/$03.50

2

Ecological Economics will, in the end, be what *Ecological Economists* do. A fair amount of space in the journal (especially in the first few years) will be devoted to introspective discussions of what the field is or should be, its historical roots, and where it is going or should be going (see Paul Ehrlich's and John Proops' contributions in this issue).

In studying the relationships between ecosystems and economic systems a large measure of "conceptual pluralism" is warranted (Richard Norgaard's article in this issue is an eloquent description of this idea). There is probably not one *right* approach or paradigm, because, like the blind men and the elephant, the subject is too big and complex to touch it all with one limited set of perceptual tools. The Journal will therefore pursue a strategy of pluralism.

Rather than reiterate the detailed list of issues that concern *Ecological Economics* (this list can be found in the journal's aims and scope statement and in more detail in Proops' article), I'd like to briefly discuss what I see as a fundamental question that underlies the need for an *Ecological Economics* and on which these other issues depend.

TECHNOLOGICAL OPTIMISM VS. PRUDENT PESSIMISM

Current economic paradigms (capitalist, socialist, and the various mixtures) are all based on the underlying assumption of continuing and unlimited economic growth. This assumption allows problems of intergenerational, intragenerational, and interspecies equity and sustainability to be ignored (or at least postponed), since they are seen to be most easily solved by additional growth. Indeed, most conventional economists define "health" in an economy as a stable and high *rate of growth*. Energy and resource limits to growth, according to these paradigms, will be eliminated as they arise by clever development and deployment of new technology. This line of thinking is often called "technological optimism".

An opposing line of thought (often called "technological pessimism") assumes that technology will *not* be able to circumvent fundamental energy and resource constraints and that eventually economic growth will stop. It has usually been ecologists or other life scientists that take this point of view (a notable exception among economists is Daly, 1977), largely because they study natural systems that *invariably do* stop growing when they reach fundamental resource constraints. A healthy ecosystem is one that maintains a stable level. Unlimited growth is cancerous, not healthy, under this view.

The technological optimists argue that human systems are fundamentally different from other natural systems because of human intelligence. History has shown that resource constraints can be circumvented by new ideas. Technological optimists claim that Malthus' dire predictions about population pressures have not come to pass and the "energy crisis" of the late 1970s is behind us.

The technological pessimists argue that many natural systems also have "intelligence" in that they can evolve new behaviors and organisms (including humans themselves). Humans are therefore a part of nature, not apart from it. Just because we have circumvented local and artificial resource constraints in the past does not mean we can circumvent the fundamental ones that we will eventually face. Malthus' predictions have not come to pass *yet* for the entire world the pessimists would argue, but many parts of the world are in a Malthusian trap now, and other parts may well fall into it.

This debate has gone on for several decades now. It began with Barnett and Morse's (1963) *Scarcity and Growth* and really got into high gear with the publication of *The Limits to Growth* by Meadows et al. (1972) and the Arab oil embargo in 1973. There have been thousands of studies over the last 15 years on various aspects of our energy and resource future and different points of view have waxed and waned. But the bottom line is that there is still an enormous amount of uncertainty about the impacts of energy and resource constraints. In the next 20 to 30 years we may begin to hit *real* fossil fuel supply limits. Will fusion energy or solar energy or conservation or some as yet unthought of energy source step in to save the day and keep economies growing? The technological optimists say yes and the technological pessimists say no. Ultimately, no one knows. Both sides argue as if they were certain but the most insidious form of ignorance is misplaced certainty.

Whatever turns out to be the case, a more ecological approach to economics and a more economic approach to ecology will be beneficial in order to maintain our life support systems and the aesthetic qualities of the environment. But there are vast differences in the specific economic and environmental policies we should pursue today, depending on whether the technological optimists or pessimists are right. Given this fundamental uncertainty about such a fundamentally important piece of information, what should we do? This is a key area of research for *Ecological Economics*.

The optimists argue that unless we believe that the optimistic future is possible and behave accordingly it will never come to pass. The pessimists argue that the optimists will bring on the inevitable leveling and decline sooner by consuming resources faster and that to sustain our system we should begin to conserve resources immediately. *Ecological Economics* will attempt to reduce our ignorance about the real energy, environmental, and economic state of the world (see, for example, Kümmel, 1989), develop methodological and ideological options for better understanding of our dilemma (see Christensen's article), and look for the optimal social paths and more effective social instruments given our very real and, unfortunately very large, ignorance (see Hansen's and Perrings' articles).

4

Real State of the World

Current Policy	Optimists Right	Pessimists Right
Technological Optimist Policy	High	Disaster
Technological Pessimist Policy	Moderate	Tolerable

Fig. 1. Payoff matrix for technological optimism vs. pessimism.

We can cast this optimist/pessimist choice in a classic (and admittedly oversimplified) game theoretic format using the "payoff matrix" shown in Fig. 1. Here the alternative policies that we can pursue today (technologically optimistic or pessimistic) are listed on the left and the real states of the world are listed at the top. The intersections are labelled with the results of the combinations of policies and states of the world. For example, if we pursue the optimistic policy and the world really does turn out to conform to the optimistic assumptions then the payoffs would be high. This high potential payoff is very tempting and this strategy has paid off in the past. It is not surprising that so many would like to believe that the world conforms to the optimist's assumptions. If, however, we pursue the optimistic policy and the world turns out to conform more closely to the pessimistic technological assumptions then the result would be "Disaster". The disaster would come because irreversible damage to ecosystems would have occurred and technological fixes would no longer be possible.

If we pursue the pessimistic policy and the optimists are right then the results are only "Moderate". But if the pessimists are right and we have pursued the pessimistic policy then the results are "Tolerable".

Within the framework of game theory, this simplified game has a fairly simple "optimal" strategy. If we *really* do not know the state of the world then we should choose the policy that is the maximum of the minimum outcomes (i.e. the MaxiMin strategy in game theory jargon). In other words, we analyze each policy in turn, look for the worst thing (minimum) that could happen if we pursue that policy, and pick the policy with the largest (maximum) minimum. In the case stated above we should pursue the pessimist policy because the worst possible result under that policy ("Tolerable") is a preferable outcome to the worst outcome under the optimist policy ("Disaster").

One must conclude that too little attention is currently being given to policies based on technologically pessimistic assumptions. Pursuing these policies (or at least having them worked out in detail and available as part of the policy dialog) might be our most prudent long-run alternative, given our present large uncertainty about the true energy and environmental state of the world.

Ecological Economics will encourage elaboration of these prudently pessimistic policies and issues, and compare them to alternative optimistic policies while trying to help reduce our uncertainty about the real state of the world vis à vis the ability of technology to circumvent fundamental resource and energy limits.

The more specific issues of concern to the Journal, in my view, all revolve around this central question of limits: the ability of technology to circumvent them, and the long run costs of the technological "cures". Do we adapt to limits with technologies that have potentially large but uncertain future environmental costs or do we limit population and per capita consumption to levels sustainable with technologies which are known to be more environmentally benign? Must we always increase supply or can we also reduce demand? Is there an optimal mix of the two?

If the limits are not really there then conventional economics' relegation of energy and environmental concerns to the side of the stage is probably appropriate, and detailed energy analyses are nothing more than interesting curiosities. If the limits *are* there then energy and environmental issues are pushed much more forcefully to center stage and the tracking of energy and resource flows through ecological and economic systems becomes much more useful and important.

Issues of sustainability are ultimately issues about limits. If economic growth is sustainable indefinitely by technology then all environmental problems can (in theory at least) be fixed technologically. Issues of equity and distribution (between subgroups and generations of our species and between our species and others) are also issues of limits. We do not have to worry so much about how an expanding pie is divided, but a constant or shrinking pie presents real problems. Finally, dealing with uncertainty about limits is the fundamental issue. If we are unsure about future limits the prudent course is to assume they exist. One does not run blindly through a dark landscape that *may* contain crevasses. One assumes they are there and goes gingerly and with eyes wide open, at least until one can see a little better.

EDITORIAL POLICY

Ecological Economics is a new field formed at the intersection of two older ones. Our policy (at least until the field becomes established) will be to send papers out for review to one "ecologist", one "economist" and one of the associate editors (since they were chosen for their superior integrative ability and are therefore assumed to already be *ecological economists*). We expected (and our experience so far has confirmed this) that we would often get conflicting reviews from the "ecologist" and the "economist." The "bad" review in these cases is not taken as damning, but rather is used to inform the author of the problems his or her work causes with the other "camp" so that to the greatest extent possible they can be addressed. Since we support conceptual pluralism, expect to find a wide range of approaches and ideas in the journal, rather than a coherent and consistent single point of view.

We have divided the journal into four main sections containing different categories of papers: (1) Commentary; (2) Methodological and Ideological Options; (3) Analysis; and (4) Book Reviews. This format allows enough latitude to address all major issues of concern appropriately, without confusing a personal opinion with an analytical result. In addition, we will have a 'Letters to the Editor" section for discussion of controversial issues.

Ecological Economics is an open niche waiting to be filled, a fertile field waiting to be sown and harvested. It will require the best of both ecology and economics, and a good measure of innovative ideas. It may one day surpass both its parents in stature and wisdom. We hope you will participate in this challenging debate about our ecological economic future.

ACKNOWLEDGEMENTS

I would like to thank Herman Daly for his central role in getting this journal started (and for reviewing this manuscript): it would not have happened without him. I would also like to thank David Pearce and Ann-Mari Jansson for their especially important efforts in forming the journal, and all the members of our editorial advisory board.

The journal benefited greatly from a series of conferences and workshops devoted to integrating ecology and economics. The first was the Wallenberg Symposium on integration of economy and ecology held in Stockholm, Sweden, in September, 1982 (Jansson, 1984). The European Centre for Research and Documentation in Social Sciences (the Vienna Center) sponsored a pair of workshops on ecology and economics in Stockholm in 1986 and in Barcelona, Spain in September, 1987. Papers presented at these two workshops eventually resulted in several of the articles appearing in the journal. There was a session at the 1987 Ecological Society of America Meeting in Columbus, Ohio on ecological economics that also contributed several papers to the journal.

Announcements of upcoming meetings of the International Society for Ecological Economics and related events will be published in this journal and in the Society's newsletter.

REFERENCES

Barnett, H.J. and Morse, C., 1963. Scarcity and Growth: The Economics of Natural Resource Availability. Johns Hopkins, Baltimore, Md.

Daly, H.E., 1977. Steady-State Economics. Freeman, San Francisco, Calif.

Jansson, A.M. (Editor), 1984. Integration of Economy and Ecology: An Outlook for the Eighties. Univ. of Stockholm Press, Stockholm.

Kümmel, R., 1989. Energy as a factor of production and entropy as a pollution indicator in macroeconomic modelling. Ecol. Econ., 1 (in press).

Meadows, D.H., Meadows, D.L., Randers, J. and Behrens, W.W., 1972. The Limits to Growth. Universe, New York, N.Y.

[3]

Ecological Economics, 1 (1989) 335–361 335
Elsevier Science Publishers B.V., Amsterdam – Printed in The Netherlands

VALUATION AND MANAGEMENT OF WETLAND ECOSYSTEMS

ROBERT COSTANZA [1], STEPHEN C. FARBER [2] and JUDITH MAXWELL [3]

[1] *Coastal and Environmental Policy Program, Center for Environmental and Estuarine Studies, Chesapeake Biological Laboratory, University of Maryland, Solomons, MD 20688-0038 (U.S.A.)*
[2] *Economics Department, Louisiana State University, Baton Rouge, LA 70803 (U.S.A.)*
[3] *School of Natural Resources, 2021 Coffey Road, The Ohio State University, Columbus, OH 43210-1085 (U.S.A.)*

ABSTRACT

Costanza, R., Farber, S.C. and Maxwell, J., 1989. Valuation and management of wetland ecosystems. *Ecol. Econ.*, 1: 335–361.

We recently completed a study of wetland values in coastal Louisiana that employed both willingness-to-pay and energy analysis-based methodologies and were able to bracket a range of values within which we feel fairly confident the true value lies. However, a large amount of uncertainty remains. Our current estimates of the total present value of an *average* acre of natural wetlands in Louisiana are US $2429–6400 per acre (assuming an 8% discount rate) to $8977–17000 per acre (assuming a 3% discount rate). At the lowest value, the current annual rate of loss of Louisiana wetlands (50 sq miles per year) is worth about $77 million. At the largest value it is worth about $544 million.

In this paper we (a) discuss the fundamental theoretical and practical problems underlying natural resource valuation; (b) summarize our methods and findings for Louisiana wetlands; and (c) elaborate on some of the more recalcitrant problems attending applied natural resource valuation, including discounting and dealing with uncertainty and imprecision.

The discount rate makes more difference in the final result than any other one factor, and yet there is much disagreement about the appropriate approach to discounting natural resources. We discuss the discounting problem as applied to natural resources and argue for lower discount rates for valuing renewable natural resources than apply for other aspects of the economy.

It now seems clear that no reasonable amount of effort will produce very precise estimates of wetland values, and we suspect this is also the case for several other classes of natural resources. We elaborate a Wetlands Assurance Bonding system to address these problems.

BACKGROUND

Imperfect markets and prices

In market economies, prices are relied on to provide signals regarding resource scarcity. These prices are considered to provide a true measure of

0921-8009/89/$03.50

economic value only if the market is characterized by a large number of buyers and sellers and by private property rights which are enforceable and transferable. The consumption choice must be made from a basket of 'rival' goods and services, that is, the choice to consume one good comes at the expense of some other good. If these conditions hold, prices can be relied on to direct the allocation of scarce resources to their highest valued use. Unfortunately, for the many ecosystem goods and services that humans *do* care about, such markets are of limited usefulness and/or fail to perform efficiently. The absence of efficient markets for these outputs is the major cause of what can be called 'inefficient' habitat modification. This is the conversion from those land use activities that have large, real, but uncapturable benefits (i.e., natural ecosystems) to land use activities that have smaller but capturable income streams. In this most prevalent case, individual preferences diverge from those of society as a whole and collective action is warranted.

Even when the preferences for the resources provided by existing natural ecosystems are strong, their common property nature makes it impossible to exclude those who do not pay for enjoying or using them. As a result there is no incentive to conserve such resources and overuse and even exhaustion can occur when utilization or harvest rates exceed the population growth rates of species, as in a fishery, or rates of forage production in common grazing areas. For some resources such as camping sites and scenic views, utilization levels result in congestion and subsequent declines in resource quality (Cicchetti and Smith, 1973). For congestible goods, exclusion results in efficient use only if consumers pay for their use in accordance with their own valuation for that use plus congestion costs imposed on others. Because of obstacles to both collecting payment and in eliciting true evaluations, public or collective management is usually required.

Lack of provision for equity and sustainability

Another deficiency of markets is that the choices and prices observed are a function of types and levels of personal endowments. The distribution of endowments and the relative importance imparted to these endowments in the marketplace can cause significant bias in environmental valuations from the individual, societal and regional viewpoint. For example, threatened species will be valued very differently by the local population in poor countries characterized by dependence on natural resource trade to secure foreign exchange and in rich countries characterized by use of imported natural resources. Unfortunately, when consumers and producers are geographically separated, consumers are able to internalize the benefits of natural resource trade while externalizing the cost of habitat destruction.

Markets may also fail to encourage ecologically sound management when very long time horizons are involved, resulting in intergenerational inequity and irreversible damage to ecosystems. The choice of interest rate is critical in determining the optimal harvest rate for renewable resources and in turn determines their renewability. Clark (1973) has shown that the high discount (or interest) rates used by individuals to assure short-term profit maximization may cause overexploitation and exhaustion of species characterized by slow growth rates. However, even if the discount rate were zero, i.e. future values equal current values, the short lifespan of humans will result in management practices which favor current values and incomes, even if such practices have a potential to cause high social costs to future generations. For example, fluorocarbons permit packaging under pressure and a finer spray than that provided by the alternative pump spray. These benefits are directly reflected in market prices and are quite modest when compared to the catastrophic cost which would result from ozone depletion. Page (1978) contends that the inability to estimate the probability of ecocatastrophy creates indifference to the huge asymmetry between current benefits and the potential for future catastrophic costs. This makes even political solutions difficult.

Where the allocation of scarce ecological resources is concerned there will invariably be a clash between individual preferences and social benefits. Markets are just one of many arenas for resolution of these disputes. Public resource management, legislation, and regulatory agencies offer alternative methods or forums for directing management decisions. In spite of the absence of market prices, environmental decision making increasingly emphasizes the quantification of benefits and costs. This has resulted in a proliferation of new resource value concepts and valuation methods.

Willingness to pay and extending existing markets

For the individual, one estimate of the economic value of an increment in any good or service is the maximum amount that he or she is willing to pay (WTP) for it. Conversely, the value of a decrement is the minimum amount that the individual is willing to accept (WTA) for it. The prices formed in well functioning markets are one source of WTP and WTA estimates of marginal increments or decrements of goods and services. Where markets fail to provide appropriate measures of environmental values, the WTP and WTA concepts of economic value are not invalidated, but alternative 'pseudomarkets' must be used to elicit these values from individuals.

The notion that an alternative chosen will be at the expense of some opportunity foregone is central to economic decision making. For example, the cost of providing a scenic view can be directly derived from the net value of outputs and uses foregone such as timber harvest and dispersed grazing. This is referred to as an *opportunity cost*. For scenic view preservation to be economically efficient, the scenic view must be preferred over other uses. In other words, its value must exceed the cost of providing it, including opportunity costs.

Ecological goods and amenities are valued by individuals for a variety of reasons: *utilitarian (or use) value* refers to the value of using an ecosystem's products and amenities to derive both current and future benefits; these benefits include commercial outputs such as timber, outdoor activities and experiences, wildlife, and aesthetics (for examples of raw material evaluation see Bartlett (1984), who discusses valuation assumptions and methods for range forage). Individuals may also be willing to pay now for the option of using a resource in the future. Such an option price includes an amount equivalent to the expected use value plus a premium, similar to a risk premium, which a person would pay over and above the expected use value. This premium is referred to as *option value*, and is due either to uncertainty surrounding the individual's preferences or to uncertainty regarding the price or availability of the resource. This premium may be positive, negative, or zero (as in the case of preference uncertainty) but it will always be positive in the case of supply availability for a risk averse person – see Greenley et al. (1981), Bishop (1982) and Brookshire et al. (1983) for the theory and empirical studies of option value. The passage of time will likely reduce the uncertainty surrounding resource usefulness. When resource use is irreversible, individuals would be willing to sacrifice current irreversible use until uncertainty about its cost has been reduced. They would be willing to pay for increased information. This payment is termed *quasi-option value* (Arrow and Fisher, 1974; Conrad, 1980). It is not attributable to risk aversion, like option value, but is due to the value of information; this value arises in the case of resource use decisions that create irreversible damages, such as species extinction or large-scale deforestation. A final, pure non-use value is what a person may be willing to pay simply to know that a resource exists even when there is no intention of use. This *existence value* has nothing to do with preserving options for future use or paying to delay use until more information is available (see Randall and Stoll, 1980, and Brookshire et al., 1983).

In practice, the measurement of these value concepts has remained difficult and largely limited to the valuation of environmental commodities and amenities which produce direct benefits to humans. An alternative approach is Norton's (1986) concept of *contributory value*, which assigns value to environmental resources not due to their *direct* value to humans, but according to their *indirect* role in maintaining and accentuating the ecosystem processes which support these direct benefits. These include the maintenance of atmospheric and aquatic quality, the amelioration and control of climate, flood control, the maintenance of a genetic library, and the supportive role of food webs and nutrient cycling. Contributory value recognizes both the long time horizons involved in many ecosystem processes and the synergism which can result from the interaction of two or more species creating benefits of which neither is individually capable.

Though empirically elusive, contributory value does provide a useful framework for conceptualizing how natural ecosystems might be evaluated. However, as Randall (1986) contends, human preferences are focussed more on life forms than on life processes. This bias is further distorted by the fact that humans, in general, will assign higher preferences to species with commercial value, to wild relatives of domesticated species and to those which are most familiar and/or easy to empathize with, such as large mammals. Lovejoy (1986) refers to this bias against invertebrates as vertebrate chauvinism, while others point to interspecies inequity (Costanza and Daly, 1987). If it is accepted that each species, no matter how uninteresting or lacking in direct usefulness, has a role in natural ecosystems (which do provide many direct benefits to humans), it is possible to shift the focus from the imperfect perceptions of individuals to the contributory value of ecosystems as expressed through their ecological relationships. One might argue that this contributory value is an estimate of the value individuals would place on environmental services if they were fully informed about the functioning of the environment in their behalf.

Ecosystem function and economic value

Assessing the contributory value of ecosystems involves the ability to understand and model the ecosystem's role in an integrated ecologic–economic system and its response to perturbations. The models must be at a level of detail and resolution that allows the assessment of impacts (marginal products) on economically important ecosystem commodities and amenities. Several types of ecological modeling can be used for this purpose, which we define under the general heading of 'ecological–economic' models. They range from relatively simple, static, linear input–output models (Isard, 1972; Hannon, 1973, 1979; Costanza and Neill, 1984; Costanza and Hannon, 1990) to multiple regression models (Farber and Costanza, 1987) to more sophisticated nonlinear, dynamic spatial simulation models (Costanza et al., 1986). Braat and Van Lierop (1986) provide a summary of ecological–economic models currently in use.

The point that must be stressed is that the economic value of ecosystems is connected to their physical, chemical, and biological role in the overall system, *whether the public fully recognizes that role or not*. Standard economics has too often operated on the assumption that the only appropriate measures of value are the current public's subjective preferences. This yields appropriate values only if the current public is *fully informed* (among a host of other provisios). The public is most likely far from being fully informed about the ecosystem's true contribution to their own well being, and they may therefore be unable to directly value the ecosystem's services (Constanza, 1984). However, scientists may be able to derive estimates of the values that a fully informed public would produce by analyzing the structure and function of ecosystems. Economists also tend to assume that local optimizing of independent individuals will produce optimal results for the society. We have noted that this only works when there are perfect markets and that perfect markets are the exception rather than the rule in the natural resource area. Therefore, once appropriate values for ecosystem services are derived, that information must be inserted into the decision making process in order to correct the market signals.

WETLAND VALUATION

This section provides an example of the methods and problems in deriving empirical estimates of natural wetland values (details are available in Costanza and Farber, 1985a,b; and Farber and Costanza, 1987). Two different wetlands valuation techniques were used: willingness-to-pay (WTP) valuation and energy analysis (EA) valuation. These methodologies are thoroughly explained elsewhere (Costanza and Farber, 1985a,b; Farber and Costanza, 1987). We provide a brief summary here.

WTP valuation refers to valuing the particular dimensions of benefits or projects by determining society's willingness-to-pay (WTP) for those particular benefits. It requires a listing of the types of benefits and an estimate of the WTP for each one. Our analysis of the WTP for wetlands concentrated on four major categories of benefits of wetlands: commercial fishing and trapping, recreation, and storm protection. Waste treatment benefits are partially included in the other benefit estimates to the extent that water quality affects recreation, fishing, and trapping values. We were not able, as part of this analysis, to place values on the existence and option value of wetlands.

The methodology for estimating commercial productivity consisted of estimating the marginal productivity of an acre of wetlands. Our estimates concentrated on the following commercial products: shrimp, menhaden, oysters, blue crab, and furs. The critical problem in estimating the marginal productivity of wetlands was to separate the effect of human effort from the effect of the intrinsic wetland productivity, when we can only observe the total effect as reflected in harvests. Failure to make this separation results in a potentially very large overestimate of the contribution of the wetlands to commercial production. A second problem in this estimation procedure is to distinguish between the average and marginal productivity of the wetlands. This is important if there exist decreasing returns to wetlands productivity (i.e. if the productivity of a unit area of wetlands depends on the amount of remaining wetlands). Perhaps average productivity is appropriate for valuing very large wetlands projects, but valuation of small projects should use marginal productivity.

The estimation of WTP for recreational value is also complex. Two techniques can be used to make this valuation. First, one can simply ask recreational users what they would be willing to pay to use the wetlands in the project area. The problem with this technique is that respondents may engage in strategic responses. For example, if they think they may have to actually pay what they say they are willing to pay, they may state a value lower than their true value. On the other hand, if they think their response may positively impact the probability of implementing a project, they may state a value higher than their true value. A second technique is to estimate recreational users' WTP based on observations of what it actually costs them to use the project area. This technique is called the travel cost method and was our primary means of assessing the recreational value of wetlands.

The value of the wetlands for hurricane protection was obtained from a methodology which determined the reduction in expected property damages in populated areas along a gradient relative to distance from the coast. In principle, people would be willing to pay for a wetlands project according to the reduction in expected property damages attributable to the project.

The energy analysis valuation technique looks at the total biological productivity of wetland vs. adjacent open water ecosystems as a measure of their total contributory value. Primary plant production is the basis for the food chain which supports the production of economically valuable products such as fish and wildlife. It is converted to an equivalent economic value based on the cost to society to replace this energy source with fossil fuel as measured by the overall energy efficiency of economic production. This technique is comprehensive and does not require a detailed listing of all the specific benefits of wetlands, but it may overestimate their value if some of the wetland products and services are not useful (directly or indirectly) to society.

We acknowledge that the overall level of precision of our current estimates of total wetland values is not as high as we would like (due mainly to cost and data constraints), especially for important categories such as option and existence values. We suggest methods for dealing with this uncertainty in a later section.

Willingness to pay-based wetland value estimates

Commercial fishery production value of wetlands. The commercial value of wetlands for fish and wildlife harvesting is attributable to the fact that wetlands provide food and habitat necessary for the production and survival of various species. This section summarizes estimates of the value of wetlands for the harvesting of shrimp, blue crab, oysters, menhaden, and furs.

Attempts to estimate the productivity of wetlands must address the problem of separating the productivity of the wetlands themselves from the productivity of human inputs which are used in harvesting those wetlands. The problem can be outlined as follows. Suppose the harvest from a given ecological system, Q, is a function of the level of some environmental variable, W (for example, wetland acreage), and some level of human effort, M:

$$Q = \mathrm{f}(M, W) \tag{1}$$

Also, the level of human effort will be a function of the price per unit of biomass harvested, P, the cost per unit of human effort, C, and the resource abundance, which, in turn, is dependent on the level of the environmental variable:

$$M = \mathrm{g}(P, C, W) \tag{2}$$

Any change in W will result in a change in both M and Q. The productivity of the environment alone is the change in Q, holding M constant. This is referred to as the Marginal Productivity (MP) of the environmental variable. Likewise, the MP of human effort is the change in Q, holding W constant.

Simply estimating (1) will not control for the effect of changes in W on the level of human effort across observations. In addition, simply observing Q/W, the Average Product (AP) of the environmental variable will more than likely overestimate the marginal productivity of the environmental variable since there are probably decreasing returns to the environmental variable when human effort is held constant; i.e., AP > MP. More importantly, the average product implicitly includes the productivity of the human effort embodied in the dependent variable Q.

A conceptual problem also arises in the estimation of the system composed of (1) and (2). It is difficult to specify the proper environmental level (W) for migratory species because it is not clear which environment or set of environments they are dependent on and for how long. It is easiest to estimate this system for more stationary species because: (a) the environmental linkage is clearer; and (b) there will be more observations over which to estimate the system of equations.

The economic value of a unit of the environment, V, for example, an acre of wetland, is the product of MP and the dockside price, P:

$$V = \text{MP} * P \tag{3}$$

Estimates of this value (V) based on the average value of harvest per unit of environment (AP) are inaccurate since they do not account for the difference between AP and MP. Human inputs have costs and productivity, so AP will most likely overestimate the social value of a unit of the environment. Another measure has been $[(Q * B) - (M * C)]/W$, the net rent to harvesters. In a perfectly competitive harvesting industry, which is probably close to what prevails, this value is approximately zero; therefore, it will most likely underestimate the social value of a unit of the environment.

Lynne et al. (1981) developed a model of catch in which catch in year t, Q_t, depends on marsh acreage in year $t-1$, W_{t-1}, catch in year $t-1$, Q_{t-1}, and effort in year t, M_t:

$$Q_t = \beta_0 + \beta_1(\ln W_{t-1})M_t + \beta_2(\ln W_{t-1})M_t^2 + \beta_3 Q_{t-1} + \epsilon_t \tag{4}$$

The marginal productivity of marshland is then the derivative of (4) with respect to W. The economic value (V) of that marginal acre of marsh is then the marginal productivity times the dockside market value of catch.

In what follows wc present summaries of our estimates of marginal productivities of marshlands with respect to commercial fishery production. We made estimates only for shrimp, menhaden, oysters, and blue crab. These species account for approximately 95% of commercial fishery harvest in Louisiana (USDC, 1983).

In our study, brown and white shrimp catch in offshore and inshore waters in Louisiana was measured using National Marine Fisheries Service (NMFS) data for subareas of Louisiana from 1963 to 1976. These data are by area of catch, not landing. There were 24 inshore subareas and four offshore areas designated by NMFS prior to 1976. Catch is measured in heads-off pounds. Effort is measured in 24-hour days. Marsh area was measured for years 1955 and 1978 by the U.S. Fish and Wildlife Service for 7.5′ quad sheets (see Costanza et al., 1983). Although data were collected on both saline and fresh marsh, this study uses the sum of the two. Area data for years between these two years were estimated by simple linear interpolation.

---

* acre ≈ 0.4047 ha.

* lb, pound (avdp) ≈ 0.454 kg.

TABLE 1

Estimated marginal productivities per acre of marsh for brown and white, inshore and offshore shrimp (heads-off pounds/acre)

Type of model	Inshore		Offshore	
	brown	white	brown	white
Non-lagged	1.60	1.44	0.90	1.23
Lagged	1.25	0.86	–	–

lb/acre ≈ 1.12 kg/ha.

Our simplest estimates of the model excluded the lagged catch value. Separate regressions were performed for brown and white, and for inshore and offshore shrimp. There was no consideration of possible changes in the structure of the equations over time. We fit equation (4) for both the lagged and non-lagged case to estimate the values of the parameters β_1 and β_2. All the parameters and equations were significant with R^2 ranging from 0.67 to 0.90.

The marginal productivity of marsh based on equation (4) is then given by:

$$\mathrm{MP_m} = (\beta_1 + \beta_2 M)M/W \tag{5}$$

For inshore areas, the sample means of M and W for brown shrimp were 1426 days and 18 249 ha, respectively. The marginal productivity estimates based on these data are summarized in Table 1.

Unfortunately, there are not sufficient data to estimate the model employed above for menhaden, oysters, or crabs. For menhaden, we assumed that the marginal and average products of estuarine area (marsh plus open water) are equal for menhaden harvest. The entire 1983 Gulf Coast catch was 2036 million lb. Using total Gulf Coast estuarine area of 14 million acres, this implies an average and marginal productivity of approximately 145 lb/acre. This estimate could be biased upward because marginal product is generally lower than average product. It could also be biased downward since we divide through by the sum of marsh plus open water area. If marsh is more productive of menhaden per acre than open water (as we suspect it is) then this procedure underestimates the per-acre production of marsh. In lieu of better data, however, we feel our current estimate is the best that can be done.

We used the results from a study of the blue crab productivity of western Florida salt marshes for estimating the marginal product of Louisiana wetlands for blue crab. Lynne et al. (1981) estimated a bioeconomic model for blue crab harvesting that is similar to the system outlined above. They estimated that the marginal productivity of the Florida salt marsh is 2.3 lb

TABLE 2

Acres of marsh open water and total recorded pounds of oyster meat harvested from 1948 to 1978

State	(a) Area of marsh and open water (million)	(b) Recorded total harvest (million lb)
La.	7.3	283.5
Fla.	3.0	78.1
Texas	2.7	66.1
Miss.	0.6	47.7
Ala.	0.4	33.2
Total	14.0	508.6

Source: Allen et al. (1984, p. 120).

of blue crab per acre per year. Although they do not specifically derive the average salt marsh productivity, one can use their figures to derive an average productivity of approximately 28 lb of blue crab per acre of salt marsh per year. In contrast, they estimate that the marginal productivity of effort is 214 lb per trap per year, while the average productivity of traps is 435 lb per year. This illustrates the inaccuracy of using average productivities to measure environmental values.

We would have liked to estimate a model for oysters similar to the one for shrimp above. Data were by area of oyster landing rather than area of catch. Without data on the origins of oyster harvest it was not possible to relate harvest to the associated level of the environmental variables (marsh area).

The results of several other studies were therefore used to estimate the marginal product of wetlands for oysters. Batie and Wilson (1978) estimated the oyster productivity of Virginia wetlands using an equation similar to (1) and found a marginal product of 1.66 lb/acre in the county with the greatest wetlands area in their sample. Aggregate data presented in Allen et al. (1984) and shown in Table 2 can be used to estimate average oyster productivity of estuarine areas. This table shows estuarine area (marsh plus open water) in acres and pounds of oyster meat harvested as reported between 1948 and 1978 in five Gulf Coast states. Using the total values, the annual recorded harvest per acre of marsh plus open water over the 30-year period was 1.21 lb. A more sophisticated estimate of marginal product is obtained by regressing harvest in Table 2 (H) on estuarine acreage (A) shown in that table. The resulting least-squares equation is:

$$\underset{}{H} = \underset{(2.3)}{2.03} + \underset{(3.4)}{35.60A} \qquad F = 35.44 \tag{6}$$

TABLE 3

Summary of estimated economic value of wetland productivity for commercial fishery harvest.

(a) Species	(b) Basis	(c) Annual MP estimate (lb/acre)	(d) 1983 ex-vessel price [a] ($/acre)	(e) Value of annual MP ($/acre)
Shrimp	Marsh Area			
brown inshore		1.60	$2.10	$3.36
white		1.44	2.10	3.02
brown offshore		0.90	2.10	1.89
white		1.23	2.10	2.58
Menhaden	Marsh and open water area	145.00 [b]	0.04	5.80
Oyster	Marsh and open water area	6.00	1.34	8.04
Blue crab	Salt marsh area	2.30	0.29	0.67
Total				$25.36

[a] USDC (1983).
[b] Assuming MP-average product.

Since the harvest data are for a 30-year period, the annual marginal product of estuarine area implied by equation (6) is 1.19 lb of oyster meat per acre. This estimate is roughly equal to the cruder average product estimate above.

The data in Table 2 are only for recorded harvests collected by NMFS. This includes oysters used only for canning. Sack and counter oysters are unreported. Lindall et al. (1972, p. 139) found that the total oyster production is five times the reported harvest. We assume a canning oyster marginal product of 1.20 lb, so the total marginal product is estimated to be 6.00 lb per acre of estuarine area per year.

Table 3 summarizes the commercial fishery productivities of marsh and estuarine areas by the four primary species. Column (b) shows the environmental variable being evaluated. For example, shrimp productivity was estimated by using the total of fresh and salt marsh acreage. Column (c) shows our annual marginal productivity estimates. Column (d) shows the 1983 ex-vessel price per pound. We assumed all shrimp were valued at the same price per pound. Column (e) is derived from columns (c) and (d). It shows the economic value of the marginal acre, and is the product of columns (c) and (d). For example, the estimated economic value of the annual marginal productivity for brown inshore shrimp was $3.36 per acre of marsh. The sum of all these economic values is $25.36 per acre of marsh per year. Discounting at 8% gives a present value per acre of $317. Discounting at 3% gives a present value per acre of $845.

Fur trapping value of wetlands. Muskrat and nutria accounted for 78% of the value of Louisiana trapping in 1977 (Davis, 1978, p. 87). The muskrat is primarily a brackish-to-intermediate marsh species. In this environment, the muskrat yield is approximately 0.98 pelts per acre. Freshwater marshes, the primary habitat of nutria, yield 0.88 pelts per acre (Davis, 1978, p. 85).

There is some difficulty placing a price on these pelts. The recent increase in the value of the dollar has reduced prices to less than one-half their 1979–81 value. We used the 1980–81 price of $6 for eastern muskrat pelts and $7 for eastern nutria pelts as expected average prices and assumed these prices to be constant over time. Using the pelt productivity values above, the annual value of pelt productivity is $12.04 per acre. At a 8% discount, this generates a present value of $151 per acre; at 3%, a present value of $401 per acre.

Recreation value of wetlands. Wetlands have values as recreational areas. They are used for fishing, hunting, photographing, boating, etc. These are non-commercial uses of wetlands. A survey of recreational users was undertaken on various days over a 1-year period to determine willingness-to-pay to preserve wetlands for recreational purposes in Terrebonne Parish, Louisiana. The survey was designed to utilize the travel cost method of evaluating consumer surplus from use of a site, and the contingent valuation method. The details of the survey and data are contained in Costanza and Farber (1985b) and Farber and Costanza (1987). Here we summarize the method and results.

The sampling procedure consisted of placing self-addressed, stamped questionnaires on windshields of all vehicles parked in the morning at 27 boat launch facilities in Terrebonne Parish on various dates throughout the period July 1984 to June 1985. The sum of the average number of vehicles per day across all sites was 563.29 on weekends and 132.1 on weekdays.

A total of 7837 questionnaires were distributed, and 1126 were returned for a response rate of 14.4%. There were 6248 questionnaires distributed on weekends, with a 15.0% response rate; and 1589 on weekdays with a 11.7% response rate.

There was no explicit attempt to determine non-response bias. However, we thought that persons placing a higher value on these particular wetlands would be more likely to return questionnaires. This could mean that response rates may decline with distance from the site. In order to test this, we instituted a lottery with several prizes ($50, $30, and $20) on weekends in

February and March, 1985. The response rate for weekend samples increased from 18.5% in the pre-lottery period to 24.3% in the lottery period.

In order to implement the travel cost methodology, seven rings of 35-mile * increments in radii were constructed centered at Dulac, Louisiana. Each parish or county of Louisiana, Texas, Mississippi and Alabama was placed in one of the rings or in a rest-of-world (ROW) category. The localized use of these wetlands is apparent from the fact that 78% of the respondents came from ring 1, and 98% from rings 1 through 3. This localized use may make the travel cost methodology inadequate for determining willingness-to-pay.

We estimated the value of travel time by determining the total cost of travel time to the typical user group in the sample. The typical user group consisted of 2.72 persons, with one male head, 0.66 female spouses, 0.51 children, and 0.55 non-family members. The average wage rate of male respondents in the sample was $13.37. Using the fact that a previous study found southern female wages to be 70% those of males, the average spouse wage was assumed to be $9.36. The non-family member was assumed to be male. Children were assumed to have zero wages. Weighting these wages by the number of members yielded average total hourly wages of the typical user group of $26.90. The estimated annual WTP using this travel cost method was $3.9 million/year.

A second method was to use respondents' answers to the direct question regarding their willingness-to-pay for the preservation of the Terrebonne Parish wetlands (contingent valuation). In particular, persons were asked what they would be willing to pay annually for the sake of their entire household. The mean response in the sample was $103.48 per household annually.

The number of different households using these wetlands annually must be estimated indirectly. An independent survey of recreational saltwater fishermen (Bertrand, 1980) found that 110 373 licensed fishermen used the LaFourche/Terrebonne area at least once in the 1982–83 season. Since Terrebonne constitutes approximately one-half of the total LaFourche/Terrebonne wetlands (Costanza and Farber, 1985b), we assumed only 55 186 of these persons used the Terrebonne area. Multiplying this by the annual WTP per household ($103.48) gives an annual total WTP of $5.7 million. This is slightly above the travel cost annual estimates. However, since the direct question referred to the head of household's WTP and several family members may have licenses, this direct estimate is not too far from the travel cost estimate. For example, if we assume the 2.17 members of a typical

mile ≈ 1.609 km.

family user unit are licensed, the $103.48 amounts to $47.69 per person. The resulting annual WTP is then $2.6 million, only slightly less than the travel cost method result.

Depending on assumptions made about population growth, the present value estimates range from $34.2 million in the no growth situation to $40.8 million if population grows at a 1.3% annual rate when the discount rate is 8%. Assuming the population growth case, this amounts to $46 per acre of estuarine area (890 000 acres) using a 8% discount rate, and $181 per acre using a 3% discount rate.

Storm protection value of wetlands. Wetlands provide storm protection for urbanized areas in several ways. The marshes create surface friction for both tidal surges and winds. They also aid in reducing the heat source of energy for the storms. The result is that marshes help reduce tidal surge levels and wind velocities of storms. A very important value of coastal marshes is therefore their value in protection against personal and property damage due to storms

Costanza and Farber (1985b) contains our analysis of the hurricane protection value of wetlands for protection from storm surge and wind damage. Farber (1987) contains a more detailed analysis of the value of coastal wetlands for protection from wind damage only. We used U.S. Army Corps of Engineering estimates of property damages resulting from four recent Gulf Coast hurricanes, and adjusted these to 1983 dollars using a construction price index. These damage estimates included both wind and flooding damages. Damages were given by county. By measuring the distance of the center of a county from the coast, and controlling for population size, hurricane strength, distance from the path of the hurricane, and probability of hurricane incidence, we estimated the increase in expected property damages resulting from being closer to the landfall of a hurricane.

If Terrebonne wetlands receded by one mile, expected damages in a four-parish area would increase by $5 752 816 annually. The loss of a 207-ft wide strip running the length of Terrebonne parish coastline would increase expected damages by $128.30 per acre of the coastal strip annually. Discounting these values by 8% yields a present value of the strip of $71.9 million; and a present value of 1 acre in the coastal strip of $1604. Assuming population grows at 1.3% annually, the present value of such a strip for storm protection is $1915 per acre, or a total of $85.9 million for the entire strip. This is a relevant value for consideration of projects designed to stop rapid, wide-area recession and coastal erosion. It is not really appropriate for evaluating projects designed to affect erosion in areas that are not direct coastal areas; unless, of course, these internal areas eventually have an impact on coastal recession.

Another way of looking at the protection value of Terrebonne wetlands is to determine how much higher expected property damages would be if they were permitted to continue receding at their present rates. Using recent recession rates (approximately 12 ft/year), the present discounted value (at 8%) of increased expected property damages lies between \$2.1 and \$3.1 million. This is relevant in determining whether to initiate projects directed toward stopping long-term recession.

Energy analysis of wetland values

The theoretical basis for energy analysis as an economic value estimation tool is discussed in Costanza and Farber (1985b) and Turner et al. (1988). The method looks at the total amount of energy captured by natural ecosystems as an estimate of their potential to do useful work for the economy. It yields an estimate of a comprehensive (in that it should include all possible useful outputs) upper bound on the economic value of the products of natural systems. It is an upper bound because not all of the work done by the system is necessarily useful to the economy.

Gross primary production.

The energy analysis methodology can be quite complicated (cf. Costanza, 1980, Costanza and Herendeen,1984; Costanza and Neill, 1984). For the purposes of this study we employ a simplified technique that is readily calculable (we discuss its shortcomings later). This technique uses the Gross Primary Production (GPP) of the whole ecosystem as an index of the solar energy captured by the system, and converts this energy value into dollars using a single dollar–energy conversion factor (described below). GPP is a measure of the solar energy that is used by the plants in the system to fix carbon into organic molecules. This 'primary' production is then used to power all the plants and animals in the system. The plants and animals in the system also moderate water flow, sedimentation and other variables. GPP for an ecosystem can be thought of as analogous to GNP for an economy: both are crude (but essential) measures of overall system performance that say nothing about the internal distribution of production and must therefore be used with caution. GPP and GNP measure the value of inputs (or outputs) of ecological and economic systems, respectively.

The energy analysis procedure can be summarized as follows:

(1) Determine by field measurements and laboratory experiments the GPP of the natural area in question, under the with and without project conditions.
(2) Convert this estimate (usually measured in grams of carbon fixed per time unit or the heat equivalent energy content of the carbon) to fossil fuel equivalents (FFE) by considering the fuel efficiency of each source.

(3) Convert the FFE value into dollars using an economy-wide ratio of economic value per unit of energy, usually the ratio of GNP to total-economy energy use (measured in FFE).

All three steps involve uncertainty. Below we discuss the steps in more detail, pointing out the potential sources of error.

GPP measurement methods. Gross Primary Production (GPP) in plants is usually measured by analysis of gas exchange. During photosynthesis plants take up carbon dioxide from the air and fix it into higher energy organic molecules. They also give off oxygen as a by-product. GPP is a measure of how much carbon plants take up (or conversely, how much oxygen they give off) and, therefore, how much high-energy organic matter they create. The measurement is usually done with an infrared gas analyzer that detects carbon dioxide concentration differences for terrestrial plants, or with oxygen meters for submerged aquatic plants. Like most field measurements, GPP measurement is much more complicated than the simple description given above. Hopkinson (1978) gives a discussion of the technique and some of the problems and inaccuracies. Despite problems, GPP remains a popular and useful index of overall ecosystem energy capture. Table 4 gives some examples of GPP estimates for Louisiana wetlands and aquatic habitats.

Conversion to fossil fuel equivalents. GPP estimates are frequently stated in grams of carbon or calories of plant biomass per unit area per unit time. The first step in converting this to a measure of equivalent economic value is to convert it to energy units more directly relevant as input to the economy, i.e.

TABLE 4

Gross primary production (GPP) estimates for Louisiana wetland and open water habitats.

Habitat type	Gross primary production (cal m^{-2} $year^{-1}$)
Salt marsh	48 000
Brackish marsh	70 300
Fresh marsh	48 500
Average marsh	55 600
Salt aquatic	6 600
Brackish aquatic	5 100
Fresh aquatic	9 300
Average aquatic	7 000
Coastal plankton	3 600

All values are directly from Hopkinson (1978). cal, calorie (International Table) = 4.1868 J (def).

TABLE 5

Energy quality conversion factors (from Odum and Odum, 1976)

Type of energy	(a) Calorie cost (calories of heat to make 1 FFE calorie)	(b) Fossil-fuel equivalents (FFE calories/per heat calorie) (1/column a)
Heat from sun's rays, uncollected	10000	0.0001
Sunlight	2000	0.0005
Gross plant production	20	0.05
Wood, collected	2	0.05
Coal and oil, delivered for use	1	1.0
Energy in elevated water	0.33	3.0
Electricity	0.25	4.0

fossil fuels. Fossil fuels are a much more concentrated, higher quality form of energy than plant biomass. One way of seeing this is to consider how much extra energy is required to upgrade biomass to fossil fuel; for example, in a biogas process. Another way is to consider the relative number of calories of biomass that would have to be burned in a power plant to produce the same amount of electricity as a given quantity of oil. Both of these methods have been used to estimate the 'energy quality factor' of biomass relative to fossil fuel. An approximate average is 0.05 cal biomass/cal fossil fuel (Odum and Odum, 1976), indicating that unprocessed biomass, such as that measured by GPP, is about 20 times less concentrated than fossil fuel. Table 5 lists energy quality conversion factors for various energy forms.

Conversion to economic value. One can look at the overall ratio of the value of economic output to energy input in the economy as a crude way to convert plant production to an equivalent economic value. This step is certainly the most controversial, with critics arguing that energy consumption and economic value are not necessarily related (Huettner, 1982). But recent studies provide supportive evidence that total direct and indirect energy consumption (embodied energy) and dollar values are indeed highly correlated in the U.S. economy (Costanza, 1980, 1984; Cleveland et al., 1984; Costanza and Herendeen, 1984). We therefore use a conversion factor based on these studies to give a crude estimate of the economic value of ecosystem production from their GPP estimates converted to FFE.

Habitat interdependence. The GPP technique outlined above does not account for the interdependence between habitats or differences in productivity within the same habitat type. For example, all salt marsh is assumed to have the same GPP, regardless of what other habitats it is adjacent to or to the special conditions of the site. This is an approximation, but the level of current knowledge is such that it is the best available approximation.

Louisiana wetland value estimates via energy analysis. Table 6 lists the gross primary production estimates for relevant Louisiana wetlands and aquatic systems and their estimated economic value using the simplified energy analysis methods outlined above. The values range from \$47 acre^{-1} year^{-1} for open ocean (coastal plankton) to \$914 acre^{-1} year^{-1} for brackish marsh. The relevant numbers are the change in value from wetland systems to open water systems, since this is the major impact of coastal erosion. These are listed in column (c). They range from \$509 acre^{-1} year^{-1} (for fresh marsh to fresh aquatic conversion) to \$847 acre^{-1} year^{-1} for brackish marsh to brackish aquatic conversion, with an average of \$631 acre^{-1} year^{-1}. The

TABLE 6

Gross primary production and EA-based economic value estimates for relevant Louisiana wetland and marine habitats

Habitat type	Total energy captured measured by GPP [a] (kcal m^{-2} year^{-1})	Annual equivalent dollar value [b] (\$ acre^{-1} year^{-1})	Net marsh-aquatic change in annual value (\$ acre^{-1} year^{-1})	Present value (\$ acre^{-1}) assuming specified discount rate [d] 8%	3%
Salt marsh	48000	624			
Salt aquatic	6600	86	538	6700	18000
Brackish marsh	70300	914			
Brackish aquatic	5130	67	847	10602	28200
Fresh marsh	48500	630			
Fresh aquatic	9300	121	509	6400	17000
Coastal plankton	3600	47	Average 631	7900	21000
Spoil banks [c]	13000	169			

[a] GPP is gross primary production. Values are from Hopkinson 1979.
[b] Based on conversion factors of 0.05 coal equivalent (CE) kcal/GPP kcal (Table 5), and 15000 CE kcal/1983 dollar (from Costanza, 1980) and 4047 m^2 acre^{-1}. The overall conversion factor from GPP (in kcal m^{-2}) to estimated economic value (in \$ acre^{-1} year^{-1}) is therefore: $(0.05 \times 4047)/15000 = 0.013$.
[c] Estimated from values for upland systems.
[d] Rounded to nearest \$100.

present value of an infinite stream of these values using 8% and 3% discount rates are given in columns (d) and (e), respectively. These yield values for average marsh/aquatic conversions of \$7900/acre and \$21 000/acre, respectively.

Summary wetland value estimates

The estimation of the economic value of natural wetlands is a difficult and complex task, but it is essential to rational management. We have employed both willingness-to-pay (WTP) and energy analysis (EA) techniques to improve this estimate. Table 7 summarizes our findings.

One problem in communicating our findings is that individual elements of the overall estimates are of varying precision and yet they must be added to produce a total average value. In Table 7 we list totals for the WTP-based analysis. We have not included any estimate for option and existence values, which studies in other areas have shown to be potentially large components of the total. This indicates that our total WTP estimate is probably still very conservative.

Our 'best estimate' values are given as a range in Table 7. These are \$2429–6400 per acre (assuming an 8% discount rate) and \$8977–17 000 per acre (assuming a 3% discount rate). Which discount rate may be most appropriate under given conditions is discussed further on, as are methods for dealing effectively with the current range of uncertainty in wetland valuation by using a assurance bonding fund system.

TABLE 7

Summary of wetland value estimates (1983 dollars)

Method	Per-acre present value (\$) at specified discount rate	
	8%	3%
WTP based		
commercial fishery	317	846
trapping	151	401
recreation	46	181
storm protection	1915	7549
Total	2429	8977
Option and existence values	?	?
EA-based GPP conversion	6400–10 600	17 000–28 200
'Best estimate'	2429– 6 400	8 977–17 000

DISCUSSION OF CURRENT VALUATION RESULTS

This section discusses what we perceive as the potential estimation problems that we encountered in valuing wetlands and outlines future studies that would be most effective in improving the estimates.

WTP-based estimates

First, the estimates of commercial values of wetlands may be overstated for some species since we used the average, rather than marginal, product of the marsh. Second, recreational value may be underestimated. The travel cost method works well if a site attracts persons from a wide range of distances. However, our evidence is that there is very intensive localized use of the Terrebonne wetlands. Since travel costs to local users are small, our estimate of their willingness-to-pay for access is also small. However, there may be no better techniques at the moment since directly asking persons their willingness-to-pay is plagued with many problems. Third, the value of wetlands for hurricane protection is important but our estimation methodology is crude. We feel it is very important to spend more effort in improving the accuracy of the flood damage benefits of wetlands. The estimation methodology we used probably overstates hurricane protection value since some of the hurricanes studied passed over coastal areas with significantly more upland area than those passing over Louisiana wetlands. Fourth, loss of wetland reduces habitats and food sources and reduces natural waste treatment capacity. We would need to know the WTP for loss of treatment capacity. Finally, we were unable to measure the value placed on wetlands by persons who do not directly use the wetland and/or who do not consume products produced by wetlands. For example, some people may be willing to pay to preserve wetlands in order to preserve the option of using them in the future. Also, people may obtain pleasure from knowing the wetlands exist; perhaps because of indirect pleasure they receive from such things as photographs, literature, etc. pertaining to those wetlands. These values may be considerable. These option and existence values would be good topics for future research. We attempted to estimate these through a statewide survey; however, the response rate was so low that we realized we would not have enough funds to complete the estimation.

EA-based estimates

The EA estimate may be an upper bound on the total value of wetlands. In practice there is enough imprecision in the data and uncertainty in the methods to make it difficult to tell whether the actual numbers are over or underestimates of the true value. It was encouraging that the EA based estimate was higher than the total WTP based estimate by an amount that seemed reasonable, given the known omissions from the WTP estimate. But more research on the general relationship of energy use to economic activity, and the specific relationship of GPP to economic value are needed to improve the quality of this estimate, and to determine its role in the overall valuation procedure.

DISCOUNTING

Often the present vs. future issue is thought to be objectively decided by discounting. But discounting at best only reflects the subjective valuation of the future to presently existing individual members of human society. Discounting is simply a numerical way to operationalize the value judgment that: (a) the near future is worth more than the distant future to the present generation of humans, and (b) beyond some point the worth of the future to the present generation of humans is negligible. Economists tend to treat discounting as rational, optimizing behavior based on people's inherent preferences for current over future consumption.

There is evidence, however, that discounting behavior may be symptomatic of a kind of semi-rational, sub-optimizing behavior known as a 'social trap'. A social trap is any situation in which the short-run, local reinforcements guiding individual behavior are inconsistent with the long-run, global best interest of the individual or society (Platt, 1973; Cross and Guyer, 1980; Costanza, 1987). We go through life making decisions about which path to take based largely on the 'road signs', the short-run, local, reinforcements that we perceive most directly. These short-run reinforcements can include monetary incentives, social acceptance or admonishment, and physical pleasure or pain. Problems arise, however, when the road signs are inaccurate or misleading. In these cases we can be trapped into following a path that is ultimately detrimental because of our reliance on the road signs. Discounting may allow individuals to give too little weight to the future (or other species, other groups or classes of humans, etc.) and thus helps to set the trap. Economists, while recognizing that individual behavior may not always lead to optimal social behavior, generally assume that discounting the future is an appropriate thing to do. The psychological evidence indicates, however, that humans have problems responding to reinforcements that are not immediate (in time and space), and can be led into disastrous situations *because* they discount too much.

It can therefore be argued that the discount rate used by the government for public policy decisions on common property resources (like wetlands) should be significantly lower than the rate used by individuals for private investment decisions. The government should have greater interest in the future than individuals currently in the market because continued social existence, stability, and harmony are public goods for which the government is responsible, and for which current individuals may not be willing to fully pay (Arrow, 1976).

Discounting future value by the rate of interest also provides a tight link between ecological destruction and macroeconomic policy. Any exploited species whose natural rate of population growth is less than the real rate of interest is under threat of extinction, even in the absence of common property problems. While Paul Voelker and the Federal Reserve probably do not worry about the effect of U.S. interest rate policy on deforestation in the Amazon or destruction of Louisiana wetlands, such links really do exist, and they probably should not.

In terms of our wetland valuation problem all this merely increases the uncertainty concerning the total present value of wetlands, because the appropriate discount rate is uncertain and it makes a big difference in the results. We have stated estimates for a range of discount rates (3%–8%) in order to demonstrate how much uncertainty is introduced by uncertainty in the discount rate, and have given arguments for why a lower discount rate may be more appropriate for wetland valuation decisions. Below we consider a method to deal with this uncertainty.

DEALING WITH IMPRECISE VALUES USING AN ASSURANCE BONDING SYSTEM

One fundamental problem with our current methods of wetlands management is that those parties that damage and destroy wetlands are not charged for the true social cost of that damage or destruction. Two reasons often given for this are: (a) we don't know what to charge them and/or (b) charging them anything implies that wetlands can be sold and they will just pay the money and continue on their merry destructive ways. Therefore we cannot accept any charging scheme and must simply prevent all destruction of wetlands.

These ideas have guided wetlands management over the last several decades and the results have been abysmal. Wetland destruction has accelerated, not abated. Canal dredging and other hydrologically disruptive activities have resulted in a current land loss rate of over 100 km^2/year in coastal Louisiana (Craig et al., 1979; Gagliano et al., 1981; Scaife et al., 1983). To understand why it has not worked we must understand the structure of the short term reinforcements facing the various players in the game of wetlands management. The situation is a 'social trap' because the narrow, short term incentives of those damaging the wetlands are inconsistent with the long term good of the system (Costanza, 1987).

To turn this trap into a trade-off one should charge the parties responsible the full cost of the ultimate environmental damage, at the time the damage is done. To do this one needs to know the economic value to society of coastal marshes and the amount of marsh destroyed by each activity. Since there is much uncertainty involved in these estimates the 'worst case' costs should be assumed and the burden of proof that the damages are in fact less than the worst case shifted to the parties who benefited or stand to benefit (see Costanza and Perrings, 1990, for a more complete discussion of this approach).

For example, our study concluded that each acre of coastal wetlands in Louisiana has a present value to society of roughly \$2500–\$17000 per acre. This range of values was due to uncertainties in the valuation procedures and the discount rate. Increasing the accuracy of the valuation estimates is an expensive proposition, and one that would stress the research budget of the state.

To effectively eliminate this trap one could charge the parties responsible for marsh destruction (ie. oil companies for dredging access canals through wetlands or developers wishing to convert wetlands to other uses) the \$17 000 per acre worst-case cost. These fees would go into an assurance bond to be returned to the developers in the event that damages are less than the worst case, or to be used for mitigating environmental damages by purchasing marshland elsewhere, backfilling canals, freshwater diversion, etc. (Costanza and Perrings, 1990). It would allow managers much more flexibility than the current 'mitigation banking' schemes because it is not limited to simple acre for acre tradeoffs. The responsible parties could lower the fee or secure a return of the bond by proving that the damages are actually less than the worst case assumption (by funding independent studies) or by minimizing the amount of wetlands they damage in the process of accomplishing their goal (by directional drilling, immediate backfilling, etc.). In either case the cause of wetland conservation would be served without unduly hindering the search for oil and gas, by converting the trap to a trade-off. Wetland developers would have strong economic incentives to minimize their damage to wetlands, and to fund additional needed research into the functions of wetlands (in order to narrow the range of uncertainty in wetland valuation estimates). Money would be held in the bond to be paid back to developers if future research aimed at reducing the uncertainty of the valuation estimates proves that they were overcharged.

SUMMARY AND CONCLUSIONS

Markets for ecological goods and services are far from perfect and we cannot rely on the free market to efficiently allocate these resources. The current system, which misallocates these resources, is better described as a social trap. Escaping from the trap involves turning it into an economic trade-off by making long run social costs, risks, and uncertainty incumbent on individuals and firms in the short run using fees and subsidies. Quantifying the proper level of fees and subsidies should be tied to models of the ecological impact of activities, but the burden of proof as to the magnitude of these damages should fall on the parties that stand to profit from them, not the general public. This addresses the distribution and incentive issues inherent in the problem in an equitable way. A flexible ecological cost charging and assurance bonding scheme can be designed that induces ecotechnological innovation by making it the most economically attractive option in the short run (as well as the long run). Implementation of such a scheme could go a long way toward allowing the development of a more ecological economics.

ACKNOWLEDGEMENTS

This research was funded in part by the Coastal Protection Section of the Louisiana Department of Natural Resources and the Terrebonne Parish Commission. Dr. Donald Boesch of the Louisiana Universities Marine Consortium and Dr. Donald Davis of Nichols State University provided much useful input data, encouragement, and advice. We are grateful to D. Pearce, K. Roberts, D. Chambers, K.J. Meyer-Arendt, D. Boesch, D. Davis, and J. Edmonson and J. Bartholomew for useful comments on earlier drafts.

REFERENCES

Allen, R.L., Turner, R.E. and Day, J.W., 1984. Oyster management and environmental influences in the Gulf of Mexico, 1880–1978. Center for Wetland Resources, Louisiana State University, Baton Rouge, La.

Arrow, K.J., 1976. The rate of discount for long-term public investment. In: H. Ashley, R.L. Rudman and C. Shipple (Editors), Energy and the Environment: A Risk Benefit Approach. Pergamon, New York, pp. 113–141.

Arrow, K.J. and Fisher, A.C., 1974. Environmental preservation, uncertainty, and irreversibility. Q. J. Econ., 55: 313–319.

Bartlett, E.T., 1984. Estimating benefits of range for wildland management and planning. In: G.L. Peterson and A. Randall (Editors), Valuation of Wildland Benefits. Westview, Boulder, Colo., pp. 143–157.

Batie, S.S. and Wilson, J.R., 1978. Economic values attributable to Virginia's coastal wetlands as inputs in oyster production. South. J. Agric. Econ., 10: 111–117.

Bertrand, A.L., 1980. Marine recreational finfisherman in Louisiana. Coastal Ecology and Fisheries Institute, Louisiana State University, Baton Rouge, La., 15 pp.

Bishop, R., 1982. Option value: an exposition and extension. Land Econ., 58: 1–15.

Braat, L.C. and Van Lierop, W.F.J., 1985. 1986. Economic–ecological modeling: an introduction to methods and applications. Ecol. Modelling, 31: 33–44.

Brookshire, D.S., Eubanks, L.S. and Randall, A., 1983. Estimating option prices and existence values for wildlife resources. Land Econ., 59: 1–15.

Cicchetti, C.J. and Smith, V.K., 1973. Congestion, quality, deterioration, and optimal use: Wilderness recreation in the Spanish Peaks primitive area. Soc. Sci. Res., 2: 15–30.

Clark, C.W., 1973. The economics of overexploitation. Science, 181: 630–634.

Cleveland, C.J., Costanza, R., Hall, C.A.S. and Kaufmann, R., 1984. Energy and the United States economy: a biophysical perspective. Science, 255: 890–897.

Conrad, J.M., 1980. Quasi option value and the expected value of information. Q. J. Econ., 94: 813–820.

Costanza, R., 1980. Embodied energy and economic valuation. Science, 210: 1219–1224.

Costanza, R., 1984. Natural resource valuation and management: Toward an ecological economics. In: A.-M. Jansson (Editor), Integration of Economy and Ecology: An Outlook for the Eighties. University of Stockholm Press, Stockholm, pp. 7–18.

Costanza, R., 1987. Social traps and environmental policy. BioScience, 37: 407–412.

Costanza, R. and Daly, H.E., 1987. Toward an ecological economics. Ecol. Modelling, 38: 1–7.

Costanza, R. and Farber, S.C., 1985a. Theories and methods of valuation of natural systems: a comparison of willingness-to-pay and energy analysis based approaches. Man Environ. Space Time, 4: 1–38.

Costanza, R. and Farber, S.C., 1985b. The economic value of coastal wetlands in Louisiana. Final Report to the Louisiana Department of Natural Resources. Center for Wetland Resources, Louisiana State University, Baton Rouge, La.

Costanza, R. and Hannon, B., 1990. Multicommodity flows in ecosystem analysis: Dealing with the 'mixed units' problem In: B.C. Patten and S.E. Jørgensen (Editors), Complex Ecology. Prentice Hall, Englewood Cliffs, NJ (in press).

Costanza, R. and Herendeen, R.A., 1984. Embodied energy and economic value in the United States economy: 1963, 1967, and 1972. Resour. Energy, 6: 129–163.

Costanza, R. and Neill, C., 1984. Energy intensities, Interdependence, and value in ecological systems: a linear programming approach. J. Theor. Biol., 106: 41–57.

Costanza, R. and Perrings, C.H., 1990. A flexible assurance bonding system for improved environmental management. Ecol. Econ. (in press).

Costanza, R, Neill, C., Leibowitz, S.G., Fruci, J.R., Bahr, L.M. and Day, J.W., 1983. Ecological models of the Mississippi Deltaic Plain Region: Data collection and presentation. FWS/OBS-82/68, Division of Biological Services, Fish and Wildlife Services, Washington, D.C., 342 pp.

Costanza, R., Sklar, F.H. and Day, J.W., Jr., 1986. Modeling spatial and temporal succession in the Atchafalaya/Terrebonne marsh/estuarine complex in South Louisiana. In: D.A. Wolfe (Editor), Estuarine Variability. Academic Press, New York, pp. 387–404.

Craig, N.J., Turner, R.E. and Day, J.W., Jr., 1979. Land loss in coastal Louisiana (U.S.A.). Environ. Manag., 3: 133–144.

Cross, J.G. and Guyer, M.J., 1980. Social Traps. University of Michigan Press, Ann Arbor, Mich.

Davis, W., 1978. Wetlands trapping in Louisiana. Geosci. Man, 19: 81–92.

Farber, S.C., 1987. The value of coastal wetlands for protection of property against hurricane wind damage. J. Environ. Econ. Manage., 14: 143–151.

Farber, S. and Costanza, R., 1987. The economic value of wetlands systems. J. Environ. Manage., 24: 41–51.

Gagliano, S.M., Meyer-Arendt, K.J. and Wicker, K.M., 1981. Land loss in the Mississippi River Deltaic Plain. Trans. Gulf Coast Assoc. Geol. Soc., 31: 295–299.

Greenley, D.A., Walsh, R.G. and Young, R.A., 1981. Option value: empirical evidence from a case study of recreation and water quality. Q. J. Econ., 95: 657–673.

Hannon, B., 1973. The structure of ecosystems, J. Theor. Biol., 41: 535–546.

Hannon, B., 1979. Total energy costs in ecosystems. J. Theor. Biol., 80: 271–293.

Hopkinson, C.S., Jr., 1978. The relation of man and nature in Barataria Basin, Louisiana, Ph.D. dissertation, Louisiana State University, Baton Rouge, La., 236 pp.

Huetner, D.A., 1982. Economic values and embodied energy (with reply by R. Costanza). Science, 216: 1141–1143.

Isard, W., 1972. Ecologic–economic analysis for regional development. Free Press, New York, 270 pp.

Lindall, N., Hall, J.R., Sykes, J.E. and Arnold, E.L., 1972. Louisiana coastal zone: analyses of resources and resource development needs in connection with estuarine ecology. National Marine Fisheries Service, St. Petersburg, Fla., 315 pp.

Lovejoy, T.E., 1986. Species leave the ark one by one. In: B.G. Norton (Editor), The Preservation of Species. Princeton University Press, Princeton, NJ., pp. 13–27.

Lynne, G.D., Conroy, P.D. and Prochaska, F.J., 1981. Economic valuation of marsh areas for marine production processes (Florida). J. Environ. Econ. Manage., 8: 175–186.

Norton, B.G., 1986. On the inherent danger of undervaluing species. In: B.G. Norton (Editor), The Preservation of Species. Princeton University Press, Princeton, N.J., pp. 110–137.

Odum, H.T. and Odum, E.P., 1976. Energy Basis for Man and Nature. McGraw-Hill, New York, 297 pp.

Page, T., 1978. A generic view of toxic chemicals and similar risks. Ecol. Law Q., 7: 207–244.

Platt, J., 1973. Social traps. Am. Psychol., 28: 642–651.

Randall, A., 1986. Human preferences, economics, and the preservation of species. In: B.G. Norton (Editor), The Preservation of Species. Princeton University Press, Princeton, N.J., pp. 79–109.

Randall, A. and Stoll, J., 1980. Consumer's surplus in commodity space. Am. Econ. Rev., 70: 449–555.

Scaife, W.W., Turner, R.E. and Costanza, R., 1983. Coastal Louisiana recent land loss and canal impacts. Environ. Manage., 7; 433–442.

Turner, M.G., Costanza, R., Springer, T.M. and Odum, E.P., 1988. Market and nonmarket values of the Georgia landscape. Environ. Manage., 12: 209–217.

USDC 1983. Fisheries of the United States. U.S. Department of Commerce, 117 pp.

[4]

Ecological economics: a new approach to understanding and managing the interactions of humans and nature

Is a swamp worth more than a shopping mall? Perhaps not, at first blush. But what if we discover that the swamp is cleaning sewage and trapping atmospheric carbon? Does its 'value' increase? If so, by how much? How many such valuable services does it take for the swamp to be worth more than the shopping mall?

Answers to questions like these may be hard to come by, but we've been making things more difficult than we have to. By viewing ecological problems as a battle between economic interests and environmental interests, we force groups to take sides to their own (and society's) mutual detriment. But what if environmental interests could be incorporated into economic planning? What if environmental assets were routinely considered in our economic accounting system? Could economic forces then be used to preserve the environment?

If we are ever to find workable long-term solutions to our environmental problems, we need a completely new conception of the relationship between economics and ecology, one that regards the economic subsystem as a part of the larger ecological life-support system. Such a conception must go beyond the narrow boundaries of the traditional academic disciplines to extend and integrate the study and management of 'nature's household' (ecology) and 'humankind's household' (economics). It must acknowledge that in the long run a healthy economy can only exist in symbiosis with a healthy ecology.

Ecological economics is beginning to be put into practice by a recently formed worldwide, multidisciplinary group called the International Society for Ecological Economics. They are in the forefront of a growing realization: that the most obvious danger of excluding nature from economics is that nature is the economy's life-support system, and that by ignoring it we may inadvertently damage it beyond repair. Current economic systems do not have built-in methods for incorporating concern about the sustainability of our ecological life-support system, nor do they adequately account for the value of ecological systems in contributing to our well-being.

Nature by the numbers

One of the more important manifestations of this problem is that it creates major misperceptions about how well the economy is doing. Gross National Product (the total 'value' of all the nation's goods and services in a given year), as well as other related measures of national economic performance have come to be extremely important as policy objectives, political issues and benchmarks of the general welfare. Yet GNP as presently defined ignores the contribution of nature to production, often leading to peculiar results.

For example, a standing forest provides real economic services for people: by conserving soil, cleaning air and water, providing habitat for wildlife, and supporting recreational activities. But as GNP is currently figured, only the value of harvested timber is calculated in the total. On the other hand, the billions of dollars that Exxon spent on the *Valdez* cleanup – and the billions spent by Exxon and others on the more than 100 other oil spills in the last 16 months – all actually *improved* our apparent economic performance. Why? Because cleaning up oil spills creates jobs and consumes resources, all of which add to GNP. Of course, these expenses would not have been necessary if the oil had not been spilled, so they shouldn't be considered 'benefits'. But GNP adds up all production without differentiating between costs and benefits, and is therefore not a very good measure of economic health.

In fact, when resource depletion and degradation are factored into economic trends, what emerges is a radically different picture from that depicted by conventional methods. Herman Daly and John Cobb have attempted to adjust GNP to account mainly for depletions of natural capital, pollution effects, and income distribution effects by producing an 'index of sustainable economic welfare' (ISEW). Figure 1 shows two versions of their index compared to GNP over the period from 1950 to 1986. What is strikingly clear is that while GNP rose over this interval, ISEW remained relatively unchanged since about 1970. When factors such as loss of farms and wetlands, costs of mitigating acid rain effects, and health costs caused by increased pollution are accounted for, the economy has not improved at all. If we continue to ignore natural ecosystems, we may drive the economy down while we think we are building it up. By consuming our natural capital, we endanger our ability to sustain income.

A sustainable economy

'Sustainability, does not necessarily mean a stagnant economy, but we must be careful to distinguish between 'growth' and 'development'. Economic growth, which is an increase in quantity, cannot be sustainable indefinitely on a finite planet. Economic development, which is an improvement in the quality of life without necessarily causing an increase in quantity of resources consumed, may be sustainable. Sustainable growth is an impossibility. Sustainable development must become our primary long-term policy goal.

Sustainability has been variously construed, but a useful definition is the amount of consumption that can be sustained indefinitely without degrading capital stocks – including 'natural capital' stocks. In a business, capital stock includes long-term assets such as buildings and machinery that serve as the means of production. Natural capital is the soil and atmospheric structure, plant and animal biomass, etc. that, taken together, forms the basis of all ecosystems. This natural capital stock uses primary inputs (sunlight) to produce the range of ecosystem services.

To achieve sustainability, we must incorporate ecosystem goods and services into our economic accounting. The first step is to determine values for them comparable to those of economic goods and services. For example: we know what it costs to

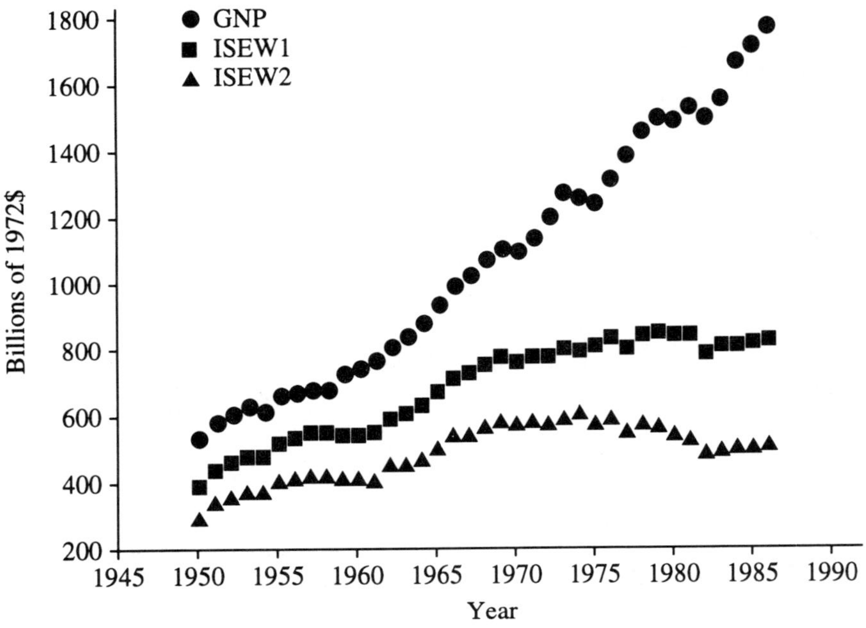

Figure 1: Herman Daly of the University of Maryland and John J. Cobb of the Claremont School of Theology calculated an 'Index of Sustainable Economic Welfare' (ISEW) that adjusts GNP to account for pollution effects, environmental services and other ecological factors. A second version (ISEW2) also includes adjustments for depletion of non-renewable resources and long-term environmental damage. By this adjusted measure, Americans are much less 'wealthy' than they seem.

Source: Daly and Cobb, 'For the Common Good: Redirecting the Economy Toward Community, the Environment, and a Sustainable Future'; Beacon Press, Boston.

build and run sewage treatment plants. Since natural ecosystems perform these same services for free, they are worth at least the amount we would pay for corresponding human-produced services.

In determining values we must also consider how much of our ecological life-support systems we can afford to lose. To what extent can we substitute manufactured for natural capital, and how much of our natural capital is irreplaceable? For example, could we replace the radiation screening services of the ozone layer if it were destroyed?

Some argue that we cannot place economic value on such 'intangibles' as human life, environmental aesthetics, or long-term ecological benefits. But, in fact, we do so every day. When we set construction standards for highways, bridges and the like, we value human life – acknowledged or not – because spending more money on construction would save lives. To preserve our natural capital, we must confront these often difficult choices and valuations directly rather than denying their existence.

Because of the inherent difficulties and uncertainties in determining values, ecological economics acknowledges several different independent approaches. The conventional economic view defines value as the expression of human preferences, with the preferences taken as given and with no attempt to analyse their origins or patterns of long-term change. For goods and services with few long-term impacts (like tomatoes or bread) that are traded in well-functioning markets with adequate information, market ('revealed preference') valuations work well.

But ecological goods and services (like wetland sewage treatment or global climate control) are long term by nature, are generally not traded in markets (no one owns the air or water), and information about their contribution to individual well-being is poor. To determine their value, economists try to get people to reveal what they would be willing to pay for ecological goods and services in hypothetical markets. For example, we can ask people the maximum they would pay to use national parks, even if they don't have to actually pay it. The quality of results in this method depends on how well informed people are; and it does not adequately incorporate long-term goals since it excludes future generations from bidding in the markets.

An alternative method for determining ecological values assumes a biophysical basis for value. This theory suggests that in the long run humans come to value things according to how costly they are to produce, and that this cost is ultimately a function of how organized they are relative to their environment. To organize a complex structure takes energy, both directly in the form of fuel and indirectly in the form of other organized structures like factories. For example, a car is a much more organized structure than a lump of iron ore, and therefore it takes a lot of energy (direct and indirect) to organize iron ore into a car. The amount of solar energy required to grow forests can therefore serve as a measure of their energy cost, their organization, and hence their value.

The point that must be stressed is that the economic value of ecosystems is connected to their physical, chemical, and biological role in the long-term, global system – whether the present generation fully recognizes that role or not. If it is accepted that each species, no matter how seemingly uninteresting or lacking in immediate utility, has a role in natural ecosystems (which do provide many direct benefits to humans), it is possible to shift the focus away from our imperfect short-term perceptions and derive more accurate values for long-term ecosystem services. We may be able to estimate the values contributed by, say, maintenance of water and atmospheric quality to long-term human well-being [see box].

Putting a price on swampland

How can we calculate the value of ecosystems? One of us (Costanza) and Steve Farber of Louisiana State University recently completed a study of the value of coastal wetlands in Louisiana (Table 1). We used two different valuation techniques: willingness-to-pay (WTP) and energy analysis (EA).

WTP valuation estimates individuals' willingness-to-pay for the benefits of wetlands – in this case, for four major categories: commercial fishing, trapping, recreation, and storm protection. We did not include two other categories of willingness-to-pay: to preserve wetlands because they may one day visit them (option value) or simply to know that wetlands exist (existence value) even though we recognize that they are significant.

To estimate recreation values, for example, two techniques were used. The first simply asked recreational users what they would be willing to pay to use the wetlands. The problem with this technique is that respondents may answer 'strategically'. For example, if they think they may actually have to pay what they say, they may give a value lower than their true value. On the other hand, if they think their response may increase the probability of implementing a project they desire, they may state a value higher than their true value. The second technique (which was the primary means used) estimates WTP from what it actually costs users to travel there, such as plane fare, boat rental, gas and mileage costs and so forth.

The EA technique uses the solar energy captured by ecosystems as a measure of their value. To estimate this energy in wetlands we measured the Gross Primary Production (GPP) or the amount of solar energy captured and stored in plants. GPP is the basis for the food chain which supports the production of economically valuable products such as fish and wildlife. By converting GPP to a value based on what it would cost to produce the same energy with fossil fuels we can put a dollar value on this energy. This technique does not require a detailed listing of all the specific benefits of wetlands, but it may overestimate their value if some of the wetland products and services are not useful (directly or indirectly) to society.

Depending on the method of valuation and the discount rate assumed (the discount rate converts future annual values into their equivalent value in the present), our 'best estimate' of the economic value of Louisiana coastal wetlands lies between \$2500 and \$17 000 for every acre of marsh. The market value, exclusive of mineral rights, is about \$500 an acre.

Table 1 Summary of Wetland Value Estimates (1983 dollars)

Method		Per acre present value at specified discount rate 8%	3%
Willingness-to-pay based			
Commercial fishery		\$ 317	\$ 846
Trapping		151	401
Recreation		46	181
Storm protection		1915	7549
	Total	\$2429	\$8977
Option and existence values		?	?
Energy analysis based			
GPP conversion		6400–10 600	17 000–28 200
'Best estimate'		\$2429–6400	\$8977–17 000

Source: R. Costanza, S.C. Farber and J. Maxwell (1989), 'Valuation and management of wetland ecosystems', *Ecological Economics*, 1: 335–62.

Toward ecological economics

Current systems of regulation are not very efficient at managing environmental resources for sustainability, particularly in the face of uncertainty about long-term values and impacts. They are inherently reactive rather than proactive. They include legal confrontation, obfuscation, and government intrusion into business. Rather than encouraging long-range technical and social innovation, they tend to suppress it. They do not mesh well with the market signals that firms and individuals use to make decisions and do not effectively translate long-term global goals into short-term local incentives.

We need to explore promising alternatives to our current command and control environmental management systems, and to modify existing government agencies and other institutions accordingly. The enormous uncertainty about local and trans-national environmental impacts needs to be incorporated into decision-making. We also need to better understand the sociological, cultural, and political criteria for acceptance or rejection of policy instruments.

One example of an innovative policy instrument currently being studied is a flexible environmental assurance bonding system designed to incorporate environmental criteria and uncertainty into the market system, and to induce positive environmental technological innovation.

In addition to direct charges for known environmental damages, a company would be required to post an assurance bond equal to the current best estimate of the largest potential future environmental damages; the money would be kept in interest-bearing escrow accounts. The bond (plus a portion of the interest) would be returned if the firm could show that the suspected damages had not occurred or would not occur. If they did the bond would be used to rehabilitate or repair the environment and to compensate injured parties. Thus, the burden of proof would be shifted from the public to the resource-user and a strong economic incentive would be provided to research the true costs of environmentally innovative activities and to develop cost-effective pollution control technologies. This is an extension of the 'polluter pays' principle to 'the polluter pays for uncertainty as well'.

Ecological economic thinking leads us to conclude that instead of being mesmerized into inaction by scientific uncertainty over our future, we should acknowledge uncertainty as a fundamental part of the system. We must develop better methods to model and value ecological goods and services, and devise policies to translate those values into appropriate incentives. If we continue to segregate ecology and economics we are courting disaster.

GOALS, AGENDA, AND POLICY RECOMMENDATIONS FOR ECOLOGICAL ECONOMICS*

Robert Costanza
Director, Maryland International Institute for Ecological Economics
Center for Environmental and Estuarine Studies
University of Maryland
Box 38, Solomons, MD 20688-0038 USA

Herman E. Daly
Environment Department
The World Bank
1818 H. Street, NW
Washington, D.C. 20433 USA

and

Joy A. Bartholomew
Director, Washington Area Office
Center for Policy Negotiation
490 Chippingwood, Suite 1
Port Republic, MD 20676 USA

ABSTRACT

This introductory chapter: 1) Summarizes the state and goals of the emerging transdisciplinary field of *ecological economics*, particularly as regards issues of sustainability; 2) provides a working agenda for research, education and policy for the coming decade to ensure sustainability; 3) provides some policy guidelines and recommendations for achieving these goals.

This chapter represents, to the extent possible, the "sense of the meeting" or consensus of the workshop which produced it. This does not mean that all the workshop participants agree with all that is said here; we can only offer one perspective. The following chapters by individual workshop participants elaborate the themes we describe and give more detailed and varied perspectives.

OVERVIEW OF THE BOOK

The book is divided into three major parts following this introductory chapter. Part I focuses on defining the basic world view of ecological economics, along with how (and why) it differs from conventional approaches. The ten papers in the section cover a broad range of perspectives. Boulding, Daly, and Hardin set the stage with incisive discussions of the root causes of the problems facing humanity and definitions of some basic ecological economic principles to build on. Page, Christensen, Norgaard and Howarth, and Norton offer perceptive insights into the problems of sustainability, discounting, and valuation. Martinez-Alier outlines some of the historical precedents for ecological economics. Funtowicz and Ravetz, and Perrings round out the section with their unique contributions on the role of uncertainty in an *ecological economic* world view and develop appropriate ways to deal with this uncertainty.

Part II of the book focuses on accounting, modeling, and analysis of ecological economic systems. It begins with El Serafy's discussion of the environment as capital. Peskin, Hueting, and Faber and Proops offer different perspectives on and methods for incorporating natural capital and services into national income accounting. Hannon and Ulanowicz extend and generalize these concepts to deal with ecosystems and combined ecological

* Reprinted from: pp. 1-20 In R. Costanza, ed. 1991. *Ecological Economics: The Science and Management of Sustainability*. New York: Columbia University Press.

economic systems. Braat and Steetskamp offer a more elaborate modeling system for regional analysis and Cleveland rounds out the section with an analysis of resource scarcity from an ecological economics perspective.

Part III of the book deals with institutional changes necessary to achieve sustainability, and includes case studies. The first five papers in the section deal with incentives and instruments. Colin Clark offers an analysis of the perverse incentives that work against sustainability, while Costanza and Farber deal with methods to alter incentives to assure sustainability. Cumberland, and d'Arge and Spash apply these concepts to intergenerational transfers, while Zylicz attacks international transfers. Following the papers on transfers, two papers, by Mary Clark and Zucchetto, discuss the role of education in furthering the goals of ecological economics and sustainability. The section ends with five papers that offer case studies of ecological economic problems and approaches. Mitsch defines the field of ecological engineering and compares the experiences of the United States and China. Jansson takes an ecological economic look at the Baltic Sea region, Tiezzi et al. look at integrated agro-industrial ecosystems, and Cavalcanti looks at the Brazilian situation. Finally Goodland et al. offer a detailed analysis and policy recommendations for the management of moist tropical forests.

While the chapters overlap to some degree in their coverage of certain basic themes, the multiple perspectives enrich the reader's understanding of the pluralistic nature of *ecological economics*.

AN ECOLOGICAL ECONOMIC WORLD VIEW

Increasing awareness that our global ecological life support system is endangered is forcing us to realize that decisions made on the basis of local, narrow, short-term criteria can produce disastrous results globally and in the long run. We are also beginning to realize that traditional economic and ecological models and concepts fall short in their ability to deal with global ecological problems.

Ecological economics is a new *transdisciplinary* field of study that addresses the relationships between ecosystems and economic systems in the broadest sense. These relationships are central to many of humanity's current problems and to building a sustainable future but are not well covered by any existing scientific discipline.

By *transdisciplinary* we mean that *ecological economics* goes beyond our normal conceptions of scientific disciplines and tries to integrate and synthesize many different disciplinary perspectives. One way it does this is by focusing more directly on the problems, rather than the particular intellectual tools and models used to solve them, and by ignoring arbitrary intellectual turf boundaries. No discipline has intellectual precedence in an endeavor as important as achieving sustainability. While the intellectual tools we use in this quest are important, they are secondary to the goal of solving the critical problems of managing our use of the planet. We must transcend the focus on tools and techniques so that we avoid being "a person with a hammer to whom everything looks like a nail." Rather we should consider the task, evaluate existing tools' abilities to handle the job, and design new ones if the existing tools are ineffective. *Ecological economics* will use the tools of conventional economics and ecology as appropriate. The need for new intellectual tools and models may emerge where the coupling of economics and ecology is not possible with the existing tools.

How Is Ecological Economics Different from Conventional Approaches?

Ecological economics (EE) differs from both conventional economics and conventional ecology in terms of the breadth of its perception of the problem, and the importance it attaches to environment-economy interactions. It takes this wider and longer view in terms of space, time and the parts of the system to be studied.

Figure 1.1 illustrates one aspect of the relationship: the domains of the different subdisciplines. The upper left box represents the domain of "conventional" economics, the interactions of economic sectors (like mining, manufacturing, or households) with each other. The domain of "conventional" ecology is the lower right box, the interactions of ecosystems and their components with each other. The lower left box represents the inputs from ecological sectors to economic sectors. This is the usual domain of *resource* economics and environmental impact analysis: the use of renewable and nonrenewable natural resources by the economy. The upper right box represents the "use" by ecological sectors of economic "products." The products of interest in this box are usually unwanted by-products of production and the ultimate wastes from consumption. This is the usual domain of *environmental* economics and environmental impact analysis: pollution and its mitigation, prevention and mediation. *Ecological economics* encompasses and transcends these disciplinary boundaries. *Ecological economics* sees the human economy as part of a larger whole. Its domain is the entire web of interactions between economic and ecological sectors.

Table 1.1 presents some of the other major differences between *ecological economics* (EE) and conventional economics (CEcon) and conventional ecology (CEcol). These issues are covered in more detail and from a number of different perspectives in Part I of this book. The basic world view of CEcon is one in which individual human consumers are the central figures. Their tastes and preferences are taken as given and are the dominant determining force. The resource base is viewed as essentially limitless due to technical progress and infinite substitutability. Ecological economics takes a more holistic view with humans as one component (albeit a very important one) in the overall system. Human preferences, understanding, technology and cultural organization all co-evolve to reflect broad ecological opportunities and constraints. Humans have a special place in the system because they are responsible for understanding their own role in the larger system and managing it for sustainability. This basic world view is similar to that of CEcol, in which the resource base is limited and humans are just another (albeit seldom studied) species. But EE differs from CEcol in the importance it gives to humans as a species, and its emphasis on the mutual importance of cultural and biological evolution.

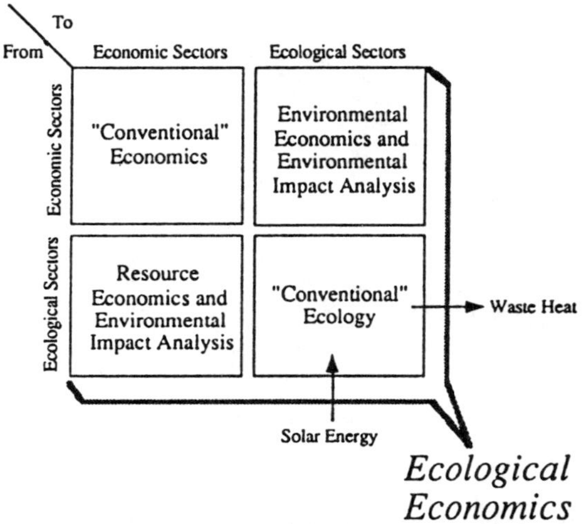

FIGURE 1.1 Relationship of domains of *Ecological Economics* and conventional economics and ecology, resource and environmental economics, and environmental impact analysis.

TABLE 1.1 Comparison of "Conventional" Economics and Ecology with *Ecological Economics*

	"Conventional" Economics	"Conventional" Ecology	Ecological Economics
Basic World View	**Mechanistic, Static, Atomistic** Individual tastes and preferences taken as given and the dominant force. The resource base viewed as essentially limitless due to technical progress and infinite substitutability	**Evolutionary, Atomistic** Evolution acting at the genetic level viewed as the dominant force. The resource base is limited. Humans are just another species but are rarely studied.	**Dynamic, Systems, Evolutionary** Human preferences, understanding, technology and organization co-evolve to reflect broad ecological opportunities and constraints. Humans are responsible for understanding their role in the larger system and managing it sustainably
Time Frame	**Short** 50 yrs max, 1-4 yrs. usual	**Multiscale** Days to eons, but time scales often define non-communicating sub-disciplines	**Multi-Scale** Days to eons, multiscale synthesis
Space Frame	**Local to International** Framework invarient at increasing spatial scale, basic units change from individuals to firms to countries	**Local to Regional** Most research has focused on smaller research sites in one ecosystems, but larger scales have become more important	**Local to Global** Hierarchy of scales
Species Frame	**Humans Only** Plants and animals only rarely included for contributary value	**Non-Humans Only** Attempts to find "pristine" ecosystems untouched by humans	**Whole Ecosystem Including Humans** Acknowledges interconnections between humans and rest of nature
***Primary* Macro Goal**	**Growth of National Economy**	**Survival of Species**	**Ecological Economic System Sustainability**
***Primary* Micro Goal**	**Max Profits (firms) Max Utility (indivs)** All agents following micro goals leads to macro goal being fulfilled. External costs and benefits given lip service but usually ignored	**Max Reproductive Success** All agents following micro goals leads to macro goal being fulfilled.	**Must Be Adjusted to Reflect System Goals** Social organization and cultural institutions at higher levels of the space/time hierarchy ameliorate conflicts produced by myopic pursuit of micro goals at lower levels
Assumptions About Technical Progress	**Very Optimistic**	**Pessimistic or No Opinion**	**Prudently Skeptical**
Academic Stance	**Disciplinary** Monistic, focus on mathematical tools	**Disciplinary** More pluralistic than economics, but still focused on tools and techniques. Few rewards for integrative work.	**Transdisciplinary** Pluralistic, focus on problems

The concept of *evolution* is a guiding notion for both ecology and ecological economics (see Boulding, this volume). Evolution is the process of change in complex systems through selection of transmittable traits. Whether these traits are the shapes and programmed behavioral characteristics of organisms transmitted genetically or the institutions and behaviors of cultures which are transmitted through cultural artifacts, books and tales around the campfire, they are both evolutionary processes. Evolution implies a dynamic and adapting nonequilibrium system, rather than the static equilibrium system often assumed in conventional economics. Evolution does *not* imply change in a particular direction (i.e., progress).

Ecological economics uses an expanded definition of the term "evolution" to encompass both biological and cultural change. Biological evolution is slow relative to cultural evolution. The price human cultures pay for their ability to adapt rapidly is the danger that they have become too dependent on short-run payoffs and thereby usually ignore long-term payoffs and issues of sustainability. Biological evolution imposes a built-in long-run constraint that cultural evolution does not have. To ensure sustainability, we may have to reimpose long-run constraints by developing institutions (or using the ones we have more effectively) to bring the global, long-term, multispecies, multiscale, whole systems perspective to bear on short-term cultural evolution.

The issue of humans' role in shaping the combined biological and cultural evolution of the planet is of critical importance. Humans are conscious of the processes of biological and cultural evolution and cannot avoid being anthropocentric. But in the long run, if humans are to manage the whole planet effectively, we must develop the capacity to take a broader *biocentric* perspective and to treat our fellow species with respect and fairness. We must also recognize that most natural systems are self-regulating and that the best "managerial strategy" is often to leave them alone.

The time frame, space frame, and species frame of EE all tend to be broader than CEcon and are more similar to the "frames" of CEcol. But there is an explicit recognition of the need for integrated, multiscale analysis. This view is also beginning to take hold in CEcol but it is all but absent from CEcon. In practice, CEcol all but ignores humans, CEcon ignores everything but humans, and EE tries to manage the whole system and acknowledges the interconnections between humans and the rest of nature. We must acknowledge that the human system is a subsystem within the larger ecological system. This implies not only a relationship of interdependence, but ultimately a relation of dependence of the subsystem on the larger parent system. The first questions to ask about a subsystem are: How big is it relative to the total system, how big can it be, and how big should it be? These questions of scale are only now beginning to be asked (see Daly, this volume).

The presumed goals of the systems under study are also quite distinct, especially at the macro (whole system) level. The macro goal of EE is sustainability of the combined ecological economic system. CEcol's macro goal of species survival is similar to sustainability, but is generally confined to single species and not the whole system. CEcon emphasizes growth rather than sustainability at the macro level. At the micro level, EE is unique in acknowledging the two-way interdependencies between the micro and macro levels. The conventional sciences tend to view all macro behavior as the simple aggregation of micro behavior. In EE, social organization and cultural institutions at higher levels of the space/time hierarchy ameliorate conflicts produced by myopic pursuit of micro goals at lower levels, and vice versa.

Perhaps the key distinctions between EE and the conventional sciences lie in their academic stances, and their assumptions about technical progress. As already noted, EE is transdisciplinary, pluralistic, integrative, and more focused on problems than on tools.

CEcon is very optimistic about the ability of technology to ultimately remove all resource constraints to continued economic growth. CEcol really has very little to say directly about technology, since it tends to ignore humans altogether. But to the extent that it has an opinion, it would be pessimistic about technology's ability to remove resource constraints because all other existing natural ecosystems that don't include humans are observed to be resource limited. EE is prudently skeptical in this regard. Given our high level of uncertainty about this issue, it is irrational to *bank on* technology's ability to remove resource constraints. If we guess wrong then the result is disastrous—irreversible destruction of our resource base and civilization itself. We should, at least for the time being, assume that technology will *not* be able to remove resource constraints. If it does, we can be pleasantly surprised. If it does not, we are still left with a sustainable system. EE assumes this prudently skeptical stance on technical progress.

A RESEARCH AGENDA FOR ECOLOGICAL ECONOMICS

To achieve sustainability, several steps are necessary including innovative research. This research should not be divorced from the policy and management process, but rather integrated with it. The research agenda for ecological economics that we suggest below is a snapshot, a first guess, intended to begin the process of defining topics for future ecological economic research rather than be the final word. The list of topics can be divided into five major parts: 1) sustainability: maintaining our life support system; 2) valuation of natural resources and natural capital; 3) ecological economic system accounting; 4) ecological economic modeling at local, regional, and global scales; and 5) innovative instruments for environmental management. Some background on each of these topics is given below, followed by a nonprioritized list of the major research questions.

Sustainability: Maintaining Our Life-Support System

Background

"Sustainability" does not imply a static, much less a stagnant, economy, but we must be careful to distinguish between "growth" and "development." Economic growth, which is an increase in quantity, cannot be sustainable indefinitely on a finite planet. Economic development, which is an improvement in the quality of life without necessarily causing an increase in quantity of resources consumed, may be sustainable. Sustainable growth is an impossibility. Sustainable development must become our primary long-term policy goal (see Boulding, this volume, and Daly, this volume, for more on these ideas).

The most obvious danger of ignoring the role of nature in economics is that nature is the economy's life support system, and by ignoring it we may inadvertently damage it beyond it's ability to repair itself. Indeed, there is much evidence that we have already done so. Several authors have stressed the fact that current economic systems do not *inherently* incorporate any concern about the sustainability of our natural life support system and the economies which depend on it (e.g., Costanza and Daly 1987; Hardin, this volume, C. Clark, this volume). Pearce (1987) discusses the reasons for the inability of existing forms of economic organization (free market, mixed, planned) to guarantee sustainability. In an important sense, sustainability is merely justice with respect to future generations. This includes future generations of other species, even though our main interest may be in our own species.

Sustainability has been variously construed (cf. Pezzey 1989; World Commission on Environment and Development 1987) but a useful definition is the amount of consumption that can be continued indefinitely without degrading capital stocks—including "natural capital" stocks (see El Serafy, this volume). In a business, capital stock includes long-term assets such as buildings and machinery that serve as the means of production. Natural capital is the soil and atmospheric structure, plant and animal biomass, etc., that, taken together, forms the basis of all ecosystems. This natural capital stock uses primary inputs (sunlight) to produce the range of ecosystem services and physical natural resource flows. Examples of natural capital include forests, fish populations and petroleum deposits. The natural resource flows yielded by these natural capital stocks are, respectively, cut timber, caught fish, and pumped crude oil. We have now entered a new era in which the limiting factor in development is no longer manmade capital but remaining natural capital. Timber is limited by remaining forests, not sawmill capacity; fish catch is limited by fish populations, not by fishing boats; crude oil is limited by the accessibility of remaining petroleum deposits, not by pumping and drilling capacity. Most economists view natural and manmade capital as substitutes rather than complements. Consequently, neither factor can be limiting. Only if factors are complementary can one be limiting. Ecological economists see manmade and natural capital as fundamentally complementary and therefore emphasize the importance of limiting factors and changes in the pattern of scarcity. This is a fundamental difference that needs to be reconciled through debate and research.

Definitions of sustainability are also obviously dependent on the time and space scale we are using. Rather than trying to determine the *correct* time and space scale for sustainability we need to concentrate on how the different scales interact and how we might construct *multiscale* operational definitions of sustainability.

While acknowledging that the sustainability concept requires much additional research, we devised the following working definition of sustainability: *Sustainability* is a relationship between dynamic human economic systems and larger dynamic, but normally slower-changing ecological systems, in which 1) human life can continue indefinitely, 2) human individuals can flourish, and 3) human cultures can develop; but in which effects of human activities remain within bounds, so as not to destroy the diversity, complexity, and function of the ecological life support system.

Major Research Questions

- What do we mean by (and how do we quantify) "health" and "sustainability" in ecological and economic systems?
- What is the hierarchy (in time and space) of goals for these systems and how is sustainability defined at different levels in the hierarchy? What conflicts arise between setting overall system sustainability goals and providing subgroup, or cultural, autonomy?
- What are the sustainable levels of population and per capita resource use, and what are the paths to achieve these?
- What kinds of actions can benefit the future without harming the present?
- How can sustainability criteria be incorporated in quantitative indices of national income, wealth, and welfare? (See also "Ecological Economic Modeling at Local, Regional and Global Scales" below.)
- What is the degree of substitutability between natural and manmade capital, and ecological and economic services, and how does this influence sustainability?
- Do the basic assumptions underlying current economic and ecological paradigms need to be revised to incorporate sustainability criteria and what are the implications of alternative assumptions?
- How can basic ecological models and principles be incorporated into operational definitions of sustainability?
- What can we learn from the study of historical human societies and natural systems that have proven to be sustainable about the general characteristics of sustainable systems?
- How can we design better institutions and instruments to assure sustainability?
- What are the conditions by which international trade may be made both economically equitable and environmentally sustainable for all parties?

Valuation of Ecosystem Services and Natural Capital

Background

To achieve sustainability, we must incorporate ecosystem goods and services into our economic accounting. The first step is to determine values for them comparable to those of economic goods and services. In determining values, we must also consider how much of our ecological life support systems we can afford to lose. To what extent can we substitute manufactured for natural capital, and how much of our natural capital is irreplaceable (El Serafy, this volume)? For example, could we replace the radiation screening services of the ozone layer which are currently being destroyed?

Some argue that we cannot place economic value on such "intangibles" as human life, environmental aesthetics, or long-term ecological benefits. But, in fact, we do so every day. When we set construction standards for highways, bridges and the like, we value human life—acknowledged or not—because spending more money on construction would save lives. To preserve our natural capital, we must confront these often difficult choices and valuations directly rather than denying their existence.

Because of the inherent difficulties and uncertainties in determining values, ecological economics acknowledges several different independent approaches. There is no consensus on which approach is right or wrong—they all tell us something—but there is agreement that better valuation of ecosystem services is an important goal for ecological economics.

The conventional economic view defines value as the expression of individualistic human preferences, with the preferences taken as given and with no attempt to analyze their origins or patterns of long-term change. For goods and services with few long-term impacts (like tomatoes or bread) that are traded in well-functioning markets with adequate information, market ("revealed preference") valuations work well.

But ecological goods and services (like wetland sewage treatment or global climate control) are long-term by nature, are generally not traded in markets (no one owns the air or water), and information about their contribution to individual's well-being is poor. To determine their value, economists try to get people to reveal what they would be willing to pay for ecological goods and services in hypothetical markets. For example, we can ask people the maximum they would pay to use national parks, even if they don't have to actually pay it. The quality of results in this method depends on how well informed people are; it does not adequately incorporate long-term goals since it excludes future generations from bidding in the markets. Also, it is difficult to induce individuals to reveal their true willingness to pay for natural resources when the question is put directly. Contingent referenda (willingness to be taxed as a citizen along with other citizens, as opposed to willingness to pay as an individual) is superior to ordinary willingness to pay studies in this regard.

In practice, valuation or shadow pricing of environmental functions may require some collectively set quantitative standard. Then shadow prices can be calculated subject to the constraint represented by that standard (see Hueting, this volume).

An alternative method for estimating ecological values assumes a biophysical basis for value (see Costanza 1980; Cleveland et al. 1984; Costanza et al. 1989; Costanza, this volume; Cleveland, this volume). This theory suggests that in the long run humans come to value things according to how costly they are to produce, and that this cost is ultimately a function of how organized they are relative to their environment. To organize a complex structure takes energy, both directly in the form of fuel and indirectly in the form of other organized structures like factories. For example, a car is a much more organized structure than a lump of iron ore; therefore, it takes a lot of energy (directly and indirectly) to organize iron ore into a car. The amount of solar energy required to grow forests can therefore serve as a measure of their energy cost, their organization, and hence, according to this theory, their value.

The point that must be stressed is that the economic value of ecosystems is connected to their physical, chemical, and biological role in the long-term, global system—whether the present generation of humans fully recognizes that role or not. If it is accepted that each species, no matter how seemingly uninteresting or lacking in immediate utility, has a role in natural ecosystems (which *do* provide many direct benefits to humans), it is possible to shift the focus away from our imperfect short-term perceptions and derive more accurate values for long-term ecosystem services. Using this perspective we may be able to better estimate the values contributed by, say, maintenance of water and atmospheric quality to long-term human well-being. Obviously, these services are vital and of infinite value at some level. The valuation question relates to marginal changes, incremental tradeoffs between, say, forested land and agricultural land on a scale of hundreds of acres rather than hundreds of square miles. The notion of safe minimum standards championed by a few economists seems relevant to the protection of critical levels of natural capital against excess myopic marginal conversion, or large-scale conversion, into manmade capital. Of course, in a perfect system, marginal valuations would become prohibitive if the safe minimum standard were transgressed. But systems are far from perfect and redundancy in the interest of prudence is not extravagance.

Major Research Questions

- How do we measure the value of ecosystem services and natural capital? Under what conditions can values be translated to single scales e.g., money, utility or energy?
- Do measures based on subjective preferences (contingent valuation, contingent referenda, willingness to pay) have any relationship to values based on ecosystem functioning and energy flows?
- What is the appropriate discount rate to apply to ecosystem services?
- What (or where) are the thresholds of irreversible degradation for natural resources?

Ecological Economic System Accounting

Background

Gross National Product, as well as other related measures of national economic performance have come to be extremely important as policy objectives, political issues and benchmarks of the general welfare. Yet GNP as presently defined ignores the contribution of nature to production, often leading to peculiar results.

For example, a standing forest provides real economic services for people: by conserving soil, cleaning air and water, providing habitat for wildlife, and supporting recreational activities. But as GNP is currently figured, only the value of harvested timber is calculated in the total. On the other hand, the billions of dollars that Exxon spent on the Valdez cleanup—and the billions spent by Exxon and others on the more than 100 other oil spills in the last 16 months—all actually *improved* our apparent economic performance. Why? Because cleaning up oil spills creates jobs and consumes resources, all of which add to GNP. Of course, these expenses would not have been necessary if the oil had not been spilled, so they shouldn't be considered "benefits." But GNP adds up all production without differentiating between costs and benefits, and is therefore not a very good measure of economic health.

In fact, when resource depletion and degradation are factored into economic trends, what emerges is a radically different picture from that depicted by conventional methods. For example, Herman Daly and John Cobb (Daly and Cobb 1989) have attempted to adjust GNP to account mainly for depletions of natural capital, pollution effects, and income distribution effects by producing an "index of sustainable economic welfare" (ISEW). They conclude that while GNP in the United States rose over the 1956-1986 interval, ISEW remained relatively unchanged since about 1970. When factors such as loss of farms and wetlands, costs of mitigating acid rain effects, and health costs caused by increased pollution, are accounted for, the US economy has not improved at all. If we continue to ignore natural ecosystems, we may drive the economy down while we think we are building it up. By consuming our natural capital, we endanger our ability to sustain income. Daly and Cobb acknowledge that many arbitrary judgments go into their ISEW, but claim nevertheless that it is less arbitrary than GNP as a measure of welfare. John Cobb and his group at Claremont have continued work on the index and their procedure is worth mentioning as a model for scholarly debate. Cobb sent the ISEW to a number of standard economists for criticism, offering an honorarium and contracting to publish their criticisms along with a revised version of the ISEW that would take account of their criticism, or else explain why that could not or should not be done. The result has been a fruitful interchange and better mutual understanding.

There are a number of additional promising approaches to accounting for ecosystem services and natural capital being developed (see El Serafy, Hannon, Hueting, Peskin, Faber and Proops, and Ulanowicz, this volume) and this area promises to be a major focus of research in ecological economics. The approaches are based on differing assumptions, but share the goal of attempting to quantify ecological economic interdependencies and arriving at overall system measures of health and performance. The economist Wassily Leontief (1941) was the first to attempt detailed quantitative descriptions of complex systems to allow a complete accounting of system interdependencies. Leontief's input-output (I-O) analysis has become a standard conceptual and applied tool in economic accounting. Isard (1972) was the first to attempt combined ecological economic system I-O analysis. Combined ecological economic system I-O models have been proposed by several other authors as well (Daly 1968; Victor 1972; Cumberland 1987). Ecologists have also applied I-O analysis to the accounting of material transfers in ecosystems (Hannon 1973, 1976, 1979, this volume; Costanza and Neill 1984; Costanza and Hannon 1989). We refer to the total of all variations of the analysis of ecological and/or economic networks as *network analysis*.

Network analysis holds the promise of allowing an integrated quantitative treatment of combined ecological economic systems and the "pricing" of commodities in ecological and/or economic systems (Costanza, this volume; Hannon, this volume; Costanza and Hannon 1989; Ulanowicz 1980, 1986, this volume; Wulff et al. 1989). This kind of analysis may provide the basis for a quantitative and general index of system health applicable to both ecological and economic systems.

Major Research Questions

- How can we create better systems of national, regional and global accounting to include natural resource depletion and ecological impacts?
- How can we develop systems for accounting for and managing transnational environmental impacts?
- How can we develop network based measures of system health that are applicable to both ecological and economic systems?
- How can we use network based measures of system interdependence (such as energy intensities) to evaluate components in both ecological and economic systems?

Ecological Economic Modeling at Local, Regional, and Global Scales

Background

Since ecosystems are being threatened by a host of human activities, protecting and preserving them requires the ability to understand the direct and indirect effects of human activities over long periods of time and over large areas. Computer simulations are now becoming important tools to investigate these interactions and in all other areas of science as well. Without the sophisticated global atmospheric simulations now being done, our understanding of the potential impacts of increasing CO_2 concentrations in the atmosphere due to fossil fuel burning would be much more primitive. Computer simulations can now be used to understand not only human impacts on ecosystems, but also our economic dependence on natural ecosystem services and capital, and the interdependence between ecological and economic components of the system (see, for example, Braat, this volume; Costanza et al. 1990).

Several recent developments make such computer simulation modeling feasible, including the accessibility of extensive spatial and temporal data bases and advances in computer power and convenience. Computer simulation models are potentially one of our best tools to help understand the complex functions of integrated ecological economic systems.

But even with the best conceivable modeling capabilities, we will always be confronted with large amounts of uncertainty about the response of the environment to human actions (see Funtowicz and Ravetz, this volume). Learning how to effectively manage the environment in the face of this uncertainty is critical (see Perrings, this volume).

The research program of ecological economics will pursue an integrated, multiscale, transdisciplinary, and pluralistic, approach to quantitative ecological economic modeling, while acknowledging the large remaining uncertainty inherent in modeling these systems and developing new ways to effectively deal with this uncertainty.

Major Research Questions

- What are appropriate model structures for a range of urban, agricultural, and natural subsystems, at several hierarchical scales?
- How can these models best be tested, scaled and integrated?
- How can existing data sources (i.e., remote sensing images, national accounting data) best be utilized in building, calibrating and testing ecological economic models at multiple scales?
- What role does biological diversity play in the health and sustainability of ecological economic systems?
- How can simulation modeling results best be used in system accounting and natural ecosystem valuation?
- What are the most appropriate roles of simulation, analytical, and optimization models? What should be their relationship to accounting frameworks?
- How are changes in the quality and cost of natural resources, i.e., rain forests, tropical seas, or grasslands to be measured? How do such changes affect economic welfare?
- Are there general system principles which govern the economy-ecology relationship?
- What viewpoints, modeling mechanisms system variables and other tools or techniques from economic models can be usefully applied to ecosystem models, and vice versa.

- How can intergenerational distribution be addressed analytically as well as ethically?
- What is the appropriate role of chaotic modeling in analyzing ecological economic problems with large degrees of uncertainty?
- How can we develop a philosophy of modeling which is open to the emergence of novelty and consistent with the evolutionary, dynamic, whole systems, multiscale paradigm?
- How do we model the interactions among local, regional, and global levels of ecological economic systems?

Innovative Instruments for Environmental Management

Background

Current systems of regulation are not very efficient at managing environmental resources for sustainability, particularly in the face of uncertainty about long-term values and impacts. They are inherently reactive rather than proactive. They induce legal confrontation, obfuscation, and government intrusion into business. Rather than encouraging long-range technical and social innovation, they tend to suppress it. They do not mesh well with the market signals that firms and individuals use to make decisions and do not effectively translate long-term global goals into short-term local incentives.

We need to explore promising alternatives to our current command and control environmental management systems, and to modify existing government agencies and other institutions accordingly. The enormous uncertainty about local and transnational environmental impacts needs to be incorporated into decision-making. We also need to better understand the sociological, cultural, and political criteria for acceptance or rejection of policy instruments.

One example of an innovative policy instrument currently being studied is a flexible environmental assurance bonding system designed to incorporate environmental criteria and uncertainty into the market system, and to induce positive environmental technological innovation (Perrings 1989; Costanza and Perrings 1990; Perrings, this volume).

In addition to direct charges for known environmental damages, a company would be required to post an assurance bond equal to the current best estimate of the largest potential future environmental damages; the money would be kept in interest-bearing escrow accounts. The bond (plus a portion of the interest) would be returned if the firm could show that the suspected damages had not occurred or would not occur. If they did, the bond would be used to rehabilitate or repair the environment and to compensate injured parties. Thus, the burden of proof would be shifted from the public to the resource-user and a strong economic incentive would be provided to research the true costs of environmentally damaging activities and to develop cost-effective pollution control technologies. This is an extension of the "polluter pays" principle to "the polluter pays for uncertainty as well." Other innovative policy instruments include tradeable pollution and depletion quotas at both national and international levels. Also worthy of mention is the newly emerging Global Environmental Facility of the World Bank that will provide concessionary funds for investments that reduce global externalities.

Major Research Questions

- What regulatory or incentive-based instruments are most appropriate for assuring sustainability?
- How can government and other institutions be modified to better account and respond to environmental impacts?
- What is the appropriate role for economic incentives and disincentives in managing ecological economic systems?
- What sociological, political, ethical, or other factors have limited acceptance of economic incentive-based instruments, and can these factors be addressed?
- How can we develop experimental economics in order to predict behavioral responses to new management instruments? What role might computer modeling play in this development?
- What is the impact of social security systems for limiting population growth?
- How do we equitably limit world population without oppressive programs?

- How do we develop mechanisms to lengthen the time horizons of institutions at all levels?
- What institutions are most effective at preserving the pool of genetic information; preserving the ecological knowledge of indigenous peoples; and facilitating cultural adaptations to environmental and/or technological change?
- What international institutions are available or necessary to assure local and global sustainability?
- Why are excise taxes on materials and energy (which are relatively effective and simple to conceptualize and design) so hard to implement politically, and can the obstacles to implementing these mechanisms be removed?

POLICY RECOMMENDATIONS

The following represents a limited set of policy recommendations on which the workshop participants reached general consensus. It is not prioritized, nor is it comprehensive, nor does it imply that all the participants were in complete agreement. But it does represent the spectrum of policy recommendations that the workshop participants felt comfortable with as a starting point for further discussion.

Sustainability as the Goal

We should institute a consistent goal of sustainability in all institutions at all levels from local to global. We should strive to address prevailing values and decision-making processes by increasing the awareness of institutions and persons about ecological sustainability. We should promote long-term thinking, the use of a systems approach in decision-making, and use of "ecological auditors" (i.e., trained environmental professionals) by public and private institutions whose activities affect the environment.

For example, the World Bank is an important global institution that directly affects economic policy, and those policies severely affect the environment, especially in developing nations. We recommend that the bank and similar institutions require that all projects meet the following criteria: For renewable resources, the rate of harvest should not exceed the rate of regeneration (sustainable yield) and the rates of waste generation from projects should not exceed the assimilative capacity of the environment (sustainable waste disposal). For nonrenewable resources, the rates of waste generation from projects shall not exceed the assimilative capacity of the environment and the depletion of the nonrenewable resources should require comparable development of renewable substitutes for that resource. These are safe, minimum sustainability standards; and once met, the bank should then select projects for funding that have the highest rates of return based on other, more traditional economic criteria.

We recognize that this policy will be difficult at first, and that the policies will likely shift as more information is developed about managing for sustainability. However, there is a need for major institutions not only to affirm, but to operationalize the goal of sustainability, because of the global scope of their programs and because of the impact their example will provide for smaller institutions worldwide. We recognize that goal setting is an ethical issue, and that it is absurd to ignore the normative preconditions of policy, however necessary it may be to avoid mixing normative and positive statements in analysis. Both economists and ecologists, if they want to talk about policy, must offer much more explicit ethical support for their goals, whether sustainability or growth.

Maintaining Natural Capital to Assure Sustainability

A minimum necessary condition for sustainability is the maintenance of the total natural capital stock at or above the current level. While a lower stock of natural capital may be sustainable, given our uncertainty and the dire consequences of guessing wrong, it is best to at least provisionally assume that the we are at or below the range of sustainable stock levels and allow no further decline in natural capital. This "constancy of total natural capital" rule can thus be seen as a prudent minimum condition for assuring sustainability, to be abandoned only when solid evidence to the contrary can be offered. There is disagreement between technological optimists (who see technical progress eliminating all resource constraints to growth and development) and technological skeptics (who do not see as much scope for this approach and fear irreversible use of resources and damage to natural capital). By maintaining total system natural capital at current levels (preferably by using higher severance and consumption taxes), we can satisfy both the skeptics (since resources will be conserved for future generations) and the optimists (since this will raise the price of natural capital resources and more rapidly induce the technical change they predict). By limiting physical growth, only development is allowed and this may proceed without endangering sustainability.

Improving Our Use of Policy Instruments

We need to use a wide variety of policy instruments including regulation, property rights, permits, marketable permits, fees, subsidies and bonds to assure sustainability. Criteria for use of policy instruments are: equity, efficiency, scientific validity, consensus, frugality and environmental effectiveness. We should institute regulatory reforms to promote appropriate use of financial, legal and social incentives. We may use market incentives where appropriate in allocation decisions. In decisions of scale, individual freedom of choice must yield to democratic collective decision making by the relevant community.

Economic Incentives: Linking Revenues and Uses

We should implement fees on the destructive use of natural capital to promote more efficient use, and ease up on income taxes, especially on low incomes in the interest of equity. Fees, taxes and subsidies should be used to change the prices of activities that interfere with sustainability versus those that are compatible with it. This can be accomplished by using the funds generated to support an alternative to undesirable activities that are being taxed. For example, a tax on all greenhouse gases, with the size of the tax linked to the impact of each gas could be linked to development of alternatives to fossil fuel. Gasoline tax revenues could be used to support mass transit and bike lanes. Current policies that subsidize environmentally harmful activities should be stopped. For example, subsidies on virgin material extraction should be stopped. This will also allow recycling options to effectively compete. Crop subsidies that dramatically increase pesticide and fertilizer use should be eliminated, and forms of positive incentives should also be used. For example, debt for nature swaps should be supported and should receive much more funding. We should also offer prestigious prizes for work that increases awareness of, or contributes to, sustainability issues, such as changes in behavior that develop a culture of maintenance (i.e., cars that last for 50 years) or promotes capital and resource saving improvements (i.e., affordable, efficient housing and water supplies).

Ecological Economic Research

While economics has developed many useful tools of analysis, it has not directed these tools toward the thorny questions that arise when considering the concept and implementation of sustainability. In particular, we need to better understand preference formation, and especially time preference formation. We also needs to understand how individual time preferences and group time preferences may differ, and how the preferences of institutions that will be critical to the success or failure of sustainability are established. We have heretofore paid too little attention to ecological feedbacks. An understanding of these will be critical to the implementation of sustainability goals, whatever they may be. We need to concentrate on the valuation of important non-market goods and services provided by ecosystems. We need to better understand the effects of various regulatory instruments that can be utilized to attain sustainability. This may require experimental testing of behavior in a laboratory context. Most importantly, we need to study how positive sustainability incentives can be employed to induce reluctant participants to lengthen their time horizons and think globally about their resource policies.

We also need to develop an ecological history of the planet (to complement the existing human economic history) that would contain trends of resource use, development and exhaustion, changes in science and technology, etc. We should promote the use (as one of a bundle of decision-making tools) of broad benefit/cost analyses that includes the consideration of all market and non-market costs and benefits.

Ecological Economics Education

Our education system is currently characterized by overspecialization and disciplinary isolation. We need to develop transdisciplinary curricula and job and academic support systems for both specialists and generalists. This needs to be combined with an emphasis on the value of general education and personal development, versus the more narrow training of professional technical specialists.

We need to develop an ecological economics core curriculum and degree granting programs that embody the skills of both economics and ecology. This implies a curriculum with some blending of physical, chemical and biological sciences and economics. Within this curriculum quantitative methods are essential, but they should be problem directed rather than just mathematical tools for their own sake.

There is a need to develop a capacity for experimentation that provides ecological economics with a solid empirical base built upon creative and comprehensive theory. We need to develop extension programs that can effectively transfer information among both disciplines and nations.

We should promote at all levels education that weaves together fundamental understanding of the environment with human economic activities and social institutions, and promotes research that facilitates this interweaving process. Particularly, awareness by the media of the common benefits of sustainability should be promoted to insure accuracy in reporting, and the media should be encouraged to use opportunities to educate others through mechanisms such as special reports and public service announcements. We should promote education of broadly-trained environmental scientists, whose jobs will be to provide on-going environmental assessment as an addition to the decision-making processes of various institutions, and as an addition to the assessments now being provided by economic analysts. The ISEE and other international institutions can (and should) provide a vehicle to help students and others focus on "big picture" questions and problems.

Institutional Changes

Institutions with the flexibility necessary to deal with ecologically sustainable development are lacking. Indeed, many financial institutions are built on the assumption of continuous exponential growth and will face major restructuring in a sustainable economy. Many existing institutions have fragmented mandates and policies, and often have not optimally used market and non-market forces to resolve environmental problems. They also have conducted inadequate benefit/cost analyses by not incorporating ecological costs; used short-term planning horizons; inappropriately assigned property rights (public and private) to resources; and made inappropriate use of incentives.

There is a lack of awareness and education about sustainability, the environment, and causes of environmental degradation. In addition, much environmental knowledge held by indigenous peoples is being lost, as is knowledge of species, particularly in the tropics. Institutions have been slow to respond to new information and shifts in values, for example, concerns about threats to biodiversity or the effects of rapid changes in communications technologies. Finally, many institutions do not freely share or disseminate information, do not provide public access to decision making, and do not devote serious attention to determining and representing the wishes of their constituencies.

Many of these problems are a result of the inflexible bureaucratic structure of many modern institutions. Experience (i.e., Japanese industry) has shown that less bureaucratic, more flexible, more peer-to-peer institutional structures can be much more efficient and effective. We need to de-bureaucratize institutions so that they can effectively respond to the coming challenges of achieving sustainability.

REFERENCES

Cleveland, C. J., R. Costanza, C. A. S. Hall, and R. Kaufmann. 1984. Energy and the United States Economy: A Biophysical Perspective. *Science* 225:890-897.
Costanza, R. 1980. Embodied Energy and Economic Valuation. *Science* 210:1219-1224.
Costanza, R. and H. E. Daly. 1987. Toward an Ecological Economics. *Ecological Modelling* 38:1-7
Costanza, R. and B. M. Hannon. 1989. Dealing with the "Mixed Units" Problem in Ecosystem Network Analysis. In F. Wulff, J. G. Field, and K. H. Mann, eds., *Network Analysis of Marine Ecosystems: Methods and Applications*, pp. 90-115. Coastal and Estuarine Studies Series. Heidelberg: Springer-Verlag.
Costanza, R. and C. Neill. 1984. Energy Intensities, Interdependence, and Value in Ecological Systems: A Linear Programming Approach. *Journal of Theoretical Biology* 106:41-57
Costanza, R. and C. H. Perrings. 1990. A Flexible Assurance Bonding System for Improved Environmental Management. *Ecological Economics* 2:57-76.
Costanza, R., S. C. Farber, and J. Maxwell. 1989. The Valuation and Management of Wetland Ecosystems. *Ecological Economics* 1:335-361.
Costanza, R., F. H. Sklar, and M. L. White. 1990. Modeling Coastal Landscape Dynamics. *BioScience* 40:91-107
Cumberland, J. H. 1987. Need Economic Development be Hazardous to the Health of the Chesapeake Bay? *Marine Resource Economics* 4:81-93.
Daly, H. 1968. On Economics as a Life Science. *Journal of Political Economy* 76:392-406.
Daly, H. E. and J. B. Cobb, Jr. 1989. *For The Common Good: Redirecting the Economy Toward Community, the Environment, and a Sustainable Future*. Boston: Beacon.
Hannon, B. 1973. The Structure of Ecosystems. *J. Theo. Biology* 41:535-46.
Hannon, B. 1976. Marginal Product Pricing in the Ecosystem. *J. Theo. Biology* 56:256-267.
Hannon, B., 1979, Total Energy Costs in Ecosystems. *J. Theo. Biology*, 80:271-293.
Isard, W. 1972. *Ecologic-Economic Analysis for Regional Development*. New York: The Free Press.
Leontief, W. 1941. *The Structure of American Economy, 1919–1939*. New York: Oxford University Press.
Pearce, D. 1987. Foundations of an Ecological Economics. *Ecological Modelling*. 38:9-18.
Perrings, C. 1989. Environmental Bonds and the Incentive to Research in Activities Involving Uncertain Future Effects. *Ecological Economics* 1:95-110.
Pezzey, J. 1989. Economic Analysis of Sustainable Growth and Sustainable Development. Environment Department Working Paper No. 15. Washington, D.C.: The World Bank.
Ulanowicz, R. E.: 1980. An Hypothesis on the Development of Natural Communities. *J. theor. Biol.* 85: 223-245.
Ulanowicz, R. E. 1986. *Growth and Development: Ecosystems Phenomenology*. New York: Springer-Verlag.
Victor, P. A. 1972. *Pollution, Economy and Environment*. Toronto: University of Toronto Press
World Commission on Environment and Development. 1987. *Our Common Future*. Oxford: Oxford University Press.
Wulff, F., J. G. Field and K. H. Mann. 1989. *Network Analysis of Marine Ecosystems: Methods and Applications*. Coastal and Estuarine Studies Series. Heidelberg: Springer-Verlag.

Natural Capital and Sustainable Development

ROBERT COSTANZA

Director, Maryland International Institute for Ecological Economics
Center for Environmental and Estuarine Studies
University of Maryland
Box 38, Solomons, MD 20688, U.S.A.

HERMAN E. DALY*

Environment Department
The World Bank
1818 H. Street, NW
Washington, D.C. 20433, U.S.A.

Abstract: *A minimum necessary condition for sustainability is the maintenance of the total natural capital stock at or above the current level. While a lower stock of natural capital may be sustainable, society can allow no further decline in natural capital given the large uncertainty and the dire consequences of guessing wrong. This "constancy of total natural capital" rule can thus be seen as a prudent minimum condition for assuring sustainability, to be relaxed only when solid evidence can be offered that it is safe to do so.*

We discuss methodological issues concerning the degree of substitutability of manufactured for natural capital, quantifying ecosystem services and natural capital, and the role of the discount rate in valuing natural capital. We differentiate the concepts of growth (material increase in size) and development (improvement in organization without size change). Given these definitions, growth cannot be sustainable indefinitely on a finite planet. Development may be sustainable, but even this aspect of change may have some limits. One problem is that current measures of economic well-being at the macro level (i.e., the Gross National Product) measure mainly growth, or at best conflate growth and development. This urgently requires revision.

Finally, we suggest some principles of sustainable development and describe why maintaining natural capital stocks is a prudent and achievable policy for insuring sustainable development. There is disagreement between technological optimists (who see technical progress as eliminat-

Resumen: *Una condición mínima para el crecimiento sostenido es el mantenimiento del stock del capital natural total al presente nivel o por encima del mismo. Si bien un stock de capital natural menor podría ser sostenible, la sociedad no permite mayores declinaciones en el mismo debido a la gran incertidumbre y a las consecuencias lamentables que podría tener el adivinar erradamente. Esta regla "de constancia del capital natural total" puede por lo tanto ser considerada una prudente condicion mínima para asegurar sostenibilidad económica, que solo podría ser relajada cuando se den sólidas evidencias en contrario.*

Discutimos temas metodológicos que conciernen el grado de sostenibilidad económica de capital manufacturado por capital natural, cuantificación de los servicios del ecosistema y capital natural, y el rol de la tasa de descuento en la valoración de capital natural. Diferenciamos entre los conceptos de crecimiento (crecimiento material en tamaño) y desarrollo (mejoramiento en la organización sin cambio en tamaño). Dadas estas definiciones, el crecimiento no puede ser mantenido indefinidamente en un planeta limitado. El desarrollo puede ser sostenido, pero incluso este aspecto del cambio puede tener límites. Uno de los problemas es que las variables corrientemente usadas para medir el bienestar a nivel global (es decir el Producto Nacional Bruto) miden principalmente crecimiento, o como máximo relacionan entre si crecimiento y desarrollo. Esto requiere una revisión en forma urgente.

Finalmente, proponemos algunos principios de desarrollo

Paper submitted December 7, 1990; revised manuscript accepted August 5, 1991.

* *The views presented here are those of the author and should in no way be attributed to the World Bank.*

ing all resource constraints to growth and development) and technological skeptics (who do not see as much scope for this approach and fear irreversible use of resources and damage to natural capital). By maintaining natural capital stocks (preferably by using a natural capital depletion tax), we can satisfy both the skeptics (since resources will be conserved for future generations) and the optimists (since this will raise the price of natural capital depletion and more rapidly induce the technical change they predict).

sostenible y describimos porque el mantenimiento del stock de capital natural representa una política prudente y posible para asegurar un desarrollo sostenido. Existe un desacuerdo entre optimistas tecnológicos (que ven el progreso tecnológico como eliminando todos los límites, en cuanto a recursos, sobre el crecimiento y desarrollo) y escépticos tecnológicos (que no ven espacio suficiente para esta posibilidad y temen un uso irreversible de los recursos y un daño al capital natural). Manteniendo los stocks de capital natural (preferentemente usando un impuesto al uso exhaustivo de capital natural) podemos satisfacer tanto a los escépticos (dado que la recursos van a ser conservados para generaciones futuras) como a los optimistas (dado que esto va a incrementar el precio del uso exhaustivo de capital natural e inducirá más rápidamente los cambios técnicos que ellos predicen).

What Is Natural Capital?

Since "capital" is traditionally defined as produced (manufactured) means of production, the term "natural capital" needs explanation. It is based on a more functional definition of capital as "a stock that yields a flow of valuable goods or services into the future." What is functionally important is the relation of a stock yielding a flow—whether the stock is manufactured or natural is in this view a distinction between kinds of capital and not a defining characteristic of capital itself. For example, a stock or population of trees or fish provides a flow or annual yield of new trees or fish, a flow that can be sustainable year after year. The sustainable flow is "natural income"; the stock that yields the sustainable flow is "natural capital." Natural capital may also provide services such as recycling waste materials, or water catchment and erosion control, which are also counted as natural income. Since the flow of services from ecosystems requires that they function as whole systems, the structure and diversity of the system is an important component in natural capital.

We also need to differentiate between natural capital and income and natural resources. There are at least two possibilities here: (1) natural capital and natural income are simply the stock and flow components, respectively, of natural resources, and (2) natural capital and natural income are aggregates of natural resources in their separate stock and flow dimensions, and forming these aggregates requires some relative valuation of the different types of natural resource stocks and flows. Capital and income, in this view, have distinct evaluative connotations relative to the more physical connotations of the term "resources." We prefer the latter definition because it emphasizes the aggregate nature of terms such as "capital" and "income" while acknowledging that this aggregation is both a strength and a weakness.

We can differentiate two broad types of natural capital: (1) renewable or active natural capital, and (2) nonrenewable or inactive natural capital. Renewable natural capital is active and self-maintaining using solar energy. Ecosystems are renewable natural capital. They can be harvested to yield ecosystem goods (such as wood) but they also yield a flow of ecosystem services when left in place (such as erosion control and recreation). Nonrenewable natural capital is more passive. Fossil fuel and mineral deposits are the best examples. They generally yield no services until extracted. Renewable natural capital is analogous to machines and is subject to entropic depreciation; nonrenewable natural capital is analogous to inventories and is subject to liquidation (El Serafy 1989).

In addition, we can differentiate two broad types of human-made capital. One is the factories, buildings, tools, and other physical artifacts usually associated with the term "capital." A second is the stock of education, skills, culture, and knowledge stored in human beings themselves. The latter type is usually referred to as "human capital" while the former we will call simply "manufactured capital." Thus we have three broad types of capital: natural, human, and manufactured, corresponding roughly to the traditional economic factors of production of land, labor, and capital. In addition, we have the important distinction between renewable and nonrenewable natural capital, and for some purposes we can lump both human and manufactured capital together as "human-made capital."

Figure 1 elaborates these concepts and their interconnections. Manufactured capital (MC), human capital (HC), and renewable natural capital (RNC) decay at significant rates by the second law of thermodynamics and must constantly be maintained. Nonrenewable natural capital (NNC) also decays, but the rate is so slow relative to MC and RNC that this can be ignored. NNC

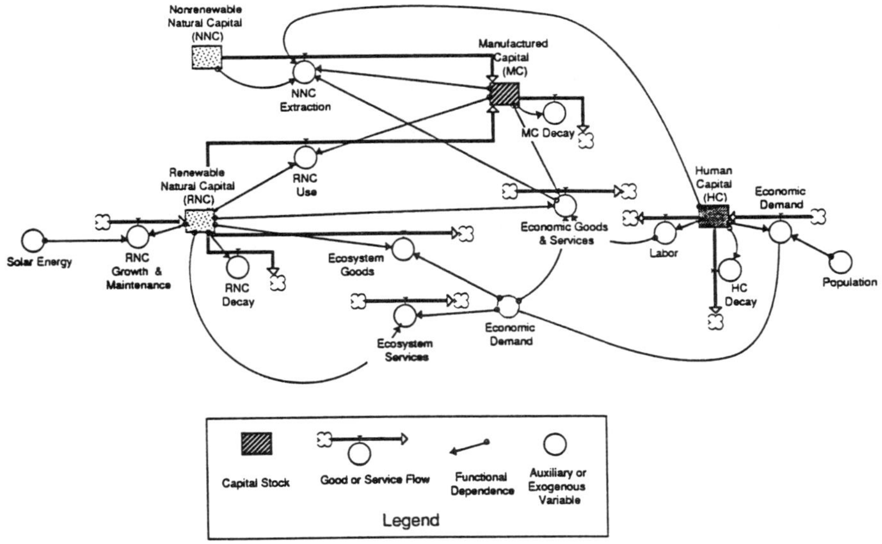

Figure 1. ***Types of natural and human-made capital stocks, good and service flows, and their interdependence.***

can be viewed as a long-term inventory that will sit quietly until extracted and used, but once it is used it is gone. RNC produces both ecosystem goods (portions of the RNC itself) and ecosystem services, and renews itself using its own capital stock and solar energy. Excessive harvest of ecosystem goods can reduce RNC's ability to produce services and to maintain itself. MC, RNC, ecosystem services, and NNC interact with HC and economic demand to determine the level of "economic" (marketed) goods and services production. The form of this interaction is very important to sustainability, and it is not well understood (more on this later). Total income in the context of Figure 1 is a combination of traditional marketed economic goods and services, and nonmarketed ecosystem goods and services.

The concept of sustainability is implicit in the definition of income (following Hicks), so natural income must be sustainable; that is, any consumption that requires the running down of natural capital cannot be counted as income. This should at least be true for RNC. Since NNC must run down with use, a logical way to maintain constant income is to maintain as constant the total natural capital (TNC = RNC + NNC), which implies some reinvestment of the NNC consumed into RNC (as has been suggested by El Serafy [1989] for national income accounting [more on this later]).

Hence constancy of total natural capital (TNC) is the key idea in sustainability of development. It is important for operational purposes to define sustainable development in terms of constant or nondeclining TNC, rather than in terms of nondeclining utility (e.g., Pezzey 1989). While there are admittedly problems in measuring TNC, utility is beyond all hope of measurement. Aggregated, discounted future utility is what is really needed to operationalize the utility-based definition of sustainability, and that is even more of a will-o'-the-wisp. Also, an important motivation behind the sustainable development discussion is that of a just bequest to future generations. Utility cannot be bequeathed, but natural capital can be. Whether future generations use the natural capital we bequeath to them in ways that lead to happiness or to misery is beyond our control. We are not responsible for their happiness or utility—only for conserving for them the natural capital that can provide happiness if used wisely.

In the past, only manufactured stocks were considered as capital because natural capital was superabundant in that mankind's activities operated at too small a scale relative to natural processes to interfere with the free provision of natural goods and services. Expansion of manufactured and human capital entailed no opportunity cost in terms of the sacrifice of services of natural capital. Manufactured and human capital were the limiting factors in economic development. Natural capital was a free good. We are now entering an era, thanks to the enormous increase of the human scale, in which natural capital is becoming the limiting factor. Human economic activities can significantly reduce the capacity of natural capital to yield the flow of ecosystem goods and services and NNC upon which the very productivity of human-made capital depends.

Of course the classical economists (Smith, Malthus, Ricardo) emphasized the constraints of natural resources on economic growth, and several more recent economists, especially environmental and ecological economists, have explicitly recognized natural resources as an important form of capital that produces major contributions to human well-being (cf., Scott 1955; Daly 1968, 1973, 1977; Page 1977; Randall 1987; Pearce & Turner 1989). But environmental economics has, until now, been a tiny subfield far from the mainstream of neoclassical economics, and the role of natural resources within the mainstream has been de-emphasized almost to the point of oblivion. We believe that, if we are to achieve sustainability, the economy must be viewed in its proper perspective, as a subsystem of the larger ecological system of which it is a part, and that environmental and ecological economics need to become much more pervasive approaches to the problem (Costanza et al. 1991).

Why Is Accounting for Natural Capital So Important?

Natural capital produces a significant portion of the real goods and services of the ecological economic system, so failure to adequately account for it leads to major misperceptions about how well the economy is doing. This misperception is important at all levels of analysis, from the appraisal of individual projects to the health of the ecological economic system as a whole. Let us concentrate on the level of national income accounting, however, because of the importance of these measures to national planning and sustainability.

There has been much recent interest in improving national income and welfare measures to account for depletion of natural capital and other mismeasures of welfare (cf. Ahmad et al. 1989). Daly and Cobb (1989) have produced an index of sustainable economic welfare (ISEW) that attempts to account mainly for depletions of natural capital, pollution effects, and income distribution effects. Figure 2 shows two versions of their index compared to GNP over the 1950 to 1986 interval. What is strikingly clear from Figure 2 is that while GNP has been rising over this interval, ISEW has remained relatively unchanged since about 1970. When depletions of natural capital, pollution costs, and income distribution effects are accounted for, the economy is seen to be not improving at all. If we continue to ignore

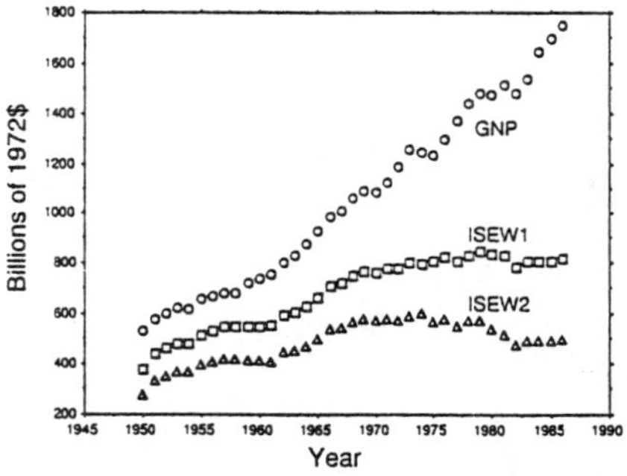

Figure 2. U.S. GNP compared with the Index of Sustainable Economic Welfare (ISEW, from Daly & Cobb 1989) for the interval 1950 to 1986. ISEW2 includes corrections for depletion of nonrenewable resources and long-term environmental damage; ISEW1 does not.

natural capital, we may well push welfare down while we think we are building it up.

Substitutability Between Natural and Man-made Capital

In addition to the former smallness of the human scale, a further reason for the neglect of natural capital has been the tenet of neoclassical economic theory that human-made capital is a near-perfect substitute for natural resources, and hence for the natural capital that generates the flow of natural resources. In the words of Nordhaus and Tobin (1972):

> The prevailing standard model of growth assumes that there are no limits on the feasibility of expanding the supplies of non-human agents of production. It is basically a two-factor model in which production depends only on labor and reproducible capital. Land and resources, the third member of the classical triad, have generally been dropped ... the tacit justification has been that reproducible capital is a near perfect substitute for land and other exhaustible resources.

The mathematical form assumed for the production function can also imply more substitutability than is there in reality. For example, even if natural capital is explicitly included in the production function, it makes little difference as long as the production function is a form (such as the Cobb-Douglas function) in which natural resources can approach zero with output remaining constant, and as long as reproducible (manufactured) capital or labor (human capital) are increased by a compensatory amount. In more technical terms, the elasticity of substitution of human-made for natural capital was assumed to be constant and high.

This assumption of near-perfect substitutability (high constant elasticity of substitution) has little support in logic or in fact. It was motivated more by mathematical convenience than anything else, except perhaps the hubris-driven technological dream of being independent of nature. Consider the following list of objections to the tenet of near-perfect substitutibility of human-made for natural capital:

1. If human-made capital were a perfect substitute for natural capital, then natural capital would also be a perfect substitute for human-made capital. But if the latter were the case there would be no reason to develop and accumulate human-made capital in the first place! Why does one need human-made capital if one already has an abundance of a near-perfect substitutes? Historically, we developed human-made capital as a complement to natural capital, not as a substitute. It should be obvious that the human-made capital of fishing nets, refineries, saw mills, and the human capital skill to run them does not substitute for, and would in fact be worthless without, the natural capital of fish populations, petroleum deposits, and forests.
2. Manufactured capital is itself made out of natural resources, with the help of human capital (which also consumes natural resources). Creation of the "substitute" requires more of the very thing that it is supposed to substitute for!
3. A physical analysis of "production" reveals that it is really a transformation process—a flow of natural resource inputs is transformed into a flow of product outputs by two agents of transformation, the stock of laborers (human capital) and the stock of manufactured capital at their disposal. Natural resources are that which is being transformed into a product (the material cause of production); manufactured and human capital are that which is effecting the transformation (the efficient cause of production). The relationship is overwhelmingly one of complementarity, not substitutability. The overwhelming reason for increasing the stock of human-made capital is to process a larger flow of natural capital, not to make possible a reduced flow. It is possible to reduce the waste of materials in process by investing capital in the recycling of prompt scrap, but this is marginal and limited.

The point is that the substitution of human-made physical capital for natural capital in the production of a given good is very limited, and that on the whole natural capital and human-made capital are complements in the production of any given good. There may remain considerable substitutability between human and manufactured capital (the two agents), or among various particular forms of natural capital (aluminum for copper, glass for aluminum), or even between NNC and RNC. That is not in dispute. Nor are we disputing the possibility of substituting a technically superior product that requires less energy and materials to render the same human service (e.g., cars that get more miles per gallon and light bulbs that give more lumens per watt). The latter is efficiency-increasing technical progress (development) as opposed to throughput-increasing technical progress (growth). But for any given product embodying any given level of technical knowledge, human-made capital and natural capital are, in general, complements, not substitutes.

Valuation of Natural Capital

The issue of valuation of natural capital is difficult but essential for many purposes, including aggregation and determining the optimal scale of human activities. The valuation of natural capital involves allocation of matter-energy across the boundary separating the economic subsystem from the ecosystem, and could be referred to as *macro-allocation.* By contrast *micro-allocation* is the allocation among competing uses of matter-energy that has already entered the economic subsystem—allocation proper. The logic defining the two optima is the same—the optimum is at the point where marginal costs equal marginal benefits. But the nature of the cost and benefit functions in the two cases is very different.

The cost and benefit functions relevant to the micro-allocation problem are those of individuals bent on maximizing their own private utility both as consumers and producers. The market coordinates and balances these individualistic maximizing efforts and in so doing determines a set of relative prices that measure opportunity cost. Individuals are allowed to appropriate matter-energy from the ecosystem as required for their individualistic purposes. Since the benefits of such expropriation are mostly private while the costs are largely social, there is a tendency to overexpand the scale of the economy—or to "allocate" too much of the matter-energy of the total ecosystem to the economic subsystem. Therefore the macro-allocation or scale problem should be viewed as a social or collective decision rather than an individualistic market decision. This means that the cost and benefit functions of macro-allocation are at the level of social preferences. A social preference function may give considerable weight to individual utility but is certainly not reducible to that alone. It has a community dimension. The value of community (with other people and other species, both present and future) must be counted in the cost and benefit functions associated with macro-allocation (Daly & Cobb 1989). These community costs and benefits are not captured in micro-allocation market prices.

How then are these nonmarket social costs and benefits measured? One approach is to imagine the valuation to be done by a different *Homo economicus* than the neoclassical pure individualist. This broader *Homo economicus* (call him *H-e* 2 to differentiate him from the neoclassical *H-e* 1) is a person in community rather than a pure individualist. *H-e* 2 is also fully informed about how the economy is related to the ecosystem and is constituted in his very identity by the relations of community with both future generations and other species with whom he shares a place in the sun. *H-e* 2 would value natural capital according to its relative long-term potential for supporting life and wealth in general. This long-term potential is closely associated with the low entropy matter-energy embodied in the natural capital. Therefore we offer as one hypothesis for investigation the idea that natural capital could be evaluated in proportion to its embodied energy (Costanza 1980; Cleveland et al. 1984). The willingness to pay of *H-e* 2 (person in community) is hypothesized to be in accordance with this long-run capacity to support life and wealth.

But it will be objected that this *H-e* 2 is not the "real" one. The "real" one (*H-e* 1) is generally ignorant of ecological relations, short-sighted, and individualistic. The "willingness to pay" of this more usual *H-e* 1 is the more common approach to the valuation of natural capital. Both concepts of *H-e* are abstractions from real people. For the micro-allocation problem we think people generally behave like the traditional individualistic *H-e* 1. But when confronted with the macro-allocation problem we think most people would behave more like *H-e* 2, the person in community. Therefore valuation of natural capital, we submit, should be done by individuals acting in an entirely different mode from that in which they operate in consumer markets. *H-e* 1 is different from *H-e* 2, but both are equally real as different aspects of real human beings relevant to different purposes. At any rate this is the interpretation we offer for the two methods of valuation we discuss here: the willingness-to-pay approach and the energy analysis approach.

Because natural capital is not captured in existing markets, special methods must be used to estimate its value. These range from attempts to mimic market behavior using surveys and questionnaires to elicit the preferences of current resource users (i.e., willingness-to-pay [WTP] to methods based on energy analysis [EA] of flows in natural ecosystems which do not depend on current human preferences at all). More complete discussions are given in Farber and Costanza (1987) and Costanza et al. (1989).

There are also problems common to valuing any kind of capital, including human-made capital. One can generally not value capital directly. The two options in use for MC are to value the net stream of services produced by the capital, or to value the cost of forming the capital. With reference to Figure 1, for RNC this corresponds to estimating the present value of ecosystem goods and services production (with, for example, WTP) or to valuing the cost of RNC production (with, for example, EA). Table 1 summarizes results from a recent study of average wetland values in coastal Louisiana (a state containing 40% of the coastal wetlands in the United States) as an example. Details of the methods, especially their conceptual and empirical assumptions and uncertainties, are contained in Farber and Costanza (1987) and Costanza et al. (1989).

Discounting

Often the present-vs.-future issue is thought to be objectively decided by discounting. But discounting at best only reflects the subjective valuation of the future to presently existing individual members of human society. Discounting is simply a numerical way to operationalize the value judgment that (1) the near future is worth more than the distant future to the present generation of humans, and (2) beyond some point the worth of the future to the present generation of humans is negligible. Economists tend to treat discounting as rational, optimizing behavior based on people's inherent preferences for current over future consumption.

There is evidence, however, that discounting behavior may be symptomatic of a kind of semirational, suboptimizing behavior known as a "social trap." A social trap is any situation in which the short-run, local reinforcements guiding individual behavior are inconsistent with the long-run, global best interest of the individual or society (Platt 1973; Cross & Guyer 1980; Costanza 1987). We go through life making decisions about which path to take based largely on the "road signs," the short-run, local reinforcements that we perceive most directly. These short-run reinforcements can include monetary incentives, social acceptance or admonishment, and physical pleasure or pain. Problems arise, however, when the road signs are inaccurate or misleading. In these cases we can be trapped into following a path that is ultimately detrimental because of our reli-

Table 1. Summary of wetland Renewable Natural Capital (RNC) value for coastal wetlands in Louisiana. Estimates (1983 dollars).

Method	*Per-acre present value at specified discount rate* 8%	3%
WTP based		
Commercial fishery	$ 317	$ 846
Trapping	151	401
Recreation	46	181
Storm protection	1,915	7,549
Total	$2,429	$8,977
Option and existence values	?	?
EA based		
GPP conversion	$6,400–10,600	$17,000–28,200
"Best estimate"	$2,429–6,400	$8,977–17,000

ance on the road signs. Discounting may allow individuals to give too little weight to the future (or other species, other groups or classes of humans, etc.) and thus helps to set the trap. Economists, while recognizing that individual behavior may not always lead to optimal social behavior, generally assume that discounting the future is an appropriate thing to do. The psychological evidence indicates, however, that humans have problems responding to reinforcements that are not immediate (in time and space) and can be led into disastrous situations because they discount too much.

It can therefore be argued that the discount rate used by the government for public policy decisions (like valuing natural capital) should be significantly lower than the rate used by individuals for private investment decisions. The government should have greater interest in the future than individuals currently in the market because continued social existence, stability, and harmony are public goods for which the government is responsible, and for which current individuals may not be willing to fully pay (Arrow 1976).

Discounting future value by the rate of interest also provides a tight link between ecological destruction and macroeconomic policy. Any exploited species whose natural rate of population growth is less than the real rate of interest is under threat of extinction, even in the absence of common property problems. While Alan Greenspan and the Federal Reserve probably do not worry about the effect of U.S. interest rate policy on deforestation in the Amazon or destruction of Louisiana wetlands, such links really do exist, and they probably should be broken.

In terms of the natural capital valuation problem, all this merely increases the uncertainty concerning the total present value because the appropriate discount rate is uncertain and makes a big difference in the results. In the wetland valuation example mentioned above, estimates for a range of discount rates (3–8%) were given to demonstrate how much uncertainty is introduced by uncertainty in the discount rate. We've also given arguments for why a lower discount rate may be more appropriate for natural capital valuation decisions. Indeed there is a reasonable case to be made for a zero discount rate in decisions taken on behalf of society at large (Page 1977; Georgescu-Roegen 1981), since society, unlike the individual, is quasi-immortal. A zero discount rate gives infinite or very large values for any indefinitely sustainable stream of income. The wants of future generations will be just as immediate to them as ours are to us. And if the fears of many climatologists and ecologists prove correct, productivity growth will be negative in the long run, so that equity would even require discounting at a negative rate—that is, future resources should be valued more highly than present resources.

Another possibility (Hannon 1985) is that the appropriate discount rate for natural capital should be linked to the natural growth and decay rates (see Fig. 1). RNC will not produce a stream of benefits into the indefinite future unless it is constantly supplied with new energy to maintain it against entropic decay. If this energy were not put into the natural capital stock in question it could be used to maintain some other natural capital stock. The "natural" discount rate might therefore be tied to the average natural decay rate (probably somewhere on the order of 1–3% per year). This is an issue for further research.

Growth, Development, and Sustainability

Improvement in human welfare can come about by pushing more matter-energy through the economy or by squeezing more human want satisfaction out of each unit of matter-energy that passes through. These two processes are so different in their effect on the environment that we must stop conflating them. It is better to refer to throughput increase as *growth*, and efficiency increase as *development*.* Growth is destructive of natural capital and beyond some point will cost us more than it is worth—that is, sacrificed natural capital will be worth more than the extra man-made capital whose production necessitated the sacrifice. At this point growth has become anti-economic, impoverishing rather than enriching. Development, that is qualitative improvement does not occur at the expense of natural capital. There are clear economic limits to growth, but not to development. This is not to assert that there are no limits to development, only that they are not so clear as the limits to growth, and consequently there is room for a wide range of opinion on how far we can go in increasing human welfare without increasing resource throughput. How far can development substitute for growth? This is the relevant question, not how far can human-made capital substitute for natural capital, the answer to which, as we have seen, is "hardly at all."

Some people believe that there are truly enormous possibilities for development without growth. Energy efficiency, they argue, can be vastly increased (Lovins 1977; Lovins & Lovins 1987); so can the efficiency of water use. Potential efficiency increases for other materials are not so clear. Others (Costanza 1980; Cleveland et al. 1984; Hall et al. 1986; Gever et al. 1986) believe that the coupling between growth and energy use is not so loose. This issue arises in the Brundtland Commission's Report (WCED 1987), which recognizes on the

* *This distinction is explicit in the dictionary's first definition of each term.* To grow *means literally "to increase naturally in size by the addition of material through assimilation or accretion."* To develop *means "to expand or realize the potentialities of; bring gradually to a fuller, greater, or better state."* (The American Heritage Dictionary of the English Language).

one hand that the scale of the human economy is already unsustainable in the sense that it requires the consumption of natural capital, and on the other hand calls for further economic expansion by a factor of 5 to 10 to improve the lot of the poor without having to appeal too much to the "politically impossible" alternatives of serious population control and redistribution of wealth. The big question is, how much of this called-for expansion can come from development and how much must come from growth? This question is not addressed by the Commission. But statements from the leader of the WCED, Jim MacNeil (1990), that "The link between growth and its impact on the environment has also been severed" (p. 13), and that "the maxim for sustainable development is not 'limits to growth'; it is 'the growth of limits,'" indicate that WCED expects the lion's share of that factor of 5 to 10 to come from development, not growth. They confusingly use the word "growth" to refer to both cases, saying that future growth must be qualitatively very different from past growth. When things are qualitatively different it is best to call them by different names. Hence our distinction between growth and development. Our own view is that WCED is too optimistic—that a factor of 5 to 10 increase cannot come from development alone, and that if it comes mainly from growth it will be devastatingly unsustainable. Therefore the welfare of the poor, and indeed of the rich, depends much more on population control, consumption control, and redistribution than on the technical fix of a 5- to 10-fold increase in total factor productivity.

We acknowledge, however, that there is a vast uncertainty on this critical issue of the scope for economic development from increasing efficiency. We have therefore devised a policy that should be sustainable regardless of who is right in this debate. We save its description for the final section. First some general principles of sustainable development.

Toward Operational Principles of Sustainable Development

The concept of sustainable development has received much attention lately, but research into how the concept might be operationalized is only beginning (Pearce & Turner 1989; Daly 1990; Costanza 1991). Below we sketch out the broad outlines of some operational principles of sustainability, while acknowledging that we still have a long way to go (both scientifically and politically) to achieve them. All the more reason to get started.

Weak sustainability is the maintaining intact of the sum of human-made and total natural capital. Even that is not done currently. Strong sustainability is the maintaining intact of natural capital and man-made capital separately. Weak sustainability would require the pricing of natural capital, which as we have just argued itself requires a given scale, that is, the holding constant of natural capital at some level, which is to say strong sustainability. So we can concentrate on strong sustainability, maintaining total natural capital intact. What does this mean operationally?

(1) The main principle is to limit the human scale to a level which, if not optimal, is at least within the carrying capacity of the remaining natural capital and therefore sustainable. Once carrying capacity has been reached, the simultaneous choice of a population level and an average "standard of living" (level of per capita resource consumption) becomes necessary. Sustainable development must deal with sufficiency as well as efficiency and cannot avoid limiting physical scale.

(2) Technological progress for sustainable development should be efficiency-increasing rather than throughput-increasing. Limiting the scale of resource throughput by high resource taxes would induce this technological shift, as discussed further below.

(3) RNC, in both its source and sink functions, should be exploited on a profit-maximizing sustained-yield basis, and in general stocks, should not be driven to extinction since they will become ever more important as NNC runs out. Specifically this means that:
   (a) harvesting rates should not exceed regeneration rates; and
   (b) waste emissions should not exceed the renewable assimilative capacity of the environment.

(4) NNC should be exploited, but at a rate equal to the creation of renewable substitutes. Nonrenewable projects should be paired with renewable projects and their joint rate of return should be calculated on the basis of their income component only, since that is what is perpetually available for consumption in each future year. It has been shown (El Serafy 1989) how this division of receipts into capital to be reinvested and income available for current consumption depends on the discount rate (rate of growth of the renewable substitute) and the life expectancy of the NNC (reserves divided by annual depletion). The faster the growth of the renewable substitute and the longer the life expectancy of the NNC, the greater will be the income component and the less the capital set-aside. "Substitute" here should be interpreted broadly to include any systemic adaptation that allows the economy to adjust to the depletion of the nonrenewable resource in a way that maintains future income at present levels (e.g., recycling).

Specific application of principle (3) might, for example, involve such requirements as no net depletion of aquifers or of topsoil (on the input side) and no net increase in soil acidity, salinization, or toxification (on the waste output side). Principle (1), general respect for carrying capacity, can be straightforwardly applied in rangelands, but can also be extended to industrial projects by requiring that all natural capital used by the industry be maintained without depletion.

These principles move us some distance toward operationalizing the basic notion that we should satisfy the needs of the present without sacrificing the ability of future populations to meet their needs. But they clearly fall far short of an operational blueprint complete with measurements. However, as argued in the following section, the principles are operational enough to guide some important policy changes without precise measures of assimilative capacities and sustainable yields. Uncertainty itself is one of the critical factors that must be addressed in designing sustainable policies.

A Fail-Safe Policy Proposal to Achieve Sustainability

We end with a policy proposal that is simple in concept (though not in implementation) and that accomplishes much toward the end of sustainable development. In spite of the disagreement over how much to expect from development without growth, both sides should be able to agree on the following. Strive to hold throughput (consumption of TNC) constant at present levels (or lower truly sustainable levels) by taxing TNC consumption, especially energy, very heavily. Seek to raise most public revenue from such a natural capital depletion (NCD) tax, and compensate by reducing the income tax, especially on the lower end of the income distribution, perhaps even financing a negative income tax at the very low end. Technological optimists who believe that efficiency can increase by a factor of ten should welcome this policy, which raises natural resource prices considerably and would powerfully encourage just those technological advances in which they have so much faith. Skeptics who lack that technological faith will nevertheless be happy to see the throughput limited since that is their main imperative in order to conserve resources for the future. The skeptics are protected against their worst fears; the optimists are encouraged to pursue their fondest dreams. If the skeptics are proven wrong and the enormous increase in efficiency actually happens, then they will be even happier (unless they are total misanthropists). They got what they wanted, but it just cost less than they expected and were willing to pay. The optimists, for their part, can hardly object to a policy that not only allows but offers strong incentives for the very technical progress on which their optimism is based. If they are proved wrong at least they should be glad that the rate of environmental destruction has been slowed.

Implementation of this policy does not hinge upon the precise measurement of natural capital. The valuation issue remains relevant in the sense that our policy recommendation is based on the perception that we are at or beyond the optimal scale. The evidence for this perception consists of the greenhouse effect, ozone layer depletion, acid rain, and general decline in many dimensions of the quality of life. It would be helpful to have better quantitative measures of these perceived costs, just as it would be helpful to carry along an altimeter when we jump out of an airplane. But we would all prefer a parachute to an altimeter if we could take only one thing. The consequences of an unarrested free fall are clear enough without a precise measure of our speed and acceleration. But we would need at least a ballpark estimate of the value of natural capital depletion in order to determine the magnitude of the suggested NCD tax. This, we think, is possible, especially if uncertainty about the value of natural capital is incorporated in the tax itself, using, for example, the refundable assurance bonding system proposed by Costanza and Perrings (1990).

The political feasibility of this policy is an important and difficult question. It certainly represents a major shift in the way we view our relationship to natural capital and would have major social, economic, and political implications. But these implications are just the ones we need to expose and face squarely if we hope to achieve sustainability. Because of its logic, its conceptual simplicity, and its built-in market incentive structure leading to sustainability, the proposed NCD tax may be the most politically feasible of the possible alternatives to achieving sustainability.

We have not tried to work out all the details of how the NCD tax would be administered. In general, it could be administered like any other tax, but it would probably require international agreements or at least national ecological tariffs to prevent some countries from flooding markets with untaxed natural capital or products made with untaxed natural capital. By shifting most of the tax burden to the NCD tax and away from income taxes, the NCD tax could actually simplify the administration of the taxation system while providing the appropriate economic incentives to achieve sustainability.

Acknowledgments

This paper was originally prepared for a workshop on natural capital organized by Barry Sadler for the Canadian Environmental Assessment Research Council (CEARC) and held in Vancouver, British Columbia, Canada, March 15 and 16 1990. We thank the participants at the workshop for feedback on early drafts of the paper, as well as John Cumberland, Dennis King, Colin Clark, and one anonymous reviewer for detailed and helpful suggestions on a subsequent draft.

Literature Cited

Ahmad, Y. J., S. El Serafy, and E. Lutz. 1989. Environmental accounting for sustainable development. A UNEP—World Bank Symposium. The World Bank, Washington, D.C.

Arrow, K. J. 1976. The rate of discount for long-term public investment. In H. Ashley, R. L. Rudman, and C. Shipple, editors. Energy and the environment: a risk benefit approach. Pergamon Press, New York.

Cleveland, C. J., R. Costanza, C. A. S. Hall, and R. Kaufmann. 1984. Energy and the United States economy: a biophysical perspective. Science 255:890–897.

Costanza, R. 1980. Embodied energy and economic valuation. Science 210:1219–1224.

Costanza, R. 1987. Social traps and environmental policy. BioScience 37:407–412.

Costanza, R. editor. 1991. Ecological economics: the science and management of sustainability. Columbia University Press, New York. 525 pp.

Costanza, R., H. E. Daly, and J. A. Bartholomew. 1991. Goals, agenda, and policy recommendations for ecological economics. Pages 1–21 in R. Costanza, editor. Ecological economics: the science and management of sustainability. Columbia University Press, New York. 525 pp.

Costanza, R., S. C. Farber, and J. Maxwell. 1989. The valuation and management of wetland ecosystems. Ecological Economics 1:335–362.

Costanza, R., and C. Perrings. 1990. A flexible assurance bonding system for improved environmental management. Ecological Economics 2:57–76.

Cross, J. G., and M. J. Guyer. 1980. Social traps. University of Michigan Press, Ann Arbor, Michigan.

Daly, H. E. 1968. On economics as a life science. Journal of Political Economy 76:392–406.

Daly, H. E. 1973. Toward a steady-state economy. W.H. Freeman and Co., San Francisco, California.

Daly, H. 1977. Steady-state economics: the political economy of bio-physical equilibrium and moral growth. W.H. Freeman and Co., San Francisco, California.

Daly, H. E. 1990. Toward some operational principles of sustainable development. Ecological Economics 2:1–6.

Daly, H. E., and J. B. Cobb, Jr. 1989. For the common good: redirecting the economy toward community, the environment, and a sustainable future. Beacon Press, Boston, Massachusetts. 482 pp.

El Serafy, S. 1989. The proper calculation of income form depletable natural resources. Pages 10–18 in Y. J. Ahmad, S. El Serafy, and E. Lutz, editors. Environmental accounting for sustainable development. A UNEP—World Bank Symposium. The World Bank, Washington, D.C.

Farber, S., and R. Costanza. 1987. The economic value of wetlands systems. Journal of Environmental Management 24:41–51.

Georgescu-Roegen, N. 1981. Energy, matter, and economic valuation: where do we stand? Pages 43–79 in H. E. Daly and A. F. Umaña, editors. Energy, economics, and the environment: conflicting views of an essential interrelationship. AAAS Selected Symposium 64. Westview Press, Boulder, Colorado.

Gever, J., R. Kaufmann, D. Skole, and C. Vörösmarty. 1986. Beyond oil: the threat to food and fuel in the coming decades. Ballinger, Cambridge, Massachusetts. 304 pp.

Hall, C. A. S., C. J. Cleveland, and R. Kaufmann. 1986. Energy and resource quality: the ecology of the economic process. John Wiley & Sons, New York. 577 pp.

Hannon, B. 1985, Ecosystem, flow analysis. Canadian Journal of Fisheries and Aquatic Sciences 213:97–118.

Lovins, A. B. 1977. Soft energy paths: toward a durable peace. Ballinger, Cambridge, Massachusetts.

Lovins, A. B., and L. H. Lovins. 1987. Energy: the avoidable oil crisis. The Atlantic (December): 22–30.

MacNeil, J. 1990. Sustainable development economics, and the growth imperative. Background Paper No. 3, Workshop on the Economics of Sustainable Development, January 23. Washington, D.C.

Nordhaus, W., and J. Tobin. 1972. Is growth obsolete? National Bureau of Economic Research, Columbia University Press, New York.

Page, T. 1977. Conservation and economic efficiency: an approach to materials policy. Resources for the Future, Washington, D.C. 266 pp.

Pearce, D. W., and R. K. Turner. 1989. Economics of natural resources and the environment. Wheatsheaf, Brighton, U.K.

Pezzey, J. 1989. Economic analysis of sustainable growth and sustainable development. Environment department working paper No. 15. The World Bank, Washington, D.C.

Platt, J. 1983. Social traps. American Psychologist 28:642–651.

Randall, A. 1987. Resource economics. 2nd ed. John Wiley & Sons, New York.

Scott, A. D. 1955. Natural resources: the economics of conservation. University of Toronto Press. Toronto, Canada.

WCED. 1987. Our common future: report of the world commission on environment and development. Oxford University Press, Oxford, England.

[7]

Toward an Operational Definition of Ecosystem Health

ROBERT COSTANZA

Ecosystem health is a normative concept: a bottom line. It represents a desired endpoint of environmental management, but the concept has been difficult to use because of the complex, hierarchical nature of ecosystems. Without an adequate operational definition of the desired endpoint, effective management is unlikely. This chapter investigates some of the operational definitions of ecosystem health, weighs their advantages and disadvantages, suggests alternatives that synthesize these past definitions, and suggests research paths aimed at allowing these new definitions to be put into practice.

Concept definitions of ecosystem health can be summarized as:

- Health as homeostasis
- Health as the absence of disease
- Health as diversity or complexity
- Health as stability or resilience
- Health as vigor or scope for growth
- Health as balance between system components

All of these concepts represent pieces of the puzzle, but none is comprehensive enough to serve our purposes here. Hence I wish to elaborate on the concept of ecosystem health as a comprehensive, multiscale, dynamic, hierarchical measure of system resilience, organization, and vigor. These concepts are embodied in the term "sustainability," which implies the system's ability to maintain its structure (organization) and function (vigor) over time in the face of external stress (resilience). A healthy system must also be defined in light of both its context (the larger system of which it is part) and its components (the smaller systems that make it up).

WHY DO WE NEED CONCEPTS FOR MANAGING ECOSYSTEMS?

All complex systems are, by definition, made up of a number of interacting parts. In general, these components vary in their type, structure, and function within the whole system. Thus a system's behavior cannot be summarized simply by adding up the behavior of the individual parts. Contrast a simple physical system (say an ideal gas) with a complex biological system (say an organism). The temperature of the gas is a simple aggregation of the kinetic energy of all the individual molecules in the gas. The temperature, pressure, and volume of the gas are related by simple relationships with little or no uncertainty. An organism, however, is composed of complex cells and organ systems. The state of an organism cannot be surmised simply by adding up the states of the individual components, since these components are themselves complex and have different, noncommensurable functions within the overall system. Indicators that might be useful for understanding heart function—pumping rate and blood pressure, for instance—are meaningless for skin or teeth.

But to understand and manage complex systems, we need some way of assessing the system's overall performance (its relative "health"). The EPA has recently begun to shift the stated goals of its monitoring and enforcement activities from protecting only "human health" to protecting overall "ecological health." Indeed, EPA's Science Advisory Board (SAB 1990:17) recently stated:

> EPA should attach as much importance to reducing ecological risk as it does to reducing human health risk. These very close linkages between human health and ecological health should be reflected in national environmental policy. When EPA compares the risks posed by different environmental problems in order to set priorities for Agency action, the risks posed to ecological systems must be an important part of the equation.

Although this statement gives the concept of ecological health importance as a primary EPA goal, it begs the question of what ecosystem health *is*, while tacitly defining it as analogous to human health. The dictionary definitions of health are: "1. the condition of being sound in mind, body, and spirit; 2. flourishing condition or well-being." These definitions are rather vague. In order to meet the mandate for effectively managing the environment we must construct a more rigorous and operational definition of health that is applicable to all complex systems at all levels of scale, including organisms, ecosystems, and economic systems. As the preceding chapters make clear, there is a wide range of opinion about how to proceed with this daunting task. Some interesting possibilites have been proposed, however, and I think we are off to a good start.

In its simplest terms, then, health is a measure of the overall performance of a complex system that is built up from the behavior of its parts. Such measures of system health imply a *weighted* summation or a more complex operation over the component parts, where the weighting factors incorporate an assessment of the relative importance of each component to the functioning of the whole. This assessment of relative importance incorporates "values," which can range from subjective and qualitative to objective and quantitative as we gain more knowledge about the system under study. In the practice of human medicine, these weighting factors or values are contained in the body of knowledge and experience embodied in the medical practitioner.

Figure 1 shows the progression from directly measured "indicators" of a component's status, through "endpoints" that are composites of these indicators, to health with the help of "values." Measures of health are inherently more difficult, more comprehensive, require more modeling and synthesis, and involve less precision, but are more relevant than the endpoints and indicators from which they are built. It remains to determine which general approaches to developing these measures of health for ecosystems are most effective. I begin with a review of current approaches and end with a synthesis incorporating the best features of these systems along with some new ideas.

CURRENT CONCEPTS OF ECOSYSTEM HEALTH

Concepts of ecosystem health can be derived by analogy with concepts of human health (Rapport 1989; Chapter 8 of this volume). Both human individuals and ecosystems are complex systems composed of interacting parts in a complex balance of interdependent function. But humans are warm-blooded, homeostatic systems and human physicians have a compendium of known

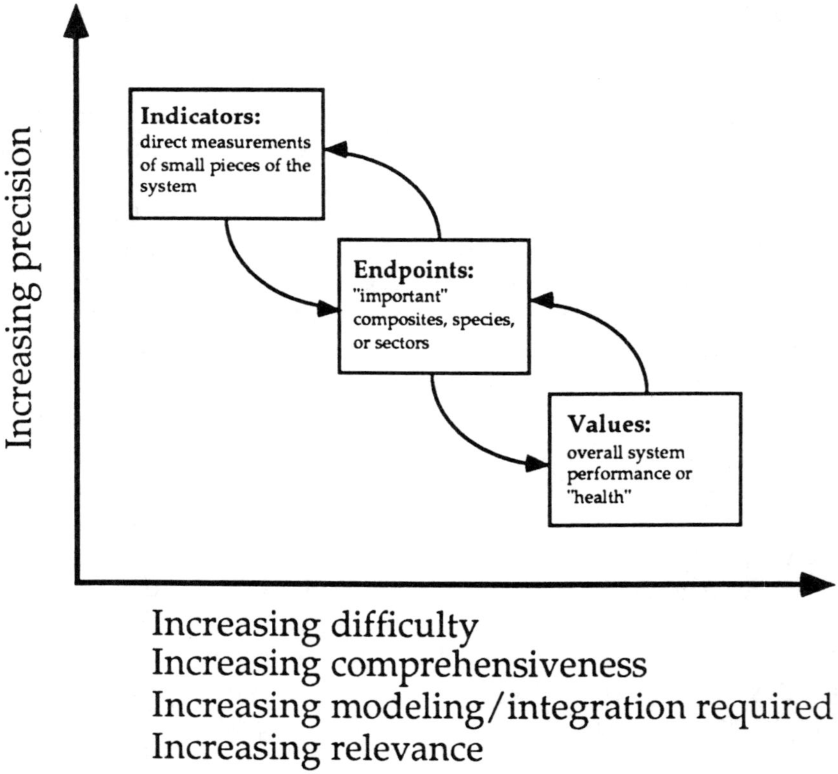

FIGURE 1. *Relationship of indicators, endpoints, and values*

diseases, a wide body of reference data on the "standard human," and many diagnostic tools (Schaeffer et al. 1988; Chapter 9 of this volume). None of these aids are available for ecosystems. There is, however, a large body of literature on the related concepts of ecosystem stability and resilience (reviewed in Pimm 1984 and Holling 1986). In the following discussion I make use of several terms and concepts that have emerged in this ecological literature over the past forty years. They are summarized and defined in Table 1 (an expanded version of a table appearing in Pimm 1984).

What we are after is a general concept of *complex system health* that draws on ideas from human health practice and ecosystem (and economic system) theory and practice but is equally applicable to evaluating the health of any complex system at any scale—from cells to organs to organisms to populations to ecosystems and economic systems.

Health as Homeostasis

The simplest and most popular definition of system health is health as homeostasis: Any and all changes in the system represent a decrease in health. It is popular because it does not require a weighted synthesis of the raw indicators. If any one indicator is seen to change beyond the range of "normal variation," the system's health is deemed to have suffered. The only complication is differentiating internal natural variation from that induced by outside stress. This approach works moderately well for organisms, especially warm-blooded vertebrates, since they are homeostatic and there is a very large population from which to determine "normal ranges." But for ecosystems, economic systems, and other nonhomeostatic systems with small populations, it works less well or not at all.

First of all, we cannot assume that all change is bad (or at least not equally bad). Even in homeostatic organisms one must be able to attach some relative importance (based on overall system function or health) to each indicator in order to get any idea of *how*

TABLE 1. *Definitions of Key Variables*

Variable	*Definition*
Stability	
Homeostasis	Maintenance of steady state in living organisms by use of feedback control processes.
Stable	A system is stable if and only if variables all return to initial equilibrium after being disturbed. A system is locally stable if this return applies to small perturbations and globally stable if it applies to all possible perturbations.
Sustainable	A system's ability to maintain structure and function indefinitely. All nonsuccessional (climax) ecosystems are sustainable, but they may not be stable. (See Resilience below.) Sustainability is a policy goal for economic systems.
Resilience	1. How fast the variables return to equilibrium following perturbation; not defined for unstable systems (Pimm 1984). 2. A system's ability to maintain structure and patterns of behavior in the face of disturbance (Holling 1986).
Resistance	The degree to which a variable is changed following perturbation.
Variability	The variance of population densities over time or allied measures such as standard deviation or coefficient of variation (SD/mean).
Complexity	
Species richness	The number of species in a system.
Connectance	The number of interspecific interactions divided by possible interspecific interactions.
Interaction strength	The mean magnitude of interspecific interaction: size of the effect of one species' density on growth rate of another species.
Evenness	The variance of species abundance distribution.
Diversity indices	Measures combining evenness and richness with a particular weighting for each; one important member of this family is the information-theory index, *H*.
Ascendency	An information-theory measure combining average mutual information (a measure of connectedness) and the system's total throughput as a scaling factor (see Chapter 11).
Others	
Perturbation	Change to a system's inputs or environment beyond normal range of variation.
Stress	Perturbation with negative effect on a system.
Subsidy	Perturbation with a positive effect on a system.

Source: Adapted from Pimm (1984) and Holling (1986).

much health has changed. Gaining ten pounds is not as bad as developing a heart murmur which is not as bad as developing cancer, even though all of these can be considered departures from homeostasis. Moreover ecosystems are complicated by the process of succession. If conditions change sufficiently, there will be replacement of one ecosystem with another that is better adapted to the new conditions. This represents radical change for the first system, and unless one can assess the relative value of the larger system before and after succession, then all successional changes must be considered harmful. But nature (even with no human intervention) is in a constant state of adjustment, change, and succession, not in a state of stasis or equilibrium. We must therefore look a little deeper for an adequate definition of ecosystem health.

Health as Absence of Disease

Health is often defined as the absence of disease. But to operationalize this definition one must first define disease. The dictionary defines it as "any departure from health." Thus defining health as absence of disease just restates the problem in the negative. If we can define health, we can also define nonhealth or disease and vice versa. It also casts the problem in terms that are much too black or white. We desire a continuous measure of relative health, not a binary index of healthy or not healthy.

For organisms, a more useful definition of disease is possible: "a particular destructive process in the body, with a specific cause and characteristic symptoms; a specific illness, ailment, or malady." Disease can thus be thought of as a stress to the system, a perturbation with certain negative effects. One can catalog and eliminate all anthropogenic stresses on an ecosystem, but without an independent definition of health it is impossible to know which of these stresses really cause problems (are negative versus positive) and to what degree. If one uses the homeostatic definition of health, then any stress that causes any change in the system is a disease—and this seems much too severe and unrealistic. In fact, as C. S. Holling (1986, 1992) points out, ecosystem health may be related more to the ability of systems to *use* stress creatively than to their ability to resist it completely. More on this later.

Health as Diversity or Complexity

A third possible definition of ecosystem health is linked to the system's diversity or complexity. The idea is that diversity or complexity are predictors of stability or resilience and that these are measures of health. (See Table 1.) This linkage has been a subject of much controversy in the ecological literature, and the tide has turned several times. But because diversity is so easy to measure in ecosystems it has come to be a prime *de facto* indicator of health. According to Stewart Pimm (1984) there are several interesting aspects of the problem that have yet to be investigated. Recent advances in network analysis (Wulff et al. 1989; Chapter 11 of this volume) hold some promise in allowing a more sophisticated view of the *organization* of systems, not just their number of parts as in diversity measures. More on this later.

Health as Stability or Resilience

Stability and the related concept of resilience have much to recommend them as general measures of health. Healthy organisms have the ability to withstand disease organisms. They are resilient and recover quickly after a perturbation. Hence this leads to a definition of health as the ability to recover from stress. The greater this ability the healthier the system. A problem with this definition is that it says nothing about the system's operating level or degree of organization. A dead system is more stable than a live system because it is more resistant to change. But it is certainly not healthier. Thus an adequate definition of health should also say something about the system's level of activity and organization as well. There is a related, but in many respects more appealing definition of resilience as "the ability of a system to maintain its structure and patterns of behavior in the face of disturbance" (Holling 1986). This definition stresses the adaptive nature of ecosystems rather than the speed with which they can shrug off perturbations. Systems are healthy if they can absorb stress and use it creatively rather than simply resisting it and maintaining their former configurations. Southern pine forests, for example, are adapted to deal with frequent fires as a necessary part of their overall functioning. Efforts to suppress this stress are counterproductive and lead to larger, more destructive fires in the long run.

Health as Vigor or Scope for Growth

It has been hypothesized that a system's ability to recover from stress (or to utilize it) is related to its overall metabolism or energy flow (Odum 1971) or to its "scope for growth" (Bayne et al. 1987)—the difference between the energy required for system maintenance and the energy available to the system for all purposes. Both measures attempt to get at the system's capability to respond to generalized stress as well as its overall level of activity and organization and thus are one step deeper than stability or resilience alone. They are intended to be predictors of activity-weighted resilience and, ultimately, health.

Health as Balance between Components

Another concept that has wide acceptance in Eastern traditional medicine is the idea that a healthy system is one that maintains the proper balance between system components. This idea of balance is deeply ingrained in ecological theory as well, but it has usually been used as a general explanation for existing distributions (the ecosystem is in balance) rather in any predictive or diagnostic way. How do we know if the system is out of balance unless we have some overall indicator of health against which to judge?

TOWARD A PRACTICAL DEFINITION

How can we create a practical definition of system health that is applicable with equal facility to complex systems at all scales? Let us first lay out the minimum characteristics of such a definition. First, an adequate definition of ecosystem health should integrate the concepts of health mentioned above. Specifically it should be a combined measure of system resilience, balance, organization (diversity), and vigor (metabolism). Second, the definition should be a comprehensive description of the system. Looking at only one part of the system implicitly gives the remaining parts zero weight. Third, the definition will require the use of weighting factors to compare and aggregate different components in the system. It should use weights for components that are linked to the functional dependence of the system's sustainability on the components, and the weights should be able to vary as the system changes to account for "balance." And fourth, the definition should be hierarchical to account for the interdependence of various time and space scales.

At a recent workshop attended by a wide range of participants including scientists, philosophers, managers, environmentalists, and industry representatives the following working definition of ecosystem health was arrived at (see the Introduction to this volume): An ecological system is healthy and free from "distress syndrome" if it is stable and sustainable—that is, if it is active and maintains its organization and autonomy over time and is resilient to stress. Ecosystem health is thus closely linked to the idea of sustainability, which is seen to be a comprehensive, multiscale, dynamic measure of system resilience, organization, and vigor. This definition is applicable to all complex systems from cells to ecosystems to economic systems (hence it is comprehensive and multiscale) and allows for the fact that systems may be growing and developing as a result of both natural and cultural influences. According to this definition, a diseased system is one that is not sustainable and will eventually cease to exist. The time and space frame are obviously important in this definition. Individual organisms are not sustainable indefinitely, but the populations and ecosystems of which they are part may be sustainable indefinitely. Distress syndrome refers to the irreversible processes of system breakdown leading to death (Rapport 1981). To be healthy and sustainable, a system must maintain its metabolic activity level as well as its internal structure and organization (a diversity of processes effectively linked to one another) and must be resilient to outside stresses over a time and space frame relevant to that system.

What does this mean in practice? Table 2 lays out the three main components of this proposed concept of system health (resilience, organization, and vigor) along with related concepts and measurements in various fields.

The following preliminary form for an overall system health index (HI) is proposed:

$$HI = V*O*R$$

where: HI = system health index, also a measure of sustainability

TABLE 2. *Indices of Vigor, Organization, and Resilience in Various Fields*

Component of health	*Related concepts*	*Related measures*	*Field of origin*	*Probable method of solution*
Vigor	Function Productivity Throughput	GPP, NPP, GEP GNP Metabolism	Ecology Economics Biology	Measurement
Organization	Structure Biodiversity	Diversity index Average mutual information predictability	Ecology Ecology	Network analysis
Resilience		Scope for growth	Ecology	Simulation modeling
Combinations		Ascendancy	Ecology	

V = system vigor, a cardinal measure of system activity, metabolism, or primary productivity

O = system organization index, a 0–1 index of the relative degree of the system's organization, including its diversity and connectivity

R = system resilience index, a 0–1 index of the relative degree of the system's resilience

This formulation leads to a comprehensive index incorporating the three major components outlined above. In essence, it is the system's vigor or activity weighted by indices for relative organization and resilience. In this context, eutrophication is unhealthy in that it usually represents an increase in metabolism that is more than outweighed by a decrease in organization and resilience. Artificially eutrophic systems tend toward lower species diversity, shorter food chains, and lower resilience.

Naturally eutrophic systems have developed higher diversity and organization along with higher metabolism and are therefore healthier. To operationalize these concepts (especially organization and resilience) the *HI* will require a heavy dose of systems modeling. We turn now to a summary of the available tools.

Network Analysis

Ecology is often defined as the study of the relationships between organisms and their environment. The quantitative analysis of interconnections between species and their abiotic environment has therefore been a central issue. The mathematical analysis of interconnections is important in other fields as well. Practical quantitative analysis of interconnections in complex systems began with the economist Wassily Leontief (1941) using what has come to be called input/output (I-O) analysis. Recently these concepts, sometimes called flow analysis, have been applied to the study of interconnections in ecosystems (Hannon 1973, 1976, 1979, 1985a, 1985b, 1985c; Costanza and Neill 1984). Related ideas were developed from a different perspective in ecology, under the heading of compartmental analysis (Barber et al. 1979; Finn 1976; Funderlic and Heath 1971). Walter Isard (1972) was the first to attempt a combined ecological/economic system I-O analysis, and combined ecological/economic mass-balance models have been proposed by several others (Daly 1968; Cumberland 1987). We refer to the total of all variations of the analysis of ecological and economic networks as *network analysis*.

Network analysis holds the promise of allowing an integrated, quantitative, hierarchical treatment of all complex systems, including ecosystems and combined ecological/economic systems. One promising route is the use of "ascendancy" (Ulanowicz 1980, 1986) and related measures (Wulff et al. 1989; Chapter 11 of this volume) to measure the degree of organization in ecological, economic, or any other networks. Measures like ascendency go several steps beyond the traditional diversity indices used in ecology. They estimate not only how many different species there are in a system but, more important, how those species are organized. This kind of measure may provide a necessary input for a quantitative and general index of system health applicable to both ecological and economic systems.

Another promising avenue of research in network analysis has to do with its use for "pricing" commodities in ecological or economic systems. The mixed-units problem arises in any field that tries to analyze interdependence in complex systems that have many different types and qualities of interacting parts. Ecology and economics are two such fields. Network analysis in ecology has avoided this problem in the past by arbitrarily choosing one commodity flowing through the system as an index of interdependence (carbon, enthalpy, nitrogen, and the like). This strategy ignores the interdependencies between commodities and assumes that the chosen commodity is a valid tracer for relative value or importance in the system. This assumption is unrealistic and severely limits the comprehensiveness of an analysis whose major objective is to deal comprehensively with whole systems.

There are evolving methods for dealing with the mixed-units problem based on analogies to the calculation of prices in economic input/output models. Starting with a more realistic commodity-by-process description of ecosystem networks that allows for joint products, one can use *energy intensities* to ultimately convert the multiple commodity description into a pair of matrices that can serve as the input for standard (single-commodity) network analysis. The new single-commodity description incorporates commodity and process interdependencies in a manner analogous to the way economic value incorporates production interdependencies in economic systems (Costanza and Hannon 1989; Chapter 12 of this volume). This analysis would allow objective valuation of components of ecosystems and combined ecological/economic systems as a complement to subjective evaluations and better overall measures of *vigor* and *organization* in the system.

Simulation Modeling

Evaluating the health of complex systems demands a pluralistic approach (Norgaard 1989, Rapport 1989) and an ability to integrate and synthesize the many different perspectives that can be taken. Probably no single approach or paradigm is sufficient because, like the blind men and the elephant, the subject is too big and complex to touch it all with one limited set of perceptual tools. Rather, we must extend our view to cover the diversity of approaches that may shed light on the problem and must also develop the ability to use *all* of the available light to understand the system.

We need an integrated, multiscale, transdisciplinary, and pluralistic approach to quantitative modeling of systems (including organisms, ecosystems, and ecological/economic systems). While this approach has frequently been suggested (Norgaard 1989), it is difficult to operationalize with traditional funding mechanisms. Such an approach would allow the relationships between scales and modeling approaches to be directly investigated and would result in a deeper understanding of the systems under study. It would produce new ways of *scaling*—or using information at one scale to build understanding and models at other scales. This kind of scaling is essential to developing quantitative measures of system health, especially in addressing the resilience component of the system health index proposed here.

Quantifying resilience implies an ability to predict the dynamics of the system under stress. Predicting these ecosystem impacts requires sophisticated computer simulation models that represent a synthesis of the best available understanding of the way these complex systems function (Costanza et al. 1990). Beyond its use in health indices, this modeling capability is essential for regional ecosystem management and also for modeling the response of regional and global ecosystems to regional and global climate change, sea level rise, acid precipitation, toxic waste dumping, and a host of other potential impacts. Several recent developments make this kind of modeling feasible—not only the improved accessibility of extensive spatial and temporal data bases from remote sensing, aerial photography, and other sources (including EPA's new EMAP program), but also advances in computer power and convenience that make it possible to build and run predictive models at the necessary levels of spatial and temporal resolution.

CONCLUSION

There is no silver bullet that will allow us to assess ecosystem health quickly, cheaply, precisely, and without ambiguity. There is no health meter with probes that can be inserted into ecosystems to yield a digital readout of health. Assessing health in a complex system—from organisms to ecosystems to economic systems—requires a good measure of judgment, precaution, and humility, but also a good measure of systems analysis and modeling in order to put all the individual pieces together into a coherent picture. Human health assessment likewise requires systems analysis, but the compendium of known diseases available, the huge body of reference data on the "standard human," and many types of diagnostic tools available make human health assessment possible without resort to sophisticated computer modeling. Not that it does not require sophisticated analysis, but this analysis is embodied in the "expert system" of medical practitioners. To generalize this expertise and apply it to all kinds of systems requires systems modeling.

I have proposed a general index of system health made up of three components: vigor, organization, and resilience. Vigor can be measured directly in most cases. I have suggested that network analysis and simulation modeling are two of the most promising avenues for the development of the organization and resilience components of the proposed index. Both are relatively expensive to implement because of their large data requirements. But developments like EPA's Environmental Monitoring and Assessment Program (EMAP) that are designed to collect much of the data necessary to implement these analyses, along with remote sensing data and more capable and friendly computers, make implementing these methods finally feasible.

The idea is also amenable to direct empirical testing. One approach might be to apply various versions of the health index to systems for which we already have general agreement on health status—for example, humans or other organisms. One could then see which version did the best job of replicating our agreed-on health rankings in these systems as a test of their effectiveness. The best indices could then be applied to ecological systems with at least some confidence that they do represent the general health of the system. None of this will be easy or simple, but it is time to begin the messy, difficult, and absolutely essential task of assessing the health of ecological systems.

References

Barber, M., B. Patten, and J. Finn. 1979. "Review and Evaluation of I-O Flow Analysis for Ecological Applications." In J. Matis, B. Patten and G. White (eds.), *Compartmental Analysis of Ecosystem Models*. Vol. 10 of *Statistical Ecology*. Bertonsville, Md.: International Cooperative Publishing House.

Bayne, B. L. et al. 1987. *The Effects of Stress and Pollution on Marine Animals*. New York: Praeger.

Costanza, R. 1987a. "Simulation Modeling on the Macintosh Using STELLA." *BioScience* 37:129–132.

———. 1987b. "Social Traps and Environmental Policy." *BioScience.* 37:407–412.

———. 1989a. "What is Ecological Economics?" *Ecological Economics* 1:1–7.

———. 1989B. "Model Goodness of Fit: A Multiple Resolution Procedure." *Ecological Modelling* 47:199–215.

Costanza, R., and H. E. Daly. 1987. "Toward an Ecological Economics." *Ecological Modelling* 38:1–7.

Costanza, R., and B. M. Hannon. 1989 "Dealing with the 'Mixed Units' Problem in Ecosystem Network Analysis." In F. Wulff, J. G. Field, and K. H. Mann (eds.), *Network Analysis of Marine Ecosystems: Methods and Applications*. Coastal and Estuarine Studies Series. Heidelberg: Springer-Verlag.

Costanza, R., and C. Neill. 1984. "Energy Intensities, Interdependence, and Value in Ecological Systems: A Linear Programming Approach." *Journal of Theoretical Biology* 106:41–57.

Costanza, R., and F. H. Sklar. 1985. "Articulation, Accuracy, and Effectiveness of Mathematical Models: A Review of Freshwater Wetland Applications." *Ecological Modelling* 27:45–68

Costanza, R., S. C. Farber, and J. Maxwell. 1989. "The Valuation and Management of Wetland Ecosystems." *Ecological Economics* 1:335–361.

Costanza, R., F. H. Sklar, and M. L. White. 1990. "Modeling Coastal Landscape Dynamics." *BioScience* 40:91–107.

Costanza, R., M. H. Sagoff, J. A. Bartholomew, and B. Haskell. 1991. *Summary Report: Workshop on Ecosystem Health and Environmental Management*. College Park, Md.: Maryland Sea Grant.

Cumberland, J. H. 1987. "Need Economic Development Be Hazardous to the Health of the Chesapeake Bay?" *Marine Resource Economics.* 4:81–93.

Daly, H. 1968. "On Economics as a Life Science." *Journal of Political Economy.* 76:392–406.

Farber, S., and R. Costanza. 1987. "The Economic Value of Wetlands Systems." *Journal of Environmental Management* 24:41–51.

Finn, J. 1976. "The Cycling Index." *Journal of Theoretical Biology* 56:363–73.

Funderlic, R., and M. Heath. 1971. *Linear Compartmental Analysis of Ecosystems*. ORNL-IBP-71-4. Oak Ridge, Tenn.: Oak Ridge National Laboratory.

Hannon, B. 1973. "The Structure of Ecosystems." *Journal of Theoretical Biology* 41:535–46.

———. 1976. "Marginal Product Pricing in the Ecosystem." *Journal of Theoretical Biology* 56:256–267.

———. 1979. "Total Energy Costs in Ecosystems." *Journal of Theoretical Biology* 80:271–293.

———. 1985a. "Ecosystem Flow Analysis." *Canadian Bulletin of Fisheries and Aquatic Sciences* 213:97–118.

———. 1985b. "Conditioning the Ecosystem." *Mathematical Biology* 75:23–42.

———. 1985c. "Linear Dynamic Ecosystems." *Journal of Theoretical Biology* 116:89–98.

Hannon, B., R. Costanza, and R. A. Herendeen. 1986. "Measures of Energy Cost and Value in Ecosystems." *Journal of Environmental Economics and Management* 13:391–401.

Hannon, B., R. Costanza, and R. Ulanowicz. 1991. "A General Accounting Framework for Ecological Systems." *Theoretical Population Biology* 40:78-104.

Holling, C. S. 1973. "Resilience and Stability of Ecological Systems." *Annual Review of Ecology and Systematics* 4:1–23.

———. 1986. "The Resilience of Terrestrial Ecosystems: Local Surprise and Global Change." In W. C. Clark and R. E. Munn (eds.), *Sustainable Development of the Biosphere.* Cambridge: Cambridge University Press.

———. 1992. "The Role of Forest Insects in Structuring the Boreal Forest." In H. H. Shugart (ed.), *A Systems Analysis of the Global Boreal Forest.* Cambridge: Cambridge University Press.

Isard, W. 1972. *Ecologic-Economic Analysis for Regional Development.* New York: Free Press.

Karr, J. R. 1981. "Assessment of Biotic Integrity Using Fish Communities." *Fisheries* 6:21–27.

Leontief, W. 1941. *The Structure of American Economy, 1919–1939.* New York: Oxford University Press.

May, R. M. 1973. *Stability and Complexity in Model Ecosystems.* Princeton: Princeton University Press.

———. 1977. "Thresholds and Breakpoints in Ecosystems with a Multiplicity of Stable States." *Nature* 269:471–477.

Norgaard, R. B. 1989. "The case for Methodological Pluralism." *Ecological Economics* 1:37–57.

Odum, H. T. 1971. *Environment, Power and Society.* New York: Wiley.

O'Neill, R. V., D. L. DeAngelis, J. B. Waide, and T.F.H. Allen. 1986. *A Hierarchial Concept of Ecosystems.* Princeton: Princeton University Press.

Pimm, S. L. 1984. "The Complexity and Stability of Ecosystems." *Nature* 307:321–326.

Rapport, D. J. 1989. "What Constitutes Ecosystem Health?" *Perspectives in Biology and Medicine* 33:120–132.

Rapport, D. J., H. A. Regier, and T. C. Hutchinson. 1985. "Ecosystem Behavior Under Stress." *American Naturalist* 125:617–640.

Schaeffer, D. J., E. E. Herricks, and H. W. Kerster. 1988. "Ecosystem Health: 1. Measuring Ecosystem Health." *Environmental Management* 12:445–455.

Science Advisory Board (SAB). 1990. *Reducing Risk: Setting Priorities and Strategies for Environmental Protection*. SAB-EC-90-021. Washington: EPA.

Turner, M. G., R. Costanza, and F. H. Sklar. 1989. "Methods to Compare Spatial Patterns for Landscape Modeling and Analysis." *Ecological Modelling* 48:1–18.

Turner, M. G., R. Costanza, T. M. Springer, and E. P. Odum. 1988. "Market and Nonmarket Values of the Georgia Landscape." *Environmental Management* 12:209–217.

Ulanowicz, R. E. 1980. "An Hypothesis on the Development of Natural Communities." *Journal of Theoretical Biology* 85: 223–245.

———. 1986. *Growth and Development: Ecosystems Phenomenology*. New York: Springer-Verlag.

Wulff, F., J. G. Field, and K. H. Mann. 1989. *Network Analysis of Marine Ecosystems: Methods and Applications*. Coastal and Estuarine Studies Series. Heidelberg: Springer-Verlag.

ESSAY 15B
Valuation of Ecological Systems

Robert Costanza, University of Maryland

The issue of valuation is inseparable from the choices and decisions we have to make about ecological systems. Some argue that valuation of ecosystems is either impossible or unwise, that we cannot place a value on such "intangibles" as human life, environmental aesthetics, or long-term ecological benefits. But, in fact, we do so every day. When we set construction standards for highways, bridges and the like, we value human life—acknowledged or not—because spending more money on construction can save lives. Another frequent argument is that we should protect ecosystems for purely moral or aesthetic reasons, and that we do not need valuations of ecosystems for this purpose. But there are equally compelling moral arguments that may be in direct conflict with the moral argument to protect ecosystems; for example, the moral argument that no one should go hungry. All we have done is to translate the valuation and decision problem into a new set of dimensions and a new language of discourse, one that, in my view, makes the valuation and choice problem more difficult and less explicit.

So, while ecosystem valuation is certainly difficult, one choice we do *not* have is whether or not to do it. Rather, the decisions we make as a society about ecosystems *imply* valuations. We can choose to make these valuations explicit or not; we can undertake them using the best available ecological science and understanding or not; we can do them with an explicit acknowledgment of the huge uncertainties involved or not; but as long as we are forced to make choices we are doing valuation. The valuations are simply the relative weights we give to the various aspects of the decision problem.

I believe that society can make better choices about ecosystems if the valuation issue is made as explicit as possible. This means taking advantage of the best information we can muster and making uncertainties about valuations explicit too. It also means developing new and better ways to make good decisions in the face of these uncertainties. Ultimately, it means being explicit about our goals as a society, in both the short term and the long term. Society has begun to do this with the recent growing consensus that sustainability is the appropriate long-range, global goal (WCED 1987).

Sustainability and the Valuation of Natural Capital

Sustainability has been variously construed, but one useful definition is the amount of consumption that can be sustained indefinitely without degrading capital stocks—including "natural capital" stocks (Pearce and Turner 1989; Costanza and Daly 1992). Since "capital" is traditionally defined as produced (manufactured) means of production, the term "natural capital" needs explanation. It is based on a more functional definition of capital as "a stock that yields a flow of valuable goods or services into the future." What is functionally important is that the stock yields a flow—whether the stock is manufactured or natural is in this view a distinction between kinds of capital and not a defining characteristic of capital itself. For example, a stock or population of trees or fish provides a flow or annual yield of new trees or fish, a flow that can be sustainable year after year. The sustainable flow is "natural income;" the stock that yields the sustainable flow is "natural capital." Natural capital may also provide services like recycling of waste materials or water catchment and erosion control, which are also counted as natural income. Since the flow of services from ecosystems requires that they function as whole systems, the structure and diversity of the ecosystem is a critical component of natural capital.

To achieve sustainability, we must incorporate natural capital, and the ecosystem goods and services that it provides, into our economic and social accounting and our systems of social choice. In estimating these values we must consider how much of our ecological life-support systems we can afford to lose. To what extent can we substitute manufactured for natural capital, and how much of our natural capital is irreplaceable? For example, could we replace the radiation screening services of the ozone layer if it were destroyed, or the pollination services of honeybees if they were eliminated?

Because natural capital is not captured in existing markets, special methods must be used to estimate its value. These range from attempts to mimic market behavior using surveys and questionnaires to elicit the preferences of current resource users (i.e., willingness to pay), to methods based on energy analysis of flows in natural ecosystems, which do not depend on current human preferences at all (Farber and Costanza 1987, Costanza et al. 1989). Because of the inherent difficulties and uncertainties in determining these values, we are better off with a pluralistic approach that acknowledges and utilizes these different, independent approaches.

The point that must be stressed is that the economic value of ecosystems is connected to their physical, chemical, and biological role in the long-term, global system—whether the present generation of individuals fully recognizes that role or not. If it is accepted that each species, no matter how seemingly uninteresting or lacking in immediate utility, has a role in natural ecosystems (which *do* provide many direct benefits to humans), it is possible to shift the focus away from our imperfect short-term perceptions and toward the goal of developing more accurate values for long-term ecosystem services. Ultimately, this will require the collaborative construction of dynamic evolutionary models of linked ecological–economic systems that adequately address long-term responses and uncertainties.

Toward an Ecological Economics

Valuation of natural capital will always involve large uncertainties. How do we make good decisions in the face of this uncertainty? Current systems of direct environmental regulation attempt to directly enforce specific behavior from the top down in an effort to control pollution. They are not very efficient at managing environmental resources for sustainability, particularly in the face of uncertainty about long-term values and impacts. They are inherently reactive rather than proactive. They induce legal confrontation, obfuscation, and government intrusion into business in a way that reduces efficiency. Rather than encouraging long-range technical and social innovation, they tend to suppress it. They do not mesh well with the market signals that firms and individuals use to make decisions and do not effectively translate long-term global goals into short-term local incentives.

We need to explore promising alternatives to our current command-and-control environmental management systems, and modify existing government agencies and other institutions accordingly. The enormous uncertainty about local and transnational environmental impacts needs to be incorporated into decision making. We also need to better understand the sociological, cultural, and political criteria for acceptance or rejection of policy instruments.

One example of an innovative policy instrument currently being studied is a flexible environmental assurance bonding system designed to incorporate environmental criteria and uncertainty into the market system and to stimulate positive environmental technological innovation (Costanza and Perrings 1990).

In addition to paying direct charges for known environmental damages, a company would be required to post an assurance bond equal to the current best estimate of its largest potential future environmental damages; the money would be kept in interest-bearing escrow accounts. The bond (plus a portion of the interest) would be returned if the firm could show that the suspected damages had not occurred or would not occur. If damages occurred, the bond would be used to rehabilitate or repair the environment and to compensate injured parties. Thus, the burden of proof would be shifted from the public to the resource user, and a strong economic incentive would be provided to determine the true costs of environmentally innovative activities and to develop cost-effective pollution control technologies. Ecological economic thinking leads one to conclude that instead of being mesmerized into inaction by scientific uncertainty over our future, we should acknowledge uncertainty as a fundamental part of the system. We must develop better methods to model and value ecological goods and services, and devise policies to translate those values into appropriate incentives. If we continue to segregate ecology and economics, we are courting disaster.

ELSEVIER

Ecological Economics 15 (1995) 193–196

ECOLOGICAL ECONOMICS

Commentary

Defining and predicting sustainability

Robert Costanza [a,*], Bernard C. Patten [b]

[a] International Institute for Ecological Economics, Center for Environmental and Estuarine Studies, University of Maryland, Box 38, Solomons, MD 20688-0038, USA

[b] Institute of Ecology, University of Georgia, Athens, GA 30602-2202, USA

Received 21 December 1994; accepted 23 June 1995

Abstract

This paper attempts to separate the definition of sustainability (which is argued to be quite straightforward) from related issues concerning: (1) which system, subsystem, or characteristics are to be sustained; (2) for how long they are to be sustained; and (3) when we can assess whether the system has actually been sustained. We argue that because we can only assess sustainability after the fact, it is a prediction problem more than a definition problem. We also propose that in order for evolutionary adaptation to occur, there must be an ordered, hierarchical relationship between the expected (finite) life spans of systems and their space and time scales.

Keywords: Sustainability

1. Introduction

There is much discussion these days about how one "defines" sustainability, sustainable development, and related concepts (cf. WCED, 1987; Pezzey, 1989; Costanza, 1991; Pearce and Atkinson, 1993). Critics argue that the concept is useless because it cannot be "adequately defined." Much of this discussion is misdirected because: (1) it casts the problem as definitional, when in fact it is more one of prediction of what will last, and of achieving consensus on what we want to last, and (2) it fails to account for the range of interrelated time and space scales over which the concept must apply.

The basic idea of sustainability is quite straightforward: *a sustainable system is one which survives or persists.*

But there are three additional complicating questions: (1) ***What system or subsystems or characteristics of systems persist?*** (2) ***For how long?*** (3) ***When do we assess whether the system or subsystem or characteristic has persisted?***

This paper attempts to address these questions by acknowledging that sustainability can only be assessed after the fact, that one must look at systems and subsystems as hierarchically interconnected over a range of time and space scales, and that each of these systems and subsystems has a necessarily finite life span.

2. When?

Biologically, sustainability means avoiding extinction and living to survive and reproduce. Eco-

* Tel.: (+1-410) 326-7213; fax: (+1-410) 326-7354; e-mail: costza@cbl.cees.edu.

Elsevier Science B.V.
SSDI 0921-8009(95)00048-8

nomically, it means avoiding major disruptions and collapses, hedging against instabilities and discontinuities. Sustainability, at its base, always concerns temporality, and in particular, longevity.

The problem is that, like "fitness" in evolutionary biology, determinations of sustainability can only be made *after the fact*. An organism alive right now is fit to the extent that its progeny survive and contribute to the gene pool of future generations. The assessment of fitness today must wait until tomorrow. The assessment of sustainability must also wait until after the fact.

What passes as *definitions* of sustainability are therefore often *predictions* of actions taken today that one hopes will lead to sustainability. For example, keeping harvest rates of a resource system below rates of natural renewal should, one could argue, lead to a sustainable extraction system—but that is a prediction, not a definition. It is, in fact, the foundation of MSY-theory (maximum sustainable yield), for many years the basis for management of exploited wildlife and fisheries populations (Roedel, 1975). As learned in these fields, a system can only be known to be sustainable after there has been time to observe if the prediction holds true. Usually there is so much uncertainty in estimating natural rates of renewal, and observing and regulating harvest rates, that a simple prediction such as this, as Ludwig et al. (1993) correctly observe, is always highly suspect, especially if it is erroneously thought of as a definition.

Similarly, the sustainability of any economic system can only be observed after the fact. Many elements of sustainability definitions are really predictions of system characteristics that one hopes lead to sustainability, not really elements of a definition. Like all predictions, they are uncertain and should rightly be the subject of much elaboration, discussion, and disagreement.

3. What system?

A second question has to do with what system or subsystem or characteristics of these systems one is interested in sustaining. A particular ecological system? A particular species or the total of all species (biodiversity)? The current economic system? A particular culture? A particular business or industry? Here, definitions of sustainability usually end up as a list of preferred characteristics, most often pertaining to the global socioeconomic system in the context of its ecological life support system. For example, most definitions of sustainable development (WCED, 1987; Pezzey, 1989; Costanza, 1991) contain elements of: (1) a sustainable *scale* of the economy relative to its ecological life-support system; (2) an equitable *distribution* of resources and opportunities between present and future generations; and (3) an efficient *allocation* of resources that adequately accounts for natural capital.

It is important that we achieve consensus on these characteristics as desirable social goals. This process will be aided by separating this consensus-building

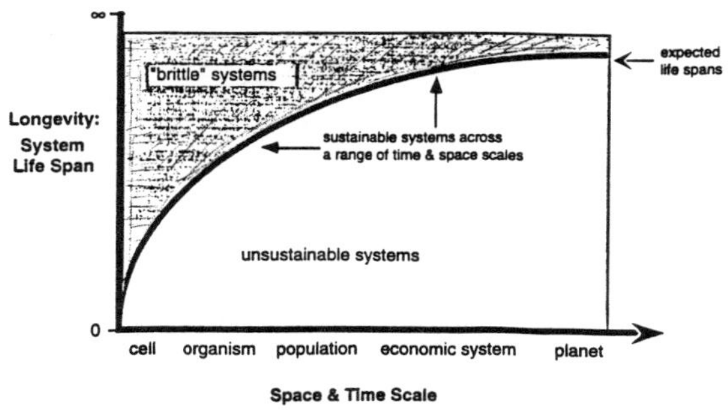

Fig. 1. Sustainability as scale (time and space) dependent concepts.

process from the definition of sustainability and the other related questions we elaborate here. For example, in addition to their desirability as social goals, the three general characteristics listed above also are predictors of the necessary characteristics that will allow the system to be sustained. They are thought to be both necessary conditions (predictors) for sustainability and desirable social goals as well. But choosing particular systems or subsystems and specific characteristics as the objects to sustain (presumably forever) hides the hierarchical interactions between systems and subsystems over a range of scales in space and time. This brings us to the final question of spatial and temporal extent.

4. How long?

The third problem is that when one says a system has achieved sustainability, one has to specify the time span involved. Some would argue that sustainability means "maintenance forever." But nothing lasts forever, not even the universe as a whole. Sustainability thus cannot mean an infinite life span or nothing would be sustainable. Instead, we argue it means a life span that is consistent with the system's time and space scale. Fig. 1 indicates this relationship by plotting a hypothetical curve of system life expectancy on the *y* axis vs. time and space scale on the *x* axis. We expect a cell in an organism to have a relatively short life span, the organism to have a longer life span, a population of organisms to have an even longer life span, an economic system to have an even longer life span, and the planet as a whole to have a longer life span. But no system (even the universe) is expected to have an infinite life span. A sustainable system in this context is thus one that attains its full expected life span within the nested hierarchy of systems within which it is embedded. We refer to this nested hierarchy of systems and subsystems over a range of time and space scales as the "metasystem."

Individual humans are sustainable in this metasystem if they achieve their "normal" maximum life span. At the population level, average life expectancy is often used as an indicator of health and well-being of the population, but the population itself is expected to have a much longer life span than any individual, and would not be considered to be sustainable if it were to crash prematurely, even if all the individuals in the population were living out their full "sustainable" life spans. As a thought experiment, what would happen to sustainability if all individual humans actually lived forever? As we argue below, immortality of any subsystem is not sustainable because it cuts off evolutionary adaptation.

Since ecosystems experience succession as a result of changing climatic conditions and internal developmental changes, they too have a limited (albeit very long) life span. The key is differentiating between changes due to normal life span limits and changes that cut short the life span of the system.

Under this definition, anything that reduces a system's natural longevity also reduces its sustainability. Thus, in humans, factors like cancer, AIDS, accidents, and a host of other causes decrease sustainability. Humans' interventions in ecosystems frequently have deleterious consequences:

- cultural eutrophication of water bodies decreases the longevity of oligotrophic states, degrades water quality, and accelerates the arrival of dystrophic senescence;
- commercial lumbering ahead of sustainable schedules necessitates later sacrifice of non-extractive social values when "saw timber" forestry must be converted to a "pulp and chip" industry, and remnant old-growth forests must be harvested to "preserve jobs";
- high-technology agriculture can only be sustained through exogenous subsidies of energy, fertilizers, pesticides, and gene pools.

These and other uses of natural capital interrupt normal function and both truncate natural longevity and hasten senescent decline. The exact consequences depend on the nature and state of the impacted system and the kind and severity of disturbance.

More formally, this aspect of sustainability can be thought of in terms of the system and its component parts' longevity (Patten and Costanza, 1995): A system is sustainable if and only if it persists in nominal behavioral states as long as or longer than its expected natural longevity or existence time; and-Neither component- nor system-level sustainability, as assessed by the longevity criterion, confers sustainability to the other level.

But one can now ask: why should small-scale systems have shorter life spans than larger-scale systems? Why don't cells or individual organisms last forever? We suggest that this is an outcome of the nested hierarchical interrelationship of systems across scales (the metasystem) that is necessary for evolutionary adaptation. Evolution cannot occur unless there is limited longevity of the component parts so that new alternatives can be selected. And this longevity has to be increasing hierarchically with scale as shown schematically in Fig. 1. Larger systems can attain longer life spans because their component parts have shorter life spans which allows the system to adapt to changing conditions. But without "death" at the lower scale, there can be no evolutionary change at the higher scale. Sustaining life requires death.

Systems with an improper balance of longevity across scales can become either "brittle" when their parts last too long and they cannot adapt fast enough (Holling, 1992) or "unsustainable" when their parts do not last long enough and the higher level system's longevity is cut unnecessarily short.

5. Conclusions

We have separated the problem of *defining* sustainability from three other, more basic questions, and have provided some tentative answers to those questions in order to motivate further discussion:

Q1. **What system** or subsystems or characteristics of systems persist?

A1. A nested hierarchy of systems over a range of time and space scales must be considered (the metasystem). Within the socioeconomic subsystem, a social consensus on *desired* characteristics which are consistent with the relationship of these subsystems with other subsystems in the hierarchy (notably ecosystems) must be arrived at. These characteristics also function as predictors of what kind of system will actually be sustainable.

Q2. For **how long**?

A2. All systems are of limited longevity, so sustainability cannot mean "maintenance forever." To maintain a sustainably evolving metasystem, we hypothesize that a particular relationship between the longevity of component subsystems and their time and space scales (Fig. 1) may be necessary.

Q3. **When** do we assess whether the system or subsystem has persisted?

A3. This can only be done after the fact, so the emphasis shifts to methods to enable us to better predict what configurations will persist, and to policies and instruments to deal with the remaining uncertainty. Given the huge uncertainties involved in the scale of the socioeconomic system, it is of particular importance in this regard to select policies that are precautionary (Costanza and Perrings, 1990; Costanza and Cornwell, 1992) in that they do not take unnecessary risks with sustainability and they do not count on hoped-for technological fixes for their success.

Acknowledgements

We wish to thank Buzz Holling, Simon Levin, and one anonymous reviewer for their helpful suggestions on a earlier version of this manuscript.

References

Costanza, R. (Editor), 1991. Ecological Economics: The Science and Management of Sustainability. Columbia University Press, New York, NY.

Costanza, R. and Cornwell, L., 1992. The 4P approach to dealing with scientific uncertainty. Environment, 34: 12–20, 42.

Costanza, R. and Perrings, C., 1990. A flexible assurance bonding system for improved environmental management. Ecol. Econ., 2: 57–76.

Holling, C.S., 1992. Cross-scale morphology, geometry and dynamics of ecosystems. Ecol. Monogr., 62: 447–502.

Ludwig, D., Hilborn, R. and Walters, C., 1993. Uncertainty, resource exploitation, and conservation: lessons from history. Science, 260: 17, 36.

Patten, B.C. and Costanza, R., 1995. A rigorous definition of sustainability. In preparation.

Pearce, D.W. and Atkinson, G.D., 1993. Capital theory and the measurement of sustainable development: an indicator of "weak" sustainability. Ecol. Econ., 8: 103–108.

Pezzey, J., 1989. Economic Analysis of Sustainable Growth and Sustainable Development. Environment Department Working Paper No. 15. The World Bank, Washington, DC.

Roedel, P.M. (Editor), 1975. Optimum Sustainable Yield as a Concept in Fisheries Management. Special Publication No. 9, American Fisheries Society, Washington, DC, 89 pp.

WCED (World Commission on Environment and Development), 1987. Our Common Future. Oxford University Press, Oxford.

PART II

MATERIAL AND ENERGY FLOWS IN ECOLOGICAL AND ECONOMIC SYSTEMS

[10]

Embodied Energy and Economic Valuation

Robert Costanza

The thesis that available energy both limits and governs the structure of human economies is not new. In 1886, Boltzmann suggested that life is primarily a struggle for available energy. Soddy stated in 1933: "If we have available energy, we may maintain life and produce every material requisite necessary. That is why the flow of energy should be the primary concern of economics" (*1*, p. 56). The flow of energy has not been the primary concern of mainstream economists, although the importance of energy to the functioning of economic systems has by now been recognized by almost everyone. The debate now focuses on the nature and details of the energy connection, and the conclusions are critically important to several aspects of national policy. In this article, the earlier input-output analyses of energy-economy linkages are extended by incorporating the energy costs of labor and government services and solar energy inputs.

Summary. Input-output analysis has been adapted to calculate the total (direct plus indirect) energy required to produce goods and services in the U.S. economy; this quantity has been termed the embodied energy. Usually, the energy required to produce labor and government services and the solar energy input to the economy are ignored by analysts. The former omission can be traced to the assumption that traditional primary factors of economic production—land, labor, and capital—are independent. A strong case can be made that these input factors are not independent and that energy is required for their production. Embodied energies can be calculated in this case by using input-output data. The results of such an analysis show that there is a strong relation between embodied energy and dollar value for a 92-sector U.S. economy if the energy required to produce labor and government services is included.

The flow of energy is the primary concern of what has come to be known as energy analysis (*2–4*). An important aspect of energy analysis is the determination of the total (direct and indirect) energy required for the production of economic or environmental goods and services. This total has been termed the embodied energy. For example, the energy embodied in an automobile includes the energy consumed directly in the manufacturing plant plus all the energy consumed indirectly to produce the other inputs to auto manufacturing, such as glass, steel, labor, and capital. A problem immediately apparent from this definition is the choice of procedures for calculating indirect energy requirements. Embodied energy values are thus contingent on methodological considerations.

Input-output (I-O) analysis is well suited to calculating indirect effects in a

The author is a postdoctoral research associate at the Coastal Ecology Laboratory, Center for Wetland Resources, Louisiana State University, Baton Rouge 70803.

systematic and all-inclusive accounting framework. Hannon (*5*) and Herendeen and Bullard (*6*) adapted this technique to calculate embodied energy. Controversy still exists concerning the relevant system boundaries for such calculations (*3*).

System Boundaries

The choice of system boundaries is critical because it determines the distinction between net inputs and internal transactions. Net inputs are considered to be independent and exogenously determined, whereas internal transactions are endogenous and interdependent. The net inputs are what economists refer to as primary factors. In the national income accounts, they are "value added." The I-O technique, in essence, distributes a net input vector through a matrix of internal interactions to balance against a net output vector.

Most recent embodied energy calculations based on national I-O tables have employed the standard definitions of economic I-O boundaries (*6*). With these definitions, the net input (or value added) vector includes labor, government services, capital services, and energy and other natural resources (raw materials). The corresponding financial categories are employee compensation, indirect business taxes, and property-type income. The sum of these net inputs, in dollar units, is the gross national product (GNP). Energy (fossil fuels, nuclear fuels, and solar) is a small component of the GNP in dollar units. This has led several people to conclude that energy is a minor component in economic production, a conclusion that would be accurate if the components of the net input vector as currently defined (GNP) were mutually independent, as is usually assumed.

Most proposals to increase the "energy efficiency" of economic activity are ultimately based on the assumption of mutual independence of primary factors, since increasing energy efficiency entails substituting other primary factors (capital, labor, government services, or other natural resources) for fuel inputs. The question is: Are the components of the net input vector as currently defined really independent? Are the conventional primary factors—capital, labor, natural resources, and government services—free from indirect energy costs? A strong case can be made for the contention that they are not (*7–9*). In this article, I present the case for the interdependence of the currently defined primary factors, detail a method for using I-O data to calculate embodied energies so as to take account of this interdependence, and interpret the results.

Primary Factors

From a physical perspective, the earth has one principal net input—solar energy. Although very small amounts of meteoric matter also enter the earth's atmosphere, and deep residual heat may continue to drive crustal movement, there is no stream of spacecraft carrying workers, government mandates, and capital structures onto the planet. Thus, practically everything on the earth can be considered to be a direct or indirect product of past and present solar energy. The same cannot be said for the other "primary" factors. Fossil fuels and other natural resources represent millions of years of embodied sunlight. Environmental flows (such as winds, rain, and rivers) represent embodied sunlight of more recent origin. Humans, under this view, are the product of millions of years of solar-powered R & D and are maintained by an agriculture that uses both current sunlight and fossil sunlight. From this perspective, industrial capital is obviously created by the economic process and is not a net (or primary) input.

As Georgescu-Roegen points out: "On paper, one can write a production function any way one likes, without regard to dimensions or to other physical constraints" (*10*, p. 97). Doing just this has allowed some economists to ignore critical real interdependences and to conclude, for example, that "There are presently extensive possibilities of substitution between resources and other factors [capital]" (*11*, p. 64). Georgescu-Roegen goes on to say: "In actuality, the increase of capital implies an additional depletion of resources." Odum (*9*) has pointed out that the currently defined primary factors are really interdependent by-products of our one observable net input—solar energy.

How can this interdependence of primary factors be taken into account in an analytical model? In an I-O framework, one can simply expand the boundaries so that the net input to the model coincides with the net input to the real system. In practice, most of the interdependences can be captured by considering households and government to be endogenous sectors. This represents a return to Leontief's concept of a "closed" economic system (*12*), with the system boundaries, in this case, placed so that only current solar energy and the energy embodied in fuels and other natural resources enter as a net input.

In a closed Leontief model, households and government are treated like any other sector, with technical coefficients based on the household and government consumption (inputs) used to produce labor and government service outputs. As with standard I-O analysis, this is strictly an accounting of inputs and outputs. The question of whether the current standard of living and level of government spending is good or bad, too high or too low, necessary or wasteful is not and need not be asked in this format.

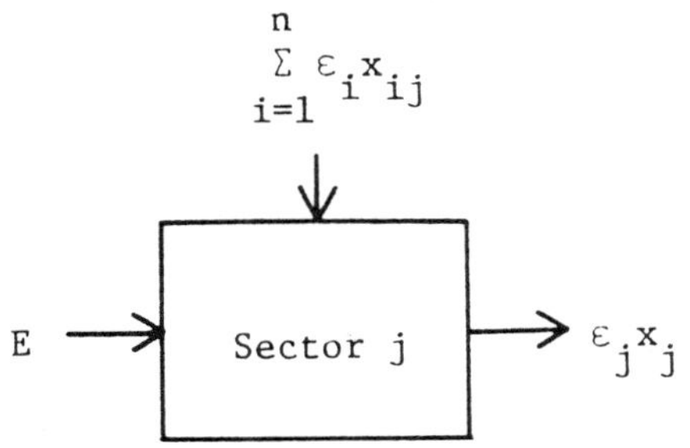

Fig. 1. Single-sector energy balance.

Input-Output–Based Energy Accounting

The I-O technique for calculating embodied energy involves defining a set of energy balance equations (one for each sector) and solving the resulting set of simultaneous linear equations for the energy intensity coefficient vector ϵ, which is the energy required directly and indirectly to produce a unit commodity flow.

Figure 1 shows the basic energy balance for a sector, where x_{ij} is the transaction from sector i to sector j, x_j is the total output of sector j, ϵ_j is the embodied energy intensity per unit of x_j, and E_j is the external direct energy input to sector j. Thus the energy balance for the jth sector is

$$E_j = \epsilon_j x_j - \sum_{i=1}^{n} \epsilon_i x_{ij} \quad (1)$$

In matrix notation for all n sectors

$$\boldsymbol{E} = \boldsymbol{\epsilon}(\hat{\boldsymbol{x}} - \boldsymbol{x}) \quad (2)$$

where $\boldsymbol{E}$ is a row vector of direct external energy inputs, $\hat{\boldsymbol{x}}$ is a diagonalized vector of gross output flows, and $\boldsymbol{x}$ is the n by n transactions matrix. One can solve for ϵ as

$$\boldsymbol{\epsilon} = \boldsymbol{E}(\hat{\boldsymbol{x}} - \boldsymbol{x})^{-1} \quad (3)$$

More detailed expositions of the technique and examples can be found in (*6*), (*13*), and (*14*).

The modifications to include labor and government in the model require expanding the transactions matrix ($\boldsymbol{x}$) to include two more sectors, households and government (Fig. 2). These sectors receive goods and services from the other sectors in proportion to personal consumption expenditures and government expenditures. They provide services to the other sectors in proportion to employee compensation, indirect business taxes, and some percentage of property-type income. The modifications and approximations are discussed in greater detail in (*14*), along with the method employed for estimating solar energy inputs based on land and water use. With household and government sectors considered endogenous, the GNP as currently defined is no longer the net input and output of the model. Personal consumption and government expenditures are now internal transactions, leaving gross capital formation, net inventory change, and net exports as the new net output. Likewise, wages and taxes are internal payments, leaving capital consumption allowances and payments to land and resources as the new net input. To be complete, gross capital formation should include human and government capital formation as well. This implies that some consumption categories in the current model (such as spending on education) would be better handled as capital formation categories. Data on these categories for the U.S. economy have recently been calculated by Kendrick (*15*), but have not been incorporated here. The effects of this omission will be discussed later.

Input-output methodology does not include capital stocks explicitly, since a static equilibrium is assumed. The flows produced by stocks and the flows necessary to maintain and expand stocks are included (as gross capital formation), so stocks are taken into account implicitly. However, even this picture is somewhat distorted, because by convention gross capital formation is credited to the industries producing the capital, not to those utilizing it. This distortion is correctable, and modifications of the I-O model that give a more accurate picture of capital flows have been constructed (*16*). These modifications were not included in the results presented here; they have been shown to cause only a 7 to 8 percent change in the average energy intensity (*16*).

Solar energy inputs were added to the E vector after correcting for the lower thermodynamic usefulness of direct sunlight in comparison with fossil fuel. Electricity represents an upgraded, more useful form than fossil fuel, requiring, directly and indirectly, about 4 British thermal units (Btu's) of fossil fuel per Btu of electricity to produce (*6*). Likewise, fossil fuel represents an upgraded, more useful form than the solar energy that produced it. To account for this difference in quality, an I-O model of the biosphere showing the complete production relations from sunlight to fossil fuel would be necessary. Since such a model does not yet exist, an approximation based on the conversion of sunlight to tree biomass to electricity in a wood-burning power plant was used. This yielded a conversion factor of 2000 Btu's of solar energy per Btu of fossil fuel (*17*). The total solar input for the United States was estimated at 103×10^{18} Btu's of solar energy per year [from data in (*18*) and (*19*)] or the functional equivalent of 51.5×10^{15} Btu's of fossil fuel per year. Solar energy was assumed to enter the economy through the agriculture, forestry, and fisheries sectors, according to their relative land areas. This distribution is crude and will need to be improved as better data become available. For example, the solar inputs to industrial sectors via the hydrologic cycle in providing water for processing and for carrying away wastes are not properly allocated with this approximation.

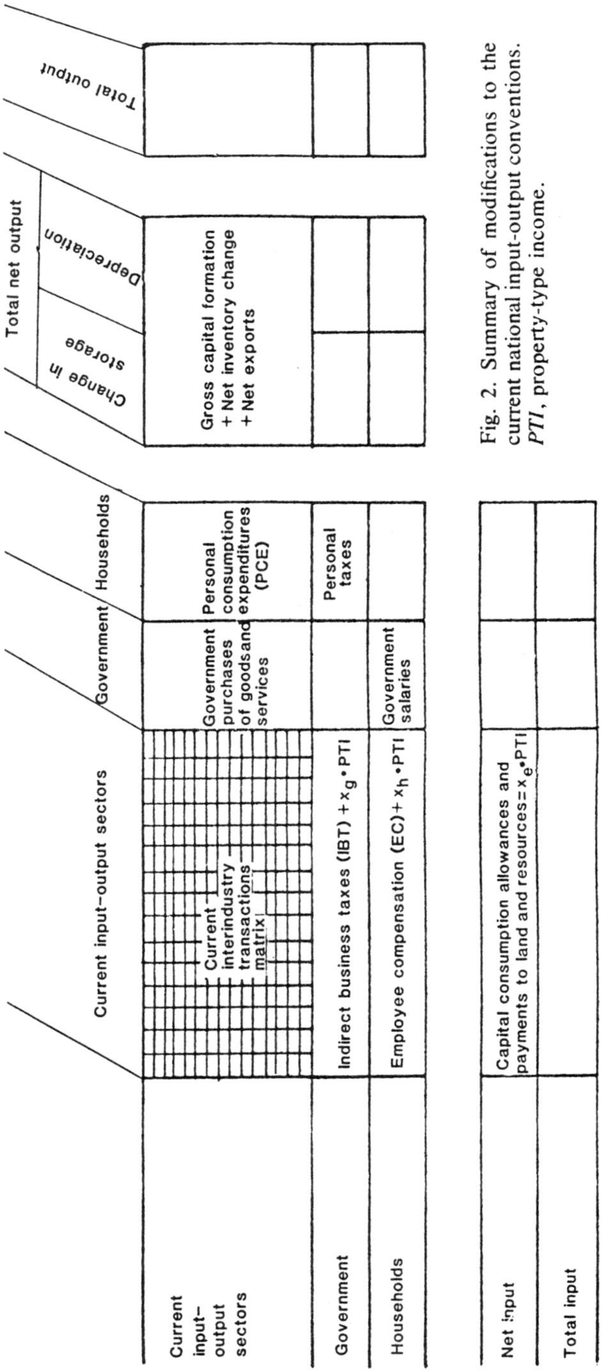

Fig. 2. Summary of modifications to the current national input-output conventions. *PTI*, property-type income.

Table 1. Embodied energy intensities for selected sectors evaluated for the 1967 data base (A) excluding labor and government energy costs and solar energy inputs, (B) including solar energy inputs, (C) including labor and government energy costs, and (D) including both labor and government energy costs and solar energy inputs. Numbers in parentheses are Bureau of Economic Affairs sector equivalents.

Sector	Embodied energy intensity (Btu's of fossil fuel per dollar)			
	A	B	C	D
1. Coal mining (7)	5,143,600	5,172,000	5,455,600	5,807,500
2. Crude petroleum and natural gas (8)	2,920,300	2,929,200	3,188,600	3,469,050
4. Electric utilities (68.01)	505,500	513,900	796,220	1,099,950
6. Other agricultural products (2)	81,567	775,090	381,090	1,385,400
10. Iron and ferroalloy ores mining (5)	65,904	99,605	406,060	800,800
14. New construction (11)	54,804	230,245	389,770	913,950
21. Apparel (18)	38,845	295,135	371,107	974,600
33. Paints and allied products (30)	107,100	160,680	425,290	809,300
73. Air transportation (65.05)	122,630	143,910	452,230	814,700
75. Transportation services (65.07)	5,672	11,615	346,970	706,750
79. Wholesale and retail trade (69)	29,302	43,265	411,490	814,350
91. Government			717,160	1,393,050
92. Households			358,350	738,050

Results of Modifications to System Boundaries

The 90-sector model of energy input and output maintained by the Energy Research Group at the University of Illinois was used to determine the effects of making the above modifications. The model is based on 1967 financial transactions in the U.S. economy. Physical flow I-O data would be preferred for embodied energy calculations, but are not available in the required form at the national level. Calculations made with financial data are nevertheless useful, because they yield information on the direct and indirect energy required to produce a dollar's worth of each of the commodities in the economy.

Selected embodied energy intensities (in Btu's of fossil fuel per dollar) were calculated for each of four possible alternatives, with the results shown in Table 1. The complete calculations may be found in (*13*). Alternative A is calculated with the conventional economic I-O boundaries and yields essentially the same results as those of Herendeen and Bullard (*6*). Alternative B includes solar energy inputs; alternative C includes labor and government as endogenous sectors; and alternative D includes the modifications of alternatives B and C together.

Figure 3 shows frequency plots for the four alternatives, which indicate the reduction in variance of the energy intensities when labor and government are included. Including solar energy did not increase or decrease the variance greatly, but this may be due to the rather crude method used in this study to estimate the distribution of solar energy to the economic sectors. A low variance indicates a more constant relationship from sector to sector of direct-plus-indirect energy consumption and dollar value of output.

The results were put in a regression format to highlight relationships and for significance testing. The calculated energy intensity for each sector (in Btu's per dollar) was multiplied by the sector's dollar output to yield the direct-plus-indirect energy input (in Btu's). This was used as the independent variable, with total dollar output as the dependent variable. Figure 4 shows the results for each of the four alternatives. The primary energy sectors (sectors 1 to 7) were found to be outliers, and the regression results excluding them are also presented. The regression lines are indicated in Fig. 4 along with the r^2 values, equations, and t statistics on the parameters (in parentheses below the parameter values). Table 2 lists the r^2 values, F statistics, and significance levels for each of the alternatives.

Table 2. Regression analysis results for direct plus indirect energy consumption (embodied energy) versus dollar value of output for 92 U.S. economy sectors evaluated for the 1967 data base: (A) excluding labor and government energy costs and solar energy inputs, (B) including solar energy inputs, (C) including labor and government energy costs, and (D) including both labor and government energy costs and solar energy inputs.

Alternative	Including energy sectors 1 to 7			Excluding energy sectors 1 to 7		
	r^2	F	Significance level of F-test	r^2	F	Significance level of F-test
A	.0210	1.89	0.1729	.5539	100.57	0.0001
B	.0629	5.90	0.1710	.2042	20.78	0.0001
C	.7809	313.73	0.0001	.9907	8633.95	0.0001
D	.8535	512.74	0.0001	.9454	1401.31	0.0001

The results indicate a significant relationship between embodied energy and dollar output when labor and government are included as endogenous sectors (alternatives C and D). Several problems still exist, but the trend is clear. As more of the indirect energy costs are taken into account, the ratio of embodied energy to dollars becomes more nearly constant from sector to sector. The primary input sectors (sectors 1 to 7) are the important exceptions to this rule. Their departure from the regression lines in Fig. 4, C and D, has several possible interpretations. One interpretation is that the energy intensities for these sectors are high because they represent the points of entry of available energy into the economy.

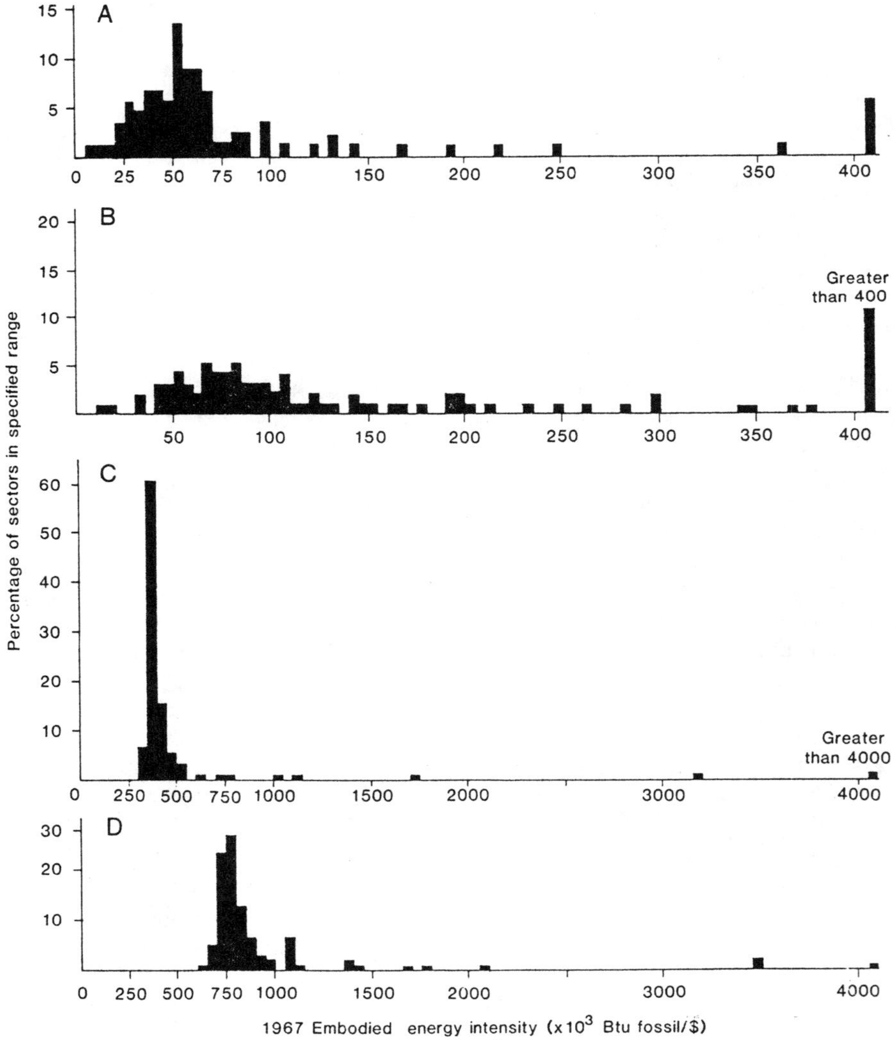

Fig. 3. Frequency plots of embodied energy intensity (in 10^3 Btu's per dollar) by sector for 92 U.S. economy sectors evaluated for the 1967 data base (A) excluding labor and government energy costs and solar energy inputs, (B) including solar energy inputs, (C) including labor and government energy costs, and (D) including both labor and government energy costs and solar energy inputs.

Their degree of departure from the line is an indication of the net energy yield or "energy profit" they provide. In other words, their direct and indirect production costs in energy terms are much less than the energy embodied in their outputs, the difference being the amount brought into the economy from outside.

Ratios of Energy to GNP

Discussions of energy and economics frequently include time series or international comparison plots showing the relation of fossil, nuclear, and hydro energy to GNP or GDP (gross domestic product). The strong historical and international link between these variables is unmistakable. Several authors have suggested that "decoupling" energy and GNP is possible and would allow the economy to continue to grow while decreasing energy consumption (*20, 21*). Calculations based on the conventional system boundaries (Figs. 3A and 4A) are often used or implied in support of this idea. If the sector-to-sector differences in embodied energy intensities implied in these calculations were real, then it might be possible to simply shift production from high energy intensity sectors to low energy intensity sectors to lower energy use without sacrificing economic activity. This conclusion would follow from the underlying assumption that the currently defined primary factors are independent. But because it takes available energy to produce labor and government services, capital, and other natural resources, the assumption of independence is not warranted. The results presented in Fig. 3, C and D, and Fig. 4, C and D, reflect the implications of an attempt to relax the independence assumption and lead to the conclusion that decoupling energy and economic activity by simply shifting production between sectors is not a real possibility. The possibility for large changes in energy efficiency is small since, all things considered, total energy efficiency is fairly constant from sector to sector. Any reductions in direct energy consumption are offset by increases in indirect energy consumption through increased use of labor, land, or capital.

Actually, Fig. 4, C and D, lead to the conclusion that energy consumption is highly related to gross capital formation plus net inventory change plus net exports because these quantities are the net output from the economy under the revised boundary definition. The GNP includes these quantities, as well as personal consumption and government expenditures. The extent to which gross capital formation, net exports, and net inventory change are separable from the GNP as a whole represents the latitude for decoupling energy and GNP. I suspect that this latitude is small, especially if human and government capital formation are included as part of gross capital formation—as Kendrick (*15*) has suggested—and not as consumption. Inclusion of human and government capital formation would also significantly decrease the mean embodied energy intensity, since it would increase the redefined net output from the economy. For alternative D the mean would drop from 12.20×10^5 to 1.88×10^5 Btu's of fossil fuel per 1967 dollar (*14*).

Double Counting

Slesser (*22*) commented that including labor costs in embodied energy calculations would involve double counting. This criticism was directed against a specific method of including labor costs, and it remains a valid criticism of that method. If the conventional system boundaries for calculation of embodied energy are used, and then the energy necessary to support labor is simply added on, the same energy has indeed been counted twice. If the energy costs of labor are to

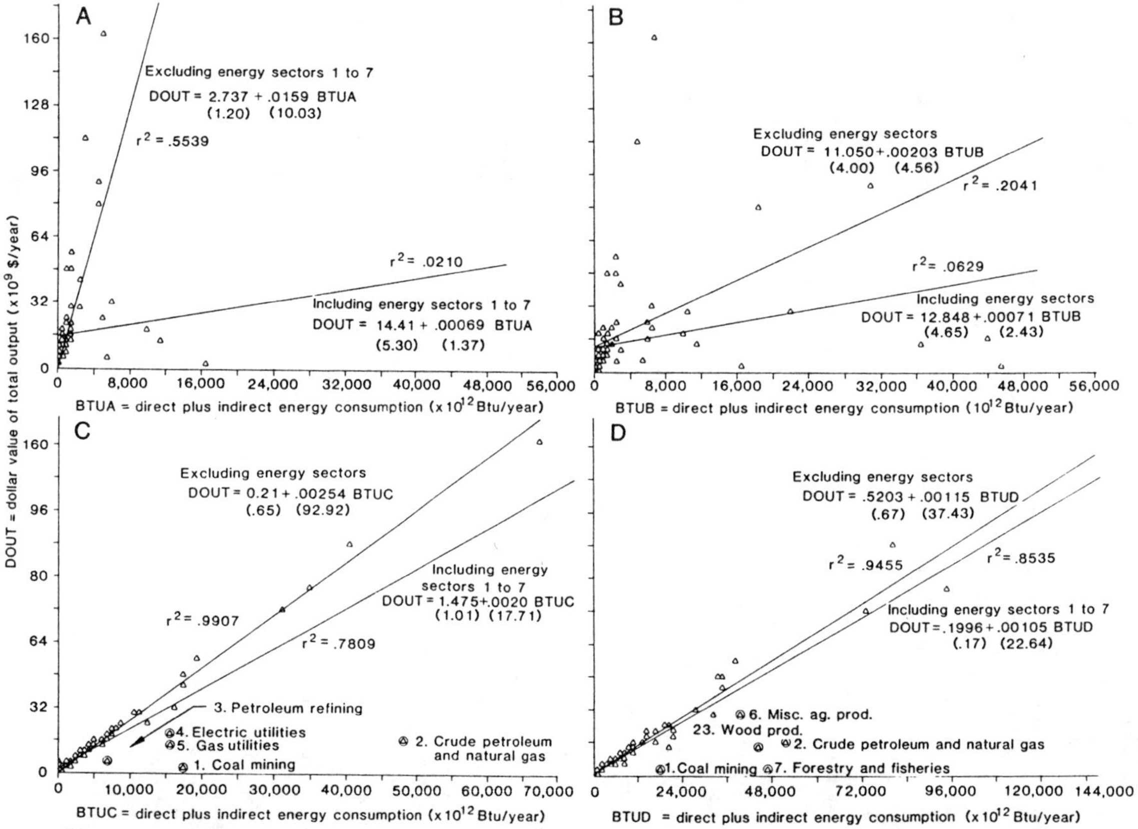

Fig. 4. Plots of direct plus indirect energy consumption (embodied energy) versus dollar value of output for 92 U.S. economy sectors evaluated for the 1967 data base (A) excluding labor and government energy costs and solar energy inputs, (B) including solar energy inputs, (C) including labor and government energy costs, and (D) including both labor and government energy costs and solar energy inputs. The primary energy sectors (sectors 1 to 7) were found to be outliers, and regression results excluding them are also presented.

be included without double counting, the system boundaries have to be changed. The net output with the revised boundaries does not include the support of labor, which is now an internal transaction (see Fig. 2). The total energy budget is now allocated to gross capital formation, net inventory change, and net exports. The total energy requirement is equal to the total energy input, and the energy cost of labor is accounted for. However, in any I-O accounting system, gross flows and net flows must be kept straight. One can never add up internal transactions in an I-O table and expect them to equal net inputs or outputs. With the expanded boundaries, net output and input are no longer equal to GNP, but rather to GNP minus labor and government transactions.

Embodied Energy Theory of Value

Several authors have proposed various forms of an energy theory of value (*1, 8, 23, 24*). The idea is summarily dismissed by neoclassical economists (*25–27*) on the ground that energy is only one of a number of primary inputs to the production process. This dismissal is unwarranted if the traditional primary factors are in reality interdependent. The results presented in this article indicate that if there are interdependences among the currently defined primary factors, then calculated embodied energy values that take this into account show a very good empirical relation to market-determined dollar values. Herendeen (*28*) has shown that, with the I-O method, the necessary and sufficient condition for the energy intensity vector to be constant is that the value-added vector (in dollars) and the direct-energy input vector (in Btu's) be proportional. If all factors other than energy are moved from the net input vector to the transactions matrix, this proportionality is to be expected.

The question might be asked whether the same thing we have done with energy could not be done with any of the other currently defined primary factors and thus support capital, labor, or government service theories of value. The answer is that on paper this could be done. We must look to physical reality to determine which factors are net inputs and which are internal transactions. No one would seriously suggest that labor creates sunlight.

An embodied energy theory of value thus makes theoretical sense and is empirically accurate only if the system boundaries are defined in an appropriate way. It is really a cost-of-production theory with all costs carried back to the solar energy necessary directly and indirectly to produce them. The results indicate that there is no inherent conflict between an embodied energy (or energy cost) theory of value and value theories based on utility. The empirical equivalence of these estimates—one from the cost or supply side, and one from the benefit or demand side—supports basic economic principles grounded in optimization while giving them a biophysical basis. The flow of energy *is* the primary concern of economics.

Conclusions

The results presented here indicate that, with the appropriate perspective and boundaries, market-determined dollar values and embodied energy values are proportional for all but the primary energy sectors. The required perspective is an ecological or "systems" view that considers humans to be a part of, and not apart from, their environment. A few economists have already taken this perspective (*29–31*), and the implications for a new ecological economics that links the natural and social sciences are great (*32*). The concept of embodied energy may help to provide such a link as an empirically accurate common denominator in ecological and economic systems. With the appropriate boundaries, embodied energy values are accurate indicators of market values where markets exist. Because they are based on physical flows, they may also be used to determine "market values" where markets do not exist—for example, in ecological systems. This is one way of "internalizing" all factors external to the existing market system and solving the natural resource valuation problem. From the ecological perspective, markets can be viewed as an efficient energy allocation device that humans have developed to solve the common problem facing all species—survival.

What does all this imply for national policy? The most important implication is that the physical dimensions of economic activity are not separable from limitations of energy supply. The universally appealing notion of unlimited economic growth with reduced energy consumption must be put firmly to rest beside the equally appealing but impossible idea of perpetual motion. It is easy to think you can get a "free lunch" by looking only at small parts of the system in isolation. When the whole system is analyzed, however, it becomes clear that all you can do is transfer the cost of your lunch to another segment of the system.

These conclusions should not be interpreted as pessimistic. Several authors, notably Daly (*31*), have pointed out the inadequacy of GNP and other yardsticks of physical economic production as measures of social welfare. Indeed, there is nothing inherently appealing about what Boulding (*30*) has called the "cowboy economy," the adolescent phase of rapid, self-conscious, often painful growth. If we are to manage our future wisely, we must be aware of the physical limitations on economic activity and learn to live well within our energy budget.

References and Notes

1. F. Soddy, *Wealth, Virtual Wealth and Debt: The Solution of the Economic Paradox* (Dutton, New York, 1933).
2. M. W. Gilliland, *Science* **189**, 1051 (1975).
3. ______ Ed., *Energy Analysis: A New Public Policy Tool* (Westview Press, Boulder, Colo., 1978).
4. D. E. Gushee, *Energy Accounting as a Policy Analysis Tool* (Congressional Research Service, Washington, D.C., 1976).
5. B. Hannon, *J. Theor. Biol.* **41**, 575 (1973).
6. R. A. Herendeen and C. W. Bullard, *Energy Costs of Goods and Services, 1963 and 1967* (Document 140, Center for Advanced Computation, University of Illinois, Champaign-Urbana, 1974).
7. H. T. Odum, *Ambio* **2**, 220 (1973).
8. ______, in *Ecosystem Modeling in Theory and Practice*, C. A. S. Hall and J. W. Day, Eds. (Wiley, New York, 1977), pp. 173–196.
9. ______, in (*3*), pp. 55–87.
10. N. Georgescu-Roegen, in *Scarcity and Growth Reconsidered*, V. K. Smith, Ed. (Johns Hopkins Press, Baltimore, 1979), pp. 95–105.
11. J. E. Stiglitz, in *ibid.*, pp. 36–66.
12. W. W. Leontief, *The Structure of American Economy, 1919, 1929; An Empirical Application of Equilibrium Analysis* (Harvard Univ. Press, Cambridge, Mass., 1941).
13. R. Costanza, *Energy Costs of Goods and Services in 1967 Including Solar Energy Inputs and Labor and Government Service Feedbacks* (Document 262, Center for Advanced Computation, University of Illinois, Champaign-Urbana, 1978).
14. ______, thesis, University of Florida, Gainesville (1979).
15. J. W. Kendrick, *The Formation and Stocks of Total Capital* (National Bureau of Economic Research, New York, 1976).
16. K. Kirkpatrick, *Effect of Including Capital Flows on Energy Coefficients, 1963* (Technical memo 26, Energy Research Group, University of Illinois, Urbana, 1974).
17. H. T. Odum, F. C. Wang, J. Alexander, M. Gilliland, *Energy Analysis of Environmental Values: A Manual for Estimating Environmental and Societal Values According to Embodied Energies* [Report to the Nuclear Regulatory Commission, contract NRC-04-77-123 (Center for Wetlands, University of Florida, Gainesville, 1978)].
18. T. H. Vonder Haar and V. E. Suomi, *Science* **163**, 667 (1969).
19. M. I. Budyko, in *Climatic Change*, J. Gribben, Ed. (Cambridge Univ. Press, New York, 1978), pp. 85–113.
20. R. Stobaugh and D. Yergin, Eds., *Energy Future: Report of the Energy Project at the Harvard Business School* (Random House, New York, 1979).
21. A. B. Lovins, *Soft Energy Paths: Toward a Durable Peace* (Ballinger, Cambridge, Mass., 1977).
22. M. Slesser, *Science* **196**, 259 (1977).
23. F. Cottrell, *Energy and Society: The Relation Between Energy, Social Change and Economic Development* (McGraw-Hill, New York, 1955).
24. B. Hannon, *Ann. Am. Acad. Polit. Soc. Sci.* **410**, 139 (1973).
25. D. A. Huettner, *Science* **192**, 101 (1976).
26. M. R. Langham and W. W. McPherson, *ibid.*, p. 8.
27. H. M. Peskin, *ibid.*, p. 9.
28. R. A. Herendeen, *On the Concept of Energy Intensity in Ecological Systems* (Document 271, Energy Research Group, University of Illinois, Champaign-Urbana, 1980).

29. N. Georgescu-Roegen, *The Entropy Law and the Economic Process* (Harvard Univ. Press, Cambridge, Mass., 1971).
30. K. E. Boulding, in *Environmental Quality in a Growing Economy*, H. Jarrett, Ed. (Johns Hopkins Press, Baltimore, 1966), pp. 3–14.
31. H. E. Daly, *Steady-State Economics* (Freeman, San Francisco, 1977).
32. E. P. Odum, *Science* **195**, 1289 (1977).
33. The input-output calculations on which this article is based were performed at the University of Illinois with the assistance of the Energy Research Group as part of a joint effort with the Center for Wetlands, University of Florida. The project was funded in part by DOE contract EY-76-S-05-4398 (H. T. Odum, principal investigator). This material was presented at the AAAS annual meeting, San Francisco, 3 to 8 January 1980, and will appear in an expanded form in the AAAS proceedings volume: *Energetic and Ecological Economics*, H. E. Daly, Ed. I thank H. E. Daly, B. M. Hannon, M. W. Gilliland, J. Bartholomew, J. W. Day, R. E. Turner, S. E. Bayley, and an anonymous reviewer for reviewing drafts and providing helpful comments, and the Center for Wetland Resources, Louisiana State University, for providing support during the preparation of this article.

Resources and Energy 6 (1984) 129–163. North-Holland

EMBODIED ENERGY AND ECONOMIC VALUE IN THE UNITED STATES ECONOMY: 1963, 1967 and 1972

Robert COSTANZA*

Louisiana State University, Baton Rouge, LA 70803, USA

Robert A. HERENDEEN

University of Illinois, Champaign, IL 61801, USA

Received October 1983, final version received February 1984

An economy can be said to operate on an energy theory of value if economic value can be shown to be proportional to an appropriate energy indicator. We have investigated this hypothesis for an 87 sector breakdown of the U.S. economy for the years 1963, 1967 and 1972. Input–output (I–O) models of the economy, modified to include households and government as endogenous sectors, were used to calculate each sector's direct plus indirect (embodied) energy consumption based on various estimates of the distribution of direct energy inputs to the sectors. Dollar value of sector output is highly correlated with this energy indicator (though not with direct energy consumption or with embodied energy calculated excluding labor and government energy costs). We also test explicitly the criticism that this result is merely a mathematical artifact of incorporating household and government sectors, thus making the system more 'closed'. Application of these tests to a 4-sector example implies that the mathematical artifact argument is not valid (except for a specific, limited case). Application of the tests to the full 87 sector model also indicates that the mathematical artifact argument is not valid. We conclude that embodied energy, calculated in the way we suggest, is a good predictor of economic value, at least for the relatively large aggregates of marketed goods and services that appear in I–O tables.

1. Introduction

An economy can be said to operate on an energy theory of value if economic value can be shown to be proportional to an appropriate energy indicator. One of us previously found evidence of such proportionality [Costanza (1980)], while the other challenged that result [Herendeen (1981)]. This paper represents a partial resolution of our differences.

We present further analysis of the type used in Costanza (1980), and address specifically the major remaining technical criticism raised in Herendeen (1981): that the observed proportionality is merely a mathematical artifact of the manipulation of the data. The other major technical criticism, having to do with double counting [Huettner (1982)], has already

*This research was funded, in part, by the National Science Foundation under Grant PRA-8003845, and by the Illinois Department of Energy and Natural Resources under Grant ENR-80.260. We thank B.M. Hannon, C.J. Cleveland, M.J. Lavine, T.J. Butler and H.E. Daly for reviewing earlier drafts and providing useful comments.

been disposed of [Costanza (1982)]. We find that the 'mathematical artifact argument', while holding in one limited situation, is in general invalid. This conclusion is based on empirical calculations. We have not been successful at finding a closed form proof.

The basic idea behind the analysis is: if proportionality is found to result from acceptable manipulations and computations with acceptable data, then it is a valid 'revealed' result. The major issue is that of data manipulation.

Our energy indicator is embodied energy, calculated using the energy input–output (I–O) method developed by Bullard and Herendeen (1975). This method uses the standard assumptions [linearity, constant coefficients, etc., cf. Carter and Brody (1970)] of I–O analysis, and is applied to an 87-sector breakdown of the U.S. economy for the years 1963, 1967 and 1972.

Features of this analysis are: (1) the energy costs of labor and government services are included by considering households and government to be endogenous sectors [Costanza (1980, 1982)]; (2) analysis of the mathematical artifact argument; and (3) use of two alternative measures of the distribution of direct energy inputs to the system. The first measure follows previous practice and assumes energy enters the economy only through the 'energy sectors'. The second measure assumes direct energy input occurs at the point of consumption, not the point of physical entry. The second method is more consistent with the treatment of transportation sectors in I–O analysis.

Embodied energy costs are calculated for each year and compared with the corresponding dollar value of output of the sectors. The accuracy of embodied energy as a predictor of sector dollar output is investigated. The differences between the results based on the two measures of direct energy input are interpreted, both from an empirical and a theoretical perspective.

2. Input–output methods

Any economic or ecological system can be divided into a number of interacting components or processes that consume, produce and exchange energy, organized material, information and services (or 'commodities' for

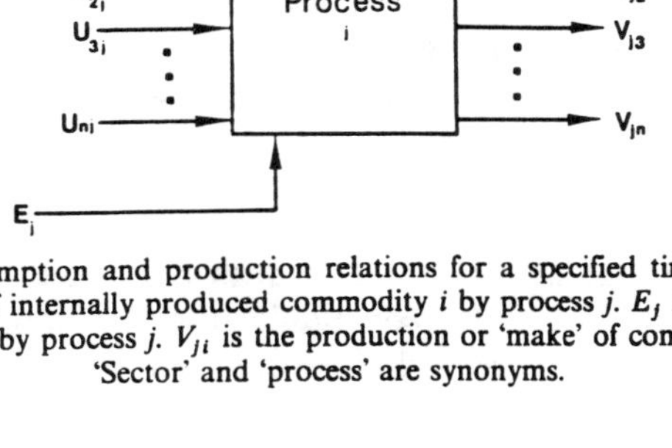

Fig. 1. Process j consumption and production relations for a specified time interval. U_{ij} is the consumption or 'use' of internally produced commodity i by process j. E_j is the use of externally produced commodities by process j. V_{ji} is the production or 'make' of commodity i by process j. 'Sector' and 'process' are synonyms.

short). Fig. 1 is a diagram of a typical process, J, which uses or consumes internally produced commodities (U_{iJ}) and externally produced commodities (E_J) in order to produce or make its output commodities (V_{Ji}). Various mathematical formulations are possible starting with this picture [cf. Ritz (1979), Carter and Brody (1970), Hannon et al. (1983), Costanza and Neill (1984)]. These approaches all share the assumptions of scale and time independent production functions. Costanza (1980) and Bullard and Herendeen (1975) did not allow for 'joint products', produced when an individual process has more than one output commodity. Our approach allows for joint products. For the purposes of this study the following formulation is employed. An embodied energy balance equation can be written for each process in the form:

$$E_J + \sum_{i=1}^{n} \varepsilon_i U_{iJ} = \sum_{i=1}^{n} \varepsilon_i V_{Ji}, \tag{1}$$

where ε_i represents the embodied energy intensity of each of the n commodities in the system and E_J represents the direct energy input to process J. It is assumed that the energy intensity for a commodity is a single number representing the average over the processes which produce it.

In matrix notation for a system with n commodities and m processes one can write:

$$\boldsymbol{E} + \boldsymbol{\varepsilon U} = \boldsymbol{\varepsilon V}^T, \quad \text{where} \tag{2}$$

$\boldsymbol{E}$ $= m$ dimensional row vector of direct energy inputs,
$\boldsymbol{U}$ $= n \times m$ matrix of the use of commodities by processes,
$\boldsymbol{V}^T = n \times m$ matrix of the production of commodities by processes,
$\boldsymbol{\varepsilon}$ $= n$ dimensional row vector of embodied energy intensities.

Given data on $\boldsymbol{U}$, $\boldsymbol{V}$ and $\boldsymbol{E}$ we wish to solve eq. 2 for the embodied energy intensity vector, $\boldsymbol{\varepsilon}$. If $m = n$ this is possible using standard matrix manipulation techniques:

$$\boldsymbol{\varepsilon} = \boldsymbol{E}(\boldsymbol{V}^T - \boldsymbol{U})^{-1} = \boldsymbol{E}\boldsymbol{V}^{T-1}(\boldsymbol{I} - \boldsymbol{U}\boldsymbol{V}^{T-1})^{-1}. \tag{3}$$

There are potential problems with this formulation, in that it can yield negative energy intensities. We believe (as will be pointed out) that these arise mainly as a result of deficiencies in the data, and are best handled by using preliminary runs to pinpoint problems. For example, preliminary runs on the U.S. economy produced negative intensities for three sectors (out of 88), one of which was Radio and TV broadcasting. On closer inspection it was discovered that this sector consumed all of its own output, according to the Bureau of Economic Analysis I–O data base we used. This was obviously done as an accounting convenience and does not reflect the real situation. This sector was aggregated with communications to eliminate the problem. Similar steps were taken for the other two problem sectors (business services and state and local government enterprises).

Most energy I–O modeling assumes the standard I–O accounting convention that places households and government outside the boundaries of the economic system (they are assumed to be exogenous). This accounting stance can lead to major distortions of energy cost calculations since labor and government provide services to the economy whose energy costs would be ignored. In this study we employed I–O models which included households and government as endogenous sectors (rows and columns in $\boldsymbol{U}$ and $\boldsymbol{V}$) in order to capture their energy cost contributions. Specific methods for doing this followed Costanza (1980) and will be discussed in detail further on.

Once modified $\boldsymbol{U}$ and $\boldsymbol{V}$ matrices were formed that included households and government as endogenous sectors and 'problem' sectors were rectified, the matrix $(\boldsymbol{V}^T-\boldsymbol{U})$ was inverted and energy intensities were calculated as a function of various estimates of the direct energy input vector, $\boldsymbol{E}$. The different $\boldsymbol{E}$ vectors reflected different measures of the distribution of direct energy inputs to the economy. The resulting energy intensities were then evaluated in terms of their relationship to market prices for the sectors. Since $\boldsymbol{U}$ and $\boldsymbol{V}$ are measured in constant 1972 dollars for the economy, and direct energy inputs are in Btu's, the energy intensities have the units Btu/$. If the energy embodied in a commodity (Btu/physical unit) is proportional to its price ($/physical unit) then the energy intensities expressed as Btu/$ should all be constant.

To test for this, the total energy embodied in sector inputs was regressed on dollar value of sector outputs. A high degree of correlation between these variables indicates a relatively constant energy intensity (Btu/$) and a high correlation between embodied energy and economic value across sectors.

3. I–O data

Eighty-eight sector $\boldsymbol{U}$ and $\boldsymbol{V}$ matrices were obtained from the Energy Research Group (ERG), University of Illinois, for the years 1963, 1967 and 1972. These data were aggregated and modified from the original I–O data available through the Bureau of Economic Analysis (BEA). Staff at the ERG invested considerable time and effort making the three year's data as compatible as possible, so that valid comparisons between years could be made. As mentioned earlier, three problem sectors remained in the data and these were first eliminated by aggregation to an 85 sector model. Household and Government sectors were then added yielding revised 87 sector matrices for all three years.

Inputs to the Government and Household sectors (columns 86 and 87 of the revised $\boldsymbol{U}$ matrix) were developed from data on government expenditures (GE) and personal consumption expenditures (PCE) available as components of final demand. Inputs of government services to households ($U_{86,87}$) were estimated as personal taxes (PT) and household services to government

Table 1
Government salaries, personal taxes, and household and government gross investment for 1963, 1967 and 1972 ($\times 10^9$ 1972\$).

	1963	1967	1972
Government salaries[a]	71.76	92.34	119.40
Personal taxes[a]	68.22	84.26	95.70
Household gross investment[b]	280.82	338.76	471.66
Government gross investment[b]	129.14	151.94	213.58

[a]From U.S. Bureau of the Census (1976).
[b]Values for 1963 and 1967 based on estimates in Kendrick (1976). Values for 1972 based on Eisner et al. (1981) and Kendrick (1976). See table 2.

($U_{87,86}$) as government salaries (*GS*). Values for these components for all three years are listed in table 1. 'Self sales' of households and government ($U_{86,86}$ and $U_{87,87}$) were assumed to be zero, since these values have no effect on the energy intensities. The inputs of government and household services to the other sectors (rows 86 and 87 of the revised U matrix) were estimated as indirect business taxes (*IBT*) and employee compensation (*EC*) respectively, both of which are also available in the I–O data base as components of value added. These modifications leave property type income (*PTI*) as the financial net input and gross capital formation (*GCF*), plus net inventory change (*NIC*), plus net exports (*NE*), plus estimates of household and government capital formation as the net output in financial terms. This net output will be referred to simply as revised net output (*RNO*) henceforth.

In a zero growth economy with no net exports this boundary definition would leave gross capital formation (including human and government capital formation) as the only non-zero components of *RNO*. At steady state, *RNO* is just enough to counteract depreciation, the system's tendency (by the second law of thermodynamics) to evolve toward a higher state of entropy if net energy inputs were cut off. It is worthwhile to note the magnitude of these adjustments to GNP. The ratio of *RNO* to 'normal' GNP was 63.1%, 63.8% and 75.0% in the three years, respectively.

Only two additional entries in the V matrix were required, $V_{86,86}$ and $V_{87,87}$. These represent the total output of the Government and Household sectors, respectively, exclusive of 'self-sales'. These values include estimates of gross household and government investment (capital formation), which were available in Kendrick (1976) and Eisner et al. (1981) (table 2), as well as data on *IBT*, *PT*, *EC*, and *GS*. The estimated total outputs of the government and household sectors are listed in table 3. The complete revised 87 sector U and V matrices in 1972\$ for 1963, 1967 and 1972 are available from the first author on request.

Table 2
Total gross investment for 1963, 1967 and 1972 (10^9 1972$).[a]

Year	Kendrick				Eisner
	Business	Government	Households	Total	Total
1963	115.48	129.14	280.82	525.44	512.95
% of total	21.98	24.58	53.44	—	—
1967	155.05	151.94	338.76	645.75	667.41
% of total	24.01	23.53	52.46	—	—
1972	204.68	213.58	471.66	—	889.93
% of total	23.00	24.00	53.00	—	—

[a]Kendrick (1976) provides business, government, and household components for gross investment, but his series stops at 1969. To extend the series to 1972, data on total gross investment from Eisner et al. (1981) was used. Eisner's totals agree well with Kendrick's for 1963 and 1967, but sector breakdowns were not provided. The average percent of total for each sector from the 1963 and 1967 Kendrick data was therefore used to estimate the breakdown of the Eisner total for 1972.

Table 3
Total government and household output, 1963, 1967 and 1972 (10^9 1972$).[a]

	1963	1967	1972
Government			
Indirect business taxes (IBT)	69.32	89.14	106.94
Personal taxes (PT)	68.22	84.26	95.70
Gov't gross investment (GGI)	129.14	151.94	213.58
Government total	266.67	325.06	416.22
Households			
Employee compensation (EC)	433.40	494.21	692.35
Government salaries (GS)	71.76	92.34	119.40
H'hold gross investment (HGI)	280.82	338.76	471.66
Household total	785.98	925.31	1283.41

[a]*Source:* See tables 1 and 2.

The remaining data necessary to complete the analysis were estimates of the direct energy input from nature to the 87 sectors (***E*** vectors) for each of the three years. There is considerable debate on the appropriate ***E*** vector for this analysis. In this analysis we used ***E*** vectors containing only fossil fuel, hydro and nuclear energy inputs, ignoring direct environmental energy inputs. The alternate ***E*** vectors used in this study for all three years are listed in table 4, along with the revised sector definitions in terms of their BEA I–O codes. Alternative 1 (DIRECT) consisted of fossil, nuclear and hydro energy

Table 4

Alternative direct energy input vectors used in this study. DIRECT assumes direct energy input at the point of physical entry into sectors, while DEC assumes direct energy consumption as the point of entry into sectors. Units are Btu per year.

			1963		1967		1972	
No.	I–O Code	Sector name	DIRECT	DEC	DIRECT	DEC	DIRECT	DEC
(1)	700	Coal mining	0.12476E+17	0.11557E+14	0.14794E+17	0.12398E+14	0.14172E+17	0.19053E+14
(2)	800	Crude petro gas	0.30384E+17	0.20272E+14	0.37459E+17	0.35012E+14	0.42336E+17	0.46075E+14
(3)	3101	Petro refin. prod.	0.10654E+16	0.14101E+15	0.12523E+16	0.16994E+15	0.17309E+16	0.23470E+15
(4)	6801	Electric utilities	0.16987E+16	0.32782E+15	0.23902E+16	0.45569E+15	0.34343E+16	0.83297E+15
(5)	6802	Gas utilities	0.71640E+15	0.70079E+14	0.11730E+16	0.99366E+14	0.14512E+16	0.13315E+15
(6)	100	Livestock		0.43954E+15		0.53604E+15		0.34777E+15
(7)	200	Misc. ag. products		0.67037E+15		0.71976E+15		0.12962E+16
(8)	300	Forest, fish products		0.31733E+14		0.49352E+14		0.11743E+15
(9)	400	Ag., for., fish services		0.94095E+13		0.11610E+14		0.60442E+14
(10)	500	Iron ore mining		0.85677E+14		0.93147E+14		0.15258E+15
(11)	600	Nonferr. mining		0.86759E+14		0.80027E+14		0.14255E+15
(12)	900	Stone clay mining		0.12601E+15		0.14442E+15		0.22576E+15
(13)	1000	Chem. mineral mining		0.11624E+15		0.15588E+15		0.19545E+15
(14)	1100	New construction		0.77198E+15		0.11946E+16		0.17365E+16
(15)	1200	Maint. rep. const.		0.48258E+15		0.26876E+15		0.79916E+15
(16)	1300	Ordnance		0.49506E+14		0.11523E+15		0.86169E+14
(17)	1400	Food		0.11292E+16		0.12699E+16		0.14582E+16
(18)	1500	Tobacco		0.21757E+14		0.26066E+14		0.29803E+14
(19)	1600	Fabric and mills		0.33952E+15		0.39455E+15		0.46058E+15
(20)	1700	Textile goods		0.41723E+14		0.63472E+14		0.10627E+15
(21)	1800	Apparel		0.93899E+14		0.11505E+15		0.22885E+15
(22)	1900	Fab. textile prod.		0.10792E+14		0.29194E+14		0.33303E+14
(23)	2000	Wood products		0.15084E+15		0.27445E+15		0.44330E+15
(24)	2100	Wood containers		0.36555E+13		0.62667E+13		0.82064E+13
(25)	2200	H'hold furniture		0.37908E+14		0.39658E+14		0.63837E+14
(26)	2300	Furn., fixtures		0.19212E+14		0.24641E+14		0.46659E+14
(27)	2400	Paper products		0.12520E+16		0.14284E+16		0.17869E+16
(28)	2500	Paperboard cont.		0.48485E+14		0.78269E+14		0.11506E+15
(29)	2600	Printing, publishing		0.10252E+15		0.13806E+15		0.21809E+15

Table 4 (continued)

No.	I–O Code	Sector name	1963 DIRECT	1963 DEC	1967 DIRECT	1967 DEC	1972 DIRECT	1972 DEC
(30)	2700	Chem. products		0.37821E+16		0.38254E+16		0.43613E+16
(31)	2800	Plastics		0.46940E+15		0.68742E+15		0.94899E+15
(32)	2900	Drugs, toil. prep.		0.27175E+15		0.12015E+15		0.18503E+15
(33)	3000	Paints		0.79557E+14		0.51586E+14		0.65851E+14
(34)	3102	Paving		0.21103E+15		0.28791E+15		0.39162E+15
(35)	3103	Asphalt		0.22213E+15		0.23050E+15		0.35914E+15
(36)	3200	Rubber products		0.22514E+15		0.29330E+15		0.45013E+15
(37)	3300	Leather products		0.28141E+14		0.21437E+14		0.22528E+14
(38)	3400	Footwear		0.15926E+14		0.24162E+14		0.30726E+14
(39)	3500	Glass products		0.28714E+15		0.31809E+15		0.41369E+15
(40)	3600	Stone clay products		0.10039E+16		0.12178E+16		0.13650E+16
(41)	3700	Prim. ir., stl. manufact.		0.42033E+16		0.44632E+16		0.43979E+16
(42)	3800	Prim. nonferr. metals		0.10206E+16		0.12944E+16		0.15481E+16
(43)	3900	Metal containers		0.20246E+14		0.38784E+14		0.58753E+14
(44)	4000	Heating, plumbing		0.11421E+15		0.14649E+15		0.18674E+15
(45)	4100	Screw mach. products		0.65586E+14		0.11460E+15		0.15158E+15
(46)	4200	Fab. metal. products		0.13279E+15		0.17981E+15		0.23877E+15
(47)	4300	Engines, turbines		0.45802E+14		0.43359E+14		0.49350E+14
(48)	4400	Farm machinery		0.44383E+14		0.52192E+14		0.64680E+14
(49)	4500	Const., mining eq.		0.54005E+14		0.75505E+14		0.94025E+14
(50)	4600	Mat. handling eq.		0.10751E+14		0.15047E+14		0.24343E+14
(51)	4700	Metalworking eq.		0.50082E+14		0.73236E+14		0.91708E+14
(52)	4800	Spec. ind. mach.		0.29132E+14		0.41292E+14		0.60529E+14
(53)	4900	Gen. ind. mach.		0.67760E+14		0.79103E+14		0.10558E+15
(54)	5000	Mach. shop products		0.23945E+14		0.50987E+14		0.60141E+14
(55)	5100	Ofc. comput. mach.		0.24032E+14		0.30755E+14		0.55097E+14
(56)	5200	Service ind. mach.		0.15349E+14		0.34577E+14		0.84507E+14
(57)	5300	Elec. ind. apparat.		0.80819E+14		0.10948E+15		0.14726E+15
(58)	5400	H'hold appliance		0.53164E+14		0.63704E+14		0.73778E+14
(59)	5500	Elec. light eq.		0.27975E+14		0.43128E+14		0.62908E+14
(60)	5600	R–TV commun. eq.		0.84589E+14		0.95244E+14		0.12282E+15

(61)	5700	Electronic comp.	0.55087E+14	0.83169E+14	0.11751E+15
(62)	5800	Electrical equipment	0.21783E+14	0.31764E+14	0.46196E+14
(63)	5900	Motor veh. and eq.	0.32010E+15	0.35971E+15	0.45230E+15
(64)	6000	Aircraft and parts	0.13051E+15	0.17568E+15	0.16596E+15
(65)	6100	Transport equipment	0.53549E+14	0.66796E+14	0.99986E+14
(66)	6200	Prof. scient. supplies	0.23448E+14	0.35886E+14	0.57473E+14
(67)	6300	Optical supplies	0.37645E+14	0.28433E+14	0.61267E+14
(68)	6400	Misc. manufact.	0.66204E+14	0.60653E+14	0.12028E+15
(69)	6501	Railroad	0.74905E+15	0.68421E+15	0.81490E+15
(70)	6502	Local transport	0.30822E+15	0.23872E+15	0.23257E+15
(71)	6503	Motor fgt. transport	0.56182E+15	0.51467E+15	0.86260E+15
(72)	6504	Water transport	0.67356E+15	0.70659E+15	0.91699E+15
(73)	6505	Air transport	0.67056E+15	0.12717E+16	0.16780E+16
(74)	6506	Pipe line transport	0.14064E+15	0.14865E+15	0.16362E+15
(75)	6507+73	Tran. busnss. serv.	0.42100E+15	0.38006E+15	0.37657E+15
(76)	66+67	Communications	0.21318E+15	0.22361E+15	0.22758E+15
(77)	6803	Water sanit. serv.	0.16664E+15	0.10875E+15	0.61226E+14
(78)	6900	Whole, retail trade	0.26494E+16	0.34762E+16	0.45105E+16
(79)	7000	Finance, insurance	0.47596E+15	0.37788E+15	0.57143E+15
(80)	7100	Real estate	0.11789E+15	0.29615E+15	0.63482E+15
(81)	7200	Hotels, pers. serv.	0.29341E+15	0.61436E+15	0.62392E+15
(82)	7500	Auto repair	0.10802E+15	0.29491E+15	0.15420E+15
(83)	7600	Amusements	0.69586E+14	0.84822E+14	0.13009E+15
(84)	7700	Med., educ. services	0.81560E+15	0.13727E+16	0.15619E+16
(85)	78+79	Govt. enterprises	0.19701E+15	0.35080E+15	0.31099E+15
(86)	—	Government	0.23369E+16	0.39163E+16	0.43813E+16
(87)	—	Households	0.18993E+17	0.22037E+17	0.27140E+17

Table 5

Domestic primary fossil fuel, hydro and nuclear energy use (10^{15} Btu/yr). Prod. is gross output by sector, primary is total primary energy use based on *w*, which is a factor that prevents double counting, e.g., when adding crude and refined petroleum. Primary is production times *w*.[a]

	1963			1967			1972		
Sector	Prod.	*w*	Primary	Prod.	*w.*	Primary	Prod.	*w.*	Primary
(1) Coal mining	12.48	1	12.48	14.79	1	14.79	14.17	1	14.17
(2) Crude petro, gas	30.38	1	30.38	37.75	1	37.75	42.34	1	42.34
(3) Refined petro	19.86	0.054	1.07	23.19	0.054	1.25	27.56	0.063	1.73
(4) Electric util.	3.13	0.543	1.70	4.16	0.575	2.39	5.99	0.573	3.43
(5) Gas utilities	13.19	0.054	0.72	17.35	0.064	1.12	20.85	0.070	1.45
Total			46.34			57.30			63.12

[a]*Sources:* Production: Hannon and Casler (1981). *w*: Hannon et al. (1983).

Table 6

Weighting factors for energy types for 1963, 1967 and 1972 (Btu primary/Btu energy type delivered for use).[a]

Sector	1963	1967	1972
(1) Coal mining	1.0141	1.0116	1.0227
(2) Crude petro, gas	1.0578	1.0564	1.0601
(3) Refined petro	1.1497	1.1192	1.1487
(4) Electric util.	3.8181	3.7542	3.7714
(5) Gas utilities	1.1684	1.1515	1.1496

[a]*Source:* Hannon and Casler (1981).

into the 'primary' energy sectors (sectors 1–5). No other sectors receive energy input from nature under this alternative. Estimates for total primary energy use for the three years are derived in table 5. The weighting factor *w* is necessary in table 5 to avoid double counting, since most refined petroleum and natural gas utilities output is made from crude, and a large part of electricity is made from coal or crude (see Bullard and Herendeen (1975)]. Alternative 2 (DEC) uses estimates of direct fossil fuel, hydro and nuclear consumed (burned) by sector. All sectors use such energy, and the total use by sector is a weighted sum of the five fuel types used in this model. The weighting factors used were calculated previously by Hannon and Casler (1981). They reflect, for example, the primary (i.e., coal or crude) fossil energy required to produce a unit of refined petroleum (about 1.15 Btu/Btu in 1972). The weighting factors for each of the three years are given in table 6.

4. Results of I–O analysis

One question to answer at the outset is: what is a proper index of proportionality in this case? There are several possible measures of dispersion of the energy intensities that could be used to measure the 'constancy' of energy intensities across sectors, and there are several ways of regressing total dollar output on total embodied energy input across sectors to test for 'proportionality'. In the results given below, we calculate and discuss both the coefficient of variation (*COV*, equal to the standard deviation divided by the mean) of the equally-weighted entries of the energy intensity vector, and a simple linear regression (including an intercept term) of total dollar output on embodied energy input. We manipulate the regressions to determine the effects of the high magnitudes of some observations on the results.

Tables 7, 8 and 9 list the results of the I–O energy analysis for 1963, 1967 and 1972, respectively for the alternative E vectors listed in table 4. Each table lists the calculated energy intensity vector (in Btu/1972$), the total energy embodied in sector inputs (in Btu, calculated by multiplying the calculated energy intensity by total dollar input), and the dollar output from the sector (in 1972$) for each of the three years. The total dollar output was regressed on total embodied energy input both including and excluding the primary energy sectors (sectors 1–5), and the household and government sectors (sectors 86–87). The results are plotted in fig. 2, and are summarized in table 10, which lists the R^2 statistic for each alternative along with the coefficient of variation for the energy intensity vector. All regressions were significant at the 0.001 level. Fig. 2 is a log–log plot because the range of values for dollar output and embodied energy input spanned over four orders of magnitude (the regressions were run on the untransformed data). The R^2 statistic is reported both including and excluding the government and household sectors (86–87) in the regression, since these sectors are much larger than the other sectors and could unduly weight the R^2 values. R^2 values excluding these sectors are also more directly comparable with previously calculated R^2 values based on an I–O model with exogenous household and government sectors.

The results of the present analysis confirm and expand previous studies [Costanza (1980)] and generally provide evidence supportive of a strong cross-sectional relationship between embodied energy and dollar value, especially if the DEC energy input vector is used. A precondition for this conclusion is the accounting for government and household energy costs by making them endogenous sectors. Exclusion of the household and government sectors from calculation of energy intensities [the treatment used by Bullard and Herendeen (1975) and others] yields much poorer values for R^2 and *COV*, both here and in the previous study [Costanza (1980)]. While the use of endogenous household and government sectors has been criticized [Herendeen (1981), Huettner (1982)], we now feel that the criticisms are less valid based on previously published arguments [Costanza (1982)], and the tests presented in a following section.

Table 7

I–O energy analysis results for 1963. I–O code refers to the BEA sector definitions included in our 87 order sectors. Results for both direct energy input vectors listed in table 4 are given.

				DIRECT		DEC	
No.	I–O Code	Sector name	Dollar output ($1972)	Emb. energy intensity (Btu/$)	Emb. energy input (Btu)	Emb. energy intensity (Btu/$)	Emb. energy input (Btu)
(1)	700	Coal mining	0.45192E+10	0.33482E+07	0.26358E+16	0.63087E+05	0.27396E+15
(2)	800	Crude Petro, Gas	0.12704E+11	0.25680E+07	0.15021E+16	0.39437E+05	0.49192E+15
(3)	3101	Petro refin. prod.	0.21345E+11	0.15907E+07	0.31180E+17	0.57309E+05	0.14857E+16
(4)	6801	Electric utilities	0.18119E+11	0.46095E+06	0.66390E+16	0.63177E+05	0.82548E+15
(5)	6802	Gas utilities	0.12830E+11	0.80180E+06	0.95969E+16	0.48425E+05	0.56882E+15
(6)	100	Livestock	0.39909E+11	0.70934E+05	0.27976E+16	0.68612E+05	0.22717E+16
(7)	200	Misc ag. products	0.29978E+11	0.10849E+06	0.30880E+16	0.86713E+05	0.18217E+16
(8)	300	Forest, fish prod.	0.32475E+10	0.40713E+05	0.13222E+15	0.34161E+05	0.79205E+14
(9)	400	Ag., for., fish serv.	0.18513E+10	0.72427E+05	0.13371E+15	0.78750E+05	0.13588E+15
(10)	500	Iron ore mining	0.95751E+09	0.12146E+06	0.11654E+15	0.16260E+06	0.68676E+14
(11)	600	Nonferr. mining	0.17408E+10	0.87019E+05	0.15426E+15	0.13715E+06	0.15344E+15
(12)	900	Stone clay mining	0.21678E+10	0.10239E+06	0.23301E+15	0.12294E+06	0.14900E+15
(13)	1000	Chem. mineral min.	0.53601E+09	0.11531E+06	0.67799E+14	0.24915E+06	0.44278E+14
(14)	1100	New construction	0.99193E+11	0.95084E+05	0.94317E+16	0.99810E+05	0.91285E+16
(15)	1200	Maint., rep. const.	0.31773E+11	0.84607E+05	0.26882E+16	0.98678E+05	0.26527E+16
(16)	1300	Ordnance	0.62571E+10	0.82085E+05	0.51798E+15	0.92019E+05	0.53170E+15
(17)	1400	Food	0.93125E+11	0.86350E+05	0.80363E+16	0.91963E+05	0.74567E+16
(18)	1500	Tobacco	0.94895E+10	0.63627E+05	0.60399E+15	0.64834E+05	0.59328E+15
(19)	1600	Fabric and mills	0.14634E+11	0.10230E+06	0.14946E+16	0.14885E+06	0.18195E+16
(20)	1700	Textile goods	0.29788E+10	0.11397E+06	0.33650E+15	0.16321E+06	0.43986E+15
(21)	1800	Apparel	0.21328E+11	0.84969E+05	0.18113E+16	0.10629E+06	0.21695E+16
(22)	1900	Fab. textile prod.	0.26834E+10	0.98741E+05	0.26509E+15	0.12543E+06	0.32698E+15
(23)	2000	Wood products	0.15498E+11	0.70161E+05	0.10951E+16	0.74446E+05	0.10128E+16
(24)	2100	Wood containers	0.50771E+09	0.97659E+05	0.48474E+14	0.10588E+06	0.48877E+14
(25)	2200	H'hold furniture	0.50171E+10	0.88545E+05	0.44433E+15	0.10252E+06	0.47719E+15
(26)	2300	Furn., fixtures	0.22884E+10	0.98974E+05	0.22470E+15	0.11358E+06	0.23889E+15
(27)	2400	Paper products	0.13932E+11	0.13647E+06	0.18848E+16	0.20013E+06	0.15097E+16

(28)	2500	Paperboard cont.	0.53877E+10	0.11229E+06	0.60401E+15	0.13965E+06	0.70393E+15
(29)	2600	Printing, publ.	0.22277E+11	0.72120E+05	0.14813E+16	0.99252E+05	0.17472E+16
(30)	2700	Chem. products	0.15070E+11	0.14927E+06	0.22644E+16	0.41587E+06	0.21898E+16
(31)	2800	Plastics	0.48515E+10	0.15337E+06	0.72501E+15	0.32036E+06	0.10519E+16
(32)	2900	Drugs, toil, prep.	0.92067E+10	0.80633E+05	0.77944E+15	0.12806E+06	0.95747E+15
(33)	3000	Paints	0.29374E+10	0.14512E+06	0.42782E+15	0.16193E+06	0.41728E+15
(34)	3102	Paving	0.47990E+09	0.53258E+06	0.24151E+15	0.55917E+06	0.42066E+14
(35)	3103	Asphalt	0.67291E+09	0.33115E+06	0.21305E+15	0.45168E+06	0.64656E+14
(36)	3200	Rubber products	0.10258E+11	0.92649E+05	0.96175E+15	0.14142E+06	0.12365E+16
(37)	3300	Leather products	0.13717E+10	0.87659E+05	0.12010E+15	0.10520E+06	0.11607E+15
(38)	3400	Footwear	0.45717E+10	0.78989E+05	0.36151E+15	0.91168E+05	0.40189E+15
(39)	3500	Glass products	0.39034E+10	0.95633E+05	0.37249E+15	0.15867E+06	0.32766E+15
(40)	3600	Stone clay prod.	0.11844E+11	0.14695E+06	0.17163E+16	0.17774E+06	0.10711E+16
(41)	3700	Prim. ir., stl. manu.	0.31470E+11	0.20178E+06	0.62055E+16	0.25113E+06	0.35003E+16
(42)	3800	Prim. Nonferr. met.	0.17338E+11	0.93197E+05	0.16445E+16	0.16910E+06	0.18883E+16
(43)	3900	Metal containers	0.32559E+10	0.13025E+06	0.42096E+15	0.15556E+06	0.48264E+15
(44)	4000	Heating, plumbing	0.10454E+11	0.11806E+06	0.12199E+16	0.14537E+06	0.13785E+16
(45)	4100	Screw mach. prod.	0.62784E+10	0.98934E+05	0.62118E+15	0.11837E+06	0.67945E+15
(46)	4200	Fab. metal prod.	0.98429E+10	0.95259E+05	0.94597E+15	0.11961E+06	0.10492E+16
(47)	4300	Engines, turbines	0.27782E+10	0.98931E+05	0.27535E+15	0.11682E+06	0.27769E+15
(48)	4400	Farm machinery	0.37282E+10	0.10612E+06	0.39701E+15	0.12389E+06	0.41871E+15
(49)	4500	Const., mining eq.	0.51551E+10	0.98196E+05	0.50736E+15	0.11451E+06	0.53597E+15
(50)	4600	Mat. handling eq.	0.18164E+10	0.96104E+05	0.17484E+15	0.10581E+06	0.18288E+15
(51)	4700	Metal working eq.	0.59703E+10	0.90545E+05	0.55230E+15	0.96586E+05	0.54690E+15
(52)	4800	Spec. ind. mach.	0.44549E+10	0.96015E+05	0.42403E+15	0.99457E+05	0.41440E+15
(53)	4900	Gen. ind. mach.	0.60436E+10	0.98349E+05	0.59433E+15	0.10778E+06	0.59384E+15
(54)	5000	Mach. shop prod.	0.30583E+10	0.82801E+05	0.25735E+15	0.93780E+05	0.26887E+15
(55)	5100	Ofc. comput. mach.	0.38901E+10	0.75530E+05	0.29296E+15	0.84144E+05	0.30097E+15
(56)	5200	Service ind. mach.	0.31348E+10	0.10576E+06	0.32763E+15	0.12044E+06	0.35887E+15
(57)	5300	Elec. ind. apparat.	0.69020E+10	0.97717E+05	0.67844E+15	0.11143E+06	0.70247E+15
(58)	5400	H'hold appliance	0.43252E+10	0.11635E+06	0.48735E+15	0.14461E+06	0.54528E+15
(59)	5500	Elec. light eq.	0.35760E+10	0.98840E+05	0.35236E+15	0.10564E+06	0.35520E+15
(60)	5600	R–TV commun. eq.	0.12866E+11	0.84156E+05	0.10918E+16	0.94874E+05	0.11527E+16
(61)	5700	Electronic comp.	0.32643E+10	0.11613E+06	0.37029E+15	0.14826E+06	0.41406E+15
(62)	5800	Electrical equip.	0.26465E+10	0.72630E+05	0.20097E+15	0.95951E+05	0.24174E+15
(63)	5900	Motor veh. and eq.	0.48812E+11	0.10100E+06	0.49309E+16	0.12024E+06	0.55516E+16
(64)	6000	Aircraft and parts	0.17895E+11	0.84633E+05	0.15166E+16	0.93023E+05	0.15447E+16
(65)	6100	Transport equip.	0.59529E+10	0.11039E+06	0.65088E+15	0.12807E+06	0.70176E+15

Table 7 (continued)

No.	I–O Code	Sector name	Dollar output ($1972)	DIRECT Emb. energy intensity (Btu/$	DIRECT Emb. energy input (Btu)	DEC Emb. energy intensity (Btu/$)	DEC Emb. energy input (Btu)
(66)	6200	Prof., scient. supp.	0.47672E+10	0.76158E+05	0.37245E+15	0.85691E+05	0.40100E+15
(67)	6300	Optical supplies	0.25066E+10	0.78960E+05	0.19892E+15	0.11313E+06	0.24192E+15
(68)	6400	Misc. manufact.	0.77409E+10	0.87555E+05	0.67037E+15	0.10632E+06	0.74791E+15
(69)	6501	Railroad	0.13290E+11	0.11620E+06	0.15338E+16	0.13297E+06	0.10012E+16
(70)	6502	Local transport	0.60762E+10	0.11998E+06	0.72731E+15	0.10264E+06	0.31698E+15
(71)	6503	Motor fgt. transp.	0.20881E+11	0.10288E+06	0.21408E+16	0.88388E+05	0.12776E+16
(72)	6504	Water transport	0.51844E+10	0.10497E+06	0.54417E+15	0.20519E+06	0.39006E+15
(73)	6505	Air transport	0.51653E+10	0.19475E+06	0.10027E+16	0.19566E+06	0.33679E+15
(74)	6506	Pipe line transp.	0.86848E+09	0.20938E+06	0.18139E+15	0.23352E+06	0.61644E+14
(75)	6507+73	Tran. busnss. serv.	0.41016E+11	0.58045E+05	0.23767E+16	0.60623E+05	0.20536E+16
(76)	66+67	Communications	0.18463E+11	0.53738E+05	0.10068E+16	0.53487E+05	0.79926E+15
(77)	6803	Water sanit. serv.	0.18640E+10	0.97664E+05	0.18180E+15	0.13494E+06	0.84464E+14
(78)	6900	Whole, retail tr.	0.16029E+12	0.78682E+05	0.12553E+17	0.75686E+05	0.94214E+16
(79)	7000	Finance, insurance	0.53882E+11	0.69144E+05	0.36737E+16	0.72121E+05	0.33454E+16
(80)	7100	Real estate	0.97834E+11	0.36986E+05	0.36188E+16	0.31943E+05	0.30078E+16
(81)	7200	Hotels, pers. serv.	0.21192E+11	0.70594E+05	0.14829E+16	0.71663E+05	0.12108E+16
(82)	7500	Auto repair	0.15962E+11	0.66835E+05	0.10627E+16	0.62136E+05	0.87967E+15
(83)	7600	Amusements	0.11168E+11	0.63041E+05	0.69840E+15	0.65972E+05	0.66003E+15
(84)	7700	Med., educ. serv.	0.54205E+11	0.66290E+05	0.35904E+16	0.69334E+05	0.29390E+16
(85)	78+79	Govt. enterprises	0.15223E+11	0.36464E+05	0.10998E+16	0.38929E+05	0.76945E+15
(86)	—	Government	0.26667E+12	0.61572E+05	0.16419E+17	0.64401E+05	0.14837E+17
(87)	—	Households	0.78598E+12	0.78484E+05	0.61687E+17	0.78159E+05	0.42438E+17

Table 8

I–O energy analysis results for 1967. I–O code refers to the BEA sector definitions included in out 87 order sectors. Results for both direct energy input vectors listed in table 4 are given.

No.	I–O Code	Sector name	Dollar output ($1972)	DIRECT Emb. energy intensity (Btu/$)	DIRECT Emb. energy input (Btu)	DEC Emb. energy intensity (Btu/$)	DEC Emb. energy input (Btu)
(1)	700	Coal mining	0.51574E+10	0.33649E+07	0.25460E+16	0.64562E+05	0.32083E+15
(2)	800	Crude petro, gas	0.15634E+11	0.25915E+07	0.17124E+16	0.35719E+05	0.54261E+15
(3)	3101	Petro refin. prod.	0.24785E+11	0.15828E+07	0.35249E+17	0.48503E+05	0.15787E+16
(4)	6801	Electric util.	0.23380E+11	0.47244E+06	0.86409E+16	0.62285E+05	0.10074E+16
(5)	6802	Gas utilities	0.16546E+11	0.79260E+06	0.11964E+17	0.40677E+05	0.59398E+15
(6)	100	Livestock	0.40270E+11	0.71002E+05	0.28273E+16	0.76724E+05	0.25093E+16
(7)	200	Misc. ag. products	0.31625E+11	0.10131E+06	0.30801E+16	0.92440E+05	0.20960E+16
(8)	300	Forest, fish prod.	0.24560E+10	0.44682E+05	0.10971E+15	0.43337E+05	0.57043E+14
(9)	400	Ag., for., fish serv.	0.27762E+10	0.53711E+05	0.14881E+15	0.58709E+05	0.15089E+15
(10)	500	Iron ore mining	0.11899E+10	0.96058E+05	0.11417E+15	0.15435E+06	0.90050E+14
(11)	600	Nonferr. mining	0.14700E+10	0.94792E+05	0.13913E+15	0.14548E+06	0.13322E+15
(12)	900	Stone clay min.	0.24875E+10	0.12169E+06	0.30784E+15	0.12349E+06	0.16793E+15
(13)	1000	Chem. mineral min.	0.75400E+09	0.91931E+05	0.76674E+14	0.26672E+06	0.55304E+14
(14)	1100	New construction	0.10943E+12	0.93495E+05	0.10231E+17	0.10278E+06	0.10052E+17
(15)	1200	Maint., rep. const.	0.32933E+11	0.89000E+05	0.29310E+16	0.96067E+05	0.28950E+16
(16)	1300	Ordnance	0.11058E+11	0.89455E+05	0.98754E+15	0.10544E+06	0.10436E+16
(17)	1400	Food	0.10418E+12	0.85253E+05	0.88694E+16	0.94688E+05	0.85897E+16
(18)	1500	Tobacco	0.94198E+10	0.67196E+05	0.63303E+15	0.71669E+05	0.64888E+15
(19)	1600	Fabric and mills	0.17469E+11	0.94944E+05	0.16529E+16	0.14047E+06	0.20342E+16
(20)	1700	Textile goods	0.41112E+10	0.96984E+05	0.39678E+15	0.14448E+06	0.52646E+15
(21)	1800	Apparel	0.25402E+11	0.83963E+05	0.21298E+16	0.10517E+06	0.25504E+16
(22)	1900	Fab. textile prod.	0.36096E+10	0.89649E+05	0.32411E+15	0.11629E+06	0.39206E+15
(23)	2000	Wood products	0.17440E+11	0.76547E+05	0.13394E+16	0.82897E+05	0.11792E+16
(24)	2100	Wood containers	0.65619E+09	0.78856E+05	0.51646E+14	0.86202E+05	0.50165E+14
(25)	2200	H'hold furniture	0.58430E+10	0.85940E+05	0.50240E+15	0.97078E+05	0.52876E+15
(26)	2300	Furn., fixtures	0.30734E+10	0.92535E+05	0.28422E+15	0.10282E+06	0.29172E+15
(27)	2400	Paper products	0.16666E+11	0.12518E+06	0.20607E+16	0.19344E+06	0.17429E+16
(28)	2500	Paperboard cont.	0.67423E+10	0.10483E+06	0.70571E+15	0.13894E+06	0.85535E+15

Table 8 (continued)

No.	I–O Code	Sector name	Dollar output ($1972)	DIRECT: Emb. energy intensity (Btu/$	DIRECT: Emb. energy input (Btu)	DEC: Emb. energy intensity (Btu/$)	DEC: Emb. energy input (Btu)
(29)	2600	Printing, publ.	0.27299E+11	0.63553E+05	0.16741E+16	0.90160E+05	0.19956E+16
(30)	2700	Chem. products	0.19596E+11	0.13388E+06	0.26890E+16	0.34706E+06	0.26699E+16
(31)	2800	Plastics	0.69912E+10	0.13876E+06	0.95225E+15	0.28107E+06	0.12454E+16
(32)	2900	Drugs, toil. prep.	0.12466E+11	0.74873E+05	0.98012E+15	0.99608E+05	0.11882E+16
(33)	3000	Paints	0.33135E+10	0.10702E+06	0.35560E+15	0.14830E+06	0.45119E+15
(34)	3102	Paving	0.68071E+09	0.42451E+06	0.27284E+15	0.52987E+06	0.54190E+14
(35)	3103	Asphalt	0.73172E+09	0.25845E+06	0.18563E+15	0.42060E+06	0.61599E+14
(36)	3200	Rubber Products	0.14002E+11	0.89194E+05	0.12554E+16	0.13313E+06	0.15710E+16
(37)	3300	Leather products	0.14014E+10	0.80810E+05	0.11337E+15	0.96380E+05	0.11381E+15
(38)	3400	Footwear	0.50479E+10	0.79040E+05	0.39933E+15	0.91822E+05	0.44006E+15
(39)	3500	Glass products	0.47454E+10	0.90319E+05	0.42790E+15	0.14439E+06	0.36331E+15
(40)	3600	Stone clay prod.	0.13149E+11	0 12918E+06	0.16862E+16	0.18570E+06	0.11874E+16
(41)	3700	Prim. ir., stl. manu.	0.37787E+11	0.21405E+06	0.78418E+16	0.23206E+06	0.40587E+16
(42)	3800	Prim. nonferr. met.	0.20903E+11	0.90525E+05	0.19348E+16	0.17533E+06	0.23364E+16
(43)	3900	Metal containers	0.41825E+10	0.13094E+06	0.52817E+15	0.14682E+06	0.56090E+15
(44)	4000	Heating plumbing	0.13860E+11	0.11904E+06	0.16304E+16	0.13602E+06	0.17147E+16
(45)	4100	Screw mach. prod.	0.10697E+11	0.11123E+06	0.11765E+16	0.12507E+06	0.12097E+16
(46)	4200	Fab. metal prod.	0.12700E+11	0.95600E+05	0.12176E+16	0.11235E+06	0.12514E+16
(47)	4300	Engines, turbines	0.38923E+10	0.10116E+06	0.39351E+15	0.11150E+06	0.38985E+15
(48)	4400	Farm machinery	0.51897E+10	0.10551E+06	0.54770E+15	0.11603E+06	0.54951E+15
(49)	4500	Const., Mining eq.	0.69695E+10	0.10158E+06	0.70487E+15	0.10940E+06	0.68531E+15
(58)	4600	Mat. handling eq.	0.27344E+10	0.96807E+05	0.26395E+15	0.10412E+06	0.26949E+15
(51)	4700	Metalworking eq.	0.87130E+10	0.93225E+05	0.81896E+15	0.94872E+05	0.76819E+15
(52)	4800	Spec. ind. mach.	0.61370E+10	0.93093E+05	0.56649E+15	0.95897E+05	0.54928E+15
(53)	4900	Gen. ind. mach.	0.82119E+10	0.97053E+05	0.79875E+15	0.10453E+06	0.78657E+15
(54)	5000	Mach. shop prod.	0.50452E+10	0.94660E+05	0.47795E+15	0.90373E+05	0.41062E+15
(55)	5100	Ofc. comput. mach.	0.61726E+10	0.79552E+05	0.48305E+15	0.88986E+05	0.50803E+15
(56)	5200	Service ind. mach.	0.47235E+10	0.94739E+05	0.44937E+15	0.11019E+06	0.48639E+15
(57)	5300	Elec. ind. apparat.	0.97929E+10	0.95199E+05	0.92460E+15	0.10663E+06	0.93304E+15

(58)	5400	H'hold appliance	0.55475E+10	0.10094E+06	0.55317E+15	0.12188E+06	0.59980E+15
(59)	5500	Elec. light eq.	0.44630E+10	0.81863E+05	0.37052E+15	0.98723E+05	0.40352E+15
(60)	5600	R–TV commun. eq.	0.17860E+11	0.75700E+05	0.13676E+16	0.84884E+05	0.14429E+16
(61)	5700	Electronic comp.	0.70304E+10	0.95567E+05	0.65919E+15	0.11964E+06	0.73469E+15
(62)	5800	Electrical equip.	0.33222E+10	0.76134E+05	0.26054E+15	0.99505E+05	0.30860E+15
(63)	5900	Motor veh. and eq.	0.50531E+11	0.98568E+05	0.49888E+16	0.11167E+06	0.52922E+16
(64)	6000	Aircraft and parts	0.25355E+11	0.88363E+05	0.22422E+16	0.92609E+05	0.21948E+16
(65)	6100	Transport equip.	0.91262E+10	0.10358E+06	0.94193E+15	0.11562E+06	0.98377E+15
(66)	6200	Prof. scient. supp.	0.62214E+10	0.78362E+05	0.49372E+15	0.88470E+05	0.52386E+15
(67)	6300	Optical supplies	0.44417E+10	0.63995E+05	0.29171E+15	0.88226E+05	0.36673E+15
(68)	6400	Misc. manufact.	0.95030E+10	0.83480E+05	0.78296E+15	0.97971E+05	0.86005E+15
(69)	6501	Railroad	0.15829E+11	0.10838E+06	0.16642E+16	0.11586E+06	0.10858E+16
(70)	6502	Local transport	0.60168E+10	0.91023E+05	0.54694E+15	0.92953E+05	0.32009E+15
(71)	6503	Motor fgt. transp.	0.24930E+11	0.11922E+06	0.29615E+16	0.84520E+05	0.15856E+16
(72)	6504	Water transport	0.54772E+10	0.12468E+06	0.67912E+15	0.22274E+06	0.50519E+15
(73)	6505	Air transport	0.99192E+10	0.16093E+06	0.15923E+16	0.19190E+06	0.62647E+15
(74)	6506	Pipe line transp.	0.12297E+10	0.19262E+06	0.23638E+15	0.19072E+06	0.85387E+14
(75)	6507+73	Tran. busnss. serv.	0.56911E+11	0.57173E+05	0.32494E+16	0.61166E+05	0.30831E+16
(76)	66+67	Communications	0.25239E+11	0.50929E+05	0.13110E+16	0.53733E+05	0.11623E+16
(77)	6803	Water sanit. serv.	0.19664E+10	0.81045E+05	0.15910E+15	0.97541E+05	0.82646E+14
(78)	6900	Whole, retail tr.	0.19587E+12	0.78347E+05	0.15274E+17	0.80762E+05	0.12257E+17
(79)	7000	Finance, insurance	0.64810E+11	0.66035E+05	0.42150E+16	0.70166E+05	0.40825E+16
(80)	7100	Real estate	0.12185E+12	0.37161E+05	0.45281E+16	0.31341E+05	0.35228E+16
(81)	7200	Hotels, pers. serv.	0.25535E+11	0.79694E+05	0.20009E+16	0.85126E+05	0.15176E+16
(82)	7500	Auto repair	0.19938E+11	0.72487E+05	0.14410E+16	0.75280E+05	0.12007E+16
(83)	7600	Amusements	0.11993E+11	0.65174E+05	0.77281E+15	0.69126E+05	0.73289E+15
(84)	7700	Med., educ. serv.	0.65499E+11	0.73980E+05	0.48421E+16	0.80598E+05	0.39017E+16
(85)	78+79	Govt. enterprises	0.18544E+11	0.36668E+05	0.12946E+16	0.59465E+05	0.94593E+15
(86)	—	Government	0.32506E+12	0.65952E+05	0.21438E+17	0.71659E+05	0.19377E+17
(87)	—	Households	0.92531E+12	0.79136E+05	0.73226E+17	0.79741E+05	0.51748E+17

Table [illegible]

I–O energy analysis results for 1972. I–O code refers to the BEA sector definitions included in our 87 order sectors. Results for both direct energy input vectors listed in table 4 are given.

				DIRECT		DEC	
No.	I–O Code	Sector name	Dollar output ($1972)	Emb. energy intensity (Btu/$)	Emb. energy input (Btu)	Emb. energy intensity (Btu/$)	Emb. energy input (Btu)
(1)	700	Coal mining	0.54424E+10	0.30608E+07	0.24739E+16	0.69555E+05	0.35977E+15
(2)	800	Crude petro, gas	0.17819E+11	0.25791E+07	0.23035E+16	0.35763E+05	0.61237E+15
(3)	3101	Petro refin. prod.	0.29581E+11	0.16047E+07	0.43304E+17	0.57363E+05	0.18744E+16
(4)	6801	Electric util.	0.31665E+11	0.56190E+06	0.14336E+17	0.70907E+05	0.16013E+16
(5)	6802	Gas utilities	0.20138E+11	0.89265E+06	0.16526E+17	0.46244E+05	0.81828E+15
(6)	100	Livestock	0.43339E+11	0.76938E+05	0.33577E+16	0.78979E+05	0.31169E+16
(7)	200	Misc. ag. products	0.35080E+11	0.84628E+05	0.29846E+16	0.95657E+05	0.20657E+16
(8)	300	Forest., fish prod.	0.19705E+10	0.89878E+05	0.17710E+15	0.11603E+06	0.11120E+15
(9)	400	Ag., for., fish serv.	0.35657E+10	0.11432E+06	0.40732E+15	0.10110E+06	0.29998E+15
(10)	500	Iron ore mining	0.12325E+10	0.12528E+06	0.15425E+15	0.19404E+06	0.86259E+14
(11)	600	Nonferr. mining	0.22700E+10	0.94867E+05	0.21743E+15	0.13463E+06	0.16709E+15
(12)	900	Stone clay min.	0.28471E+10	0.11979E+06	0.36057E+15	0.13700E+06	0.18466E+15
(13)	1000	Chem. mineral min.	0.77460E+09	0.13102E+06	0.10612E+15	0.32819E+06	0.50899E+14
(14)	1100	New construction	0.12958E+12	0.97375E+05	0.12618E+17	0.10996E+06	0.12513E+17
(15)	1200	Maint. rep. const.	0.36417E+11	0.10117E+06	0.36843E+16	0.11196E+06	0.32780E+16
(16)	1300	Ordnance	0.70841E+10	0.93187E+05	0.66035E+15	0.10010E+06	0.62904E+15
(17)	1400	Food	0.11830E+12	0.82543E+05	0.97809E+16	0.93817E+05	0.96640E+16
(18)	1500	Tobacco	0.92269E+10	0.61078E+05	0.56356E+15	0.66434E+05	0.58318E+15
(19)	1600	Fabric and mills	0.17632E+11	0.10556E+06	0.18508E+16	0.15881E+06	0.23013E+16
(20)	1700	Textile goods	0.59584E+10	0.10304E+06	0.61396E+15	0.14847E+06	0.77802E+15
(21)	1800	Apparel	0.30183E+11	0.90078E+05	0.27220E+16	0.11295E+06	0.31890E+16
(22)	1900	Fab. textile prod.	0.49226E+10	0.95506E+05	0.47190E+15	0.12081E+06	0.56762E+15
(23)	2000	Wood products	0.21511E+11	0.10921E+06	0.23495E+16	0.10523E+06	0.18274E+16
(24)	2100	Wood containers	0.46570E+09	0.10373E+06	0.48469E+14	0.11040E+06	0.43175E+14
(25)	2200	H'hold furniture	0.72816E+10	0.91088E+05	0.66507E+15	0.10152E+06	0.67988E+15
(26)	2300	Furn., fixtures	0.37275E+10	0.99734E+05	0.37128E+15	0.11273E+06	0.37401E+15
(27)	2400	Paper products	0.19833E+11	0.13485E+06	0.26414E+16	0.19738E+06	0.20739E+16
(28)	2500	Paperboard cont.	0.79097E+10	0.11350E+06	0.89645E+15	0.14349E+06	0.10201E+16

(29)	2600	Printing, publ.	0.29635E+11	0.66760E+05	0.20634E+16	0.99577E+05	0.23375E+16
(30)	2700	Chem. products	0.24041E+11	0.14883E+06	0.36042E+16	0.31147E+06	0.29066E+16
(31)	2800	Plastics	0.96840E+10	0.13690E+06	0.12981E+16	0.25998E+06	0.14891E+16
(32)	2900	Drugs, toil. prep.	0.17228E+11	0.78111E+05	0.14007E+16	0.89680E+05	0.14551E+16
(33)	3000	Paints	0.36101E+10	0.11988E+06	0.43596E+15	0.15717E+06	0.51958E+15
(34)	3102	Paving	0.90260E+09	0.49398E+06	0.42526E+15	0.54128E+06	0.76830E+14
(35)	3103	Asphalt	0.94700E+09	0.33993E+06	0.33095E+15	0.49245E+06	0.88694E+14
(36)	3200	Rubber products	0.20648E+11	0.94741E+05	0.19762E+16	0.13244E+06	0.23236E+16
(37)	3300	Leather products	0.10524E+10	0.98537E+05	0.10363E+15	0.12340E+06	0.10726E+15
(38)	3400	Footwear	0.45291E+10	0.86354E+05	0.39160E+15	0.10133E+06	0.42949E+15
(39)	3500	Glass products	0.55834E+10	0.10568E+06	0.58988E+15	0.15913E+06	0.47392E+15
(40)	3600	Stone clay prod.	0.15267E+11	0.13260E+06	0.20283E+16	0.18380E+06	0.14353E+16
(41)	3700	Prim. ir., stl. manuf.	0.36440E+11	0.19237E+06	0.68477E+16	0.24561E+06	0.43238E+16
(42)	3800	Prim. nonferr. met.	0.23874E+11	0.10709E+06	0.25788E+16	0.19467E+06	0.30697E+16
(43)	3900	Metal containers	0.48236E+10	0.12594E+06	0.60382E+15	0.16010E+06	0.70933E+15
(44)	4000	Heating, plumbing	0.15304E+11	0.11467E+06	0.17484E+16	0.13787E+06	0.19174E+16
(45)	4100	Screw mach. prod.	0.11135E+11	0.11566E+06	0.12766E+16	0.13942E+06	0.13839E+16
(46)	4200	Fab. metal prod.	0.14141E+11	0.10223E+06	0.14483E+16	0.12486E+06	0.15265E+16
(47)	4300	Engines, turbines	0.54095E+10	0.97906E+05	0.53047E+15	0.11380E+06	0.56789E+15
(48)	4400	Farm machinery	0.55662E+10	0.92672E+05	0.52504E+15	0.10770E+06	0.54721E+15
(49)	4500	Const., mining eq.	0.78886E+10	0.95367E+05	0.76050E+15	0.10937E+06	0.78055E+15
(50)	4600	Mat. handling. eq.	0.28090E+10	0.98438E+05	0.27679E+15	0.11012E+06	0.28584E+15
(51)	4700	Metalworking eq.	0.71480E+10	0.96626E+05	0.70102E+15	0.10010E+06	0.64497E+15
(52)	4800	Spec. ind. mach.	0.58633E+10	0.95709E+05	0.56651E+15	0.10375E+06	0.55945E+15
(53)	4900	Gen. ind. mach.	0.81320E+10	0.10447E+06	0.84541E+15	0.11067E+06	0.80321E+15
(54)	5000	Mach. shop prod.	0.44433E+10	0.10850E+06	0.48114E+15	0.10450E+06	0.41001E+15
(55)	5100	Ofc. comput. mach.	0.80508E+10	0.76523E+05	0.62702E+15	0.84903E+05	0.64663E+15
(56)	5200	Service ind. mach.	0.84954E+10	0.90200E+05	0.76970E+15	0.10334E+06	0.80278E+15
(57)	5300	Elec. ind. apparat.	0.10392E+11	0.95838E+05	0.99378E+15	0.11107E+06	0.10096E+16
(58)	5400	H'hold appliance	0.66589E+10	0.88272E+05	0.59249E+15	0.11020E+06	0.66218E+15
(59)	5500	Elec. light eq.	0.55221E+10	0.81844E+05	0.46823E+15	0.10078E+06	0.51565E+15
(60)	5600	R–TV commun. eq.	0.17950E+11	0.80753E+05	0.14589E+16	0.91074E+05	0.15286E+16
(61)	5700	Electronic comp.	0.83929E+10	0.88982E+05	0.74143E+15	0.10832E+06	0.78013E+15
(62)	5800	Electrical equip.	0.42767E+10	0.81532E+05	0.35898E+15	0.10419E+06	0.41254E+15
(63)	5900	Motor veh. and eq.	0.65080E+11	0.90038E+05	0.58900E+16	0.10616E+06	0.64995E+16
(64)	6000	Aircraft and parts	0.17021E+11	0.90362E+05	0.15429E+16	0.98020E+05	0.15118E+16
(65)	6100	Transport equip.	0.12763E+11	0.99941E+05	0.12764E+16	0.11448E+06	0.13630E+16
(66)	6200	Prof. scient. supp.	0.69807E+10	0.83314E+05	0.58633E+15	0.90597E+05	0.58678E+15

Table 9 (continued)

No.	I–O Code	Sector name	Dollar output ($1972)	DIRECT Emb. energy intensity (Btu/$)	DIRECT Emb. energy input (Btu)	DEC Emb. energy intensity (Btu/$)	DEC Emb. energy input (Btu)
(67)	6300	Optical supplies	0.65269E+10	0.69182E+05	0.45995E+15	0.81939E+05	0.48720E+15
(68)	6400	Misc. manufact.	0.11979E+11	0.93679E+05	0.11121E+16	0.10652E+06	0.11485E+16
(69)	6501	Railroad	0.15067E+11	0.10987E+06	0.16607E+16	0.12441E+06	0.10647E+16
(70)	6502	Local transport	0.74063E+10	0.13874E+06	0.10232E+16	0.95782E+05	0.47643E+15
(71)	6503	Motor fgt transp.	0.29993E+11	0.10629E+06	0.31862E+16	0.90985E+05	0.18652E+16
(72)	6504	Water transport	0.73075E+10	0.15265E+06	0.10977E+16	0.24494E+06	0.83384E+15
(73)	6505	Air transport	0.13134E+11	0.16748E+06	0.21983E+16	0.19162E+06	0.83686E+15
(74)	6506	Pipe line transp.	0.16167E+10	0.16596E+06	0.26829E+15	0.16157E+06	0.97559E+14
(75)	6507+73	Tran. busnss. serv.	0.70346E+11	0.72104E+05	0.50988E+16	0.67547E+05	0.44079E+16
(76)	66+67	Communications	0.36078E+11	0.43236E+05	0.17161E+16	0.47483E+05	0.15946E+16
(77)	6803	Water sanit. ser.	0.25822E+10	0.95565E+05	0.24677E+15	0.98433E+05	0.19295E+15
(78)	6900	Whole. retail tr.	0.26493E+12	0.77371E+05	0.20498E+17	0.79248E+05	0.16485E+17
(79)	7000	Finance, insurance	0.77886E+11	0.65656E+05	0.51122E+16	0.67301E+05	0.46664E+16
(80)	7100	Real estate	0.17458E+12	0.32605E+05	0.56923E+16	0.31021E+05	0.47807E+16
(81)	7200	Hotels, pers. serv.	0.30504E+11	0.86630E+05	0.26303E+16	0.82911E+05	0.18934E+16
(82)	7500	Auto repair	0.24340E+11	0.79060E+05	0.19243E+16	0.77333E+05	0.17281E+16
(83)	7600	Amusements	0.12745E+11	0.73535E+05	0.93693E+15	0.75976E+05	0.83663E+15
(84)	7700	Med., educ. serv.	0.84900E+11	0.77769E+05	0.66026E+16	0.79814E+05	0.52143E+16
(85)	78+79	Govt. enterprises	0.18919E+11	0.41237E+05	0.15300E+16	0.57458E+05	0.10576E+16
(86)	—	Government	0.41622E+12	0.55567E+05	0.23128E+17	0.58533E+05	0.19981E+17
(87)	—	Households	0.12834E+13	0.71033E+05	0.91163E+17	0.69804E+05	0.62447E+17

Table 10

Summary statistics for embodied energy estimates calculated using the alternative direct energy input vectors shown in table 4. R^2 estimates are for a linear regression of dollar output by sector on embodied energy input (see tables 7–9 for listings of these series and fig. 2 for plots). All R^2 values are significant at the 0.001 level. Coefficient of variation (*COV*) estimates are for the embodied energy intensity vectors listed in tables 7–9.

Year	Sectors included in statistics	DIRECT R^2	DIRECT *COV*	DEC R^2	DEC *COV*
1963	1–87	0.800	2.35	0.981	0.67
	6–87	0.986	0.69	0.981	0.67
	1–85	0.239	2.34	0.858	0.67
	6–85	0.884	0.69	0.858	0.67
1967	1–87	0.814	2.43	0.984	0.64
	6–87	0.987	0.69	0.984	0.64
	1–85	0.251	2.42	0.866	0.64
	6–85	0.873	0.69	0.866	0.64
1972	1–87	0.805	2.25	0.978	0.64
	6–87	0.986	0.61	0.978	0.64
	1–85	0.247	2.24	0.851	0.64
	6–85	0.876	0.61	0.851	0.64

The present study also indicates the relative merits (as a predictor of market value) of calculations of embodied energy based on alternative treatments of the direct energy input vector, ***E***. We also find that the results for the three different years are very similar, indicating a stable pattern over the time interval of the data.

Comparison of the various alternatives in table 10 brings out some interesting points. The R^2 values for alternative 1, (DIRECT) including only sectors 6–87 or 6–85 in the regression, are much higher than with the primary energy sectors (1–5) included, and are very close to those for alternative 2 (DEC) with or without the primary energy sectors. Alternative 1 represents direct energy input to the economy (specifically to the primary energy sectors) while alternative 2 represents consumption of that energy distributed through the economy. Distribution is the key word here, since this is the major difference between the two alternatives. The primary energy sectors distribute energy to the rest of the economy, and if this distribution function is factored out by excluding the primary energy sectors from the regression or by predistributing the energy by looking at consumption rather than production (i.e., alternative 2), then higher correlations result. The degree of departure of the energy sectors from the regression line in alternative 1 (fig. 2) can thus be viewed as a measure of the net energy input to the system.

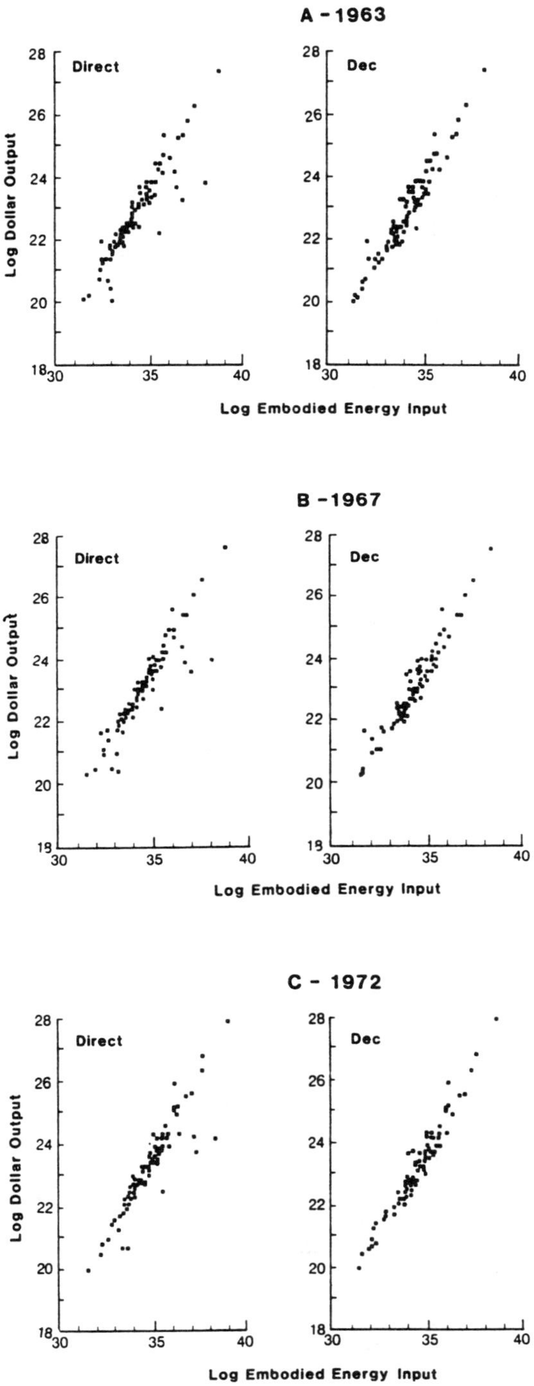

Fig. 2. Log–log plots of embodied energy inputs vs. dollar output for the 87 sector data, for three years and two alternative direct energy input vectors.

The primary energy sectors functions are like the transportation sectors, which alse require special treatment in I–O analysis based on the difference between the services they provide and their physical inputs and outputs. If a strictly physical interpretation were applied to the transportation sectors, they would receive almost all goods produced in the whole economy as inputs and redistribute them as output, masking information on transfers of goods between sectors. For this reason, the transportation sectors in I–O analysis are thought of as providing transportation services that are purchased by the producing sector, preserving the connection between the producing and consuming sector but adding a 'transportation margin'. For analogous reasons, the primary energy sectors should be thought of as providing a 'transportation service' in moving primary energy from nature to the consuming sectors. The DEC energy input vector incorporates this interpretation.

In a previous article [Herendeen (1981)] it was shown that the necessary and sufficient conditions for constant energy intensities in an I–O analysis are that the direct energy input vector be proportional to the dollar value of net input (the remaining components of value added). With the boundaries and approximations used in this study, the dollar value of net input is equal to property type income (*PTI*), and there is, in fact a relatively high correlation between *PTI* and direct energy consumption (DEC) across sectors. This explains the relatively constant energy intensities calculated for alternative 2. For alternative 1, however, this correlation is very low, since only the energy sectors (1–5) have direct energy inputs under this alternative. The energy intensities are still relatively constant, however, except for the energy sectors (1–5). The distributive function of the energy sectors is responsible for this phenomenon. In the appendix we prove that if and only if the sum of the energy rows (1–5 in our case) of U is proportional to net dollar input (PTI in our case) then ε is constant except for the energy sectors.

5. The effects of adding labor and government sectors: The mathematical artifact argument

Several critics of this approach have argued that closing the input–output matrix as we do here must inevitably lead to a reduction in the variance of the energy intensities, or, in the terms of this paper, an inevitably high correlation between economic value and embodied energy [Herendeen (1981), Huettner (1982), Reister (personal comment)]. (This is not worrisome, of course, if inclusion of the household and government sectors is uncontroversial.) In this section we present the mathematical artifact argument in some detail, establish several theorems which aim in the right direction, and finally present results of some empirical tests.

The manipulations we have performed 'close' the matrix by converting two parts of final demand to producing sectors whose outputs (labor and government services), previously a part of value added, are now listed as a consumed input by all sectors. The rank of the I–O matrix is increased by two, while the 'closedness' increases. We define closedness as

$$1-\left(\sum_{i=1}^{n} Y_i \Big/ \sum_{i=1}^{n} X_i\right), \tag{4}$$

where

Y_i = net output of sector i,
X_i = gross output of sector i.

Closedness thus varies between 0 (possible only for a trivial one-sector system) and 1 (for a system with no net output at all).

The new inputs (labor and government services) tend to be fairly large fractions of all inputs, and are non-zero for almost every sector. Therefore one suspects a homogenizing effect on the energy intensities (ε's), which has been stated thus [Herendeen (1981, p. 671)]:

> 'The intuitive argument that inclusion of labor and government as producing as well as consuming sectors ought to force the ε's in the direction of a common value is this: every economic sector pays wages (and practically every one pays taxes), and these expenditures are a large fraction of the expenditures for all inputs. (Labor costs are typically 30%–50% of the total, Bureau of Economic Analysis, 1980). Thus the inclusion of labor requires every sector to have a large input flow from the same sector. Referring to fig. 1, we see that the reason that the ε's can be different is that each sector can, in principle, have a different input mix. Inclusion of the (necessarily large) labor input to all sectors reduces that possibility.'

To demonstrate this argument, we will use the 4×4 example shown in table 11. In the language of table 11, we ask what happens to the coefficient of variation (standard deviation divided by the mean) of ε_1, ε_2, and ε_3 as L_1, L_2, and L_3 increase from zero up to their maximum allowable values, equal to total value added before the inclusion of labor. In this example we make endogenous only one sector (labor), vs. two (labor and government) in the actual data, since this simplifies the discussion and does not cause any loss of generality. The inputs to the labor sector (personal consumption) expand in such a way that their total just equals the production of labor. For discussion, we will use the normalized labor ($\boldsymbol{l}=\boldsymbol{L}\boldsymbol{V}^{T-1}$) and energy input ($\boldsymbol{e}=\boldsymbol{E}\boldsymbol{V}^{T-1}$) vectors. We can test the following hypotheses:

Hypothesis 1 (*the 'strong hypothesis'*). Starting with $l_1=l_2=l_3=0$, use of any admissable positive l_i will always decrease the coefficient of variation of the 3 ε's. We will call the coefficient of variation of the ε's '*COVE*'. Thus *COVE3* is the coefficient of variation of the 3 ε's in our example.

Table 11
Example 4×4 input–output table. All units are dollars except for the direct energy inputs, which are Btu's.

Sector	1	2	3	Personal consumption (*PC*)	Net output	Total output
1	1	1	2	$0.3(L_1+L_2+L_3)$	$6-(PC_1)$	10
2	1	2	1	$0.4(L_1+L_2+L_3)$	$6-(PC_2)$	10
3	1	3	1	$0.3(L_1+L_2+L_3)$	$5-(PC_3)$	10
Wages	L_1	L_2	L_3	0	0	$L_1+L_2+L_3$
Profits	$7-L_1$	$4-L_2$	$6-L_3$	0	0	$17-(L_1+L_2+L_3)$
Energy	E_1	E_2	E_3	E_4		

For above: ($\boldsymbol{l}=\boldsymbol{L}/10$, $\boldsymbol{G}=\boldsymbol{UV}^{T-1}\Lambda$ $\boldsymbol{e}=\boldsymbol{EV}^{T-1}$)

I–G =	0.9	−0.1	−0.2	−0.3
	−0.1	0.8	−0.1	−0.4
	−0.1	−0.3	0.9	−0.3
	l_1	l_2	l_3	1
e =	$0.1E_1$	$0.1E_2$	$0.1E_3$	$0.1E_4$

Table 12
Coefficient of variation of the first three epsilons (*COVE3*) for various combinations of the normalized direct energy input vector (*e*) and the normalized labor vector (*l*). See table 11 for details.

Labor input l_1 l_2 l_3 l_4	Closed-ness	Normalized energy input ($e=EV^{T-1}$) (1111)	(1000)	(0100)	(0010)	Proportional to 1st row of *G*
(1) *No labor* 0 0 0 0	0.43	0.1300	0.7425	0.9688	0.6886	0.2066
(2) *'Actual'* 0.5 0.2 0.2 0	0.79	0.1043	0.4573	0.4189	0.2516	0.0744
(3) *Prop. to VA* 0.37 0.21 0.32 0	0.79	0.0458	0.3600	0.4251	0.3282	0.0582
(4) *Constant* 0.3 0.3 0.3 0	0.79	0.1300	0.3108	0.4929	0.3349	0.1320
(5) *Mirror image* 0.1 0.4 0.4 0	0.79	0.2927	0.1663	0.5975	0.4500	0.3272

Conclusion 1. This hypothesis is false by counter-example. In table 12 we see that it is violated for $e=(1, 1, 1, 1)$, and $l=(0.1, 0.4, 0.4, 0)$. However, from table 12 the hypothesis appears true for the restricted case of $\boldsymbol{e}$ having just one non-zero element and also not satisfying Hypothesis 3 below.

Hypothesis 2. Use of a labor vector $\boldsymbol{l}$ such that normalized profits are proportional to $\boldsymbol{e}$, results in $COVE3=0$.

Conclusion 2. This hypothesis is true in general, and was proved previously [Herendeen (1981)].

Hypothesis 3. Use of any $\boldsymbol{l}$ whose first three entries are proportional to the first three entries of $\boldsymbol{e}$ results in the same value for *COVE3*.

Conclusion 3. This hypothesis is true in general, and is proved in the appendix.

Hypothesis 4. By examining certain values from $\boldsymbol{G}(=\boldsymbol{U}\boldsymbol{V}^{T-1})$, $\boldsymbol{l}$, and $\boldsymbol{e}$ it is possible to predict when *COVE3* will decrease without actually calculating it.

Conclusion 4. This hypothesis is as yet unproven.

Hypothesis 5 (the 'weak hypothesis'). While it can be shown by hypothesis 1–3 above that *COVE3* can be reduced to zero, remain unchanged, or increase on the addition of some positive $\boldsymbol{l}$, and while Hypothesis 4 is unproven, it is still true that for a wide class of reasonable $\boldsymbol{l}$ it will very likely decrease.

Conclusion 5. This is the strongest statement that can now be made of the mathematical artifact argument, and is obviously sensitive to the definitions of 'wide class', 'very likely', and 'reasonable $\boldsymbol{l}$'. At this point we see no way to proceed except by empirical test applied to the 4×4 example and to the actual 87-sector data.

What, then, are reasonable values for $\boldsymbol{l}$, besides those obtained by the analysis of the first section of this paper? We choose several options and illustrate them by reference to the 4×4 example. We then proceed to the 87-sector data.

(1) $\boldsymbol{l}=\boldsymbol{0}$ This is the base case. The labor sector is assumed to be exogenous.
(2) $\boldsymbol{l}$=actual values used, as in the previous section. For the 4×4 example, we (arbitrarily, in this case) pick $\boldsymbol{l}=(0.5, 0.2, 0.2)$.
(3) $\boldsymbol{l}$ proportional to the normalized value added (profit including labor costs). In the example this would give $\boldsymbol{l}$ proportional to (0.7, 0.4 0.6). This assumes that labor is a constant fraction of value added, sector by sector.
(4) $\boldsymbol{l}$=constant fraction of total inputs. This assumes that a fixed fraction of the value of output is spent on labor. Both 3 and 4 have some justification in reality. Labor is usually the largest component of value added.
(5) $\boldsymbol{l}$=mirror image of the actual $\boldsymbol{l}$ in 2. This is an attempt to use an $\boldsymbol{l}$ which is 'opposite' from or inversely correlated with the actual one. This could be done in many ways. By mirror image we mean that $l_{i,\mathrm{mirror}}$ is set

equal to $l_{\text{mean}}-(l_{i,\text{actual}}-l_{\text{mean}})$, where l_{mean} denotes the average labor input. In the example, $l_{\text{mean}}=(0.5+0.2+0.2)/3=0.3$. Then $l_{1,\text{mirror}}=0.3-(0.5-0.3)=0.1$, $l_{2,\text{mirror}}=0.3-(0.2-0.3)=0.4$, etc. Caution is needed to avoid allowing the $l_{i,\text{mirror}}$ to get too large. In this particular example this doesn't happen.

In the example (table 12) we have constrained all 'options' so that $L_1+L_2+L_3=9$, which corresponds to a constant closedness of $1-8/(30+9)=0.79$ vs. $1-17/30=0.43$ for $L_1=L_2=L_3=0$.

In fig. 3 we present the results shown in table 12. In fig. 3a there seems to be only one systematic pattern: that for any non-zero values of $\boldsymbol{l}$ the coefficient of variation of all the ε's (*COVE3*) decreases relative to that for $l_1=l_2=l_3=0$, as long as only one entry in $\boldsymbol{e}$ is non-zero. However, for $\boldsymbol{e}=(1,1,1,1)$, this is no longer true. Otherwise, there is apparently no connection between the options. The 'mirror image' can produce a *COVE3* that is greater or smaller than that for the 'actual'.

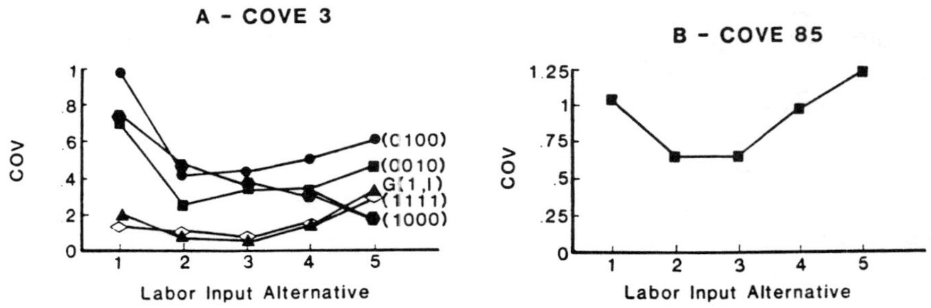

Fig. 3. Coefficients of variation (*COV*) for alternative labor input vectors for the 4×4 example (A) and the 87 sector model using 1967 data (B). Labels on A are the normalized direct energy input vector used for each plot. Labor input alternatives are: (1) no labor (labor sector is exogenous); (2) the 'actual' labor vector; (3) labor proportional to value added; (4) labor proportional to total input; (5) labor is the 'mirror image' of actual labor input. Note that the order of these alternatives is arbitrary.

Based on this limited example, we come to the following empirical conclusion: For $\boldsymbol{e}$ containing only one non-zero element, *COVE3* is reduced as $\boldsymbol{l}$ is increased from $\boldsymbol{0}$. Otherwise, no conclusion can be made about *COVE3* based on the relationship of the two $\boldsymbol{l}$ vectors, unless they satisfy hypothesis 2 (in which case *COVE3*$=0$) or hypothesis 3 (in which case *COVE3* is unchanged). Thus, for a general $\boldsymbol{e}$ with many non-zero elements, even the weak hypothesis is not true, and the mathematical artifact argument appears false.

One additional aspect needs mention. The most general formulation of the energy intensity problem allows for the possibility that energy inputs can occur for any sector, so that $\boldsymbol{E}$ is not constrained. In the U.S. economy there are several energy sectors (e.g., coal, refined petroleum), which are the only ones with $\boldsymbol{E} \neq \boldsymbol{0}$. However, these sectors consume little energy (usually an exception is electric utilities) and pass the bulk of their input on as energy to be consumed or sequestered by their customers. If the purpose of $\boldsymbol{E}$ is to show where energy is finally consumed, then $\boldsymbol{E}$ should actually be the same as the energy rows of $\boldsymbol{U}$, or DEC in the 87-sector examples, which includes non-zero entries for all sectors.

In this case it is particularly easy to calculate $\boldsymbol{\varepsilon}$. In the appendix we prove that if and only if $\boldsymbol{e} = k\boldsymbol{G}_e$ (where $\boldsymbol{G}_e$ means the energy row of $\boldsymbol{G}$), then

$$\boldsymbol{\varepsilon} = k[(\boldsymbol{I} - \boldsymbol{G})^{-1} - \boldsymbol{I}]. \tag{5}$$

Except for the $-\boldsymbol{I}$ in the bracket this is identical to calculating $\boldsymbol{\varepsilon}$ when $\boldsymbol{e}$ is zero for all sectors except an entry k in the eth column.

For this special case, one might suspect a connection with the case of having only one non-zero element in $\boldsymbol{e}$, for which we can make a definite statement about the behavior of *COVE3* as $\boldsymbol{l}$ increases from zero. However, applying eq. 5 to the 4×4 example quickly shows that for $\boldsymbol{e}$ equal to the first row of $\boldsymbol{G}$, *COVE3* is 0.327 for the mirror image labor case vs. 0.207 for $\boldsymbol{l} = 0$ (see table 12). Even for this special case, the mathematical artifact argument does not hold.

6. 87-sector tests

We performed the tests outlined in the previous section for the full 87-sector model. Since there was little variation in the overall findings between the three years, we limited our tests to only one year's I–O model: 1967. The results of using labor input vectors 1–5 above for the 1967 87-sector data are given in table 13, and plotted in fig. 3b. Table 13 indicates that adding a labor vector does not in itself guarantee a lower coefficient of variation of the ε's, or a higher R^2 between embodied energy and dollar output. The mirror image labor vector, for example, produced a lower R^2 (0.013) and a higher *COV* (1.22) than vector 1 ($\boldsymbol{l} = \boldsymbol{0}$, $R^2 = 0.394$, *COVE85* = 1.02). Labor vectors 3 and 4 produced less variation in the ε's than vector 1, but more than vector 2 (the actual input). Vector 4 was not a significant improvement on vector 1, but vector 3 (labor input proportional to total value added) was. This is to be expected since the actual labor vector is a relatively large and constant component of value added.

Table 13

Results of alternative labor vector tests on the full 87 sector model. Tests were performed on the 1967 data with DEC energy input vector. For comparison with the 4×4 system, statistical indicators are calculated for sectors 1–85 only.

Labor vector	R^2	*COVE85*
(1) $l=0$	0.394	1.02
(2) $l=$actual	0.866	0.64
(3) $l\ \alpha$ value added	0.832	0.65
(4) $l\ \alpha$ total input	0.457	0.97
(5) $l\ \alpha$ mirror image	0.013	1.22

7. Conclusions

We conclude from this analysis that the mathematical artifact argument is not valid for a 'reasonable' set of labor vectors. The reduction in *COVE85* and the high degree of correlation between embodied energy and dollar value found using the 'actual' labor vector are therefore representative of real relationships and constraints in the economy and are not simply artifacts of the method used to incorporate labor and government energy costs. If they were artifacts, we would expect *COVE* to decrease dramatically on addition of any large labor vector, which tables 12 and 13 and fig. 3 show is not the case.

It seems that the only remaining objections to this analysis are philosophical ones concerning the propriety of removing humans from their 'controlling' position outside the economy and making them endogenous and therefore themselves 'controlled' to a larger extent [cf. Daly (1981)]. This is analogous to the 'positive vs. normative' debate in economics. We believe that there is no one universally correct position on either of these questions, but that the answer is dependent on the intended uses of the analysis. In the case of calculating a static measure of total energy cost it seems appropriate to consider humans to be endogenous, since they have already made their energy consumption choices and we merely want to look at the repercussions of them. For making projections into the future, however, it is still debatable whether humans should be considered endogenous, exogenous, or some complex combination of the two.

In any case, our analysis has definitely strengthened the case that embodied energy (calculated the way we suggest) is a good, non-trivial, static correlate of the economic value of the relatively large aggregates of goods and services that make up the entries in I–O tables. This does not imply that: (1) the market is perfect; (2) this relationship would continue to hold at the level of individual microeconomic transactions; or (3) absolutely no improvements in energy efficiency are possible. It is a relationship that applies to large aggregates, analogous to the way that the gas laws apply only to large assemblages of molecules. The gas laws are, nonetheless, very powerful tools when used to predict the overall behavior of ideal gasses, and we think that embodied energy may be an equally powerful tool to help predict the overall behavior of economic systems.

Appendix

Two theorems regarding predicting certain attributes of the energy intensities from propertiesof EV^{T-1} and G.

Theorem 1. If and only if EV^{T-1} is proportional to the pth row of G then

$$\varepsilon = c[(I-G)^{-1}-I]_p, \tag{A.1}$$

where c is the constant of proportionality and the subscript p means the pth row.

Proof of sufficiency. Assume $(EV^{T-1})_k = c(G)_{pk}$, $c=$constant.. Substituting in eq. (3):

$$(\varepsilon)_l = \sum_k (EV^{T-1})_k (I-G)^{-1}_{kl} = c\sum_k (G)_{pk}(I-G^{-1})_{kl},$$

$$(\varepsilon)_l = c[G(I-G)^{-1}]_{pl}. \tag{A.2}$$

For any invertible matrix $(I-G)$,

$$(I-G)(I-G)^{-1} = I \quad \text{and} \quad G(I-G)^{-1} = (I-G)^{-1} - I. \tag{A.3}$$

Substituting eq. (A.3) into (A.2) proves sufficiency.

Proof of necessity. Rewrite eq. (3):

$$EV^{T-1} = \varepsilon(I-G). \tag{A.4}$$

Assume

$$(\varepsilon)_l = d[I-G)^{-1} - I]_{pl}, \qquad d=\text{constant}. \tag{A.5}$$

Substituting eq. (A.5) in eq. (A.4):

$$(EV^{T-1})_k = d\sum_l [(I-G)^{-1} - I]_{pl}(I-G)_{lk},$$

$$(EV^{T-1})_k = d\{[(I-G)^{-1} - I](I-G)\}_{pk}. \tag{A.6}$$

Substituting eq. (A.3) in eq. (A.6):

$$(EV^{T-1})_k = d[G(I-G)^{-1}(I-G)]_{pk},$$

$$EV^{T-1} = d(G)_p, \qquad \text{which was to be proved.}$$

Theorem 2. For **G** *of the form*

$$\begin{pmatrix} G_{1,1} & \dots & G_{1,n} & G_{1,n+1} \\ \vdots & & \vdots & \vdots \\ G_{n,1} & \dots & G_{n,n} & G_{n,n+1} \\ l_1 \, l_2 & \dots & l_n & l_{n+1} \end{pmatrix}.$$

For $m=n$ or $n+1$ the following is true:

If the first m entries of EV^{T-1} *are proportional to the first m entries of* l *(i.e., to* $l_1, l_2, \dots, l_m$*), then the coefficient of variation of the first m elements of*

$$\varepsilon = EV^{T-1}(I-G)^{-1} \tag{A.7}$$

is independent of the magnitude of l.

Proof (of sufficiency only). We will prove that under the conditions above, when $l_1, l_2 \dots l_m$ are multiplied by a constant, the first m elements of ε are multiplied by a constant. Therefore any normalized dispersion index of the ε_i, including the coefficient of variation,[1] is unchanged.

Assume that the first n elements of EV^{T-1} are equal to the corresponding elements of l, i.e., of the $(n+1)$th row in **G** (there is no loss of generality of assuming equality rather than just proportionality, as we will show below).

We can then write

$$EV^{T-1} = (G)_{n+1} + (0, 0, \dots, (EV^{T-1})_{n+1} - (G)_{n+1,n+1}). \tag{A.8}$$

Using eq. (3) and applying Theorem 1 to the first term on the right-hand side,

$$\varepsilon = [(I-G)^{-1} - I]_{n+1} + ((EV^{T-1})_{n+1} - (G)_{n+1,n+1})(I-G)^{-1}_{n+1}. \tag{A.9}$$

The second term on the right-hand side is just a scalar times the $(n+1)$th row of $(I-G)^{-1}$.

[1]

$$COVM \equiv \left[\sum_{i=1}^{m}\left(\varepsilon_i - \frac{1}{m}\sum_{i=1}^{m}\varepsilon_i\right)^2 \Big/ m\right]^{\frac{1}{2}} \Big/ \frac{1}{m}\sum_{i=1}^{m}\varepsilon_i.$$

Now assume that the first n elements of $\boldsymbol{l}$ are multiplied by β. Following the same steps as above leads to

$$\varepsilon' = \frac{1}{\beta}[(\boldsymbol{I}-\boldsymbol{G}')^{-1} - \boldsymbol{I}]_{n+1}$$

$$+\left((\boldsymbol{E}\boldsymbol{V}^{T-1})_{n+1} - \frac{1}{\beta}(\boldsymbol{G}')_{n+1,n+1}\right)(\boldsymbol{I}-\boldsymbol{G}')^{-1}_{n+1}, \qquad \text{(A.10)}$$

where the primes refer to this second case. $\boldsymbol{G}'$ is identical to $\boldsymbol{G}$ except that all $n+1$ elements of the $(n+1)$th row have been multiplied by β. Rewriting eq. (A.10):

$$\varepsilon' = \overbrace{\left(\frac{1}{\beta} + (\boldsymbol{E}\boldsymbol{V}^{T-1})_{n+1} - \frac{1}{\beta}(\boldsymbol{G}')_{n+1,n+1}\right)}^{A}[(\boldsymbol{I}+\boldsymbol{G}')^{-1} - \boldsymbol{I}]_{n+1}$$

$$+\left((\boldsymbol{E}\boldsymbol{V}_{T-1})_{n+1} - \frac{1}{\beta}(\boldsymbol{G}')_{n+1,n+1}\right)(\boldsymbol{I})_{n+1,n+1}. \qquad \text{(A.11)}$$

The term A is a scalar and can be factored out of the first term on the right-hand side of eq. (A.11). The question which still remains is how $[(\boldsymbol{I}-\boldsymbol{G})^{-1} - \boldsymbol{I}]$ and $[(\boldsymbol{I}-\boldsymbol{G}')^{-1} - \boldsymbol{I}]$ are related. It turns out that their terms are proportional.

We show this by brute force examination of the elements of the inverses.

For an invertible matrix $(\boldsymbol{I}-\boldsymbol{G}')$,

$$(I-G')^{-1}_{n+1,j} = \frac{1}{\det(\boldsymbol{I}-\boldsymbol{G}')}(-1)^{n+1+j} \cdot \det \text{ of } (\boldsymbol{I}-\boldsymbol{G}')$$

$$\text{with} \begin{pmatrix} j\text{th row} \\ (n+1)\text{th column} \end{pmatrix} \text{removed} \qquad \text{(A.12)}$$

[Noble (1969, pp. 200, 210)].

For $j<n$, the numerator of the right-hand side of eq. (A.12) is just β times the numerator of the expression for the inverse of $(\boldsymbol{I}-\boldsymbol{G})$.

Using eq. (A.12), and expanding $\det(\boldsymbol{I}-\boldsymbol{G}')$ by its $(n+1)$th row:

$$[(\boldsymbol{I}-\boldsymbol{G}')^{-1}-\boldsymbol{I}]_{n+1,n+1}$$

$$=\frac{1}{\det(\boldsymbol{I}-\boldsymbol{G}')}\left\{\begin{array}{l}\text{det of } (\boldsymbol{I}-\boldsymbol{G}') \text{ with } \begin{pmatrix}(n+1)\text{th row}\\(n+1)\text{th column}\end{pmatrix}\text{removed}\\ -\left(\sum_{j=1}^{n}(-1)^{n+1+j}\beta l_j\cdot\text{det of } (\boldsymbol{I}-\boldsymbol{G}')\right) \text{ with } \begin{pmatrix}n+1\text{th row}\\j\text{th column}\end{pmatrix}\text{ removed}\\ +(1-\beta l_{n+1}) \text{ det of } (\boldsymbol{I}-\boldsymbol{G}') \text{ with } \begin{pmatrix}n+1\text{th row}\\n+1\text{th column}\end{pmatrix}\text{removed}\end{array}\right\} \tag{A.13}$$

In eq. (A.13), none of the determinants inside the brackets contains the $(n+1)$th row of $\boldsymbol{I}-\boldsymbol{G}'$; therefore all terms are the same as the corresponding ones of $\boldsymbol{I}-\boldsymbol{G}$. In addition, the only terms not linear in β cancel out. The results is that numerator of eq. (A.13) is also just β times the numerator for a similar expansion of $[(\boldsymbol{I}-\boldsymbol{G})^{-1}-\boldsymbol{I}]_{n+1,n+1}$.

This establishes that the $n+1$ elements of $[(\boldsymbol{I}-\boldsymbol{G})^{-1}-\boldsymbol{I}]$ and $[(\boldsymbol{I}-\boldsymbol{G}')^{-1}-\boldsymbol{I}]$ are proportional. Combining this with the fact that the factor A in eq. (A.11) is a constant independent of column, proves the theorem for $m=n$. The existence of the second term on the right-hand side of eq. (A. 11), which is non-zero only for the $n+1$th element of ε, prevents the theorem from applying to $m=n+1$ if the $(n+1)$th elements of $\boldsymbol{EV}^{T-1}$ and $\boldsymbol{l}$ are not proportional.

On the other hand, if all $n+1$ entries in $\boldsymbol{EV}^{T-1}$ are proportional to those of $\boldsymbol{l}$, the second term on the right-hand side of eq. (A.11) is zero and the theorem applies for $m=n+1$. This completes the proof.[2]

One can wonder why the theorem applies only for $m=n$ or $n+1$, but not a smaller number. The reason seems to be that there would be more than one non-zero element in the second term of eq. (A.8) and that other rows of $(\boldsymbol{I}-\boldsymbol{G})^{-1}$ besides the $(n+1)$th would be involved in the right-hand term of eq. (A.10), which would then not be easily factorable.

The case of $m=n$ corresponds exactly to the notion of

(1) starting with an $n\times n$ system to which labor is exogenous,
(2) adding a labor sector which has fixed input coefficients (i.e., fixed values of the $(n+1)$th column of $(\boldsymbol{G})$,
(3) constraining the values of the labor input coefficients (the l_i) to the proportional to $\boldsymbol{EV}^{T-1}$ as states, and yet to vary in absolute magnitude.

[2]Since we chose our initial $\boldsymbol{l}$ to have its first n elements equal to those of $\boldsymbol{EV}^{T-1}$, the theorem is only strictly proved when we note that the above arguments could be used to compare the results of using two multiplicative factors, say β_1 and β_2. Comparing the results for the two values of β would yield the same conclusion as we quote here.

David Reister [personal communication (25 April 1983)] has obtained a similar but more limited result. In the language of our proof, he

(1) assumes that $G_{n+1}, G_{n+1}=0$,
(2) looks at one row of $(\boldsymbol{I}-\boldsymbol{G})^{-1}$ at a time, which is equivalent to $\boldsymbol{E}\boldsymbol{V}^{T-1}$ having only one non-zero entry,
(3) assumes that $(\boldsymbol{E}\boldsymbol{V}^{T-1})_j$ is proportional to the jth column sum of $(\boldsymbol{I}-\boldsymbol{G})$.

He finds in this case that for the first n rows of $(\boldsymbol{I}-\boldsymbol{G})^{-1}$, the fractional deviation of each entry from the row mean decreases as the constant of proportionality in his assumption 3 increases.

This result is what is claimed in the mathematical artifact argument, but Reister's assumptions are too restrictive. In particular, use of $\boldsymbol{E}\boldsymbol{V}^{T-1}$ containing many non-zero elements is common. But, all of these proofs, his and ours, admittedly cover special cases.

*This research was funded, in part, by the National Science Foundation under Grant PRA-8003845, and by the Illinois Department of Energy and Natural Resources under Grant ENR-80.260. We thank B.M. Hannon, C.J. Cleveland, M.J. Lavine, T.J. Butler and H.E. Daly for reviewing earlier drafts and providing useful comments.

References

Bullard, C.W. and R.A. Herendeen, 1975, The energy costs of goods and services, Energy Policy 3, 268–278.

Carter, A.P. and A. Brody, eds., 1970, Input-output analysis (Elsevier, New York).

Costanza, R., 1980, Embodied energy and economic valuation, Science 210, 1219–1224.

Costanza, R., 1982, Economic values and embodied energy: reply to D.A. Huettner, Science 216, 1141–1143.

Costanza, R. and C. Neill, 1981, The energy embodied in the products of the biosphere, in: W.J. Mitsch, R.W. Bosserman and J.M. Klopatek, eds., Energy and ecological modeling (Elsevier, New York) 745–755.

Costanza, R. and C. Neill, 1984, Energy intensities, interdependence, and value in ecological systems: A linear programming approach, Journal of Theoretical Biology 106, 41–57.

Daly, H.E., 1981, Unresolved problems and issues for further research, Postscript in: H.E. Daly and A.F. Umana, eds., Energy, economics, and the environment: conflicting views of an essential interrelationship (Westview, Boulder, CO) 165–186.

Eisner, R., E.R. Simons, P.J. Pieper and S. Bender, 1981, Total incomes in the United States, 1946 to 1976: A summary report (International Association for Research in Income and Wealth, Gouvieux, France).

Hannon, B. and S. Casler, 1981, Calculation of the energy and labor intensities of U.S. commodities, 1974, and a comparison to 1963, 1967, and 1972, Document no. 315, Energy Research Group (University of Illinois, Champaign, IL).

Hannon, B., T. Blazeck, D. Kennedy and R. Illyes, 1983, A comparison of energy intensities 1963, 1967, and 1972, Resources and Energy 5, no. 1, 83–102.

Herendeen, R.A., 1981, Energy intensities in economic and ecological systems, Journal of Theoretical Biology 91, 607–620.

Herendeen, R.A. and C.W. Bullard, 1974, Energy costs of goods and services, 1963 and 1967, CAC document no. 140, Energy Research Group (University of Illinois, Urbana, IL).

Huettner, D.A., 1982, Economic values and embodied energy, Science 216, 1141–1143.

Kendrick, J.W., 1976, The formation and stocks of total capital (National Bureau of Economic Research, New York).

Leontief, W.W., 1941, The structure of American economy, 1919, 1929: An empirical application of equilibrium analysis (Harvard University Press, Cambridge, MA).

Nobel, B., 1969, Applied linear algebra (Prentice-Hall, Englewood Cliffs, NJ).
Ritz, P.M., 1979, The input–output structure of the U.S. economy, 1972, Survey of Current Business, Feb., 34–72.
Searle, S., 1966, Matrix algebra for the biological sciences (Wiley, New York).
U.S. Bureau of the Census, 1976, Statistical abstract of the United States (U.S. Government Printing Office, Washington, DC).

[12]

J. theor. Biol. (1984) **106**, 41–57

Energy Intensities, Interdependence, and Value in Ecological Systems: A Linear Programming Approach

ROBERT COSTANZA AND CHRISTOPHER NEILL

Coastal Ecology Laboratory, Center for Wetland Resources, Louisiana State University, Baton Rouge, Louisiana 70803, U.S.A.

(*Received* 28 *January* 1983, *and in revised form* 18 *July* 1983)

Many authors have applied input–output techniques to the analysis of energy and material flows in ecosystems. These applications are important contributions to our understanding of interdependence in ecological systems, but they suffer from reliance on "single commodity" flow matrices (i.e. enthalpy or carbon) and they do not address the problem of joint products, which is particularly significant for ecological applications. In this paper a general linear programming model is developed and used to describe and analyze interdependence in multicommodity ecosystems with joint products. The model is applied to data for Silver Springs and embodied energy intensities for the ecosystem products are calculated. The effects of different assumptions concerning the treatment of waste heat and joint products on the energy intensities are also discussed, as are potential applications to resource management problems that require a measure of relative value.

1. Introduction

The concept of value can play a major role in both ecology and economics. Both fields are involved in the study of the complex interdependence between physically dissimilar components. The concept of value allows comparisons to be made between these dissimilar components. The "valuation problem" for any system is therefore analogous to answering the question: what weighting or conversion factors can be used to compare essentially dissimilar, non-commensurable items, such as cars, swamps, and eagles? Is there a common denominator useful in linking all system components and making the cost/benefit calculations necessary to predict surviveability?

The weighting factors in modern economic systems are prices. Several alternatives have been proposed as the analog of prices for ecological systems. The most common is calorimetric energy content (Odum, 1971). Any proposed valuation or weighting system must satisfy the basic accounting constraint: the sum of the values of inputs (weighting factors times

0022–5193/84/010041 + 17 $03.00/0

quantities) must equal the sum of values of outputs for all transformation processes. This conservation constraint holds in dollars for economic entities, for calorimetric energy (by the first law of thermodynamics), and for mass (more accurately, for the total mass and energy). However, the use of first law accounting in ecology does not guarantee a "value" solution analogous with prices. The problem with first law accounting is the existence of the second law of thermodynamics, which states that the "usefulness" or availability of calorimetric energy decreases in any transformation. As Georgescu-Roegen (1971) has pointed out, it is low-entropy matter and energy that are "useful" and therefore necessary for economic value. An accounting that recognizes the second law is more appropriate for ecological and economic systems, since it allows value calculations that take into account usefulness or availability. It is the purpose of this paper to extend the development of such an accounting.

One form of second law accounting assumes, like all of classical thermodynamics, that all processes are reversible (Clapp, 1981; Ross, 1978). Reversible processes occur infinitely slowly and at maximum (Carnot) efficiency. Processes in the real world occur at finite rates, however, and are irreversible. Useful accountings of energy flows in ecological systems must therefore incorporate concepts of time, irreversibility, and power (Odum & Pinkerton, 1955; Prigogine, 1980). Accounting systems that do this are called irreversible second law accountings.

In irreversible systems the notion of "dissipative structures" is important (Prigogine, 1980). A dissipative structure is one that maintains its own ordered structure by dissipating gradients elsewhere in the system. The concept of "value" is hypothesized to correspond most closely with "degree of organization." Quantifying the degree of organization of dissipative structures (like cars, swamps, and eagles) is no simple matter. One approach, through information theory, is to estimate the degree of departure of the structure from a random arrangement of its elements (Gatlin, 1972; Ulanowicz, 1980; Jorgensen, 1982). While promising, this approach is not yet fully operational for complex structures, because the data and computations necessary to investigate all possible levels of organization are formidable.

Since creating and maintaining organized structures requires the dissipation of energy, a second approach to estimating the degree of organization in real, irreversible systems is to calculate the calorimetric energy required directly and indirectly to produce the structure. This dissipated energy is then said to be "embodied" in the organized structure (Costanza, 1980). Embodied energy serves as an index of order in the same sense that measuring the energy required to pump water into a reservoir is an index of the available energy stored in the elevated water. Embodied energy has also been shown to correlate well with economic value given appropriate assumptions (Costanza, 1980). Using this approach we can calculate theoretically the energy embodied in the structure of plants, animals, soil, water, and all other ecological "goods and services" once we know the detailed web of transformations that lead to their production.

One approach to this complex calculation is to use systems of linear equations to represent the transformations, and the well-known mathematical techniques of input–output analysis to solve them. This has been attempted by Hannon (1973, 1976, 1979) for selected ecosystems but, as Herendeen (1980) points out, the results were somewhat confusing. We will show that Hannon was really performing a first law accounting and will go on to demonstrate how an irreversible second law accounting that allows for joint products may be performed using the Silver Springs, Florida, ecosystem data originally published by Odum (1957).

2. Joint Products

Joint products refer to the interdependent by-products of most real transformation processes. For the purposes of discussion we can divide all production processes into two fundamental types: sorting and assembly. A production process is defined here as one that increases the degree of organization of some of its "products" while dissipating the order of at least some of its inputs. Sorting is a fundamental anti-entropic activity involving the splitting of a mixed substance into its components; assembly involves combining inputs into an organized product with lower entropy. If all production processes of interest were of the pure assembly type, then joint products might not present a problem, but the existence of sorting implies that joint products are unavoidable. All industries in the U.S. economy produce joint products. The mining industry, for example, produces refined minerals but also spent ore. The pulp produced by the timber industry and the sulfur removed from crude oil during refining are examples of joint products that are marketable. Other joint products are considered waste, such as air and water pollutants, and have no market value.

All ecological processes also produce joint products. Trees produce oxygen, water vapor, and waste heat as well as tree biomass. Waste heat is the most ubiquitous of joint products and requires special treatment, as discussed below. Although joint products seem to reflect the physical nature of economic and ecological processes (it is impossible to produce iron without also producing spent iron ore or to produce a tree without producing oxygen), they complicate mathematical description and analysis and have often been ignored.

Waste heat is an unavoidable by-product of all transformation processes. To understand its special role we must define a third fundamental process already alluded to—dissipation of an existing gradient. Dissipation is not a production process (since it proceeds spontaneously in the direction of increasing entropy) but is required to drive all production processes (which produce low entropy structures). The second law of thermodynamics requires that the amount of disorder produced by dissipation be greater than or equal to the amount of order created by sorting and assembly for irreversible processes in an isolated system. To sort or assemble at a finite rate, fuel, capital, labor, etc. must be "consumed" or "dissipated", by allowing the gradients to dissipate in a controlled way at a finite rate (cf. Odum & Pinkerton, 1955; Prigogine, Allen & Herman, 1977).

We can thus divide joint products into two distinct groups depending on their origin as the result of sorting or dissipation. This distinction is critical because the products of a purely dissipative process have no order and therefore no ability to perform work, no available embodied energy and no "value," while the products of sorting do.

For example, a temperature gradient could be allowed to dissipate without doing any work, in which case the only product would be uniform heat. The available energy embodied in the original gradient would disappear. On the other hand, we could insert an engine between the high temperature source and low temperature sink, and the available energy embodied in the original temperature gradient could be used to produce another gradient (sorting or assembly "work" via the engine). We could say that the dissipation of the original gradient was a necessary cost of production, and the original gradient could be said to be "embodied" in the products of the engine.

In real, irreversible systems, gradients are frequently not dissipated completely. For example, the exhaust from an automobile engine is above environmental temperatures and thus still has some available energy. It is immediately dissipated and lost without doing any work when the exhaust is released to the environment. Since this is a necessary cost of driving the production process at a finite rate, we might conclude that the energy embodied in the entire gradient should be embodied in the outputs. Alternatively, we could reason that only the gradient between the engine combustion temperature and the exhaust temperature be embodied in the outputs. We will discuss the implications of these alternatives on the resulting calculations.

3. Methods

The problem is to trace the flow of a primary resource (energy) through a complex web of multicommodity biological and chemical transformations to determine the amount required directly and indirectly to produce each of the components of an ecological system. This problem is analogous to the study of interdependence and the imputation of value to primary factors in economics. The economic problem was first explicitly formulated by Walras (1896) and empirical applications began with Leontief's (1941) Nobel prize-winning work. Leontief's approach has come to be known as input–output (I–O) analysis. I–O analysis has been applied to the study of energy and material flow in ecosystems (Hannon, 1973; Richey *et al.*, 1978) and in economic systems (Bullard & Herendeen, 1975; Costanza, 1980) and we refer the reader to these works for more detailed descriptions of the technique. I–O analysis can be shown to be a special case of the more general Linear Programming (LP) analysis (Dorfman, Samuelson & Solow, 1958). I–O analysis results when two simplifying assumptions are imposed on the LP model: (1) no joint products; (2) no alternative production technologies (i.e., there is a unique combination of inputs for each output).

Since it is just these two assumptions that we wish to relax, the LP approach provides the appropriate analytical framework. We proceed by developing the LP model, noting correspondence with the I–O model where appropriate.

A general equilibrium model of an economy that allows joint products and alternative production technologies was first proposed by von Neumann (1945). In the von Neumann model there are m commodities (denoted by $C_1, C_2, \ldots, C_m$) and n processes or activities for transforming commodities (denoted by $Q_1, Q_2, \ldots, Q_n$). Each transformation process can be indicated by its input commodity requirements and its jointly produced outputs, for example for process j:

$$Q_j = \begin{bmatrix} U_{1j}, U_{2j}, \ldots, U_{nj} \\ V_{j1}, V_{j2}, \ldots, V_{jn} \end{bmatrix}$$

or (U_{ij}, V_{ji}), $i = 1, m$; $j = 1, n$, where U_{ij} = the input of commodity i to process j, V_{ji} = the output of commodity i from process j and one discrete time period or accounting unit is implied. Figure 1 illustrates this general production relation.

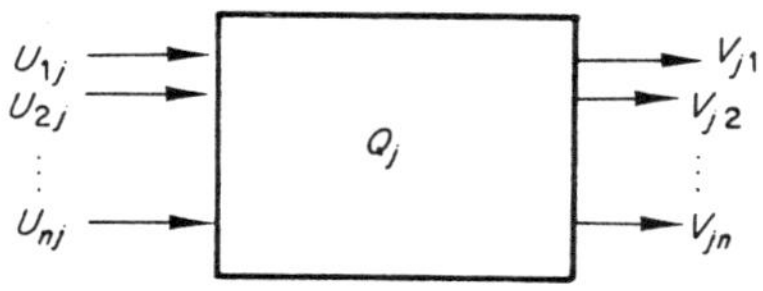

FIG. 1. General production relations. U_{ij} is the input of commodity i to process j. V_{ji} is the output of commodity i from process j.

In the Leontief system there would be only one V_{ji} for each process (j) and each commodity (i) would correspond to one process ($V_{ji}=0$ if $i \neq j$). We will assume a linear transformation process, or one where:

$$\begin{bmatrix} \lambda U_{1j}, \lambda U_{2j}, \ldots, \lambda U_{nj} \\ \lambda V_{j1}, \lambda V_{j2}, \ldots, \lambda V_{jn} \end{bmatrix}$$

or (λU_{ij}, λV_{ji}) holds for all λ.† Next we set up a system of m linear equations (one for each commodity) which balance the total input of each commodity to all processes against the total output of each commodity from all processes. Note that m does not necessarily equal n, that is, there can be a different number of commodities and processes. Thus we have:

$$\begin{array}{l} U_{11} + U_{12} + \ldots + U_{1n} + Y_1 = V_{11} + V_{21} + \ldots + V_{n1} \\ U_{21} + U_{22} + \ldots + U_{2n} + Y_2 = V_{12} + V_{22} + \ldots + V_{n2} \\ \vdots \\ U_{m1} + U_{m2} + \ldots + U_{mn} + Y_m = V_{1m} + V_{2m} + \ldots + V_{mn} \end{array} \tag{1}$$

An "open" system allows for imports (commodities that are inputs from outside the system boundaries) and exports (commodities that are outputs to outside the system boundaries). We develop an open system by denoting imports and exports of commodity i by $U_{i,n+1}$ and $V_{n+1,i}$, respectively, and net exports by $Y_i = V_{n+1,i} - U_{i,n+1}$. Any change in the storage of a commodity (net accumulation or depletion) is included as a net export. Also, depreciation of an already produced commodity (as distinct from losses in the process of production) is considered to be a net export, since it represents a loss of the commodity to the system. This is an important distinction, since it implies that at steady state the net input to the system is just enough to maintain all the internal stocks of commodities against depreciation.

The left side of each equation in (1) represents the demand for each commodity (as the sum of input requirements for all processes plus exports or "final demand") while the right side represents the supply of each commodity (from internal production plus imports). Note, for comparison, that in the Leontief model the right-hand side of each equation is set equal to the total output of each commodity, and supply is implicitly assumed to meet or exceed demand.

Next we define two sets of technical coefficients: $A_{ij} = U_{ij}/X_j$ = gross input coefficient, the amount of commodity i required as input for process

† In practice we require that λ be small for the static equilibrium assumption. For dynamic applications we would require a more complex functional relation (probably nonlinear) relating inputs to outputs. As long as we limit applications to static accounting applications the linearity assumption is acceptable, however.

j per unit activity of process j. These are the Leontief technical coefficients. $B_{ij} = V_{ji}/X_j$ = gross output coefficient, the amount of commodity i produced as output from process j per unit activity of process j. X_j = some measure of the activity level of process j.† Thus we can rewrite equation (1) as:

$$\begin{array}{l} A_{11}X_1 + A_{12}X_2 + \ldots + A_{1n}X_n + Y_1 = B_{11}X_1 + B_{12}X_2 + \ldots + B_{1n}X_n \\ A_{21}X_1 + A_{22}X_2 + \ldots + A_{2n}X_n + Y_2 = B_{21}X_1 + B_{22}X_2 + \ldots + B_{2n}X_n \\ \vdots \qquad \vdots \qquad \vdots \qquad \vdots \qquad \vdots \qquad \vdots \qquad \vdots \\ A_{m1}X_1 + A_{m2}X_2 + \ldots + A_{mn}X_n + Y_m = B_{m1}X_1 + B_{m2}X_2 + \ldots + B_{mn}X_n \end{array} \tag{2}$$

In matrix notation we can indicate equations (2) as

$$\mathbf{AX} + \mathbf{Y} = \mathbf{BX} \tag{3}$$

or

$$(\mathbf{B} - \mathbf{A})\mathbf{X} = \mathbf{Y} \tag{4}$$

where $\mathbf{A}$ is a $n \times m$ matrix of gross input coefficients, $\mathbf{B}$ is a $n \times m$ matrix of gross output coefficients. If there are no joint products and $m = n$, $\mathbf{B}$ is the identity matrix. $\mathbf{X}$ is a m dimensional column vector of process activity levels. $\mathbf{Y}$ is a n dimensional column vector of "net exports" (including "exports" or losses due to depreciation and any net accumulation over the time interval).

Since we do not necessarily have equal numbers of commodities and processes or a one-to-one correspondence between commodities and processes, the above system of equations is not necessarily solvable using standard linear algebra manipulations and is best handled as a linear programming problem. Certain assumptions can be imposed to allow I–O models to handle joint products but these either (1) can lead to negative relative weights or (2) require that we know the relative weights *a priori*, both of which are unacceptable for our purposes. The former (commodity-technology assumption) assumes that joint products require the same inputs as when they are produced as the sole output from a process. Thus, one simply transfers the inputs required for the sole output process away from the joint output process. This can lead to "negative inputs" and negative relative weights. The second assumption (the market shares assumption)

† The appropriate activity measure in input–output analysis is the total output of the one commodity produced by each sector. In the LP model the appropriate activity measure is not obvious and there are several possibilities. We could choose a "main" product output, multiply all the outputs by weighting factors and add, etc. In our examples we use the first alternative but others are certainly possible. We have not investigated the effects of using different activity measures on the results.

assigns inputs to joint products based on the percentage of the total value of the output that each joint product represents (Ritz, 1979). To arrive at this percentage (market share), we must already know the relative weights to apply to the joint outputs. For economic applications market prices are used to determine market shares, but in ecological examples it is just these relative weights that we are trying to calculate and we cannot use them *a priori* to obtain a solution.

Linear programming allows a more general and flexible formulation of the problem. LP uses a system of linear inequalities (rather than equations) that represent constraints on the system's behavior combined with an objective function, that represents the direction of system evolution within the constraints. Systems of linear inequalities have many possible (feasible) solutions but only the solution that maximizes (or minimizes) the objective function is optimal. The choice of objective function is therefore critical to the definition of the problem and its solution. LP formulations have another desirable characteristic for this application. They consist of both a "primal" problem and a sort of mirror image problem implicit in the primal called the "dual". The dual problem is of considerable importance since it can be used to determine the "shadow prices" or implied valuations for ecological commodities. We can formulate the generalized von Neumann model as a classic primal/dual LP pair (Dorfmann *et al.*, 1958), with objective functions consistent with (but not identical to) Hannon's (1979) hypothesis† and also with Oster & Wilson's (1978) hypothesis of "maximum egronomic efficiency" and Odum's (1971) "maximum power" hypothesis.

Primal

Minimize

$$P = \mathbf{EX} \tag{5}$$

(primary resource cost of all processes) subject to:

$$(\mathbf{B} - \mathbf{A})\mathbf{X} \geq \mathbf{Y} \tag{6}$$

(materials balance constraints, one for each commodity) and

$$\mathbf{X} \geq 0 \tag{7}$$

(non-negativity constraints on the process activity levels).

† Hannon (1979, p. 271) states: "In brief, the hypotheses are that while the components of an ecosystem strive to maximize their total direct and indirect energy storage within the constraints of their production characteristics, the overall system strives to minimize the metabolized energy per unit of stored biomass energy."

Dual

Maximize

$$P' = \mathbf{eY} \tag{8}$$

("value" of net output) subject to

$$\mathbf{e}(\mathbf{B}-\mathbf{A}) \leq \mathbf{E} \tag{9}$$

(value balance constraints, one for each process) and $\mathbf{e} \geq 0$ (non-negativity constraints), where P is the value of the primal objective function, P' is the value of the dual objective function, $\mathbf{B}$ is an $n \times m$ matrix of commodity outputs per unit activity level and $\mathbf{A}$ is an $n \times m$ matrix of commodity inputs per unit activity level. $\mathbf{Y}$ is an $n \times 1$ vector of commodity net exports, $\mathbf{X}$ is a $m \times 1$ vector of process activity levels, $\mathbf{E}$ is a $1 \times m$ vector of net primary resource inputs by process, per unit activity level, and $\mathbf{e}$ is a $1 \times n$ vector of energy intensities (relative weights or shadow prices) per unit of commodity.

For ecological systems the primary (exogenous) resources ($\mathbf{E}$ vector) are direct solar energy and the solar energy embodied in other primary inputs (i.e., commodities which are not also produced inside the system). The $\mathbf{e}$ vector can thus be interpreted as the direct and indirect energy cost (embodied energy) per unit commodity with allowances for joint products and alternative production technologies. The system adjusts the process activity levels ($\mathbf{X}$) and the relative weights or embodied energy intensities ($\mathbf{e}$) in order to minimize the total primary resource (energy) cost of production, which also maximizes the total value (relative weights times quantities) of the net exports from the system.

4. Results

To demonstrate the LP model, we employ the same example system as Hannon (1973, 1976, 1979) and Herendeen (1981). Data on biomass and nitrogen flows for the Silver Springs, Florida, ecosystem were obtained originally by Odum (1957).

Table 1 shows the flow data for Silver Springs. Inputs (the upper entry) and outputs (the lower entry in parentheses) of commodities (listed along the left of the table) to and from processes (listed along the top of the table) are shown. Export of biomass was divided proportionally among all biomass commodities and not allocated solely to producers, as in Herendeen (1981). The flow network is shown diagrammatically in Fig. 2. Each commodity in the tables and figure is kept separate and we seek the conversion of weighting factors that would allow us to compare them.

TABLE 1

Input–output table for Silver Springs, Florida.

Commodity (units)	Processes: Primary producers	Herbivores	Carnivores	Top carnivores	Decomposers	Export (import)	Total demand (supply)
Plant biomass (g)	0	748·4	0	0	874·2	460·3	2082·9
	(1962·9)	(0)	(0)	(0)	(0)	(120)	(2082·9)
Herbivore biomass (g)	0	0	85·1	0	170·7	72·6	328·4
	(0)	(328·4)	(0)	(0)	(0)	(0)	(328·4)
Consumer biomass (g)	0	0	0	4·7	6·9	3·3	14·9
	(0)	(0)	(14·9)	(0)	(0)	(0)	(14·9)
Top carnivore +	0	0	0	0	80·6	22·9	103·5
decomposer biomass (g)	(0)	(0)	(0)	(1·3)	(102·2)	(0)	(103·5)
Nitrogen (g)	121·7†	0	0	0	0	4415·6§	4537·3
	(0)	(0)	(0)	(0)	(70·3)‖	(4467·0)‡	(4537·3)
Heat (kcal)	0	0	0	0	0	407 986	407 986
	(401 167)	(1890)	(316)	(13)	(4600)	0	(407 986)
Sun (kcal)	410 000	0	0	0	0	0	410 000
	(0)	(0)	(0)	(0)	(0)	(410 000)	(410 000)

Upper numbers are inputs and lower numbers (in parentheses) are outputs of commodities listed along the left to processes listed along the top. All flows are $/m^2$yr.

† Nitrogen comprises 6·2% of plant biomass by weight. Net primary production is 2082·9 g/m^2yr.

§ Net output of N obtained by difference (total input-uptake).

‖ Nitrogen produced by decomposers is 6·2 percent of biomass input to that sector. Assume all N in decomposing biomass is regenerated.

‡ $3{\cdot}395 \times 10^8$ g/yr inflow in spring water distributed over an area of $7{\cdot}6 \times 10^4$ m^2.

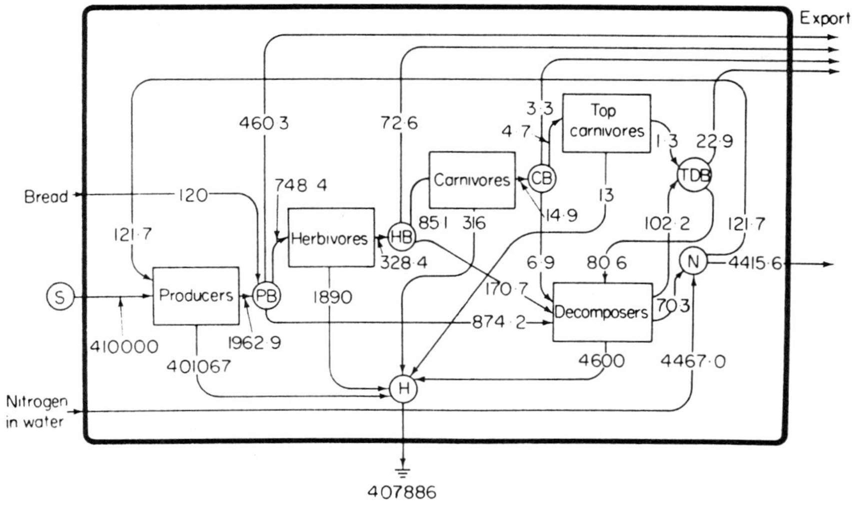

FIG. 2. Transactions diagram for the Silver Springs ecosystem. Boxes represent production processes. Circles represent commodities. PB = plant biomass: HB = herbivore biomass; CB = carnivore biomass; TDB = top carnivore + decomposer biomass; N = nitrogen; all g/m^{2}yr. H = waste heat; S = sunlight (both kcal/m^{2}yr).

The table and figure correspond to the mathematical description outlined earlier. Table 1 lists the demand or use of each ecological commodity (U_{ij}) as the sum of inputs to internal processes and export. For example, of the total 2082·9 g/m^{2}yr plant biomass available for use, 748·4 g/m^{2}yr was used as input to herbivores (U_{12}), 874·2 g/m^{2}yr was consumed by decomposers (U_{15}) and 460·3 g/m^{2}yr was exported (U_{16}). Table 1 also shows the supply characteristics of each commodity in the system as the sum of internal production and imports. For example, of the total 4537·3 gN/m^{2}yr produced or imported into the system, 70·3 gN/m^{2}yr was produced internally by decomposers (V_{55}) and 4467·0 gN/m^{2}yr was imported into the system in the inflowing water (V_{65}).

In Fig. 2 each process is represented by a box and each commodity by a circle. Looking at the inputs and outputs to a circle is equivalent to looking at the corresponding commodity rows in Table 1. Looking at a box in the figure is equivalent to looking at the corresponding process column in Table 1. The system receives a solar energy input of 410 000 kcal m^{2}yr. The input of 120 g/m^{2}yr of bread thrown into the system by tourists was considered a net import of plant biomass.

The essence of the valuation problem is finding a set of weighting or conversion factors that would allow us to add and balance process inputs and outputs (boxes in Fig. 2 or columns in Table 1) while maintaining our ability to add and balance commodities (circles in Fig. 2 or rows in Table 1).

Table 1 and Fig. 2 show waste heat as a secondary joint product of all processes. Decomposers produce their own biomass, nutrients, and waste heat as joint products. Other joint products, such as feeding or nesting sites, may be included in the model as data permit.

The treatment of waste heat is critical since it determines whether a first law, a reversible second law, or an irreversible second law analysis results.

TABLE 2

Energy intensities (in kcal/g) for the Silver Springs ecosystem for various values of the quality factor for waste heat

Quality factor for waste heat†	Plant biomass	Herbivore biomass	Consumer biomass	Top carnivore + decomposer biomass	Nitrogen
0·0	297·05	676·95	3866·32	13 978·24	1422·20
0·01	294·16	670·44	3829·35	13 844·66	1408·60
0·0428	284·68	694·02	3707·73	13 405·31	1363·91
0·1	287·17	611·71	3495·85	12 639·84	1286·07
0·5	152·67	350·80	2014·19	7 287·07	741·78
1·0	4·50	4·50	4·50	4·53	0·0

† This is operationally equivalent to Herendeen's (1981) α.

Table 2 shows the energy intensities which are analogous to shadow prices, that result from application of the LP model.† The quality factor or "value" of waste heat was varied over the range from zero to one. (Different quality factors for heat were handled by converting the heat to solar equivalents (by multiplying by the chosen quality factor) and decreasing the input of solar energy by that amount.) A quality factor of one for waste heat implies a first law accounting since no distinction is made between dissipation and production. A quality factor of zero for waste heat implies a reversible second law accounting since the heat outflow is assumed to be completely dissipated and thus valueless. An intermediate quality factor implies an irreversible second law accounting since waste heat is assumed to be incompletely dissipated and to still contain some available energy and some "value".

† The ZX3LP subroutine of the IMSL library was used to perform the analysis on the IBM 370/3033 at LSU. The subroutine uses a revised simplex technique.

5. Discussion

This paper demonstrates the application of linear programming techniques to the valuation problem in ecological systems. Joint products, which are unavoidable in any system that contains sorting or dissipation activity, can be dealt with in the LP format, but simply casting the data in this formal structure does not guarantee intelligible results. The distinction between dissipation (change in structure in the direction of increasing entropy) and production (sorting and assembly, or change in structure in the direction of decreasing entropy) is critical. If dissipation products (such as waste heat) are not distinguished from production products, then a first law accounting results. If they are distinguished, then a more useful second law accounting results. Hannon (1973, 1976, 1979), following established conventions in ecology, used a quality factor of one for waste heat and therefore obtained constant energy intensities. Herendeen (1981) attempted to draw the distinction between dissipation and production by eliminating respiratory heat flow from the production matrix (see also Ulanowicz, 1972). Herendeen's results show increasing energy intensities moving up the food chain as we might expect. Our results extend Herendeen's analysis by allowing for non-dissipative joint products. As a first step we include nitrogen in the system. Contrary to Herendeen's expectation the inclusion of nitrogen did not tend to decrease the variance in energy intensities but rather increased it.

Herendeen's α factor is operationally equivalent to the quality factor for waste heat. A value of $\alpha = 1$ implies a first law accounting and energy intensities equal to the calorimetric values for the commodities. A value of $\alpha = 0$ implies a reversible second law accounting. An intermediate value for α may be more appropriate for real irreversible systems since it implies that the dissipation products are not completely degraded or that all the dissipated potential is not embodied in the products.

When waste heat is the main dissipation product the Carnot ratio using the source-sink temperature gradient may be an appropriate independent measure of α. For example, we might define an index of α as:

$$\alpha' = 1 - ((T_2 - T_1)/T_2) = T_1/T_2 \tag{9}$$

where T_1 = temperature of the source and T_2 = temperature of the sink.

The implication of this formulation is that waste heat (at sink temperature T_1) still has work potential relative to the universe, which is at a still lower temperature (≈ 3 K). For our Silver Springs example, we calculated a value for α' based on $T_2 = 7000$ K (effective temperature of sunlight) and $T_1 = 300$ K (average temperature of the earth) as $\alpha' = 1 - ((7000\text{–}300)/7000) = 0{\cdot}0428$.

The energy intensities based on this α value are included in Table 2. These show an average variation from the intensities calculated with $\alpha = 0$ of 0·96%. Thus, assuming that $\alpha = 0$ does not lead to significant numerical error in this example since more than 95% of the available energy in sunlight is degraded by the time it emerges as 300 K waste heat.

The problem with this formulation is that Carnot ratios are based on reversible (infinitely slow) reactions. The question of what percentage of the dissipated gradient is embodied in the products is still not adequately addressed in this formulation (100% embodiment is assumed implicitly). Odum & Pinkerton (1955) have suggested and defended with theoretical arguments an embodiment ratio closer to 50%. In our example, an $\alpha = 0{\cdot}5$ would lead to energy intensities with an average variation of 48·1% compared to $\alpha = 0$.

Inspection of Table 2 shows that, except for values close to zero (second law case), changes in the value of α change the absolute values of the energy intensities more than their relative values. Thus, questions about relative energy intensities are not as dependent on the choice of α as are questions of absolute energy intensities. This may prove useful in resource management applications, since we could "scale" the model using known resource prices without changing the relative energy intensities significantly. It also means that the choice of α does not significantly affect questions about relative economic value (Costanza, 1980) since changing α affects mainly the absolute, not the relative, energy intensities.

6. Zero Energy Intensities and Activity Levels

While the non-negativity constraints in the LP model prevent negative energy intensities, an unequal number of commodities and processes invariably leads to either zero activity levels for some processes or zero energy intensities for some commodities. These results are interpretable within the framework of linear programming as indicating an uncompetitive process or the existence of "slack" or unused capacity in the system (cf. Dorfman, Samuelson & Solow, 1958). We avoided this result by aggregating top carnivore and decomposer biomass (since they are both at the "top" of the food chain). This allowed an equal number of commodities (four biomass types and nitrogen) and processes (five tropic levels) and produced positive nonzero activity levels and energy intensities for all components. An equal number of commodities and processes does not guarantee this result, however. The "structure" of the data must also be such that all processes and commodities are part of what the LP model deems to be the optimal system. In our Silver Springs example, it was possible to change individual entries in the I–O table slightly and cause processes and commodities to be eliminated from the optimal solution. Since Silver Springs is a stable ecosystem that has persisted in essentially the same condition for many years, one would expect its structure to be very close to optimal. An optimization model that does not reproduce this conclusion brings into question the model, the data, or both.

One interpretation is that the model is correct and any failure to reproduce the real system is caused by imprecise data. Since the ecological data used to construct I–O tables are admittedly very imprecise, this assumption seems reasonable. Given this assumption, the LP model could be used as a consistency check on the data. One way to handle this problem would be to specify a range of certainty for each individual entry in the I–O table and use a Monte Carlo approach to determine which combinations of numbers randomly selected from within these ranges lead to all non-zero energy intensities and activity levels. An exercise like this could be used to construct ranges on the resulting energy intensities and activity levels.

Since the I–O model does not constrain energy intensities to be nonnegative, the same data that produce zero energy intensities (with $m = n$) in the LP model will produce negative energy intensities in an I–O formulation. If the I–O formulation (with $m = n$) produces all positive energy intensities, its results will be identical to an LP formulation using the same data. As noted previously, the I–O and LP models are very similar, but the LP model makes the optimization aspects of the problem more visible.

7. Resource Management Applications

Input–output type models that summarize ecological transformations have been suggested as potentially useful to determine "shadow prices" for nonmarketed ecological commodities (Daly, 1968; Isard, 1972; Victor, 1972; Ayres, 1978; Costanza, 1980, 1982). This approach to shadow pricing has some potential advantages over the currently more popular "willingness-to-pay" formulations (Freeman, 1979). Most importantly, one does not have to interject humans into transactions in which they play no "direct" role and therefore exhibit irrelevant preferences. For example, people's willingness-to-pay for detritus is not meaningful since they do not use it directly. We must either survey detritivores about their preferences or carry the chain of production relations forward to the point where economically important commodities with well-defined markets are produced.

Linear programming models represent a well-developed, comprehensive way of detailing a complex set of production relations. As we have shown, they are applicable to ecological systems with joint products. The "shadow prices" that they produce are also interpretable as the direct and indirect primary resource cost of each product. Since sunlight is the major net input to the biosphere we may be able to use embodied solar energy as a common denominator linking ecological and economic systems (Costanza, 1980; Costanza & Neill, 1981). Such a common denominator would obviously be very useful for a broad range of resource management applications.

For realistic applications we would require detailed transactions tables for the ecological systems of the U.S. and the world. While these tables would always be inaccurate and incomplete (just as economic I–O tables always are), they would at least serve as a framework in which to summarize the extent of our current quantitative knowledge on ecological transactions, interdependence, and value. They would also be valuable in pinpointing areas for further research.

This work was supported, in part, by NSF Project No. PRA-8003845, titled "Use of embodied energy values in the analysis of energy/economy trade-off decisions: an exploratory analysis". M. J. Lavine and R. Costanza were the principal investigators. We wish to thank B. Hannon, R. Herendeen, R. Ulanowicz, F. Sklar, and R. E. Turner for reviewing earlier drafts and providing useful comments. All remaining errors and omissions are, of course, the responsibility of the authors. This is contribution #LSU-CEL-83-02 from the Coastal Ecology Laboratory, Louisiana State University, Baton Rouge, Louisiana 70803, U.S.A.

REFERENCES

AYRES, R. N. (1978). *Resources, Environment, and Economics: Applications of the Materials/Energy Balance Principle.* New York: Wiley.

BULLARD, C. W. & HERENDEEN, R. A. (1975). *Energy Policy* **3,** 268.

CLAPP, R. E. (1981). *J. theor. Biol.* **92,** 15.

COSTANZA, R. (1980). *Science* **210,** 1219.

COSTANZA, R. (1984). *Proceedings of the Wallenberg Symposium,* Stockholm, Sweden, Sept. 1–3, 1982 (in press).

COSTANZA, R. & NEILL, C. (1981). In: *Energy and Ecological Modelling* (Mitsch, W. J., Bosserman, R. W. & Klopatek, J. M., eds). pp. 745–755. New York: Elsevier.

DALY, H. E. (1968). *J. pol. Econ.* **76,** 392.

DORFMAN, R., SAMUELSON, P. A. & SOLOW, R. M. (1958). *Linear Programming and Economic Analysis.* New York: McGraw Hill.

FINN, J. R. (1976). *J. theor. Biol.* **56,** 363.

FREEMAN, A. M. (1979). *The Benefits of Environmental Improvement.* Baltimore: Johns Hopkins University Press.

GATLIN, L. L. (1972). *Information Theory and the Living System.* New York: Columbia University Press.

GEORGESCU-ROEGEN, N. (1971). *The Entropy Law and the Economic Process.* Cambridge: Harvard University Press.

HANNON, B. (1973). *J. theor. Biol.* **41,** 535.

HANNON, B. (1976). *J. theor. Biol.* **56,** 253.

HANNON, B. (1979). *J. theor. Biol.* **80,** 271.

HERENDEEN, R. A. (1981). *J. theor. Biol.* **91,** 607.

ISARD, W. (1972). *Ecologic–Economic Analysis for Regional Development.* New York: The Free Press.

JORGENSEN, S. E. (1982). In: *Energetics and Systems* (Mitsch, W. J., Ragade, R. K., Bosserman, R. W., Dillon, J. A., eds). pp. 61–72. Ann Arbor: Ann Arbor Science.

LEONTIEF, W. W. (1941). *The Structure of American Economy, 1919, 1929: An Empirical Application of Equilibrium Analysis.* Cambridge: Harvard University Press.

ODUM, H. T. (1957). *Ecol. Monogr.* **27,** 55.

ODUM, H. T. (1971). *Environment, Power, and Society.* New York: Wiley.

ODUM, H. T. & PINKERTON, R. C. (1955). *Am. Sci.* **43,** 331.

OSTER, G. F. & WILSON, E. O. (1978). *Caste and Ecology in the Social Insects. Monographs in Population Biology* No. 12. Princeton: Princeton University Press.

PATTEN, B. C. (1982). In: *Energetics and Systems* (Mitsch, W. J., Ragade, R. K., Bosserman, R. W., Dillon, J. A., eds). pp. 109–118. Ann Arbor: Ann Arbor Science.

PRIGOGINE, I. (1980). *From Being to Becoming.* San Francisco: Freeman.

PRIGOGINE, I., ALLEN, P. M. & HERMAN, R. (1977). In: *Goals in a Global Community* (Lazslo, E. & Bierman, J., eds). New York: Pergamon Press.

RICHEY, J. E., WISSMAR, R. C., DEROL, A. H., LIKENS, G. E., EATON, J. S., WETZEL, R. G., ODUM, W. E., JOHNSON, H. M., LOUCKS, O. L., PRENTKI, R. T.& RICH, P. H. (1978). *Science* **202,** 1183.

RITZ, P. M. (1979). *Survey of Current Business.* February 1979. 34–72.

ROSS, M. (1978). In: *Energy Analysis: A New Public Policy Tool* (Gilliland, M. W., ed.). pp. 43–54. Boulder: Westview.

ULANOWICZ, R. E. (1972). *J. theor. Biol.* **34,** 239.

ULANOWICZ, R. E. (1980). *J. theor. Biol.* **85,** 223.

VICTOR, P. A. (1972). *Pollution, Economy and Environment.* Toronto: University of Toronto Press.

VON NEUMANN, J. (1945). *Rev. Econ. Stud.* **13,** 1.

WALRAS, L. (1896). *Elements d'Economic Politique.* Lausanne.

JOURNAL OF ENVIRONMENTAL ECONOMICS AND MANAGEMENT 13, 391–401 (1986)

Measures of Energy Cost and Value in Ecosystems

BRUCE HANNON

Geography Department, University of Illinois at Urbana-Champaign, Urbana, Illinois 61801

ROBERT COSTANZA

Coastal Ecology Institute, Center for Wetland Resources, Louisiana State University, Baton Rouge, Louisiana 70803

AND

ROBERT A. HERENDEEN

Illinois Natural History Survey, University of Illinois at Urbana-Champaign, Urbana, Illinois 61801

Received September 26, 1983; revised October 8, 1985

The physical output of ecological processes have different values even though they may be measured in the same physical units. Using linear input–output theory, we derive a set of weights based on direct and indirect energy requirements for ecosystem commodities which uniquely converts them into commensurable unit costs. Under certain conditions, these costs are equal to values or prices. Using this system, behavioral theories can be better posed for experimental verification. © 1986 Academic Press, Inc.

Components of an ecosystem exchange physically measurable quantities with each other, in much the same way as sectors of an economy do. While these exchanges can be physically measured in a number of ways (e.g., by mass, enthalpy, or carbon content), these measures will not necessarily capture the system-wide cost of the exchange. Energy cost is defined here as a weighting factor times the physical quantity exchanged, representing the total system-wide energy required for the exchange. In economics, the relevant weighting factors are called prices and either they are determined by decentralized markets (prevalent in western economies) or they are set by a central authority (prevalent in socialist economies). The connection between unit energy cost (or energy intensity as we prefer to call it) is made later in the paper.

We can physically measure the ecosystem exchanges and the inputs of resources to a system. But what are the unit costs of exchange in an ecosystem where there are no agents to set or reveal them? In this paper we will show that a unique set of unit costs in the ecosystem can be determined by an appropriate allocation of the net input to the ecosystem through the web of system exchanges. In this process of unit cost determination, we will use an input–output description of an ecosystem and use available energy as the only net resource input (a thermodynamically closed system; one in which only energy flows across the boundary).

We will demonstrate how the two basic, alternative assumptions of modern linear input–output formalization collapse to one, yielding the basis for a unique set of energy prices for ecosystem exchanges. The development of this theoretical concept

0095-0696/86 $3.00

is important because it allows us to experimentally (e.g., using microcosms) check various behavioral hypotheses based on the value system.

I. THEORETICAL DEVELOPMENT

In this section we first review input–output economics' treatment of the joint production problem and the two alternative assumptions usually used to handle it. We then obtain two expressions for energy intensities based on these assumptions. For arbitrary commodity weightings, the two results are different, but if the weightings are proportional to the system energy intensities, we show that the two assumptions yield identical sets of energy intensities. Finally we give an example of how the energy intensities can be used to pose testable behavioral hypotheses about light-constrained ecosystems.

Theory — Standard *I*– *O* Economics

In previous articles [1–3], the system interchange composed of processes exchanging with other processes was described by a single matrix. This matrix, combined with a vector of total outputs of each of the processes, allowed an approximation of the direct and indirect energy cost of a unit of process output. Major problems arise because each process may produce more than one type of output and some of these outputs are also made in other processes, a situation called the production of joint commodities. The proper assignment of input costs to these joint commodities is an unresolved problem in economics. The problem can be resolved by assumption, of course, and that is the way we intend to handle it; fortunately as we shall see here, the available assumptions can be uniquely restricted.

A modern [4–7] formulation of input–output theory is designed to accomodate if not resolve the joint products problem. Production and consumption are given by two distinct matrices: one which gives the use of the n commodities by the m processes (called the "Use" matrix or $\mathbf{U}$, an $n \times m$ matrix) and the other which gives the production of commodities by the processes (called the "Make" matrix or $\mathbf{V}$, an $m \times n$ matrix). Each commodity is measured in the same units throughout $\mathbf{U}$ and $\mathbf{V}$, but the units need not be the same for all the commodities. For example, the commodity flow "algal biomass" from the process "algae" may be measured in grams but the algal oxygen flow can be measured in cubic centimeters. It is therefore always dimensionally possible to form the total commodity output vector q but not the total process output vector g. This incommensurability problem for g is the basic difficulty to which this paper is devoted.

In this section we first review input–output economics' treatment of the joint production problem and the two alternative assumptions usually used to handle it. We then obtain expressions for energy intensities based on these two assumptions. For arbitrary commodity prices, the two results are different, but for the assumption that price is proportional to energy intensity, we show that the two results are identical.

For a set of process outputs to be summable dimensionally, each output commodity must be separately weighted. These weighting factors should in some way represent the relative importance of each commodity to the system, thereby converting the various outputs to a consistent unit of measure. Let us assume for now that the weighted commodity flows are commensurate and that **g** is somehow measurable. The basic physical commodity balance equations are

$$\mathbf{q} = \mathbf{Ui} + \mathbf{e}, \tag{1a}$$

$$\mathbf{q} = \mathbf{V}^{\mathrm{T}}\mathbf{i}, \quad \text{where T indicates transpose,} \tag{1b}$$

$$\mathbf{g} = \mathbf{Vi} \tag{1c}$$

where

$\mathbf{q}$ = commodity output vector
$\mathbf{g}$ = process output vector
$\mathbf{e}$ = net system output vector
$\mathbf{U}$ = use matrix (commodity × process)
$\mathbf{V}$ = make matrix (process × commodity) [6].

All quantities are marginal for a fixed time period. In addition, i = vector of 1's.

We want to solve for **q** as a function of **e**. But to do this we must first transform the system from one with joint or multiple outputs to an equivalent system in which each sector has only one output.

We can manipulate Eqs. (1) under one of two assumptions: The process-technology or the commodity-technology assumption.

The process-technology assumption allocates inputs to joint outputs in proportion to the "market share" or proportion of total output each joint product represents [9]. This assumption requires that the outputs be in communsurable units (i.e., dollars), an assumption that does not hold for ecosystem flows measured in physical units.

The commodity-technology assumption allocates inputs to joint products based on their proportions in a "major" producing sector for each commodity [9]. These inputs in "minor" producing sectors are proportionally reassigned to the "major" producing sector to eliminate the joint product. A problem with this technique is that it can lead to "negative inputs" if the input proportions to the major and minor sectors are very different.

These two assumptions are defined more explicitly and compared in Table I.

It can be seen that the two assumptions also share this feature: a commodity requires the same direct inputs per unit of its output, regardless of what sector(s) it is produced in.

Both Eqs. (2) and (3) relate total output (say of steel) required for the economy to produce net output (say of shoes). (Steel is required indirectly, to produce shoes, if not directly.) The numerical results for **q** from Eqs. (2) and (3) will differ, depending on which technology assumption is used [9].

Theory — Energy Intensities

Energy intensities in ecosystems can be calculated in a way similar to the economic argument used so far [3].

We assume that energy "enters" in specific processes (e.g., autotrophs) and that the processes (e.g., trophic levels) exchange materials in a way describable by

TABLE I

Comparison of Assumptions

Process-technology assumption

Rewriting Eq. (1a),

$$\mathbf{q} = \mathbf{U}\hat{\mathbf{g}}^{-1}\hat{\mathbf{g}}\mathbf{i} + \mathbf{e}$$

where $\hat{\mathbf{g}}$ is a diagonal matrix with the elements of $\mathbf{g}$ the diagonal. Substitute from Eq. (1c).

$$\mathbf{q} = \mathbf{U}\hat{\mathbf{g}}^{-1}\mathbf{V}\mathbf{i} + \mathbf{e},$$

and rewriting,

$$\mathbf{q} = \mathbf{U}\hat{\mathbf{g}}^{-1}\mathbf{V}\hat{\mathbf{q}}^{-1}\hat{\mathbf{q}}\mathbf{i} + \mathbf{e}.$$

Now define $\mathbf{U}\hat{\mathbf{g}}^{-1} = \mathbf{B}$

$$\mathbf{V}\hat{\mathbf{q}}^{-1} = \mathbf{D}.$$

Then

$$\mathbf{q} = \mathbf{B}\mathbf{D}\mathbf{q} + \mathbf{e}$$

$$\mathbf{q} = (\mathbf{I} - \mathbf{B}\mathbf{D})^{-1}\mathbf{e} \qquad (2)$$

Assuming that $\mathbf{B}$ and $\mathbf{D}$ are constant is the process-technology assumption. $\mathbf{B}$ = constant means that the inputs to each process are proportioned to its total output (assuming that the output is in commensurate units). $\mathbf{D}$ = constant is the market-shares assumption, which states that when anyone consumes 1 unit of a commodity, that unit was produced by the several processes that produce it in constant proportions.

Commodity-technology assumption

Rewriting Eq. (1a),

$$\mathbf{q} = \mathbf{U}\hat{\mathbf{g}}^{-1}\hat{\mathbf{g}}\mathbf{V}^{T-1}\mathbf{V}^{T}\mathbf{i} + \mathbf{e}$$

$$= \mathbf{B}(\mathbf{V}^{T}\hat{\mathbf{g}}^{-1})^{-1}\mathbf{V}^{T}\mathbf{i} + \mathbf{e}$$

Substitute from (1b)

$$\mathbf{q} = \mathbf{B}(\mathbf{V}^{T}\hat{\mathbf{g}}^{-1})^{-1}\mathbf{q} + \mathbf{e}$$

Define $\mathbf{V}^{T}\hat{\mathbf{g}}^{-1} = \mathbf{C}$. Then

$$\mathbf{q} = \mathbf{B}\mathbf{C}^{-1}\mathbf{q} + \mathbf{e}$$

$$\mathbf{q} = (\mathbf{I} - \mathbf{B}\mathbf{C}^{-1})^{-1}\mathbf{e}. \qquad (3)$$

Assuming that $\mathbf{B}$ and $\mathbf{C}$ are constant is the commodity-technology assumption. $\mathbf{B}$ = constant means the same as before. $\mathbf{C}$ = constant is the production shares assumption, which says that when a process produces 1 unit of output (assuming that the output is in commensurate units), the various commodities produced in that process have fixed proportions.

---

input–output matrices as discussed above. In practice, we use this approach only as a linear approximation for small changes about an initial equilibrium condition.

Energy intensity is defined as the total system input energy necessary to facilitate production of a unit of a commodity. In this sense the intensity can be thought of as an energy cost. Most of the energy intensity of a good actually represents dissipated free energy, but here it is considered an implied property of the final good, and therefore a congenial quantity, in that, for a process:

$$(\text{energy intensities}) \times (\text{flows in}) + (\text{any directly acquired energy})$$

$$= (\text{energy intensities}) \times (\text{flows out}).$$

Because commodities in ecosystems are measured in different physical units (i.e., gram of biomass) the vector $\mathbf{g}$ is not necessarily calculable and the process-technology assumption is not directly applicable. However, it is indirectly applicable by

TABLE II

Comparison of Assumptions for Ecosystems

Process-technology assumption

The derivation of energy intensities here is not as simple as for the economic case, because we first have to obtain a *process* energy intensity vector $\mathbf{E}^{\mathrm{P}}$, (using the process technology assumption) and then convert it to a commodity energy intensity (without changing the assumption).

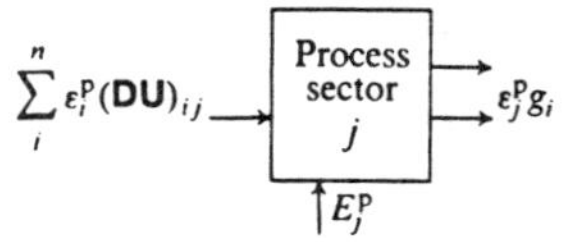

FIG. 2. A graphic representation of the process-technology assumption and energy balance across a typical process.

Figure 2 represents the conservation of embodied energy across process j. It is necessary to use the market shares assumption ($\mathbf{D}$ is constant) to "connect" process outputs to commodity inputs in the term $\mathbf{DU}$. We have assumed for the moment that g is self-consistent. $\boldsymbol{\varepsilon}^{\mathrm{P}}j$ is the energy intensity of the *process* output. Solving, as before:

$$\boldsymbol{\varepsilon}^{\mathrm{P}} = \mathbf{E}^{\mathrm{P}}\hat{\mathbf{g}}^{-1}(\mathbf{I} - \mathbf{DB})^{-1}. \tag{6}$$

We want the energy intensity of commodities, and therefore must convert process output to commodity output. We cannot assume $\mathbf{C}$ = constant here since we have already assumed $\mathbf{D}$ = constant (assuming both $\mathbf{C}$ and $\mathbf{D}$ to be constants is inadmissably restrictive). Then

$$\varepsilon_j^{\mathrm{c}} = \frac{\partial E}{\partial q_j} = \sum_{i=1}^{h} \frac{\partial E}{\partial q_i}\frac{\partial q_i}{\partial q_j}$$

$$= \sum_{i=1}^{n} \varepsilon_i^{\mathrm{P}} D_{ij} = (\boldsymbol{\varepsilon}^{\mathrm{P}}\mathbf{D})_j$$

or

$$\boldsymbol{\varepsilon}^{\mathrm{c}} = \boldsymbol{\varepsilon}^{\mathrm{P}}\mathbf{D}, \quad \text{and}$$

$$\boldsymbol{\varepsilon}^{\mathrm{c}} = \mathbf{E}^{\mathrm{P}}\hat{\mathbf{g}}^{-1}\mathbf{D}(\mathbf{I} - \mathbf{BD})^{-1}. \tag{7}$$

Commodity-technology assumption

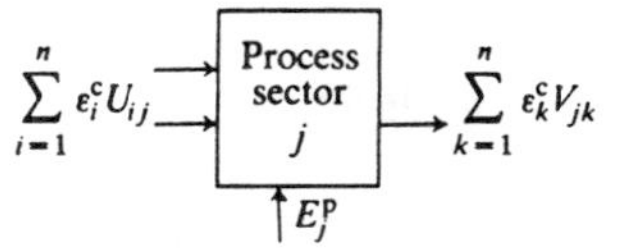

FIG. 1. Graphic representation of the commodity-technology assumption and energy balance across a typical process.

Figure 1 represents graphically the conservation of embodied energy, i.e., of energy intensities times flows across process j.

Matrices $\mathbf{U}$ and $\mathbf{V}$ are the "use" and "make" matrices mentioned previously. $\varepsilon_j^{\mathrm{c}}$ is the energy intensity under the commodity technology assumption (measured in calories/unit). E_j is the energy input to sector j from outside the system (in a fixed time period). In the figure, $\varepsilon_k^{\mathrm{c}}$ is assumed to be independent of j; this is the commodity technology assumption.

The balance equation implied by Fig. 1 is

$$\boldsymbol{\varepsilon}^{\mathrm{c}}(\mathbf{V}^{\mathrm{T}} - \mathbf{U}) = \mathbf{E}^{\mathrm{P}}.$$

Post multiplying by $\hat{\mathbf{g}}^{-1}$ (assuming g makes sense dimensionally) yields

$$\boldsymbol{\varepsilon}^{\mathrm{c}}(\mathbf{V}^{\mathrm{T}}\hat{\mathbf{g}}^{-1} - \mathbf{U}\hat{\mathbf{g}}^{-1}) = \mathbf{E}^{\mathrm{P}}\hat{\mathbf{g}}^{-1} \tag{4}$$

or

$$\boldsymbol{\varepsilon}^{\mathrm{c}}(\mathbf{C} - \mathbf{B}) = \mathbf{E}^{\mathrm{P}}\hat{\mathbf{g}}^{-1}.$$

Thus

$$\boldsymbol{\varepsilon}^{\mathrm{c}} = \mathbf{E}^{\mathrm{P}}\hat{\mathbf{g}}^{-1}\mathbf{C}^{-1}(\mathbf{I} - \mathbf{BC}^{-1})^{-1}. \tag{5}$$

Equation (5) should be compared with its economic counterpart, Eq. (2). Note that in Eq. (4), $\mathbf{E}^{\mathrm{P}}$ is the counterpart of other process inputs in $\mathbf{U}$ with two differences: $\mathbf{E}^{\mathrm{P}}$ comes from outside the system and hence there is no counterpart in $\mathbf{V}$ (in energy terms). By definition the energy intensity associated with $\mathbf{E}^{\mathrm{P}}$ is one.

---

assuming a set of weights to allow the formation of g and then investigating the properties of these weights. We describe more explicitly and compare the process- and commodity-technology assumptions for ecosystems in Table II.

Since Eqs. (5) and (7) describe commodity energy intensities for different technology assumptions, we need to use more complete notation.

The commodity energy intensities we wish to calculate, under the two technology assumptions, are

$$\text{commodity technology:} \quad \boldsymbol{\varepsilon}(c, c) = \mathbf{E}^{P}\hat{\mathbf{g}}^{-1}\mathbf{C}^{-1}(\mathbf{I} - \mathbf{B}\mathbf{C}^{-1})^{-1} \tag{8}$$

$$\text{process technology:} \quad \boldsymbol{\varepsilon}(c, p) = \mathbf{E}^{P}\hat{\mathbf{g}}^{-1}\mathbf{D}(\mathbf{I} - \mathbf{B}\mathbf{D})^{-1} \tag{9}$$

where for example, the notation $\boldsymbol{\varepsilon}(c, p)$ means commodity base, process technology. Conditions for invertibility can be derived in a way similar to that of Hawkins and Simon [8].

Equations (8) and (9) yield different values for the energy intensities. Both sets of intensities can be shown to satisfy energy closure, i.e., that energy coming into the system equals embodied energy leaving it embodied in net system output). That is,

$$E^{T} = \sum_{i=1}^{n} E_i^{P} = \sum_{i=1}^{n} \varepsilon_i e_i = \text{total energy into the system.} \tag{10}$$

When Are the Intensities Calculated by Both Methods Equal?

We will show that Eqs. (8) and (9) yield the same values when specific weightings are used for the flows in $\mathbf{U}$ and $\mathbf{V}$. In order to address this, we first derive general expressions for the effects of changing weights. Assume that the use and make matrices change thus (primes denote the new values):

$$\mathbf{U}' = \hat{\mathbf{p}}\mathbf{U}$$
$$\mathbf{V}' = \mathbf{V}\hat{\mathbf{p}},$$

where $\hat{\mathbf{p}}$ is a diagonal matrix containing the (commodity) weights. Then it follows that

$$\mathbf{g}' = \mathbf{V}\mathbf{p}$$
$$\mathbf{q}' = \hat{\mathbf{p}}\mathbf{q}$$
$$\mathbf{B}' = \hat{\mathbf{p}}\mathbf{U}\widehat{(\mathbf{V}\mathbf{p})}^{-1}$$
$$\mathbf{D}' = \mathbf{V}\hat{\mathbf{p}}\widehat{(\hat{\mathbf{p}}\mathbf{q})}^{-1} = \mathbf{V}\hat{\mathbf{p}}\hat{\mathbf{p}}^{-1}\hat{\mathbf{q}}^{-1} = \mathbf{V}\hat{\mathbf{q}}^{-1} = \mathbf{D}$$
$$\mathbf{C}' = \hat{\mathbf{p}}\mathbf{V}^{T}\widehat{(\mathbf{V}\mathbf{p})}^{-1}.$$

We substitute these primed values into (8) and (9) to produce expressions involving the $\mathbf{p}$ which have the relation to the desired energy intensities, $\varepsilon = \boldsymbol{\varepsilon}'\hat{\mathbf{p}}$. Note that since $E_i \geq 0$ for all i, for physical reality, $p_i > 0$ for all i.

We find that the commodity-technology energy intensity $\boldsymbol{\varepsilon}(c, c)$ (Eq. (8)) is unchanged. This seems reasonable when we note that it is not *necessary* to specify a process output g in the derivation of $\boldsymbol{\varepsilon}(c, c)$. On the other hand, the expression for the process-technology energy intensities does change:

$$\boldsymbol{\varepsilon}(c, p) = \mathbf{E}^{P}\widehat{(\mathbf{V}\mathbf{p})}^{-1}\mathbf{D}\left(\mathbf{I} - \hat{\mathbf{p}}\mathbf{U}\widehat{(\mathbf{V}\mathbf{p})}^{-1}\mathbf{D}\right)^{-1}\hat{\mathbf{P}}. \tag{11}$$

Equation (11) is the general expression for the process technology energy intensity when commodity flows are given new weightings $\mathbf{p}$. It reduces to Eq. (9), as it should, when $\mathbf{p} = \mathbf{i}$.

In economic systems an alternative set of weights inherently exists: the monetary commodity prices $\mathbf{p}^c$. In earlier work [2, 5] we used this combined system with $\mathbf{g} = \mathbf{V}\mathbf{p}^c$ in Eqs. (8) and (9) to calculate the commodity-based process technology energy intensities $\boldsymbol{\varepsilon}^c$. We did this because in the economy the physical flows are generally not measured and reported, only the already priced dollar flows are, and because the commodity-technology assumption yielded some negative $\boldsymbol{\varepsilon}^c$ values. We now realize that such negative values are mainly a result of flaws in the original data acquisition and aggregation and can be eliminated by judicious further aggregation,[1] or by better data [16].

To summarize, Eqs. (8) and (10) give different values for energy intensities. For a particular choice of weightings $\mathbf{p}$, Eq. (10) becomes identical to Eq. (8). The choice that accomplishes this is the equality of weighting to the energy intensity itself, i.e., in Eq. (10), let $\mathbf{p} = \boldsymbol{\varepsilon}$.

THEOREM. *A sufficient condition for the equality of energy intensities calculated using the commodity-technology assumption (Eq.* (8)) *and the process-technology assumption (Eq.* (10)) *is that the commodity weightings in the process-technology assumption are the energy intensities, i.e.,* $\mathbf{p} = \boldsymbol{\varepsilon}$.

Proof. Rewriting Eq. (11),

$$\boldsymbol{\varepsilon}\left[\hat{\mathbf{p}}^{-1}\mathbf{D}^{-1}\widehat{\mathbf{V}\mathbf{p}} - \mathbf{U}\right] = \mathbf{E}^{P}, \tag{12}$$

and reducing the commodity-technology equation for $\mathbf{E}^P$ (Eq. (8)) gives

$$\boldsymbol{\varepsilon}[\mathbf{V}^{T} - \mathbf{U}] = \mathbf{E}^{P}. \tag{13}$$

These two equations are identical if

$$\boldsymbol{\varepsilon}\mathbf{V}^{T} = \boldsymbol{\varepsilon}\hat{\mathbf{p}}^{-1}\mathbf{D}^{-1}\mathbf{V}\mathbf{p}. \tag{14}$$

The RHS of this equation reduces to $\boldsymbol{\varepsilon}\mathbf{V}^T$ if $\mathbf{p} = \boldsymbol{\varepsilon}$ (sufficiency), thus

$$\begin{aligned}
\boldsymbol{\varepsilon}\hat{\mathbf{p}}^{-1}\mathbf{D}^{-1}\widehat{\mathbf{V}\mathbf{p}} &= \boldsymbol{\varepsilon}\hat{\boldsymbol{\varepsilon}}^{-1}\mathbf{D}^{-1}\widehat{\mathbf{V}\boldsymbol{\varepsilon}} && \text{assuming } \mathbf{p} = \boldsymbol{\varepsilon}, \\
&= \mathbf{i}\mathbf{D}^{-1}\widehat{\mathbf{V}\boldsymbol{\varepsilon}}, \\
&= \boldsymbol{\varepsilon}\mathbf{V}^{T}\widehat{\mathbf{i}\mathbf{D}^{-1}}, \\
&= \boldsymbol{\varepsilon}\mathbf{V}^{T} && \text{since } \mathbf{i}\mathbf{D}^{-1} = \mathbf{i}\hat{\mathbf{q}}\mathbf{V}^{-1} = \mathbf{q}\mathbf{V}^{-1} = \mathbf{i}\mathbf{V}\mathbf{V}^{-1} = \mathbf{i}.
\end{aligned}$$

But does Eq. (14) hold for any other $\mathbf{p}$? We can easily show by many 3×3 counterexamples that other $\mathbf{p}$ also exist. In each case, however, at least one element of each of the additional $\mathbf{p}$ was negative. Thus we suspect that the only "real" solution (i.e., all $p_i > 0$) is $\mathbf{p} = \boldsymbol{\varepsilon}$, but we are unable to complete the proof. Of course in a system with multiple inputs of non-produced commodities (the usual way in which an economy is viewed) we have several possible vectors of positive definite prices, one for each non-produced input.

In other words, if we choose to weight the commodity outputs by their energy intensities to form a process output value, we find the difference in the energy

[1] For example, the radio and TV broadcasting sector consumed all of its own product according to the 1972 I–O tables. This was one of 3 obvious data lapses that explained the negative energy intensities obtained via the commodity-technology assumption. Stone [9] has a detailed explanation for the occurrence of negative elements.

intensities provided by the two principle assumptions of I–O analysis disappear: the simpler result from the commodity-technology assumption suffices.

What significance does this have for ecosystem modeling? We have shown that using weightings which are equal to energy intensities results in only one method (Eq. (8)) for computing those energy intensities.[2] There is certainly something suggestive and attractive about the notion of commodity weighting in an ecosystem being proportional to energy intensity. It allows use of embodied energy as the "fundamental" unit of transaction between components of ecosystems in a manner analogous to the way dollar values are used to track exchanges in economic systems. This analogy does not hold for "raw" calorie energy content.

ENERGY COSTS AND VALUE

Finally, under what conditions can we think of the energy intensities (which are actually "costs") as "prices" or "unit values" in exchange in an ecosystem? Both Sraffa [10] and Samuelson [11] have shown that unless the *present* cost of historic capital (biomass in our case) formation is included in the calculation of the cost, then they cannot say that the costs equal value in exchange (price) in an economic system. These authors calculate the present value of historic costs in economic systems by enlarging these historic costs, depending on their age, by an "interest" rate (the time cost of capital), and adding them on to the current cost. So, they argue, that cost is price in economic systems only if they add to the costs calculated from current inputs, those historic capital costs of capital items used up in the current period, weighted by their age using an interest rate [12]. But the present-day value of capital created several periods ago is influenced by two other phenomena: first the physical, irreparable damage suffered by the capital item over time and second, the existence of a new, more efficient capital item which accomplishes the same end result as the older capital. For value balance to occur at the end of each period, the interest or appreciation rate suggested by Sraffa and Samuelson should just overcome the loss of value of the capital item due to these two effects. Thus the present value of historic capital is its present replacement value. In the case of our ecosystem, that value is the direct and indirect energy cost of producing the biomass *in the present period*. Thus, if we include in the energy inputs to the system the energy required for the present period's production of replacement biomass, we should have satisfied the capital-aging problem.

In the most general equilibrium solution described in economics, both the levels of demand and of supply are functions of the price and the quantity involved in exchange. The intersection of these two functions determines the equilibrium price (and quantity). This price represents the lowest possible direct and indirect energy per unit output achievable in the system. We have defined our system so that the solution to this problem is simplified, although this procedure might restrict the utility of our approach.

Another theorem [10] from economics allows prices to be calculated in the absence of knowledge of consumer preferences. These conditions are: (1) a known distribution among the processes of a single input factor (energy in our case); (2) constant, linear production coefficients (Eqs. (8) or (9) with constant **B**, and **C** or

[2] We also note that this means that we must define **U** and **V** as square matrices, i.e., the number of commodities and of processes must be equal.

D)[3]; and (3) the absence of joint production of commodities (the result of applying the process-technology or commodity-technology assumption).

Such a set of assumptions allows the formation of new biomass considered as a net output (a "profit") and disconnects demand from the determination of price or unit value in the system. Cost is linearly proportional to total production and production technique *alone* determines price. The quantity produced is determined only by the collective demand for the various commodities.

This set of assumptions allows the price (ε) of the various system commodities to be determined by the normalized coefficients of the use and production matrices. The columns in the **BD** and $\mathbf{BC}^{-1}$ matrices are said to be "technological" descriptors of the production processes of their respective commodities. As long as none of these technologies change (or change little) the prices in the ecosystem are constant (or nearly constant). But under the assumptions given above this means that each set of normalized production process inputs is independent of the level of production (no economics of scale) and it means that each species (and perhaps even each different age cohort in each species) should be defined as a separate process. Otherwise the technological descriptors will change simply due to shifts in the population balance between various species (e.g., algae) collected into the same process. This is a definitional or aggregational problem and it requires more data (on each subspecies) to allow separate process definition.

Prices in the ecosystem can be viewed in terms of the opportunity costs for the components (processes). While ecosystems do not have the level of "consciousness" and choice apparently available in economic systems, and exchanges are not tracked with an easily observable common currency, the concepts of cost, benefit, and "choice" are still important in an evolutionary sense. Any ecosystem faces a scarcity of primary resource (solar energy) in the long run and intermediate resources (nutrients, water, etc.) in the short run. Competition requires an optimal allocation of these resources and a balancing of costs (measured in the units of E^{T}) and benefits (in the same units). These measures of embodied energy can be used to quantify and summarize the complex trade-offs between foraging and predator avoidance faced by organisms in ecosystems. In the ecosystem, natural "unconscious" natural selection chooses the optimal allocation. Humans seem capable of improving (though some would argue just speeding up) this unconscious process by applying conscious modeling and forethought. The completely "rational" consumer is, however, only an idealization and "choice" via natural selection seems to play an important role in both ecological and economic systems. The energy prices we define are merely a convenient index of the results of this process that may be useful in understanding ecosystem and economic system behavior.

Utilizing the Energy Prices

The ultimate quest of this exercise is to provide a value base for ecosystem exchanges so that the behavior pattern of the components can be modeled. When such behavior is understood, the future course of ecosystem development may be

[3] It is possibly that the full production potential is not reached by every component at all times. The marginal energy costs can be determined empirically by Eq. (8) or (12), by letting the $\mathbf{V}^{T}$, $\mathbf{U}$, and $\mathbf{E}^{P}$ be the matrices and vector of *change* in their respective elements between two consecutive time periods [13].

better predicted when the system is subjected to predetermined changes in the basic inputs or outputs.

We can proceed with the above set of assumptions regarding the connection between cost and price. We can, for example, posit a behavioral hypothesis such as the following:

Define the net output vector **e**, in a given time period, to be composed of three independent vectors:

(1) The vector of commodity depreciation. The depreciation rates of the "closed system" commodities are exactly countered at the steady state by the input of energy to the system. The depreciation rates can be determined experimentally by suddenly removing the energy input and observing the initial rates of change of the commodity stocks. As experience is gained from such observations, theoretical descriptions of the depreciation rates can be made (such as, these being equal to a constant times the stock level). These depreciation rates may also be thought of as the "basal" or "resting" metabolism rates of each of the processes. These rates would be represented by the commodity flows required in the ecosystem which would occur if the system's components were producing only enough to satisfy their minimum needs (i.e., no flows for predators, for predation, or for reproduction).

(2) The vector of total new additions of each of the commodities.

(3) The vector of commodity net exports from the system. These would be commodity exports less the imports of the same commodities.

Note that we define the commodities as organized substances produced (ordered) by the system. The only non-produced commodity used by the system is light energy. We note that an ecosystem cannot long have commodity net exports. Therefore, let us assume that our system is thermodynamically closed, i.e., our system has light as its only input and heat and light as its only net outputs. We can then perform controlled experiments on this ecosystem to see if it is, for example, maximizing Q, where $Q = \varepsilon(\mathbf{e}^2 - \mathbf{e}^1)$, where $\mathbf{e}^2$ is the vector of the change in net biomass formation rate and $\mathbf{e}^1$ is the vector of change in the depreciation rates and ε is derived from Eq. (13) for the initial state. The maximizing procedure is constrained by the given amount of light increase, the temperature of the environment surrounding the system, and a series of equations which set the maximum flow rate for each commodity as determined from the physical aspects of the given system (e.g., niche size). The change in the net system output $\mathbf{e}^1$ and $\mathbf{e}^2$ can also be experimentally determined. Their difference vector can be compared to the same vector determined from the optimization program. This procedure allows for changes in the output of each of the commodities (Eq. (3)).

We note that this specification of an optimizing program is such that if it is an accurate predictor of the resulting net output, then the concept of ε as a measure of ecosystem exchange value is upheld.

We might also specify columns and rows of U and V respectively for a large number of possible processes in an ecosystem and let the optimizing program select the appropriate mix of components as it tries to maximize $\varepsilon\mathbf{e}$. This is similar to the linear programming approach suggested by Costanza and Neil [14]. Other behavior patterns in economics are demonstrated by Simon [15].

We have recently begun the construction of small (1000 ml) aquatic ecosystems in which all exchanges can either be directly measured or imputed from direct measurement. We will be able to control all of the system inputs and outputs. We should then be able to measure the energy costs and test for behavioral strategies using an actual system. It is this blend of system theory and real experiments on living systems which we believe will be fruitful for ecological and, perhaps, economic understanding.

ACKNOWLEDGMENTS

We thank R. Gorden of the Illinois Natural History Survey, who, with R. Costanza, was Principal Investigator of Grant (ENR-80.260) "Modeling of Economic and Ecological Systems" from the Illinois Department of Energy and Natural Resources, which supported this work. We also thank J. Finn and two anonymous reviewers for their helpful suggestions on earlier drafts.

REFERENCES

1. W. Leontief, "The Structure of the American Economy, 1919–1939," Oxford Univ. Press, New York (1941); National Bureau of Economic Research, Input–output analysis: An appraisal, *in* "Studies in Income and Wealth," Vol. 18, Arno, New York (1955).
2. R. Herendeen and C. Bullard, Energy costs of goods and services, *Energy Policy* **3** (1975).
3. B. Hannon, The structure of ecosystems, *J. Theoret. Biol.* **41**, Part 3, 535–546 (1973); B. Hannon, Total energy costs in ecosystems, *J. Theoret. Biol.* **80**, 271–293 (1979); R. Herendeen, On the concept of energy intensity in ecological systems, *J. Theoret. Biol.* **91**, 607–620 (1981).
4. H. Gigantes, "Contributions to Input-Output Analysis" (A. Carter and A. Brody, Eds.), 2 Vol., especially Chaps. 14, 17, American Elsevier, New York (1970).
5. B. Hannon, T. Blazeck, D. Kennedy, and R. Illyes, A comparison of energy intensities, 1963, 1967, and 1972, *Energy Resources*, **5**, 83–102 (1983).
6. P. M. Ritz, "Definitions and Conventions of the 1972 Input–Output Study," Bureau of Economic Analysis, U.S. Dept. of Commerce, BEA.-SP80-034, (1980).
7. P. Flaschel, Input–output technology assumptions and the energy requirements of commodities, *Resources Energy* **4**, No. 4, 359–390 (1982).
8. D. Hawkins, and H. Simon, Note: Some conditions on macro economic stability *Econometrica* **17**, Nos. 3, 4, 245–248 (1949).
9. R. Stone, Input–output relationships, 1954–1966, *in* "A Programme for Growth," Vol. 3, pp. 11–22, MIT Press, Cambridge, Mass. (1963).
10. P. Sraffa, "Production of Commodities by Means of Commodities," Cambridge Univ. Press, London (1960).
11. P. A. Samuelson, Abstract of a theorem concerning substitutability in open leontief models, *in* "Activity Analysis of Production and Allocation," (T. C. Koopmans, Ed). pp. 142–146 Wiley, New York (1951); (This theorem was proven independently by Georgescu-Rogen). See also: A new theorem on nonsubstitution, *in* "The Collected Papers of P. A. Samuelson" (J. E. Stiglitz, Ed.), Vol. I, Chap. 37, MIT Press, Cambridge, Mass. (1966).
12. B. Hannon, "Discounting in Ecosystems," Energy Research Group, Doc. 312, University of Illinois, Urbana (1982).
13. B. Hannon and T. Blazeck, "Marginal Energy Cost of Goods and Services," Energy Research Group, Doc. 320, University of Illinois, Urbana (1981).
14. R. Costanza and C. Neill, Energy intensities, interdependence, and value in ecological systems: A linear programming approach, *J. Theoret. Biol.* **106**, 41–57 (1984).
15. H. Simon, Theories of decision making in economic and behavioral sciences, *Amer. Econ. Rev.* **49**, 253–283 (1959); O. Williamson, Firms and markets, *in* "Modern Economic Thought" (S. Weintraub, Ed.), Chap. 10, Univ. of Pennsylvania Press, Philadelphia (1977).
16. R. Costanza and R. A. Herendeen, Embodied energy and economic value in the U.S. economy: 1963, 1967, and 1972, *Resources Energy* **6**, 129–164 (1984).

[14]

DEALING WITH THE "MIXED UNITS" PROBLEM IN ECOSYSTEM NETWORK ANALYSIS

Robert Costanza
Chesapeake Biological Laboratory
University of Maryland
Solomons, Maryland, 20688-0038
USA

Bruce Hannon
Geography Department
and Illinois Natural History Survey
University of Illinois
Urbana, IL 61801, USA

INTRODUCTION

Ecology is often defined as the study of the relationships between organisms and their environment. The quantitative analysis of interconnections between species and their abiotic environment has therefore been a central issue. The mathematical analysis of interconnections is also important in several other fields. Practical quantitative analysis of interconnections in complex systems began with the economist Wassily Leontief (1941) using what has come to be called **Input-Output (I-O) Analysis.** More recently, these concepts, sometimes called **Flow Analysis**, have been applied to the study of interconnections in ecosystems (Hannon 1973, 1976, 1979, 1985a,b,c; Costanza & Neill 1984). Related ideas were developed from a different perspective in ecology, under the heading of **Compartmental Analysis** (Barber *et al.* 1979, Patten & Finn, 1979; Funderlic & Heath, 1971; Hett & O'Neill, 1971). We refer to the total of all variations of the analysis of ecological or economic networks as **Network Analysis** (See Field *et al.* 1989, Chapter 1 of this volume for distinctions among the various forms of network analysis).

In this chapter we: 1) discuss the necessity to deal with multiple commodities (not just carbon, energy, or nitrogen) and joint products (processes that produce more than one type of commodity as output) for a more realistic treatment of ecosystem networks; 2) develop the mathematical form for a general multicommodity system capable of dealing with joint products; and 3) present and briefly discuss a detailed example of these applications.

We find that multicommodity, hierarchial, I-O (flow) analysis can be used to calculate a set of unique net input intensity factors, that can then be used to form more comprehensive and realistic input matrices for the kinds of compartmental analysis used elsewhere in this book. We can think of this as a form of preprocessing that yields a hybrid commodity (embodied energy). This new commodity has the desired characteristic of conservation necessary for compartmental analysis but it also incorporates the production interdependencies (i.e. the ammounts of each commodity required to produce other commodities) between the original commodities.

COMMENSURABILITY

A fundamental issue in any field that deals with the interconnections between dissimilar components is *commensurability* : the ability to measure the components in the same addable (commensurable) units. Both economics and ecology must deal with this "apples and oranges" or mixed units issue, although we feel its importance in ecology has not yet been fully appreciated.

Flow and compartmental analysis differ fundamentally in terms of: (1) their concentration on outputs vs. inputs (respectively) and; (2) what things they require to "add up". The fundamental reasons for these distinctions are summarized in following sections. To obtain a comprehensive understanding of ecosystem interdependence one needs to understand *both* input and output relationships. We therefore seek a way to integrate these approaches.

Flow (output) analysis requires for most of its results only that total output of each commodity in the system equal total input, without ever requiring the addition of different commodities (i.e. apples and oranges, or carbon and nitrogen). Compartmental (input) analysis, on the other hand, requires a "conservative" unit of measure, such as mass or energy or carbon content. A conservative unit is one that obeys the rule that total inputs to any process equal total outputs. One must therefore be able to *add* process inputs and outputs and in real processes these are usually different, noncommensurable commodities. For example,the very different commodities CO_2, water, light energy, and nutrients are all required in the process of photosynthesis to produce the commodity plant biomass. The usual simplification in ecological compartment analysis is to arbitraily choose one commodity (such as carbon) which is conservative and declare that this commodity is a valid tracer for all others. This approach can be misleading, however. Imagine using only the weight (mass) of the interconnecting flows in an economic system to analyze interdependence. Bulk commodity industries like sand and gravel would be given much more "weight" (pun intended) than they deserve under this approach at the expense of service and other less massive industries. Likewise, choosing any one commodity in an ecosystem to analyze interdependence can be misleading.

Before compartmental analysis can yield comprehensive and realistic results for ecosystems one must calculate and apply an appropriate set of intensity factors analogous to prices in economic systems. This chapter demonstrates several related techniques for doing this.

METHODS

Flow Accounting

In the analysis of complex dynamic systems, it is necessary to develop consistent definitions and categorizations of all the identifiable flows. We start with the diagram shown in Figure 5.1.

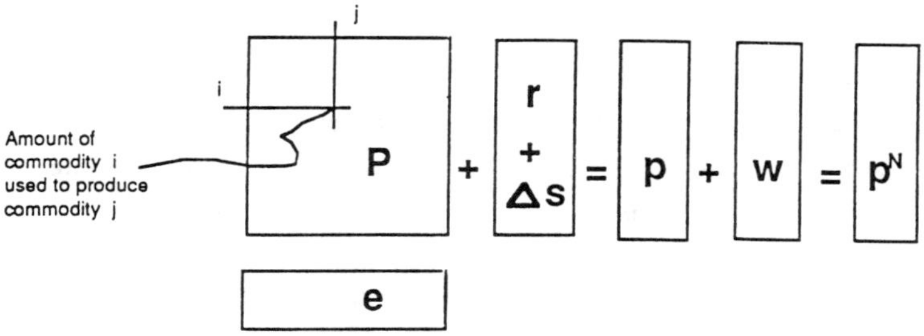

Figure 5.1. Ecosystem flow accounting diagram

A **commodity** is defined as some identifiable unit moving through the system. It can be a simple element (like carbon) or a complex structure (like plant biomass) or even the results of a service (like aerated sediments). Commodities are transformed (produced, consumed, or combined into more complex commodities) in **processes**. Biomass, for example, is produced by the photosynthetic process, which combines (consumes) water, carbon dioxide, sunlight and nutrients into plant material.

In Figure 5.1, **P** is known as the production matrix. (Throughout this Chapter we use bold lowercase letters to indicate vectors and bold uppercase letters to indicate matrices.) It summarizes the direct interdependences between the system's commodities and processes. Its elements are the amount of commodity *i* which is used by process *j* in the given time period. For example, p_{ij} could be the daily amount of nitrogen (*i*) consumed in the photosynthetic process of a particular plant species (*j*). This is a multicommodity system since different, noncommensurable commodities are listed along the rows. The row sums may be calculated (since they are all the same commodity) but the column sums cannot (since that would require adding, for example, nitrogen, sunlight, carbon dioxide, and water).

We begin with a system without joint products, or one in which each process (column) is assumed to produce only one commodity. This ignores, for example, the oxygen produced by photosynthesis as a joint product along with the biomass. Later we relax this requirement.

The vector **r** *is the net output of commodities from the system*. It is composed of two types of commodities: 1) the net export (export minus import) of each produced commodity, during the given period; and 2) the amount of biomass made during the given period used in rebuilding the depreciated stock (we use the basal metabolism as a surrogate for this commodity flows). The importance of this distinction will become clearer later on. Suffice it to say here that it is critical to a general description that allows the desired quantities to be calculated for both open and closed systems. The **Δs** is a vector of net changes in stock during the time period (zero at steady state).

The vector **p** is the total output of commodities by the system. The elements of **p** are the row sums of **P**, plus **r**, and **Δs**. In other words the total amount of each commodity produced equals the sum of the amounts sent to other internal processes, net exports, and change in stock. Excluded from the row summing is the amount of the commodity **i** which is depreciated (given off as heat in non-basal respiration). These "waste heat" or depreciation flows are the elements of the vector **w**. If the vectors **w** and **p** are added, the result is the total input vector $\mathbf{p}^N$. The vector **e** is the net input vector, the amounts of commodities absorbed by the processes of the system but not produced by it, during the given time period.

Flow Analysis

Flow analysis proceeds in the following way given these definitions. Let **s** be a vector of stocks; s_i is the amount of commodity **i** held as a stock in the system. As the time period becomes infinitesimal, the commodity balance along the row becomes:

$$ds_i/dt = p_i - \sum_j p_{ij} - r_i = p^n{}_i - w_i - \sum_j p_{ij} - r_i \qquad (1)$$

Note that the depreciation vector is excluded from the balance in equation 1. This exclusion indicates that **w** has zero *value* to the ecosystem when compared to **p**. In other words **w** and **p** are different commodities. Let us assume that the flow between two components in **P** divided by the **receiving** component is a constant matrix **G'**. That is: $g'_{ij} = p_{ij}/s_j$. Now equation 1 can be rewritten:

$$ds_i/dt = p_i - \sum g'_{ij} s_j - r_i \qquad (2)$$

or in vector-matrix form:

$$\mathbf{ds/dt} = \mathbf{p} - \mathbf{G's} - \mathbf{r} \qquad (3)$$

Equation 1 or 2 could be used in microcosm research to determine the flows (via **G**) from the stock level changes. Assuming an *n* component system and assuming that the outputs **r** can be measured, there are n^2 unknowns. The stock and net output vectors must be measured over at least *n* different ranges to provide sufficient data to determine **G** uniquely.

If we assume further that the ratio of the stock to flow for each component is a constant diagonal matrix **B**, then the elements of this stock/flow matrix are $b_{ii} = s_i/p_i$ and equation 3 can be further rewritten as:

$$\mathbf{B}(d\mathbf{p}/dt) = \mathbf{p} - \mathbf{G'Bp} - \mathbf{r} = (\mathbf{I}-\mathbf{G'B})\mathbf{p} - \mathbf{r}$$

and if we combine the two assumptions, $g_{ij} = p_{ij}/p_j$ and

$$d\mathbf{p}/dt = \mathbf{B}^{-1}(\mathbf{I}-\mathbf{G})\mathbf{p} - \mathbf{B}^{-1}\mathbf{r} \qquad (4)$$

This is the "standard" form for the dynamic equation of the flow analysis approach. It could also be referred to as the recipient-controlled dynamic flow equation. The stability of future **p** when the system is subjected to changes in **r** depends entirely on the matrix which multiplies **p** in equation 4. If the eigenvalues of that matrix are negative, **p** is stable. Since **B** and **G** are always positive, the eigenvalues of the matrix are always positive and future **p** will always respond to changes in **r** in an unstable manner. Equation 4 can be made to respond stably by modifying **r** to include a feedback control in addition to the desired change in **r**. The feedback control can be a function of **p**, and/or the derivative or integral of **p**. The controls can be thought of in two ways: first, they give the ecosystem manager the appropriate coordinated steps to be taken in advance or following the desired changes in **r**; secondly, the ecosystem could be thought of as possessing certain types of these feedback controls. In this case, control theory could be coupled with ecosystem experiment to discern the mathematical form of the natural controls. The details of these control theory approaches are discussed by Hannon (1985a,b,c). If $d\mathbf{p}/dt = 0$, equation 4 becomes:

$$\mathbf{p} = (\mathbf{I}-\mathbf{G})^{-1}\mathbf{r} \qquad (5)$$

which is independent of the stock level. Equation 5 is the steady state relationship between the net and the total output. In an ecosystem with no material flows across the boundary, equation 5 indicates the amount of total output required to make up for the structural depreciation (basal metabolism).

Compartmental Analysis

In compartmental analysis, the inputs to a process are summed and the total output (in this case, $\mathbf{p}^N$ since the non-metabolic heat cannot be considered part of the stock change) is removed, leaving the change in the stock level. The inputs include the net input of non-produced commodities from outside the system. In a form similar to equation 1, the balance equation for the compartmental approach is:

$$ds_i/dt = \Sigma p_{ij} + e_i - p^n_j \qquad (6)$$

We now assume that the intercompartmental flow divided by the stock of the donor compartment is the constant matrix, G" whose elements are $g''_{ij} = p_{ij}/s_i$. Equation 6 can now be written

$$ds_i/dt = \Sigma s_i g''_{ij} + e_i - p^n_j$$

or in vector-matrix form:

$$\mathbf{ds/dt = sG'' + e - p^n} \qquad (7)$$

Again, we assume that the stock to total output flow ratio is the constant matrix **B'**, whose elements are $b'_{ij} = s_i/p_i^N$. The two assumptions lead, as before, to the "standard" dynamical form of the compartmental analysis approach (donor-controlled):

$$\mathbf{dp^n/dt = - p^n(I\text{-}G^*)B'^{-1} + eB'^{-1}} \qquad (8)$$

where $g_{ij}^* = p_{ij}/p_i^N$.

The matrix which multiplies $\mathbf{P^N}$ determines the stability of the total output in response to changes in **e**. Since **B** and **G** are both positive matrices, the eigenvalues of the critical matrix are always negative, and the predictive solutions to equation 8 are always stable. However, because the method involves the summing of commodities of different qualities, the value of equation 8 is limited to systems measured in commensurable units. As we have pointed out commensurable units can be achieved by ignoring everything in the system except one commodity, or through the use of a weighting function (see below).

The steady state version of compartmental analysis is:

$$\mathbf{p^n = e(I\text{-}G^*)^{-1}} \qquad (9)$$

which is similar to equation 5 in the flow analysis approach, except that here the equation is based on the net input **e** (rather than net output **r**) and a "donor controlled coefficient matrix **G*** (rather than the "recipient controlled" coefficient matrix **G**).

To fully understand the physical meaning of the compartmental approach, we draw a picture which represents the balance given by the steady state version (equation 9):

Figure 5.2 clearly reveals both forms of the mixed commodity problem in compartmental analysis. The production matrix **P** is summed down the columns, adding together different commodities of different qualities. Even though these commodities may be measured in the same physical units, they cannot be added together because of their differences in quality. For the same reasons, the quantity $\mathbf{p^N}$ cannot exist. It is obtained by adding physical units representing both valuable structures and waste heat.

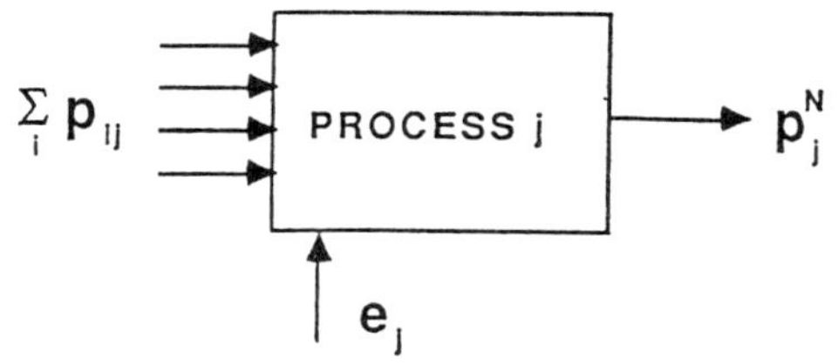

Figure 5.2. Balance diagram for the compartmental analysis approach, where Σp_{ij} represents the amount of commodity i used in process j, e_j = net input of the jth process, and p_j^N is a hypothetical quantity produced by process j.

To allow the addition required in the compartmental analysis approach, a weighting function must introduced. Let this function be the vector ϵ. We assume that the ecosystem acts as though it is perfectly competitive in the economic sense: no producer or consumer acting alone is significant enough to affect the ϵ values; information about the stocks and flows in the system is "communicated" directly or indirectly to every process in the system. Such conditions produce a unique set of weighting factors. Then, the diagram in Figure 5.2 becomes:

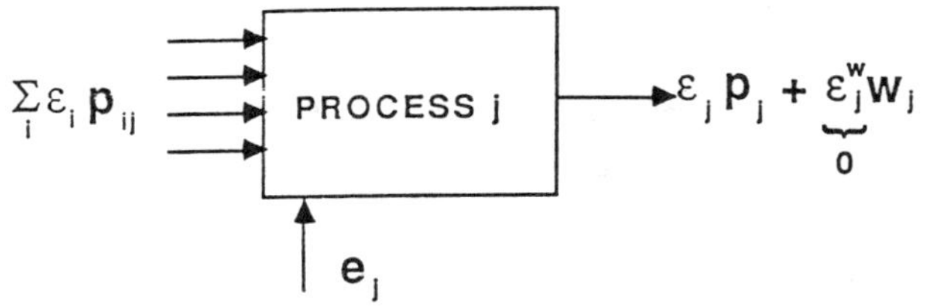

Figure 5.3. Weighted balance for the compartmental analysis approach. Symbols as in Fig 5.2. and where $\Sigma\epsilon_i$ is a weighting factor for commodity i, and ϵ_j, ϵ_j^W are weighting factors for process j and its associated metabolic loss W_j, respectively.

In Figure 5.3, $\epsilon^W = 0$ means that the non-basal metabolic heat has no value to the system or, in other words, no value relative to the commodity flows represented in **P** or **r**. The equation which represents the balance shown in Figure 5.3 is:

$$\Sigma\epsilon_i p_{ij} + e_j = \epsilon_j p_j$$

or in vector-matrix form:

$$\epsilon \mathbf{p} + \mathbf{e} = \epsilon \mathbf{D} \mathbf{p} \qquad (10)$$

where $\mathbf{D_p}$ is the diagonalized $\mathbf{p}$ vector

$$\epsilon = \mathbf{e}(\mathbf{Dp}- \mathbf{p})^{-1}$$

and since

$$\mathbf{G} = \mathbf{pD_p}^{-1}$$

then

$$\epsilon = \mathbf{eD_p}^{-1}(\mathbf{I}-\mathbf{G})^{-1} \tag{11}$$

Equation 10 is the solution for the needed weighting factors which allows a recognition of commodity quality in the compartmental analysis approach. It is derivable directly from the flow analysis approach: the **p** and **G** in equation 10 are the total output vector and the constant flow coefficients matrix used in the flow analysis approach. The analogy is obviously extendable to the dynamic case.

In compartmental analysis, the weighting factors, ϵ are usually implicitly assumed to be one. This is not likely to ever be a valid assumption, since, at minimum, from the second law of thermodynamics one would expect some waste heat production. If the waste heat w_j is included in the p_j, the resulting ϵ are all ones (Hannon, 1985a). The ϵ therefore, may be thought of as weighting factors among a diverse set of flows, each of whose thermodynamic quality is the same along its row in $\mathbf{Pi} + \mathbf{r}$. The quantity $\epsilon_i p_i$ is directly comparable to the quantity $\epsilon_j p_j$: the ϵ are like economic "prices" but they arise from thermodynamic and production considerations.

When the compartmental analysis approach is weighted using net input intensity factors to more closely represent reality, it turns into the flow analysis approach. Consequently, we have combined the two approaches into one: if the desire is to calculate the stock and total output change due to a net output change, the flow analysis approach is the more directly useful one. When the ϵ vector is introduced into the standard compartmental approach, the resulting output vector is identical to the one obtained from the flow analysis approach.

The flow analysis approach requires that a given commodity have the same value everywhere in the system. Otherwise, summing along the rows in a matrix of physical units would not be appropriate. This assumed uniformity of commodity weighting is a result of a broader assumption of system competition. For a system to be competitive in this sense, it must have many, small consumers and producers each possessing all the current information about the variables which affect them. Under these conditions, no single consumer can directly affect the unit weight of a commodity.

Under certain conditions, these values can be calculated on the basis of the net inputs alone, as occurs in equation 10. If each producer has only one type of output, if all producers of the same commodity use the same inputs per unit output (common production recipe), and if the system has only one net input, then the ϵ in equation 10 are the commodity unit values (Samuelson 1966). The system produces all the desired quantities of each commodity at that unit value. We can always reduce the system to one net input (see the global ecosystem discussion and Table 5.7, below*). We can also deal with systems in which each producer (process) has multiple commodity outputs, or in other words where there are joint products (see Figure 5.4, below).

Joint Products in Flow Analysis

In the discussion so far, we have avoided reference to ecological processes which produce more than one useful output. Our analysis recognized that each process produced only two types of output: **p** and **w**. Only one of these, **p**, is considered usable by the system; **w** is therefore a "product" which is not absorbed by any other process in the system. It is dropped from consideration or equivalently, it is assigned an ϵ which is zero. Now we complicate the picture a little further (attempt to better approximate reality) by introducing the multiple (useful) output format. The result is parallel to the

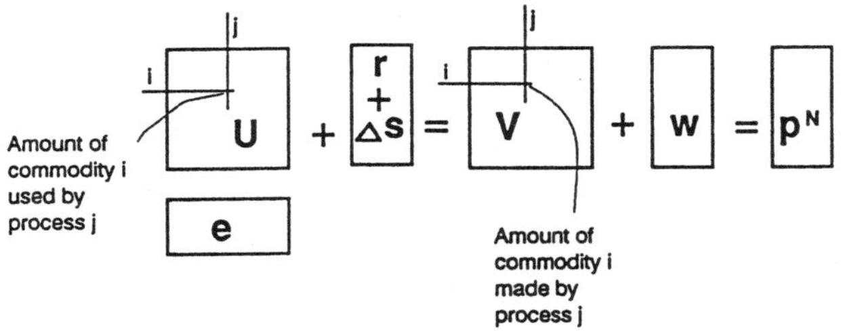

Figure 5.4. Multiproduct ecosystem flow accounting diagram where **U** is an input matrix, **e** is a vector of inputs required by the processes, **r** is a vector of output commodities, and Δs the changes in biomasses of commodities; **V** is an output matrix, **w** a product not absorbed by any other process, and $\mathbf{p}^N$ a vector of usable commodities produced.

previous development: the column-summing and row-summing approaches become equivalent under the appropriate assumptions. In Figure 5.4, we show the expanded accounting system.

Interpret the diagram in Figure 5.4 as follows: the ith row sum of **U** plus the ith element of **r** plus Δs_i equals the ith row sum of **V** (which is equal to the ith element of **p**, the total output without the non-basal respiration), all for the given time period. The additional step taken in the multiple product formulation is the elaboration of the **p** vector into the "Make" or output matrix, **V**. Two assumptions are possible for the linear model. One of them requires summing down the columns of **U** which we have argued

*All tables are shown at the end of the chapter.

above is not appropriate. Under conditions of perfect competition, each commodity has a similar unit value or weight to each of its consumers, and summing commodity flows along the rows is appropriate.

A row from the accounting diagram in Figure 5.4 can be stated in continuous time as:

$$\Sigma V_{ij} = \Sigma U_{ij} + r_i + ds_i/dt \quad (12)$$

or in vector-matrix form,

$$\mathbf{Vi} = \mathbf{Ui} + \mathbf{r} + \mathbf{ds/dt} \quad (13)$$

where i is a vector of ones. Rewriting equation 13 and solving for ds/dt gives;

$$\mathbf{ds/dt} = \mathbf{(V\text{-}U)i - r} \quad (14)$$

or

$$\mathbf{ds/dt} = \mathbf{(I\text{-}UV^{-1})Vi - r}$$

With the stock-flow assumption used above, Equation 14 becomes;

$$\mathbf{dp/dt} = \mathbf{B^{-1}(I\text{-}UV^{-1})p - B^{-1}r} \quad (15)$$

By a procedure identical to equation 10, the ϵ or net input intensities are (with dp/dt = 0)

$$\epsilon = \mathbf{e(V\text{-}U)^{-1}} \quad (16)$$

$$\epsilon = \mathbf{e((I\text{-}UV^{-1})V)^{-1}} \quad (17)$$

The intensities are evaluated below for the global system. Equations 15 and 16 (or 17) are the multiple input-output equivalent of the output flow analysis approach.

It is important to note that in the joint product flow analysis formulation it is possible to have negative entries in the $(V\text{-}U)^{-1}$ matrix (the commodities required directly and indirectly as input to processes). These negative values are a consequence of joint production. A negative value in the $(V\text{-}U)^{-1}$ matrix implies that the column process directly or indirectly *produces* (rather than requires) the row commodity. The less significant joint production is in the system, the fewer and smaller will be the negative elements in the $(V\text{-}U)^{-1}$ matrix.

The existence of negatives in the $(V\text{-}U)^{-1}$ matrix may also give rise to negative elements in the net input intensity vector (ϵ). Negative energy intensities would imply that production of an additional unit of the commodity in question would require less energy (directly and indirectly) and not more energy. We argued elsewhere (Hannon *et al.* 1985) that these negative intensities are most likely the result of poor data or poor system specification, and can be eliminated by better data or better specification of the system.

If all positive intensities are obtained for a system using equation 16 or 17, it is possible to combine them with an additional assumption to derive a commodity by commodity flow matrix (**P**) and coefficient matrix (**G**) whose elements are guaranteed to be non-negative and that can then be analysed using the methods described earlier. The first step is to calculate "evaluated" **U** and **V** matrices. These matrices are defined as:

$$\mathbf{U^*} = \mathbf{D\epsilon U} \tag{18}$$

$$\mathbf{V^*} = \mathbf{D\epsilon V} \tag{19}$$

where $\mathbf{D\epsilon}$ means the ϵ vector diagonalized.

A characteristic of the **U*** and **V*** matrices is that they are in commensurable units and both their row and column totals are meaningful. They are analogous to dollar flow matrices in economic applications. From the definition of ϵ the total evaluated commodity inputs to each process should equal the total evaluated commodity outputs, or:

$$\mathbf{iU^*} + \mathbf{e} = \mathbf{iV^*}$$

The column-summing assumption is a way of allocating inputs to joint products in order to derive an equivalent single-product system (Hannon *et al.* 1985). In the context of the multiple input and output view, this assumption is related to compartmental analysis, except that the production matrix **U** and the use matrix **V** have been weighted first by ϵ. It assumes that input commodities are allocated to output commodities in proportion to the proportion which the output commodity represents of the *total* output of the process. This situation of course requires that we can calculate the total output of processes which in turn requires that we measure these outputs in commensurable units. Given that we know **V*** from the previous analysis, we can calculate a matrix to perform this allocation:

$$\mathbf{Q} = \mathbf{V^*}(\mathbf{D_{iV^*}})^{-1} \tag{20}$$

The elements of **Q** are simply the percentages which each commodity flow represents of the total input to each process. A commodity by commodity flow matrix (**P**) can then be calculated as:

$$\mathbf{P} = \mathbf{UQ}^{T} \tag{21}$$

Standard flow analysis techniques as outlined above can then be applied to the system, and will yield the same ϵ as that obtained using equation 16 or 17 (Hannon *et al.* 1986).

Similarly, one can calculate a process by process flow matrix (call it **P***) as:

$$\mathbf{P^*} = \mathbf{Q^{*T}U} \tag{22}$$

where **Q*** is a matrix of the percentages which each commodity flow represents of the total outputs of that commodity (from the evaluated **V*** matrix).

HIERARCHICAL NET INPUT INTENSITIES USING A GLOBAL MULTICOMMODITY INPUT-OUTPUT MODEL

Multicommodity flow analysis is employed to calculate the net input intensity factors that can then be used to weight different commodities to make them commensurable. If there is more than one net input to the system, however, this method does not yield complete weightings. For example, consider an ecosystem with boundaries defined such that there are net inputs of both sunlight and water. In such a case we could calculate sunlight intensities *and* water intensities but would have no way of comparing or adding the two. One approach to this problem is to define an hierarchial series of models with ever more expansive boundaries. At the level of the whole globe, there is effectively only one net input - sunlight. A global multicommodity flow analysis model can thus be used to evaluate the relative solar energy intensities of commodities at this scale. These estimates can then be used at lower levels to put different net inputs into the same units. If we can calculate the solar energy cost of fresh water via the hydrologic cycle at the global level we can use that information to equilibrate net inputs of water and sunlight at the ecosystem level. We can speak of the net input of sunlight and the sunlight "embodied" in the water, and produce a single set of more detailed net input intensities at the ecosystem level.

Of course, the level of detail of the description of the global system will limit the number of different commodities that can be evaluated. A description with only aggregate nitrogen cannot be used to evaluate the different species of nitrogen. The nine process by nine commodity global model in the following section is intended only as a simplified example. Practical applications would require a more elaborate global model with probably several hundred commodities and processes. This more detailed level of description would allow distinctions between, say, ammonia and nitrate, different levels of water purity, and perhaps regional differences (i.e. fresh water in high rainfall vs. desert areas).

Tables 5.1 and 5.2 are examples of a global multicommodity flow table set up in the multiple output, commodity-process format discussed earlier. Table 5.1 shows the inputs of the the commodities listed along the left, to the processes listed along the top. This is the **U** matrix. Note that the units for the commodities are different (they are not commensurable) so one cannot add down the columns of **U**. The outputs of each commodity from each process are listed in Table 5.2. This is the **V** matrix. Note that conservation holds for each commodity but not for the processes, which are each measured in different units. The total output of each commodity from all the processes which produce it (the row sum of **V**) is equal to the total input of that commodity to all the processes that use it (the row sum of **U**), including the amount of commodity that is "depreciated" or exported (**r**). Processes (columns in **V**) that contain more than one entry represent "joint products." At the global level joint products are significant and unavoidable.

Using the methods described earlier we can calculate the direct and indirect use matrix, $(\mathbf{V}-\mathbf{U})^{-1}$, and the net input (in this case sunlight) intensity factors. This matrix and vector are shown in Table 5.3. Note that Table 5.3 contains many negatives. This reflects the fact that joint products are significant. There is no guarantee that using this method will produce an all-positive ϵ vector Appropriate data for **U** and **V** have to be provided to yield an all-positive ϵ vector.

Tables 5.4 and 5.5 are the evaluated **U** and **V** matrices ($\mathbf{U}^*$ and $\mathbf{V}^*$ using equations 15 and 16) in embodied solar energy units. Note that the total inputs to processes listed in Table 5.4 equal the total outputs from processes listed in Table 5.5. Table 5.6 is the commodity input distribution matrix (**Q**) calculated from $\mathbf{V}^*$ using equation 21.

Table 5.7 is the commodity by commodity flow matrix (**P**) calculated from **U** and **Q** using equation 22. Table 5.7 shows the amount of each row commodity required to produce a unit of column commodity in the global process taken as a whole. In Table 5.7 each commodity is measured in its own units. It is a simple matter to convert this table into a commensurable table by multiplying through each commodity by its energy intensity. The result is Table 5.8, which is a commodity by commodity flow matrix with all flows in embodied solar energy units. Since column sums equal row sums for this matrix, compartmental analysis is directly applicable (the $\mathbf{G}^*$ and $(\mathbf{I}-\mathbf{G}^*)^{-1}$ matrices and all of the network indices outlined elsewhere in this book can be calculated from Table 5.8)

There is an additional way of looking at this system to make it a closer analog to the usual starting point for compartmental analysis. Table 5.8 shows the interdependence among *commodities* within the global *process* taken as a whole. We might also want to investigate the interdependence among the different global *processes* with the *commodities* aggregated and treated as a single hybrid commodity. To do this we apply equation 22 to the global **U** and $\mathbf{Q}^*$ matrices and multiply through by the energy intensities. The results are shown in Table 5.9. This matrix indicates the flow of a single hybrid commodity (again measured in embodied solar energy units) between the global processes. This hybrid commodity incorporates the interdependencies in the disaggregated commodities through the calculation of the energy intensities.

Tables 5.8 and 5.9 are interesting for what the say about the relative importance of the various commodities and processes in the global system. For example, Table 5.8 indicates the importance of fresh water as an input to the production of manufactured goods. Fresh water represents 252.24 of a total of 757.65 x 10^{18} solar calories/yr (or 33%) of direct inputs to manufactured goods. This is slightly more than fossil fuels (29%) and turns out to be the most significant single input. Fresh water is an even more significant input to agricultural products and natural products.

Looking at the total input row in Table 5.8 indicates the relative importance of the hydrologic and carbon cycles in the global system. Water is three and carbon is two orders of magnitude larger than manufactured goods in terms of total inputs.

Table 5.9 yields a related but unique picture. Here the surface ocean and atmosphere (the two main processes in the hydrologic cycle) dominate the total input and output figures. The urban economy is shown to be very dependent on inputs from soil, atmosphere, and deep geology (for fossil fuels).

Whether one uses the commodity by commodity (table 5.8) or process by process (table 5.9) matrices as the starting point for further analysis depends on what questions are of interest. If the questions center on the interdependence between commodities (i.e. the effect of changes in the carbon cycle on the nitrogen cycle) then the commodity by commodity matrix is most appropriate. If the questions center on the interdependence between processes (i.e. the degree of dependence of the shallow ocean on land-based processes) then the process by process matrix is most appropriate. For calculating total system interdependence measures (i.e. Finn's (1976) cycling index or Ulanowicz's (1980) ascendency it is not clear which starting point is preferable. One can speak of a "commodity ascendency" and also of a "process ascendency." Each of these may reveal different aspects of system organization.

Ascendency of the Global System

By way of example, we have calculated both full and internal ascendency (A) capacity (C) and relative ascendancy (A/C) for the commodity by commodity (table 5.8) and process by process (table 5.9) descriptions of the global system (see Kay *et al.* 1989, Chapter 2 of this volume for a description of the methods for these calculations). The results are given in Table 5.10. They indicate a relative ascendency of .477 to .495. This means about half of the capacity of the global system for flow organization is being utilized. The differences between relative ascendency (A/C) for the commodity by commodity and process by process descriptions and between full and internal variants of the measures seem minor. Both the total ascendency and capacity are significantly lower for the process by process than for the commodity by commodity descriptions, however (on the order of 25%). Total system throughput is slightly less for the process by process than the commodity by commodity description and this may account for the discrepency, since ascendency and capacity both include T as a factor. At any rate, relative ascendency (A/C) seems to be a more stable and reliable quantity and would thus be preferable for comparisons between different systems and for the same system over time.

SUMMARY AND CONCLUSIONS

In this paper we have compared compartmental and flow analysis and have shown that flow analysis is the more appropriate approach if the system is not in commensurable units. Comprehensive analysis of ecosystems must include several different commodities measured in physical (noncommensurable) units. Flow analysis can be used to derive a set of unique intensity factors that perform the same function as prices in economic systems. They allow physical flows to be put in commensurable units and the "mixed units" problem to be solved.

We have also elaborated methods to deal with hierarchial intensity factors and joint products in ecosystems, and to convert commodity by process joint product systems to equivalent commodity by commodity single process systems and process by process single commodity systems. We have given a detailed description of how this works out for the global system, including what are probably the first attempted calculations of the ascendancy and relative ascendancy of the biosphere as a whole. While no conclusions can be drawn from these calculations alone, the methods discussed allow a more realistic and comprehensive treatment of ecosystem interdependence and can form the basis for comparative analysis of whole system performance once comparable calculations have been performed for enough systems.

REFERENCES

Barber, M., B. Patten & J. Finn 1979. Review and evaluation of I-O flow analysis for ecological applications, in: Matis, J., B. Patten & G.White, (Eds)*Compartmental Analysis of Ecosystem Models,* Vol 10 of Statistical Ecology, Internatl Coop. Publish. House, Bertonsville, Md.

Costanza, R. & C. Neill 1981. The energy embodied in the products of the biosphere. pp. 745-755 in: Mitsch, W. J., R. W. Bosserman, and J. M. Klopatek, (Eds) *Energy and Ecological Modeling.* Elevier, Amsterdam.

Costanza, R. & C. Neill 1984. The energy embodied in the products of ecological systems: a linear programming approach. J. Theor. Biol. 106: 41-57

Finn, J. 1976. The cycling index. J. Theor. Biol. 56: 363-73

Funderlic, R & M. Heath 1971. Linear Compartmental Analysis of Ecosystems. Oak Ridge Natl Lab, ORNL-IBP-71-4.

Hannon, B. 1973. The structure of ecosystems, J. Theor. Biol. 41:535-46.

Hannon, B. 1976. Marginal product pricing in the ecosystem. J. Theor. Biol. 56:256-267.

Hannon, B. 1979. Total energy costs in ecosystems. J. Theor. Biol. 80:271-293.

Hannon, B. 1985a. Ecosystem flow analysis. In: Ulanowicz, R.E. & T.Platt (Eds), *Ecosystem theory for biological oceanography,* Can. Bull. Fish. Aquat. Sci. 213: 97-118.

Hannon, B. 1985b. Conditioning the ecosystem. Mathematical Biology, 75: 23-42.

Hannon, B. 1985c. Linear dynamic ecosystems. J. Theor. Biol. 116: 89-98.

Hannon, B. 1986. Ecosystem control theory, submitted.

Hannon, B., R. Costanza, & R. Herendeen 1986. Energy cost and value in ecosystems. J. Environ. Ecol. Manage. 13: 391-401.

Hett, J & R. O'Neill 1971. Systems analysis of the aleut ecosystem. US-IBP, deciduous forest biome Memo Report, 71-16, September.

Hippe, P. 1983. Environ analysis of linear compartmental systems: The dynamic time invariant case. Ecol. Mod. 19:1-26.

Kay, J J., L. Graham & R. E. Ulanowicz 1989. A detailed guide to network analysis. In: Wulff, F., J.G. Field & K. H. Mann (Eds), *Network Analysis in Marine Ecology: Methods and Applications*. Lecture notes on coastal and estuarine studies. Springer-Verlag, New York.

Kercher, J. 1983. Closed-form solutions to sensitivity equations in the frequency and time domains for linear models of ecosystems. Ecol. Model. 18: 209-221. .

Leontieff, W. 1941. *The Structure of American Economy. 1919, 1929: An empirical application of equilibrium analysis.* Harvard University Press. Cambridge.

Samuelson, P. 1966. A new theorem on non-substitution, in: Stiglitz, J., (ed.), *The Collected Papers of P. A. S.*, 1, MIT Press, Cambridge, Mass., Chapter 37.

Stone, R. 1963. Input-output relationships 1954-1966; A programme for growth, MIT Press, Cambridge, Mass. 1-41.

Ulanowicz, R. 1980. An hypothesis on the development of natural communities. J. Theor. Biol.. 85: 223-245.

Vernberg, J. F. 1978. *Physiological Ecology of Organisms*. Columbia University Press, N.Y.

THEORETICAL POPULATION BIOLOGY 40, 78–104 (1991)

A General Accounting Framework for Ecological Systems: A Functional Taxonomy for Connectivist Ecology

BRUCE HANNON

Department of Geography and Illinois Natural History Survey, University of Illinois, Urbana, Illinois 61801

AND

ROBERT COSTANZA AND ROBERT ULANOWICZ

Chesapeake Biological Laboratory, Center for Environmental and Estuarine Studies, University of Maryland, Solomons, Maryland 20688-0038

Received February 1, 1990

Accounting of material and energy flows has long been an important tool in ecosystem ecology. But each material is usually handled separately and independently. The connections *between* materials, energy, plants, animals, etc. have not been incorporated into the accounting framework, and "service" or information flows (such as flower pollination by bees) are usually ignored. We develop a general accounting framework that addresses this deficiency. In our framework, each connection (both physical and informational) can be unambiguously assigned, quantified, and qualified, and an input–output balance is easily checked and maintained for each product. Costly independent data collections can be integrated into this common framework to amplify their original usefulness and provide the investigator or ecosystem manager with enhanced understanding of the entire ecosystem from which they were taken. The integrated data also allow various ecosystem models to be constructed efficiently, without unnecessary and costly duplication of effort. We present detailed guidelines for construction of such a framework, followed by examples and applications.

Contents

0040-5809/91 $3.00

I. Introduction

A. *What Is an Accounting System?*

In biology, species are identified and classified according to a general system first devised by Linnaeus. The assignment of any particular species to a place in the hierarchic system is based on genetic and morphological similarities between organisms. Classifications are often debated and reassignments are occasionally made, but progress in biology without such a system would not be possible.

In ecology, although functional connections between the many species and their environment have been observed for decades, there is no accepted general accounting system for noting and comparing these connections. We propose a functional taxonomy for quantitative ecology—a general ecological accounting system. It is a framework in which the quantified connections between organisms (individual species, collections of species) and their abiotic environment can be placed and balanced, without ambiguity, omission, or double counting exchanges, at any scale which an investigator chooses. By connections we mean any kind of exchange of product (e.g., nectar from a plant, pollination time from an insect) between ecological processes (e.g., insect and plant). A connectivist ecology is one in which the choice of process definition is largely discretionary, but once the choice is made, the interconnection flows are determined and are of primary importance in the ensuring system description. This is in contrast to the Linnaean taxonomy, in which the place of an organism in the system is determined by its structure and evolutionary history, and flows between it and the rest of the system are of secondary importance at best.

This general ecological accounting system is the product of years of debate among ecological modelers, and it also benefits from years of debate and experience gained in national economic accounting.

B. *Why Use an Accounting System?*

The principal advantage of a universal accounting system in ecology is that it allows the material, energy, and service flows between all the parts of an ecosystem to be systematically placed in a common framework. Ecologists have long been involved in material and energy flow accounting (Hannon, 1973; Finn, 1976), but in the past each type of material (e.g., nitrogen) or energy was accounted for independently of all the rest. To qualify as eco*system* accounting, the interconnections between all the material and energy (and service) flows must also be included. This is the purpose of the framework proposed below.

The concept of a common framework also appreciates the value of extant data bases (gathered for unrelated purposes) in that they can be incorporated and commensurately scaled into the same framework as current data. Together, old and new data can reside in a framework that provides the format for evaluation of whole ecosystem function (e.g., Hannon and Joiris, 1989).

In more detail, the use of an ecological accounting system could therefore assure ecosystem analysts and managers that a research effort on a particular ecosystem was done: 1. with full awareness of the system boundary (in space and time); 2. such that balance of materials, energy, and service flows for each compartment of the ecosystem under study was achieved; 3. with quantified connection to the rest of that ecosystem of any particular species of special interest; 4. in a way that allowed the compilation of data from various researchers of differing interests into a framework of growing utility.

The first known accounting framework for physical systems was developed in the 18th century by Turgot and Quesnay. The first large system accounting framework in which quantified interconnecting flows were measured was in the field of economics. Kuznets (1946) defined the concept of net output of an economy (Gross National Product) as a way of quantitatively comparing the activity levels of the economies of various countries. Leontieff (1941) defined a matrix structure for collecting the flows between various producing sectors so that he could determine the total output required to produce a unit of net output of each sector of the whole economy. This procedure is of crucial importance in planned economies and was of great use to the U.S. government just prior to and during World War II. Many countries (especially Japan) use the Leontieff system to look for production "bottlenecks" and to plan the development of their economies in specified areas. Stone (1963) refined the Leontieff approach to allow unambiguous accounting of multiple inputs *and* outputs. With Stone's contribution, the *economic* accounting procedure concept was essentially complete. The use of such accounting systems for public policy (Koopmans, 1951) and their theoretical implications for ecology (Amir, 1979) have been reported.

We have been guided in our development of an *ecological* accounting system by the experience of these economists. However, the consequences of the laws of thermodynamics are more apparent in ecological systems. With this recognition, we have modified the economic approach in an attempt to create a more comprehensive, less arbitrary accounting system that incorporates thermodynamic constraints and that simultaneously meets the needs of ecologists and economists. An added benefit is the ability to integrate economic and ecological data for analysis, planning, and management of large regional systems and for global change studies, as so elegantly recommended by Roughgarden (1989).

II. Development of Issues Involving Accounting Systems in Ecology

Quantifying a population's food sources and losses in terms of biomass and numbers can lead to useful insights. However, when the interaction of living organisms with their non-living surroundings are measured, it is only natural to seek a physical yardstick. The fact that a significant portion of an organisms' surroundings consists of other living populations leads us to seek consistency by applying the same physical yardstick to interbiotic transfers.

Lindeman (1942) first constructed a budget of the flows connecting the biotic and non-living components of a senescent Michigan lake ecosystem. Lindeman's work is considered by many to be the prototype of modern ecosystems accounting schemes. It emphasized the relational or connectivist view of ecology. Not only is a population related to its physical surroundings, but it is connected *in the same terms* to other populations. Through Lindeman, ecology experienced a hierarchical leap from the study of populations to a consideration of the wider scope and scale of ecosystems.

Also important were the units in which Lindeman's accounting ultimately were reported—those of energy. Energy is a physical characteristic and can be used to express the physical nature of a biological system in a way that is *non-reductionistic*. Furthermore, energy is a construct that derives from the phenomenological science of thermodynamics. By accounting for all energy entering and leaving each population, one is recapitulating the first law of thermodynamics—that energy is neither created nor destroyed. But the first law begs the invocation of the second, which says (in one of its myriad of equivalent forms) that useful output from any process cannot occur without the degradation of some of the process input into less useful forms. The inviolability of the second law impresses a pyramidal form upon any discernible trophic chain of energetic transfers. The amounts of energy available to be passed on to higher trophic links must become progressively smaller.

Eugene Odum (1953, 1959) recognized the hierarchical shift implied by Lindeman's budgets and did more than anyone else to popularize the ecosystems perspective in quantitative terms. Howard Odum also pressed for further applications of the second law in ecology (Odum and Pinkerton, 1955). Howard Odum was also intrigued by the cycles that appear in most community budgets. He argued (Odum, 1971) that such cycles are indicative of the cybernetic processes at work in structuring ecosystems. Those components and pathways that are more effective than others at recycling materials and energy unto themselves will eventually grow at the relative expense of those other members. Systems develop and evolve in the same sense as do their components.

The shift towards whole system budgets afforded other connectivist insights. Connecting elements together in an overall budget made it possible to trace indirect causes in quantitative terms. However, the number and complexity of such indirect linkages easily overwhelms one's perceptual capacities. So to make any progress in evaluating indirect effects one must resort to systematic analytical techniques. Of course, the question of indirect effects is hardly limited to ecology. It is a significant issue in economics as well. It was an economist (Leontieff, 1941) who first successfully applied the techniques of matrix algebra to the task of accounting for indirect effects. Some economists (Daly, 1968) have suggested that ecological flows be included in the Leontieff approach.

Hannon (1973) demonstrated how Leontieff's methods could be applied to ecological budgets. There followed copious efforts to apply "input–output" analysis to various ecosystems and to modify the analytical techniques to address better various issues of ecological concern. Patten et al. (1976) combined input–output analysis with general systems theory to extend the notion of an ecological niche to include indirect impacts and effects. Barber (1978) emphasized the probabilistic nature of ecological transfers and spotlighted the Markovian assumptions underlying the Leontieff approach. Finn (1976) studied the indirect effects that many system components exert upon themselves and showed how to estimate the fraction of the total system activity that is devoted to recycle.

Amir (1979) laid out the economist's views on equilibrium in ecological systems, including the interpretations of value, cost, and price. Ulanowicz and Kemp (1979) remarked how the algebraic powers of the matrix of normalized transfers (the technical coefficients of economics) provide information on how much medium traverses trophic pathways of various lengths. They used the successive matrix powers to transform arbitrary webs of trophic interactions into Lindeman-like chains or pyramids of flows.

Matis and Patten (1981) attempted to incorporate the contents, or stocks, associated with the system components into the analysis of indirect effects and sketched out what they called "environ analysis." Unlike the standard input–output analysis of systems that must balance around each component, environ analysis treats systems that are unbalanced and change via an assumed set of linear dynamics. Hannon (1986) examined the stability of such linear systems and evaluated several control strategies (either endogenous or externally applied) that could guide the system towards particular configurations.

Virtually all of the early work in ecosystem accounting focused on the exchange of a single medium. That is, budgets were cast in terms of energy, or carbon, or nitrogen; but seldom was there an attempt to treat systems wherein more than one medium was flowing, or to include connections that involved no physical exchange (e.g., the effect of pheromones, shading, pollination). Implicit in single medium analyses are the assumptions that all inputs to a compartment have equal effect upon the recipient population, and that only one product issues from each compartment (usually its biomass as food to predators.) The latter assumption is not valid because organisms produce by-products such as feces, urine, detritus, and other exudates. How does one treat these multiple products that issue from a population or process? But perhaps even more problematic is the likelihood that the various foods consumed by each predator differ in their utilities to the consumer. How do we weight the various inputs to a compartment to reflect their relative utilities? Fortunately, one solution to both these difficulties is suggested by recent work in input–output theory.

In economics, one view of the origin of prices is that they account for the cumulative value added to a particular item at every step in the economic process from raw materials to finished product.[1] In ecology it is sometimes possible to make analogous calculations (Costanza and Neill, 1984). If a system has only one external input of a type not produced in the system, it is then possible to trace back through the network to identify the amounts of that input medium that were necessary to create any given connection. That is, one can estimate the portion of the input that has been "embodied" into each connection. It has been shown (Costanza, 1980; Costanza and Herendeen, 1984) how all the energies contributing to various economic products are correlated to their market prices. In the special case of a network with but a single medium (e.g., all energy flows), a particular transfer between higher trophic levels may yield value when directly measured (a certain number of calories). However, the de facto value of the flow in a systems context would reflect more the amount of the external input (e.g., sunlight) that went into creating the given flow. The ratio of the latter quantity to the former is called an "intensity" and can be used to weight the various inputs to a population so as to allow a legitimate comparison among these inputs.

Similarly, intensities can be calculated for an ecosystem description which has multiple outputs as well as multiple inputs. That procedure is more complex (Costanza and Hannon, 1989) and requires the accounting system described below.

Amir (1987) has discussed the use of an ecological accounting system, both static and dynamic, to elaborate on the formal connections between ecology, thermodynamics, and economics. He points out that the "intensities" of which we speak are measured in terms of an external input and that we therefore must choose which external input should form the basis of the intensities. In the development of the general accounting system,

[1] This is the view we take in our paper. Amir (1979) points out the other economic theories on the origin of prices.

however, we are not proposing the use of intensities or any other kind of model. We view the accounting system as a necessary underpinning for any kind of ecosystem model which claims to be consistent with any other kind. The accounting system which we propose forms the basis for consistent comparison of model results. Amir points out that these intensities are reminiscent of economic prices which arise from ecological resource allocation problems, just as they do in economics.

III. A General Accounting Framework

A. *Desiderata*

We can now set forth, in general terms, the minimum desired criteria for an accounting framework capable of handling both ecological and economic systems. These can be summarized as (1) generality; (2) comprehensiveness; (3) uniqueness; and (4) quality control. These are described in more detail below.

Generality

The accounting framework should exhibit a high degree of universality or generality, in the sense that its usefulness should not be limited to any particular system or temporal or spatial scale. It should be applicable to both ecological and economic systems, on spatial and temporal scales ranging from microcosms to the planet as a whole. We desire this characteristic so as to begin to make valid comparisons between divergent systems and to start to bridge the wide chasm that currently exists between ecology and economics. We wish to be able to combine data from different geographic regions of the same ecosystem into the same framework, for a given time period.

Comprehensiveness

The accounting framework should exhibit a high degree of comprehensiveness, in the sense that it should; at least in theory, be able to include the full range of phenomena that occur in a system. We understand that practical limitations will often limit the achievable comprehensiveness of the accounting, but the accounting framework itself should not be the impediment. The accounting system should be able to handle processes which have several different types of inputs and outputs. The system equally should be able to include simultaneously a physical exchange and a non-physical exchange between processes. For example, when a bee visits a plant, it receives nectar (physical exchange) and provides cross pollination from other flowers (non-physical exchange). Both types of exchanges should be included in the accounting system.

Uniqueness

The accounting framework should provide a unique and unambiguous place for each measurable type of connection. The physical or thermodynamic quality of the connection must be recognized and treated consistently and the system boundaries should be physically definable in a discoverable way.

Quality control

The accounting framework should exhibit an ability to deal with information of varying quality in a simple and consistent way. The precision of the data for each connection should carry its own mark of reliability and the change in that mark should be specified as the data are mingled arithmetically with other data.

B. *The Art of Choosing Stocks and Flows*

When asked to list the important components of the system, it is extremely rare that two investigators will spontaneously enumerate the same elements. Of course, the subjective biases that determine what is actually measured will color the ensuing analysis. Critics of systems ecology are always quick to cite the relative nature of the results from network analyses. It is our opinion that in the end the ambiguities associated with which components to include in the accounting scheme (the lexical decisions) pale in comparison to the insights into system structure and function one obtains by performing the budgetary exercise. To be more specific, we *hypothesize* that the qualitative conclusions drawn when the accounting techniques are applied to ecosystems will differ very little (if at all) whenever the same ecosystem is parsed in different ways by various investigators. More important is the application of a consistent, systematic, and comprehensive framework of accounting for exchanges and storages, much as the one described below. We can also put this question to the test by reparsing and reanalyzing the ecological system if the accounting framework allows this kind of manipulation to be done conveniently. Of course, the different scales used by independent investigators must be considered when the data is transposed into a common framework.

Such apology having been made, it is nonetheless useful to elaborate the *art* of choosing the elements to include in the accounting. As in general systems theory, we feel the delimitation of the system is strictly at the discretion of the observer; i.e., the system boundaries and list of internal elements may be chosen at will. That is not to say that all choices are equally good.

Common sense should prevail in defining the boundaries of the system. Ideally, the physical boundaries are chosen to minimize the amount and diversity of exchanges across them. Then the exogenous transfers can be more easily monitored. Interfaces that inhibit certain classes of transfers, such as air–water or water–land, are often convenient for this purpose. Topographic features, such as watershed or airshed boundaries, often work nearly as well. The duration and frequency of sampling for data also place hierarchical boundaries on the system description every bit as important and restrictive as the demarcation of spatial domain. The definition of temporal limits devolves into monitoring strategy, and space does not permit a full discussion of these issues (see, for example, Schubel et al., in press). Suffice it to say that the duration of data acquisition should be long enough to characterize statistically the slower biotic processes and the most frequent sampling will be required by those populations exhibiting rapid changes.

The temporal limits are thus inexorably connected with the choice of compartments. What are the important processes and products of the ecosystem? The answer, of course, will be colored by the inclinations of the investigator or the source of funding for the accounting endeavor. Certainly, the experienced investigator will rarely omit the visibly most abundant species in the system. Activity level is another criterion for selection of budget items. Microbial populations usually have small standing stocks, but engender a disproportionate fraction of system activity. Often a species of marginal ecological importance will be included into the accounting by virtue of its economic, aesthetic, recreational, or political usefulness, or, in the case of endangered species, its rarity per se. As will be discussed below, value is not always synonymous with magnitude.

Then there is the delicate issue of control. It may happen that a seemingly insignificant species is exerting a powerful control upon ecosystem processes. Control is a dynamical attribute, and as such is beyond the scope of this paper. But we would be foolish to exclude an item that is known to exert strong control on significant processes. Conversely, an ecologist is always at risk of excluding a species that, unknown to the observer, is exhibiting control upon the system. Such negligence may not be as tragic as it seems. For practical reasons not every agency can be included in the accounting process, and the investigator is forced to assume that the influences of these unknown dynamics are implicit in the chosen processes.

While the finitude of resources for research may abridge the number of compartments that can be included in the scheme, the availability of historical data conversely may allow the inclusion of some species into the budget that otherwise would be too costly or impossible to monitor under the duration of the project. In fact, the reader would probably be surprised by the quantity of data extant on his/her ecosystem of interest. Quite often, all that is necessary to piece together a system budget of surprisingly good resolution is a couple of man-years of expert effort and persistence (cf. Costanza et al., 1983; Baird and Ulanowicz, 1989).

Finally, there is no reason to regard the lexical choices an investigator makes at the outset of an accounting project as cast in stone. Accounting projects allow for iterative reevaluation as more data accrue. Often the investigator may begin with order-of-magnitude guesses as to the intensity of various processes and use these estimates to gauge the values to be attached to each flow. As a result, certain processes might be dropped from further consideration or aggregated with more important elements.

C. *Quantifying the Flows*

Once the system boundary in space and time has been identified, and the processes with their input and output products have been chosen, one can begin the accounting procedure. There are six distinct types of connections, in addition to the stocks, that must be identified in analyzing any ecosystem: 1. the non-produced inputs; 2. the net outputs; 3. the product use record; 4. the product production record; 5. the total output; and 6. the waste heat flows. These product flows are shown in Fig. 1.

1. *The Non-produced Inputs*

We distinguish here between imported/exported products made within the defined ecosystem, and imports of special products which are not made within this system. One thinks of the import of the non-produced products as a constraint on the system's activity level. These are the products which are sometimes deemed as scarce or growth-limiting in some sense. Sunlight is a non-produced import but not the only possible one. For example,

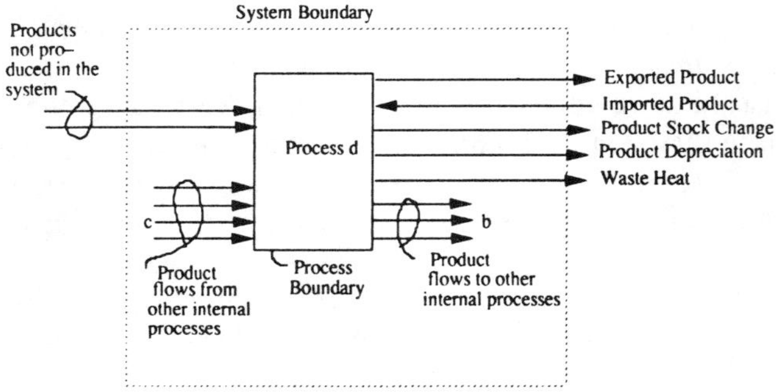

FIG. 1. The product flows into and out of a typical process in an ecosystem. Product flows are mainly distinguished as going to other processes inside the system boundary or, crossing the boundary. Products imported from outside the system are separated depending on whether they are made in the system or not.

sunlight contains blue, red, and infrared radiation, all of which may be used by the ecosystem. While we sometimes think of infrared radiation as extraneous, it is possible to define this radiation as a product *within* the ecosystem. If the ecologist chooses not to define it in this way, then infrared radiation should be included as a non-produced input to the system.

Ambient heating is also an input to any system. In what sense is the flow of heat through the ecosystem an important theoretical consideration? Ambient heating, from an economic point of view, is very important. The departure from some ideal standard results in a drop in the value of agricultural output and an increase in fossil fuel use. From the ecologic point of view, the heat flow is also very important, since temperature is a primary controlling factor in many life processes. However, heat flows are largely cyclical and within a given range, they are predictable. To this extent, heat flows are not of primary importance in ecosystem studies. They are of course important in detailed studies of the variations in organism development in the ecosystem. We recommend that heat flows be included as a measured net inputs to the system.

2. *The Net Outputs*

The net output flows are connections from the defined ecosystem across the system boundary to itself at a future time and/or to other ecosystems. There are three kinds of net output flows which must be accommodated in our accounting system.

First, we have the import and export of products made and/or used by the processes in the defined system. For example, in an aquatic ecosystem, one of the processes is likely to be algae, and one of its output products would be "algal biomass". Some of this biomass could be washed from the system (export) or into the system (import) during a flood.

The second kind of net output flow is the change in the storage level of a particular product which occurs during the designated time period. Since we have assumed a static picture of the ecosystem, we must include the changes in stocks explicitly as flows. These flows might be thought of as flows across the time boundary of the chosen period. For example, an increase in storage will be used in the next or later time periods.

Thus, the requirements are not very surprising for the experienced ecologist. But there remains a third net output flow across the ecosystem boundary that is harder to describe. If, as we have just assumed, the stock change is a flow across the time boundary of the system, what about the change of stock due to the natural decay and stock replacement processes inherent in all products of the ecosystem as required by the second law of thermodynamics? Everyone is aware of the decay processes associated with death. These same processes are at work in the living system, but they are countered by the simultaneous restorative or anabolic processes we call life.

Thus, when one observes a quantity of living substance perceived to be of constant stock over the chosen time period, one is really seeing the balanced result of the decay and replacement processes. During the study time period, a certain amount of the living product actually decayed into its component parts and some of that lost stock was replaced. This decay–replacement process is known to occur because the products of decomposition and the net absorption of energy are both evident. If the stock size of the organism does not change during the chosen time period, what is lost or gained by the organism? It is known from thermodynamics that the *order* of the structure of the organism was lost for that stock of product which decayed during the time period. Yet, for the case where the total product stock size did not change, that lost order was exactly made up by what we call the replacement process. One must record the contribution of this replacement process in some manner. It is a product contribution across the time boundary of the system in the same manner as is the net change of a product stock.

Decay rates can be measured directly by isolating a sample of the product in question and observing the loss of order with time. Frequently this isolation is not possible or practical, however, and an estimate of the magnitude of the decay rate for living products (e.g., biomass) must be substituted. The basal metabolism of living products can be used as an estimate of decay rates, since it represents the replacement flow required just to compensate for decay processes when the organism is at rest.

In a similar way, abiotic products in the ecosystem (e.g., solution ammonia) might also degrade during the time period, and in the process, give off heat. We need to know what the normal degradation rate would have been for this substance at the system temperature. Such data for most substances can be found in standard chemical reference handbooks. We accept these standard data as the *replacement* rate of the non-living substances in question. If one wishes to account for the waste heat associated with the decomposition of these abiotic compounds, one could add another process to the accounting system which describes the input and output of the compound and its degradation (therefore its replacement rate) and record the associated waste heat. Of course, some of the non-living substances might already be at their lowest energy state, at equilibrium with the system environment (e.g., carbon dioxide), and no decay need be considered.

The assignment of the basal or standard metabolism to the net output of the framework to represent the replacement of the depreciated stock is explict acknowledgement of the second law of thermodynamics. The remainder of the respiratory flows are not counted as a part of the net output since they are not of the same quality as the flows along that row of the matrix. These flows are recorded only to provide a check on the balance of the total flow of that substance in the system. The assignment process does not double count any of the flows.

3. *The Product Use Record*

We have chosen the "Use" and "Make" matrices approach (Stone, 1963) and modified it to meet the special problems involved with ecological flows. The "Use" matrix is the record of which process uses what product. The "Make" matrix is the product production record and is discussed in the next section.

The first accounting step is to record where each product is used and by which process. A "Use" or U matrix is constructed as follows: Each process is placed at the head of a column in the U matrix; each product is placed at the beginning of a row in this matrix. The use of a product (e.g., product "c") by a particular process (e.g., process "d") for the chosen time period (i.e., the flow of "c" into "d"), is the number placed on the cell which lies at the intersection of row "c" and column "d". The quantities of the substances consumed by predators for example, appear in the U matrix. The picture of the U matrix appears in Fig. 2.

The units of measure of product *c* must be the same wherever product *c* is used, but these need not be the same as the measure for any of the other products. For example, product *c* may be measured in grams-carbon per square meter and product *d* may be measured in kcal per square meter. So long as the units are consistent along the row of *U*, the products may be measured in any units.

It is clear to ecologists that the inputs to a particular species may vary in type and quantity with time, with age of the individuals in that species, and with the availability of resources. It is theoretically possible to include

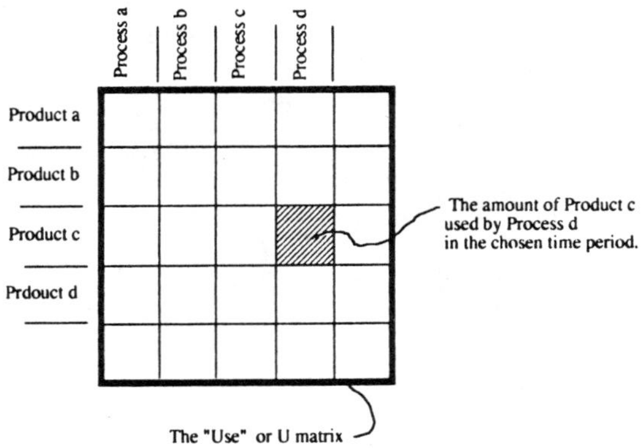

FIG. 2. The uses of products by the various processes are tabulated in the Use or U matrix.

such variation in a single descriptive Use matrix by devising a column for each time, age, and resource condition. This matrix is then controlled by a time-varying vector of factors, each between zero and one, which select the proper portions of each of the columns involved with that species. The Make matrix (discussed below) may require a similar modification.

Besides allowing greater convenience in data gathering, the tolerance of the U matrix for any kind of unit of measure lets the experimentalists incorporate units of "service" into the matrix. For example, the pollination of flowers by bees may be measured in "pollination bee-seconds" per square meter for the chosen time period. We know that if some pollutant reduced the bee population by half, flower productivity would decrease. But there is hardly any physical transfer from bees to flowers, except that measurable by the service units of pollination. The "bee-seconds" measure is the collective visitation time spent by bees in flowers. In the U matrix, the process *plant* would have "used" so many bee-seconds of pollination service. So the term "product" as we use it here may mean an actual physical product *or* a service. Negative services, such as the effect of allelopathic chemicals, can also be included.

4. *Product Production Record*

In the general accounting system, a second matrix is needed to show where the products are made. Such a matrix is called a "Make" or V matrix and it has the same configuration as the U matrix: the column heads are the processes and the product names are shown at the beginning of each row. The quantified list of substances produced by prey for example, are listed in the production matrix. The elements of the V matrix are for example, the amount of product *b* which is produced or made by process *d*; see Fig. 3.

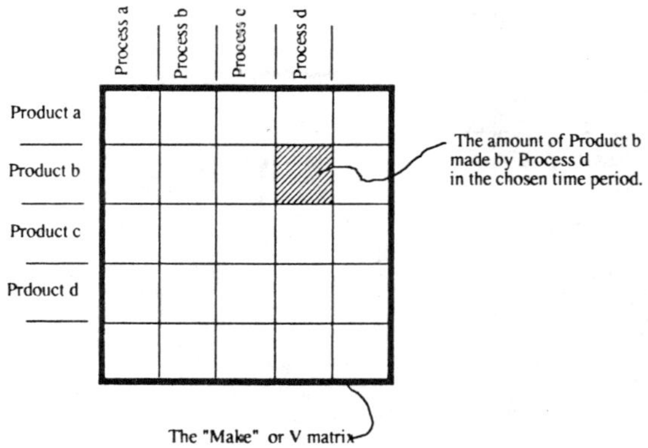

FIG. 3. The products made by the various processes are tabulated according to where they are made.

The units of a product must be consistent across the row of the V and U matrix but can vary from product to product.

The products of a species or an organism in the ecosystem can vary with the available portions of the net input. For example, at various times of the year, energy, water, and nitrogen may be in short supply. Since the organism requires these inputs in fixed proportion for growth, the rate of biomass and the type and amount of excretion products will vary. A variety of vectors can be assigned to a particular organism or species and a time-varying control vector, whose zero to one factors depend on the mix of net inputs, can be used to the appropriate mix of outputs through time.

5. *The Total Output Flow*

The sum of the entries in a row of U plus the corresponding row of the net outputs is the total output flow for that product. This sum is also equal to the sum of the corresponding row of the V or "Make" matrix. The balance here provides a check on the various product entries.

6. *The Waste Heat Flow*

The respiratory or total waste heat is composed of the basal metabolic heat from the process and the organism's muscle and bone friction, prey-seeking or predator-avoidance effort, and reproductive effort. To complete the accounting procedure, we collect all of the heat given off by each process into a vector. We consider this heat as lost to the system due to its lack of utility to any of the other organisms in the system. If some of this heat were used by certain components in the ecosystem, then that quantity of heat would be classed as a product produced and used by the appropriate components in the U and V matrices. If some of this "waste" heat could be used as a measure of reproductive service for example, then that quantity of heat would appear in the U and V matrices as used and made by the same component. All of the "waste" heat could be assigned in this manner. Note that the waste heat flow defined in this section is not associated with the basal metabolic processes: those substances representing basal metabolism have been assigned to represent the decay processes and appear in the net output.

To complete the accounting framework, we augment Figs. 2 and 3 with the matrices of product inputs and outputs to the system. Since the non-produced inputs to the system are products used by the system, they are best assembled at the lower edge of the U matrix. The produced import and export products, the changes in product stocks, and the depreciation products are all products of the system but they cross the system boundary. We therefore associate the matrix of these three types of flows (the net outputs matrix) with the U (Use) matrix on its right-hand side for convenience in balancing. The waste heat from the processes of the system is

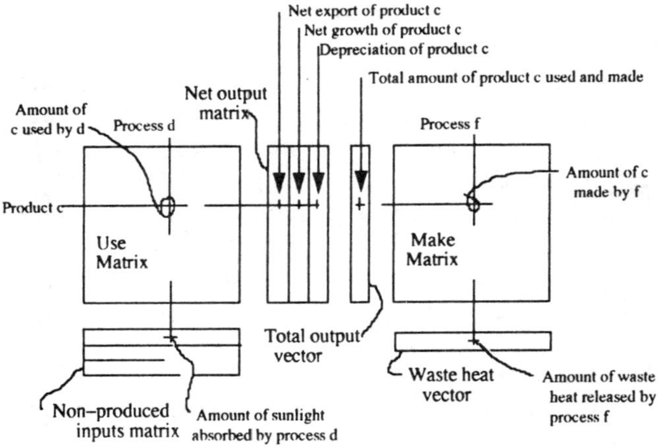

FIG. 4. The general accounting system describing the assignment of all product flows to where they are made and used.

tabulated at the bottom edge of the V (Make) matrix as a notational reminder that they have been accounted for. The complete ecological accounting system therefore looks as shown in Fig. 4.

As a matter of accounting convenience, the U and V matrices are overlaid in tabular form and kept in the same table, with the Make or V matrix entries shown immediately below the Use or U matrix entries. Also note that the U and V matrices will most likely be rectangular and not square, because the number of products used will not necessarily equal the number of products made.

The general accounting procedure is shown in the following examples.

D. *Examples*

The following simplified examples will serve to illustrate the accounting system. We have chosen to use simplified examples rather than data from actual systems. The application of a simplified form of the accounting system to the Southern North Sea ecosystem has been published (Hannon and Joiris, 1989; Costanza and Hannon, 1989). Our goal in this paper is to demonstrate the full accounting system in the simplest possible form so that each of the principles can be clearly explained. We know of no ecosystem for which a sufficient amount of data has been collected and codified for application of the full accounting procedure.

The first example is a hypothetical ecosystem consisting of three internal processes (abiotic chemical processes, primary producer processes, and consumer processes) and five products (nutrients, plant biomass, animal biomass, waste heat, and sunlight). The "use" or inputs, "make" or out-

TABLE I

Hypothetical Ecosystem Network Illustrating the General Accounting Framework

Products (units)		Internal Processes			External Processes			Totals
			Biotic processes		Net Outputs			
		Abiotic Chemical Processes	Producers	Consumers	Change in stock	Exports/ imports	Depre- ciation	
Internally produced								
Nutrients	use	20	10	0	0	5	2	37
(g/*t*)	make	20	5	5	—	7	—	37
	stock	500	0	0	—	—	—	500
Plant biomass	use	1	5	6	1	0	1	14
(g/*t*)	make	0	14	0	—	0	—	14
	stock	0	100	0	—	—	—	100
Animal biomass	use	1	1	5		0	1	8
(g/*t*)	make	0	0	8	—	0	—	8
	stock	0	0	10	—	—	—	10
Waste heat	use	—	—	—	—	—	100	100
(Cal/*t*)	make	5	50	45	—	—	—	100
Externally produced								
Sunlight	use	0	100	0	—	—	—	100
(Cal/*t*)	make	—	—	—	—	100	—	100

puts, and "stock" of each of these products by (or in) each of the internal processes are shown in table I and Fig. 5. The table and figure are equivalent representations of the system. Figure 6 shows the nutrient product flows isolated from the system. Most network analysis in ecosystems has in the past concentrated on just such a one-product abstraction of the system. Our general accounting framework is intended to take more of the full complexity of ecological networks into account as shown in Fig. 5 and table I.

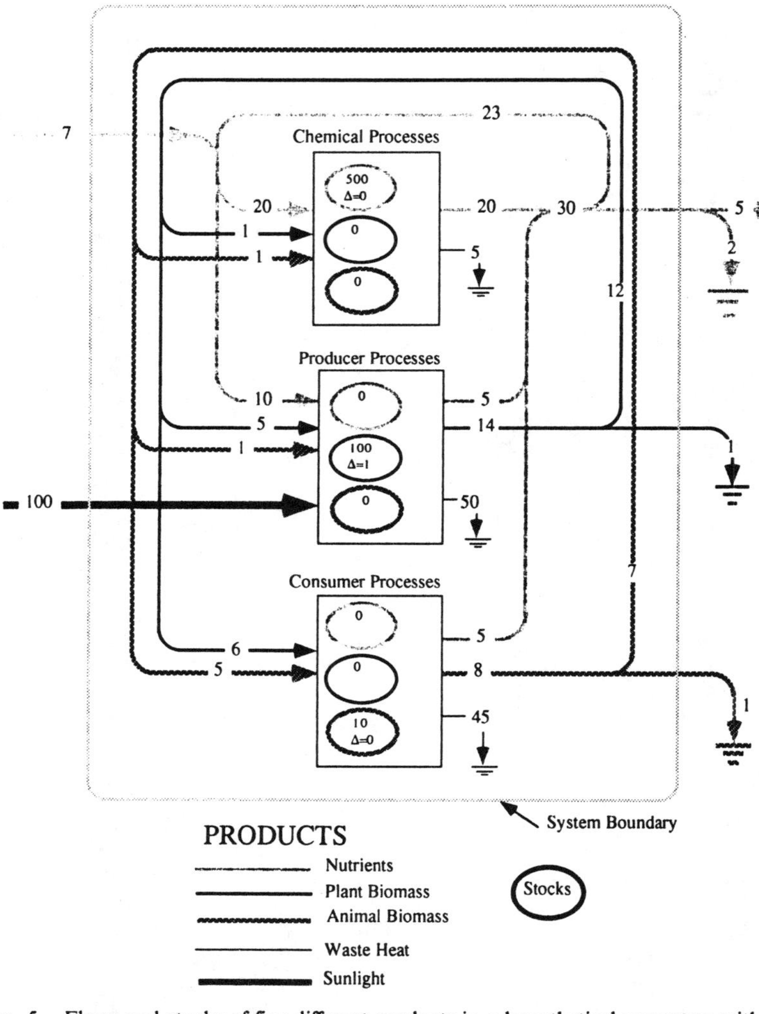

FIG. 5. Flows and stocks of five different products in a hypothetical ecosystem with three internal processes.

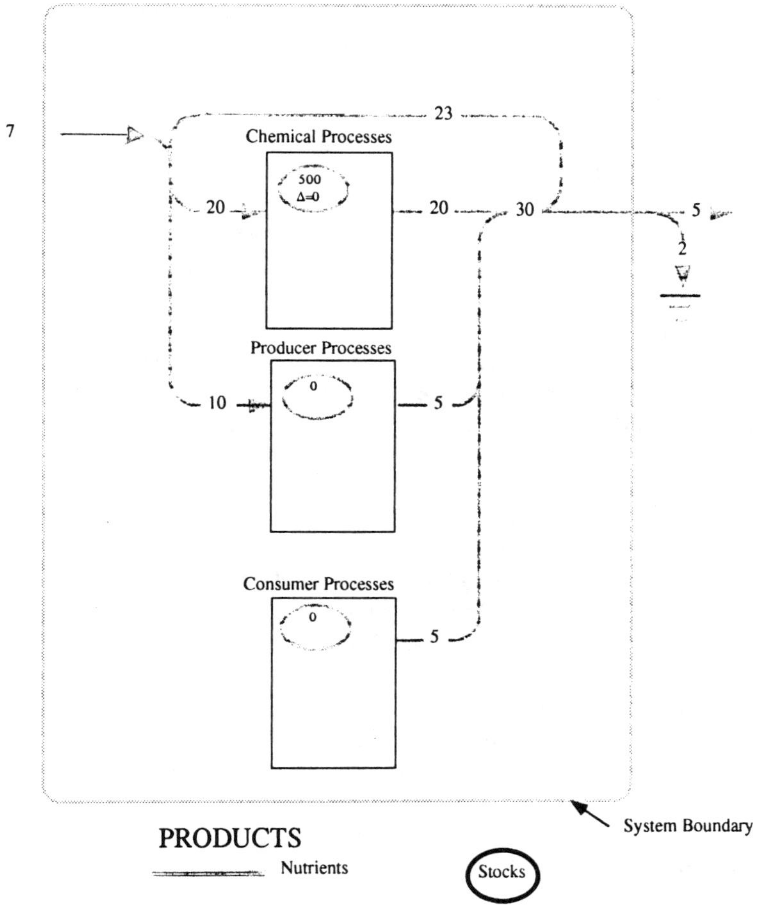

FIG. 6. Hypothetical ecosystem flows and stocks of the single product "nutrients".

Table I represents a particularly compact, yet easily readable representation of the complex flows shown in Fig. 5. For example, one can read from Fig. 5 that abiotic chemical processes use 20 g per unit time of nutrients, primary producers use 10, and consumers use 0. Nutrients are "made" by all three processes, since plants and animals release nutrients when they die and decompose. In contrast, plant and animal biomass are "made" only by producers and consumers, respectively.

A fourth internal product is waste heat. This products is unique in that it is made by all the internal processes but is used by none of them. In addition to the four internal products, one "external" product is noted for this ecosystem. This is sunlight, which is used by producers to drive the system and is not made anywhere in the system. Any product that is not produced anywhere in the system under study but is necessary for the system's survival is called an externally produced product.

There are also three "external processes" shown, change in stock, exports/imports, and depreciation replacement, along with their use and make of the system's products. As already mentioned, a change in stock is equivalent to an export to another time period, and depreciation is equivalent to export from the system. So, taken together, these three external processes represent net outputs from the system of one kind or another.

Note that for this system (and for any system) mass and energy balance are maintained for each product. For example the total use of nutrients in the system of 37 g/t (use by internal processes plus use by external processes in the form of change in stock, exports and depreciation) is equal to the total production of nutrients by internal processes plus imports (also 37 g/*t*). Product use must balance product make for each product in the system.

"Products" in our accounting system can also be services or information. To illustrate this we present an example system in which bee pollination services are an important product (table II). In this example the products are bee biomass, honey, plant biomass, and been pollination effort, in addition to the ubiquitous waste heat and sunlight. The internal processes are bees, and two species of plants that the bees pollinate. Bees in this system produce four different products; (1) bee biomass (7 g/*t*); (2) honey (35 g/*t*); (3) pollination effort (10 bee s/*t*); and waste heat (5 Cal/*t*). Note that both bee biomass and honey are used and made exclusively by bees. Bee pollination effort is used more by plant 1 (6 bee s/*t*) than by plant 2 (3 bee s/*t*). Plant 1 also has twice the biomass stock of plant 2 (200 vs. 100) and uses more sunlight (40 vs. 30 Cal/*t*).

E. *Data Quality Control*.

All numerical estimates have some uncertainty associated with them, and the normal assumption that they are measured with total precision is an inaccurate approximation. In the case of well-established experimental or field data, there are standard statistical techniques available for representing data quality and how varying quality of data affects results of accounting systems and models on them (cf. Bullard and Sebald, 1977). But statistically valid samples are usually available for only a very small percentage of the entries needed in the proposed accounting system. What we need is some other means to communicate and manipulate data quality when that quality falls below the level that standard statistics can deal with. We need a way to use all the scarce information available on systems connections in a clear and straightforward way. In the absence of such a

TABLE II

Hypothetical Ecosystem Network Illustrating the Accounting of Service Type Products

Products (units)		Internal processes			External processes			Totals
		Bees	Plant 1	Plant 2	Change in stock	Net outputs exports/ imports	Depre- ciation	
				Internally produced				
Bee biomass	use	5	0	0	1	0	1	7
(g/*t*)	make	7	0	0	—	0	—	7
	stock	35	0	0	—	—	—	35
Honey	use	30	0	0	0	0	5	35
(g/*t*)	make	35	0	0	—	0	—	35
	stock	0	100	0	0	0	0	100
Plant biomass	use	5	25	35	3	0	5	73
(g/*t*)	make	0	33	40	—	0	—	73
	stock	0	200	100	—	—	—	300
Bee pollination	use	0	6	3		0	1	10
Effort	make	10	0	0	—	0	—	10
(bee s/*t*)	stock	10	0	0	—	—	—	10
Waste heat	use	—	—	—	—	—	70	70
(Cal/*t*)	make	5	30	35	—	—	—	70
				Externally produced				
Sunlight	use	0	40	30	—	—	—	70
(Cal/*t*)	make	—	—	—	—	70	—	70

system, once a number is obtained and exported to the general scientific community it is labelled either "good" or "bad," and the record of its degree of quality is all but forgotten except by the experts familiar with the details of the measurement methods. What is needed is a formal, systematic way of communicating to the non-expert the "degree of goodness" or "quality" associated with each number. This can be imagined as composed of its degrees of precision and accuracy; that is, how little "spread" or scatter there is in its underlying data, and how reliable it is as an estimate of what it is measuring. Thus, we can think of all quantitative measurements as having associated truth-value modifiers, which we will call the "grades" of numbers. We chose this term since everyone is familiar with the grading process through their academic experience, and the process of grading quantitative measurements is conceptually similar to grading students or grading almost anything else. Also, stating a grade with each number connotes the evaluative and qualitative nature of the measure of uncertainty we propose, which is in keeping with its correct interpretation.

Such systems for grading and manipulating data of sub-statistical quality are currently under development (e.g., Funtowitz and Ravitz, 1989). We lack the space to adequately treat them here, except to say that they are a necessary adjunct to the proposed accounting system to allow information the *quality* of numerical estimates to be carried through the accounting and subsequent manipulations of complex systems built up from measurements of highly varying quality. They will ultimately allow a more honest and rational use of our numerical resources.

IV. Uses of the General Accounting System

The accounting framework described above allows the collection of ecosystem data in a form that is useful for a number of analytical purposes. Some of these uses and their importance are described in detail in a number of recent works (e.g.) Hannon and Joiris, 1989, Costanza and Hannon, 1989, Fasham, 1984; Hannon, 1986; MacDonald, 1983; Ulanowicz, 1986; and Wulff *et al.*, 1989). Below we briefly describe some examples that demonstrate existing and potential uses, but the presence of a consistent accounting framework should allow an explosion of new uses not mentioned or conceived of here.

Most uses of the framework require some assumptions about the functional relationships between process inputs and outputs. The examples below are organized in order of increasing sophistication of these assumptions, from static, linear ones, to dynamic, nonlinear ones, to more elaborate optimization functions.

A. *Network Analysis and Energy Intensities*

The "mixed units" problem is a critical one in both ecology and economics. We have elaborated an accounting system which allows multiple products, but most analytical work requires (or at least is much more convenient) when only a single product is tracked. One area of research therefore is the conversion of the full multi-product network into an equivalent single-product network. Work in this area has so far centered on various ways to calculate intensity factors (analogous to prices in economic systems) that allow all the system's products to be converted into a common currency (Hannon, Costanza, and Herendeen, 1986; Hannon and Costanza, 1985, Costanza, and Hannon, 1989). If the system under study has only one non-produced input (usually sunlight for ecological systems) and there are an equal number of products and processes it becomes possible to calculate the input intensities that represent the amount of the non-produced input "embodied" in each of the system's products (Costanza and Hannon, 1989). These energy intensities can then be used to convert the system into a single product network (i.e., in "embodied sunlight") that is amenable to further network analysis. The range of possible network analysis that can be performed on single product ecological networks is given in a recent compendium (Wulff *et al.*, 1989).

The general accounting framework will also allow analysis of different but connected geographical ecosystems. The matrix of use and make for the first ecosystem would be arranged in the manner stated above. The use matrix of the second, adjoining ecosystem would be appended to the use matrix of the first one, centered on the extended diagonal of the first. Any exchanges between the two ecosystems would be placed in the appropriate cell in the matrix to the right of or below the first matrix. The vectors of net and total output and of net input of the first matrix would be extended in length to accommodate those same vectors from the second system. The combined result could then be analyzed as though it were a single system matrix. For example, the above mentioned energy intensities would then reflect the combination of the two systems with possibly differing intensities for the same product from each system.

B. *Simulation Modeling*

Another possible use for the data in our accounting framework is as the basis for ecological simulation models. These models require that a dynamic mathematical function be used to link process inputs and outputs. The mathematical form of these "production functions" is an active area of research that would itself benefit from the existence of a consistent data format like the proposed accounting system.

Ecosystem simulation has been by far the most popular form of analysis of whole ecosystems. Thousands of ecosystem simulation models have been constructed over the years and we could not begin to summarize them here. Most of these modeling studies involved using either an explicit or an implicit, ad hoc accounting framework as a preliminary step. Our point is that the proposed framework will provide a consistent base from which to start, a minimum ideological baggage, and a minimum of unnecessary duplication of data collection. This step would facilitate ecosystem modeling of all kinds.

C. *Optimization*

Network analysis, simulation, and the related techniques help to portray the effects of the entire system upon individual processes and product flows. But the data required by energy budgets also can be used to gauge how the system as a whole is acting. In order to quantify such system tendencies some investigators have attempted to formulate objective functions that might portray some overall preferred state or goal. For example, H. T. Odum (1971) placed great stress on the maximization of useful output as a criterion for a population's survival (an idea which has much earlier been articulated by Lotka (1922)). Odum suggested that the Lotka maximum power principle also might be applicable to the ecosystem in aggregate. Hannon (1979) and Hannon *et al.* (1986) have posited that the scalar product of the energy intensities with the net outputs of each system is an appropriate objective function.

Ulanowicz (1980, 1986) defined the network "ascendency" as an appropriate objective function. It is calculated entirely from the exchanges transpiring among the system elements and with their environment. Ascendency is purported to rise monotonically as the system grows and develops.

Fontaine (1981), Loehle (1988), and Herendeen (1991) have attempted to compare the efficacies of the various objective functions as descriptors of system development, but to date, there is no agreement as to the best quantitative description of system development. The problem in comparing the various whole-system hypotheses has been a paucity of data on exchanges and storages in actual ecosystems. The potentially enormous advantages resulting from the discovery of a principle for ecosystem development should highlight the urgent need for more data collected under the accounting schema described above.

Amir (1987) also describes a dynamic optimization process for ecosystems in mathematical detail. He discusses the use of a biowealth function which is said to be maximized by the ecosystem resource allocation solution.

V. Summary and Conclusions

We have elaborated the need for and style of a general accounting system as an ecological research tool. When field ecologists investigate one portion of a large ecosystem, they usually design their own research strategy. In so doing, they may miss the opportunity to significantly augment the future work of other scientists by slight changes in their research strategy. They may also leave off some stock or flow measurement which was unimportant to their own needs. By reviewing their research proposal and checking it against the requirements of a general accounting system, these scientists are assuring themselves that their work will be in a form usable to others. In this way, their research is contributing to a network of understanding of the larger ecosystem. As the research progresses on the pieces of the larger system, the time approaches when they and other scientists will be able to synthesize the collective information into a model of the larger system function.

Acknowledgments

The authors thank Craig Loehle and G. A. Swanson for their useful comments.

References

Amir, S. 1979. Economic interpretations of equilibrium concepts in ecological systems, *J. Soc. Biol. Struct.* **2**, 293–314.

Amir, S. 1987. Energy pricing, biomass accumulation, and project appraisal, *in* "Environmental Economics: The Analysis of a Major Interface" (G. Pillet and T. Murota, Eds.), pp. 53–103, Leimbreger, Geneva.

Baird, D., and Ulanowicz, R. E. 1989. The seasonal dynamics of the Chesapeake Bay ecosystem, *Ecol. Monographs* **59**(4), 329–364.

Barber, M. 1978. A retrospective Markovian model for ecosystem resource flow, *Ecol. Model* **5**, 125–35.

Bullard, C., Sebald, A. 1977. Effects of parametric uncertainty and technological change on input–output models, *Rev. Econ. Stat.* **59**(1), 75–81.

Costanza, R. 1980. Embodied energy and economic valuation, *Science* **210**, 1219–1224.

Costanza, R., and Herendeen, R. A. 1984. Embodied energy and economic value in the United States economy: 1963, 1967, and 1972, *Resour. Energy* **6**, 129–164.

Costanza, R., and Neill, C. 1984. The energy embodied in the products of ecological systems: a linear programming approach, *J. Theor. Biol.* **106**, 41–57.

Costanza, R., Neill, C., Leibowitz, S. G., Fruci, J. R., Bahr, L. M., Jr., and Day, J. W., Jr. 1983. "Ecological Models of the Mississippi Deltaic Plain Region: Data Collection and Presentation." U. S. Fish and Wildlife Service, Division of Biological Services, Washington, DC FWS/OBS-82/68.

COSTANZA, R., AND HANNON, B. 1989. Dealing with the "mixed" units problem in ecosystem analysis, *in* "Flow Analysis of Marine Ecosystems" (F. Wulff, J. G. Field, and K. H. Mann, Eds.), Chap. 5, Ecological Studies Series, Springer-Verlag, Berlin/New York.

DALY, H. 1968. Economics as life science, *J. Polit. Econ.* **76**, 392–401.

FASHAM, M. J. R. 1984. "Flows of Energy and Materials in Marine Ecosystems," Plenum, New York.

FINN, J. 1976. Measure of ecosystem structure and function derived from the analysis of flows, *J. Theor. Biol.* **56**, 363–380.

FONTAINE, T. D. 1981. A self-designing model for testing hypotheses of ecosystem development, *in* "Progress in Ecological Engineering and Management by Mathematical Modelling" (S. E. Jorgensen, Ed.), pp. 281–291, Elsevier, Amsterdam.

FUNTOWITZ, S., AND RAVITZ, J. 1989. "Uncertainty and Quality in Science for Policy," Kluwer, Amsterdam.

HANNON, B. 1973. The structure of ecosystems, *J. Theor. Biol.* **41**, 535–546.

HANNON, B. 1979. Total energy costs in ecosystems, *J. Theor. Biol.* **80**, 271–93.

HANNON, B. 1986. Ecosystem control theory, *J. Theor. Biol.* **121**, 417–437.

HANNON, B. M., AND COSTANZA, R. 1985. Ecosystems with multiple products. *ISEM Journal* **7**, 27–49.

HANNON, B., COSTANZA, R., AND HERENDEEN, R. 1986. Measures of energy cost and value in ecosystems, *J. Environ. Econ. Management* **13**, 391–401.

HANNON, B., AND JOIRIS, C. 1989. A seasonal analysis of the Southern North sea ecosystem, *Ecology* **70**(6), 1916–1934.

HERENDEEN, R. 1991. Do economics-like principles predict ecosystem behavior under changing resource constraints? *in* "Theoretical Studies Ecosystems: The Network Perspective" (T. Burns and M. Higashi, Eds), pp. 261–287, Cambridge Univ. Press.

KOOPMANS, T. C. (Ed.) 1951. "Activity Analysis of Production and Allocation," Wiley, New York.

KUZNETS, S. 1946. Problems of interpretation of national accounts, *in* "National Income: A Summary of Findings," pp. 111–129, National Bureau of Economic Research, New York.

LEONTIEFF, W. 1941. "The Structure of the American Economy, 1919–1939," Oxford Univ. Press, New York.

LINDEMAN, R. L. 1942. The trophic–dynamic aspect of ecology, *Ecology* **23**, 399–418.

LOEHLE, C. 1988. Evolution: The missing ingredient in systems ecology, *Amer. Nat.* **132**, 884–899.

LOTKA, A. J. 1922. Contribution to the energetics of evolution, *Proc. Natl. Acad. Sci. U.S.A.* **8**, 147–155.

MACDONALD, N. 1983. "Trees and Networks in Biological Models," Wiley, Chichester.

MATIS, J. H., AND PATTEN, B. C. 1981. Environ analysis of linear compartmental systems: The static, time invariant case, *Bull. Int. Stat. Inst.* **48**, 527–565.

ODUM, E. P. 1953. "Fundamentals of Ecology," Saunders, Philadelphia.

ODUM, H. T. 1971. "Environment, Power, and Society," Wiley, New York.

ODUN, E. P., AND ODUM, H. T. 1959." Fundamentals of Ecology," 2nd ed., Saunders, Philadelphia.

ODUM, H. T., AND PINKERTON, R. C. 1955. Time's speed regulator: The optimum efficiency for maximum power output in physical and biological systems, *Amer. Sci.* **43**, 331–343.

PATTERN, B., BOSSERMAN, R., FINN, J. AND CALE, W. 1976. Propagation of cause in ecosystems, *in* "Systems Analysis and Simulation in Ecology," Vol. 4, pp. 457–479, Academic Press, New York.

ROUGHGARDEN, J., 1989, The U.S. needs an ecological survey, *Bioscience* **39**(1), 5.

SCHUBEL, J., *et al.*, in press, Report of the Chesapeake Bay Panel, Marine Environmental Monitoring Committee, National Research Council, Washington, DC.

STONE, R. 1963. Input–output relationships 1954–1966, *in* "A Programme for Growth," Vol. 3, pp. 11–22, MIT Press, Cambridge, MA.

ULANOWICZ, R. E. 1980. An hypothesis on the development of natural communities. *J. Theor. Biol.* **85**, 223–245.

ULANOWICZ, R. E. 1986. "Growth and Development: Ecosystems Phenomenology," Springer-Verlag, New York.

ULANOWICZ, R., AND KEMP, W. 1979. Toward canonical trophic aggregation, *Amer. Nat.* **114**, 871–883.

WULFF, F., FIELD, J. G., AND MANN, K. H. 1989, "Network Analysis in Marine Ecology," Ecological Studies Series, Springer-Verlag, Berlin/New York.

PART III

ECOLOGICAL AND ECONOMIC SYSTEMS MODELLING AND ANALYSIS

[16]

Ecological Modelling, 27 (1985) 45–68
Elsevier Science Publishers B.V., Amsterdam – Printed in The Netherlands

ARTICULATION, ACCURACY AND EFFECTIVENESS OF MATHEMATICAL MODELS: A REVIEW OF FRESHWATER WETLAND APPLICATIONS

ROBERT COSTANZA and FRED H. SKLAR

Coastal Ecology Laboratory, Center for Wetland Resources, Louisiana State University, Baton Rouge, LA 70803 (U.S.A.)

(Accepted 6 September 1984)

ABSTRACT

Costanza, R. and Sklar, F.H., 1985. Articulation, accuracy and effectiveness of mathematical models: a review of freshwater wetland applications. *Ecol. Modelling*, 27: 45–68.

Eighty-seven mathematical models of freshwater wetlands and shallow water bodies were classified by wetland type, location, and degree of nonlinearity, and rated by three new indices: articulation; accuracy; and effectiveness. Articulation measures the size and complexity of the model in the three modes of components, space, and time. Accuracy combines measures of goodness-of-fit in each mode. Effectiveness measures explanatory power as a combination of articulation and accuracy. For the models reviewed accuracy was seen to fall with increasing articulation, probably as a result of increasing complexity and cost. Effectiveness, however, rose to a maximum at intermediate articulation and then fell, reflecting the fact that highly accurate models tended to be low in articulation (they said much about little), while highly articulate models tended to be low in accuracy (they said little about much). These methods for ranking models may prove useful for further analysis and the results of this analysis may provide a useful guide to model builders concerned with maximizing the effectiveness of their models using limited resources.

INTRODUCTION

Mathematical models are essential tools for understanding and managing ecosystems. There are a large number of models in the international literature on freshwater wetlands alone, and the list for general ecosystems models is enormous.

Contribution ≠LSU-83-10.

0304-3800/85/$03.30

One of the most fundamental questions facing scientists is: how does one evaluate alternative explanations (models), given that an essentially infinite number of models are possible and no one model can ever achieve perfection? In this paper we (a) develop several methods for classifying models and several scales for ranking models; (b) apply them to mathematical models of freshwater wetlands; and (c) interpret the results.

The task can be thought of as a systematic literature review. To access, evaluate, and use modeling information, periodic literature reviews are necessary. An effective review must be more than a list, however. It must organize and summarize the information in a convenient and useful way. In this review we summarize the models by:

(1) wetland type;
(2) geographical area;
(3) degree of nonlinearity;
(4) a measure of model complexity we call the 'degree of articulation' in terms of components, space, and time;
(5) where possible, indices of 'descriptive accuracy' and 'effectiveness'.

The review is limited to models that use some kind of formal mathematical description, either explicit equations or system diagrams with implied equations. The review is also limited to freshwater wetlands and shallow bodies of water. Shallow is taken to mean a maximum depth of 3 m or less. Rivers and other flowing water systems are also excluded.

While this review is not exhaustive, even of this limited subset of ecosystems, it covers 87 published works that span the modeling spectrum. Our organizational scheme provides a compact and accessible guide to this literature, and a method for classifying the models in terms that are useful for further analysis. First we briefly discuss some theoretical and philisophical points.

Mathematical tools

The mathematical tools available for ecological modeling can be classified in several ways, but the most frequently used classification is into linear and nonlinear categories. This distinction is important since linear systems theory is a well-developed branch of mathematics, while there is no corresponding body of theory on nonlinear systems (cf. Patten, 1976).

With the development of inexpensive high speed computing, nonlinear systems began to receive more attention. Computer algorithms are the tools associated with nonlinear systems instead of the more traditional theorems and proofs associated with linear theory. For example, the diagrammatic languages developed by Odum (1971) and Forrester (1961) are tools for developing computer programs to simulate nonlinear differential equation systems on computers. Even with readily available computers, however, nonlinear systems of equations are usually more difficult to manipulate than linear systems, and the more nonlinear a system of equations is, the more troublesome and difficult it usually is. This extra 'cost' must be compensated for by some 'benefits' in terms of a better description of the system. For this reason we looked at the 'degree of nonlinearity' of the models (measured as the percentage of nonlinear terms in the model equations) as one index of their mathematical difficulty.

Modes of articulation

To 'articulate' in language is to 'divide into syllables or words meaningfully arranged'. The term articulation is a useful concept for the discussion of ecosystem models since models are simplifications or divisions of the continuum that is nature. The simplification or 'dividing into words' can be accomplished in three modes: components; space; and time. Ecosystem models can be classified according to their degree of articulation in these.

Dynamic models are those articulated in time: spatial models are articulated in space; and compartment models are articulated in the system components (state variables). Of course, models may be articulated in all three modes at once. The more articulated a model is, the more expensive it is to build and run. Since no practical model can be maximially articulated in all three modes simultaneously, there are trade-offs among the modes. The optimal solution is determined by the relative importance of articulation in each mode to specific questions the model is designed to address.

Descriptive accuracy

The terms descriptive and predictive recur in the modeling literature. In general, descriptive refers to models that describe an existing structure or known behavior of a system. Predictive refers to models that are used to extrapolate the structure or behavior of a system outside the existing data boundaries. Most mathematical models combine both functions, since prediction is usually accomplished by mathematically manipulating the descriptive model. Another way of thinking of the relationship is that descriptive models are the mathematical tools available to model builders for interpolation, while prediction requires extrapolation beyond the existing data.

One reason for the abundance and diversity of both descriptive and predictive models of ecosystems is that no single model can claim a high degree of accuracy over a broad range of ecosystem structure or behavior. This is to be expected, because ecosystems are complex phenomena. The range of ecosystem structure and behavior cannot be totally captured in a single, cost-effective model. It is more useful to maintain a family of descriptive models (mathematical tools) and the predictions based on them (model uses), since each model has its own areas of accuracy and applicability.

The degree of accuracy with which a particular model can describe the historical structure or behavior of an ecosystem is measurable in a number of ways (Jørgensen 1982). Statistical indices of 'goodness-of-fit' (like R-squared) are useful in this regard. Frequently, however, the data necessary to calculate these statistical indices are not available, and other less formal methods must be used.

Although predictive accuracy is the goal of most models, descriptive accuracy is all one can measure before the fact. Descriptive accuracy is usually taken as at least a necessary (though not a sufficient) condition for predictive accuracy. As such, it is a useful concept for classifying model performance.

METHODS

We supplemented our existing knowledge of the wetland modeling literature with a systematic computer literature search and use of previous SCOPE wetland modeling reviews (i.e. Mitsch et al., 1982). While we cannot claim to have found via this method every reference that exists on freshwater wetland models, we do think that we achieved a relatively thorough review. Using this review, we compiled a bibliography and additional data for each reference. Wetland type (Table I), geographical location, and degree of nonlinearity were cataloged for each model (see Table II). In addition, indices of articulation, descriptive accuracy, and effectiveness, as described below, were computed for those models with sufficient information.

TABLE I

Wetland types used in this study

Number	Wetland type [a]
(1)	Forested swamp
(2)	Bottomland hardwood forest
(3)	Emergent marsh
(4)	Floating marsh
(5)	Shallow ponds and lakes (3 m or less)
(6)	Bogs and fens
(7)	Tundra
(8)	Combinations of the above

[a] After Mitsch et al. (1982).

Articulation indices

To compare the degree of articulation of the models, we constructed indices for the three major modes of articulation: components, space, and time. The index for each mode, we thought, should have a 'diminishing return' form, to reflect the fact that initial articulation effort is more productive than later effort, and that infinite effort asymptotically approaches a maximum articulation. We calculated the index for both the model and the data in all cases, since it is possible to construct a very articulate model with very inarticulate (or even nonexistent) data.

We used the following equation for the articulation index since it is a popular and simple form that exhibits the desired diminishing return behavior (although other equation forms that also exhibit diminishing returns would probably work just as well):

$$A_i = \frac{N_i - 1}{k_i + (N_i - 1)} \times 100 \tag{1}$$

where A_i = articulation index for mode i; N_i = number of divisions in mode i; k_i = scaling factor for mode i.

The number of divisions in each mode are: the number of components or state variables for the component mode (N_c), the number of time steps for the time mode (N_t), and the number of spatial units (i.e., pixels) for the space mode (N_a). The scaling factor was chosen to reflect the relative degree of difficulty of increasing the number of divisions in the mode, and an idea of the maximum size of the most articulated existing models in each mode. The scaling factors chosen for components, time, and space, respectively, were:

$k_c = 50$

$k_t = 1000$

$k_s = 5000$

These parameter values indicate that adding a component (state variable) to a model is much more difficult than adding a time step, which is in turn more difficult than adding a pixel of spatial resolution. For example, a model with 50 state variables, 1000 time steps, and 5000 spatial units would have an articulation index of 50 for each mode, and 50 average. The same average articulation could be achieved by a model with 200 state variables, 2340 time steps, and 1 spatial unit.

The distinction between the articulation index of the model and data is critical. It is relatively easy to run a simulation model with 10 000 time steps (or infinite time steps on an analog computer) but it is very difficult to collect supportive data at this frequency. In many cases, the articulation of the data is the limiting factor.

Descriptive accuracy

An index of descriptive accuracy was calculated as the percentage of the total (historical) variation that was explainable by the model, averaged over all three modes and stated as a fraction between 0 and 1. The average value was used to standardize the index across all three modes of articulation and to estimate model accuracy as a percentage of the total maximum accuracy possible.

Our ability to calculate this index varies from study to study. In many cases the necessary information was not available. In most of the remaining cases, only a rough estimate of the descriptive accuracy of the model was possible. In only a few cases there was either enough information to precisely calculate the index or it has already been calculated and reported. We noted which of these three situations applied for each model.

Two situations arose frequently: (a) curves showing the model's behavior in time would be given, with the associated data points; or (b) the steady-state values for the model components would be given with average values for the real system. In the first case we estimated the descriptive accuracy of the model by using a small digitizer connected to a microcomputer to replicate the model and data time series. We then calculated the coefficient of determination (R^2) for each component and took the average; the error associated with this procedure was about 5–10% (based on the precision of the digitizer). In the second case we simply calculated the percent deviation between the model and the data as:

$$1 - \frac{|\text{model} - \text{data}|}{\text{data}} \qquad (2)$$

and took the average over the components or spatial units.

Neither of these procedures gives very precise estimates, and this must be remembered when interpreting the results.

Effectiveness

The best model is the one that explains the most. A model with a high descriptive accuracy does not explain much if its accuracy is limited in articulation, however. For example, a one component model may have high descriptive accuracy for that one component, but say nothing about the rest of the system. Similarly, a highly articulated model which does not fit the data explains little.

To rank the models we developed an index of effectiveness or explanatory power. This index was calculated as the coefficient of determination (if calculatable) for each mode multiplied by the minimum of the data or model articulation index for that mode, and then averaged over the three modes. The most effective model under this scheme is one that balances the costs of added articulation with the benefits of increased accuracy to do the best job of explaining all the modes of the system.

RESULTS

Our review turned up 87 models in 59 different studies that were (a) sufficiently documented and (b) within the limits of our review. There were several additional models that were tangential to the topic, too general to allow calculation of indices, redundant with models we had already reviewed, or lacked readily available documentation. The reviewed models are a representative, though not an exhaustive, sample.

Tables II–IV summarize the results of our review. Table II lists the reviewed models, sorted according to wetland type (as given in Table I), and lists the location, principal modeling unit, and the raw scores used for calculating the articulation indices and other parameters for each model. Many of the reviewed models had missing values for some of the data. These are indicated by a dash (–) in Table II and in subsequent tables.

Table II indicates that the majority of the modeling effort has been focused on shallow lakes (30 models), forested swamps (18 models), and emergent marshes (14 models). Floating marshes (5 models), tundra (4 models) and bogs and fens (2 models) are noticeably underrepresented. Except for some of the shallow lake models, the modeled systems are all in the United States.

The principal modeling component (PMC) is listed for those models that dealt with mainly one accounting unit that cycled through the internal modeling components. For example, there were 13 hydrologic models (PMC = water), 13 biomass models, 4 carbon models, 4 energy models, and 10 phosphorus models. There were several models that dealt in multiple units and these were labled PMC = general.

Table II lists the number of components or state variables in the model (MCA) and the data (DCA), the number of spatial units or pixels in the model (MSA) and the data (DSA), and the number of time intervals in the model (MTA) and the data (DTA) for each study. 'Analog' models or data are given a value of 99999. Different types of models have characteristic values for these variables, but these are more easily seen after the articulation indices based on them are calculated.

TABLE II

Reviewed models sorted by wetland type (see Table I), showing the date and location of the study and raw scores used to calculate indices

Author	Year	Region	State	Nation	PMC	MCA	DCA	MSA	DSA	MTA	DTA	PCNL	FIT	FIT-CALC	CFM	SFM	TFM
(1) *Forested swamp*																	
Brown	1978.1	Green Swamp	FL	U.S.A.	Water	4	2	1	1	22500	108	41.6	0.94	1	1	0	1
Brown	1978.2	Cypress dome	FL	U.S.A.	Biomass	10	5	1	1	1	24	15.8	0.00	0	0	0	0
Brown	1978.3	Floodplain	FL	U.S.A.	Biomass	9	4	1	1	1	24	15.8	0.00	0	0	0	0
Costanza	1975.1	Green Swamp	FL	U.S.A.	General	7	7	1	99999	1	1	26.0	0.00	0	0	0	0
Costanza et al.	1983.1	Deltaic Plain	LA	U.S.A.	General	110	110	1	273	1	1	0.0	0.00	0	0	0	0
Ewel and Deghi	1978.0	Gainesville	FL	U.S.A.	Phosphorus	15	15	1	2	10000	1	19.0	0.00	0	0	0	0
Florschutz	1978.0	Southwest	FL	U.S.A.	Phosphorus	4	4	1	1	99999	1	10.0	0.00	0	0	0	0
Littlejohn	1977.0	Naples Bay	FL	U.S.A.	Water	2	2	1	12	99999	–	0.0	0.00	0	0	0	0
Mitsch	1983.0	Cypress Dome	FL	U.S.A.	Biomass	8	7	1	4	9999	6	41.7	–	–	–	–	–
Nessel	1978.0	Waldo	FL	U.S.A.	Phosphorus	14	1	1	1	1	0	40.0	0.00	0	0	0	0
Ogawa	1977.0	Southern	IL	U.S.A.	General	15	15	1	1	1	1	50.0	0.00	0	0	0	0
Paschal et al.	1979.0	Dismal Swamp	NC	U.S.A.	Mice	11	11	1	100	26	4	50.0	0.16	1	1	0	1
Patten and Matis	1982.0	Okefenokee	GA	U.S.A.	Water	4	4	1	1	1	1	0.0	0.00	0	0	0	0
Rykiel	1977b.1	Okefenokee	GA	U.S.A.	Water	2	2	1	1	1	1	0.0	0.00	0	0	0	0
Rykiel	1977a.2	Okefenokee	GA	U.S.A.	Water	8	8	1	1	1	1	0.0	0.00	0	0	0	0
Sklar	1983.0	Barataria	LA	U.S.A.	Water	1	1	1	4	768	24	45.2	0.50	1	1	0	1
Wharton et al.	1976.0	General	G	U.S.A.	General	17	0	1	0	99999	0	75.0	0.00	0	0	0	0
Wiemhoff	1977.0	Southern	IL	U.S.A.	Water	2	2	1	1	104	1	0.0	0.00	0	0	0	0
(2) *Bottomland hardwood forest*																	
Botkin et al.	1972.0	Hubbard Brook	NH	U.S.A.	Trees	13	13	99999	99999	200	1	20	0.3	1	1	0	0
Costanza et al.	1983.2	Deltaic Plain	LA	U.S.A.	General	16	1	1	273	1	1	0	0.0	0	0	0	0
Kuenzler et al.	1980.1	Creeping Swamp	NC	U.S.A.	Carbon	7	7	1	1	1	1	0	–	–	–	–	–
Kuenzler et al.	1980.2	Creeping Swamp	NC	U.S.A.	Phosphorus	9	9	1	1	1	1	0	–	–	–	–	–
Odum and Brown	1975.0	Green Swamp	FL	U.S.A.	General	35	1	1	99999	1	1	80	0.0	0	0	0	0
Phipps	1979.1	White River	AR	U.S.A.	Trees	25	25	4356	4356	200	1	43	0.0	0	0	0	0
Phipps	1979.2	White River	AR	U.S.A.	Trees	25	25	4356	4356	200	1	43	0.0	0	0	0	0
Phipps	1979.3	White River	AR	U.S.A.	Trees	25	25	4356	4356	200	1	43	0.0	0	0	0	0
Phipps	1979.4	White River	AR	U.S.A.	Trees	25	25	4356	4356	200	1	43	0.0	0	0	0	0
(3) *Emergent marsh*																	
Bayley and Odum	1976.0	Everglades	FL	U.S.A.	General	4	2	1	1	99999	1	25	0.00	0	0	0	0
Burns and Taylor	1979.0	Kissimmee R.	FL	U.S.A.	Water	1	1	135	1	99999	1	0	0.00	0	0	0	0
Burns and Taylor	1979.1	Kissimmee R.	FL	U.S.A.	Phosphorus	7	7	1	1	99999	1	8	0.88	1	1	0	0
Cleveland et al.	1981.0	Southern	LA	U.S.A.	Area	4	4	1	273	100	3	43	0.00	0	0	0	0
Costanza	1975.0	Green Swamp	FL	U.S.A.	General	7	7	1	99999	1	1	26	0.00	0	0	0	0

Costanza et al.	1983.3	Deltaic Plain	LA	U.S.A.	General	70	70	1	273	1	1	0	0.00	0	0	0	0
Costanza et al.	1983.6	Deltaic Plain	LA	U.S.A.	General	15	1	1	263	1	1	0	0.00	0	0	0	0
Flebbe	1982.1	Okefenokee	GA	U.S.A.	Carbon	5	5	1	1	1	1	0	0.00	0	0	0	0
Flebbe	1982.2	Okefenokee	GA	U.S.A.	Carbon	5	5	1	1	1	1	0	0.00	0	0	0	0
Flebbe	1982.3	Okefenokee	GA	U.S.A.	Carbon	5	5	1	1	1	1	0	0.00	0	0	0	0
Gardner et al.	1980.0	Lake Wingra	WI	U.S.A.	Water	2	2	1	1	244	244	50	0.89	1	1	0	1
Huff and Young	1980.0	Madison	WI	U.S.A.	Water	1	1	1	1	240	240	0	0.86	1	0	0	1
Stone and McHugh	1979.0	Barataria	LA	U.S.A.	Water	3	3	3025	5	99999	120	0	0.69	1	1	0	0
White et al.	1978.0	Navarre	OH	U.S.A.	Tritium	1	1	31	6	2600	28	0	0.58	1	0	1	1
(4) *Floating marsh*																	
Mitsch	1976.0	Lake Alice	FL	U.S.A.	Water	1	1	1	1	269	269	0.0	–	–	–	–	–
Mitsch	1976.1	Lake Alice	FL	U.S.A.	General	21	15	1	3	99999	7	47.8	0.7	1	1	0	1
Sklar	1983.1	Barataria	LA	U.S.A.	Biomass	7	6	1	1	7200	24	45.2	0.4	1	1	0	1
Sklar	1983.2	Barataria	LA	U.S.A.	Biomass	7	6	1	1	1	24	45.2	0.0	0	0	0	0
Sklar	1983.3	Barataria	LA	U.S.A.	Biomass	7	6	1	1	1	24	45.2	0.0	0	0	0	0
(5) *Shallow lakes*																	
Browder	1978.0	Southwest	FL	U.S.A.	General	10	15	1	60	300	1	13.0	–	–	–	–	–
Costanza et al.	1983.4	Deltaic Plain	LA	U.S.A.	General	38	38	1	273	1	1	0.0	0.00	0	0	0	0
Costanza et al.	1983.5	Deltaic Plain	LA	U.S.A.	General	14	1	1	273	1	1	0.0	0.00	0	0	0	0
Halfon	1979.0	Heart Lake	ONT	Canada	Phosphorus	4	2	1	1	300	27	0.0	0.95	1	1	0	1
Huff et al.	1973.0	Lake Wingra	WI	U.S.A.	Biomass	8	8	1	1	1750	24	50.0	0.74	1	0	0	1
Jolánkai	1982.1	Lake Balaton		Hungary	TP	1	1	1	20	1	60	0.0	0.85	1	0	0	0
Jolánkai	1982.2	Lake Balaton		Hungary	TN	1	1	1	20	1	60	0.0	0.85	1	0	0	0
Jørgensen	1982.0	Copenhagen		Denmark	Eutrophic	17	17	1	0	3650	35	35.8	0.69	2	1	0	1
Loucks and Weiler	1979.0	Lake Wingra	WI	U.S.A.	Phosphorus	18	16	1	–	–	–	50.0	–	–	–	–	–
Loucks and Weiler	1979.0	Lake Wingra	WI	U.S.A.	Phosphorus	18	16	1	–	–	–	50.0	–	–	–	–	–
Mitsch	1975.0	Cypress Pono	FL	U.S.A.	Biomass	5	5	1	4	99999	6	40.0	–	–	–	–	–
Nyholm	1978.1	Lake Ollemp		Denmark	General	7	7	1	1	360	9	50.0	0.23	1	1	0	1
Ondok and Pokorny	1982.0	S. Bohemia		Czechoslovakia	Oxygen	4	3	1	1	384	80	14.3	0.88	2	1	0	1
Richey	1977.0	Mountains	CA	U.S.A.	Phosphorus	9	7	5	6	6	6	33.3	0.50	1	1	1	0
Svirezhev and Voinov	1982.0	General		U.S.S.R.	Eutrophic	4	0	1	0	99999	0	22.2	0.00	0	0	0	0
Uhlmann and Recknagel	1982.0	General		G.D.R.	Bod	1	1	1	12	1	40	0.0	0.90	1	1	0	0
Verhagen	1978.0	De Grote Rug		The Netherlands	Biomass	8	8	1	1	9999	6	0.0	–	–	–	–	–
Walters	1980.0	General			Biomass	11	0	1	0	540	0	25.0	0.00	0	0	0	0
Walters et al.	1980.1	Lake George		Uganda	General	28	28	1	1	36500	365	50.0	0.10	1	1	0	1
Walters et al.	1980.2	Lake Wingra	WI	U.S.A.	General	28	28	1	1	36500	365	50.0	0.38	1	1	0	1
Wiegert	1971.1	Yellowstone	MT	U.S.A.	Algae-fly	6	6	1	3	360	1	50.0	0.85	0	0	0	0
Wiegert	1971.2	Yellowstone	MT	U.S.A.	Algae-fly	6	6	1	3	360	1	50.0	0.68	2	1	0	0
Wiegert	1971.3	Yellowstone	MT	U.S.A.	Algae-fly	6	6	1	3	360	1	50.0	0.78	2	1	0	0
Wiegert	1971.4	Yellowstone	MT	U.S.A.	Algae-fly	4	6	1	3	360	1	50.0	0.19	2	1	0	0
Wiegert	1971.5	Yellowstone	MT	U.S.A.	Algae-fly	2	6	1	3	360	1	50.0	0.69	2	1	0	0

TABLE II (continued)

Author	Year	Region	State	Nation	PMC	MCA	DCA	MSA	DSA	MTA	DTA	PCNL	FIT	FIT-CALC	CFM	SFM	TFM
Wheeler et al.	1978.0	Central	IL	U.S.A.	Lead	6	6	1	1	48	1	0.0	0.82	2	1	0	0
Williams	1971.1	Cedar Bog Lake	MN	U.S.A.	Energy	3	11	1	1	99999	1	0.0	0.00	0	0	0	0
Williams	1971.2	Cedar Bog Lake	MN	U.S.A.	Energy	10	10	1	1	99999	1	0.0	0.00	0	0	0	0
Williams	1971.3	Cedar Bog Lake	MN	U.S.A.	Energy	10	10	1	1	99999	1	29.0	0.00	0	0	0	0
Williams	1971.4	Cedar Bog Lake	MN	U.S.A.	Energy	10	10	1	1	99999	1	29.0	0.00	0	0	0	0
(6) *Bogs and fens*																	
Bazilevich and Tishkov	1982.0	Novgorod		U.S.S.R.	General	28	28	1	1	1	1	50	–	–	–	–	–
Silvola and Hanski	1979.0			Finland	Peat	1	0	1	0	72	0	0	0	0	0	0	0
(7) *Tundra*																	
Dauffenbach et al.	1981.0	North Slope	AK	U.S.A.	General	51	0	1	0	–	0	50.0	0.00	0	0	0	0
Douce	1978.0	Barrow	AK	U.S.A.	Biomass	5	5	1	–	99999	–	6.9	0.00	0	0	0	0
Miller et al.	1976.0	Barrow	AK	U.S.A.	Phosphoru	9	4	1	1	292	100	50.0	0.84	1	1	0	1
Tiwari	1978.0	Barrow	AK	U.S.A.	Biomass	16	16	1	–	1440	–	50.0	–	–	–	–	–
(8) *Combinations*																	
Hopkinson and Day	1980.0	Barataria	LA	U.S.A.	Water	3	3	56	15	240	65	0	0.68	2	1	1	0
Kemp and Mitsch	1979.0	General		U.S.A.	Biomass	5	0	1	0	30	0	36	0.00	0	0	0	0
Larson et Golet	1982.1	Bristol County	MA	U.S.A.	Area	11	11	1	1	2	2	0	0.00	0	0	0	0
Larson and Golet	1982.2	South Kingston	RI	U.S.A.	Area	7	7	1	1	2	2	0	0.00	0	0	0	0
Wang	1978.0	General	GA	U.S.A.	Oxygen	1	1	1	1	1	1	0	0.99	2	1	0	0

PMC, Principal Modeling Component; MCA, number of model components; DCA, number of data components; MSA, number of model spatial units; DSA, number of data spatial units; MTA, = number of model time intervals; DTA, number of data time intervals; PCNL, percent nonlinearity of the model; FIT, coefficient of determination of the model.

FITCALC = 0 if FIT is not calculatable, 1 if FIT is estimated, 2 if FIT is estimated, and (–) if FIT is missing.

CFM, SFM, and TFM, component, space, and time fit modifiers, respectively; they equal 1 if FIT was calculated for that mode and 0 otherwise.

Numbers following decimal points under year refer to multiple models in the same publication.

Estimating the percent nonlinearity (PCNL) of the models was not always easy. We entered a value of 50% if we knew the models were nonlinear but could not disentangle them sufficiently to do a more precise estimate. The maximum PCNL was 80% for a general bottomland hardwood model by Odum and Brown (1975). Linear models are those with PCNL = 0. Almost 40% of the models we reviewed were linear.

As previously noted, calculation of the descriptive accuracy of the models (FIT in Table II) was complicated by poor reportage and missing data problems. The FITCALC modifier in Table II keeps track of whether the fit was not given or calculatable (0), estimated from given information (1), calculated from given information or reported directly (2), or calculatable but missing (–). Additional fit modifier variables are given that note if the fit was calculated for components (CFM = 1), space (SFM = 1), or time (TFM = 1). These additional modifiers were important for the calculation or effectiveness. For example, if FIT was only calculatable for components (CFM = 1, SFM = 0, and TFM = 0) then effectiveness would be the product of CFM, FIT, and the minimum of the data or model component articulation index (from Table III), divided by three (the number of modes). If FIT was calculable for all three modes (CFM = 1, SFM = 1, and TFM = 1), then effectiveness was the average of the products of FIT and the minimum of the data or model articulation index in each mode.

Table III lists the articulation indices calculated using equation 1 for each model, by mode for the model and the data, listed in order of decreasing average articulation. The average articulation index (AAI) is defined as the minimum of the average model or data articulation listed in Table III. Different types of models are recognizable from their model articulation indices. For example linear, static, input–output models — like Ogawa (1977) or Costanza et al. (1983) — have zero model space and time articulation, but generally high component articulation. Spatially articulated models are rare, with the forest models of Botkin et al. (1972) and Phipps (1979) being notable exceptions. Models that are highly articulated in time are fairly common, but matching time articulation in the data is rare. The models of Mitsch (1975), Gardner et al. (1980), Huff and Young (1980) and Walters et al. (1980), are notable exceptions to this rule. Inspection of the order of the models in Table III shows the possible trade-offs between modes to achieve a high overall articulation. The models of Botkin et al. (1972) and Phipps (1979) top this list by combining high component and space articulation. These models simulate the growth of individual trees in forest plots. Costanza et al. (1983) score high purely on component articulation, while Walters et al. (1980) combine component and time articulation.

Table IV is a summary of model characteristics including the degree of nonlinearity, average articulation index, descriptive accuracy index, and

TABLE III

Articulation indices for the freshwater wetland models reviewed in this study

Model reference		Articulation mode							
Author	Date	Component		Space		Time		Average	
		M	D	M	D	M	D	M	D
Botkin et al.	1972.0	19.3548	19.3548	95.2380	95.2380	16.5972	0.0000	43.7300	38.1976
Phipps	1979.1	32.4324	32.4324	46.5526	46.5526	16.5972	0.0000	31.8607	26.3284
Phipps	1979.2	32.4324	32.4324	46.5526	46.5526	16.5972	0.0000	31.8607	26.3284
Phipps	1979.3	32.4324	32.4324	46.5526	46.5526	16.5972	0.0000	31.8607	26.3284
Phipps	1979.4	32.4324	32.4324	46.5526	46.5526	16.5972	0.0000	31.8607	26.3284
Costanza et al.	1983.1	68.5535	68.5535	0.0000	5.1593	0.0000	0.0000	22.8512	24.5709
Walters et al.	1980.1	35.0649	35.0649	0.0000	0.0000	97.3333	26.6862	44.1327	20.5837
Walters et al.	1980.2	35.0649	35.0649	0.0000	0.0000	97.3333	26.6862	44.1327	20.5837
Costanza et al.	1983.3	57.9832	57.9832	0.0000	5.1593	0.0000	0.0000	19.3277	21.0475
Costanza et al.	1983.4	42.5287	42.5287	0.0000	5.1593	0.0000	0.0000	14.1762	15.8960
Odum and Brown	1975.0	40.4762	0.0000	0.0000	95.2380	0.0000	0.0000	13.4921	31.7460
Bazilevich and Tishkov	1982.0	35.0649	35.0649	0.0000	0.0000	0.0000	0.0000	11.6883	11.6883
Jørgensen	1982.0	24.2424	24.2424	0.0000	0.0000	78.4900	3.2882	34.2441	9.1769
Browder	1978.0	15.2542	21.8750	0.0000	1.1662	23.0177	0.0000	12.7573	7.6804
Mitsch	1976.1	28.5714	21.8750	0.0000	0.0400	99.0099	0.5964	42.5271	7.5038
Ewel and Deghi	1978.0	21.8750	21.8750	0.0000	0.0200	90.9083	0.0000	37.5944	7.2983
Ogawa	1977.0	21.8750	21.8750	0.0000	0.0000	0.0000	0.0000	7.2917	7.2917
Gardner et al.	1980.0	1.9608	1.9608	0.0000	0.0000	19.5495	19.5495	7.1701	7.1701
Mitsch	1976.0	0.0000	0.0000	0.0000	0.0000	21.2356	21.1356	7.0452	7.0452
Huff and Young	1980.0	0.0000	0.0000	0.0000	0.0000	19.2897	19.2897	6.4299	6.4299
Paschal et al.	1979.0	16.6667	16.6667	0.0000	1.9416	2.4390	0.2991	6.3686	6.3024
Larson and Golet	1982.1	16.6667	16.6667	0.0000	0.0000	0.099	0.099	5.5889	5.5889
Williams	1971.1	3.8462	16.6667	0.0000	0.0000	99.0099	0.0000	34.2853	5.5556
Williams	1971.2	15.2542	15.2542	0.0000	0.0000	99.0099	0.0000	38.0880	5.0847
Williams	1971.3	15.2542	15.2542	0.0000	0.0000	99.0089	0.0000	38.0880	5.0847
Williams	1971.4	15.2542	15.2542	0.0000	0.0000	99.0099	0.0000	38.0880	5.0847

Miller et al.	1976.0	13.7931	5.6604	0.0000	0.0000	22.5407	9.0082	12.1113	4.8895
Stone and McHugh	1979.0	3.8462	3.8462	37.6869	0.0799	99.0099	10.6345	46.8477	4.8535
Huff et al.	1973.0	12.2807	12.2807	0.0000	0.0000	63.6231	2.2483	25.3013	4.8430
Kuenzler et al.	1980.2	13.7931	13.7931	0.0000	0.0000	0.0000	0.0000	4.5977	4.5977
Verhagen	1978.0	12.2807	12.2807	0.0000	0.0000	90.9074	0.4975	34.3960	4.2594
Rykiel	1977a.2	12.2807	12.2807	0.0000	0.0000	0.0000	0.0000	4.0936	4.0936
Brown	1978.1	5.6604	1.9608	0.0000	0.0000	95.7445	9.6658	33.8016	3.8755
Nyholm	1978.1	10.7143	10.7143	0.0000	0.0000	26.4165	0.7937	12.3769	3.8360
Sklar	1983.1	10.7143	9.0909	0.0000	0.0000	87.8034	2.2483	32.8392	3.7797
Richey	1977.0	13.7931	10.7143	0.0799	0.0999	0.4975	0.4975	4.7902	3.7706
Mitsch	1983.0	12.2807	10.7143	0.0000	0.0600	90.9074	0.4975	34.3960	3.7573
Ondok and Pokorny	1982.0	5.6604	3.8462	0.0000	0.0000	27.6934	7.3216	11.1179	3.7226
Cleveland et al.	1981.0	5.6604	5.6604	0.0000	5.1593	9.0082	0.1996	4.8895	3.6731
Larson and Golet	1982.2	10.7143	10.7143	0.0000	0.0000	0.0999	0.0999	3.6047	3.6047
Burns and Taylor	1979.1	10.7143	10.7143	0.0000	0.0000	99.0099	0.0000	36.5747	3.5714
Costanza	1975.0	10.7143	10.7143	0.0000	95.2380	0.0000	0.0000	3.5714	35.3174
Costanza	1975.1	10.7143	10.7143	0.0000	95.2380	0.0000	0.0000	3.5714	35.3174
Kuenzler et al.	1980.1	10.7143	10.7143	0.0000	0.0000	0.0000	0.0000	3.5714	3.5714
Sklar	1983.2	10.7143	9.0909	0.0000	0.0000	0.0000	2.2483	3.5714	3.7797
Sklar	1983.3	10.7143	9.0909	0.0000	0.0000	0.0000	2.2483	3.5714	3.7797
Hopkinson and Day	1980.0	3.8462	3.8462	1.0880	0.2792	19.2897	6.0150	8.0746	3.3801
Brown	1978.2	15.2542	7.4074	0.0000	0.0000	0.0000	2.2483	5.0847	3.2186
Wiegert	1971.1	9.0909	9.0909	0.0000	0.0400	26.4165	0.0000	11.8358	3.0436
Wiegert	1971.2	9.0909	9.0909	0.0000	0.0400	26.4165	0.0000	11.8358	3.0436
Wiegert	1971.3	9.0909	9.0909	0.0000	0.0400	26.4165	0.0000	11.8358	3.0436
Wiegert	1971.4	5.6604	9.0909	0.0000	0.0400	26.4165	0.0000	10.6923	3.0436
Wiegert	1971.5	1.9608	9.0909	0.0000	0.0400	26.4165	0.0000	9.4591	3.0436
Wheeler et al.	1978.0	9.0909	9.0909	0.0000	0.0000	4.4890	0.0000	4.5266	3.0303
Mitsch	1975.0	7.4074	7.4074	0.0000	0.0600	99.0099	0.4975	35.4724	2.6550
Brown	1978.3	13.7931	5.6604	0.0000	0.0000	0.0000	2.2483	4.5977	2.6362
Flebbe	1982.1	7.4074	7.4074	0.00000	0.00000	0.0000	0.00000	2.4691	2.46914

TABLE III (continued)

Articulation indices for the freshwater wetland models reviewed in this study

Model reference		Articulation mode							
Author	Date	Component		Space		Time		Average	
		M	D	M	D	M	D	M	D
Flebbe	1982.2	7.4074	7.4074	0.00000	0.00000	0.0000	0.00000	2.4691	2.46914
Flebbe	1982.3	7.4074	7.4074	0.00000	0.00000	0.0000	0.00000	2.4691	2.46914
Florschutz	1978.0	5.6604	5.6604	0.00000	0.00000	99.0099	0.00000	34.8901	1.88679
Patten and Matis	1982.0	5.6604	5.6604	0.00000	0.00000	0.0000	0.00000	1.8868	1.88679
Costanza et al.	1983.2	23.0769	0.0000	0.00000	5.15933	0.0000	0.00000	7.6923	1.71978
Costanza et al.	1983.5	10.6349	0.0000	0.00000	5.15933	0.0000	0.00000	6.8783	1.71978
Costanza et al.	1983.6	21.8750	0.0000	0.00000	4.97910	0.0000	0.00000	7.2917	1.65970
Halfon	1979.0	5.6604	1.9608	0.00000	0.00000	23.0177	2.53411	9.5594	1.49830
White et al.	1978.0	0.0000	0.0000	0.59642	0.0990	78.2561	2.62902	26.2842	0.90964
Sklar	1983.0	0.0000	0.0000	0.00000	0.05996	43.4069	2.24829	14.4690	0.76942
Bayley and Odum	1976.0	5.6604	1.9608	0.00000	0.00000	99.0099	0.00000	34.8901	0.65359
Rykiel	1977b.1	1.9608	1.9608	0.00000	0.00000	0.0000	0.00000	0.6536	0.65359

Wiemhoff	1977.0	1.9608	1.9608	0.00000	0.00000	9.3382	0.00000	3.7663	0.65359
Burns and Taylor	1979.0	0.0000	0.0000	2.61005	0.00000	99.0099	0.00000	33.8733	0.00000
Dauffenbach et al.	1981.0	50.0000	0.0000	0.00000	0.00000	–	0.00000	–	0.00000
Douce	1978.0	7.4074	7.4074	0.00000	–	99.0099	–	35.4724	–
Jolânkai	1982.1	0.0000	0.0000	0.00000	0.37856	0.0000	5.57129	0.0000	1.98329
Jolánkai	1982.2	0.0000	0.0000	0.00000	0.37856	0.0000	5.57129	0.0000	1.98329
Kemp and Mitsch	1979.0	7.4074	0.0000	0.00000	0.00000	2.8183	0.00000	3.4086	0.00000
Littlejohn	1977.0	1.9608	1.9608	0.00000	0.21952	99.0099	–	33.6569	–
Loucks and Weiler	1979.0	25.3731	23.0769	0.00000	–	–	–	–	–
Loucks and Weiler	1979.0	25.3731	23.0769	0.00000	–	–	–	–	–
Nessel	1978.0	20.6349	0.0000	0.00000	0.00000	0.0000	0.00000	6.8783	0.00000
Silvola and Hanski	1979.0	0.0000	0.0000	0.00000	0.00000	6.6293	0.00000	2.2098	0.00000
Svirezhev and Voinov	1982.0	5.6604	0.0000	0.00000	0.00000	99.0099	0.00000	34.8901	0.00000
Tiwari et al.	1978.0	23.0769	23.0769	0.00000	–	58.9996	–	27.3588	–
Uhlmann and Recknagel	1982.0	0.0000	0.0000	0.00000	0.21952	0.0000	3.75361	0.0000	1.32438
Walters	1980.0	16.6667	0.0000	0.00000	0.00000	35.0227	0.00000	17.2298	0.000000

The indices for both the models (M) and the data (D) are given for each mode, along with the average over the three modes. The models are listed in decending order starting with the largest average articulation (the minimum of the model and the data).

TABLE IV

Summary of model characteristics

Model reference		PCNL	Articulation	Descriptive accuracy	Effectiveness
Author	Date				
Walters et al.	1980.2	50.0	20.5837	0.253333	7.82181
Gardner et al.	1980.0	50.0	7.1701	0.593333	6.38138
Jørgensen	1982.0	35.8	9.1769	0.460000	6.33204
Huff and Young	1980.0	0.0	6.4299	0.286667	5.52973
Mitsch	1976.1	47.8	7.5038	0.466667	5.24333
Miller et al.	1976.0	50.0	4.8895	0.560000	4.10720
Brown	1978.1	41.6	3.8755	0.626667	3.64298
Ondok and Pokorny	1982.0	14.3	3.7226	0.586667	3.27587
Burns and Taylor	1979.1	8.0	3.5714	0.293333	3.14286
Wheeler et al.	1978.0	0.0	3.0303	0.273333	2.48485
Wiegert	1971.3	50.0	3.0436	0.260000	2.36364
Wiegert	1971.2	50.0	3.0436	0.226667	2.06061
Walters et al.	1980.1	50.0	20.5837	0.066667	2.05837
Botkin et al.	1972.0	20.0	38.1976	0.100000	1.93548
Richey	1977.0	33.3	3.7706	0.333333	1.79904
Sklar	1983.1	45.2	3.7797	0.266667	1.51189
Halfon	1979.0	0.0	1.4983	0.633333	1.42338
Hopkinson and Day	1980.0	0.0	3.3801	0.453333	0.93508
Paschal et al.	1979.0	50.0	6.3024	0.106667	0.90484
Stone and McHugh	1979.0	0.0	4.8535	0.230000	0.88462
Nyholm	1978.1	50.0	3.8360	0.153333	0.88228
Huff et al.	1973.0	50.0	4.8430	0.246667	0.55458
White et al.	1978.0	0.0	0.9096	0.386667	0.52759
Wiegert	1971.5	50.0	3.0436	0.230000	0.45098
Sklar	1983.0	45.2	0.7694	0.333333	0.37471
Wiegert	1971.4	50.0	3.0436	0.063333	0.35849

effectiveness index. Table IV indicates where the most effective modeling efforts for freshwater wetlands have been, both in terms of model types and the level of articulation of the models, since the models are listed in order of decreasing effectiveness. Only 26 of the 87 models we reviewed were complete enough to calculate accuracy and effectiveness, and only these models are listed in Table IV. Among these, it is interesting to note that the highest effectiveness scores were not for the models with the highest articulation or the highest accuracy, nor were they exclusively linear or nonlinear. The most effective models were those that achieved a balance between articulation and accuracy. Note also that the effectiveness index shown in Table IV is not simply the product of average articulation and descriptive accuracy indices shown in Table IV. It is rather the average of the products of FIT and the minimum of model or data articulation for the three modes as described above. Had we used the product of the averages instead, the results would not have been substantially different, however, although the order of some of the models would have changed.

DISCUSSION

Science can be viewed as the process of building successively 'better' descriptive and predictive models of the world. But how does one define 'better'? In the past, scientists have tended to narrow their questions in order to achieve higher accuracy. This leads to models with low articulation but high descriptive accuracy. They say much about little. More recently, scientists have begun to take a 'systems view' that looks at phenomena more comprehensively. This strategy leads to highly articulated models with low accuracy. These models say little about much.

The real effectiveness or explanatory power of a model is a function of *both* how much it attempts to explain (articulation) and how well it explains what was attempted (descriptive accuracy). The overall effectiveness index captures both of these attributes.

The 26 models for which we could calculate accuracy and effectiveness exhibit some interesting patterns in the relationship between articulation and

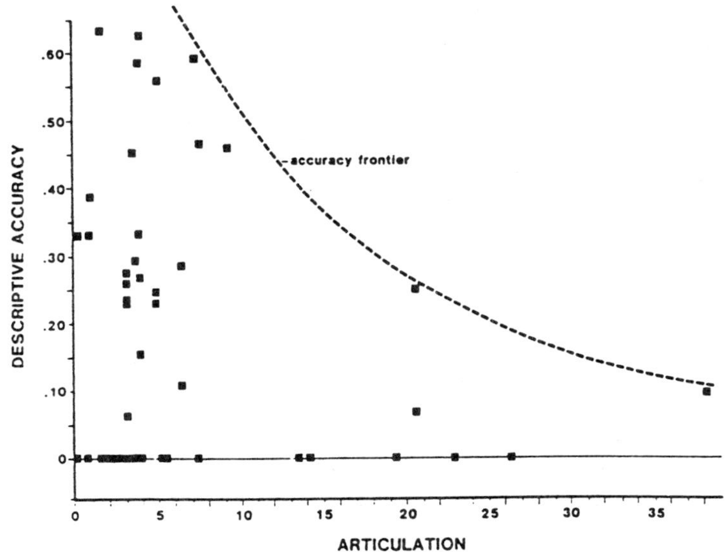

Fig. 1. Plot of articulation index vs. descriptive accuracy index for the models reviewed in this study, showing the current accuracy frontier.

these variables. Figure 1 is a plot of average articulation on the x axis vs. average descriptive accuracy on the y axis. It shows that the maximum accuracy tends to decrease with increasing articulation. This relationship is analogous to the relationship between thermodynamic efficiency and the rate of energy transformation processes (Odum and Pinkerton, 1955; Gutkowicz-Krusin et al., 1978). Efficiency is analogous to accuracy in that both are performance ratios. The thermodynamic efficiency is maximal when the rate of the energy transformation is zero (the reversible or Carnot limit) and decreases as the rate increases. Articulation is analogous to the reaction rate, and accuracy may decrease as articulation increases for reasons analogous to those that cause efficiency to decrease with reaction rate. As the thermodynamic rate increases, entropy and disorder increase and efficiency drops. Likewise, as articulation increases there are more sources of error introduced and maximum accuracy is lowered. It is important to note that the points plotted in Fig. 1 do not all fall on a particular line, but rather below an upper bound line that can be thought of as an 'accuracy frontier'. Many of the models are below the accuracy frontier (the upper bound) for their degree of articulation because they have not been 'completed' sufficiently. It may be possible to push the frontier farther out with additional effort (and cost), but we hypothesize that there is a fundamental limit to this process, such that additional articulation can only be achieved at some cost in accuracy.

Figure 2 is a plot of the articulation index on the x axis vs. model effectiveness on the y axis. The shape of this plot is determined by the shape of the accuracy vs. articulation plot and the definition of effectiveness. The upper bound line of maximum achieved effectiveness (the effectiveness frontier) in Fig. 2 is low for low articulation/high accuracy models (those that say much about little), increases to a maximum for articulation values around 25, and decreases again for high articulation/low accuracy models (those that say little about much). This implies that there is an optimum articulation for maximum model effectiveness at a point substantially below the maximum articulation.

It is important to note that this interpretation depends in large part on the scores for the one model we reviewed with high articulation (Botkin et al., 1972). It therefore cannot be stated with much force until additional data are collected. In informal conversations with ecosystem modelers on this point, however, several unpublished, high articulation models that tend to fit the pattern were mentioned. At this point it should best be considered a hypothesis with a small amount of supporting data.

If it proves accurate, the implications of Fig. 2 for model builders are obvious. There is an optimum size or complexity or articulation as we have called it beyond which the 'benefits' of additional articulation are out-

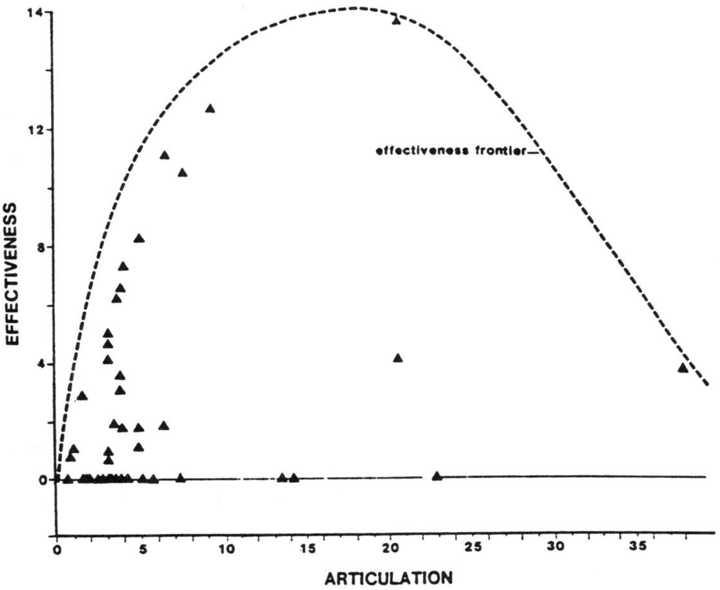

Fig. 2. Plot of articulation index vs. effectiveness index showing the current effectiveness frontier.

weighted by the 'costs' of lowered accuracy. If additional studies are supportive, it could be very useful for model builders and consumers of model output. All types of models are expensive, and ecosystem models are among the most expensive. The question of how complex or articulate to make a model is of primary concern in any modeling study. A reliable guide to solving this problem would help to wisely use the limited resources that can be devoted to ecosystem modeling.

In a more general sense, this result speaks to a fundamental question in science concerning how one should rank alternative explanations. In the past both maximum accuracy and maximum articulation (under different names) have been used as ranking criteria, without much discussion of their potential limits or possible trade-offs. For example, the model of science advocated by Popper (1959, 1972) assumes that anything less than 100% accuracy 'falsifies' a model, and that science achieves 'truth' by successively identifying and discarding 'false' models. We believe the situation is not nearly so black-and-white in most cases, as our modeling review has demonstrated. We must speak of *degrees* of accuracy and articulation and the trade-offs between them, rather than in the absolute terms of truth and falsehood when evaluating complex models. We hope that this paper stimulates more discussion on these trade-offs, and we propose 'model effectiveness' as one way to begin quantifying them and ranking models in a more realistic way.

64

ACKNOWLEDGEMENTS

This work was supported in part by grants from the National Sea Grant College Program and the Center for Energy Studies at Louisiana State University. The Center for Wetland Resources provided additional support during preparation. P. Bianchi provided large and invaluable contributions. J. Bartholomew, C. Cleveland, E. Coleman, and two anonymous reviewers provided useful comments on earlier drafts.

REFERENCES

Bayley, S., and Odum, H.T., 1976. Simulation of interrelations of the Everglades' marsh, peat, fire, water and phosphorus. Ecol. Modelling, 2(3): 169–188.

Bazilevich, N.I. and Tishkov, A.A., 1982. A conceptual-balance model of chemical element cycles in a mesotrophic bog ecosystem. In: D.O. Logofet and N.K. Luckyanov (Editors), Ecosystem Dynamics in Freshwater Wetlands and Shallow Water Bodies, Vol. 2. UNEP/SCOPE, U.S.S.R. Academy of Sciences, Moscow, pp. 236–272.

Botkin, D.B., Janak, J.F. and Wallis, J.R., 1972. Some ecological consequences of a computer model of forest growth. J. Ecol., 60: 849–872.

Browder, J.A., 1978. A modeling study of water, wetlands, and wood storks. Wading Bird Res. Rep. 7, National Audubon Society, New York, NY, 21 pp.

Brown, S.L., 1978. A comparison of cypress ecosystems in the landscape of Florida. Ph.D. Diss., University of Florida, Gainesville, FL, 569 pp.

Burns, L.A. and Taylor, R.B., 1979 Nutrient-uptake model in marsh ecosystems. Proc. Am. Soc. Civ. Eng. J. Tech. Counc., 105: 177–196.

Cleveland, C.J., Neill, C. and Day, J.W., Jr., 1981. The impact of artificial canals on land loss in the Barataria Basin, Louisiana. In: W.J. Mitsch, R.W. Bosserman and J.M. Klopatek (Editors), Energy and Ecological Modelling. Developments in Environmental Modelling, 1. Elsevier, Amsterdam/New York/Oxford, pp. 425–434.

Costanza, R., 1975. An analysis of the energy and material budgets of some major subsystem groupings of the Green Swamp and the Green Swamp as a whole. In: M.T. Brown et al. (Editors), Natural Systems and Carrying Capacity of the Green Swamp. Report to Florida Department of Administration, Division of State Planning, Contract #M74-30317. Center for Wetlands, University of Florida, Gainesville, FL, pp. 39–99.

Costanza, R., Neill, C., Leibowitz, S.G., Fruci, J.R., Bahr, L.M., Jr. and Day, J.W., Jr., 1983. Ecological models of the Mississippi Deltaic Plain Region: data collection and presentation. FWS/OBS-82/68, U.S. Fish and Wildlife Service, Division of Biological Services, Washington, DC, 342 pp.

Daeffenbach, L., Atlas, R.M. and Mitsch, W.J., 1981. A computer simulation model of the fate of crude petroleum spills in Artic tundra ecosystems. In: W.J. Mitsch, R.W. Bosserman and J.M. Klopatek (Editors), Energy and Ecological Modelling. Developments in Ecological Modelling, 1. Amsterdam. Elsevier, Amsterdam/Oxford/New York, pp. 145–155.

Douce, G.K. and Webb, D.P., 1978. Indirect effects of soil invertebrates on litter decomposition: elaboration via analysis of a tundra model. Ecol. Modelling, 4: 339–359.

Ewel, K.C. and Deghi, G., 1978. Effect sewage effluent application on phosphorus cycling in cypress domes. In: H.T. Odum and K.C. Ewel (Editors), Cypress Wetlands for Water

Management, Recycling and Conservation. Fourth Annual Report to NSF and Rockefeller Foundation. Center for Wetlands, University of Florida, Gainesville, FL, pp. 104–155.

Flebbe, P.A., 1982. Biogeochemistry of carbon, nitrogen, and phosphorus in the aquatic subsystem of selected Okefenokee Swamp sites. Ph.D. Diss., University of Georgia, Athens, GA, 348 pp.

Florschutz, E., 1978. Dwarf cypress in the big cypress swamp of southeastern Florida. In: H.T. Odum and K.C. Ewel (Editors), Cypress Wetlands for Water Management, Recycling, and Conservation. Fourth Annual Report to NSF and Rockefeller Foundation. Center for Wetlands, University of Florida, Gainesville, FL, pp. 862–909.

Forrester, J.W., 1961. Industrial Dynamics. MIT Press, Cambridge, MA, 464 pp.

Gardner, R.H., Huff, D.D., O'Neill, R.V., Mankin, J.B., Carney, J. and Jones, J., 1980. Application of error analysis to a marsh hydrology model. Water Resour. Res., 16: 659–664.

Gutkowicz-Krusin, D., Procaccia, I. and Ross, J., 1978. On the efficiency of rate processes: power and efficiency of heat engines. J. Chem. Phys., 69: 3898–3906.

Halfon, E., Unbehauen, H. and Schmid, C., 1979. Model order estimation and system identification theory and application to the modelling of ^{32}P kinetics within the trophogenic zone of a small lake. Ecol. Modelling, 6: 1–22.

Hopkinson, C.S., Jr. and Day, J.W., Jr., 1980. Modelling hydrology and eutrophication in a Louisiana swamp forest ecosystem. Environ. Manage., 4: 325–335.

Huff, D.D. and Young, H.L., 1980. The effect of a marsh on runoff. I. A water-budget model. J. Environ. Qual., 9: 633–640.

Huff, D.D., Koonce, J.F., Ivarson, W.R., Weiler, P.R., Dettmann, E.H. and Harris, R.F., 1973. Simulation of urban run off, nutrient loading, and biotic response of a shallow eutrophic lake. In: E.J. Middlebrooks, D.H. Falkenberg and T.E. Maloney (Editors), Modeling the Eutrophication Process. Ann Arbor Science, Ann Arbor, MI, pp. 33–55.

Jolánkai, G., 1982. Non-point source input modelling experiences on the catchment area of the lake Balaton, Hungary. In: D.O. Logofet and N.K. Luckyanov (Editors), Ecosystem Dynamics in Freshwater Wetlands and Shallow Water Bodies, Vol. 2. UNEP/SCOPE, U.S.S.R. Academy of Sciences, Moscow, pp. 273–296.

Jørgensen, S.E., 1982. Modelling the eutrophication of shallow lakes. In: D.O. Logofet and N.K. Luckyanov (Editors), Ecosystem Dynamics in Freshwater Wetlands and Shallow Water Bodies, Vol. 2. UNEP/SCOPE, U.S.S.R. Academy of Sciences, Moscow, pp. 125–155.

Kemp, W.M. and Mitsch, W.J., 1979. Turbulence and phytoplankton diversity: a general model of the 'paradox of plankton'. Ecol. Modelling, 7: 201–222.

Kuenzler, E.J., Molholland, P.J., Yarbro, L.A. and Smock, L.A., 1980. Distributions and budgets of carbon, phosphorus, iron, and manganese in a floodplain swamp ecosystem. Water Resour. Res. Rep. 157, Water Resources Research Institute, University of North Carolina, Chapel Hill, NC, 234 pp.

Larson, J.S. and Golet, F.C., 1982. Models of freshwater wetland change in southeastern New England. In: B. Goap, R.E. Turner, R.G. Wetzel and D.F. Whigham (Editors), Wetlands: Ecology and Management. National Institute of Ecology/International Scientific Publications, New Dehli, pp. 181–155.

Littlejohn, C.B., 1977. An analysis of the role of natural wetlands in regional water management. In: C.A.S. Hall and J.W. Day, Jr. (Editors), Ecosystem Modeling in Theory and Practice. Wiley, New York, N.Y., pp. 451–476.

Loucks, O.L. and Weiler, P.R., 1979. The effects of harvest removal of phosphorus on remineralized P sources in a shallow lake. In: J.E. Breck, R.T. Prentki and O.L. Loucks

(Editors), Aquatic Plants Lake Mangement and Ecosystem Consequences of Lake Harvesting. Proc. Conf., 14–16 February 1979, Madison, WI, pp. 191–207.

Miller, P.C., Stoner, W.A. and Tieszen, L.L., 1976. A model of stand photosynthesis for the wet meadow tundra at Barrow Alaska. Ecology, 57: 411–430.

Mitsch, W.J., 1975. Systems analysis of nutrient disposal in cypress wetlands and lake ecosystem in Florida. Diss., University of Florida, Gainsville, FL, 421 pp.

Mitsch, W.J., 1976. Ecosystem modeling of waterhyacinth management in Lake Alice, Florida. Ecol. Modelling, 2: 69–89.

Mitsch, W.J., 1983. Ecological models for management of freshwater wetlands. In: S.E. Jørgensen and W.J. Mitsch (Editors), Application of Ecological Modeling in Environmental Management, Part B. Developments in Environmental Modelling, 4B. Elsevier, Amsterdam/Oxford/New York, pp. 283–310.

Mitsch, W.J., Day, J.W. Jr., Taylor, J.R. and Madden, C.H., 1982. Models of North American freshwater wetlands. Int. J. Ecol. Environ. Sci., 8: 109–140.

Nessel, J.K., 1978. Phosphorus cycling, productivity, and community structure in the Waldo cypress strand. In: H.T. Odum and K.C. Ewel (Editors), Cypress Wetlands for Water Management, Recycling, and Conservation. Fourth Annual Report to NSF and Rockefeller Foundation. Center for Wetlands, University of Florida, Gainesville, FL, pp. 750–801.

Nyholm, N., 1978. A simulation model for phytoplankton growth and nutrient cycling in eutrophic, shallow lakes. Ecol. Modelling, 4: 279–310.

Odum, H.T., 1971. Environment, Power, and Society. Wiley Interscience, New York, NY, 317 pp.

Odum, H.T. and Brown, M.T., 1975. Southern mixed hardwood floodplain swamp. In: M.T. Brown et al. (Editors), Natural Systems and Carrying Capacity of the Green Swamp. Report to Florida Department of Administration, Division of State Planning Contract #M74-30317. Center for Wetlands, University of Florida, Gainesville, FL, pp. 296–299.

Odum, H.T. and Pinkerton, R.C., 1955. Time's speed regulator: the optimum efficiency for maximum power output in physical and biological systems. Am. Sci., 43: 331–343.

Ogawa, H., 1977. Modelling of the Heron Pond ecosystem. In: W.J. Mitsch, C.L. Dorge and J.R. Wiemhoff (Editors), Forested Wetlands for water resource Management in Southern Illinois. Res. Rep. 132, Water Resources Center, University of Illinois, Urbana, IL, 275 pp.

Ondok, J.P. and Pokorny, J., 1982. Models of the O_2 and CO_2 regimes in shallow ponds. In: D.O. Logofet and N.K. Luckyanov (Editors). Ecosystem Dynamics in Freshwater Wetlands and Shallow Water Bodies, Vol. 2. UNEP/SCOPE, U.S.S.R. Academy of Sciences, Moscow, pp. 174–189.

Paschal, J.E., Soneshine, D.E. and Richardson, J.H., 1979. A simulation model of a peromyscus leucopus population in an area of the great dismal swamp. In: P.W. Kirk, Jr. (Editors), The great dismal swamp. University Press of Virginia, VA, pp. 277–296.

Patten, B.C. (Editor), 1976. Systems Analysis and Simulation in Ecology, Vol. III. Academic Press, New York, NY, 601 pp.

Patten, B.C. and Matis, J.H., 1982. The water environs of Okefenokee swamp: an application of static linear environ analysis. Ecol. Modelling, 16: 1–50.

Phipps, R.L., 1979. Simulation of wetlands forest vegetation dynamics. Ecol. Modelling, 7: 257–288.

Popper, K.R., 1959. The Logic of Scientific Discovery. Basic Books, New York, NY, 479 pp.

Popper, K.R., 1972. Objective Knowledge: An Evolutionary Approach. Clarendon, Oxford, 380 pp.

Richey, J.E., 1977. An empirical and mathematical approach toward the development of a

phosphorus model of Castle Lake. In: C.S. Hall and J.W. Day, Jr. (Editors), Ecosystem Modeling in Theory and Practice. Wiley, Sons, New York, NY, pp. 267–288.
Rykiel, E.J., Jr., 1977a. Toward simulation and systems analysis of nutrient cycling in the Okefenokee Swamp, Georgia. Tech. Complet. Rep. USDI/OWRT Project A-060-GA. University of Georgia, Athena, GA, 139 pp.
Rykiel, E.J., Jr., 1977b. The Okefenokee swamp watershed: water balance and nutrient budgets. Ph.D. Diss., University of Georgia, Athena, GA, 170 pp.
Silvolva, J. and Hanski, I., 1979. Carbon accumulation in a raised bog: simulation on the basis of laboratory measurements of CO_2 exchange. Oecologia, 37: 273–283.
Sklar, F.H., 1983. Water budget, benthological characterization, and simulation of aquatic material flows in a Louisiana freshwater swamp. Ph.D. Diss., Louisiana State University, Baton Rouge, LA, 280 pp.
Stone, J.H. and McHugh, G.F., 1979. Hydrologic effects of canals in coastal Louisiana via computer simulations. In: Proc. 1979 Summer Computer Simulation Conference. AFIPS Press, Montvale, NJ, pp. 339–346.
Svirezhev, Y.M. and Voinov, A.A., 1982. A shallow lake as a dynamic system. In: D.O. Logofet and N.K. Luckyanov (Editors), Ecosystem Dynamics in Freshwater Wetlands and Shallow Water Bodies, Vol. 2. UNEP/SCOPE, U.S.S.R. Academy of Sciences, Moscow, pp. 156–173.
Tiwari, J.L., Hobbie, J.E., Reed, J.P., Stanley, D.W. and Miller, M.C., 1978. Some stochastic differential equation models of an aquatic ecosystem. Ecol. Modelling, 4: 3–27.
Uhlmann, D. and Recknagel, F., 1982. Dimensioning of ponds for biological waste treatment. In: D.O. Logofet and N.K. Luckyanov (Editors), Ecosystem Dynamics in Freshwater Wetlands and Shallow Water Bodies, Vol. 2. UNEP/SCOPE, U.S.S.R. Academy of Sciences, Moscow, pp. 403–420.
Verhagen, J.H.G., 1978. A model of the plankton dynamics in an eutrophic shallow lake based on field data. In: S.E. Jørgensen (Editor), State-of-the-Art in Ecological Modelling. Pergamon Press, Oxford, pp. 661–672.
Walters, C.J., 1980. Production pathways in relation to nutrient loading. In: E.D. LeCren and R.H. Lowe-McConnell (Editors), The Functioning of Freshwater Ecosystems. IBP 22, Cambridge University Press, Cambridge, pp. 229–235.
Walters, C.J., Park, R.A. and Koonce, J.F., 1980. Dynamic models of lake ecosystems. In: E.D. LeCren and R.H. Lowe-McConnell (Editors), The Functioning of Freshwater Ecosystems. Cambridge University Press, pp. 455–479.
Wang, L.K., and Vielkind, D. and Wang, M.H., 1978. Mathematical models of dissolved oxygen concentration in freshwater. Ecol. Modelling, 5: 115–123.
Wharton, C.H., Odum, H.T., Ewel, K.C., Deuver, M., Lugo, A., Boyt, R., Bartholomew, J., DeBellevue, E., Brown, S., Brown, M. and Deuver, L., 1976. Forested wetlands of Florida — their management and use. Final report to Division of State Planning, State of Florida. Center for Wetlands, University of Florida, Gainesville, FL.
Wheeler, G.L., Rolfe, G.L. and Reinbold, K.A., 1978. A simulation model for lead movement in a watershed. Ecol. Modelling. 5: 67–76.
White, G.C., Adams, L.W. and Bookhout, T.A., 1978. Simulation model of tritium kinetics in a freshwater marsh. Health Physics, 34: 45–54.
Wiegert, R.G., 1971. Simulation modelling of the algal-fly components of a thermal ecosystem: effects of spatial heterogeneity, time delays, and model condensation. In: B.C. Patten (Editor), Systems Analysis and Simulation in Ecology, Vol. III. Academic Press, New York, NY, pp. 157–181.
Wiemhoff, J.; 1977. A Hydrology Model for Heron Pond. In: W.J. Mitsch, C.L. Dorge and

J.R. Wiemhoff (Editors), Forested Wetlands for Water Resource Management in Southern Illinois. Res. Rep. 132, Water Resources Center, University of Illinois, Urbana, IL, pp. 223–272.
Williams, R.B., 1971. Computer simulation of energy flow in Cedar Bog Lake, Minnesota, based on the classical studies of Lindeman. In: B.C. Patten (Editor), Systems Analysis and Simulation in Ecology. Vol. 1. Academic Press, New York, NY, pp. 543–582.

Ecological Modelling, 47 (1989) 199–215 199
Elsevier Science Publishers B.V., Amsterdam – Printed in The Netherlands

MODEL GOODNESS OF FIT: A MULTIPLE RESOLUTION PROCEDURE

ROBERT COSTANZA

Coastal and Environmental Policy Program, Chesapeake Biological Laboratory, University of Maryland, Solomons, MD 20688-0038 (U.S.A.)

(Accepted 7 March 1989)

ABSTRACT

Costanza, R., 1989. Model goodness of fit: a multiple resolution procedure. *Ecol. Modelling*, 47: 199–215.

Quantitatively evaluating the goodness of fit of ecological simulation models is difficult, and no generally agreed upon method has evolved. This paper presents a method for quantifying the goodness of fit of spatial and/or time series data and models based on measuring the similarity of the patterns, and the idea that measurement at one resolution is not sufficient to describe complex patterns. The method yields indices that summarize the way the fit changes as the resolution of measurement changes. An expanding 'window' is used to gradually degrade the resolution of the comparison. Lack of fit can be partitioned into 'registration', 'resolution' and residual components. This allows a better understanding of the underlying patterns and type of correspondence. Multiple resolution methods yield additional information not contained in single resolution methods that is necessary to adequately evaluate the performance of complex ecological models.

INTRODUCTION

No theory or model fits reality perfectly. As Albert Einstein once said: "The laws of mathematics, as far as they refer to reality, are not certain, and as far as they are certain, do not refer to reality." What scientists really need to know is exactly how well (or how poorly) their models perform over a broad range of conditions and criteria. Because there are no generally agreed upon procedures for measuring the degree of fit between simulation models and reality, this testing and evaluation process is not often given the importance it deserves. Lack of consensus results from the fact that many levels of disaggregation are used and the range of spatial and temporal resolutions over which models must operate and be tested is very large. Standard statistical tests of goodness of fit are generally applied only at a single resolution of measurement. The thesis of this paper is that there is no

0304-3800/89/$03.50

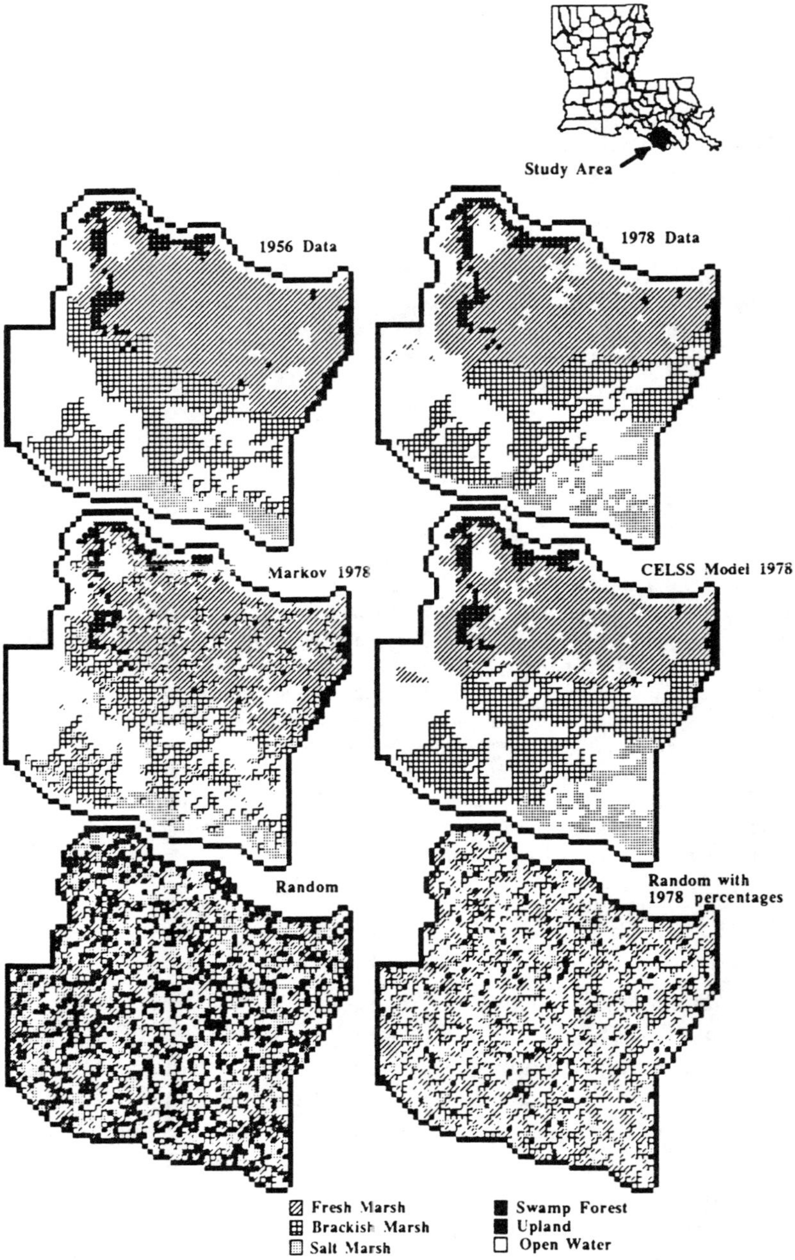

Fig. 1. Habitat distribution data and various model predictions for the Atchafalaya/Terrebonne area of coastal Louisiana. Each of the 2479 grid cells represents 1 km^2.

one 'proper' resolution, but rather a range of resolutions is necessary to adequately describe the fit of models with reality.

For relatively simple purposes there are well-established statistical measures of goodness-of-fit (i.e. R^2, χ^2). However, most ecological modeling involves quantifying the degree of matching or similarity between complex spatial and temporal patterns. Spatial pattern matching is not a straightforward statistical procedure. Even quantifying the degree to which nonspatial ecosystem modeling time series results match real patterns of ecosystem behavior is difficult and there is no universally agreed upon procedure (Gardner et al., 1980; Jørgensen, 1982). In spatial ecological analysis the literature has concentrated on determining if non-random patterns exist in point data (Ripley, 1981; Getis and Franklin, 1987), determining the optimum quadrat size based on an analysis of variance (Moellering and Tobler, 1972; Grieg-Smith, 1983), and determining whether or not two maps are statistically "different" (Pielou, 1977). But most statistical tests tend to miss or mask the details of spatial and temporal *patterns* in the data, concentrating instead on deviations from standard, random distributions. For example, a standard χ^2 test can be used to measure the fit between two land use maps, but it ignores the spatial pattern of the land use variables. It would yield information only about whether the total number of pixels in each land use category were significantly different between two maps, but not whether there was a significant difference in the pattern of two maps. The maps may both have the same total number of pixels in each land use category but be radically different in the arrangement of the pixels. The problem is more akin to the problem of matching amino acid sequences in large protein sequence data bases, which had been successfully attacked by developing "similarity scores" (Lipman and Pearson, 1985). The approach described in this paper extends the similarity scoring concept to include the possibility of performing the scoring over multiple resolutions.

The practical problems which led to the development of the procedures in this paper arose from work on spatial simulation modeling of long-term habitat succession in the Louisiana coastal zone (Sklar et al., 1985; Costanza et al., 1986, 1988). Some sample model results are shown in Fig. 1, which includes measured habitat distribution maps for 1956 and 1978 and various model predictions for 1978. We needed to gauge the models' performance in predicting the 1978 conditions from the 1956 conditions in a quantitative way that would allow parameter optimization, and we also needed an indication of the relative effectiveness of the various models. The simplest pattern sensitive goodness of fit metric under these circumstances is the percent of the cells that are correct (i.e., are the same type in both the model and data in a cell by cell comparison). The problem with this method was that it ignored 'near misses', and two maps with the same percent correct could exhibit very different patterns in their residuals (misses). One might have random misses while the other might have systematic misses, for example at the boundaries between habitat types. We wanted a method that would give some weight to near misses as well as direct hits and tell us whether the 'pattern' was being relatively well matched. Lipman and Pearson's (1985) method of handling the 'near miss' problem was to weight comparisons based on the evolutionary likelihood of one category (amino acid) changing into another. This requires a priori information on which categories are 'most simalar' to which other categories. In our case, it would have required us to determine, for example, that salt marsh is more similar to fresh marsh than it is to open-water habitat. To avoid having to make these somewhat arbitrary judgments, we developed an algorithm that uses spatial similarity in the pattern, rather than similarity between categories that must be supplied from other sources.

The method applies standard fit procedures over a number of temporal and/or spatial resolutions and uses the way the fit changes with resolution to interpret the model's performance. The procedure is first developed for categorical spatial data (the most difficult case) and then extended to interval spatial data, and to non-spatial time series data. It also borrows from ideas about edge detection as applied to problems of emulation of human vision (Rosenfeld and Kak, 1978; Marr and Hildreth, 1980) based on using moving two-dimensional 'windows' to filter the data (Spacek, 1986), but extends this idea to multiple resolutions.

Conceptually, this multiple resolution approach is similar to a "fractal dimension" (Mandelbrot, 1977, 1983) which measures the way the length of a coastline or other boundary changes as the resolution of measurement changes. For example, if we wished to determine the length of the coastline of Britain, the answer would depend on what resolution map we used (or the size of the fundamental unit of measurement). The smaller the fundamental unit of measurement (or the higher the resolution of the map) the longer the coastline measurement would be. Rather than speak of the 'length' of the coastline (which is resolution-dependent) we could alternatively speak of the way length depends on resolution. We can then develop resolution independent measures of the relationship between resolution and length. The fractal dimension is an elegantly simple example. It can be interpreted as a measure of the 'complexity' of boundaries.

The fundamental idea underlying fractals can be generalized and stated simply as: measurement at one particular resolution is always insufficient to describe complex natural phenomenon. It is necessary to measure phenomenon at several resolutions and interpret the way the results change with changing resolution to arrive at a meaningful description. The algorithm described in this paper implements this idea for model testing.

COMPONENTS OF FIT

Lack of fit between a model and data (or between any two data series) can be partitioned among three components: registration, resolution, and residual. Lack of fit due to registration has to do with the failure of the model and data to 'line up' even though their patterns may be similar. For example, two identical pictures may show very little pixel by pixel correspondence if they are slightly rotated, if one is moved slightly horizontally or vertically, or if one is a different size. By rotating, sliding, expanding or contracting the pictures (or time series), the fit may be dramatically increased. Lack of fit due to misregistration can be removed by performing the above manipulations on the data until the fit is maximized. In analyzing two data maps, spatial misregistration can be an important problem, especially when the goal is to detect small changes between the two maps. In spatial modeling work, spatial misregistration is seldom a problem since the model is designed to spatially register with the data. Temporal misregistration can be an important problem in measuring fit, however, as we discuss further on.

Once the lack of fit due to misregistration has been removed, the resolution component of fit can be analyzed. This is described by way of example in the following sections.

SPATIAL PATTERN MATCHING USING VARIABLE RESOLUTION FITTING

Two example 10 × 10 scenes with four different categories of cover (Fig. 2) are used to describe the procedure. Looking at the two scenes we can discern that the patterns are 'similar' but not identical. There is a block of category-1 cells in the upper left corner of each scene, they both have a large block of category-3 cells covering most of the right side, etc. The patterns are also certainly non-random. Humans seem to have an inate ability to recognize these kinds of pattern similarities. The problem is to systematize this ability to the point that computer algorithms can approximate it.

Pattern recognition is scale-dependent (Allen and Starr, 1985). It depends on both resolution and extent (the size of the scene). For example, Fig. 3 presents two related scenes at different scales. The enlarged view (Fig. 3a) has higher resolution, lower extent and the general pattern is not apparent. In Fig. 3b resolution has been sacrificed for increased extent and the pattern is apparent. The increased extent is not necessary to discern the pattern, however. Decreasing the resolution is often enough, as can be seen by squinting at Fig. 3a or holding it at a distance so the effective resolution is decreased.

Scene 1

1	1	1	1	2	2	2	3	3	3
1	1	1	2	2	2	3	3	3	3
1	1	2	2	2	3	3	3	3	3
3	3	2	2	3	3	3	3	3	3
1	3	3	3	3	3	3	3	3	3
1	1	1	3	3	3	3	3	3	3
2	2	2	2	2	2	2	2	3	3
3	3	3	3	3	3	3	3	3	3
3	3	3	3	2	2	3	3	3	3
3	3	3	3	2	2	2	2	3	3

Scene 2

1	1	2	2	2	2	2	2	3	3
1	1	1	1	2	3	3	3	3	3
1	1	1	2	3	3	3	3	3	3
3	1	2	2	3	3	3	4	4	4
3	3	3	3	3	3	3	3	3	3
1	1	1	3	3	3	3	3	3	3
1	1	2	2	2	2	2	2	3	3
1	2	2	3	3	2	2	3	3	3
3	3	3	3	2	2	2	3	3	3
3	3	3	3	2	2	2	2	3	3

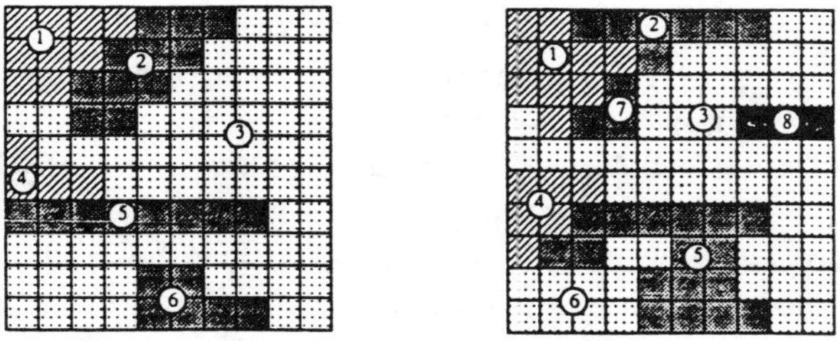

Fig. 2. Example 10 × 10 scenes with four categories.

The algorithm described in this paper decreases the resolution of comparisons by increasing the size of a sampling window that slides over scenes for which fit is calculated. The effect is similar to squinting to unfocus the scenes in order to perceive the larger pattern. Doing this with scene a makes the pattern apparent.

There are several alternative ways of measuring fit at a particular window size (resolution), depending on the nature of the data and other considerations. The multiple resolution approach does not depend on which measure of fit is used, as long as it is consistently applied at all resolutions. If numerical data are available, a standard coefficient of correlation (r^2) can be used. Categorical data are more of a problem.

For a sampling window size of 1, a convenient measure of fit for categorical data is the proportion of cells accurately matched (80% in the example 10 × 10 scenes). As the sampling window size is increased, one would like to use an analogous measure of fit. Essentially, the data are being aggregated within each sampling window and there are several possible ways to perform this aggregation. The simplest approach is 'proportional' aggregation which chooses that category which is the highest proportion of the cells within the window, randomly deciding ties. This method tends to quickly eliminate rare categories, however. Most aggregation schemes replace all the cells within the sampling window with a single category, and result in a rapid loss of information about the relative proportions of the categories. For some purposes this loss of information is acceptable, but for

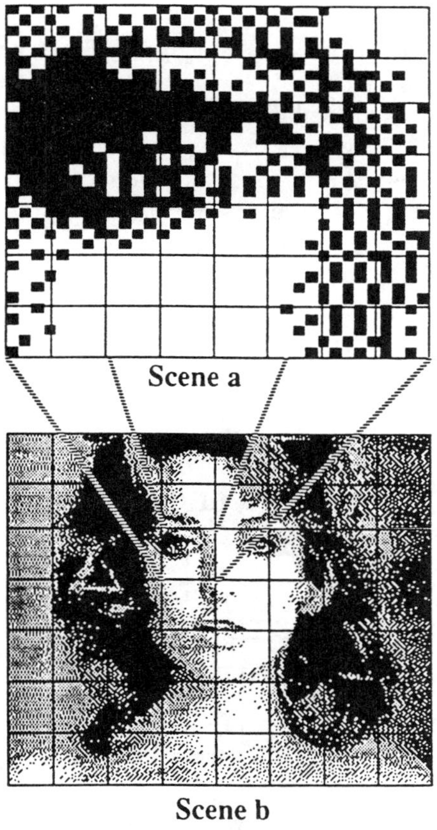

Fig. 3. Example showing the effects of resolution and extent on ability to recognize patterns. Scene a is a blowup of the right eye of what is obviously a picture of a woman in scene b, but it is only recognizable as such if we ignore some of the detail.

calculating fit, it is to be avoided if possible. A simple formula was devised that retains more of the information about the relative proportions of categories within the sample window in estimating fit while decreasing the resolution. The fit for each sampling window is estimated as 1 minus the proportion of cells that would have to be changed to make the sampling windows each have the same number of cells in each category, regardless of their spatial arrangement. For example, if a particular 2×2 window had two cells of forest and two of marsh in both scenes, the fit would be 100% regardless of how the cells were arranged within the windows. If one sampling window had one forest and three marsh, while the other had two of each category, the fit would be 75% (since one cell out of four would have to be changed to make the fit 100%). The fit for the whole scene for a particular sampling window size is the average fit over all the sampling windows of that size. The sampling window is moved through the scene one cell at a time until the entire image is covered.

The following formula for the fit at a particular sampling window size (F_w) implements this idea for aggregation. It reduces to the percent correct if the sampling window size is 1 and retains information about relative category proportions as the window size is increased:

$$F_w = \frac{\sum_{s=1}^{t_w} \left[1 - \frac{\sum_{i=1}^{p} |a_{1i} - a_{2i}|}{2w^2} \right]_s}{t_w} \qquad (1)$$

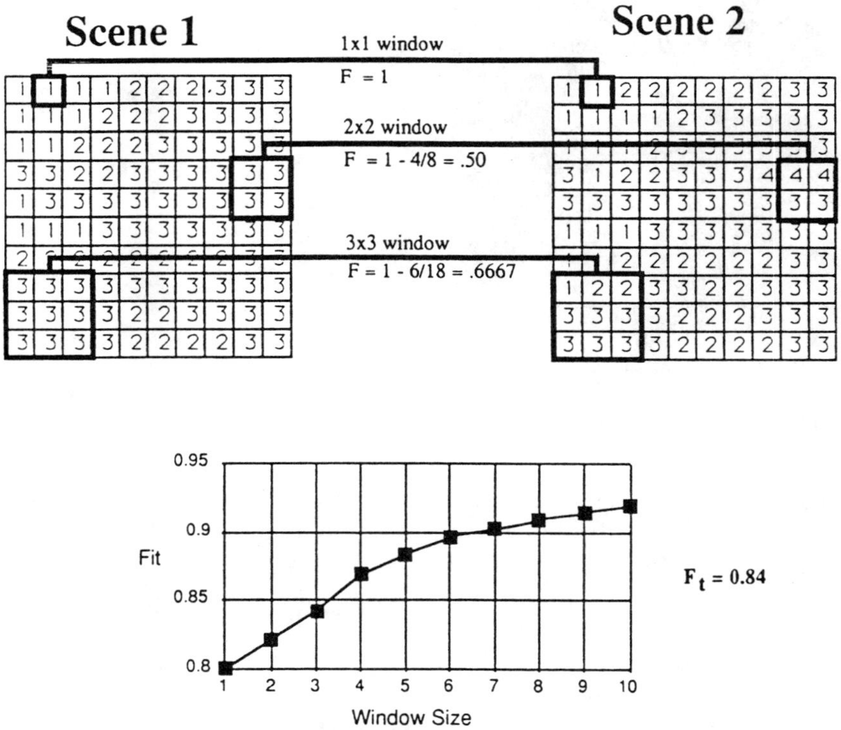

Fig. 4. Example of the multiple resolution fitting procedure for two sample 10×10 scenes with four categories. The plot shows that the two scenes match moderately well, as there is significant improvement in the fit with increasing window size. The total fit (F_t) is an exponentially weighted average over all the window sizes with $k = 0.1$. See text for further explanation.

where F_w is the fit for sampling window size w, w the dimension of one side of the (square) sampling window, a_{ki} the number of cells of category i in scene k in the sampling window, p the number of different categories (e.g., habitat types) in the sampling windows, s the sampling window of dimension w by w which slides through the scene one cell at a time, and t_w the total number of sampling windows in the scene for window size w.

One can then plot the fit between the scenes (F_w) vs. the size of the sampling window (w) as in Fig. 4. Using other aggregation methods or fit estimates would yield similar (but not identical) results, but the fundamental idea would still apply. If the plot behaves as it does for the two example scenes (it increases rapidly at first) then the pattern between the two scenes is very well matched even though the initial fit at window size 1 is relatively low. This would occur if the patterns between the scenes were similar, but the precise boundaries in the maximum resolution scenes were slightly off. Conversely, if the plot starts at a relatively low fit and is flat, then the spatial pattern is not well matched even though the initial fit might be higher than that for the two sample scenes. If the scenes were exactly identical, a perfect match over all window sizes would result. If two randomly generated scenes were compared, the expected fit would start at $1/p$ and rapidly increase to 1 as the expanding sampling window made the statistical similarity between any two random scenes apparent.

To use these measures to determine an overall degree of fit between two maps the information in the plot of window sizes vs. fit must be summarized. A weighted average of the fits at different window sizes is one possible way of summarizing the overall fit that allows more weight to be given to smaller window sizes while not totally ignoring the large window sizes. For this purpose one can use the following formula:

$$F_t = \frac{\sum_{w=1}^{n} F_w \, e^{-k(w-1)}}{\sum_{w=1}^{n} e^{-k(w-1)}} \qquad (2)$$

where F_t is a weighted average of the fits over all window sizes, F_w the fit for sampling windows of linear dimension w, k a constant, and w linear dimension of a sampling window. This formula gives exponentially less weight to the fit at lower resolution. The value of k determines how much weight is to be given to small vs. large sampling windows. If $k = 0$, all window sizes are given the same weight. At $k = 1$, only the first few window sizes will be important. The relative importance of matching the patterns precisely vs. crudely must be answered in the context of the model's objectives and the quality of the data. From previous studies on aggregation

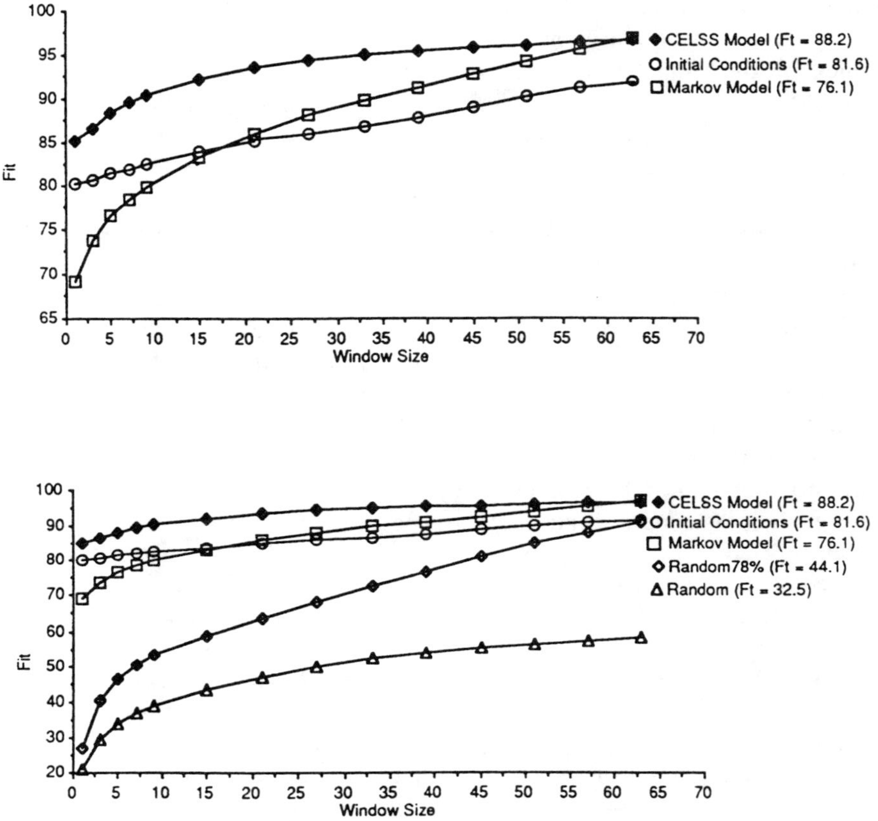

Fig. 5. Example plots of fit vs. window size for the various models in Fig. 1 compared to the 1978 data. Upper graph shows the CELSS model, the Markov model, and the initial (1956) conditions on an expanded *y* axis.

error in data and models (e.g., Gardner et al., 1982), we know that simple models may always be somewhat incorrect, but they may do a good job of matching the general patterns of the data, especially when there is high variance and uncertainty in the data. For the purposes of matching spatial patterns of land use, we have found that a value of $k \approx 0.1$ gives an 'adequate' amount of weight to the larger window sizes. For the example in Fig. 2, $k = 0.1$ yields $F_t = 0.84$.

The power of the technique in interpreting the patterns of correspondence between data and various models can be seen in Fig. 5, which shows the variable resolution procedure applied to the spatial modeling results summarized in Fig. 1. Fit vs. window size is plotted for the 1978 data compared with the 1978 CELSS simulation model prediction (labeled 'CELSS model'), and several 'null models'. The most simple-minded null model is a completely random distribution of habitats with all of the categories being equiprobable (labeled 'random equiprobable' in the figure). A slightly more reasonable null model is a random distribution but with the same overall land cover probabilities (frequencies) as the 1978 data (labeled 'random with 1978 frequencies' in the figure). A simple Markov chain model is a slightly more sophisticated null model. It incorporates the statistical trend of habitat changes in an area in the form of transition probabilities (or frequencies). In our case, we use the frequencies of transition of each habitat type into each other type over the 1956–1978 interval. The fit over various window sizes for the Markov model is labeled 'Markov model' in the figure. Finally, the 1956 initial conditions represent a null model that predicts no change (labeled 'initial conditions' on the figure).

The CELSS simulation model performs better than any of the null models, but its performance can best be judged *in relation* to the null models. The simulation model fits the 1978 data better than 'random equiprobable' ($F_t = 88.2\%$ vs. 32.5%) and 'random with 1978 frequencies' ($F_t = 88.2\%$ vs. 50%). The fit for 'random with 1978 frequencies' approaches one as window size increases indicating that the overall percentages of habitat types are the same but the pattern is not well matched.

Compared to the 'initial conditions' the CELSS model might not appear to be significantly better if only the fit at window size 1 is considered (85% vs. 81%). The initial conditions model appears to fit fairly well because only about 20% of the cells actually changed type between 1956 and 1978. But the pattern of fit is revealed by looking at the plots of fit vs. window size. The simulation model plot increases rapidly as window size increases indicating that the 'pattern' between the model and data is well matched. The initial conditions model exhibits a flatter plot indicating the pattern is not well matched. Total weighted fit (F_t) is significantly higher for the CELSS model than the initial conditions null model (88.2% vs. 81.6%).

The Markov model has a lower initial fit (69%) than the initial conditions model (81%), but the fit increases more rapidly as the window size increases. At the maximum window size it fits better than the initial conditions model since the total number of cells of each type is closer to the 1978 data. Total weighted fit for the Markov model is less than the initial conditions model (81.6% vs. 76.1%) since by randomly placing the transition cells the detailed spatial pattern is disrupted while increasing the fit at larger window sizes.

STATISTICAL SIGNIFICANCE

Since the F_t values generated by our procedure do not follow a normal distribution, one cannot calculate a statistical probability (P value). The most satisfactory approach at present seems to be to generate z values following the method of Lipman and Pearson (1985), where:

$$z = \frac{(F_t/\text{mean of randomly permutated } F_t)}{\text{standard deviation of randomly permutated } F_t}$$

The randomly permutated F_t values are generated by randomly rearranging one of the maps while retaining the same total number of pixels in each category. At least 20 random permutations should be used and Lipman and Pearson (1985) suggest the following significance guidelines:

- $z > 3$: possibly significant
- $z > 6$: probably significant
- $z > 10$: significant.

The results would be similar to comparing the CELSS model 1978 map (Fig. 1) to the Random with 1978 percentages map for several random permutations to test for significance of the fit with the 1978 data map. Because of the large number of cells involved and the highly patterned nature of the data maps, the mean of the randomly permutated F_t will generally be much lower than F_t (0.882 vs. 0.50 yielding a ratio of about 1.7) and the standard deviation of the randomly permutated F_t will be relatively low (around 0.1) yielding z scores much greater than 10 and highly significant comparisons.

TEMPORAL PATTERN MATCHING

The multiple resolution procedures are also applicable to time series rather than spatial data. In analysing time series data the sampling 'window' takes in progressively more time rather than progressively more space. In both cases, we are interested in summarizing the effects of 'smoothing' or averaging the data on goodness of fit. The procedures are also applicable to data that are ordinal, interval, or ratio rather than categorical (or nominal), by simply altering the formula for the fit at a particular window size (equation 1). For ratio and ordinal data the coefficient of correlation (r^2) can be substituted for F_w in equation (1).

An example similar to one that might occur in ecological modeling work is given in Fig. 6a, which shows hypothetical 'data' and 'model' time series. In this example the data are ratio values (meaning relative to some absolute zero, for example biomass or K) and the fit is calculated as the coefficient of determination between the data and the model (r^2).

In this example the effects of misregistration can be clearly seen. Fig. 6b is a plot of the data compared to the model output lagged by two time steps. Fig. 7a is a plot of fit versus window size (in this case the number of intervals in a moving average of the data) for the unlagged data (Fig. 6a).

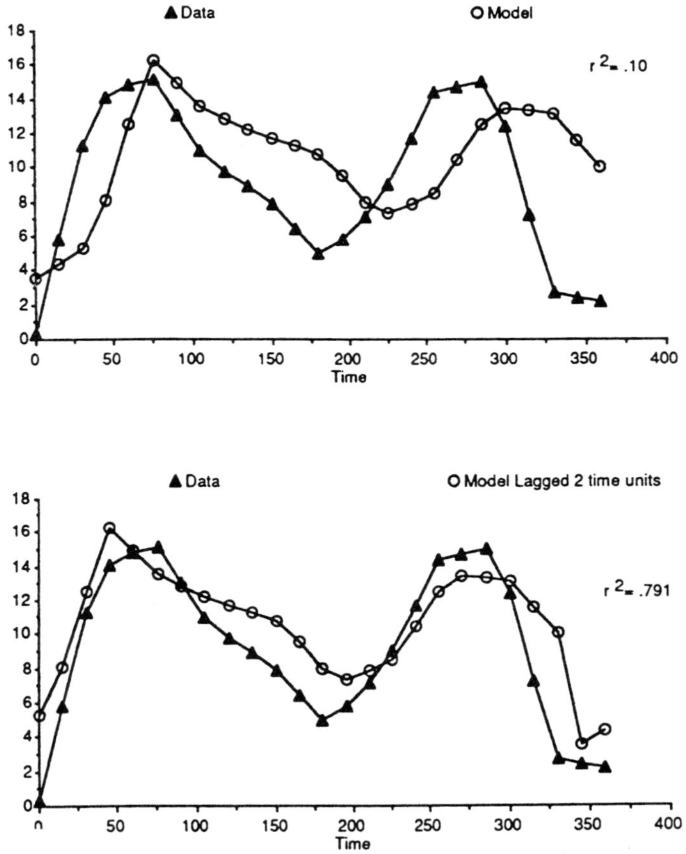

Fig. 6. Hypothetical data and model curves (top) and the same curves with the model lagged by two points.

Even though it is obvious (to human eyes) that the model and data curves in Fig. 6a are quite 'similar', the fit starts at 0.1 and decreases as the window size increases to a minimum of 0.02 before increasing again to 0.08 at a window size of 11. This occurs because there is a slight temporal misregistration in the two series. Fig. 7b is a plot of fit vs. lag for the two series. A lag of two time units increases the fit from 0.1 to almost 0.8. Figure 8 shows the fit vs. window size calculations performed after the model had been lagged by 2 units. F_t for this plot (with $k = 0.1$) is 0.804.

We need to subtract something for the model's failure in this example to get the timing right, making it necessary to lag the model by 2 units. Again, the amount to subtract is subjective and depends on how important it is to the model's purpose to precisely match the timing of the data. Small

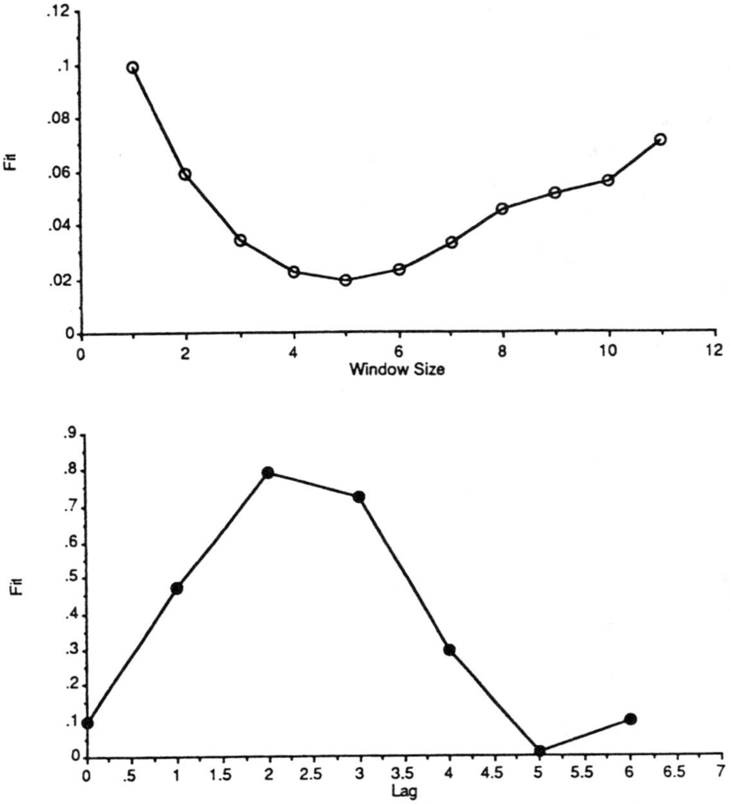

Fig. 7. Fit vs. window size of a moving average of the unlagged data and model from Fig. 6 (top) and fit vs. lag for the same data (bottom).

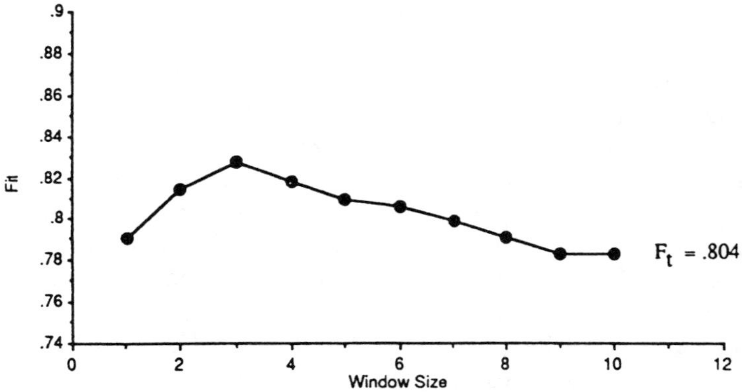

Fig. 8. Fit vs. window size for the data and model output from Fig. 6 after lagging the model by two time units.

misregistrations (low number of lags) are probably less important than large lags, so one approach would be to subtract successively more as the required lag increased. We might apply the following formula for a weighted fit over lag and window size:

$$F_{tL} = F_t \, e^{-k_L L} \quad (3)$$

where F_{tL} is the total weighted fit over lag and window size, k_L is the weighting factor for lag, L is the lag required to maximize the fit, for example, if $F_t = 0.804$, $L = 2$, and $k_L = 0.05$ then $F_{tL} = 0.728$.

DISCUSSION AND CONCLUSIONS

A simple procedure for determining the overall fit between model output and data that incorporates the effects of temporal and spatial misregistration and allows a degree of pattern matching by varying the resolution of the fit has been developed. Subjective weighting factors for the importance of precise vs. general pattern matching (k) and the importance of precise registration (k_L) must be supplied by the user, based on the purposes of the proposed model.

The procedures have many possible applications in modeling work, and also in descriptive pattern analysis. For example, one potential use of the procedures is analysis of the degree of organization of a landscape or other pattern. Organization can be defined as the degree of departure from a random pattern. While other measures (i.e. fractal dimension) yield information about the degree of departure from a random pattern, they are not sensitive to specific spatial patterns in the data. The multiple resolution fitting procedure described above can be used to directly measure the departure from a random pattern by measuring the degree of fit between a specific landscape pattern and a random one. For example, for the scenes in Fig. 2, the weighted average fits (F_t) were 0.445 for scene 1 and 0.517 for scene 2 when compared with a randomly generated pattern (using $k = 0.1$). This indicates that scene 1 is slightly more organized (farther from random, less complex, more predictable) than scene 2. The advantage of this measure over others is that it is sensitive to aperiodic patterns or clusters and is insensitive to the complexity of the patterns. This is an advantage since it is possible to have complex, aperiodic patterns that are highly non-random. The Atchafalaya/Terrebonne marsh landscape in Fig. 1 has a total weighted fit with a random scene of 0.325, indicating it is fairly highly organized.

The multiple scale procedures allow a much more sophisticated description of patterns and of the way models (particularly spatial models) fit the data. Ecological modeling cannot progress without procedures that allow better assessment of the relative successes of the models. The procedures outlined here are a modest step in that direction.

ACKNOWLEDGEMENTS

Monica G. Turner and Fred H. Sklar provided many useful ideas, criticism and support. Fred Sklar wrote the original computer code to implement the multiple resolution fitting procedure (which is available from the author on request in Basic or Fortran). Mary White and Tamer Ozmen aided in computer programming.

This research was funded in part by the U.S. Fish and Wildlife Service (a division of the U.S. Department of Interior) under Cooperative Agreement # 14-16-0009-84-921 titled: Spatial Simulation Modeling of Coastal Wetland Systems for Evaluating Management Alternatives, and by the National Science Foundation under Grant # BSR-8814272 titled: Responses of a Major Land Margin Ecosystem to Changes in Terrestrial Nutrient Inputs, Internal Nutrient Cycling, Production and Export.

Computer time on the CRAY supercomputer at the University of Illinois to run the CELSS model and the multiple resolution procedures were provided by the National Center for Supercomputer Applications and by an NSF grant on modeling landscape dynamics, Don Jameson, Principal Investigator.

REFERENCES

Allen, T.F.H. and Starr, T.B., 1982. Hierarchy: perspectives for ecological complexity. University of Chicago Press, Chicago, IL.

Costanza, R., Sklar, F.H. and Day, J.W., Jr., 1986. Modeling spatial and temporal succession in the Atchafalaya/Terrebonne marsh/estuarine complex in South Louisiana. In: D.A. Wolfe (Editor), Estuarine Variability. Academic Press, New York, pp. 387–404.

Costanza, R., Sklar, F.H., White, M.L. and Day, J.W., Jr., 1988. A dynamic spatial simulation model of land loss and marsh succession in coastal Louisiana. In: W.J. Mitsch, M. Straškraba and S.E. Jørgensen (Editors), Wetland Modelling. Developments in Environmental Modelling, 12. Elsevier, Amsterdam, pp. 99–114.

Gardner, R.H., O'Neill, R.V., Mankin, J.B. and Kumar, D., 1980. Comparative error analysis of six predator–prey models. Ecology, 61: 323–332.

Gardner, R.H., Cale, W.G. and O'Neill, R.V., 1982. Robust analysis of aggregation error. Ecology, 63: 1771–1779.

Getis, A. and Franklin, J., 1987. Second-order neighborhood analysis of mapped point patterns. Ecology, 68: 473–477.

Grieg-Smith, P., 1983. Quantitative Plant Ecology. Blackwell, Oxford.

Jørgensen, S.E., 1982. Modelling the eutrophication of shallow lakes. In: D.O. Logofet and N.K. Luckyanov (Editors), Ecosystem Dynamics in Freshwater Wetlands and Shallow Water Bodies, 2. UNEP/SCOPE, USSR Academy of Sciences, Moscow, pp. 125–155.

Lipman, D.J. and Pearson, W.R., 1985. Rapid and sensitive protein similarity searches. Science, 227: 1435–1441.

Mandelbrot, B.B., 1977. Fractals. Form, Chance and Dimension. Freeman, San Francisco, CA.

Mandelbrot, B.B., 1983. The Fractal Geometry of Nature. Freeman, San Francisco, CA.

Marr, D. and Hildreth, E., 1980. Theory of edge detection. Proc. R. Soc. London B, 207: 187–212.

Moellering, H. and Tobler, W.R., 1972. Geographical variances. Geogr. Anal., 4: 35–50.

Pielou, E.C., 1977. Mathematical Ecology. Wiley, New York.

Ripley, B.D., 1981. Spatial Statistics. Wiley, New York.

Rosenfeld, A. and Kak, A.C., 1978. Digital Image Processing. Wiley, New York.

Sklar, F.H., Costanza, R. and Day, J.W., Jr., 1985. Dynamic spatial simulation modeling of coastal wetland habitat succession. Ecol. Modelling, 29: 261–281.

Spacek, L.A., 1986. Edge detection and motion detection. Image Vision Comput., 4: 43–56.

Modeling Coastal Landscape Dynamics

Process-based dynamic spatial ecosystem simulation can examine long-term natural changes and human impacts

Robert Costanza, Fred H. Sklar, and Mary L. White

Predicting the way ecological systems respond to human modifications has been a primary goal of ecosystem ecology (Hall and DeAngelis 1985). Ecosystems represent an economic resource whose value to society is only now becoming recognized. Coastal ecosystems in particular provide valuable marketed and nonmarketed services, including fish and wildlife resources, storm protection, and recreation. The average value to society of coastal wetlands has been estimated as \$2000–\$10,000/acre, even though their market price is only \$200–\$400/acre (Costanza et al. in press, Farber and Costanza 1987, Turner et al. 1988).

Coastal ecosystems are being threatened by a host of human activities, including oil and gas exploration, urban development, and sediment diversion. The potential for sea level rise due to global greenhouse-effect warming is also of concern. Protecting and preserving these ecosystems requires the ability to predict the direct and indirect, temporal, and spatial effects of proposed human activities, the ability to separate these effects from natural changes, and the ability to appropriately modify the short-term incentive structures that guide local decision-making to better reflect these impacts (Costanza 1987a). Adequately predicting ecosystem impacts requires sophisticated computer simulation models that represent a synthesis of the best available understanding of the way these complex coastal ecosystems function.

Management options can be effective at mitigating impacts of proposed alterations

The more general objectives of landscape modeling are to predict changes in land cover patterns across large geographic regions (tens to hundreds of kilometers) over long time scales (tens to hundreds of years) as a result of various site-specific management alternatives and natural changes. Development of this capability is needed for regional ecosystem management and also for modeling regional and global ecosystem response to regional and global climate change, sea level rise resulting from atmospheric CO_2 enrichment, acid precipitation, toxic waste dumping, and a host of other potential impacts.

Two recent developments make this type of modeling feasible. First, the ready accessibility of extensive spatial and temporal databases from such sources as remote sensing and historical aerial photography make it possible to measure the behavior of real landscapes over large spatial and long temporal scales. Second, advances in computer power and convenience make it possible to build and run predictive landscape models at the necessary levels of spatial and temporal resolution.

Coastal marshes

The Atchafalaya delta and adjacent Terrebonne Parish marshes represent one of the most rapidly changing landscapes in the world. Figure 1 shows the study area. Figure 2 shows the historical sequence of Mississippi River main distributaries that have deposited sediments to form the current Mississippi deltaic plain marshes. This delta switching cycle (on average lasting 1500 years) sets the historical context of this landscape. At present, the river is in the process of changing from the current channel to the much shorter Atchafalaya River.

The US Army Corps of Engineers maintains a control structure at Old River (see Figure 1) to control the percentage of Mississippi River flow going down the Atchafalaya. For the last 40 years, this percentage has been set at approximately 30%. Sediment borne by the Atchafalaya River first filled in open water areas in the upper Atchafalaya basin, and more recently it has begun to build a delta in Atchafalaya Bay (Roberts et al. 1980, Van Heerden and Roberts 1980a,b). Atchafalaya-borne sediments are dispersed

Robert Costanza is an associate professor in the Coastal and Environmental Policy Program, Chesapeake Biological Laboratory, Center for Environmental and Estuarine Studies, University of Maryland, Solomons, MD 20688-0038. Fred H. Sklar is an assistant professor at the Belle Baruch Institute, University of South Carolina, Columbia, SC 29211. Mary L. White is a research associate at the Coastal Ecology Institute, Center for Wetland Resources, Louisiana State University, Baton Rouge, LA 70803.

to Fourleague Bay (Figure 3) and are contributing to marsh building in the eastern part of the study area as well (Baumann and Adams 1981, Baumann et al. 1984). During the next few decades, new delta is projected to form at the mouth of the river, and plant community succession will occur on the recently formed delta and in the existing marshes.

In contrast, the leveeing of the Mississippi and Atchafalaya rivers, along with the damming of distributaries, has virtually eliminated riverine sediment input to most Louisiana coastal marshes. This change has broken the deltaic cycle and greatly accelerated land loss. The overall Louisiana coastal zone has been projected to lose a net of approximately 100 km^2/yr due to sediment starvation and salt water intrusion (Gagliano et al. 1981). Only in the area of the Atchafalaya delta is sediment-laden water flowing into wetland areas and land gain occurring (Roberts et al. 1980, Van Heerden and Roberts 1980a,b).

Primary human activities that potentially contribute to wetland loss are flood control, canals, spoil banks, land reclamation, fluids withdrawal, and highway construction. There is evidence that canals and levees are an important factor in wetland loss in coastal Louisiana, but there is much disagreement about the magnitude of the indirect loss caused by them (Cleveland et al. 1981, Craig et al. 1979, Deegan et al. 1984, Leibowitz 1989, Scaife et al. 1983). Natural channels are generally not deep enough for the needs of oil recovery, navigation, pipelines, and drainage, so a vast network of canals has been built. In the Deltaic Plain of Louisiana, canals and their associated spoil banks of dredged material currently comprise 8% of the total marsh area compared to 2% in 1955. The construction of canals leads to direct loss of marsh by dredging and spoil deposition and indirect loss by changing hydrology, sedimentation, and productivity. Canals are thought to lead to more rapid salinity intrusion, causing the death of freshwater vegetation. Canal spoil banks also limit water exchange with wetlands, thereby decreasing deposition of suspended sediments.

Proposed human activities can have a dramatic impact on the distribution

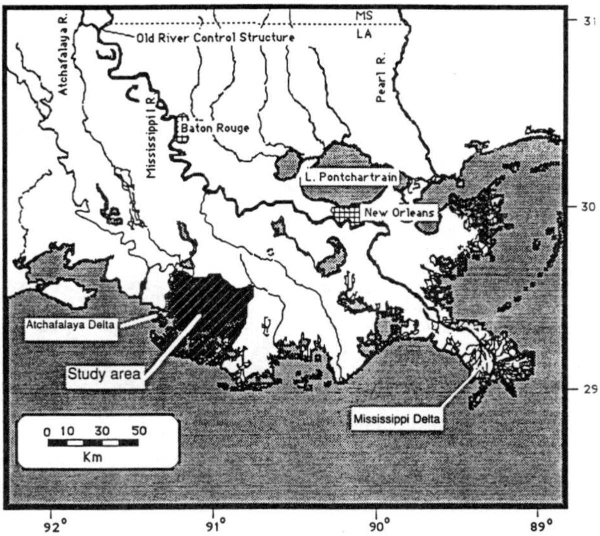

Figure 1. Map of southern Louisiana showing the Atchafalaya/Terrebonne study area.

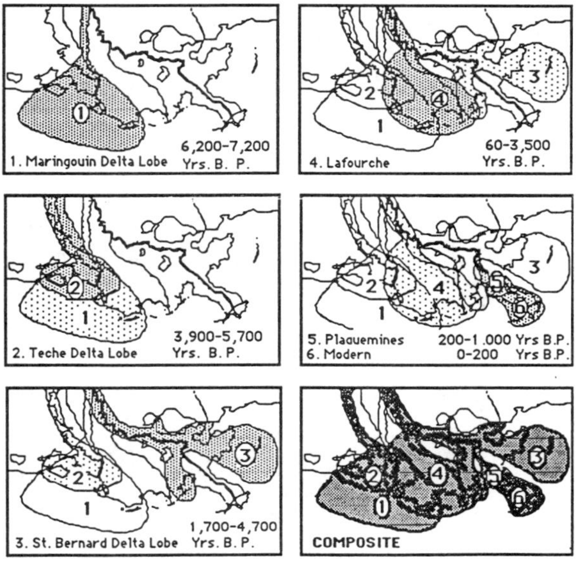

Figure 2. Historical sequence of major Mississippi River distributary changes. (After Baumann and Adams 1981.)

of water and sediments from the Atchafalaya River, and consequently on the development of the Atchafalaya landscape. For example, the Corps of Engineers is considering extending a levee along the east bank of the Atchafalaya that would restrict water and sediment flow into the Terrebonne marshes (Figure 3). This situation represents a unique opportunity to study landscape dynamics. The Atchafalaya landscape is changing rapidly enough to provide time-series observations that can be used to test basic hypotheses about how coastal landscapes develop. In addition to short-term observations, there is a uniquely long and detailed history of field and remotely sensed data available on the study area (Bahr et al. 1983, Costanza et al. 1983).

Solutions to the land loss problem in Louisiana all have far-reaching implications. Outside forces (such as rates of sea level rise) also influence the effectiveness of any proposed solution. In the past, suggested solutions have been evaluated independently of each other and in an ad hoc manner. To more objectively evaluate the many interdependent implications of the various natural changes, management strategies, and specific projects that have been suggested to remedy the coastal erosion problem, an integrated spatial simulation modeling approach was developed (Costanza et al. 1988, Sklar et al. 1985, in press). Using this approach, we first demonstrated the ability to simulate the past behavior of the system, and then we projected future conditions as a function of various management alternatives and natural changes, both individually and in various combinations. Our approach simulates both the dynamic and spatial behavior of the system, and it keeps track of several of the important landscape level variables in the system, such as ecosystem type, water level and flow, sediment levels and sedimentation, subsidence, salinity, primary production, nutrient levels, and elevation.

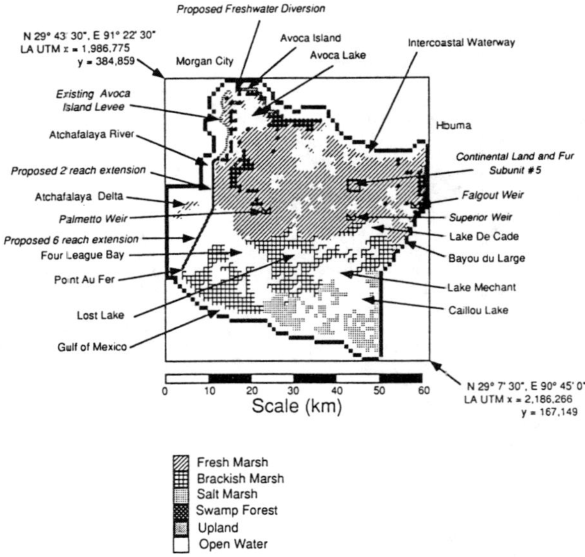

Figure 3. Atchafalaya/Terrebonne study area showing major geographic features, ecosystem types in 1983, and the location of the management options analyzed.

Process-based dynamic spatial ecosystem simulation models

Ecosystem models can be differentiated from population models in that the former include biotic and abiotic components whereas the latter include only populations of organisms. Ecosystem models tend to be more complex and realistic, and population models tend to be more simple and general. The majority of ecosystem models in the literature are designed to predict dynamic behavior while treating the system as spatially homogeneous (Costanza and Sklar 1985). Many existing ecosystem models are process based, in the sense of attempting to mimic (at least in an aggregated way) the underlying physical and ecological processes in the system, as opposed to statistical or probabilistic models, which are based directly on observed correlations in the data, generally without specifying mechanisms.

One way to extend the process-based approach to model spatial dynamics is to arrange a spatial array of point ecosystem models and connect them with fluxes of, for example, water and nutrients, employing rules to govern successional, evolutionary, or other changes in the structure of the system. This approach is somewhat analogous to that employed in general atmospheric circulation models used in long-term climate modeling (Potter et al. 1979, Schlesinger and Zhao 1989, Washington and Williamson 1977, Williams et al. 1974), but it also incorporates elements of cellular automata and expert systems modeling incorporated in the successional rules.

Richard Levins (1966) first described the fundamental trade-offs in modeling between realism, precision, and generality. No single model can maximize all three goals, and the choice of which objectives to pursue depends on the fundamental purposes of the modeling study. Our approach favors higher realism and precision (the ability to and accurately realistically depict specific processes and ecosystems) at the expense of generality (direct and easy applicability to a broad range of systems). It is a relatively expensive and time-consuming approach to modeling that requires much site-specific data and a significant amount of effort to calibrate the model to local conditions. But the payoffs are significant in light of the model's ability to simulate realistically a specific system. This approach was essential to achieve the analytical and management goals of our study.

The spatial process-based approach had been attempted in only a few previous cases for ecosystem modeling (Botkin et al. 1972, Costanza and Sklar 1985, Phipps 1979). In general, past applications were relatively successful, and their rarity is probably due to the size and complexity of the resultant models and the difficulty of assembling the necessary databases for calibrating and verifying the models. These limitations are decreasing with the increasing availability of remote sensing data and supercomputers, and we expect the relative expense of the spatial process–based approach to continue to decrease in the future.

The CELSS model

We developed a process-based spatial simulation model for the Atchafalaya/Terrebonne marsh/estuarine complex in south Louisiana (Figure 3) called the coastal ecological landscape spatial simulation (CELSS) model (Costanza et al. 1988, Sklar et al. 1989). The model consists of 2479 interconnected square cells, each representing 1 square kilometer. Each cell contains a dynamic ecosystem simulation model (Figure 4), and each cell is connected to its four nearest neighbors by the exchange of water and suspended materials (salts, nitrogen, and suspended organic and inorganic sediments). The buildup of land or the development of open water in a cell depends on the balance between net inputs of sediments and local organic peat deposition on the one hand and outputs due to erosion and subsidence on the other hand. The balance of sediment inputs and outputs is critical for predicting how marsh succession and productivity is affected by natural and human activities.

Inputs are specified in the form of time series during the simulation period. Weekly values of Atchafalaya and Mississippi river discharges, Gulf of Mexico salinity, river sediments and nutrients, rainfall, sea level, runoff, temperature, and winds are supplied to the simulation with each iteration. The location, time of construction, and characteristics of the major waterways, canals, and levees are also supplied as inputs to the simulation.

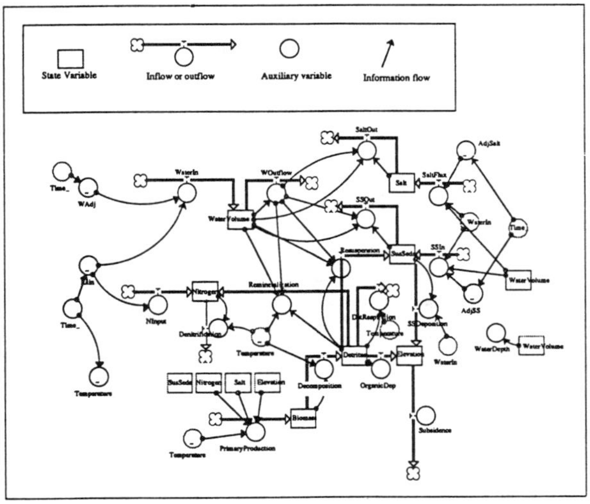

Figure 4. Diagram of a typical unit cell model in the CELSS landscape model in the STELLA modeling language (Costanza 1987b). All ecosystem types used a unit model with the same general structure, but with unique parameter settings.

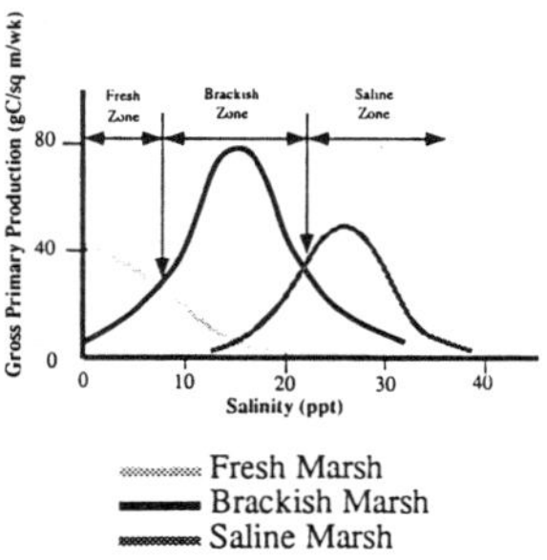

Figure 5. General relationship between gross primary production and salinity for three habitat types in the CELSS model. Data used to calibrate these relationships were taken from Conner and Day (1987).

The change in water level in each cell is determined in the model by water exchanges in both directions across all four boundaries plus surplus rainfall (precipitation minus evapotranspiration). The hydrologic component of the model is, in essence, a two-dimensional, finite-difference, mass-balance model. Although this mass-balance approach does not accurately simulate short-term hydrodynamics (because it leaves out momentum transfers, vertical dynamics, and Coriolis forces), it does approximate the major longer-term effects in our flat, shallow, and well-mixed study area.

It was necessary to give up some hydrologic precision because we needed to do continuous simulations for 58 years, which would have been prohibitively expensive using a complete hydrodynamic model, even on the fastest supercomputer. In addition, our primary goal in this model was to simulate plant community succession and productivity, conditions that respond more strongly to longer-term water flow patterns than to short-term flooding. Our results for water flow were similar to those produced for a few selected points in time by a more elaborate two-dimensional hydrodynamic model of the same area.

In our model, water can exchange

with adjacent cells via canals, natural bayous, and overland flow, or it may be prevented from exchanging with adjacent cells by the presence of levees. An overall water flow connectivity parameter (K) is adjusted during the model run to reflect the presence and size of waterways or levees at the cell boundaries. Connectivity is a function of habitat type, drainage density, waterway orientation, and levee height. If a waterway is present at a cell boundary, a large K value is used, increasing with the size of the waterway. If a levee is present, a K value of 0 is used until water level exceeds the height of the levee. The model's canal and levee network is updated each year during a simulation run (i.e., dredged canals and levees are added to the model's hydrologic structure at the beginning of the year they were built).

Water crossing from one cell to another carries both organic and inorganic sediments. This sediment is partitioned between being deposited, resuspended, lost due to subsidence, and carried to the next cell. The relative rates of each of these sediment exchanges in each location is a function of ecosystem type. Plants and nutrients within each cell also influence these exchanges and flows. Changes in other abiotic material concentrations (i.e., salts and nitrogen) are also a function of water flow between cells and concentration of materials in the cells, along with internal deposition and resuspension (Figure 4).

The primary production in a cell is related to flooding regimes, turbidity, temperature, and elevation, according to functions like the one illustrated in Figure 5, which shows the model's relationship between weekly gross primary productivity and salinity for three of the habitat types. Data to calibrate the productivity functions was taken from Conner and Day (1987). In this type of function, maximal output occurs at optimal levels of inputs, and output is reduced with increased deviation from the optimum. The response of primary production to different nitrogen concentrations was stimulated with a Michaelis-Menten type rate equation, in which production continues to increase with increasing nitrogen, but at a decreasing rate. Data to calibrate this function were taken from Hopkinson (1978).

Table 1. Analysis of variance table for selected individual parameters and interactions of parameters on total fit of the model with 1978 conditions.

Parameter	Mean square	F value	Pr > F
Individual parameters			
Water flow (fresh marsh)	2.30404601	5.31	0.0266
Sedimentation	0.12118223	0.28	0.6002
Primary production	8.31807987	19.16	0.0001
Organic matter	6.31000576	14.54	0.0005
Water flow parameters	0.00848915	0.02	0.8895
Turbulent resuspension	1.59570305	3.68	0.0625
Water flow (open water)	0.04134081	0.10	0.7592
Subsidence	3.59999056	8.29	0.0064
Two-way interactions			
Water flow (fresh marsh) and sedimentation	1.05885098	2.44	0.1264
Water flow (fresh marsh) and primary production	0.71286012	1.64	0.2076
Water flow (fresh marsh) and organic matter	0.19934273	0.46	0.5020
Water flow (fresh marsh) and turbulent resuspension	0.24456926	0.56	0.4574
Water flow (fresh marsh) and subsidence	0.51497506	1.19	0.2827
Sedimentation and primary production	2.00028590	4.61	0.0381
Sedimentation and organic matter	1.66397862	3.83	0.0574
Sedimentation and turbulent resuspension	2.91185842	6.71	0.0134
Sedimentation and subsidence	0.34385175	0.79	0.3789
Primary production and organic matter	4.65211481	10.72	0.0022
Primary production and turbulent resuspension	5.94659088	13.70	0.0007
Primary production and subsidence	2.23346004	5.15	0.0289
Organic matter and turbulent resuspension	0.54097224	1.25	0.2711
Turbulent resuspension and subsidence	0.09995870	0.23	0.6340
Water flow (open water) and subsidence	0.00524133	0.01	0.9131
Three-way interactions			
Sedimentation and primary production and turbulent resuspension	5.05771666	11.65	0.0015
Error (degrees of freedom = 39)	0.43402680		

Ecosystem succession occurs in the model (after a time lag) when the physical conditions in a cell become appropriate to a different ecosystem type. The program monitors the state variables in each cell and checks the physical environment (e.g., salinity, elevation, and water level). If the values of the state variables change to the extent that the environment in the cells is outside the range for its currently designated ecosystem type, then the cell's ecosystem type and all the associated parameter settings are switched to a new, better-adapted set. For example, if salinity in a cell that is fresh marsh rises beyond a certain threshold value and remains at this high level long enough, then the model converts the cell to brackish marsh and changes all the associated parameters.

The square cells have exchanges across their four sides. We did not use a hexagonal or triangular grid or a square one that allowed exchanges across the diagonals mainly because we wanted the simplest arrangement that would work reasonably well for our purposes and was easy to program. We used a simple Euler numerical integration technique with a variable time step. The maximal time step is one week. The model checks the rates of change of each variable, and if any of these is above a predetermined maximum it reduces the time step in increments until the rates of change are below the threshold, down to a minimum of one day.

The model was written in standard FORTRAN (3021 lines of code), and was run on a variety of computers, including a VAX 11/780, IBM 3034, and CRAY X/MP. A typical 22-year run at a weekly time step (1144 total time steps) for all 2479 cells with eight state variables each (19,832 total simultaneous difference equations) takes approximately 24 hours of CPU time on the VAX, 2 hours on the IBM, and 15 minutes on the CRAY. Most of the full-scale runs of the model were done on the CRAY, with the other computers used mainly in the early model development stages.

Apple Macintoshs were used extensively for unit model design and debugging using STELLA (Costanza 1987b), for telecommunicating with the CRAY, and for mapping, analysis, and animation of results.

Input data. Primary input data for the model were: detailed, digitized ecosystem type maps prepared by the US Fish and Wildlife Service for 1956, 1978, and 1983; the history of canal and levee construction in the area, obtained from analysis of state permit records for the 1956–1978 period; a weekly record of climate variables, including rainfall, temperature, wind, river flow, and sediment and nutrient concentrations; and water level and salinity in the Gulf of Mexico. In addition, field measurements of productivity, biomass, and nutrient uptake were available for setting parameters for the productivity component of the model.

The model was initialized using the 1956 ecosystem type map. Because no direct measurements for the initial values for the model's other state variables in each cell were available, they were set at the middle of the range for the corresponding ecosystem type.

Calibration based on ecosystem type maps. Our first objective was to replicate the behavior of the system during the period from 1956 to 1978 and quantify the degree of fit between various alternative models and the data. The CELSS model was calibrated by starting it with the 1956 ecosystem type conditions and associated values for the other variables and simulating the evolution of the area during the intervening 22 years to 1978 with a maximum of weekly time steps. A measured ecosystem type map was available for 1978 for comparison with the model's predictions. The simulated and real maps were then compared for degree of fit. The model's parameters were iteratively adjusted within predetermined ranges of uncertainty to maximize the fit. The model was then continued to 1983 (for which a third map was available), and the fit was again calculated to estimate the model's predictive accuracy.

The CELSS model contains more than 130 parameters. In calibrating the model, we first choose initial values and ranges of uncertainty for these parameters, based on available data and literature values. We then ran calibration runs of the model from 1956 to 1978 and compared the goodness of fit of the model's ecosystem type predictions with the 1978 data using visual inspection and the procedures described below. We also looked at the other variables in the model to make sure they were approximately replicating what we knew to have happened in the system. But we concentrated on the ecosystem type predictions because ecosystem type is the result (in the model as well as in the real world) of the integration of the behavior of the other variables. Ecosystem type is also the most easily and accurately observed variable in the real system at the landscape scale.

We performed a preliminary parameter optimization by manually adjusting parameters within the predetermined ranges of uncertainty to improve the ecosystem type fit. When

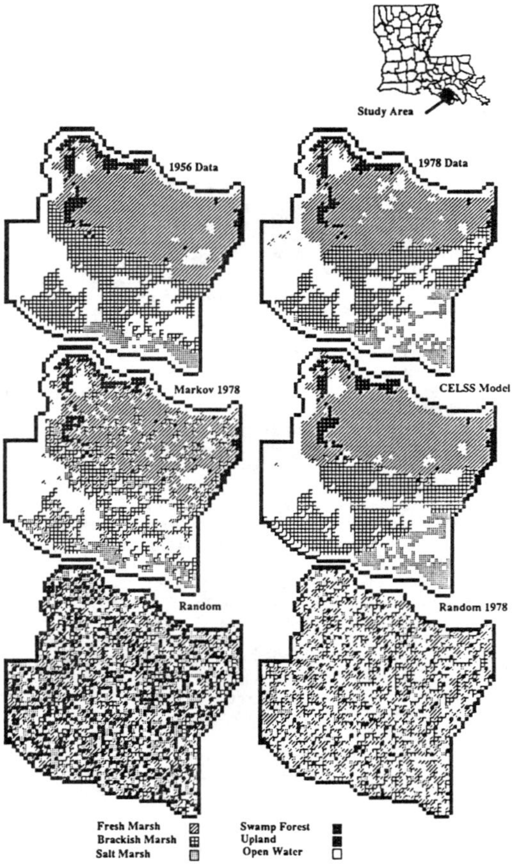

Figure 6. CELSS model and various alternative null model predictions for 1978 ecosystem type using the 1956 conditions as the starting point.

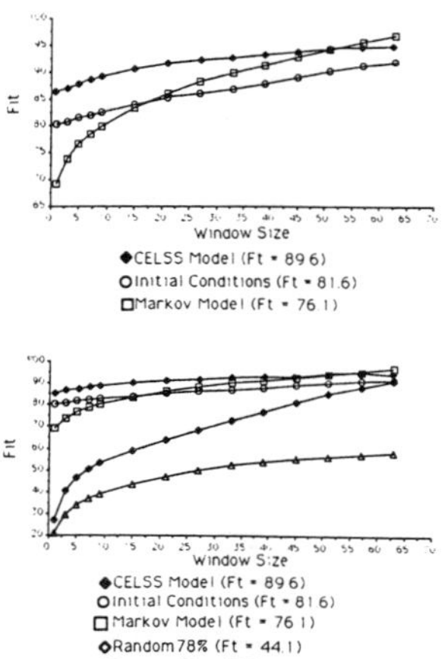

Figure 7. Example plots of fit versus window size for the various models in Figure 6 compared with the 1978 data. Upper graph shows the CELSS model, the Marov model, and the initial (1956) conditions on an expanded y-axis.

this procedure began to yield negligible improvements, we began a more formal parameter optimization procedure.

Because the model is nonlinear and has many discontinuities (due in part to the ecosystem succession algorithm), it is not amenable to traditional linear parameter optimization procedures, such as linear regression. We therefore used a procedure that is applicable to any model structure. This procedure treats the model as if it were an experiment (with the parameters as the controllable factors in the experiment) and uses traditional analysis-of-variance procedures to analyze the response of the model's fit to various combinations of changes in the parameters (factors). This method required a large number of simulation runs (one for each combination of parameter changes chosen) and was only possible for a model of this size because the speed of the supercomputer made generating the requisite number of runs feasible. A by-product of this approach is a fairly elaborate sensitivity analysis of the model's response to changes in the parameters, which gave us significant insight into the model's behavior.

Table 1 shows the results of an analysis of the variance in fit due to the manipulated parameters and combinations of parameters. These results indicate that, although the physical and hydrologic parameters (such as water flow and subsidence) are important, the biological parameters (such as primary productivity), alone and in combination with the physical parameters, contribute significantly to controlling the fit of the model. It also appeared that our decision to use a process-based, whole-ecosystem approach was justified, because no single parameter explained most of the variation in fit and the higher order interactions between physical and biological parameters were significant.

We limited the parameters manipulated in this procedure to those of which we were most unsure, and, based on preliminary sensitivity analysis, those with the largest impact on the fit. Based on an analysis of the parameters, we could derive a set of changes in the parameter settings that would maximally improve the fit. We then implemented these changes and repeated the factorial experimental procedure. We iterated this process until significant improvements in fit were no longer being made. The base case CELSS model results reflect these optimized parameter settings.

Degree of fit of predicted ecosystem type with data. For relatively simple purposes, there are well-established statistical measures of goodness of fit. For example, a standard chi-square test can determine the fit between two categorical variables, but it ignores the spatial or other patterns of the variables. It could be used to determine if the total number of cells in each land use category were significantly different between two maps, but not whether there was a significant difference in the pattern of two maps that both had the same total number of cells in each land use category.

Landscape analysis requires quantifying the degree of matching of complex spatial and temporal patterns. Spatial pattern matching is not a straightforward statistical procedure. Even quantifying the degree to which nonspatial ecosystem modeling time-series results match real patterns of ecosystem behavior is difficult and there is no agreed-on procedure (Gardner et al. 1982, Jørgensen 1982).

We used a multiple resolution approach to test the goodness-of-fit between the model and data. This approach allows a more complete analysis of the way the spatial patterns match (Costanza 1989, Turner et al. 1989). The algorithm gradually degrades the resolution with which the fit is measured by gradually increasing the size of a sampling window in which the fit is calculated. A plot of it versus window size (resolution) yields information on the way the patterns match. The total fit is estimated as a weighted average of the fit at all the window sizes, with the smaller window sizes given the most weight.

Figure 6 shows various model predictions for 1978 (including several null models) based on simulations using the 1956 conditions as the starting point. Figure 7 shows the variable resolution procedure applied to the spatial modeling results summarized in Figure 6. Fit versus window size is plotted for the 1978 data compared with the 1978 CELSS simulation model prediction (labeled "CELSS model") and with several alternative and null models.

The most simple-minded null model is a completely random distribution of habitats with all the categories being equally probable (labeled "random" in Figure 6). A slightly more reasonable null model is a random distribution but with the same

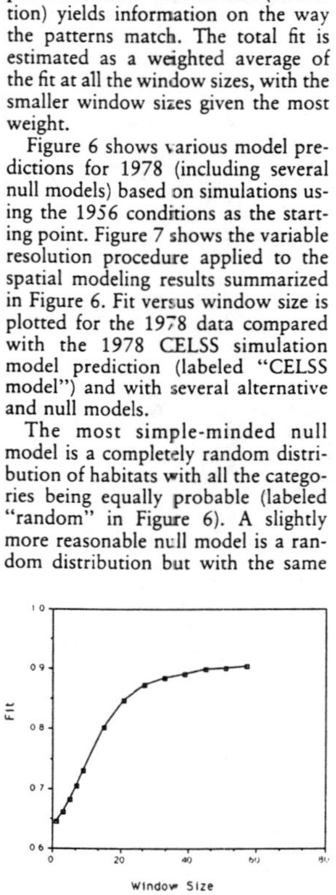

Figure 8. Comparison of CELSS model predictions for salinity with the WES two-dimensional hydrodynamic model (Donnell and Letter 1989, Letter 1982) for low-flow conditions over a range of window sizes.

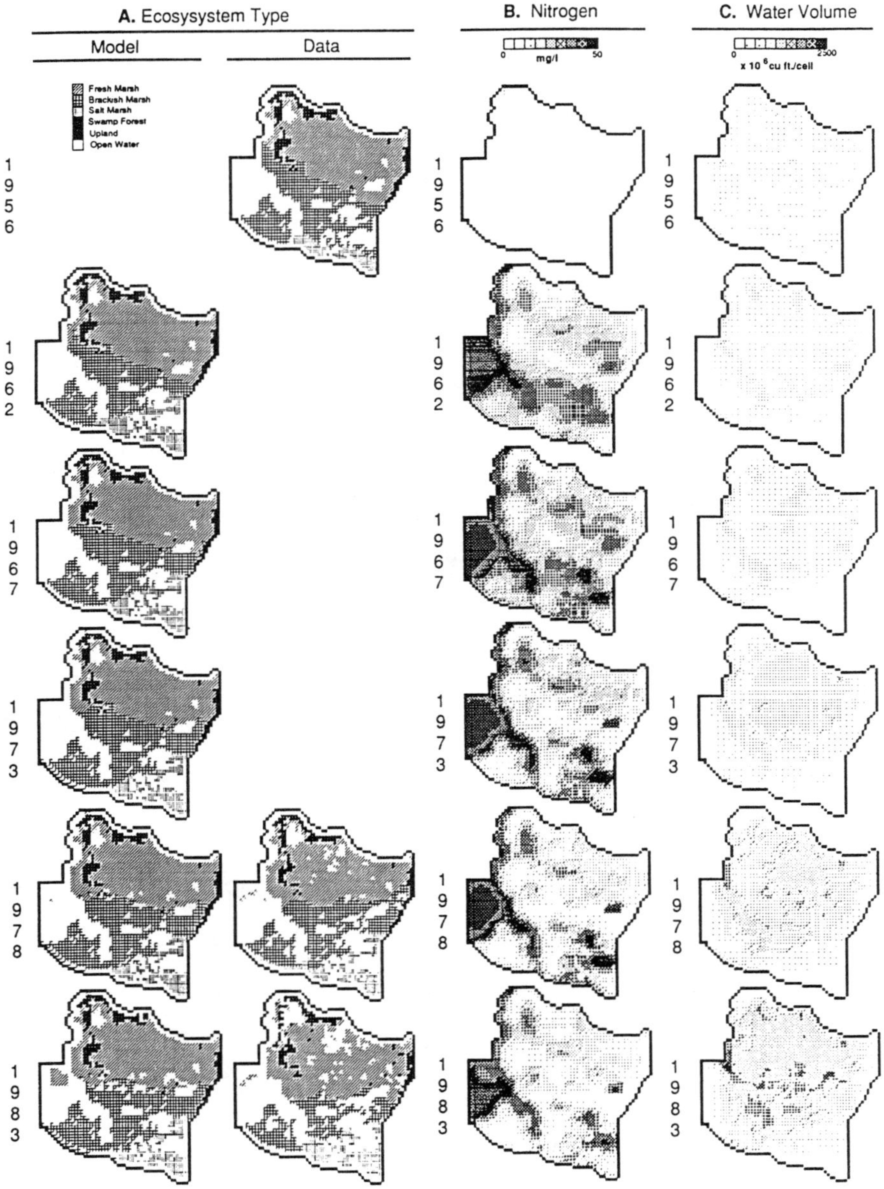
A. Ecosysystem Type
Model
Data
Fresh Marsh
Brackish Marsh
Salt Marsh
Swamp Forest
Upland
Open Water
B. Nitrogen
0
mg/l
50
C. Water Volume
0
2500
x 10 ^{6} cu ft./cell
1956
1962
1967
1973
1978
1983

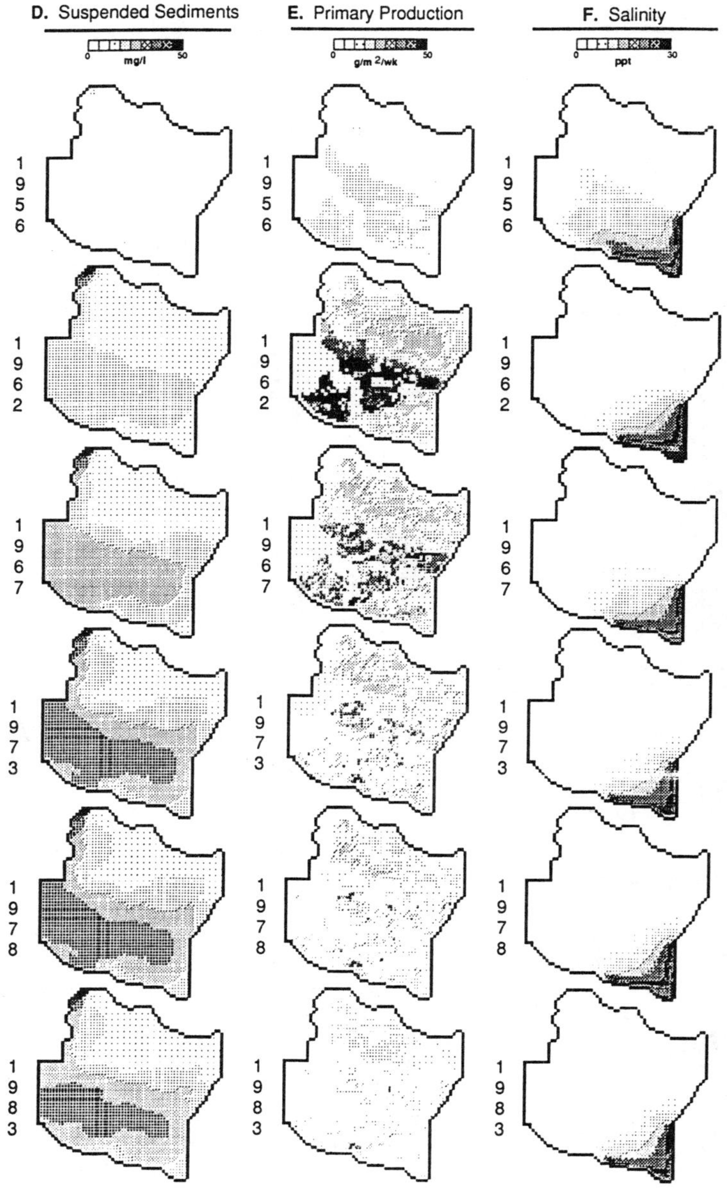

Figure 9. Sample model prediction output from the CELSS model, starting with the 1956 initial conditions. **a.** Ecosystem type distribution along with real ecosystem type data for 1978 and 1983. **b.** Nitrogen. **c.** Water volume. **d.** Suspended sediments. **e.** Primary production. **f.** Salinity for selected years.

overall land cover probabilities (frequencies) as the 1978 data (labeled "random 1978"). A simple Markov chain model is a slightly more sophisticated null model that incorporates the statistical trend in habitat changes in the area in the form of transition probabilities (or frequencies) of each habitat type into each other type during the 1956–1978 interval. The fit for various window sizes for the Markov model is labeled "Markov model." Finally, the 1956 initial conditions represent a null model that predicts no change (labeled "initial conditions").

The CELSS simulation model performs better than any of the alternative or null models, but its performance can best be judged in relation to the null models. The simulation model fits the 1978 data better than "random" (F_t = 89.6% versus 32.5%) and "random 1978" (F_t = 89.6% versus 50%). The fit for "random 1978" approaches 100% as window size increases, indicating that the overall percentages of habitat types are the same, but the pattern is not well matched.

If only the fit at window size 1 is considered, the 1956 initial conditions null model does not appear to be much worse than the CELSS model (86% versus 81%). The initial conditions null model appears to fit fairly well because only approximately 20% of the cells actually changed type between 1956 and 1978. But the pattern of fit is revealed by looking at the plots of fit versus window size in Figure 7. The CELSS model plot increases rapidly as window size increases indicating that the patterns of the model and data are similar. The initial conditions null model exhibits a flatter plot, indicating the patterns are not as similar. Total weighted fit (F_t) reflects this added pattern matching (89.6% versus 81.6%).

The Markov null model has a lower fit (69%) at window size 1 than the initial conditions null model (81%), but the fit increases more rapidly as window size increases. At the maximal window size, it fits better than the initial conditions model because the total number of cells of each type is closer to the 1978 data. Total weighted fit for the Markov model is less than the initial conditions model (81.6% versus 76.1%) because, by randomly placing the transition cells, the detailed spatial pattern is disrupted even while the fit is increased at larger window sizes.

The CELSS model is the only alternative that also predicts changes in the underlying physical and ecological processes and that links these changes in a causal way to ecosystem type changes. Thus, even if it were only as good as the alternative models at predicting ecosystem type changes, the CELSS model would be preferred for management applications because it can address the underlying reasons for habitat changes and the relative impacts of human changes on these processes.

This is not to say that the CELSS model approach to spatial ecosystem modeling is in all aspects superior to other possible approaches. Like anything else, it has advantages and disadvantages. Its advantages are the ability to deal with a large, complex ecological system in a relatively realistic way. If the goal of the modeling effort is to make specific predictions about specific management alternatives in a specific region, then these advantages are crucial.

In achieving realism, however, this approach must sacrifice some generality. The model's parameters must be calibrated to historical conditions for each application of the model. Thus, while the CELSS modeling approach can be applied to any coastal area, its specific results in one area are not directly generalizable to other areas.

We compared the CELSS model simulations for some of the physical variables with a more elaborate hydrodynamic model of the area constructed by the Corps of Engineers' Waterways Experiment Station (WES; Donnell and Letter in press, Letter 1982). The WES model deals with fewer variables (water, salt, and sediments) over much shorter time scales (maximum of one week continuous runs with time steps of minutes or seconds). It gives a more precise picture of short-term water, salt, and sediment levels and fluxes, whereas the CELSS model is more concerned with long-term ecosystem succession as driven by such factors as long-term water, salt, and sediment fluxes.

In general, the two models agree fairly well for their areas of overlap. Figure 8 shows the fit between the CELSS model and the WES model for salinity over several window sizes. The weighted average fit for this comparison was approximately 80%.

No one model can provide a complete picture of a complex phenomenon such as Louisiana's coastal marshes. Like the blind men all feeling different parts of an elephant and coming to different conclusions about what it is, we must take the results of a suite of modeling and experimental studies and integrate them to provide a reasonable overall picture.

Base case output. The CELSS model can produce a huge amount of output. Some of the most useful pieces of output are contour maps for each of the eight state variables and for internal flows (i.e., sedimentation) and ex-

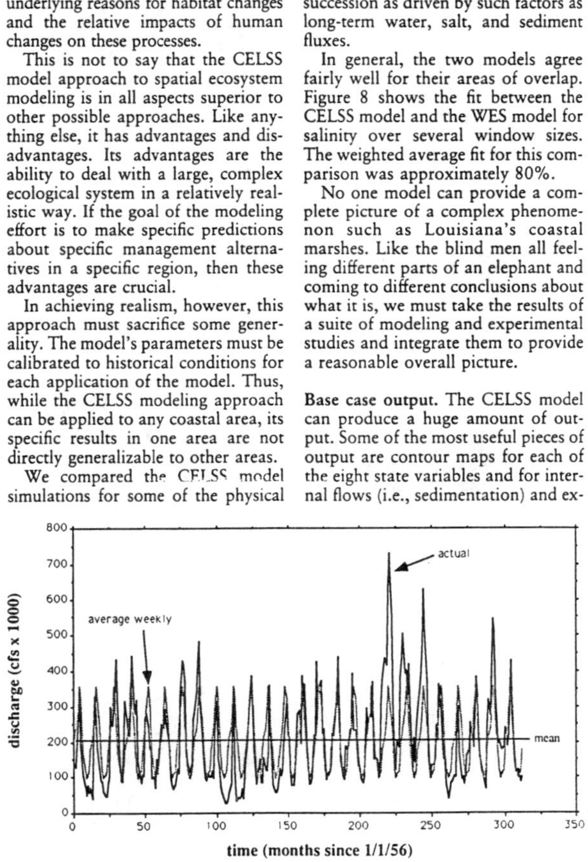

Figure 10. Atchafalaya River discharge data for 1956–1983 period. Also shown are the weekly average data and the mean for the period.

changes between cells (i.e., water flow) for each week of the simulation. The results of the model are best comprehended by viewing animations of the model's time series mapped output for each of the variables. Here, we can only present a few example snapshots of the model's output and discuss some of the findings.

Figure 9 shows some sample output from the base-case run of the CELSS model, covering the period 1956–1983. Starting with the 1956 initial conditions, the model's predictions of average annual ecosystem distribution (the ecosystem that was present in the cell for the majority of the year), salinity, suspended sediments, water volume, nitrogen, and primary production for several years are shown, along with the real ecosystem type data for 1978 and 1983 for comparison with the model's output.

The CELSS model accurately reproduced the gradual intrusion of salt into the system from the southeastern part of the study area with the concurrent freshening in the southwestern sector due to increased Atchafalaya River input (Figure 9f). It also shows a loss of elevation in the north and an increase in elevation in the south. Both of these trends are indicative of river water and sediments moving further south in recent times, as well as a lack of connectivity with the more northern fresh marsh areas due to levee construction. Predicted water volume (Figure 9c) and suspended sediments (Figure 9d) behaved in a similar way and are generally consistent with what is known about the historical behavior of these variables in the area.

Scenario analysis

Once the model was calibrated, we analyzed a series of future and historical scenarios. The scenarios can be divided into four categories: *climate scenarios,* which address the impacts of climate variations on the model's behavior; *management scenarios,* which address the impacts of various internal site-specific manipulations to the system; *historical scenarios,* which address what the system would have looked like if the environment had not been altered by human intervention or if climatic conditions had been different, and *boundary scenar-*

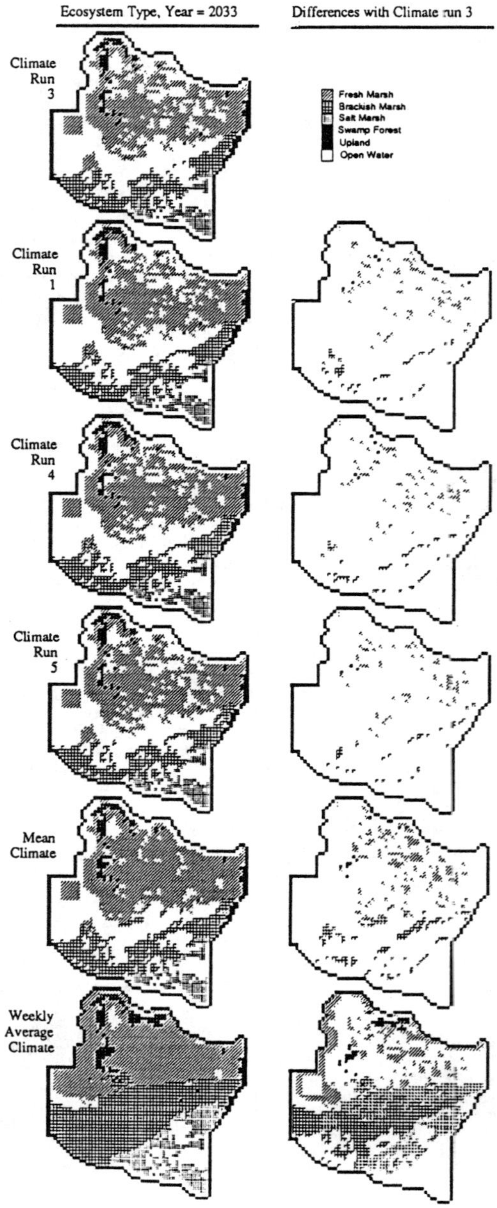

Figure 11. Ecosystem type maps for 2033 under various selected climate scenarios.

Table 2. Number of square kilometers of each ecosystem type for the three years for which data is available and for 2033 for various scenarios. Changes from the base case (in sqare kilometer) are indicated in parentheses.

	Swamp	Fresh marsh	Brackish marsh	Saline marsh	Upland	Total land	Open water
1956	130	864	632	98	13	1737	742
1978	113	766	554	150	18	1601	878
1983	116	845	347	155	18	1481	998
2033 Scenarios[*]							
Climate scenarios[†]							
Climate run 3 (climate base case)	84	871	338	120	10	1423	1056
Climate run 1	79 (−5)	874 (+3)	337 (−1)	127 (+7)	10 (0)	1427 (+4)	1052 (−4)
Climate run 4	85 (+1)	900 (+29)	355 (+17)	130 (+10)	10 (0)	1480 (+57)	999 (−57)
Climate run 5	83 (−1)	891 (+20)	332 (+6)	126 (+6)	10 (0)	1442 (+19)	1037 (−19)
Mean climate	94 (+10)	974 (+103)	402 (+64)	136 (+16)	11 (+1)	1617 (+194)	862 (−194)
Weekly average climate	128 (+44)	961 (+90)	813 (+475)	300 (+180)	11 (+1)	2213 (+790)	266 (−790)
Management scenarios							
No levee extension (base case)	100	796	410	123	15	1444	1035
Two-reach levee extension	98 (−2)	804 (+8)	399 (−11)	123 (0)	15 (0)	1439 (−5)	1040 (+5)
CLF marsh management	102 (+2)	798 (+2)	409 (−1)	123 (0)	15 (0)	1447 (+3)	1032 (−3)
Falgout Weir	104 (+4)	799 (+3)	403 (−7)	122 (−1)	16 (+1)	1444 (0)	1035 (0)
Full six-reach levee extension	103 (+3)	790 (−6)	362 (−48)	122 (−1)	15 (0)	1392 (−52)	1087 (+52)
Fresh-water diversion (FWD)	103 (+3)	803 (+7)	404 (−6)	123 (0)	15 (0)	1448 (+4)	1031 (−4)
FWD and Palmetto Weir	102 (+2)	802 (+6)	407 (−3)	123 (0)	15 (0)	1449 (+5)	1030 (−5)
FWD and Superior Weir	104 (+4)	799 (+3)	404 (−6)	123 (0)	15 (0)	1445 (+1)	1034 (−1)
FWD and Superior and Palmetto weirs	104 (+4)	792 (−4)	407 (−3)	123 (0)	15 (0)	1441 (−3)	1038 (+3)
FWD and Superior and Falgout weirs	104 (+4)	803 (+7)	407 (−3)	122 (−1)	15 (0)	1451 (+7)	1028 (−7)
Boundary scenarios[‡]							
EPA low sea level rise	104 (+4)	800 (+4)	411 (+1)	124 (+1)	15 (0)	1454 (+10)	1025 (−10)
EPA high sea level rise	89 (−11)	794 (−2)	396 (−14)	131 (+8)	15 (0)	1425 (−19)	1054 (+19)
Historical scenarios[§]							
No original Avoca Levee	84	951	350	126	13	1524	955
No effects	130	863	401	144	12	1550	929

[*]The summary maps and this table indicate the dominant habitat type for each cell (i.e., the ecosystem type present in the cell for the largest amount of time during the year). Alternatively, we could have added the total number of cells of each ecosystem type for each week of the simulated year and divided the totals by 52. Although this gives a somewhat more accurate picture of the habitat distribution, it is inconsistent with the totals from the maps.

[†]The climate analysis scenarios used a slightly different set of parameters for the model than the other scenarios. See text for details.

[‡]EPA low scenario is a 50-centimeter rise by 2100. We used 0.46 cm/yr, which is double the historical rate of eustatic sea level rise in the study area of 0.23 cm/yr. Subsidence in the study area varies horizontally from 0.57 to 1.17 cm/yr, giving historical rates of apparent sea level rise (eustatic rise plus subsidence) of 0.8 to 1.4 cm/yr. EPA high scenario is a 200-centimeter rise by 2100 (1.67 cm/yr eustatic or 2.24 to 2.84 cm/yr apparent). Base case for comparison was no levee extension.

[§]No comparisons with a base case are given for the historical scenarios because these runs started in 1956 rather than 1983.

ios, which address the impacts of natural and human-induced variations in the systems' boundary conditions (i.e., sea level rise).

Management and boundary scenarios were run by restarting the model with the real 1983 ecosystem type map (rather than the model's predicted 1983 map) to ensure maximal realism. Climate and historical scenarios were run starting with 1956, so that the full impacts of climate and historical variations could be analyzed. After 1978, canal and levee construction for oil and gas exploration slowed significantly in the area compared with the 1956–1978 period. Therefore, all scenarios assumed that no additional canals or levees were constructed after 1978, except those specifically mentioned in the scenarios.

We present summary maps of the ecosystem type in the year 2033 for comparison of alternatives (Figures 11, 13, and 14). We also further summarize the results in Table 2, which lists for each alternative the total area of each ecosystem type in 2033, along with differences between each scenario and the base case.

Climate scenarios. Predicting future marsh succession required that we provide the model with predictions of future climate and boundary conditions. By *climate* we mean all the model's external forcing functions, including rainfall, Atchafalaya River flow, wind, and sea level.

For example, Figure 10 is a plot of Atchafalaya River discharge during the 1956–1983 period showing the weekly data used in calibrating the model. To project the base case climate into the future, we selected at random one-, two-, or three-year blocks from this record, modified them by randomly increasing or decreasing each point a maximum of 10%, and added this block to the end of the projected time series. This exercise provided a series of future years that were statistically identical to the past record and included the seasonal timing of the historical signals, but allowed for some novel random variations. We produced several future climate runs with this algorithm and tested the model's response to each. Some examples are shown in Figure 11.

We were also interested in what

part of the behavior of the system was due to random, aperiodic variations in climatic variables; what part was due to the annual periodic signal; and what part was due to the mean or average signal. We therefore analyzed two additional climate scenarios. These were the weekly average climate scenario, in which each week's value for each climate variable for the entire run from 1956 to 2033 was set at the average value for that week from the 1956 to 1983 data, and the mean-climate scenario, in which the long-term average for each variable was used for all weeks. For example, Figure 10 shows both the weekly average and mean signals for Atchafalaya River discharge.

Figures 11 and 12 show the projected ecosystem type maps for the year 2033 and a summary of the land/water balance in the system during the 1956–2033 period for the various climate scenarios. These figures clearly show the major effect of differing climate assumptions on the model. The base case runs show a moderate amount of difference due to the different random components in each run, but the general behavior was approximately the same. In all other future scenarios, we used the climate run labeled 3, because this case produced intermediate results.

The degree to which the other climate scenarios affected the results was surprising. The weekly average climate scenario produced a drastic reversal in land loss in the area. The mean climate scenario produced only a moderate decrease in land loss. This result indicates that the annual flood cycle and other annual periodicities in the climate are important to the land building process, but that random, aperiodic events (such as major storms and floods) tend to have a net erosional effect on marshland. A periodic but predictable climate seems to maximize marsh building. If global climate becomes less predictable in the future due to global warming, it may bode ill for the stability of coastal marshes.

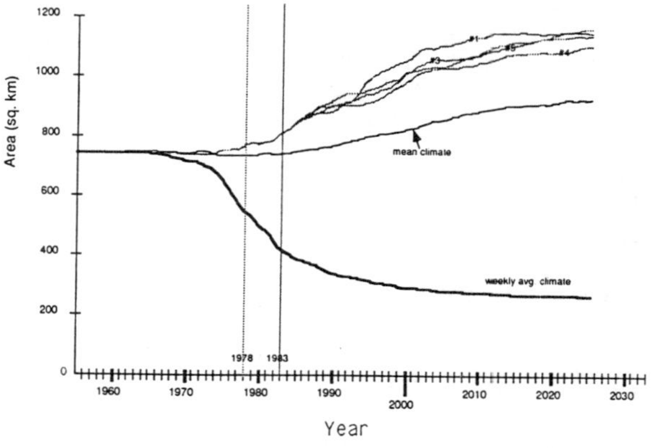

Figure 12. Summary time series of total open water area predictions under various climate scenarios.

Management alternatives. A base case run and several management alternatives were analyzed using the model. The results for 2033 for selected alternatives are summarized in Figure 13a and Table 2. The figure shows both the ecosystem type map resulting from each alternative in 2033 and the cells that are different from those in the base case run, regardless of the direction of change. All the alternatives (see Figure 3) except the base case assume the two-reach Avoca Island levee extension (a 15-kilometer extension to the current levee system on the Atchafalaya River) has been built. The results for the other management options therefore indicate the amount of remaining (unmitigated) impact from the two-reach levee extension. All alternatives used climate run 3.

Base case. The base case of the model assumed the canal network fixed as it was in 1978. As shown in Table 2, the base case run indicates a net land loss to open water of 37 km^2 from 1983 to 2033. Most of this loss occurred in fresh (-49 km^2) or saline marsh (-32 km^2) that was either converted to open water or to brackish marsh ($+63$ km^2) due to continued fresh water inputs via the Atchafalaya River.

The overall rate of land loss predicted by the model to occur after 1983 (0.75 km^2/yr) was much lower than the rates between 1956 and 1978 (6.2 km^2/yr) and between 1978 and 1983 (24 km^2/yr). There was therefore some concern that the model may be seriously underestimating the future rate of land loss.

To test the model's predictions, we performed a careful visual inspection of infrared aerial photographs taken in December 1988, which indicated that the rates of land loss have indeed slowed dramatically in the study area. Areas which appeared stressed in 1983 and which might have been expected to succeed to open water habitat have remained as marsh, as the model predicted. There were no apparent areas of significant marsh loss in the study area between 1983 and 1988, as predicted by the base case run of the model. The 1988 photographs are currently being interpreted and digitized to allow a quantitative assessment of the model's predictions, but it is clear that the model provided a better prediction of the status of the area in 1988 than predictions based on simple extrapolation of past trends. This finding underscores the effectiveness of our spatial, process-based approach to landscape modeling.

Two-reach levee extension. The model was then modified in structure to allow for the construction of the first two reaches of the proposed Avoca Island levee extension. All other model parameters were held constant and identical climate inputs were used. The predicted effects are the indirect effects of the construction and do not include the acreage directly affected by construction.

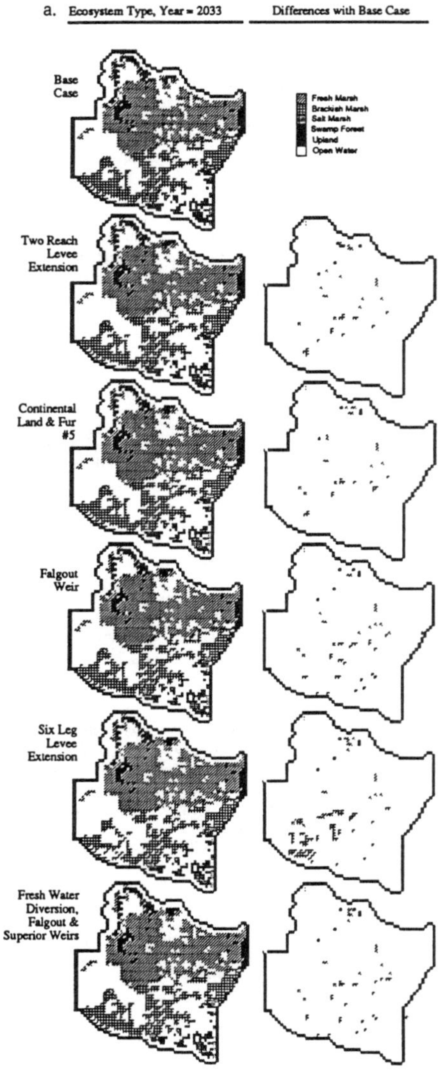

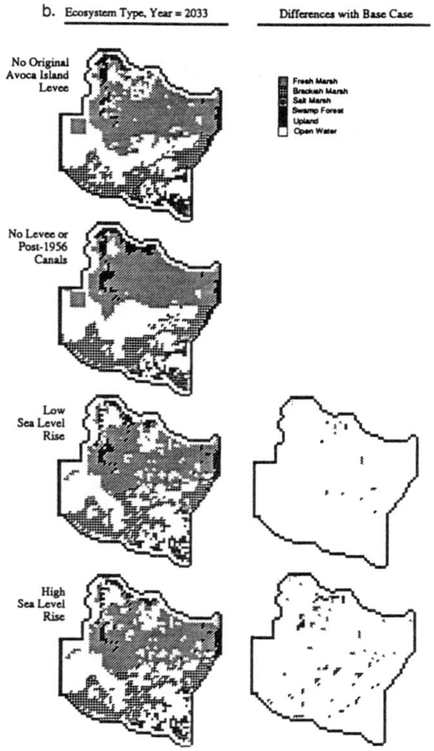

Figure 13. a. Ecosystem type maps for 2033 under various management scenarios. **b.** Ecosystem type maps for 2033 under various boundary and historical scenarios.

The result was a relatively modest net negative land loss (-5 km^2) compared to the base case, mostly from the brackish marsh category. Most of the effects were at the fresh/brackish interface, due to the redirection of fresh water by the levee extension further south in the study area. All the other management alternatives assumed the two-reach levee extension was in place, so that their ability to mitigate its effects could be estimated.

CONTINENTAL LAND AND FUR MARSH MANAGEMENT PLAN. Implementation in the model of Soil Conservation Service Treatment Unit #5 of the Continental Land and Fur proposed marsh management plan involved establishing levees and weirs to control water levels in an approximately 4-square-kilometer area (see Figure 3). The plan was installed in 1988, three years after the proposed levee extension was implemented in the model. This alternative resulted in a slight net gain of land (+3 km^2) relative to the base case. It caused modest gains in fresh marsh and swamp (+2 km^2 each) balanced by smaller losses in brackish marsh (−1 km^2) due to indirect effects on water flow patterns.

FALGOUT WEIR. Implementation of this alternative involved a run of the model with a weir at the entrance of the Falgout Canal, beginning in model year 1985. This alternative resulted in zero net gain of land relative to the base case. It caused increases in fresh marsh (probably due to reduction of salt water intrusion) and swamp, but also caused losses in brackish marsh that canceled out these gains.

FULL SIX-REACH LEVEE EXTENSION. We also analyzed the full six-reach (25 km) levee extension that had been under consideration at one time (see Figure 3). This scenario involved introducing the levee extension beginning in 1983, with completion of the final reach in 1988. This alternative results in a relatively large net loss of land (−52 km^2) relative to the base case. The majority of the loss was from the brackish marsh (−48 km^2) and, to a lesser extent, from the fresh marsh (−6 km^2). The full levee extension prevented sediment-laden water from reaching the brackish marshes bordering Four League Bay, where most of the loss occurs.

FRESH-WATER DIVERSION STRUCTURE. This run of the model included a fresh-water diversion structure located in the northwest corner of Avoca Lake (see Figure 3), installed in 1985. The fresh-water diversion structure would allow 2% of the Atchafalaya River flow to be diverted into the Terrebonne Marsh, up to a river flow of 370,000 cubic feet per second. At and above this flow, the diversion flow is turned off to prevent backwater flooding.

This alternative resulted in a net gain of land (+4 km^2) relative to the base case. The filling of Avoca Lake with sediments, which would be expected to occur with a water diversion structure, did not take place in the model. The flow of water did not allow for significant sedimentation because the turbulence is too high near the division structure. The CELSS model does not, however, currently distinguish sediment grain sizes, and it may not adequately account for large-grain sediments that fall out quickly near a diversion site. If coarse-grained sediments make up a significant fraction of the total, the net land gain under this scenario may therefore be higher than the model predicts.

PALMETTO WEIR AND FRESH-WATER DIVERSION. Implementation of this alternative involved a run of the model with a weir on Palmetto Bayou (see Figure 3). The weir was installed in model year 1985 and allowed flow one way to the south. The fresh-water diversion structure was installed as described above and run with the same limits on the river flow conditions.

This alternative resulted in a 5-square-kilometer net land gain relative to the base case and only a one-cell land gain relative to the simulation with fresh-water diversion as the only mitigation. Because the weir is preventing the newly diverted water from flowing out Palmetto Bayou, redirected water has beneficial effects in the brackish marsh. It does, however, flood some of the fresh marsh just north of the weir.

SUPERIOR WEIR AND FRESH-WATER DIVERSION. Implementation of this alternative involved a run of the model with a weir on Superior Canal at the location of an existing plug (see Figure 3). The weir was installed in model year 1985 and allowed flow one way to the south. The fresh-water diversion structure was installed as described above and run with the same limits on the river flow conditions.

This alternative resulted in a 1-square-kilometer net land gain relative to the base case. The swamp habitat in the north is prevented from succeeding to open water, and land loss occurs just to the north. The retardation of the diverted water, which is beneficial to the swamp, waterlogs the marsh in the south and causes land loss there.

FRESH-WATER DIVERSION STRUCTURE AND BOTH PALMETTO AND SUPERIOR WEIRS. This run included the fresh-water diversion structure and both the Palmetto Bayou Weir and the Superior Canal Weir, as described above. This model run illustrates the importance of cumulative impacts. In this scenario there is a net loss of land (−3 km^2) relative to the base case. This net loss occurs even though the structures each produced a predicted net gain when used individually. The effects are not additive, however. The positive effects of the sediments in the fresh water are overcome by the negative effects of waterlogging when both weirs are used, but not when either one is used by itself. There is some optimal balance of water-diversion rate and location and weir location that can best be determined by iterative simulations of a model of this type.

FRESH-WATER DIVERSION STRUCTURE AND BOTH FALGOUT AND SUPERIOR WEIRS. This scenario included the Falgout Canal Weir, the Palmetto Bayou Weir, and the fresh-water diversion structure. This alternative resulted in a net gain of land (+7 km^2) relative to the base case. This net gain occurred mainly in the swamp and fresh marsh ecosystem types, due mainly to increased sediment flows to these areas as a result of the diversion. This combination of management alternatives yielded the largest positive net land gain of those we have investigated thus far.

Boundary scenarios. One important boundary scenario was analyzed—the effect of increasing rates of future sea level rise due to global warming. Projected rates of future sea level rise are in the range of 50 to 200 cm during the next 120 years (or 0.42 to 1.67 cm/yr; Titus 1988) Coastal Louisiana has historically experienced high rates of apparent sea level rise due to regional subsidence. In the study area, this rate has ranged from 0.57 to 1.17 cm/yr (0.23 cm/yr from eustatic or general oceanic sea level rise and the remainder from subsidence; Penland et al. 1987). Thus coastal Louisiana represents an appropriate laboratory for studying the response of coastal wetlands to high rates of sea level rise (Day and Templet 1989).

We experimented with the CELSS model to study the effects on the study area of the projected higher rates of sea level rise. Figure 13b and Table 2 show the results for rates of eustatic sea level rise of 0.46 and 1.67 cm/yr (1.03 to 1.63 and 2.24 to 2.84 cm/yr apparent rates including subsidence) starting in model year 1983.

The results were somewhat surprising. Doubling the rate of eustatic sea level rise (from 0.23 to 0.46 cm/yr) actually caused a slight net gain in land in the study area (+10 km^2, or 0.7% of the total land area) relative to the base case. We believe this increase occurs because, in the presence of high sediment loads, healthy coastal marshes can keep up with moderate rates of sea level rise. In fact, the entire existing coastal marsh system in Louisiana has developed in the presence of high apparent rates of sea level rise (Day and Templet 1989). If sea level rise rates become high enough, however, the marshes can no longer keep up. The Environmental Protection Agency's higher rate of sea level rise (1.67 cm/yr eustatic, 2.24 cm/yr apparent) caused a net loss of land of 19 km^2 (or 1.3% of the total land area).

These results indicate that healthy coastal marshes with adequate sediment inputs may act as a buffer against moderate rates of sea level rise. The marshes build coastal marshland as fast as the sea can rise to inundate it.

Historical scenarios. Two historical scenarios were analyzed. We looked at how the system would have evolved if the original Avoca Island levee had not been built or if neither the levee nor the the post-1956 canals had been built. Results are summarized in Figure 13b and Table 2. These results indicate that both the original levee and the canals had a major effect on the evolution of the system. Results of these runs are not directly comparable with the base case 2033 scenario, because the base case was restarted with actual 1983 data, whereas the historical scenarios had to use model predictions for 1983. Nevertheless, it is clear that the post-1956 canals and the original levee caused increased land loss in the area compared to what would have happened without them.

Conclusions

The CELSS model simulation of long-term ecosystem changes demonstrates that spatially linked ecological and physical processes can be realistically modeled on modern supercomputers. The results of the CELSS model indicate complex and often counterintuitive behavior that, like the real system, is difficult to summarize. This observation is not surprising, given that the CELSS model trades off generality for realism. The model is most enlightening in its elaboration of the effects of specific cases. Nevertheless, a few general conclusions can be drawn from this modeling exercise.

- Past and future climate variations are important, especially severe deviations from average conditions (i.e., severe droughts, floods, and hurricanes). Random climate variations with no change in the historical trends can cause changes in the region of approximately equal magnitude to that of the human modifications analyzed. A comprehensive, process-based model such as the CELSS model is essential to separate these effects. Projected future climate changes (particularly changes in the predictability of climates) due to global warming can cause major changes in the region.

- Ecological variables, such as primary production, have significant feedback to physical and chemical processes and significantly affect the model's ability to replicate historical changes in ecosystem type distribution.

- Coastal marshes can adapt to future projected higher rates of sea level rise and serve as a buffer against future global sea level rise if the rates are moderate, sediment sources are available, and the marshes remain healthy.

- Past activities in the area that modified the hydrologic and sediment flow patterns, such as canal and levee construction, at critical stages had significant influence on the evolution of the region. Proposed future modifications seem to have smaller effects, partly because they will occur at less critical times in this landscape's evolution.

- Management options in the area can be effective at mitigating the effects of proposed human alterations, but cumulative effects make analysis of individual options in isolation risky. Process-based spatial models such as CELSS may be necessary to incorporate these cumulative effects, to effectively weigh the costs and benefits of major projects, and to design optimal coastal management strategies.

At present, ecosystem models of the size and complexity of the CELSS model are fairly new and expensive to build and run. But as we gain experience, and as supercomputers and parallel processors become more readily available, models of this type will become more practical tools for understanding and managing ecosystems. Future studies might employ parallel computers (e.g., the Connection Machine[1] or microcomputer-based transputer systems such as TransLink[2] boards) to radically improve the speed, complexity, and ease of use of spatial ecosystem models.

We are currently applying the CELSS approach at multiple scales to other coastal areas in Louisiana, Maryland, and South Carolina, and we plan to continue to modify, improve, and experiment with the existing model toward the goal of better environmental management. We hope to learn enough from these applications and experiments to allow both scaling up of this approach for global ecosystem modeling to assess the impacts of global climate change and scaling down to assess local effects in more detail.

Acknowledgments

This research was supported by the US Fish and Wildlife Service in part with funds from the US Army Corps of Engineers under cooperative agreement #14-16-0009-84-921 titled "Spatial Simulation Modeling of Coastal Wetland Systems for Evaluating Management Alternatives" (E. Pendleton, project officer) and by from the National Science Foundation under project BSR-8906269 titled "Landscape Modeling: The Synthesis

[1] Thinking Machine Corp., 215 First Street, Cambridge, MA 02112.

[2] Levco Corp., 6160 Lusk Boulevard, San Diego, CA 92121.

of Ecological Processes Over Large Geographic Regions and Long Time Scales." Computer time on the CRAY supercomputer at the University of Illinois was provided by the National Center for Supercomputer Applications (NCSA) and by an NSF grant on modeling landscape dynamics (D. Jameson, principal investigator). The NCSA staff was extremely helpful in the performance of this research. We thank J. W. Day Jr. for his critical role in the birth and success of this project and for his input on model formulation and evaluation of results, W. Kitchens for getting this project off the ground, T. Ozman, K. Sampey, S. Leibowitz, P. Nepalli, S. Nellore, M. Ahmed, and P. Templet Jr. for their contributions to computer programming and data assembly, and three anonymous reviewers for their helpful comments on earlier drafts of the manuscript.

References cited

Bahr, L. M., R. Costanza, J. W. Day Jr., S. E. Bayley, C. Neill, S. G. Leibowitz, and J. Fruci. 1983. Ecological characterization of the Mississippi Deltaic Plain Region: a narrative with management recommendations. FWS/OBS-82/69, US Fish and Wildlife Service Division of Biological Service, Washington, DC.

Baumann, R. H., and R. Adams. 1981. The creation and restoration of wetlands by natural processes in the lower Atchafalaya River system: possible conflicts with navigation and flood control management. Pages 1–24 in R. H. Stovall, ed. *Proceedings of the Eighth Annual Conference on Wetlands Restoration and Creation.* Hillsborough, FL.

Baumann, R. H., J. W. Day Jr., and C. A. Miller. 1984. Mississippi deltaic wetland survival: sedimentation versus coastal submergence. *Science* 224: 1093–1095.

Botkin, D. B., J. F. Janak, and J. R. Wallis. 1972. Some ecological consequences of a computer model of forest growth. *J. Ecol.* 60: 849–872.

Cleveland, C. J., C. Neill, and J. W. Day Jr. 1981. The impact of artificial canals on land loss in the Barataria Basin, Louisiana. Pages 425–434 in W. J. Mitsch, R. W. Bosserman, and J. M. Klopatek, eds. *Energy and Ecological Modeling.* Elsevier, Amsterdam.

Conner, W. H., and J. W. Day Jr., eds. 1987. The ecology of the Barataria Basin, Louisiana: an estuarine profile. US Fish and Wildlife Service biology report 85(7.13).

Costanza, R. 1987a. Social traps and environmental policy. *BioScience.* 37: 407–412.

______. 1987b. Simulation modeling on the Macintosh using STELLA. *BioScience.* 37: 129–132.

______. 1989. Model goodness of fit: a multiple resolution procedure. *Ecol. Model.* 47: 199–215.

Costanza, R., S. C. Farber, and J. Maxwell. In press. The valuation and management of wetland ecosystems. *Ecological Economics.*

Costanza, R., C. Neill, S. G. Leibowitz, J. R. Fruci, L. M. Bahr Jr., and J. W. Day Jr. 1983. Ecological models of the Mississippi deltaic plain region: data collection and presentation. FWS/OBS-82/68, US Fish and Wildlife Service, Division of Biological Service, Washington, DC.

Costanza, R., and F. H. Sklar. 1985. Articulation, accuracy, and effectiveness of mathematical models: a review of freshwater wetland applications. *Ecol. Model.* 27: 45–68.

Costanza, R., F. H. Sklar, M. L. White, and J. W. Day Jr. 1988. A dynamic spatial simulation model of land loss and marsh succession in coastal Louisiana. Page 99–114 in W. J. Mitsch, M. Straskraba, and S. E. Jørgensen, eds. *Wetland Modelling.* Elsevier, Amsterdam.

Craig, N. J., R. E. Turner, and J. W. Day Jr. 1979. Land loss in coastal Louisiana (U.S.A.) *Environ. Manage.* 3: 133–144.

Day, J. W. Jr., and P. H. Templet. 1989. Consequences of sea level rise: implications from the Mississippi Delta. *Coastal Management* 17: 241–257.

Deegan, L. A., H. M. Kennedy, and C. Neill. 1984. Natural factors and human modifications contributing to marshloss in Louisiana's Mississippi River deltaic plain. *Environ. Manage.* 8: 519–528.

Donnell, B., and J. V. Letter. In press. The Atchafalaya River delta. Report 11. Two dimensional model verification. Waterways Experiment Station, Vicksburg, MS.

Farber, S., and R. Costanza. 1987. The economic value of wetlands system. *J. Environ. Manage.* 24: 41–51.

Gagliano, S. M., K. J. Meyer-Arendt, and K. M. Wicker. 1981. Land loss in the Mississippi River deltaic plain. *Trans. Gulf Coast Assoc. Geol. Soc.* 31: 285–300.

Gardner, R. H., W. G. Cale, and R. V. O'Neill. 1982. Robust analysis of aggregation error. *Ecology* 63: 1771–1779.

Hall, C. A. S., and D. L. DeAngelis. 1985. Models in ecology: paradigms found or paradigms lost? *Bulletin of the Ecological Society of America* 66: 339–346.

Hopkinson, C. S. 1978. The relation of man and nature in Barataria Basin, Louisiana. Ph.D. dissertation, Louisiana State University, Baton Rouge.

Jørgensen, S. E. 1982. Modelling the eutrophication of shallow lakes. Pages 125–155 in D. O. Logofet and N. K. Luckyanov, eds. *Ecosystem Dynamics in Freshwater Wetlands and Shallow Water Bodies.* vol 2. UNEP/SCOPE, USSSR Academy of Sciences, Moscow.

Leibowitz, S. 1989. The pattern and process of land loss in coastal Louisiana: a landscape ecological analysis. Ph.D. dissertation, Louisiana State University, Baton Rouge.

Letter, J. V. Jr. 1982. The Atchafalaya River deta: extrapolation of delta growth. Waterways Experiment Station, technical report HL-82-15. Vicksburg, MS.

Levins, R. 1966. The strategy of model building in population biology. *Am. Sci.* 54: 421–431.

Penland, S., K. E. Ramsey, R. A. McBride, T. F. Moslow, and K. A. Westphal. 1987. Relative sea level rise and subsidence in Louisiana and the Gulf of Mexico. Louisiana Geological Survey, Coastal Geology Section, Baton Rouge.

Phipps, R. L. 1979. Simulation of wetland forest vegetation dynamics. *Ecol. Model.* 7: 257–288.

Potter, G. L., H. W. Ellsaesser, M. C. MacCracken, and F. M. Luther. 1979. Performance of the Lawrence Livermore Laboratory zonal atmospheric model. Pages 852–871 in W. L. Gates, ed. Report of the JOC study conference on climate models: performance, intercomparison and sensitivity studies. Global Atmospheric Research Programme Series no. 22, Washington, DC.

Roberts, H. H., R. D. Adams, and R. H. Cunningham. 1980. Evolution of the sand-dominated subaerial phase, Atchafalaya Delta, Louisiana. *Am Assoc. Pet. Geol. Bull.* 64: 264–279.

Scaife, W. W., R. E. Turner, and R. Costanza. 1983. Coastal Louisiana recent land loss and canal impacts. *Environ. Manage.* 7: 433–442.

Schlesinger, M. E., and Z. C. Zhao, 1989. Seasonal climatic changes induced by doubled CO_2 as simulated by the OSU atmospheric GCM/mixed-layer ocean model. *Journal of Climate* 2: 463–499

Sklar, F. H., R. Costanza, and J. W. Day Jr. 1985. Dynamic spatial simulation modeling of coastal wetland habitat succession. *Ecol. Modell.* 29: 261–281.

Sklar, F. H., M. L. White, and R. Costanza. In press. The Coastal Ecological Landscape Spatial Simulation (CELSS) model: structure and results for the Atchafalaya/Terrebonne study area. NWRC open file report. US Fish and Wildlife Service. Washington, DC.

Titus, J. G., ed. 1988. Greenhouse effect, sea level rise and coastal wetlands. EPA-230-05-86-013, Office of Policy, Planning, and Evaluation, Washington, DC.

Turner, M. G., R. Costanza, and F. H. Sklar. 1989. Methods to evaluate the performance of spatial simulation models. *Ecol. Modell.* 48: 1–18.

Turner, M. G., R. Costanza, T. M. Springer, and E. P. Odum. 1988. Market and nonmarket values of the Georgia landscape. *Environ. Manage.* 12: 209–217.

Washington, W. M., and D. L. Williamson. 1977. A description of the NCAR global circulation models. Pages 111–172 in J. Chang, ed. *Methods of Comparative Physics. vol. II. General Circulation Models of the Atmosphere.* Academic Press, New York.

Williams, J., R. G. Barry, and W. M. Washington. 1974. Simulation of the atmospheric circulation using the NCAR global circulation model with ice age boundary conditions. *Journal of Applied Meteorology* 11: 305–317.

Van Heerden, I. L., and H. H. Roberts. 1980a. The Atchafalaya Delta—Louisiana's new prograding coast. *Trans. Gulf Coast Assoc. Geol. Soc.* 30: 497–506.

______. 1980b. The Atchafalaya Delta—rapid progradation along a traditionally retreating coast (South Central Louisiana). *Zeitschrift Geomorphologie N.F.* 34: 186–201.

Assessing and Communicating Data Quality in Policy-Relevant Research

ROBERT COSTANZA*
Coastal and Environmental Policy Program
Center for Environmental and Estuarine Studies
University of Maryland
Solomons, Maryland 20688-0038, USA

SILVIO O. FUNTOWICZ
Commission of the European Communities
Joint Research Center
Institute of Systems Engineering and Informatics
I-21020 Ispra (VA), Italy

JEROME R. RAVETZ
The Research Methods Consultancy Ltd.
13 Temple Gardens
London NW11 0LP, UK

ABSTRACT / The quality of scientific information in policy-relevant fields of research is difficult to assess, and quality control in these important areas is correspondingly difficult to maintain. Frequently there are insufficient high-quality measurements for the presentation of the statistical uncertainty in the numerical estimates that are crucial to policy decisions. We propose and develop a grading system for numerical estimates that can deal with the full range of data quality—from statistically valid estimates to informed guesses. By analyzing the underlying quality of numerical estimates, summarized as spread and grade, we are able to provide simple rules whereby input data can be coded for quality, and these codings carried through arithmetical calculations for assessing the quality of model results. For this we use the NUSAP

KEY WORDS: Uncertainty; Data quality; NUSAP; Environmental policy; Policy-relevant research

*Author to whom correspondence should be addressed.

(numeral, unit, spread, assessment, pedigree) notational system. It allows the more quantitative and the more qualitative aspects of data uncertainty to be managed separately. By way of example, we apply the system to an ecosystem valuation study that used several different models and data of widely varying quality to arrive at a single estimate of the economic value of wetlands. The NUSAP approach illustrates the major sources of uncertainty in this study and can guide new research aimed at the improvement of the quality of outputs and the efficiency of the procedures.

The Problem of Data Quality in Policy-Relevant Research

In scientific research, as in any other sphere of activity, the maintenance of the quality of products is critical for their effective use. In matured fields of traditional science, quality control is exercised informally by the competent practitioners (Ravetz 1971). In most scientific studies, the scientists actually doing the analysis have a good working understanding of the inherent quality of their measurements and results, but there is no accepted method to communicate this knowledge of data quality to potential users of the information. When the results of research are intended to be used as inputs to public policy decisions, the users of this information must either be knowledgeable in the details of the research methods or accept the results with no idea of their quality. Usually, they lack the knowledge for performing their own assessment of quality and must do without. As a result, the policy process on very many issues is impaired. This deficiency is recognized in the courts, as when expert witnesses are used for technical questions, but the traditional criteria for the quality of personal testimony do not apply to scientific information and so the courts generally pursue the vain hope of scientific certainty. Worse yet, in the absence of a quality-assessment system, these deficiencies are largely unrecognized and their consequences are difficult to estimate. Grades for quality are routinely assigned in innumerable spheres of activity in our society; yet in the case of information, one of the most sensitive products we have, there are no standard systems for grading and hence no means for a socially effective system of quality control. This article presents a system aimed at rectifying this situation.

The standard techniques of statistics were developed to handle a different aspect of uncertainty. They assume that uncertainty is due to real, precisely measured variation in the populations being sampled. They generally assume that we have a probability distribution to work with, without asking how well we know that distribution. This article concentrates on the issue of how well we know the distribution (its quality) and how we [121]
may communicate that knowledge. The standard statistical assumptions are justifiable in the case of the traditional experimental or field sciences, but the data available in policy-related research is frequently so scattered and coarse that refined mathematical manipulations do not possess much genuine meaning when applied to them. The more basic problem is that of partitioning of the total uncertainty into that due to real variation in the population (statistical uncertainty) and that due to errors in measurement (data quality).

The achievement of scientific work of high quality requires the deployment of sophisticated craft skills, as well as the motivating force of commitment and morale. Therefore, a full specification of quality would be as complex and subtle a task as the research itself. Fortunately, from the inexpert user's point of view, the relevant aspects of quality depend more on the product than on the process. Since the product of research is information that has certain knowledge as its ideal, we can assess quality by that yardstick. The incompleteness of certainty (or the inevitable uncertainty) of scientific information can be used to define a system of quantitative estimates and qualitative grades. By this means the various aspects of the uncertainty, and hence of the quality, of scientific information can be described.

No scientific activity is free from uncertainty; we may say that the key to a science being matured in its success in the recognition, communication, and control of the various sorts of uncertainty that affect its results and predictions. These include inexactness, as expressed by significant digits, unreliability as expressed in systematic error, and others. No amount of sophisticated apparatus and computer power can replace theoretical understanding of the problems of uncertainty or the practical skills of controlling and communicating it.

When quantitative information is used to provide inputs for the policy process, as in the case of indicators in the social and environmental fields, the scientist's problems of management and communication of uncertainty are severe. First, the original data are rarely as well controlled as in the laboratory. Well-structured theories, normally expected to be available in basic or applied science, are conspicuously absent in policy-related research. Furthermore, such research is interdisciplinary, involving fields of varying states of maturity and with very different sorts of practice in their theoretical, experimental, and social dimensions. Scientists must use inputs from fields they do not know intimately, so they cannot make the same sensitive judgments of quality that they do in their own subject. The result is that the quality control on the research process is diluted; the quality assurance of results is weaker; and they command less confidence among users.

The problems of uncertainty in policy-related research are further increased in its public dimension. Science is judged by the public (including decision makers) by its performance in such sensitive areas as hazardous wastes, radioactive fallout, food additives, and reproduction engineering. All these involve much uncertainty and also inescapable social and ethical aspects. Simplicity and precision in predictions, or even in the assignment of safe limits, are not feasible; yet policy makers tend to expect straightforward information as inputs to their own decision-making process. They want their statistical indicators to provide them with certainty.

In such circumstances, the maintenance of confidence in science among policy makers and the general public becomes increasingly difficult. The issue manifests itself at several levels. The simplest is in the representation of uncertainty in quantitative estimates. For example, in risk assessments, the scientist who advises policy makers knows that a prediction like a one-in-a-million chance of a serious accident should be qualified with statements about the many sorts of uncertainty, so as to caution any user about the limits of reliability of the numerical assertions. If these are all expressed in prose, the statement becomes tedious and incomprehensible to the lay users; if they are omitted or even given in some simple statistical representation, then the same advisor can be accused of conveying a certainty that is not warranted by the facts. Lacking a means for qualifying his quantitative statements, the advisor is caught in a communications trap.

Yet another even worse dilemma is encountered whenever scientists give advice on policy-related issues. In addition to low-frequency hazards, these may concern diffused hazards, such as pesticides or food additives, or possible large-scale future environmental perturbations, such as the greenhouse effect. Such advice is usually supported by the present or expected behavior of some critical indicator. This dilemma has been stressed in a recent article by Maddox (1987) "Half-truths make sense (almost)". This was a comment on a prediction of the consequences of the greenhouse effect, using the rise in global mean temperature by 2030 AD as the indicator. Offering definite advice is a risky business: a prediction of danger will appear alarmist if nothing happens in the short run, while reassurance can be condemned if it retrospectively turns out to be incorrect. Then the credibility of science, traditionally based on its supposed infallibility, is threatened. Facing this dilemma, the scientific advisor may prudently refuse to accept low-quality expert opinions as a basis for quantitative threshold values and consequently decline to provide a definite opinion when requested by [122]
policy makers. Then science is perceived as failing to perform its public function of offering advice and assurance, and its legitimacy is again threatened. Thus, the credibility of science, based for so long on the supposed certainty of its conclusions, is endangered by *any* sort of statement on such inherently uncertain issues, be it advice or disclaimers. Is there no way to escape the horns of this dilemma, in which the credibility and the legitimacy of science are both at risk? As Maddox (1987) puts it, these are among the trials with which policy research centers must contend. "Tell the people that there is a muddle, or give them a clear message that they must man the barricades?" The World Resources Institute's solution to the dilemma (the adoption of a computer model) is described by Maddox as a "cop-out."

Thus, in policy-related research, the traditional tools for assuring quality through the control of uncertainty need to be enriched. To solve the scientific advisors' dilemma, one needs something more than bigger, faster computers and more data. Uncertainty is integral to these problems; it cannot be removed by technical means. It must be managed and effectively communicated so that it becomes a recognized input to the decision-making process. We should exhibit the structure of our uncertainty, so that the quality of our information in relation to its functions is assured. The notational system NUSAP (Funtowicz and Ravetz 1991) has been designed and developed to further the evolution toward these ends.

Science and the Management of Uncertainty

As natural science has grown and matured over the centuries, it has developed tools for the management of different sorts of uncertainty. Each particular set of tools was devised in response to a recognized problem. Quantitative measurements have been made since antiquity in such fields as astronomy, but not until the early nineteenth century was an effective *calculus of errors* created. In a separate tradition, *combinatorial probabilities* were created in the seventeenth century for the analysis of games of chance. These mathematical tools were then available in the later nineteenth century for use in all natural sciences involving random processes. A parallel development was in *statistics* from the seventeenth century onwards, involving aggregated information gathered for its importance to statecraft and commerce. These three approaches can be seen to relate to different aspects of the limits of our knowledge: errors relate to the limits of exactness of measurements made with real instruments; randomness relates to the limits of causality and determinism as observable in the natural world; and statistics relates (implicitly in its practice) to the limits of correspondence between descriptive categories and the reality to which they relate. These three approaches have all interacted with and enriched each other, so that now they are not distinct in name or subject matter.

Another way of looking at the history of the management of uncertainty is in terms of the relation between the researcher and the system under study. Combinatorial probabilities describe an abstract world, where knowledge of processes is incomplete, but where events occur totally independently of the observer and have no imprecision in themselves. The theory of errors arose from the realization of the interaction between the elements of the measurement process. These are the instruments with a limited fineness of scale and accuracy of construction and calibration, and the individual operators with their perceptual inaccuracies and distortions. In statistics there is an analogous effect; general concepts (e.g. population, income) must have operational definitions, and data collection and analysis must have safeguards against a variety of possible errors. A scientific underpinning for error theory has been provided by quantum mechanics, with its proof that each observation has a finite effect on the system and that there is a lower bound to the imprecision of related pairs of measured magnitudes.

Within the present century another approach to probability has been articulated, which formalizes personal judgements of the confidence to be placed on assertions and (in principle) allows their calculation by means of Bayes' theorem on inverse probabilities (Savage 1954). Such subjective probabilities have been applied to the analysis of complex problems in risks and the environment, where (as elicited from experts) they are used to remedy the lack of reliable statistical data and established causal theories. The formal system of those subjective probabilities is equivalent to that of fuzzy sets (Gupta and others 1979). These may be seen as managing linguistic uncertainty. Thus, old does not have a distinct boundary with not old or young. The function describing membership of human ages in the class old will have the value zero for 1 and 2, and unity for 99 and 100. An intermediate zone of ages, describable as not so old, pretty old, etc., will have intermediate values for the fuzzy-set membership function (Zadeh 1965). Since it is formally equivalent to the traditional probability calculus, fuzzy-set theory enables an elaborated computation with subjective probabilities.

These techniques have been developed mainly in connection with the study of highly articulated models of decision procedures, in the field of policy analysis
(Morgan and Henrion, 1990), rather than for the char- [123]
acterization of the highly uncertain information that is common in policy-related research. For the latter case

(which is our present concern), they are well adapted for a finer description of the inexactness or spread of estimated quantities, since they can exhibit a complete probability distribution rather than a simple mean and variance, however, such information is not at all certain. To characterize its own uncertainties (quite a real problem in the case of what are only personal opinions) leads to marked difficulties in the theory because the only means available within the framework of the theory is to produce a subjective probability distribution for a subjective probability distribution, and it is not easy to find a straightforward interpretation for such a second-order operation (Henrion 1988). In our scheme, this function is performed by a separate category, the *assessment* or *grade*, which directly expresses the reliability of the information rather than standing for its iterated probability.

All the formal approaches to probability are afflicted by the problems of applying analytical techniques for the management of the severe uncertainties in the information that is frequently the best available in policy-related research. All the traditional statistical techniques, even the non parametric methods for ordinal data, presuppose that the data are numerous and of good quality. In the face of a few coarse and scattered readings, all such techniques require many strengthening assumptions about the data for their applications to be legitimate. The significance of low-level environmental effects, as assessed by standard tests, may well depend more on computing procedures and on hypotheses about the shape of the data distributions than on the scanty data themselves. (Bailar 1988, pp. 8–12).

It is because of the inadequacy of the best attempts to apply traditional statistical techniques to the highly imperfect data so frequently encountered in policy-relevant research that we have developed the coarser, semi-qualitative approach that is advanced here. Our approach:

1. avoids the attempt to replace human judgements by formal systems or by computer programs—instead it applies simple yet robust techniques for the guidance of those judgements;

2. relies more on description and classification than on formal calculations;
3. complements the standard statistical techniques as commonly taught and practiced.

It can be useful even in cases where the data are appropriate for manipulation by the standard techniques; but we believe that it is essential in the circumstances of policy-related research.

As Bailar (1988) puts it:

> All the statistical algebra and all the statistical computations are of value only to the extent that they add to the process of inference. Often they do not aid in making sound inferences; indeed they may work the other way, and in my experience that is because the kinds of random variability we see in the big problems of the day tend to be small relative to other uncertainties. This is true, for example, for data on poverty or unemployment; international trade; agricultural production; and basic measures of human health and survival.
>
> Closer to home, random variability—the stuff of P-values and confidence limits, is simply swamped by other kinds of uncertainties in assessing the health risks of chemical exposures, or tracking the movement of an environmental contaminant, or predicting the effects of human activities on global temperature or the ozone layer. It was, in fact, this aspect of environment problems that first attracted me to the field. I have long had an interest in non-random variability, and here I see it in almost pure form [pp. 19–22].

In most discussions among scientific researchers actually performing measurements there is usually at least an implicit recognition of the relative degree of quality of various methods, but once a number is obtained and exported to the general scientific community or to an inexpert policy audience, it is implicitly presumed good. Even if it is quoted with its known imprecision (e.g., by significant digits or by mean and variance), there is no record of its quality. Only those experts familiar with the details of the measurement methods will remember it.

In the case of policy-related research, most of those using the information are not experts in its production; they will not know, or be able to understand, the technicalities of the research that allow its quality to be understood. They will at first take the information on trust, presuming it to be of good quality; if this turns out to be specious, then the credibility of all comparable information can be impaired. All experts tend to be accorded equal credibility in policy debates. When any one is discredited, the credence given to all and the credibility of science itself are diminished. The communication of data quality therefore must be clear and easily understood if it is to be at all effective.

We will use a familiar example to show how a single numerical measure is not adequate for expressing all aspects of the quality of information. A marksman shooting at a target will produce a pattern of shots. They may all cluster tightly, in which case we speak of high precision, but we are also concerned with how closely they come to the bullseye, which we describe in terms of accuracy. If the sighting apparatus is defective, the marksman's shots may well have high precision and low accuracy. (Of course, precision instruments are [124]
those with both high precision and high accuracy). In general scientific practice, the thing being measured is not accessible to such simple, naked-eye observation; and while precision can be simply measured (as by the variance of a set of readings, what we will refer to as the spread), accuracy is known only indirectly, by the accumulated experience of the behavior of the system. Under such circumstances, the equivalent to accuracy becomes the reliability of the process, or the strength of the results, or what we will refer to as the grade. Its assessment is accomplished by judgements based on craft experience rather than by counts and calculations.

It is important to appreciate that the two attributes are quite independent. Using the example of the marksman with defective sighting apparatus, one can see how there could be high precision (low spread) with low accuracy (low grade). On the other hand, there are many scientific situations where the best available data may be of relatively low precision (high spread), but can nonetheless be quite reliable as a representation of the thing being measured and therefore deserve a high grade. High quality in scientific information is not secured by the banishment of uncertainty (for that is impossible) but by its effective communication and management.

NUSAP Notational System

Our notational system is thus based on an elucidation of these two sorts of uncertainty. We start with the simplest sort, usually expressed by error bars and significant digits. Every set of data has a spread; it is an attribute of any quality, however derived; it may be considered in some contexts as a degree of precision, as a tolerance, or as a random error in a calculated measurement. It is the kind of uncertainty that relates most directly to the quantity as stated and is most familiar to students and even the lay public.

A more complex sort of uncertainty relates to the level of confidence to be placed in a quantitative statement; this relates to the accuracy that we have contrasted to precision. In statistical practice, this is usually represented by the confidence limits (at, say, 95% or 99%). In practice, such judgments are quite diverse; thus safety and reliability estimates are given as conservative by a factor of *n*. In risk analyses and futures scenarios, estimates are qualified as optimistic or pessimistic. In laboratory practice, the systematic error in physical quantities, as distinct from the random error or spread, is estimated on an historic basis. Thus, it provides a kind of assessment to act as a qualifier on the number, or alternatively (if desired) on the spread. We call this attribute the *grade* to convey the qualitative degree of goodness of a number. This assessment of grade is one level up from spread, both in its sophistication and variety. Our knowledge of the behavior of the data gives us the spread; and our knowledge of its production or intended use, gives us its grade.

We can now introduce the full notational system designed for the management of uncertainty in quantitative information. We call it NUSAP; the last three letters in the acronym refer to the spread, assessment and pedigree. The first two refer to numeral and unit. The first category encompasses the arithmetical system, and the second the base in which it is appropriately expressed. In a full NUSAP expression, there is a balance between all the elements; thus the number of significant digits in the numeral place, when combined with the scaling factor in the units place, will be coherent with the inexactness described under spread.

We arrive at the grade by means of an evaluative accounting we call the *pedigree* of the data. We have developed a matrix of items that show the boundary with ignorance (Table 1) by displaying the degrees of

Table 1. Numerical estimate pedigree matrix

Score	Theoretical, quality of model	Empirical, quality of data	Social, degree of acceptance
4	Established theory	Experimental data	Total
	Many validation tests	Statistically valid samples	All but cranks
	Causal mechanisms understood	Controlled experiments	
3	Theoretical model	Historical/field data	High
	Few validation tests	Some direct measurements	All but rebels
	Causal mechanisms hypothesized	Uncontrolled experiments	
2	Computational model	Calculated data	Medium
	Engineering approximations	Indirect measurements	Competing schools
	Causal mechanisms approximated	Handbook estimates	
1	Statistical processing	Educated guesses	Low
	Simple correlations	Very indirect approximations	Embryonic field
	No causal mechanisms	"Rule of thumb" estimates	
0	Definitions/assertions	Pure guesses	None

strength of crucial theoretical, empirical, and social components of the process. The theoretical, empirical, and social components are *quality of models, quality of data,* and *degree of acceptance* (Table 1). By scoring a particular measurement in each of these components we can describe its pedigree, and this pedigree is used to assess the measurement's grade. The three components are coded on an ordinal scale of 0–4, and their average, normalized on the scale 0–1, provides a convenient measure of the overall grade. It should be clear that this scale provides a simple and suggestive index, and not a measured quantity. Provided that it is used with that awareness, and is not embedded in complex, hyperprecise mathematical manipulations, it will function as a useful tool in the evaluation of scientific information. Thus the pedigree, in exhibiting the limits of the state-of-the-art of the field in which the information was produced, provides us with a simple gauge for an assessment of the strength of that information, or its grade.

For example (referring to Table 1), if we qualify the theoretical component of a particular measurement as having used a computational model, we are implicitly stating that we do not have a theoretical model. We thus record the absence of an effective theory and score the theoretical component as a 2. Similarly, if the empirical component is not experimental, it can be at best historical or field data, as in most environmental research, which would be scored as a 3. In the latter case, data are inherently less capable of control; so it is less effective as an input and check on the quality of the model. The components on the social side describe the evaluation of [125] the information in its particular context. Degree of acceptance of a result will be straightforward in a fully matured field where criteria of quality are agreed; a rough approximation to this is the referee's judgment on the research paper. The social degree of acceptance component is required because it represents an additional element in the overall pedigree of uncertainty. Measurements with high theoretical and empirical quality can still have high uncertainty if they have not withstood the tests of peer review and achieved scientific consensus.

NUSAP is a system because it is not simply a collection of fixed notations. Rather, it is a set of determinate categories, each of which can be filled by particular notations appropriate to the particular context of application. The names of the five categories (or boxes, or places in a string) make up the acronym NUSAP. By means of this place value representation, each category can be expressed without need for its explicit identification (this is why we refer to it as a scheme of notations). For each category, there are many possibilities for conveying particular desired meanings; thus in energy studies, kilowatts, megawatts and gigawatts are not merely the same unit with prefixes denoting a scaling increasing by a thousand. Rather, they refer to physical and accounting operations at very different levels, and they have quite different meanings as indices. Thus, writing in the NUSAP notation we do not have 1 kW = 10^{-6} GW, except in a formal arithmetical sense. Similarly, units of money have various appropriate expressions that are clearly distinguished in NUSAP. Thus, for the valuation of wetlands a common unit is: thousand dollars per acre at a particular date. So we write "$K/acre/yr" in the unit place. These cases show how NUSAP representations can convey variants of meanings that may appear not too different in ordinary practice but that are conceptually quite distinct. Any particular array of such constituents in the five places we call a notation. Given such a notation, any particular case, such as "6 1/2 $K/acre/yr" will be an "instance" of the notation.

The key distinction between NUSAP and other notational systems is its incorporation of more of the components of uncertainty, in particular the assessment of the grade of the estimate. It is not intended as a final and complete system for this purpose, but as a starting point in the evolution of our management of uncertainties in data quality to compliment our management of other forms of uncertainty.

To show the use of NUSAP for characterizing uncertainty in information in policy-related research, we take the example criticized by Maddox (1987). The chosen indicator (temperature rise consequent on greenhouse effect) as described by the World Resources Institute did not exhibit effective control of its uncertainties, and so [as Maddox (1987) said] could not command very high confidence. The original statement was of a rise between 1.6°C and 4.5°C (in average earth temperature over the next 40 yr). In NUSAP, this increase is best displayed as,

3	°C	±50%	[0.5]
numeral	unit	spread	grade

The first three places are derived directly from the quoted quantitative prediction. The range of 1.6*x* to 4.5*x* is near enough to 3 ± 50%, and it may be said that our mode of representation is more faithful to the scientific meaning of the datum. It thus displays skill in the management of uncertainty and would, therefore, tend to maintain confidence in the scientists making the prediction. We estimate a pedigree of (2, 2, 2) using the model pedigree matrix of Table 1, and this translates to [126]
a grade of [0.5] [(2 + 2 + 2)/12]. This rating comes from analyzing the World Resources Institute's model of global warming. Are there effective theoretical models for atmospheric CO_2 and its temperature effects? According to Maddox (1987), not quite; severe uncertainties exist on the time scales both of millions of years and of days. Hence we have, at best, computational models. What about the data that are injected into the models as inputs? There are some that are better than educated guesses but (as yet) not much obtained through instrumental readings, even as historic/field data. Hence we do best to call them calculated data, usually resting indirectly on measurements. Moving now to the social aspects of the pedigree, the degree of acceptance of the result seems to be medium. The criticisms of Maddox (1987) are of the policy implications of the prediction rather than of the quantity itself.

This mapping of the limits of the state-of-the-art exhibits the boundaries with our ignorance. We do not know as much as we could had there been theoretical models and historic/field data. In such a case, predictions would have had more strength, more justified urgency, and perhaps also more information on environmental consequences and remedies. As it is, our knowledge is not quite swamped by our ignorance, but it is still too weak and unfocused for effective decision making. Our ignorance in the policy aspects of the problem has scarcely been dispelled. Thus, the indicator of the World Resources Institute, when properly expressed, tells us more about our ignorance than about the biosphere.

In this way we see how relevant evaluations of quality are expressed through the assessment and pedigree categories. These are cast in terms of the characteristic uncertainties of the information, including the border with ignorance; and they can be expressed in a form most appropriate for the policy problem that defines the indicator itself.

As we have seen, the NUSAP system enables the representation of a quantity (with its uncertainties) in a variety of ways. Each form of expression corresponds to a particular type of message, depending on the content and context to be conveyed. Some expressions may contain more detailed information than others, if the loss of brevity is justified by the gain in effectiveness. The full NUSAP form, as given above, is the most general framework for such expressions. In it, the assessment box may be used to constitute the grade or degree of goodness. However, when a set of similar numbers are being compared, some of the boxes may be redundant. For many policy makers it is sufficient to use the most abbreviated form, the pair (N, A), where N (the numeral) is a representative number, and A (the assessment) is a code for the grade that describes the degree of goodness of the number, as distinct from its spread.

An Arithmetic for Data Quality

The NUSAP system is designed to enable judgements of the quality of quantitative information to be applied in a consistent manner, so that all users of that information can make the same (or roughly the same) evaluations of it. So far we have shown how the various aspects of the uncertainty of information can be described in standard codes; the system is thus established as a descriptive scheme. As such, it has a limited usefulness. The numbers by which quantitative information is described are also used for calculation, and the NUSAP system should enable the various sorts of uncertainty to be tracked through a computation. Then, from given uncertainties in the inputs, it should be possible to describe the uncertainties in the outputs of a calculation. With that accomplished, the NUSAP system would constitute a true arithmetic, a special one for the characterization, manipulation, and ultimately the control of uncertainty in quantitative information. For this first sketch of an arithmetic of uncertainty, we will restrict ourselves to the case of a small set of elementary operations. There may well be problems arising when operations are iterated many times, for which further special rules may be necessary.

An arithmetic of uncertainty will be slightly different from ordinary arithmetic in several ways. First, since it is dealing with particular properties of numbers, its operations will not necessarily mirror those affecting the numbers themselves. Moreover, we can expect that those concerning the spread will not be the same as those concerning the grade, since one is primarily a quantitative property while the other involves judgements of quality. In addition, there will be some modifications of the rules to fit special cases. These can be detected by examination of the numbers involved (this aspect of the arithmetic can be programmed on a computer, along with the basic arithmetic).

It might be thought that an arithmetic with exceptional cases is a rather odd arithmetic; hence it may be useful to show the sorts of special cases affecting ordinary arithmetic, which in themselves indicate why a special notation for uncertain quantities is necessary.

Consider two simple sums:

$$\begin{array}{r} 1{,}000{,}000 \\ +\underline{\qquad\quad 5} \\ 1{,}000{,}005 \end{array} \qquad\qquad \begin{array}{r} 1{,}000{,}000 \\ +\underline{\qquad\quad 5} \\ 1{,}000{,}000 \end{array}$$

The first of these is in conventional arithmetic; it is arithmetically correct, but probably nonsense in practice. [127]
For, except in the very rare case when the million has been counted out with perfect precision, the quantity 5 is vanishingly small in comparison with it. On the other hand, the second sum, while meaningful in practice, is formally incorrect as arithmetic; one can imagine the reaction of a schoolteacher if a pupil produced and defended such a sum! This pair of sums is the simplest representative of a large class of arithmetical operations where the numbers do not, or cannot, mean what they seem to; in technical language, we say that the zero is an ambiguous symbol, capable of standing for either a digit (although even then a strange one) or a filler of an empty place denoting a larger unit of aggregation for counting. In NUSAP notation, the sum in its simplest form would read as follows:

$$1\ \mathrm{E}6 + 5\ \mathrm{E}0 = 1\ \mathrm{E}6$$

and it is clear that the two quantities are of different orders of magnitude, incapable of addition in an ordinary sum.

Let us next consider the rules of simple arithmetic that are appropriate for spread. These follow the traditional rules of the simple calculus of errors: in sums and differences, absolute errors add; while in multiplications and divisions, proportional errors add. We could adopt the common rule that the root mean square sum of errors is to be taken, but this would introduce an inappropriate degree of complexity of calculation at this stage. Thus (with *a, b, c, d* all positive)

$$(A \pm a) + (B \pm b) = (A + B) \pm (a + b)$$
$$(A \pm a) - (B \pm b) = (A - B) \pm (a + b)$$

and

$$(C \pm c\%) * (D \pm d\%) = (C * D) \pm (c + d)\%$$
$$(C \pm c\%)/(D \pm d\%) = (C/D) \pm (c + d)\%$$

The use of percentages to express proportional spreads must be done with caution, as it is very easy to write meaningless percentages such as 102% or 700%. When spreads are as large as, or larger than, the number itself, then the expression of proportional spreads requires some skill. Quite reasonable percentages can give quite large spreads; thus spreads of ±33%, ±50% and ±67% produce variations through factors of 2, 3, and 5, respectively (since, for example, [1 + 67%]/[1 − 67%] = 5). For larger proportional spreads than those, we should use a notation for "factor of", as *F* 10, to indicate variation through that proportional range.

The rules of elementary arithmetic for the grade are nearly as simple, although there are two exceptional cases to be observed. In the case of addition and subtraction, we usually take the weighted mean of the separate grades of the numbers. This reflects the intuitive judgement that the quality of the result should be the "average" grade of the collection. The strengths or weaknesses of the separate elements are given their influence, proportional to the size of that element. Using brackets to denote the grade, we have:

$$E,[e] \pm F,[f] = (E \pm F), [(E * e + F * f)/(E + F)]$$

The two exceptional cases both apply when the two terms are nearly equal. The reason for an exceptional grade is easier to see in the case of subtraction. If we have two terms that are nearly equal, say 95 and 92, then any uncertainties in the initial terms will be magnified in their difference. This is easy to see in the case of spread; if each has a spread of ±1, then their difference will be 3 ± 2. The proportional spread goes from about ±1% for each of the initial terms, to ±66% for the difference, quite an enormous change. It is hard to imagine such a number being in any way as reliable as either of the initial terms. Hence we must construct a rule, inevitably somewhat arbitrary in its details, for reducing the grade of the difference element when its spread is so dramatically increased. This will be a more general, simple, and coarse version of the rules for distinguishing the means of statistical distributions. We divide the rule into three cases. There is no change when the ratio difference to (average) spread (both expressed as percentages or as numbers) is greater than 5. If that ratio is less than 2, the grade is reduced by 50%. In between, the reduction is linear, bearing in mind that grades are expressed to the nearest single digit only.

The exceptional rule for addition is not quite so completely automatic in its operation; it comes into play when two quantities that are derived from independent procedures are averaged or compared in some other way. In this case, there is a qualitative judgement that if two such quantities are equal, or nearly so, by some appropriate criterion, then this property serves as a corroboration of them both. Even if neither of them can be checked directly against the reality that it is intended to measure, the unlikelihood that both have come to the same erroneous estimate serves as positive evidence that they are both more likely to be correct. For this case, we can apply the above rule in the other direction: when the ratio difference to (average) spread varies between 5 and 2, the grade is increased by up to 50%.

For multiplication of numbers, the rule for grade is simple; here we adopt a weak-link principle: the grade of the product is the minimum of the grades of the factors. Thus

$$G,[g] * H,[h] = G * H,[Min(g,h)]$$

For this rule, there are no exceptional cases.

As we have been displaying the various rules for combining spreads and grades, we have been showing the way in which numbers may be expressed using the full NUSAP system. In this simple format, the difference from ordinary notation is slight; thus we have, as a sample, 5 g/s ±2, [0.6]. Should it be useful to include the pedigree in the expression, then this might be done with another sort of bracket, giving an expression like 5 g/s ±2, [0.6], {2,3,2}.

We notice that the grade almost always decreases in calculations, sometimes quite drastically. It could be that many computations that are now accepted as reasonable and as giving meaningful outputs would, under such a grading system, be seen to be of very low quality. In particular, matrix-inversion operations, involving the sums and differences of many-factored products, would be especially vulnerable. The fault, however, might not lie in the peculiarities of a grading system, but rather in a class of mathematical operations over which there has hitherto been very little effective quality control. If these grading rules turn out to be too harsh in practice, then they can easily be modified in their details, but the principle, on which effective quality control can be based, that there must be some standard procedures for quality assessment, is not to be compromised.

An Example: Valuation of Ecosystems

To demonstrate the usefulness of the proposed system, we carry it through for the example case of ecosystem valuation. We use a well-documented study of the economic value of wetlands in Louisiana (Farber and Costanza 1987, Costanza and others 1989) that employed a number of different models and methods to arrive at an estimate of the total value of the ecosystem. The results from the original study are reproduced in Table 2.

There are two overall methods whose results are presented. The willingness to pay-based method enumerates the various components of ecosystem value and derives an independent estimate for each one. These components are then added to yield the total value. For example, shrimp production value was estimated as \$10.85/acre/yr, and storm protection value as \$128.30/

Table 2. Summary of wetland value estimates (1983 dollars) for various components of wetlands contributing to their economic value, using two competing models [willingness to pay (WTP) and energy analysis (EA)] from Costanza and others (1989)

Method	Annual value per acre	Per acre present value at specified discount rate	
		8%	3%
WTP-based			
Shrimp	10.85	136	362
Menhaden	5.80	73	193
Oyster	8.04	100	268
Blue crab	0.67	8	22
Total commercial fishery	$25.37	$317	$846
Trapping	12.04	151	401
Recreation	3.07	46	181
Storm protection	128.30	1915	7549
Subtotal	168.78	$2429	$8977
Option and existence values	?	?	?
EA-based			
GPP conversion	$509–847	$6,400–10,600	$17,000–28,200
Best estimate	$169–509	$2,429–6,400	$8,977–17,000

acre/yr. Option and existence value are known to be important components of the total but no direct estimate was made for this ecosystem.

A second method (energy analysis) uses the total solar energy captured by the ecosystem as an indicator of its economic value. It is more comprehensive (in that it does not require summing individually measured components to arrive at the total), but the connection between energy captured and economic value is controversial and uncertain.

Finally, the present value of the ecosystem services are calculated using various discount rates based on the assumption that the ecosystems provide a constant stream of benefits into the indefinite future. In this case: present value = annual value/discount rate. The appropriate discount rate to use in such a situation is highly uncertain, however.

Table 3 is a recasting of these results into the NUSAP system. Here the numerical results are given only to the [129] appropriate degree of precision, and the spreads on each number are shown (using only 10% increments except for 25% and 75%). The pedigree for each number is given, based on an analysis of the individual models and methods used (see Costanza and others 1989, for a complete description of these) coded using the 0–4 system in Table 1. For example, the shrimp production estimate was based on a theoretical model relating wetland area to shrimp catch (score = 3) using historical and/or field data from National Marine Fisheries shrimp catch statistics and measured wetland area (score = 3) in a procedure (regression analysis) that has high but not total peer acceptance for the intended purpose (score = 3). Finally the grade for each estimate is given based on the average scores in the pedigree $[(3 + 3 + 3)/12 = 0.6]$. Note that grades are rounded to one digit.

Several quantities are calculated in the table using the NUSAP arithmetic described above. These are shown in bold. The total commercial fishery value is the sum of four components. Its spread is the weighted average of the percentage spreads of the components $[(1E1 * 0.1 + 6E0 * 0.2 + 8E0 * 0.3 + 1E0 * 0.4)/2.5E1) = 0.2]$. Its grade is the weighted average of its component grades $[(1E1 * 0.7 + 6E0 * 0.5 + 8E0 * 0.6 + 1E0 * 0.6)/2.5E1 = 0.6]$.

Table 3. NUSAP scores and summary grades for elements of wetland valuation problem

Element	Numeral, N	Unit, U	Spread, S	Assessment	
				Pedegree	Grade
WTP-based estimates					
Shrimp	1 E1	$/ac/yr	±10%	(3,3,3)	0.7
Menhaden	6 E0	$/ac/yr	±20%	(2,2,2)	0.5
Oyster	8 E0	$/ac/yr	±30%	(2,3,2)	0.6
Blue crab	1 E0	$/ac/yr	±40%	(3,2,3)	0.6
Total Commercial Fishery	**2.5 E1**	$/ac/yr	**±20%**		**0.6**
Trapping	1.2 E1	$/ac/yr	±30%	(2,2,2)	0.5
Recreation	3 E0	$/ac/yr	±10%	(3,4,3)	0.8
Storm Protection	1.3 E2	$/ac/yr	±20%	(2,3,2)	0.6
Subtotal	**1.7 E2**	$/ac/yr	**±20%**		**0.6**
Option and Existence Values	5 E2	$/ac/yr	±50%	(1,0,1)	0.2
Total WTP	**7 E2**	$/ac/yr	**±40%**		**0.3**
EA-based					
GPP conversion	7 E2	$/ac/yr	±25%	(3,2,1)	0.5
Average of two methods	**7 E2**	$/ac/yr	**±30%**		**0.6**
Discount rate	5 E0	%	±50%	(1,3,1)	0.4
Present value	**15 E3**	$/ac	**±80%**		**0.4**

An estimate for option and existence value is given based on studies of other areas, but, as its spread and grade indicate, for this application it is definitely an order-of-magnitude estimate. The total WTP based value reflects the quantitative importance of option and existence values and their relatively low quality. We end with a spread of ±40% and a grade of 0.3 for this estimate.

The EA-based estimate yielded a very similar quantity estimate to the WTP estimate, and this is taken as corroborating evidence since the likelihood that this would occur by chance is small. The average of the two methods is therefore of higher grade than either of the inputs [0.6 vs (0.5 and 0.3)], and we are left with a reasonably high-quality estimate of the total annual value of wetland production [7 E2 $/acre/yr ± 30% (0.6)].

Converting this to present value significantly reduces the data quality, however, because of the high uncertainty about the discount rate. The spread on the present value goes to ±80% and the grade goes down to 0.4.

The two tables present very different pictures of the situation. This is partly because in the original table, the per acre present value was calculated for each component of ecosystem value, so that the original table has three columns of figures. In the NUSAP version, there is only one column, and the quantitative information is reduced to the minimum relevant to the quality assessment. Thus (for these purposes) we do not need to calculate present values with 3% and 8% discount rates, but only to provide a discount rate of 5 ±50%, with an appropriate pedigree. Hence the numeral column of the table corresponds generally to the first column of the original table.

We notice that much more information can be provided by the NUSAP approach. For instance, if someone consulting the table wanted to know about the quality of one of the estimates, then the number 10.85 (an- [130]
nual value for shrimp) would not convey very much useful information. Clearly, this is not intended to say that an estimate of 10.88 would be seriously wrong; but whether 12 would be equally acceptable is not clear. Thus the digits by themselves do not provide an estimate of their spread; the significant digits convention breaks down here as in many other cases, but with the

NUSAP notation, the spread is given explicitly.

With the confidence that NUSAP affords in the handling of highly inexact quantities, we can include useful quantitative arguments that would otherwise be obscure or burdensome. For example, in a table of entries given to four or five digits (as the original one), there is no way to express the very inexact estimate of option and existence values. In the original table that row is left empty, with only question mark signs, but with NUSAP, this can be expressed as 5E2 ±50%, or lying between 250 and 750, thus varying through a threefold range. When added to the willingness to pay estimates, this provides a sum of 7E2 ±40%, and this compares well with the completely independent estimate of 7E2 ±25% by GPP conversion. It is then possible to invoke the principle of corroboration and to increase the grade of the common estimate.

Thus, the NUSAP representation of the series of calculations that went into the estimation of the value of wetlands offers a clear picture of the data quality. It also allows the uncertainty in the final estimate to be easily communicated, and it directs research to those areas most likely to improve the quality of that final estimate. A system such as this (should it come into general usage) would allow much saner management of our intellectual resources and much better management of our natural resources.

Acknowledgments

This article benefited from a number of informal reviews and discussions among our colleagues at Maryland, Ispra, and in the UK, including R. Ulanowicz, B. Hannon, J. Bartholomew, S. Tennenbaum, and B. deMarchi. Partial support was provided by the National Science Foundation, grant BSR-8906269 titled: "Landscape modeling: The synthesis of ecological processes over large geographic regions and long time scales," R. Costanza and F. H. Sklar, Principal Investigators, and by the Joint Research Center of the Commission of the European Communities. We are indebted to T. O'Riordan, R. Christofferson, and one anonymous reviewer for their helpful suggestions on an earlier draft.

Literature Cited

Bailar, J. C., III. 1988. Scientific inferences and environmental problems: The uses of statistical thinking. Institute for Environmental Studies, University of North Carolina at Chapel Hill.

Costanza, R., S. C. Farber, and J. Maxwell. 1989. The valuation and management of wetland ecosystems. *Ecological Economics* 1:335–361.

Farber, S., and R. Costanza. 1987. The economic value of wetlands systems. *Journal of Environmental Management* 24:41–51.

Funtowicz, S. O., and J. R. Ravetz. 1991. Uncertainty and quality in science for policy. Kluwer, Dordrecht.

Gupta, M., R. Ragade, and R. Yager (eds.). 1979. Advances in fuzzy set theory and applications. North Holland, Amsterdam.

Henrion, M. 1988. Uncertain information processing in knowledge support system. *In* A. P. Sage (ed.), Concise encyclopedia of information processing in systems and organizations. Pergamon, Oxford.

Henrion, M., and B. Fischhoff. 1986. Assessing uncertainty in physical constants. *The American Journal of Physics* 00:000.

Maddox, J. 1987. Half-truths make sense (almost). *Nature* 326:637.

Morgan, M. G., and M. Henrion. 1990. Uncertainty: A guide to dealing with uncertainty in quantitative risk and policy analysis. Cambridge University Press, New York.

Ravetz, J. R. 1971. Scientific knowledge and its social problems, Oxford University Press, New York.

Savage, L. J. 1954. The foundations of statistics. John Wiley, New York.

Zadeh, L. A. 1965. Fuzzy sets. *Information and Control* 8:338. [131]

Robert Costanza, W. Michael Kemp and Walter R. Boynton

Predictability, Scale, and Biodiversity in Coastal and Estuarine Ecosystems: Implications for Management

This paper looks at coastal and estuarine ecosystems in terms of their unique biodiversity characteristics and the implications of these characteristics for management. With the exception of coral and other reef communities, coastal and estuarine systems are generally low in species diversity. But estuaries are typically dominated by strong aperiodic physical forces (e.g. salinity changes due to freshwater inflows, storm events) and under these conditions structure is more difficult to build and maintain. Estuaries are also characterized by a high degree of organism mobility. These characteristics point to a high degree of ecosystem resilience. The general hypothesis is that the biodiversity achievable in a system is a function of the predictability and scales of its physical environment. This hypothesis is consistent with the limited data on diversity in estuaries and other systems, and can be further tested in the future via comparative analysis. These ideas are elaborated and extrapolated to the task of managing complex and coupled ecological economic systems. Biological or species diversity is put in a systems context as a scale-dependent measure of an important system characteristic. In estuaries it is the diversity of ecological processes, and in particular certain keystone processes, that are more critical and that should be the focus of management efforts. Effective management is seen as the process of escaping from social traps that occur when local, individual incentives diverge from global, long-term goals.

COASTAL AND ESTUARINE ECOSYSTEMS

Coastal and estuarine ecosystems are the vast biomes that join continental lands and oceanic islands with their surrounding seas. Most of the world population resides in the coastal zone and the density of coastal economic development is increasing. Therefore, these ecosystems are particularly important for integrating sound ecological management with sustainable economics (1).

Estuarine ecosystems are coastal indentations with "restricted connection to the ocean and remain open at least intermittently" (2). Salinities are usually intermediate between those of fresh and seawater, but in regions where evaporation is high or rainfall low, estuarine salinities may be equal to or higher than those of the ocean. Most present day estuaries were formed during the last 15 000 years of the current interglacial period, and are thus geologically ephemeral features of the landscape.

Although estuaries vary in depth from one to several hundred meters, shallowness clearly distinguishes them from the open ocean. Depending on the mode of origin and the nature of surrounding land masses, estuaries may assume a variety of sizes and forms. Coastal plain estuaries were formed with the drowning of coastal rivers with rising sea level, while others (e.g. fjords) were formed in glacial channels with terminal sills associated with moraine deposits. Others fill the chasm left from tectonic activities or formed as part of river deltas. Estuaries also include the large system of shallow coastal lagoons formed from oceanic sedimentological processes behind barrier islands, peninsulas, and spits.

One of the larger and more productive estuaries in the world is the Chesapeake Bay. Because many characteristics of the bay and its watershed have been well documented, it represents a good case study for further elaboration of some key concepts in estuarine science and management, and in particular, elaboration of issues of predictability, scale, and diversity.

Special Physical Characteristics of Coastal and Estuarine Systems

Perhaps the most distinctive feature that contrasts estuaries from other biomes is the nature and variability of the physical forces which influence these ecosystems. Within small geographic regions, many estuaries experience widely varying conditions of temperature, salinity, concentrations of a wide variety of chemicals, and plant and animal densities, much of which is mediated by water movement over relatively short time scales. [88]

For example, in the Chesapeake Bay, temperatures range from near 30° C in surface waters in late summer to zero by late winter. Ice cover is extensive in severe winters, but of only local importance in normal winters. Salinity also varies widely, from near zero in the upper reaches of tributaries to 30 ppt near the capes. Superimposed on these general gradients of temperature and salinity, significant, unpredictable, interannual variability also occurs related to normal climatic shifts from wet to dry periods. As a result, the spatial extent of various estuarine habitats undergoes periods of significant expansion and contraction.

Shifts from wet to dry periods also strongly influence the rate at which essential nutrients (such as nitrogen, phosphorus, and silica) enter the system from the surrounding watersheds. Since these elements are essential for plant growth, their availability determines, at least in part, the amount of organic matter available to support food webs. Recent measurements indicate that nutrient loading rates and algal production rates vary among years by at least a factor of two in the Chesapeake Bay.

In addition, the amount of freshwater entering the system is the primary factor determining the degree to which estuaries are vertically stratified, with lighter, fresher water near the surface and saltier, denser water near the bottom. One aspect of the bilological significance of stratification lies in the fact that the degree of stratification determines the ease with which essential gases such as oxygen can reach deep waters and support the respiratory needs of benthic communities. In turn, the degree of stratification also regulates the ease with which nutrients released from benthic communities reach euphotic surface waters and are again available to support plant growth.

Finally, catastrophic events, such as hurricanes and severe tropical storms, cause yet another, largely unpredictable scale of variability. These storms can discharge huge amounts of freshwater, nutrients and sediments into estuaries through a variety of mechanisms, and subject most organisms to some degree of stress. However, the "memory" of most estuaries with respect to these events seems to be relatively short (< 5 years) at least for lower levels of the food web. At higher trophic levels the long term impacts are not clear.

Although fluctuations in some physical features (like temperature) are damped in marine systems compared to terrestrial environments, the shallowness of estuaries makes them more susceptible to larger amplitude variations. In both marine and estuarine environments, spectral distributions for variations in many physical forces exhibit patterns which are inversely related to the square of the frequence (Fig. 1a). This so-called "red noise" distribution, which is associated with interactions between events at low and high frequencies, characterizes terrestrial processes at scales longer than 50 years (3). For higher frequencey events, which occur within the life time of many organisms in terrestrial environments, variations in physical forces tend to be distributed independently of the frequency of occurrence, producing a pattern of "white noise" (Fig. 1b). One ecological consequence is that organisms in marine environments (as opposed to estuarine) are better able to adapt their behaviors and physiologies to the more predictable physical variations in the marine habitat.

Figure 1. Comparison of variance frequency spectra for a) marine systems; and b) terrestrial systems. Source: (3).

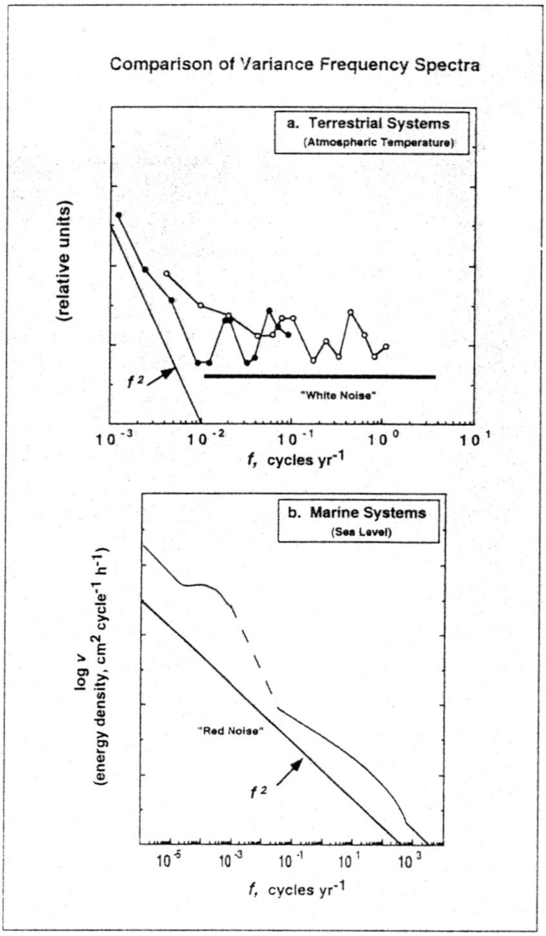

Ecological Diversity of Estuaries

The relatively large and unpredictable variations in salinity and water movement characterizing most estuaries tend to limit the number of animal and plant species capable of adapting to these rigorous conditions (2, 4). As an ecotone between fresh and marine environments, estuaries contain a mixture of freshwater and oceanic species, but both planktonic and benthic communities [89] contain substantially fewer species than do similar communities in oligotrophic lakes and in the ocean. The number of benthic faunal species in the deep sea may be comparable to that of tropical forest biomes (5), while estuarine benthos are commonly dominated by a few species, with limited taxonomic diversity in any given bottom area (2).

The relatively low taxonomic diversity of estuarine communities arises because of physiological difficulties in dealing with high-amplitude unpredictable stresses (4) and because of the high organism mobility afforded by physical processes and properties of water. Osmotic stress is a primary physiological limitation for many organisms. In an estuary organisms must adapt to continually changing salinity. Other factors such as oxygen deficiency can contribute to environmental difficulties. Estuaries do provide a means for rapid dispersion and easy mobility for resident organisms due to the buoyancy of water and the rapid hydrodynamic transport associated with tides, winds, and pressure gradients. Many coastal marine organisms have high fecundity and depend on water transport for larval dispersal, so that isolated populations are rare. Many fish and swimming invertebrates migrate long distances (10^2–10^3 km) during portions of their life-cycles. Consequently, functional replacements for a given estuarine species are virtually always available (6) so that the selective advantages of specialization are minimal. There are relatively few endemic species in estuaries; most originate from freshwater or oceanic environments, and many marine organisms require estuarine environments for a portion of their life-cycle.

For example, during each year many adult stripped bass (*Morone saxatilus*) spend a portion of the summer in coastal waters, the winter in deep waters of the coastal bays, and the spring in the tidal-freshwater portions of tributary rivers. Small-scale vertical movements also occur during summer in response to prey distributions, water temperatures, and oxygen conditions.

Other organisms, especially those without the mobility of fish and larger crustaceans, have developed physiological mechanisms to deal, often for extended periods of time, with adverse environmental conditions. The American Oyster (*Crassostrea virginica*) has often been cited as a premier example of an estuarine organism. The oyster can grow well across an extreme salinity range, feeds successfully on a broad range of algal species and detritus, stops feeding during cold periods of the year when food supplies are limited, and can survive extended periods of hypoxia or anoxia by closing tightly and switching its metabolism to a form of anaerobic respiration. On the scale of the whole estuary, reproduction is favored in some years in one location and in other locations at other times. Pelagic larval stages insure wide dispersal and colonization of available habitats and replenishment of areas that have become depopulated.

Finally, estuaries are truly open systems and this has implications for maintenance of species assemblages as well. Both the ocean and landward end of these systems are open to active and passive migrations of both indigenous and exotic species. For example, estuaries are characterized by having both anadromous (ocean dwelling but spawning in estuaries) and catadromous (freshwater dwelling but spawning in seawater) species. In addition, exotic species find their way into these systems attached to commercial ships or recreational boats. The constant exchange of fresh and saltwaters insures a constant seeding of planktonic organisms as well. Thus, despite the rigorous environment typical of estuaries and intense fishing pressure and degraded habitats in some instances, local extinctions are relatively rare and generally of short duration. Normal migrations, passive entry via river and tidal water flows, and accidental introductions insure a continual supply of normal and new species.

In addition to the physical stresses, another factor which may limit the number of species in estuarine environments is the virtual absence of the physical structures and associated habitats created by organisms, e.g. plant canopies, which typify terrestrial environments. In very shallow coastal environments, generally less than 10 m, however, rooted vascular plants (seagrasses) and attached algae, e.g. kelp, often do create complex physical structures which lead to multiple physical niches and relatively high taxonomic diversity. Similarly, reefs formed by colonial animals (oysters, mussels), in estuaries can produce complex physical structures containing relatively more species. In very stable tropical marine environments, coral reefs develop unparalleled taxonomic diversity. Coral reefs cannot survive in highly variable environments, and such high-diversity systems do not occur in estuaries.

In general, the relationship in any ecosystem between taxonomic diversity (number and distribution of species) and functional diversity (variety of ecological processes) is unclear. The basic ecological processes involved in biogeochemical cycles and trophic interactions are the same in estuarine ecosystems as in any other biome. In estuaries, however, a given species is relatively less specialized for performing a single or a limited repertoire of ecological function(s). For example, the cosmopolitan estuarine clam, *Macoma balthica*, acts as a suspension-feeder, filtering food from the overlying water in environments with low rates of organic deposition to sediments, but acts as a deposit-feeder, scavenging food from the sediments, in organic-rich environments (7). Indeed, most estuarine animals appear to be opportunistic feeders, altering their diets to focus on foods which are relatively abundant (2). Similarly, most estuarine bacteria have alternative metabolic pathways for obtaining energy (8), and the same algal species can be found dominating benthic diatom, phytoplankton or epiphytic communities under different estuarine conditions (2). One measure of the functional diversity of estuarine ecosystems is the variety of different responses displayed by organisms to the range of physical environmental changes that occur (6). Thus, the relatively large scales of physical, and attendant biological, variability in estuaries might suggest that despite low taxonomic diversity estuarine ecosystems have high functional diversity (9).

Estuarine Productivity

Estuaries and coastal marine ecosystems are cited among the most productive biomes of the world (10). One reason for the high primary productivity of estuaries is the high nutrient loading rates, characteristic of these systems, compared to agricultural systems and other biomes (11). Rates of carbon fixation in estuaries rival those reported for the most productive terrestrial environments and substantially exceed those for oceans and many lakes (Fig. 2a). While benthic algae and seagrass can contribute substantially to estuarine production in shallow and clear coastal environments, phytoplanktonic algae tend to be the dominant autotrophic group. In addition to the relatively high rates of nutrient inputs to estuaries, their shallow depth and proximity of sediments to the euphotic zone promote efficient nutrient recycling. Physical circulation, characterized by landward flow of more saline waters and particle trapping, with density-driven stratification, leads to efficient nutrient retention (13).

Secondary production of estuaries is also large compared to other biomes of the world (13). Biomass production of certain benthic suspension-feeding bivalves in estuarine ecosystems exceeds the highest protein yield of pond-cultured herbivorous fish and rivals the areal production of highly subsidized cattle farms (14). These remarkable production rates for estuarine animal tissue result, again, from the natural energy subsidy associated with hydrodynamic transport of food and wastes to and from benthic animals. Thus, food-chains associated with benthic communities in shallow estuaries are likely to be more efficient in producing animal tissue. The omnivorous diets of many estuarine animals, and particularly their ability to grow on combinations of living plant material and detrital (dead plant and animal) foods, also results in relatively high trophic efficiencies [90]
in organic-rich estuaries (13). Indeed, compared to freshwater ecosystems, the relative yield of fish per unit primary production is considerably greater in coastal marine ecosystems (Fig. 2b). This appears to be associated primarily with the mechanical boost associated with physical transport in estuaries (15). There is, therefore, considerable potential for production of human foods in coastal ecosystems (16), but the same physical processes and their associated variabilities which provide estuaries with natural work subsidies leading to high trophic efficiencies, also impair the ability of humans to cultivate the coastal seas.

In summary, we find that estuaries and other shallow coastal ecosystems represent unique biomes in which variabilities in certain physical properties, e.g. salinity, and processes, e.g. water movement, are relatively large and unpredictable. As a consequence of natural environmental stresses and the mobility afforded by buoyancy and hydrodynamic transport, taxonomic diversity in estuaries tends to be low with few endemic species. Estuarine functional diversity, however, appears to be relatively high compared to that in other biomes, especially in benthic dominated subsystems. Rates of primary production of estuarine ecosystems are among the highest in the biosphere, and trophic transfer of this production to growth of animal populations is relatively

Figure 2. Synthesis diagrams of a) nitrogen inputs vs. productivity for various ecosystem types; and b) primary production vs. fisheries yield for marine and freshwater systems. Source: (15).

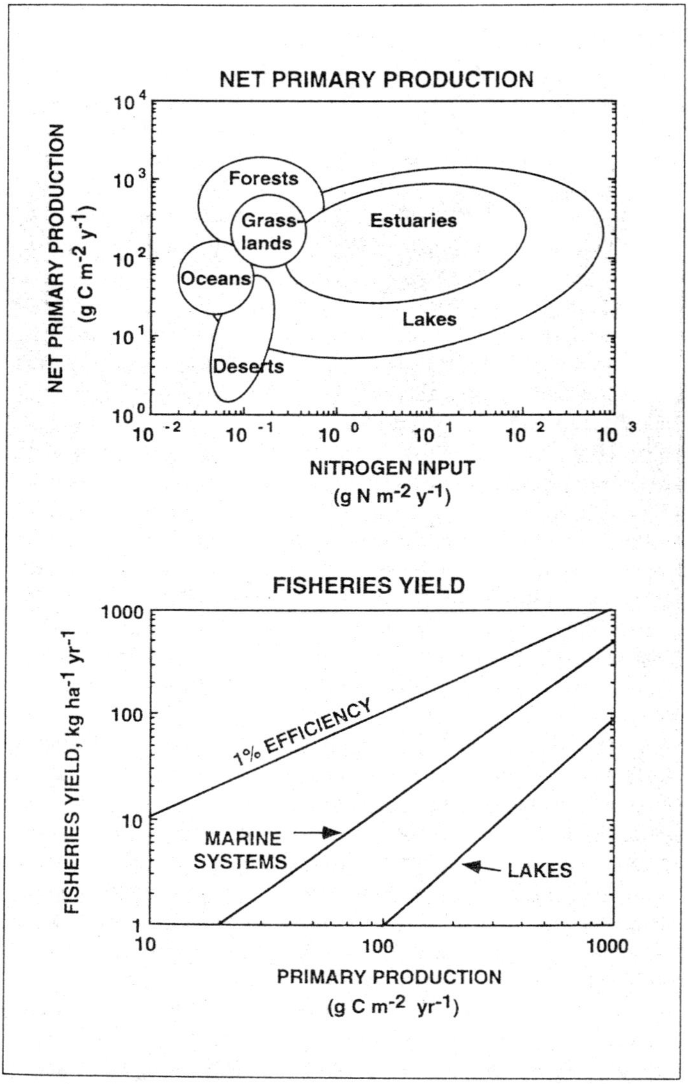

efficient. These high conversion efficiencies of sunlight to plant tissue to animal biomass in estuaries are attributable largely to the mechanical subsidy of hydrodynamic processes.

Resilience and Keystone Processes in Estuarine Ecosystems

It has been suggested that many ecosystems exhibit resilient responses to external and internal perturbations by developing mechanisms which allow them to "absorb, buffer, or generate change" (1). In this context, ecosystems contain key organisms and processes which play crucial roles to insure long-term resilience by modifying the impact on ecosystem structure resulting from environmental changes. One mechanism for conferring ecosystem resilience is to establish alternating replacement structures that are switched periodically but which avoid accumulations of excessive structure. Examples of such keystone species or processes have been cited for a variety of terrestrial ecosystems. For instance, periodic outbreaks of the spruce budworm serve to release accumulated ecological structure for temperate coniferous forests (17). Few, if any examples of these kinds of key organisms have been identified for estuarine ecosystems. The term "keystone" organisms has also been used to describe organisms that play pivotal roles in the trophic structure of an ecosystem (18). In this case, predation by keystone organisms effectively preserves community structure by relieving competitive pressure between organisms at lower trophic levels or serving to keep lower-level predation levels in check (19). This latter kind of keystone organism or process has been identified for shallow benthic ecosystems in coastal marine environments (20), but they are poorly documented for estuarine plankton systems.

In spite of the sparseness of keystone organisms in estuaries, there is strong evidence that these ecosystems are relatively resilient to perturbations, at least for time scales less than 10^3 years. Estuarine ecosystem processes have been shown to return to pre-disturbance levels within months after perturbations from major meteorological events, e.g. hurricanes, floods, droughts, and winter freezes. For example, the Chesapeake Bay experienced a 200-year event in June of 1972 when a tropical storm created an unprecedented flood in the lower watershed. Sediment loading to the Bay during the 4–5 days of the storm were equivalent to inputs from the previous decade. Sufficient freshwater was delivered to remove virtually all seawater from the estuary for several days. Despite this dramatic change in environmental conditions, plankton community production and abundance returned to prestorm levels within 2–3 months. Although there were massive mortalities of benthic faunal populations, they recovered within a year (21). Similarly, there were no apparent effects on the annual fisheries yields comparing 1972 with previous and subsequent years. Numerous other examples are well documented illustrating estuarine ecosystem resilience to major disturbances; e.g. Hurricane Hugo in North Inlet, South Carolina. A few coastal ecosystems such as coral reefs are much less resilient to environmental changes (22), but organisms in these systems are not adapted to the same kind of high-frequency/high-amplitude variations in physical and chemical environmental conditions as are those in estuaries.

It appears that this well-buffered disturbance-response displayed by various estuarine ecosystems rests on three primary factors:

i) the relatively small standing ecological structure;
ii) the high degree of organism mobility;

iii) the prevalence of generalist species.

Unlike forests, estuaries and other aquatic ecosystems contain relatively low levels of standing biomass. Hence, the time required to regenerate any losses in ecological structure is relatively short for estuarine systems. The combination of strong hydrodynamic transport and active motility insure that seed organisms are readily available to replace those lost with perturbations from both the land and marine ends of estuarine systems. Furthermore, the high degree of functional generalism among estuarine [91] organisms increases the probability that any ecological processes lost with species declines from external perturbations can be replaced by other organisms. In many estuarine ecosystems, the rapid plankton turnover resulting from hydrodynamic transport tends to keep any species from dominating the broad ecological niches of estuaries. This tends to facilitate species coexistence and stabilize community structure against internal disruptions such as overgrazing (23).

Conventional ecological views of keystone organisms may not be sufficiently inclusive for estuarine systems. There are, nevertheless, a number of key organisms and processes which play fundamental roles in the functioning of estuarine ecosystems. Although the loss of these critical ecological attributes may not jeopardize the resilience of an estuarine ecosystem, it may significantly change its ecological structure. Many of these critical processes are most evident in the benthic subsystems of estuaries. An example of such a process is nitrification-denitrification which is crucial in nature and is generally not fully recognized until after its loss has occurred.

A complex but essential component of nitrogen cycling in estuaries is the coupled process of nitrification-denitrification. In this process the reduced nitrogen salt, ammonium, which is released in microbial decomposition and animal excretion, is converted to gaseous forms—predominantly di-nitrogen gas (N_2), which comprises almost 80% of the earth's atmosphere. Whereas the reduced salts of nitrogen such as ammonium are essential for plant growth, the gaseous forms of nitrogen are virtually unavailable for use by estuarine plants. Under normal conditions the rate of nitrification-denitrification is directly proportional to the rate of nitrogen loading to the estuary (24) so that this coupled process buffers the ecosystem, maintaining an intermediate level of internal nitrogen. In all biomes of the world, including estuaries, nitrifier bacteria are highly specialized organisms with strict nutrient requirements, especially for oxygen and ammonium, necessary for growth. Thus, nitrifiers are an exception to the rule of few specialist organisms occurring in estuarine ecosystems. Because ammonium concentrations are highest in sediment porewaters, the highest rates of nitrification tend to be concentrated in surface sediments in the narrow zone into which oxygen penetrates. In contrast, denitrifier bacteria are generalists capable of numerous alternative metabolic processes for growth. To metabolize via denitrification pathways, however, they require an abundance of the nitrogen salt produced by nitrifiers (nitrate) as well as total absence of oxygen. Therefore, denitrification will not occur without nitrification and the critical coupling of nitrification and denitrification occurs only at the interface between anaerobic and aerobic environments (25).

In certain estuaries, such as those with deep channels, a high ratio of river flow to tidal flow, and/or limited turbulent mixing, and excessive inputs of nitrogen from the watershed can lead to depletion of oxygen from bottom waters. This results from nitrogen-stimulated growth of planktonic algae and decomposition of algal matter near the benthic surface at rates which consume oxygen faster than reoxygenation from the air-water interface. The anoxic conditions which ensue result in massive mortality of bottom-dwelling animals and elimination of any aerobic bacterial processes, e.g. nitrification, which might otherwise occur at the sediment surface. Hence, whereas under normal conditions a significant portion, approximately 50%, of the nitrogen entering the estuary is removed via nitrification-denitrification, under these eutrophic conditions of excessive nitrogen loading and anoxia, this nitrogen removal process is inhibited (26). However, within months after oxygen is restored to the Bay bottom, rates of nitrification-denitrification return nearly to the levels occurring prior to the anoxic disturbance. This is, therefore, another example of a key estuarine process that is susceptible to change and which controls the nature of the ecosystem, but which is quickly restored once the perturbation is removed.

TOWARD A GENERAL THEORY OF PREDICTABILITY, SCALE, AND BIODIVERSITY

Given the foregoing discussions and insights about biodiversity in estuaries, we have formulated an embryonic hypothesis about the relationship of biodiversity to the scale and predictability of the environment. This hypothesis may be useful in sorting out the value of biodiversity, both to the ecosystems themselves and to human consumers of ecosystem services, and to devising better policies and management systems (27, 28).

In the discussion that follows, we employ the 4-box model of Holling (29, 30). Holling proposes four basic functions common to all complex systems and a spiraling evolutionary path through them (Fig. 3). The functions (boxes) are: i) *Exploitation* (r-strategists, pioneers, opportunists, entrepreneurs, etc.); ii) *Conservation* (K-strategists, climax, consolidation, rigid bureaucracies, etc.); iii) *Release* (fire, storms, pests, political radicals, etc.); and iv) *Reorganization* (accessible nutrients, abundant natural resources, etc.). Within this model, systems evolve from the rapid colonization and exploitation phase, during which they capture easily accessible resources, to the conservation stage of building and storing increasingly complex structures.

Figure 3. The Holling 4-box model. Source: (29, 30).

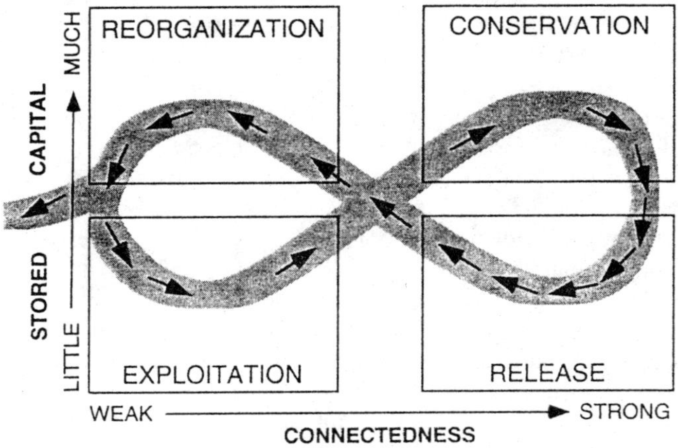

Examples of the *exploitation phase* are early successional ecosystems colonizing disturbed sites or pioneer societies colonizing new territories. Examples of the *conservation phase* are climax ecosystems or mature, large bureaucracies. The *release* or *creative destruction phase* represents the breakdown and release of these mature structures via aperiodic events like fire, storms, pests, or political upheavals. The released structure is then available for *reorganization* and uptake in the exploitation phase. The amount of ongoing release or creative destruction that takes place in the system is critical to its behavior. The *conservation phase* can often build elaborate and tightly bound structures by severely limiting creative destruction—the former Soviet Union is a good example—but these structures become brittle and susceptible to massive and widespread destruction. If some moderate level of release is allowed to occur on a more routine basis, the destruction is on a smaller scale and leads to a more resilient system. Creative destruction, in terms of shocks or surprises, seems to be crucial for system resilience and integrity. Similarly, it has been argued that episodic events, such as the Chernobyl accident, the Rhine chemical spill, the death of seals in the North Sea, are shocks to the social-cultural value system and may stimulate change towards more resilient ecological economic systems (31).

Fire climax systems such as the pine forests of Yellowstone [92] National Park are a good example of the range of possibilities for creative destruction. In its unmanaged state, Yellowstone burned over extensive areas relatively often, but because of the high frequency the amount of fuel was insufficient to allow highly destructive fires. The more frequent, small to moderate size fires would release nutrients stored in the litter and support a spurt of new growth without destroying all the old growth. On the other hand, if fires are suppressed and controlled, fuel builds up to high levels and when the fire does come it wipes out the entire forest.

Estuaries, in this context, are awash in creative destruction due to the strong physical forces of tides and currents that dominate this unpredictable environment. They are constantly reset to the exploitation phase and rarely build up enough structure to make it to the conservation phase. They are resilient, low taxonomic diversity systems. Only systems with relatively predictable environments can build and maintain a diverse set of specialist species. Tropical rainforests and coral reefs are the extreme case of both environmental predictability and biodiversity. In this view a stable environment allows biodiversity to develop, rather than the reverse argument, that high biodiversity leads to a more stable ecosystem response. But the process is seen as a feedback loop. Ecosystems in unpredictable environments at one scale can build structures at a larger scale to smooth out and stabilize that unpredictability. For example, forests build structure to smooth out lower scale unpredictability. But this process can be tampered with, e.g. the Yellowstone forest fire management policy, by artificially reducing the amount of release or creative destruction, and the system can become brittle.

In estuaries the unpredictability is at several scales, including the large scales, and the organisms usually cannot build large biostructures and therefore the system remains at a relatively low diversity. An exception which proves the rule is the case of artificial structures like bridge pilings, on which diverse biological communities do grow because of the smoothing effect of the artificial structure. To a lesser extent, seagrasses and oyster reefs are also exceptions that prove the rule. To the extent that organisms can establish and maintain fixed structure in the face of the large and unpredictable physical forces in estuaries, they can begin to counter the unpredictability and support specialization and diversity. But even oyster reefs and seagrass beds are fairly low diversity systems that occur only in special conditions within the estuaries. Oyster reefs rely on the large and unpredictable changes in salinity in estuaries to keep them free of disease organisms and intense predation. Seagrass beds are very sensitive to nutrient enrichment and turbidity.

Estuaries do have high functional diversity, however, and high resilience. Figure 4 summarizes our view of estuaries and their relationship with their physical environment. The top half of the diagram show the effects of the high variance, low predictability physical forces driving estuarine ecosystem dynamics with high efficiency secondary production and high fisheries yields. The bottom half of the diagram shows the effects of the physical forces and linkages with ecosystem dynamics on ecosystem structure, with low taxonomic diversity, moderate biomass, and high functional diversity. Large and unpredictable physical forces cause structural losses and keep high taxonomic diversity from developing, but also enhance productivity.

From this analysis of estuaries we have developed an hypothesis about the general relationship of resource predictability to scale and biodiversity. The biodiversity (or taxonomic diversity) in a system is a function of the predictability of the resource environment on the time and space scales at and above the scale of the system of interest. Smaller scale unpredictability can be filtered out by the structure of the system. All else being equal, the higher the predictability of the environmental resources and forcings, the higher the biodiversity that can potentially develop in an attempt to maximize the efficiency of use of these resources. The absolute amount of biodiversity is limited by the absolute size of the resources and forcings. The system can also be tampered with by artificially restricting the relationship between structure and predictability as in the Yellowstone and the former Soviet Union. These attempts lead to brittle systems that ultimately collapse, however.

We think that the above hypothesis is testable using comparative analysis of various systems' resource predictability, diversity, and structural dynamics over several scales. It is applicable to both [93]
economic and ecological systems and may help us to better understand the role of diversity in systems performance and value—a key issue in modern conservation policy.

MANAGING COASTAL AND ESTUARINE ECOSYSTEMS

Estuaries in general have rather low biodiversity, but are nonetheless very productive and resilient ecosystems. Because of the dominance of large, unpredictable physical forces in estuaries, and the lack of a stable base on which to build biological structure to smooth out this unpredictability, these systems are dominated by a relatively few generalist species. The economic value of estuaries focuses on these few species. For example, in the Chesapeake the American oyster, striped bass, American shad, and blue crab have been economically important species for both commercial and recreational fisheries (32–34).

Estuaries are generally open-access resources, and this fact, combined with the relatively high unpredictability of physical forces and living resource stocks, and the rapidly growing coastal population, has led to overexplotation and eventual decline of critical organisms and processes, as discussed above. How do we manage these ecosystems in light of their special ecological characteristics? Assigning private property rights has met with only very limited success in these systems because of the difficulty of preventing the use of resources by other than their owners. Leased oyster beds have been fairly successful in some locations, e.g. in Louisiana, because it is possible with relatively small enforcement costs to exclude non-owners from harvesting the oysters from these beds. But, in general, because of the unpredictability and mobility of estuarine resources, it is very difficult to assign and enforce property rights, and it is difficult to assess when the resilience of the system has been stretched to the breaking point.

A fundamental reason for the mismanagement of these systems is the inherent mismatch between the characteristics of the ecological system on the one hand and of the human institutions developed to manage it on the other. Our management institutions have largely been based on systems of private property rights adapted from terrestrial systems and agriculture, and assume a relatively high degree of predictability. But, as we have noted, these rights are difficult to define and enforce in estuaries and unpredictability is the norm. One critical feature is the incentive structures that these institutions produce. Society's response has been to develop systems of direct regulation of the potentially damaging activities like fishing. But the incentive structures these regulatory systems produce often lead to behavior that is directly counter to the long-term health of the whole system, and often even to the stated goals of the institution itself. How does this happen and how can we fix it?

SOCIAL TRAPS

This process of short-run and local incentives moving out of sync with long-term and global goals has been well studied in the last decade under several rubrics (35, 36), but one particularly effective representation is John Platt's notion of "social traps" (37–41). In all such cases the individual decision-maker may be said to be 'trapped' by the local conditions into making what turns out to be a bad decision viewed from a longer or wider perspective People go through life making decisions about which path to take based largely on road signs, i.e. the short-run, local reinforcements that we perceive most directly. These short-run reinforcements can include monetary incentives, social acceptance or admonishment, and physical pleasure or pain. In general, this strategy of following the road signs is quite effective, unless the road signs are inaccurate or misleading. In these cases we can be trapped into following a path that is ultimately detrimental because of our reliance on the road signs. For example, overfishing is a social trap because by following the short-run economic road signs, fishermen are led to exploit the resource to the point of collapse.

The elimination of social traps requires intervention; the modification of the reinforcement system. Indeed, it can be argued that the proper role of a democratic government is to eliminate social traps, no more and no less, while maintaining as much individual freedom as possible. Cross and Guyer list four broad methods by which traps can be avoided or escaped from. These are education about the long-term, distributed impacts; insurance; superordinate authority, i.e. legal systems, government, religion; and converting the trap to a trade-off, i.e. correcting the road signs.

Education can be used to warn people of long-term impacts that cannot be seen from the road. Examples are the warning labels now required on cigarette packages and the warnings of environmentalists about future hazardous waste problems. People can ignore warnings, however, particularly if the path seems otherwise enticing. For example, warning labels on cigarette packages have had little effect on the number of smokers.

The main problem with education as a general method of avoiding and escaping from traps is that it requires a significant time commitment on the part of individuals to learn the details of each situation. Our current society is so large and complex that we cannot expect even professionals, much less the general public, to know the details of all the extant traps. In addition, for education to be effective in avoiding traps involving many individuals, all the participants must be educated, and this is usually not possible.

Governments can, of course, forbid or regulate certain actions that have been deemed socially inappropriate. The problem with this direct, *command-and-control* approach is that it must be rigidly monitored and enforced, and the strong short-term incentive for individuals to try to ignore or avoid the regulations remains. A police force and legal system are very expensive to maintain, and increasing their chances of catching violators increases their costs exponentially, both the costs of maintaining a larger, better- [94]
equipped force and the cost of the loss of individual privacy and freedom.

Religion and social customs can be seen as much less expensive ways to avoid certain social traps. If a moral code of action and belief in an ultimate payment for transgressions can be deeply instilled in a person, the probability of that person's falling into the "sins" (traps) covered by the code will be greatly reduced, and with very little enforcement cost. On the other hand, the problems with religion and social customs as means to avoid social traps are that the moral code must be relatively static to allow beliefs learned early in life to remain in force later, and it requires a relatively homogeneous community of like-minded individuals to be truly effective. This system works well in culturally homogeneous societies that are changing very slowly. In modern, heterogeneous, rapidly changing societies, religion and social customs cannot handle all the newly evolving situations, nor the conflict between radically different cultures and belief systems.

Many trap theorists believe that the most effective method for avoiding and escaping from social traps is to turn the trap into a trade-off. This method does not run counter to our normal

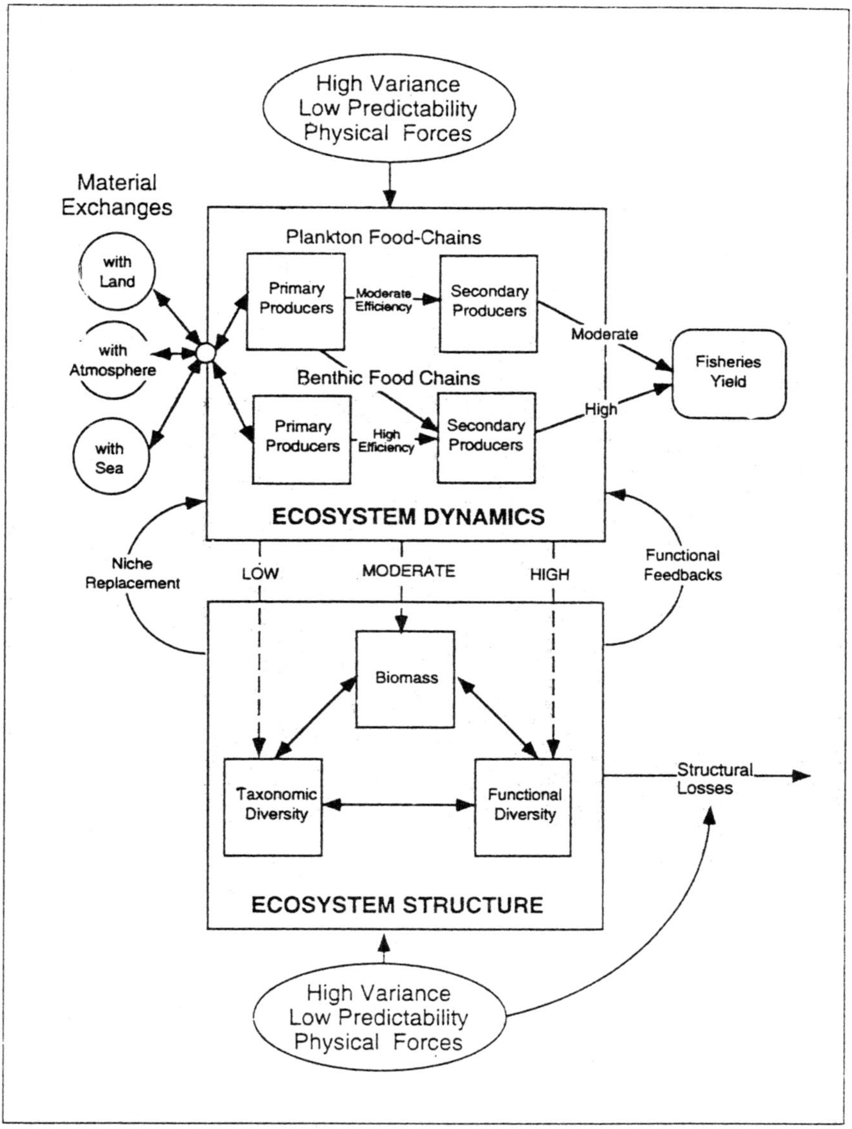

Figure 4. Conceptual diagram of the relationships between physical forcings and ecosystem structure and dynamics in estuaries.

tendency to follow the road signs; it merely corrects the signs' inaccuracies by adding compensatory positive or negative reinforcements. A simple example illustrates how effective this method can be. Playing slot machines is a social trap because the long-term costs and benefits are inconsistent with the short-term costs and benefits. People play the machines because they expect a large short-term jackpot while the machines are in fact programmed to pay off, say, USD 0.80 on the dollar in the long term. People may win hundreds of dollars playing the slots in the short run, but if they play long enough they will certainly lose USD 0.20 for every dollar played. To change this trap to a trade-off, one could simply reprogram the machines so that every time a dollar was put in USD 0.80 would come out. This way the short-term reinforcements, USD 0.80 on the dollar, are made consistent with the long-term reinforcements (USD 0.80 on the dollar), and only the dedicated aficionados of spinning wheels with fruit painted on them would continue to play.

Modifying Incentives for Improved Management

In the context of social traps, the most effective way to make global and long-term goals consistent with local, private, short-term goals is to somehow modify the local, private, short-term incentives (37–41). These incentives are any combination of the reinforcements that are important at the local level, including economic, social, and cultural incentives (42). We must design the social and economic instruments and institutions to bridge the gulf between the present and future, between the private and social, between the local and global, between the ecological and economic parts of the system.

One policy that has often been recommended, and which is consistent with this idea of modifying local incentives, is the "polluter pays principle." This principle would require the payment of pollution taxes (43) to account for the damages to ecological systems by private polluters or resource users. One factor limiting the adoption of this approach has been the high degree of uncertainty and unpredictability associated with ecological damages. How big should the tax be? If it is too low the polluters are not paying the full cost to society and will continue to overpollute. If it is too high the polluters will be subsidizing society and the cost of their products will be too high.

One way to handle this uncertainty about the true damages is the idea of a flexible environmental assurance bonding system (44, 45). This variation of the deposit-refund system is designed to incorporate environmental criteria and uncertainty into the market, and to induce positive environmental technological innovation. It

works in this way: in addition to charging for known environmental damages, an assurance bond equal to the current best estimate of the largest potential future environmental damages, would be levied and kept in an interest-bearing escrow account for a predetermined length of time. In keeping with the precautionary principle, this system requires the commitment of resources now to offset the potentially catastrophic future effects of current activity. Portions of the bond, plus interest, would be returned if and only if the agent could demonstrate that the suspected worst case damages had not occurred or would be less than originally assessed. If damages did occur, a portion of the bond would be used to rehabilitate or repair the environment, and possibly to compensate injured parties. By requiring the users of environmental resources to post a bond adequate to cover uncertain future environmental damages, with the possibility for refunds, the burden of proof and the cost of the uncertainty is shifted from the public to the resource user. At the same time, agents are not [95]
charged in any final way for uncertain future damages and can recover portions of their bond in proportion to how much better their performance actually was compared with the worst case.

Deposit-refund systems, in general, are not a new concept. They have been effectively applied to consumer policy, conservation policy, and other efficiency objectives. Deposit-refund systems can be market generated or government initiated and are often performance based. For example, deposit-refund systems are currently effectively used to encourage the proper management of beverage containers and used lubricating oils (46).

Strong economic incentives are provided by the bond to reduce pollution, to research the true costs of environmentally damaging activities, and to develop new innovative, cost-effective pollution control technologies. The bonding system is an extension of the "polluter pays principle" to "the polluter pays for uncertainty as well" or the "precautionary polluter pays principle" (4P) (43). It would allow a much more proactive, rather than reactive, approach to environmental problems because the bond is paid up front, before the damage is done. It would tend to foster prevention rather than cleanup by unleashing the creative resources of agents on finding more environmentally benign technologies since these technologies would also be economically attractive. Competition in the marketplace would lead to environmental improvement rather than degradation. The bonding system would deal more appropriately with scientific uncertainty and the inherent unpredictability of ecosystems.

The 4P approach has several potential applications. Any situation with large, true uncertainty is a likely candidate, and these situations abound in the modern world, especially in ecosystem management and especially in managing coastal and estuarine ecosystems.

References and Notes

1. Holling, C. S. 1986. The resilience of terrestrial ecosystems: local surprise and global change. In: *Sustainable Development of the Biosphere.* Clark, W. and Munn, R. (eds). Cambridge University Press, Cambridge, p. 292–317.
2. Day, J.W. Jr., Hall,C.A.S., Kemp, W.M. and A. Yañez-Arancibia, A. 1989. *Estuarine Ecology*. John Wiley, New York.
3. Steel, J. H. 1985. A comparison of terrestrial and marine ecological systems. *Nature*, 313, 355–358.
4. Slobodkin, L.B. and Sanders, H.L. 1969. On the contribution of environmental predictability to species diversity. In: *Diversity and Stability in Ecological Systems.* Brookhaven symposium in Biology No. 22. NTIS, Springfield, VA, p. 82–95.
5. Grassle, J.F. 1991. Deep-sea benthic biodiversity. *BioScience*, 41, 464–469.
6. Steele, J.H. 1991. Marine functional diversity. *BioScience*. 41, 470–474.
7. Henriksen, K., Rasmiussen, M. and Jensen, A. 1983. Effect of bioturbation on microbial nitrogen transformations in the sediment and fluxes of ammonium and nitrate to the overlying water. *Ecoll. Bull.* , 35, 193–205.
8. Fenchel, T. and Blackburn, T.H.. 1979. *Bacteria and Mineral Cycling*. Academic Press, London.
9. Powell, T.M. 1989. Physical and biological scales of variability in lakes, estuaries and the coastal ocean. In: *Perspectives in Ecological Theory*. Princeton University Press, Princeton, NJ.
10. Mann, K.H. 1982. *Ecology of Coastal Waters*. University of California Press, Berkeley.
11. Kelly, J. and Levin, S. 1986. A comparison of aquatic and terrestrial nutrient cycling and production processes in natural ecosystems. In: *The Role of the Oceans as a Waste Disposal Option*. Kullenberg, G. (ed.). D. Reidel Press, Dordrecht, The Netherlands, p. 157–176.
12. Kemp, W.M. and Boynton, W.R. 1984. Spatial and temporal coupling of nutrient inputs to estuarine primary production: the role of particulate transport and decomposition. *Bulll. Mar. Sci. 35*, 522–535.
13. Odum, E.P. 1971. *Fundamentals of Ecology*. Saunders, Philadelphia.
14. Odum, H.T. 1967. Energetics of world food production. In: *The World Food Problem: A Report of the President's Science Advisory Committee, vol 3.* The White House, Washington, DC, p. 55–94.
15. Nixon, S.W. 1988. Physical energy inputs and the comparative ecology of lake and marine ecosystems. *Limn. Oceanogr. 33*, 702–724.
16. For example, see: Ryther, J.H. 1969. Photosynthesis and fish production in the sea. *Science. 166,* 72–76.
17. Holling, C.S. 1973. Resilience and stability of ecological systems. *Ann. Rev. Ecol. Syst. 4,* 1–23.
18. Paine, R.T. 1966. Food web complexity and species diversity. *Am. Nat. 102,* 243–282.
19. Carpenter, S.R. (ed.) 1988. *Complex Interactions in Lake Communities*. Springer-Verlag, New York.
20. Dayton, P. 1971. Competition, disturbance, and community organization: the provision and subsequent utilization of space in a rocky intertidal community. *Ecol. Monogr. 41,* 351–389.
21. Chesapeake Research Consortium. 1976. *The Effects of Tropical Storm Agnes on the Chesapeake Bay Estuarine System.* Johns Hopkins Univ. Press, Baltimore, MD.
22. Jackson, J.B. C. 1991. Adaptation and diversity of reef corals. *BioScience 41*, 475–482.
23. Kemp, W.M. and Mitsch, W.J. 1979. Turbulence and phytoplankton diversity: a general model of the paradox of plankton. *Ecol. Model. 7,* 201–222.
24. Seitzinger, S.P. 1988. Denitrification in freshwater and coastal marine ecosystems. *Limnol. Oceanogr. 33*, 702–724.
25. Henriksen, K. and Kemp, W.M. 1988. Nitrification in estuarine and coastal marine sediments: methods, patterns, and regulating factors. In: *Nitrogen Cycling in Coastal Marine Environments.* Blackburn, T.H. and Sorensen, J. (eds). John Wiley, New York, p. 207–249.
26. Kemp, W.M., Sampou, P.A., Caffrey, J.M., Mayer, M., Henriksen, K. and Boynton, W.R.. 1990. Ammonium recycling versus denitrification in Chesapeake Bay sediments. *Limnol. Oceanogr. 35*, 1545–1563.
27. Norton, B. G. and Ulanowicz, R.E. 1992. Scale and biodiversity policy—a hierarchical approach. *Ambio 21,* 244–249.
28. Costanza, R., Norton B.G., and Haskell, B.J. (eds). 1992. Ecosystem Health: New goals for Environmental Management. Island Press, Washington DC, 269 p.
29. Holling, C.S. 1987. Simplifying the complex: The paradigms of ecological function and structure. *Eur. J. Operat. Res. 30*, 139–146.
30. Holling, C.S. 1992. Cross-scale morphology, geometry and dynamics of ecosystems. *Ecol. Monogr.* February.
31. Folke, C. and Berkes, F. 1992. Cultural capital and natural capital interrelations. *Beijer Discussion Paper Series No. 8.* Beijer International Institute of Ecological Economics, The Royal Swedish Academy of Sciences, Stockholm.
32. Cumberland, J.H. (ed.). 1988. *Proc. Third Ann. Conf. Econ. Chesapeake Bay Management. Annapolis, MD.* Bureau of Business and Economic Research, University of Maryland, 471 p.
33. Cumberland, J.H. (ed.). 1989. *Proc. Fourth Ann. Conf. Econ. Chesapeake Bay Management. Baltimore, MD.* Bureau of Business and Economic Research, University of Maryland, 451 p.

34. Cumberland, J.H. (ed.). 1990. *Proc. Fifth Ann. Conf. Econ. Chesapeake Bay Management, Annapolis, MD.* Bureau of Business and Economic Research, University of Maryland, 265 p.
35. Hardin, G. 1968. The tragedy of the commons. *Science. 162,* 1243–1248.
36. Axelrod, R. 1984. *Evolution of Cooperation.* Basic Books, New York.
37. Platt, J. 1973. Social traps. *Am. Psychol., 28,* 642–651.
38. Cross, J.G., and Guyer, M.J. 1980. *Social Traps.* University of Michigan Press, Ann Arbor.
39. Teger, A.I. 1980. *Too Much Invested to Quit.* Pergamon, New York.
40. Brockner, J. and Rubin, J.Z. 1985. *Entrapment in Escalating Conflicts: A Social Psychological Analysis.* Springer-Verlag, New York. 275 p.
41. Costanza, R. 1987. Social traps and environmental policy. *BioScience. 37,* 407–412.
42. Perrings, C., Folke, C. and Mä ler, K.-G. 1992. The ecology and economics of biodiversity loss: the research agenda. *Ambio 21,* 201–211.
43. Pigou, A.C. 1920. *The Economics of Welfare.* Macmillan, London.
44. Costanza, R. and Perrings, C. 1990. A flexible assurance bonding system for improved environmental management. *Ecol. Econ. 2,* 57–76.
45. Costanza, R. and Cornwell, L. 1992. The 4P approach to dealing with scientific uncertainty. *Environment 34,* 12–20, 42.
46. Bohm, P. 1981. *Deposit-refund Systems.* Resources for the Future, Inc., The John Hopkins University Press, Baltimore and London.

47. Carl Folke, AnnMari Jansson, Lisa Wainger, and Joy Bartholomew provided useful comments and suggestions on earlier drafts. The Beijer International Institute of Ecological Economics provided support during the preparation of this manuscript.

Robert Costanza is director of the Maryland International Institute for Ecological Economics (MIIEE), Center for Environmental and Estuarine Studies (CEES), University of Maryland System, Box 38, Solomons, MD 20688-0038. He is also a professor in CEES, and director of the complex systems research program at the Beijer International Institute of Ecological Economics, The Royal Swedish Academy of Sciences. He received his PhD from the University of Florida in systems ecology with a minor in economics. He is co-founder and president of the International Society for Ecological Economics (ISEE) and chief editor of the society's journal: Ecological Economics. His address: Maryland International Institute for Ecological Economics, University of Maryland, P.O. Box 38, Solomons, MD 20688-0038, USA. W. Michael Kemp is a professor at the Horn Point Environmental Lab, Center for Environmental and Estuarine Studies, University of Maryland System. He is also a research fellow in MIIEE. He received his Ph.D. from the University of Florida in systems ecology. His major interests center on nutrient cycling in estuaries, ecosystem modeling, and scaling ecological properties. His address: Horn Point Environmental Lab., Center for Environmental and Estuarine Studies, University of Maryland System, Box 775, Cambridge, MD 21613, USA. Walter R. Boynton is a professor at the Chesapeake Biological Laboratory, Center for Environmental and Estuarine Studies. He is also a research fellow in MIIEE. He received his Ph.D. from the University of Florida in systems ecology. His major interests center on comparative ecology issues at whole system levels of organization and in bringing scientific issues into the management arena. His address: Chesapeake Biological Laboratory, Center for Environmental and Estuarine Studies, University of Maryland System, Box 38, Solomons, MD 20688-0038, USA.

[96]

Modeling Complex Ecological Economic Systems

Toward an evolutionary, dynamic understanding of people and nature

Robert Costanza, Lisa Wainger, Carl Folke, and Karl-Göran Mäler

Recent understanding about system dynamics and predictability that has emerged from the study of complex systems is creating new tools for modeling interactions between anthropogenic and natural systems. A range of techniques has become available through advances in computer speed and accessibility and by implementing a broad, interdisciplinary systems view.

Systems are groups of interacting, interdependent parts linked together by exchanges of energy, matter, and information. Complex systems are characterized by strong (usually nonlinear) interactions between the parts, complex feedback loops that make it difficult to distinguish cause from effect, and significant time and space lags, discontinuities, thresholds, and limits. These characteristics all result in scientists' inability to simply add up or aggregate small-scale behavior to arrive at large-scale results (Rastetter et al. 1992, von Bertalanffy 1968). Ecological and economic systems both independently exhibit these characteristics of complex systems. Taken together, linked ecological economic systems are devilishly complex.

A comprehensive understanding of linked systems requires the synthesis and integration of several different conceptual frames

Although almost any subdivision of the universe can be thought of as a system, modelers of systems usually look for boundaries that minimize the interaction between the system under study and the rest of the universe in order to make their job easier. The interactions between ecological and economic systems are many and strong. So, splitting the world into separate economic and ecological systems is a poor choice of boundary.

Classical (or reductionist) scientific disciplines tend to dissect their subject into smaller and smaller isolated parts in an effort to reduce the problem to its essential elements. To allow the dissection of system components, it must be assumed that interactions and feedbacks between system elements are negligible or that the links are essentially linear so they can be added up to give the behavior of the whole (von Bertalanffy 1968). Complex systems violate the assumptions of reductionist techniques and therefore are not well understood using the perspective of classical science. In contrast, systems analysis is the scientific method applied across many disciplines, scales, resolutions, and system types in an integrative manner.

In economics, for example, a typical distinction is made between partial equilibrium analysis and general equilibrium analysis. In partial equilibrium analysis, a subsystem (a single market) is studied with the underlying assumption that there are no important feedback loops from other markets. In general equilibrium analysis, on the other hand, the totality of markets are studied to bring out the general interdependence in the economy. The large-scale, whole-economy, general equilibrium effects are usually quite different from the sum of the constituent small-scale partial equilibrium effects. Add to this observation the further complication that in reality equilibrium is never achieved, and one can begin to see the limitations of classical, reductionist science in understanding complex systems.

Economic and ecological analysis needs to shift away from implicit assumptions that eliminate links within and between economic and natural

Robert Costanza is director of the Maryland International Institute for Ecological Economics (MIIEE), Center for Environmental and Estuarine Studies (CEES), The University of Maryland System, Solomons, MD 20688-0038. He is also a professor in CEES and director of the complex systems research program of the Beijer International Institute of Ecological Economics (BIIEE) of the Royal Swedish Academy of Sciences. Lisa Wainger is a graduate research assistant at MIIEE, supported in part by a grant from BIIEE. Carl Folke is the deputy director of BIIEE, S-104 05 Stockholm, Sweden. He is also an assistant professor in the Department of Systems Ecology, Stockholm University, S-106 91 Stockholm, Sweden. Karl-Göran Mäler is director of BIIEE. He is also a professor at the Stockholm School of Economics, S-113 83 Stockholm, Sweden.

Table 1. The limits of analytical methods in solving mathematical problems (after von Bertalanffy 1968). The thick solid line divides the range of problems that are solvable with analytical methods from those that are difficult or impossible using analytical methods and require numerical methods and computers to solve. Systems problems are typically nonlinear and fall in the range that requires numerical methods. It should be noted that whereas some special problems that fall in the areas labeled impossible in the table are actually possible to solve using analytical methods (frequently requiring special tricks), in general one cannot depend on a solution being available. Computers have guaranteed that a solution can be found in all the cases listed in the table.

	Linear			Nonlinear		
Equations	**One equation**	**Several equations**	**Many equations**	**One equation**	**Several equations**	**Many equations**
Algebraic	Trivial	Easy	Difficult	Very difficult	Very difficult	Impossible
Ordinary differential	Easy	Difficult	Essentially impossible	Very difficult	Impossible	Impossible
Partial differential	Difficult	Essentially impossible	Impossible	Impossible	Impossible	Impossible

systems because, due to the strength of the real-world interactions between these components, failing to link them can cause severe misperceptions and indeed policy failures (Costanza 1987). Because reductionist thinking fails in the quest to understand complex systems, new concepts and methods must be devised.

Achieving a comprehensive understanding that is useful for modeling and prediction of linked ecological economic systems requires the synthesis and integration of several different conceptual frames. As Levins (1966) has described this search for robustness, "we attempt to treat the same problem with several alternative models each with different simplifications... Then, if these models, despite their different assumptions, lead to similar results we have what we call a robust theorem which is relatively free of the details of the model. Hence our truth is the intersection of independent lies" (p. 423).

Existing modeling approaches can be classified according to a number of criteria, including scale, resolution, generality, realism, and precision. The most useful approach within this spectrum of characteristics depends on the specific goals of the modeling exercise. We describe here a few examples of how one might match model characteristics with several of the possible modeling goals relevant for ecological economic systems, and we claim that a better appreciation of the range of possible model characteristics and goals can help to match characteristics and goals.

Complex-systems analysis offers great potential for generating insights into the behavior of linked ecological economic systems. These insights will be needed to change the behavior of the human population toward a sustainable pattern, one that works in synergy with the life-supporting ecosystems on which it depends. The next step in the evolution of ecological economic models is to fully integrate the two fields and not just transfer methods between them. Clark's (1976, 1981, 1985) bioeconomics work was the start of this recognition of the importance of linking the mutually interacting subparts. But much work remains to be done to bring the two fields and the technology that supports them to the point where their models can adequately interact. Transdisciplinary collaboration and cooperative synthesis among natural and social scientists will be essential (Norgaard 1989).

Computers and modeling

Until computers became available, the equations that described the dynamics of systems had to be solved analytically, severely limiting the level of complexity (as well as the resolution) of the systems that could be studied and the complexity of the dynamics that could be examined for any particular system. Table 1 shows the limits of analytical methods in solving various classes of mathematical problems in general.

Only relatively simple linear systems of algebraic or differential equations can, in general, be solved analytically. The problem is that most complex, living systems (like economies and ecosystems) are decidedly nonlinear, and efforts to approximate their dynamics with linear equations have been of only limited usefulness. In addition, complex systems often exhibit discontinuous and chaotic behavior (Rosser 1991) that can only be adequately represented with numerical methods and simulations using computers.

We differentiate here between the use of linear systems of equations to model complex-system dynamics (which does not work well) versus the use of linear systems to understand system structure (which may work reasonably well). Integrating these views of structure and dynamics is a key item for research on complex ecological economic systems.

In recent years, computers have become not only faster but also much more accessible. This ease of access has allowed researchers to develop methods to allow adaptive, evolutionary, dynamic solutions. For example, Holland and Miller (1991) describe how recent computer and machine learning (a form of artificial intelligence) advances have spawned "artificial adaptive agents," computer programs that can simulate evolution and acquire sophisticated behavioral patterns. In these programs, individual agents (e.g., processes, elements, and pieces of computer code) in networks of interacting agents reproduce themselves in the next time period based on some measure of their performance in the current time period. The system exhibits changing group behavior over time and mimics evolution. To exhibit this adaptive behavior, the actions of the agents must be assigned values, and the agents must act to increase these values over time. Algorithms like these can provide a realistic representation of ecological and economic processes.

Another useful technique is metamodeling, in which more general models are developed from detailed ones. Richard Cabe, Jason Shogren, and their colleagues (1991) have developed this technique to link models of agricultural production and economic behavior that could not normally be used together because, for one, they run at different time and space scales. Their models, which cover the entire midwestern farm belt of the United States, provide a method for a quick and cost-efficient evaluation of ecological economic policies.

Computer hardware advances such as CRAY supercomputers and Connection Machines (massively parallel supercomputers) facilitate the modeling of complex systems using advanced numerical computation algorithms (e.g., finite difference and finite element routines, cellular automata algorithms, and emerging methods that employ at least a modicum of artificial intelligence). For example, parallel computers make high spatial resolution and regional and global ecological economic models computationally feasible (Costanza et al. 1990, Costanza and Maxwell 1991) and allow the types and resolution of evolutionary and metamodeling approaches to expand dramatically. These new capabilities, linked with a more realistic and pluralistic view of the various roles and limitations of models in understanding and decision making, can dramatically increase the effectiveness of modeling.

Purposes of models

Models are analogous to maps. Like maps, they have many possible purposes and uses, and no one map or model is right for the entire range of uses (Levins 1966, Robinson 1991). It is inappropriate to think of models or maps as anything but crude, although in many cases absolutely essential, abstract representations of complex territory. Their usefulness can best be judged by their ability to help solve the navigational problems faced. Models are essential for policy evaluation, but they are often also misused because there is "the tendency to use such models as a means of legitimizing rather than informing policy decisions. By cloaking a policy decision in the ostensibly neutral aura of scientific forecasting, policy-makers can deflect attention from the normative nature of that decision..." (Robinson in press).

In the case of modeling ecological economic systems, purposes can range from developing simple conceptual models to provide a general understanding of system behavior, to detailed realistic applications aimed at evaluating specific policy proposals. It is inappropriate to judge this whole range of models by the same criteria. At minimum, the three criteria of realism (simulating system behavior in a qualitatively realistic way), precision (simulating behavior in a quantitatively precise way), and generality (representing a broad range of systems' behaviors with the same model) are necessary. Holling (1964) first described the fundamental trade-offs in modeling among these three criteria. Later, Holling (1966) and Levins (1966) expanded and further applied this classification. No single model can maximize all three of these goals, and the choice of which objectives to pursue depends on the fundamental purposes of the model. Several examples in the literature of ecological and economic models demonstrate the various ways in which trade-offs are made among realism, precision, and generality.

High-generality conceptual models. In striving for generality, models must give up some realism and/or precision. They can simplify relationships and/or reduce resolution. Simple linear and nonlinear economic and ecological models tend to have high generality but low realism and low precision (Brown and Swierzbinski 1985, Clark and Monroe 1975, Kaitala and Pohjola 1988, Lines 1989, 1990b). Examples include Holling's four-box model (Holling 1987), the ecological economy model of Brown and Roughgarden (1992), most conceptual macroeconomic models (Keynes 1936, Lucas 1975), economic growth models (Solow 1956), and the evolutionary games approach. For example, the ecological economy model (Brown and Roughgarden 1992) contains only three state variables (labor, capital, and natural resources), and the relationships among these variables are highly idealized. But the purpose of the model was not high realism or precision but rather to address some basic questions about the limits of economic systems in the context of their dependence on an ecological life-support base.

High-precision analytical models. Often one wants high precision (quantitative correspondence between data and model) and is willing to sacrifice realism and generality. One strategy here is to keep resolution high but to simplify relationships and deal with short time frames. Some models strive to strike a balance between mechanistic small-scale models that trace small fluctuations in a system and more general whole-system approaches that remove some of the noise from the signal but do not allow the modeler to trace the source of system changes. The alternative some ecologists have devised is to identify one or a few properties that characterize the system as a whole (Wulff and Ulanowicz 1989). For example, Hannon and Joiris (1987) used an economic input-output model to examine relationships between biotic and abiotic stocks in a marine ecosystem; they found that this method allowed them to show the direct and indirect connection of any species to any other and to the external environment in this system at high precision (but low generality and realism). Also using input-output techniques, Duchin's (1988, 1992) aim was to direct development of industrial production systems to efficiently reduce and recycle waste in the manner of ecological systems. Large econometric models (Klein 1971) used for predicting short-run behavior of the economy belong to this class of models, because they are constructed to fit existing data as closely as possible, at the sacrifice of generality and realism.

High-realism impact-analysis models. When the goal is to develop realistic assessments of the behavior of specific complex systems, generality and precision must be relaxed. High-realism models are concerned with accurately representing the underlying processes in a specific system, rather than with precisely matching quantitative behavior or being generally applicable. Dynamic, nonlinear, evolutionary systems models at moderate to high resolution generally fall into this category. Coastal physical-biological-chemical models (Wroblewski and Hofmann 1989), which are used to investigate nutrient fluxes and contain large amounts of site-specific data, fall into this category, as do micromodels of behavior of particular business activities. Another example is a model of coastal landscape dynamics (Costanza et al. 1990), which includes high spatial and temporal resolution and complex nonlinear process dynamics. This model divides a coastal landscape into 1-square-kilometer cells, each of which contains a process-based dynamic ecological simulation model. Flows of water, sediments, nutrients, and biomass from cell to cell across the landscape are linked with internal ecosystem dynamics to simulate long-term successional processes and responses to various human impacts in a realistic way. But the model is site specific and of only moderate numerical precision.

Moderate-generality and moderate-precision indicator models. In many types of systems modeling, the desired outcome is to accurately determine the overall magnitude and direction of change, trading off realism for some moderate amount of generality and precision. For example, aggregate measures of system performance such as standard gross national product, environmentally adjusted net national product (or green NNP), which includes environmental costs (Mäler 1991), and indicators of ecosystem health (Costanza et al. 1992) fit into this category. The microcosm systems employed by Taub (1989) allow some standardization for testing ecosystem responses and developing ecosystem performance indices. Taub (1987) notes, however, that many existing indicators of change in ecosystems are based on implicit ecological assumptions that have not been critically tested, either for their generality, realism, or precision.

Scale and hierarchy

In modeling complex systems, the issues of scale and hierarchy are central (O'Neill et al. 1989). Some claim that the natural world, the human species included, contains a convenient hierarchy of scales based on interaction-minimizing boundaries: scales ranging from atoms to molecules to cells to organs to organisms to populations to communities to ecosystems (including economic and/or human-dominated ecosystems) to bioregions to the global system and beyond (Allen and Starr 1982, O'Neill et al. 1986). By studying the similarities and differences among different kinds of systems at different scales and resolutions, one might develop hypotheses and test them against other systems to explore their degree of generality and predictability.

The term *scale* in this context refers to both the resolution (spatial grain size, time step, or degree of complication of the model) and extent (in time, space, and number of components modeled) of the analysis. The process of *scaling* refers to the application of information or models developed at one scale to problems at other scales. In both ecology and economics, primary information and measurements are generally collected at relatively small scales (i.e., small plots in ecology or individuals or single firms in economics), and that information is then often used to build models at radically different scales (i.e., regional, national, or global). The process of scaling is directly tied to the problem of aggregation (the process of adding or otherwise combining components), which in complex, nonlinear, discontinuous systems (like ecological and economic systems) is far from a trivial problem (O'Neill and Rust 1979, Rastetter et al. 1992). For example, in applied economics, basic data sets are usually derived from national accounts that contain data that are linearly aggregated over individuals, companies, or organizations. Sonnenschein (1974) and Debreu (1974) have shown that, unless one makes strong and unrealistic assumptions about the individual units, the aggregate (large-scale) relations between variables have no resemblance to the corresponding relations on the smaller scale.

Rastetter et al. (1992) describe and compare three basic methods for scaling that are applicable to complex systems. All of their methods are attempts to use information about the nonlinear small-scale variability in the large-scale models. They list partial transformations of the fine-scale mathematical relationships to coarse scale using a statistical expectations operator that incorporates the fine-scale variability; partitioning or subdividing the system into smaller, more homogeneous parts (i.e., spatially explicit modeling); and calibration of the fine-scale relationships to coarse-scale data when this data is available. They go on to suggest a combination of these methods as the most effective overall method of scaling in complex systems.

A primary reason for aggregation error in scaling complex systems is the nonlinear variability in the fine-scale phenomenon. For example, Rastetter et al. (1992) give a detailed example of scaling a relationship for individual leaf photosynthesis as a function of radiation and leaf efficiency to estimate the productivity of the entire forest canopy. Because of nonlinear variability in the way individual leaves process light energy, one introduces significant aggregation error by simply using the fine-scale relationships among photosynthesis, radiation, and efficiency along with the average values for the entire forest to get total forest productivity.

One must somehow understand and incorporate this nonlinear fine-scale variability into the coarse-scale equations using some combination of the three methods mentioned above. The statistical expectations method implies deriving new coarse-scale equations that incorporate the fine-scale variability. The problem is that incorporation of this variability often leads to equations that are extremely complex and cumbersome (Rastetter et al. 1992). The partitioning method implies subdividing the forest into many relatively more homogeneous levels or zones and applying the basic fine-scale equations for each partition. This approach requires a method for adjusting the parameters for each partition, a choice of the number of partitions (the resolution), and an understanding of the effects of the choice of resolution and parameters on the results. The recalibration method implies simply recalibrating the fine-scale equations to coarse-scale data. It presupposes that coarse-scale data are available (as more than simply the aggregation of fine-scale data). In many important cases, however, this coarse-scale data is either extremely limited or is not available. Thus, although a judicious application of all three aggregation methods is necessary, from the perspective of complex systems modeling, the partitioning approach seems to hold particular promise, because it can take fullest advantage of emerging computer technologies and databases.

From the scaling perspective, hierarchy theory is a potentially useful tool for partitioning systems in ways that minimize aggregation error. According to hierarchy theory, nature can be partitioned into naturally occurring levels, which share similar time and space scales and which interact with higher and lower levels in systematic ways. Each level in the hierarchy experiences the higher levels as constraints and the lower levels as noise. For example, individual organisms experience the ecosystem they inhabit as a slowly changing set of constraints, and the operation of their component cells and organs is what matters most to them. However, Norton and Ulanowicz (1992) suggest that what appears to be noise at a lower level could be turned into significant perturbations on the higher level. This change can happen when a critical mass of components participate in a trend, a behavioral pattern, that affects the slower processes at the higher level. The rapid and extensive human uses of fossil fuels could be seen as such a trend, causing perturbations at the global atmospheric level, which might feed back and radically alter the framework of action at the lower level.

Shugart et al. (1991) explains the relationship between scales: "Clearly, natural patterns in environmental constraints contribute substantially to the spatial pattern and temporal dynamics of particular ecosystems...these patterns, especially temporal ones, may resonate with natural frequencies of plant growth forms (i.e., phenology and longevity) to amplify environmental patterns" (p. 232). The simplifying assumptions of hierarchy theory may ease the problem of scaling by providing a common (but somewhat generalized) set of rules that could be applied at any scale in the hierarchy.

Fractals and chaos

The concept of fractals (Mandelbrot 1977) can be seen as another related approach to the problem of scaling, based on the fundamental principle of self-similarity between scales. This concept implies a regular and predictable relationship between the scale of measurement (here meaning the resolution of measurement) and the measured phenomenon. For example, the measured length of a coastline is an increasing function of the resolution at which it is measured. At higher resolutions, one can recognize and measure more of the small-scale bays and indentations in the coast and the total length measured increases.

The relationship between length and resolution usually follows a regular pattern that can be summarized in the following equation:

$$L = k\, s^{(1-D)}$$

where L equals the length of the coastline or other fractal boundary, s equals the size of the fundamental unit of measure or the resolution of the measurement, k equals a scaling constant, and D equals the fractal dimension.

Phenomena that fit this equation are said to be self-similar because, as resolution is increased, one perceives patterns at the smaller scale similar to those at the larger scale. This convenient scaling rule has proven useful in describing many kinds of complex boundaries and behaviors (Mandelbrot 1983, Milne 1991, Olsen and Schaffer 1990, Sugihara and May 1990, Turner et al. 1989). One test of the principle of self-similarity is that it can be applied to produce computer-generated shapes that have a decidedly natural and organic look to them (Mandelbrot 1977).

Certain nonlinear dynamical systems models exhibit behaviors whose phase plots ($x[t]$ versus $x[t\text{-}dt]$) are fractals. These chaotic attractors, as they are called, are one of four possible pure types of attractors that can be used to classify system dynamics. The other three are point attractors (indicating stable, non–time varying behavior), periodic attractors (indicating periodic time behavior), and noisy attractors (indicating stochastic time behavior). Real-system behavior can be thought of as representing some combination of these four basic types.

The primary questions about the range of applicability of fractals and chaotic-systems dynamics to the practical problems of modeling ecological economic systems are the influence of scale, resolution, and hierarchy on the mix of behaviors one observes in systems. This problem is key for extrapolating from small-scale experiments or simple theoretical models to practical applied models of ecological economic systems.

Resolution and predictability

The significant effects of nonlinearities raise some interesting questions about the influence of resolution (including spatial, temporal, and component) on the performance of models, in particular on their predictability. For example, the relationship between the degree of complication (the number of components included) and the predictability of models is an important input to model design. Hofmann (1991) discusses this concern in the context of scaling coastal models to the global scale. The difficulty of using aggregate models that integrate over many details of finer resolution models is that the aggregated models may not be able to represent biological processes on the space and time scales necessary. Hofmann suggests that coupled detailed models (in which the output of one model becomes the input for another) may be a more practical method for scaling models to larger systems.

Costanza and Maxwell (in press) analyzed the relationship between spatial resolution and predictability and found that, although increasing resolution provides more descriptive information about the patterns in data, it also increases the difficulty of accurately modeling those patterns. There may be limits to the predictability of natural phenomenon at particular resolutions, and scaling rules that determine how both "data" and "model" predictability change with resolution.

Predictability (Colwell 1974) measures the reduction in uncertainty about one variable given knowledge of others using categorical data. One can define spatial autopredictability (P_a) as the reduction in uncertainty about the state of a pixel in a scene, given knowledge of the state of adjacent pixels in that scene, and spatial cross-predictability (P_c) as the reduction in uncertainty about the state of a pixel in a scene, given knowledge of the state of corresponding pixels in other scenes. P_a is a measure of the internal pattern in the data, whereas P_c is a measure of the ability of a model to represent that pattern.

Some limited testing of the relationship between resolution and predictability (by resampling land-use map data at different spatial resolutions) showed a strong linear relationship between the log of P_a and the log of resolution (measured as the number of pixels per square kilometer). This fractal-like characteristic of self-similarity with decreasing resolution implies that predictability, like the length of a coastline, may be best described using a unitless dimension that summarizes how it changes with resolution. One can define a fractal predictability dimension (D_p) in a manner analogous to the normal fractal dimension that summarizes this relationship. D_p allows convenient scaling of predictability measurements taken at one resolution to other resolutions.

Cross-predictability (P_c) can be used for pattern matching and testing the fit between map scenes. In this sense, it relates to the predictability of models versus the internal predictability in the data revealed by P_a. Although P_a generally increases with increasing resolution (because more information is being included), P_c generally falls or remains stable (because it is easier to model aggregate results than fine-grain ones). Thus, we can define an optimal resolution for a particular modeling problem that balances the benefit in terms of increasing data predictability (P_a) as one increases resolution, with the cost of decreasing model predictability (P_c). Figure 1 shows this relationship in generalized form.

These results may be generalizable to all forms of resolution (spatial, temporal, and number of components) and may shed some light on chaotic behavior in systems. When looking across resolutions, chaos may be the low level of model predictability that occurs as a natural consequence of high resolution. Lowering model resolution can increase model predictability by averaging out some of the chaotic behavior, at the expense of losing detail about the phenomenon. For example, Sugihara and May (1990) found chaotic dynamics for measles epidemics at the level of individual cities, but more predictable periodic dynamics for whole nations.

Evolutionary approaches

In modeling the dynamics of complex systems, it is impossible to ignore the discontinuities and surprises that often characterize these systems and the fact that they operate far from equi-

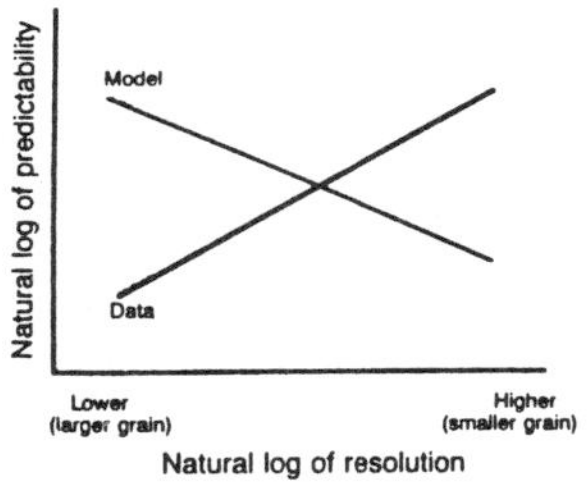

Figure 1. Hypothetical relationship between resolution and predictability of data and models, plotted on log-log axes (from Costanza and Maxwell in press). Data predictibility is a measure of the internal pattern in the data (e.g., the degree to which the uncertainty about the state of landscape pixels is reduced by knowledge of the state of adjacent pixels in the same map). Model predictability is a measure of the correspondence between data and models (e.g., the degree to which the uncertainty about the state of pixels is reduced by knowledge of the corresponding state of pixels in a model of the system). In general, data predictability rises with increasing resolution (because more internal patterns are perceived), whereas model predictability falls (because it becomes more difficult to match the high-resolution patterns). Particular types of models and data sets would fall on different lines, and certain types of models would require certain types of data. An optimal resolution occurs where the data and model predictability lines intersect.

librium in a state of constant adaptation to changing conditions (Holland and Miller 1991, Kay 1991, Lines 1990, Rosser 1991, 1992). The paradigm of evolution has been broadly applied to both ecological and economic systems (Arthur 1988, Boulding 1981, Lindgren 1991, Maxwell and Costanza in press) as a way of formalizing understanding of adaptation and learning behaviors in nonequilibrium dynamic systems. The general evolutionary paradigm posits a mechanism for adaptation and learning in complex systems at any scale using three basic interacting processes: information storage and transmission, generation of new alternatives, and selection of superior alternatives according to some performance criteria.

The evolutionary paradigm is different from the conventional optimization paradigm popular in economics in at least four important respects (Arthur 1988): evolution is path dependent, meaning that the detailed history and dynamics of the system are important; evolution can achieve multiple equilibria; there is no guarantee that optimal efficiency or any other optimal performance will be achieved, due in part to path dependence and sensitivity to perturbations and lock-in (survival of the first rather than survival of the fittest) is possible under conditions of increasing returns. Arthur (1988) notes, "conventional economic theory is built largely on the assumption of diminishing returns of the margin (local negative feedbacks),' but life itself can be characterized as a positive feedback, self-reinforcing autocatalytic process (Günther and Folke in press, Kay 1991), and we should expect increasing returns, lock-in, path dependence, multiple equilibria, and suboptimal efficiency to be the rule rather than the exception in economic and ecological systems.

genetic evolution

In biological evolution, the information storage medium is the genes, the generation of new alternatives is by sexual recombination or genetic mutation, and selection is performed by nature according to criteria of fitness based on reproductive success. The same process of change occurs in ecological, economic, and cultural systems, but the elements on which the process works are different. For example, in cultural evolution the storage medium is the culture (the oral tradition, books, films, or other storage medium for passing on behavioral norms), the generation of new alternatives is through innovation by individual members or groups in the culture, and selection is again based on the reproductive success of the alternatives generated. Reproduction is carried out by the spread and copying of the behaviour through the culture rather than by biological reproduction.

One may also talk of economic evolution, a subject of cultural evolution dealing with the generation, storage, and selection of alternative ways of producing things and allocating that which is produced. The field of evolutionary economics has grown up in approximately the last decade based on these ideas (cf. Day 1989, Day and Groves 1975). Evolutionary theories in economics have already been successfully applied to problems of technical change, to the development of new institutions, and to the evolution of means of payment.

For large, slow-growing animals like humans, genetic evolution has a built-in bias toward the long run. Changing the genetic structure of a species requires that characteristics (phenotypes) be selected and accumulated by differential reproductive success. Behaviors learned or acquired during the lifetime of an individual cannot be passed on genetically. Genetic evolution is therefore usually a relatively slow process requiring many generations to significantly alter a species' physical and biological characteristics.

Cultural evolution is potentially much faster. Technical change is perhaps the most important and fastest-evolving cultural process. Learned behaviors that are successful, at least in the short term, can be almost immediately spread to other members of the culture and passed on in the oral, written, or video record. The increased speed of adaptation that this process allows has been largely responsible for *Homo sapiens*' amazing success at appropriating the resources of the planet. Vitousek et al. (1986) estimate that humans directly control from 25% to 40% of the total primary production of the planet's biosphere, and this control is beginning to have significant effects on the biosphere, including changes in global climate and in the planet's protective ozone shield.

The costs of this rapid cultural evolution, therefore, are potentially significant. Like a car that has increased speed, humans are in more danger of running off the road or over a cliff. Cultural evolution lacks the built-in long-run bias of genetic evolution and is susceptible to being led by its hyperefficient short-run adaptability over a cliff into the abyss.

Another major difference between cultural and genetic evolution may serve as a countervailing bias, however. As Arrow (1962) has pointed out, cultural and economic evolution, unlike genetic evolution, can to some extent employ foresight. If society can see the cliff, perhaps it can be avoided.

Although market forces drive adaptive mechanisms (Kaitala and Pohjola 1988), the systems that evolve are not necessarily optimal, so the question remains: What external influences are needed, and when should they be applied to achieve an optimal economic system via evolutionary adaptation? The challenge faced by ecological economic systems modelers is to first apply the models to gain foresight and then to respond to and manage the system feedbacks in a way that helps avoid any foreseen cliffs (Berkes and Folke in press). Devising policy instruments and identifying incentives that can translate this foresight into effective modifications of the short-run evolutionary dynamics is the challenge (Costanza 1987).

Evolutionary criteria

A critical problem in applying the evolutionary paradigm in dynamic models is defining the selection criteria a priori. In its basic form, the theory of evolution is circular and descriptive (Holling 1987). Those species or cultural institutions or economic activities survive that are the most successful at reproducing themselves. But we only know which ones were more successful after the fact. To use the evolutionary paradigm in modeling, we require a quantitative measure of fitness (or more generally performance) to drive the selection process.

Several candidates have been proposed for this function in various systems, ranging from expected economic utility to thermodynamic potential. Thermodynamic potential is interesting as a performance criterion in complex systems because even simple chemical systems can be seen to evolve complex nonequilibrium structures using this criterion (Nicolis and Prigogine 1977, 1989, Prigogine 1972), and all systems are (at minimum) thermodynamic systems (in addition to their other characteristics). Therefore, thermodynamic constraints and principles are applicable across both ecological and economic systems (Eriksson 1991).

This application of the evolutionary paradigm to thermodynamic systems has led to the development of far-from-equilibrium thermodynamics and the concept of dissipative structures (Prigogine 1972). An important research question is to determine the range of applicability of these principles and their appropriate use in modeling ecological economic systems.

Many dissipative structures follow complicated transient motions. Schneider and Kay (in press) propose a way to analyze these chaotic behaviors and note that, "Away from equilibrium, highly ordered stable complex systems can emerge, develop and grow at the expense of more disorder at higher levels in the system's hierarchy." It has been suggested that the integrity of far-from-equilibrium systems has to do with the ability of the system to attain and maintain its (set of) optimal operating point(s) (Kay 1991). The optimal operating point(s) reflect a state where self-organizing thermodynamic forces and disorganizing forces of environmental change are balanced. This idea has been elaborated and described as "evolution at the edge of chaos" by Bak and Chen (1991) and Kauffman and Johnson (1991).

The concept that a system may evolve through a sequence of stable and unstable stages leading to the formation of new structures seems well suited to ecological economic systems. For example, Gallopin (1989) stresses that to understand the processes of economic impoverishment "The focus must necessarily shift from the static concept of poverty to the dynamic processes of impoverishment and sustainable development within a context of permanent change. The dimensions of poverty cannot any longer be reduced to only the economic or material conditions of living; the capacity to respond to changes, and the vulnerability of the social groups and ecological systems to change become central" (p. 394).

In a similar fashion, Robinson (1991) argues that sustainability calls for maintenance of the dynamic capacity to respond adaptively, which implies that we should focus more on basic natural and social processes than on the particular forms these processes take at any time. Berkes and Folke (in press) have discussed the capacity to respond to changes in ecological economic systems, in terms of institution building, collective actions,

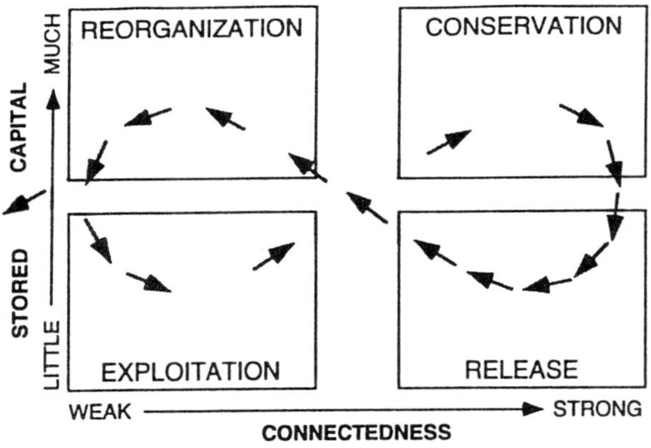

Figure 2. The four general system functions and the flow of events between them (from Holling 1987, 1992). The arrows show the speed of that flow in the ecosystem cycle; arrows close to each other indicate a rapidly changing situation and arrows far from each other indicate a slowly changing situation. The cycle reflects changes in two attributes: on the Y axis, the amount of accumulated capital (nutrients and carbon) stored in variables that are dominant keystone variables at the moment, and, on the X axis, the degree of connectedness among variables. The exit from the cycle indicated at the left of the figure indicates the stage where a flip is most likely into a less- or more-productive and organized system, that is, devolution or evolution as revolution.

cooperation, and social learning. These activities might enhance the capacity for resilience (increase the capacity to recover from disturbance) in interconnected ecological economic systems.

The Holling model

One broad conceptual application of these ideas to ecological and economic systems, with the goal of maximal generality, is the model of Holling (1987, 1992). Holling proposes four basic functions common to all complex systems and a spiraling evolutionary path through them (Figure 2). The functions (boxes) are: exploitation (e.g., r-strategists, pioneers, opportunists, and entrepreneurs), conservation (e.g., K-strategists, climax ecosystems, consolidation, and rigid bureaucracies), release (e.g., fire, storms, pests, and political upheavals), and reorganization (e.g., accessible nutrients and abundant natural resources). Within this model, systems evolve from the rapid colonization and exploitation phase, during which they capture easily accessible resources, to the conservation stage of building and storing increasingly complex structures. Examples of the exploitation phase are early successional ecosystems colonizing disturbed sites or pioneer societies colonizing new territories. Examples of the conservation phase are climax ecosystems or large, mature bureaucracies.

The release or "creative destruction" (Schumpeter 1950) phase represents the breakdown of mature structures via aperiodic events such as fire, storms, pests, or political upheavals. The released structure is then available for reorganization and uptake in the exploitation phase. The amount of ongoing creative destruction that takes place in the system is critical to its behavior. The conservation phase can often build elaborate and tightly bound structures by severely limiting creative destruction (the former Soviet Union is a good example), but these structures become brittle and susceptible to massive and widespread destruction. If some moderate level of release is allowed to occur on a more routine basis, the destruction is on a smaller scale and leads to a more resilient system. It could be argued that patterns of behavior with moderate levels of ongoing creative destruction evolved in those local communities and human cultures that managed to survive for thousands of years or more.

Creative destruction, in terms of shocks or surprises, seems to be crucial for system resilience and integrity. Similarly, it has been argued that episodic events, such as the Chernobyl accident, the Rhine chemical spill, and the death of seals in the North Sea, are shocks to the social-cultural value system and may stimulate positive change toward more resilient ecological economic systems (Berkes and Folke in press).

Fire climax systems, such as the pine forests of Yellowstone National Park, are a good example of the range of possibilities for creative destruction. In its unmanaged state, Yellowstone burned over extensive areas relatively often, but the high fire frequency kept the amount of fuel insufficient to create extremely destructive fires. The more-frequent, small- to moderate-size fires released nutrients stored in the litter and supported a spurt of new growth without destroying all the old growth. On the other hand, when fires were suppressed and controlled, fuel built up to high levels and (because control and suppression are never perfect—remember the former Soviet Union), when the fire did come it wiped out much of the forest.

The Holling four-box model may serve as a minimal ecological economic model aimed at generality (at the expense of precision and realism). It raises some interesting questions about the relationships among diversity, stability, resilience, control, creativity, surprise, and evolution in ecological and economic systems that are ripe for further analyses.

Evolutionary game theory

Evolutionary game theory is the combination of traditional game theory and evolutionary models. The evolution of evolutionary game theory is itself quite interesting, because it relied on several interacting disciplines. Game theory began with von Neuman (1928) as a mathematical exercise for analyzing parlor games. It continued with von Neuman and Morgenstern (1944), who developed the theory for applications in economics. The central idea is that a game consists of a number of players who all act rationally (i.e., use the information available to select strategies that will maximize their expected payoff). The situation when all players have picked their optimal strategies and no one can expect to increase their payoff is called a Nash equilibrium. Conventional game theory with rational players has had an enormous impact on economics, and an increasing number of economic problems are being studied using its tools.

Game theory was imported into evolutionary biology (Maynard-Smith and Price 1973, Maynard-Smith 1979, 1982) to improve understanding of biological processes. There was, however, an important change in the interpretation. Whereas economists used static, rational strategic choices on the part of the players, Maynard-Smith introduced evolution by identifying strategies with genes and the payoff with reproductive success. Reproductive strategies with high payoffs would be expected to have a proportionally higher representation in the population. A Nash equilibrium corresponds to an evolutionarily stable strategy (i.e., a strategy that would be immune to invasion by other strategies).

After this further development within evolutionary biology, evolutionary game theory was then reimported into economics when it became clear that it could be used for an improved understanding of the evolution of various economic institutions (e.g., means of payments and property rights) and of technical processes in production. Economists interested in evolutionary game theory have even started reapplying it to biological evolution (Selten 1980), and political scientists and others have developed it for the interdisciplinary analysis of the evolution of cooperation in both economic and ecological systems (Axelrod 1984).

Through research within four disciplines—mathematics, biology, economics, and political science—evolutionary game theory has developed as a rather important tool for understanding these social and biological processes in isolation. To address ecological economic systems, conventional game theory must be integrated with evolutionary game theory. This integration would include the analysis of games in which different subsets of the players have different time horizons, payoff structures, and objectives. For example, some organisms within the system may choose strategies not only with regard to reproductive success but also with regard to other goals. Some progress has been made along these lines (e.g., Banerjee and Weibull 1991), and it seems to be a fruitful area for future research.

Summary of questions and opportunities

Based on this synthesis, the major researchable questions and opportunities in modeling complex ecological economic systems can be divided into three broad, interdependent categories. These categories are listed below.

Application of the evolutionary paradigm to modeling ecological economic systems. The evolutionary paradigm provides a general framework for complex ecological economic systems dynamics. It incorporates the elements of uncertainty, surprise, learning, path dependence, multiple equilibria, suboptimal performance, lock-in, and thermodynamic constraints. In applying the evolutionary paradigm, a key feature is the choice of the measure (or multiple measures) of performance on which the system's selection process will work. Several such measures have been proposed and partially tested, but additional research and testing in this area may have a high payoff. An important research question is the range of applicability of nonequilibrium thermodynamic principles and their appropriate use in modeling ecological economic systems. Key methods include adaptive computer simulation models and integrated conventional/evolutionary game theory.

Scale and hierarchy considerations in modeling ecological economic systems. The key questions involve exactly how hierarchical levels interact with each other and how to further develop the three basic methods of scaling (statistical expectations, partitioning, and recalibration) for application to complex ecological economic systems. Additional questions concern the range of applicability of fractals and chaotic-systems dynamics to the practical problems of modeling ecological economic systems. In particular, what is the influence of scale, resolution, and hierarchy on the mix of behaviors one observes in systems? This question is key for extrapolating from small-scale experiments or simple theoretical models to practical applied models of ecological economic systems at regional and global scales.

The nature and limits of predictability in modeling ecological economic systems. The significant effects of nonlinearities raise some interesting questions about the influence of resolution (including spatial, temporal, and component) on the performance of models, in particular on their predictability. There may be limits to the predictability of natural phenomena at particular resolutions, and fractal-like rules that determine how both data and model predictability change with resolution. To test these limits, we need better measures of model correspondence with reality and long-term, aggregate-system performance that incorporate the three conflicting criteria of generality, realism, and precision.

Acknowledgments

The Beijer International Institute for Ecological Economics, a research institute of the Royal Swedish Academy of Sciences, provided support for the preparation of this article, which was presented at the workshop on Complex Ecological Economic Systems Modeling held at the Beijer Institute in Stockholm, Sweden, 27–29 July 1992. We thank C. S. Holling, J. Kay, R. E. Ulanowicz, J. Bartholomew, and four anonymous reviewers for detailed comments and suggestions on earlier drafts. We are also indebted to the other participants at the Beijer workshop (G. Brown, C. Clark, P. Dasgupta, F. Duchin, K.-E. Eriksson, S. O. Funtowicz, G. Gallopin, C. Lindgrend, B. Hannon, E. Hofmann, H. Isomäki, R. Kaufmann, V. Kaitala, M. Lines, T. Maxwell, J. McGlade, J. Robinson, C. Perrings, J. B. Rosser, J. Roughgarden, J. Shogren, and F. Taub) for their valuable input and feedback on the article. The article also benefited from interactions with faculty from the University of Maryland's

Multiscale Experimental Ecosystem Research Center, which is devoted to research on many of the topics we have identified.

References cited

Allen, T. F. H., and T. B. Starr. 1982. *Hierarchy*. University of Chicago Press, Chicago.

Arrow, K. 1962. The economic implications of learning by doing. *Review of Economic Studies*. 29: 155–173.

Arthur, W. B. 1988. Self-reinforcing mechanisms in economics. Pages 9–31 in P. W. Anderson, K. J. Arrow, and D. Pines, eds. *The Economy as an Evolving Complex System*. Addisson-Wesley, Redwood City, CA.

Axelrod, R. 1984. *Evolution of Cooperation*. Basic Books, New York.

Bak, P., and K. Chen. 1991. Self-organized criticality. *Sci. Am.* 264: 46.

Banerjee, A., and J. W. Weibull. 1991. Evolutionary selection and rational behavior. Research Papers in Economics 4, Department of Economics, University of Stockholm, Sweden.

Berkes, F., and C. Folke. In press. Investing in cultural capital for a sustainable use of natural capital. In A. M. Jansson, C. Folke, R. Costanza, and M. Hammer, eds. *Investing in Natural Capital: The Ecological Economic Approach to Sustainability*.

Boulding, K. E. 1981. *Evolutionary Economics*. Sage, Beverly Hills, CA.

Brown, G. M., and J. Roughgarden. 1992. An ecological economy: notes on harvest and growth. Beijer Discussion Paper Series 12, Beijer International Institute of Ecological Economics, Stockholm, Sweden.

Brown, G. M., and J. Swierzbinski. 1985. Endangered species, genetic capital and cost-reducing R&D. Pages 111–127 in D. O. Hall, N. Myers, and N. S. Margaris, eds. *Economics of Ecosystems Management*. Dr. W. Junk Publ., Dordrecht, The Netherlands.

Cabe, R., J. Shogren, A. Bouzaher, and A. Carriquiry. 1991. Metamodels, response functions, and research efficiency in ecological economics. Working paper 91-WP 79, Center for Agricultural and Rural Development, Iowa State University, Ames.

Clark, C. W. 1976. *Mathematical Bioeconomics*. John Wiley & Sons, New York.

_____. 1981. Bioeconomics of the ocean. *BioScience* 31: 231–237.

_____. 1985. *Bioeconomic Modelling and Fisheries Management*. John Wiley & Sons, New York.

Clark, C. W., and G. R. Munro. 1975. The economics of fishing and modern capital theory: a simplified approach. *J. Environ. Econ. Manage.* 2: 92–106.

Colwell, R. K. 1974. Predictability, constancy, and contingency of periodic phenomena. *Ecology* 55: 1148–1153.

Costanza, R. 1987. Social traps and environmental policy. *BioScience* 37: 407–412.

Costanza, R., and T. Maxwell. 1991. Spatial ecosystem modeling using parallel processors. *Ecol. Model.* 58: 159–183

_____. In press. Resolution and predictability: an approach to the scaling problem. *Landscape Ecol.*

Costanza, R., B. Norton, and B. J. Haskell, eds. 1992. *Ecosystem Health: New Goals for Environmental Management*. Island Press, Washington, DC.

Costanza, R., F. H. Sklar, and M. L. White. 1990. Modeling coastal landscape dynamics. *BioScience* 40: 91–107

Day, R. H. 1989. Dynamical systems, adaptation and economic evolution. MRG Working Paper no. M8908, University of Southern California, Los Angeles.

Day, R. H., and T. Groves, eds. 1975. *Adaptive Economic Models*. Academic, New York.

Debreu, G. 1974. Excess demand functions. *Journal of Mathematical Economics* 1: 15–23.

Duchin, F. 1988. Analyzing structural change in the economy. Pages 113–128 in M. Ciaschini, ed. *Input-Output Analysis: Current Developments*. Chapman and Hall, New York.

_____. 1992. Industrial input-output analysis: implications for industrial ecology. *Proc. Natl. Acad. Sci.* 89: 851–855.

Eriksson, K.-E. 1991. Physical foundations of ecological economics. Pages 186–196 in L. O. Hansson and B. Jungen, eds. *Human Responsibility and Global Change*. University of Güteborg Press, Güteborg, Sweden.

Gallopin, G. C. 1989. Global impoverishment, sustainable development and the environment: a conceptual approach. *International Social Science Journal* 121: 375–397.

Günther, F., and C. Folke. In press. Characteristics of nested living systems. *Journal of Biological Systems*.

Hannon, B., and C. Joiris. 1987. A seasonal analysis of the southern North Sea ecosystem. *Ecology* 70: 1916–1934.

Hofmann, E. E. 1991. How do we generalize coastal models to global scale? Pages 401–417 in R. F. C. Mantoura, J. M. Martin, and R. Wollast, eds. *Ocean Margin Processes in Global Change*. John Wiley & Sons, New York.

Holland, J. H., and J. H. Miller. 1991. Artificial adaptive agents in economic theory. *American Economic Review* 81: 365–370.

Holling, C. S. 1964. The analysis of complex population processes. *Can. Entomol.* 96: 335–347.

_____. 1966. The functional response of invertebrate predators to prey density. *Mem. Entomol. Soc. Can.* 48.

_____. 1987. Simplifying the complex: the paradigms of ecological function and structure. *European Journal of Operational Research* 30: 139–146.

_____. 1992. Cross-scale morphology, geometry and dynamics of ecosystems. *Ecol. Monogr.* 62: 447–502

Kaitala, V., and M. Pohjola. 1988. Optimal recovery of a shared resource stock: a differential game model with efficient memory equilibria. *Nat. Res. Model.* 3: 91–119.

Kauffman, S. A., and S. Johnson. 1991. Coevolution to the edge of chaos: coupled fitness landscapes, poised states, and coevolutionary avalanches. *J. Theor. Biol.* 149: 467–505.

Kay, J. J. 1991. A nonequilibrium thermodynamic framework for discussing ecosystem integrity. *Environ. Manage.* 15: 483–495.

Keynes, J. M. 1936. *General Theory of Employment, Interest and Money*. Harcourt Brace, London, UK.

Klein, L. R. 1971. Forecasting and policy evaluation using large-scale econometric models: the state of the art. Pages 133–177 in M. D. Intriligator, ed. *Frontiers of Quantitative Economics*. North-Holland Publ., Amsterdam, The Netherlands.

Levins, R. 1966. The strategy of model building in population biology. *Am. Sci.* 54: 421–431.

Lindgren, K. 1991. Evolutionary phenomena in simple dynamics. Pages 295–312 in C. G. Langton, C. Taylor, J. D. Farmer, and S. Rasmussen. *Artificial Life*. Addison-Wesley, Redwood City, CA.

Lines, M. 1989. Environmental noise and nonlinear models: a simple macroeconomic example. *Economic Notes* 19: 376–394.

_____. 1990. Stochastic stability considerations: a nonlinear example. *International Review of Economics and Business* 37: 219–233.

Lucas, R. E. 1975. An equilibrium model of the business cycle. *Journal of Political Economy* 83: 1113–45.

Mäler, K.-G. 1991. National accounts and environmental resources. *Environmental and Resource Economics* 1: 1–15.

Mandelbrot, B. B. 1977. *Fractals: Form, Chance and Dimension*. W.H. Freeman, San Francisco, CA.

_____. 1983. *The Fractal Geometry of Nature*. W.H. Freeman, San Francisco, CA.

Maxwell, T., and R. Costanza. In press. An approach to modelling the dynamics of evolutionary self-organization. *Ecol. Model.*

Maynard-Smith, J. 1979. Game theory and the evolution of behavior. *Proc. R. Soc. Lond. B* 205: 475–488.

_____. 1982. *Evolution and the Theory of Games*. Cambridge University Press, New York.

Maynard-Smith, J., and G. R. Price. 1973. The logic of animal conflict. *Nature* 246: 15–18

Milne, B. T. 1991. Lessons from applying fractal models to landscape patterns. Pages 199–235 in M. G. Turner and R. Gardner, eds. *Quantitative Methods in Landscape Ecology*. Springer-Verlag, New York.

Nicolis, G., and I. Prigogine. 1977. *Self-organization in Non-equilibrium Systems*. John Wiley & Sons, New York.

_____. 1989. *Exploring Complexity*. W.H. Freeman, New York.

Norgaard, R. B. 1989. The case for methodological pluralism. *Ecological Economics* 1: 37–57.

Norton, B. G., and R. E. Ulanowicz. 1992. Scale and biodiversity policy: a hierarchical approach. *Ambio* 21: 244–249.

Olsen, L. F., and W. M. Schaffer. 1990. Chaos versus noisy periodicity: alternative hypotheses for childhood epidemics. *Science* 249: 499–504.

O'Neill, R. V., D. L. DeAngelis, J. B. Waide, and T. F. H. Allen. 1986. *A Hierarchical Concept of Ecosystems*. Princeton University Press, Princeton, NJ.

O'Neill, R. V., A. R. Johnson and A. W. King. 1989. A hierarchical framework for the analysis of scale. *Landscape Ecol.* 3: 193–205.

O'Neill, R. V., and B. Rust. 1979. Aggregation error in ecological models. *Ecol. Model.* 7: 91–105.

Prigogine, I. 1972. Thermodynamics of evolution. *Physics Today* 23: 23–28.

Rastetter, E. B., A. W. King, B. J. Cosby, G. M. Hornberger, R. V. O'Neill, and J. E. Hobbie.

1992. Aggregating fine-scale ecological knowledge to model coarser-scale attributes of ecosystems. *Ecological Applications* 2: 55–70.

Robinson, J. B. 1991. Modelling the interactions between human and natural systems. *International Social Science Journal* 130: 629–647.

______. Of maps and territories: the use and abuse of socio-economic modelling in support of decision-making. *Technological Forecast and Social Change*.

Rosser, J. B. 1991. *From Catastrophe to Chaos: A General Theory of Economic Discontinuities*. Kluwer, Amsterdam, The Netherlands.

______. 1992. The dialogue between the economic and ecologic theories of evolution. *Journal of Economic Behavior and Organization* 17: 195–215.

Schneider, E. D., and J. J. Kay. In press. Life as a manifestation of the second law of thermodynamics. *International Journal of Mathematical and Computer Modelling*.

Schumpeter, J. A. 1950. *Capitalism, Socialism and Democracy*. Harper & Row, New York.

Selten, R. 1980. A note on evolutionary stable strategies in asymmetrical animal conflicts. *J. Theoret. Biol.* 84: 93–101.

Shugart, H. H. 1989. The role of ecological models in long-term ecological studies. Pages 90–109 in G. E. Likens, ed. *Long-Term Studies in Ecology: Approaches and Alternatives*. Springer-Verlag, New York.

Shugart, H. H., G. B. Bonan, D. L. Urban, W. K. Lavenroth, W. J. Parton, and G. M. Hornberger. 1991. Computer models and long-term ecological research. Pages 221–239 in P. G. Risser, ed. *Long-term Ecological Research: An International Perspective*. John Wiley & Sons, New York.

Solow, R. M. 1956. A contribution to the theory of economic growth. *Quarterly Journal of Economics* 70: 65–94.

Sonnenschein, H. 1974. Market excess demand functions. *Econometrica* 40: 549–563.

Sugihara, G., and R. M. May. 1990. Nonlinear forecasting as a way of distinguishing chaos from measurement error in time series. *Nature* 344: 734–741

Taub, F. B. 1987. Indicators of change in natural and human impacted ecosystems: status. Pages 115–144 in S. Draggan, J. J. Cohrssen, and R. E. Morrison, eds. *Preserving Ecological Systems: The Agenda for Long-term Research and Development*. Praeger, New York.

______. 1989. Standardized aquatic microcosm: development and testing. Pages 47–92 in A. Boudou and F. Ribeyre, eds. *Aquatic Ecotoxicology: Fundamental Concepts and Methodologies*. vol II. CRC Press, Boca Raton, FL.

Turner, M. G., R. Costanza, and F. H. Sklar. 1989. Methods to compare spatial patterns for landscape modeling and analysis. *Ecol. Model.* 48: 1–18.

Vitousek, P., P. R. Ehrlich, A. H. Ehrlich, and P. A. Matson. 1986. Human appropriation of the products of photosynthesis. *BioScience* 36: 368–373.

von Bertalanffy, L. 1968. *General System Theory: Foundations, Development, Applications*. George Braziller, New York.

von Neuman, J. 1928. Sur Theorie der Gesellschaftsspield. *Mathematische Analen* 100: 295–320.

von Neuman, J., and O. Morgenstern. 1944. *Theory of Games and Economic Behavior*. Princeton University Press, Princeton, NJ.

Wulff, F., and R. E. Ulanowicz. 1989. A comparative anatomy of the Baltic Sea and Chesapeake Bay ecosystems. Pages 232–256 in F. Wulff, J. G. Field, and K. H. Mann, eds. *Network Analysis of Marine Ecology: Methods and Applications*. Springer-Verlag, NY.

Wroblewski, J. S., and E. E. Hofmann. 1989. U.S. interdisciplinary modeling studies of coastal-offshore exchange processes: past and future. *Prog. Oceanogr.* 23: 65–99.

Landscape Ecology vol. 9 no. 1 pp 47-57 (1994)
SPB Academic Publishing bv, The Hague

Resolution and predictability: An approach to the scaling problem

Robert Costanza and Thomas Maxwell
Maryland International Institute for Ecological Economics, Center for Environmental and Estuarine Studies, University of Maryland, Box 38, Solomons, MD 20688-0038, USA

Keywords: Scaling, predictability, resolution, GIS, fractals, landscape modeling

Abstract

We analyzed the relationship between resolution and predictability and found that while increasing resolution provides more descriptive information about the patterns in data, it also increases the difficulty of accurately modeling those patterns. There are limits to the predictability of natural phenomenon at particular resolutions, and "fractal-like" rules determine how both "data" and "model" predictability change with resolution.

We analyzed land use data by resampling map data sets at several different spatial resolutions and measuring predictability at each. Spatial *auto-predictability* (P_a) is the reduction in uncertainty about the state of a pixel in a scene given knowledge of the state of adjacent pixels in that scene, and spatial *cross-predictability* (P_c) is the reduction in uncertainty about the state of a pixel in a scene given knowledge of the state of corresponding pixels in other scenes. P_a is a measure of the internal pattern in the data while P_c is a measure of the ability of some other "model" to represent that pattern.

We found a strong linear relationship between the log of P_a and the log of resolution (measured as the number of pixels per square kilometer). This fractal-like characteristic of "self-similarity" with decreasing resolution implies that predictability may be best described using a unitless dimension that summarizes how it changes with resolution. While P_a generally increases with increasing resolution (because more information is being included), P_c generally falls or remains stable (because it is easier to model aggregate results than fine grain ones). Thus one can define an "optimal" resolution for a particular modeling problem that balances the benefit in terms of increasing data predictability (P_a) as one increases resolution, with the cost of decreasing model predictability (P_c).

Introduction

We hypothesized that an important determinant of the predictability of phenomenon is the scale (resolution and extent) of the analysis. By resolution we mean "grain size" or the size of the smallest unit of measure, with increasing resolution corresponding to fine grain. We can distinguish at least two ways that resolution might affect predictability. One is the increasing difficulty of building predictive models at increasingly finer resolution. For example, the position and velocity of individual molecules in a gas is highly unpredictable, but the temperature of the gas (which is an average of these motions at a much cruder resolution) is highly predictable. Likewise, it is easier to predict general climate patterns than it is to predict the exact geographic location and timing of rainstorms (the weather).

On the other hand, finer resolution allows more

detail to be observed and internal patterns in the data to be seen that may not have been observed at cruder resolutions. One example is the warm core gyres that form in the Gulf Stream that were not observed until remote sensing images including the proper thermal bands and of sufficiently fine resolution were available. Another example is the quest by the military to obtain high enough resolution satellite images to see the features (such as tanks and airplanes) of interest to them that would not appear on lower resolution images.

Some phenomenon are known to vary in a regular way with resolution. For example, the regular relationship between the measured length of a coastline and the resolution at which it is measured is a fundamental one behind the concept of fractals (Mandelbrot 1977) and can be summarized in the following equation:

$$L = k\ s^{(1-D)} \qquad (1)$$

where:

- L = the length of the coastline or other "fractal" boundary
- s = the size of the fundamental unit of measure or the resolution of the measurement
- k = a scaling constant
- D = the fractal dimension

This convenient "scaling rule" has proved to be very useful in describing many kinds of complex boundaries and behaviors (Mandelbrot 1983, Milne 1988, Turner *et al.* 1987, 1989, Olsen and Schaffer 1990, Sugihara and May 1990). We hypothesized that this same kind of relationship might exist between resolution and predictability (and possibly other measures as well) and might be useful for developing scaling rules for understanding and modeling. We tested this hypothesis by calculating both data and model predictability for a number of landscapes at a number of different resolutions.

Measurement of predictability

Colwell (1974) applied information theoretic concepts to the problem of estimating the degree of predictability of periodic phenomena. The method is similar to autocorrelation analysis except that it is applicable to both interval and categorical data and may thus be more appropriate, for example, for comparing patterns of land cover. Predictability in this context refers to the reduction in uncertainty about one variable that can be gained by knowledge of another. For example, if the seasonal rainfall pattern in an area is predictable (*e.g.*, there is always a severe dry summer), then knowing the time of year provides information about rainfall (if it's summer, it must be dry). If there is no relationship between rainfall and season, time of year tells us little and the rainfall is relatively unpredictable from a knowledge of time of year.

These techniques can also be applied to spatial data (Turner *et al.* 1989). In this application, one is interested in the degree to which the uncertainty about the category of a particular pixel is reduced from knowledge of other aspects of the same scene, or from knowledge of aspects of other, related scenes. There are several aspects of a scene that might be used as predictors. We discuss two implementations based on (1) the state of adjacent pixels in the same scene ("auto-predictability" or P_a); and (2) the state of corresponding pixels in other, related scenes ("cross predictability" or P_c). Other combinations of these two and higher level analyses (*i.e.*, adjacent pixel pairs, triplets, etc., or multiple cross comparisons) are also possible and useful for various purposes (Turner *et al.* 1989).

The method in general can determine if there are regularities in a spatial data set, ranked on a scale from 0 (totally unpredictable) to 1 (totally predictable), and the answer can be interpreted as the degree of departure of the scene or comparison between scenes from a random (totally unpredictable) pattern.

To estimate predictability, one first assembles a contingency matrix with states or conditions of the pixels along the left axis, and corresponding states of other pixels along the top. For auto-predictability the categories in a map are listed on the left and along the top of a matrix. The numbers in the matrices represent the frequency of occurrence in the mapped data of the category (or category pair, triplet, etc. for higher level analysis) listed along the top of the matrix lying adjacent to the category listed along the left. This yields information about how predictable the patterns of adjacency are in the sample map data.

The contingency matrix can be any set of meaningful spatial relationships in the data. For example, another way of setting up the matrix is to define the predictability of one scene given another scene. For example, we might want to know the predictability of a landscape in one year given information in some previous year(s), or we might want to know the predictability of a real landscape compared to a landscape model's output. We call this the "cross" predictability, because it provides information on the predictability of a given pixel's category given knowledge of the category of the corresponding pixel in another scene.

Following Colwell (1974) we define N_{ij} to be the elements in the contingency matrix (*i.e.*, the number of times in the data that a pixel of category i was adjacent to one of category j for auto-predictability analysis). Define X_j as the column totals, Y_i as the row totals, and Z as the grand total, or:

$$X_j = \sum_{i=1}^{s} N_{ij} \qquad (2)$$

$$Y_i = \sum_{j=1}^{t} N_{ij} \qquad (3)$$

and

$$Z = \sum_i \sum_j N_{ij} = \sum_j X_j = \sum_i Y_i \qquad (4)$$

Then the uncertainty with respect to X is:

$$H(X) = - \sum_{j=1}^{t} \frac{X_j}{Z} \log \frac{X_j}{Z} \qquad (5)$$

and the uncertainty with respect to Y is:

$$H(Y) = - \sum_{i=1}^{S} \frac{Y_i}{Z} \log \frac{Y_i}{Z} \qquad (6)$$

and the uncertainty with respect to the interaction of X and Y is:

$$H(XY) = - \sum_i \sum_j \frac{N_{ij}}{Z} \log \frac{N_{ij}}{Z} \qquad (7)$$

Then define the conditional uncertainty with regard to Y with X given as:

$$H_x(Y) = H(XY) - H(X) \qquad (8)$$

Finally, define a measure of predictability (P) with the range (0,1) as:

$$P = 1 - \frac{H_x(Y)}{\log s} = 1 - \frac{H(XY) - H(X)}{\log s} \qquad (9)$$

where s is the total number of rows (categories) in the contingency matrix.

This measure gives an index scaled on the range from 0 (unpredictable or maximum uncertainty) to 1 (totally predictable or minimum uncertainty). Predictability will be minimal when all the elements in the contingency matrix (N_{ij} are equiprobable (*i.e.*, when all entries are the same), and will be maximized when only one entry in each column is non-zero. Most real spatial data will fall between these extremes.

Study areas

We applied these indices of predictability to land use data sets from the Kissimmee/Everglades Basin, Florida and the state of Maryland. Both of these data sets contained three distinct years of data over which significant changes in land use patterns had occurred.

Kissimmee/Everglades Basin, Florida

The Kissimmee/Everglades drainage basin in South Florida represents one of the most rapidly changing and intensively modified landscapes in the country. It consists of some 18,700 square miles (48,500 km^2) of land and water (Fig. 1) covering about 1/4 of the state of Florida. A set of three land use maps with 26 land use categories were prepared for the years 1900, 1953, and 1973 in order to analyze the dramatic changes that had occurred in the region during this interval (Costanza 1975, 1979). In 1900, when much of the United States had already been developed into farmland and cities, the Kissimmee/Everglades basin remained much as it had been for

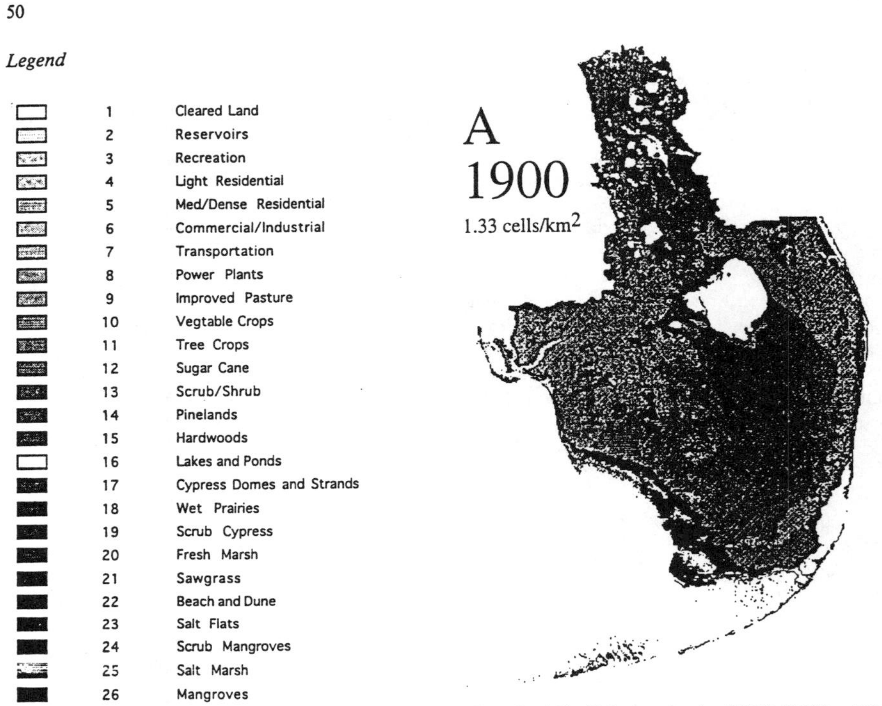

Fig. 1. South Florida land use data for A) 1900, B) 1953, and C) 1973 (from Costanza (1975)).

centuries. By 1953, the expanding US middle class and post-war economic boom had led to significant urban and agricultural development. This development accelerated into the 70s and 80s.

For the predictability analysis we used versions of the land use maps that had been manually digitized into 128 acre (0.52 km^2) rectangular cells, each 625 m by 833 m (Costanza 1979). This produced an array with overall dimensions of 576 rows by 400 columns (230,400 total cells) of which about 93,000 were inside the study area. Each cell was assigned one of 26 land use categories ranging from natural to agricultural to urban systems (Costanza 1979).

State of Maryland

The Maryland Department of State Planning has compiled digitized land use data (using 80 acre cells) for three different years (1973, 1981, and 1985) for the entire state, using 20 different land use categories. While there were significant shifts in land use in Maryland, land use had changed much less dramatically in this area over the 22-year interval between 1973 and 1985 than it had in South Florida during the 1900 to 1973 interval. Major changes involved reforestation of agricultural areas and significant increases in urban land uses, especially in the Washington/Baltimore corridor. For the state of Maryland we used a rectangular array of 345 rows by 640 columns or a total of 220,800 cells, of

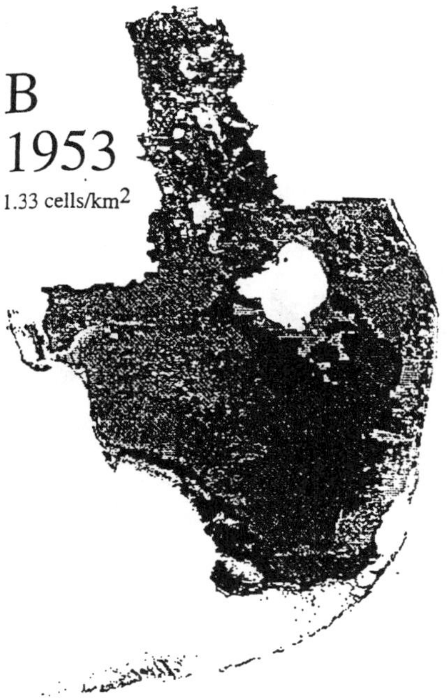

Fig. 1B.

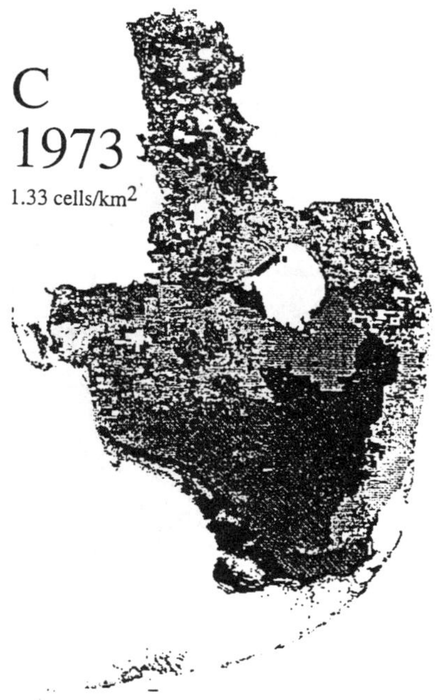

Fig. 1C.

which approximately 68,800 were within the boundaries of the state.

Software and algorithms

Land use data from the two study sites was imported into Map II™, a simple and easy to use raster-based GIS package for the Macintosh, to prepare data files for calculations using high speed parallel transputers, as discussed below. Any GIS system capable of producing raster output would be suitable, however.

Decreasing the resolution (increasing the grain) of a spatial data set involves the repetitive resampling of a specified number of small cells into larger cells. Analytically, this is accomplished by moving a resampling matrix (whose size is the number of rows and columns of the original data needed to make a single cell in the new raster) through the original raster. The cell values falling within the resampling matrix are tabulated and used to determine the value of the appropriate larger cell in the new, coarser resolution raster. We experimented with several methods of resampling or aggregating the spatial data. The first method, which we call *proportional aggregation*, assigns the cell values in the coarser grain raster according to the most dominant category found within the resampling matrix. A second method, termed *random aggregation*, assigns new categories by randomly choosing from the categories found within the resampling matrix. The major difference between the two methods is that rare categories are more likely to be preserved when the data are resampled with the random aggregation scheme. While the choice of aggrega-

52

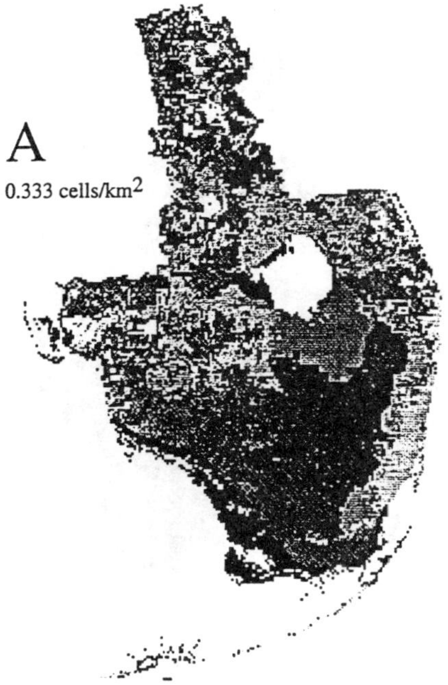

Fig. 2. Example of the random, sequential aggregation scheme applied to the 1973 South Florida data four successive times. These four aggregations, along with the original, make up the five different resolutions used in the analyses. The resolutions used for the Florida site were 1.333 (original), 0.333 (A), 0.083 (B), 0.021 (C), and 0.005 (D) cells/km^2.

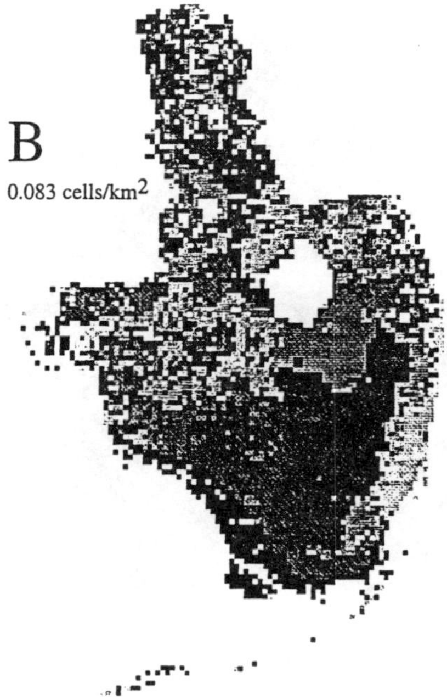

Fig. 2B.

tion scheme can be significant in many spatial analyses, we found that the aggregation scheme made little difference to the results of our particular experiments. We settled on a version of the random aggregation scheme that is both simple and suits our immediate needs. In this version aggregation takes place in steps. In each step the original map is aggregated using a 2 × 2 resampling matrix, yielding an aggregated map with 1/4 the number of cells of the original. In each 2 × 2 resampling matrix we choose the category of the northwest cell as the category for the cell in the aggregate map. This process was repeated on the new aggregate map to yield a series of maps each with 1/4 the total number of cells of the one preceding it in the series. Figure 2 shows the results of this process for the South Florida, 1973 data set. Each map in this series has 1/4 the resolution of the preceding map. For the Florida maps the resulting resolutions (in cells/km^2) were 1.333 (original), 0.333, 0.083, 0.021, and 0.005. For the Maryland maps the resulting resolutions (in cells/km^2) were 2.743 (original), 0.686, 0.171, 0.043, and 0.011.

We developed algorithms in a parallel version of the C programming language to calculate auto and cross-predictability for mapped data on Inmos Transputers (a form of RISC based parallel processor) on a Macintosh (Costanza and Maxwell 1991). Transputers are extremely fast for this sort of calculation. For example, for the South Florida data (a 576 × 400 array) calculation of auto-predictability and printing results to a text file took approximate-

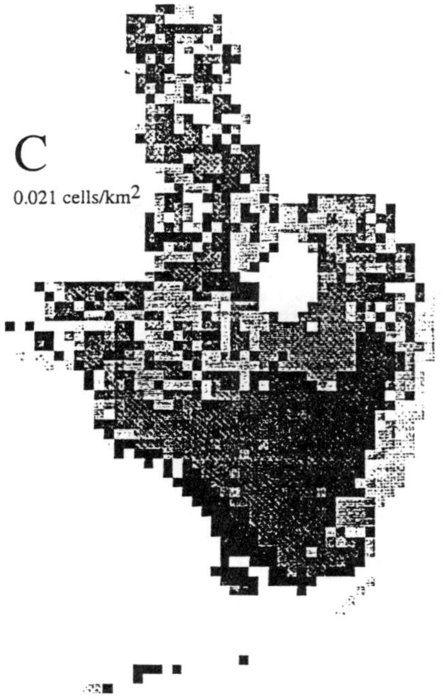

Fig. 2C.

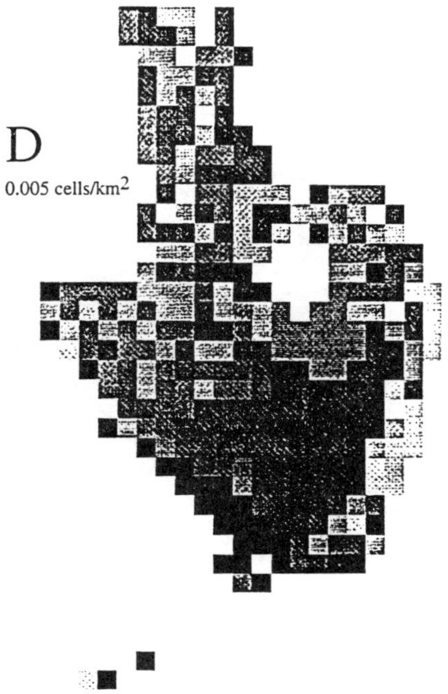

Fig. 2D.

ly 2.4 seconds using a Macintosh IIci with 4 transputers[1].

Auto-predictability experiments

We calculated P_a for both study areas for all three years and at five different resolutions. We started with the maximum resolution of the data and gradually degraded it by aggregating pixels. In each step we halved the resolution by aggregating 2×2 blocks of pixels at the previous resolution into single pixels as described above. Resolution is frequently indicated as the length of a side of a cell (pixel), with higher or finer resolution corresponding to smaller cell (pixel) sizes. For example, LANDSAT satellite data has 30-meter resolution while SPOT satellite data has finer resolution at 18 meters. In our plots we wanted higher resolution to correspond to higher (not lower) numbers so we measured resolution as the number of cells per km^2. For example, 50-meter cells would have a resolution of 400 cells/km^2, while 200-meter cells would have a resolution of 25 cells/km^2.

We fit the equation:

$$P = k\, r^{(1 - D_P)} \qquad (2)$$

[1]The algorithms also work on serial machines, only slower. Each transputer is approximately the speed of a SUN Sparc station so the 4 transputer time is about four times the speed one would expect on a Sparc station. Contact Tom Maxwell for more information about obtaining the algorithms or using transputers for spatial analysis.

Table 1. Fractal auto-predictability dimension (given as $1\text{-}D_{AP}$, scale constant (k), adjusted R^2, and degrees of freedom (df) for auto-predictability (P_a) from regression of equation 3 for both data sets. ** indicates significant at the 0.1 level, * indicates significant at the .05 level.

Site	Year	k	($1\text{-}D_{AP}$)	adj R^2	df
Kissimmee/Everglades, FL	1900	0.6364	0.111	.999**	4
Kissimmee/Everglades, FL	1953	0.6383	0.085	.988**	4
Kissimmee/Everglades, FL	1973	0.6250	0.096	.981**	4
Kissimmee/Everglades, FL	all years	0.6332	0.097	.958**	14
State of Maryland	1973	0.5189	0.031	.780*	4
State of Maryland	1981	0.5046	0.034	.780*	4
State of Maryland	1985	0.4956	0.030	.631*	4
State of Maryland	all years	0.5434	0.031	.720**	14

Table 2. Fractal cross-predictability dimension (stated as $1\text{-}D_{CP}$, scale constant (k), adjusted R^2, and degrees of freedom (df) from regression of equation 3 for cross-predictability (P_c) for both data sets. ** indicates significant at the 0.1 level, * indicates significant at the .05 level.

Site	Year	k	($1\text{-}D_{CP}$)	adj R^2	df
Kissimmee/Everglades, FL	1900/1953	0.5764	−0.11	.943**	4
Kissimmee/Everglades, FL	1953/1973	0.4936	−.017	.778*	4
State of Maryland	1973/1981	1.0790	−.006	.805*	4
State of Maryland	1981/1985	0.9296	−.004	.777*	4

where:

- P = the spatial predictability (P_a refers to auto-predictability, P_c refers to cross-predictability)
- r = the resolution measured as the number of cells/km^2
- k = a scaling factor
- D_P = the fractal predictability dimension (dimensionless)

by first transforming it into log-log form:

$$ln\,(P_1) = ln\,(k) + (1 - D_P) ln\,(r) \qquad (3)$$

and using standard linear regression analysis to solve for the parameters k and D_P.

The results are summarized in Table 1, which indicates the high R^2 for this relationship for both of the study sites.

Cross-predictability experiments

We calculated P_c for both of the study areas by comparing maps from different years. This is analogous to a simple "null model" that predicts land use patterns for one time from patterns at some previous time or times. This "model" includes no information on the underlying processes of change, but we were interested in how changing the resolution of the maps affected the predictability, and the "null model" of no change is an interesting point of reference. We fit equation 3 to the data and the results for the three sites are shown in Table 2.

Results of both the auto and cross-predictability experiments for both sites are plotted together on a log-log scale in Fig. 3. The strong linearity of the relationship for all cases is apparent, as is the fact that auto-predictability (P_a) increases with increasing resolution while cross-predictability (P_c) decreases slightly with increasing resolution, although with a smaller D_p. These results are consistent with our original hypotheses. Results for the Kissimmee/Everglades data are markedly different from those for the Maryland data. The auto-predictability of Maryland land use changed much less with resolution than the Kissimmee/Everglades land use. The slope of the regression line ($1\text{-}D_{AP}$ for the Kissimmee/Everglades data was roughly three

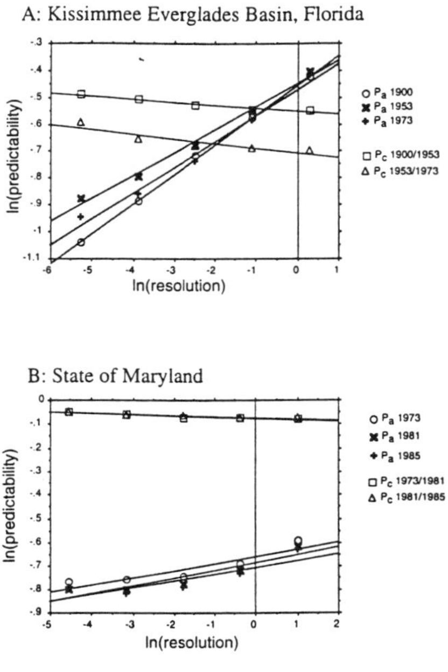

Fig. 3. Natural log of resolution vs. natural log of predictability for A) the Kississmee/Everglades, Florida, and B) the state of Maryland land use data. Plot shows both auto-predictability (P_a) indicating internal pattern in the data for three different years, and cross-predictability (P_c) indicating pattern matching between null models of prior land use maps and the particular map. The resolutions used (in cells/km^2) were: Florida: 0.005, 0.021, 0.083, 0.333, 1.333; Maryland: 0.011, 0.043, 0.171, 0.686, 2.743.

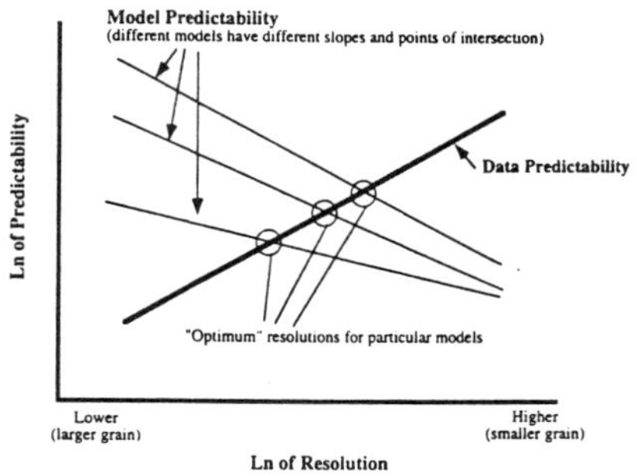

Fig. 4. Hypothetical relationship between resolution and predictability of data and models. Data predictibility is the degree to which the uncertainty about the state of landscape pixels is reduced by knowledge of the state of adjacent pixels in the same map. Model predictability is the degree to which the uncertainty about the state of pixels is reduced by knowledge of the corresponding state of pixels in output maps from various models of the system.

times that for the Maryland data. Auto-predictability varied from about 0.65 to 0.35 over the range of resolutions used for the Florida data, but only from about 0.55 to 0.45 for the Maryland data. The Kissimmee/Everglades data was also more predictable at the highest resolutions than the Maryland data.

The cross-predictability results also differ markedly between the Florida and Maryland data. The slope of the regression line ($1 - D_{cp}$ was about three times higher for the Florida data than the Maryland data. Recall that the "null models" we are comparing with "data" in this analysis were land use data from prior years. As we can see from the results, this null model is a very good predictor of land use at all resolutions if the land use did not change radically over the study interval (as was the case in Maryland). In the Florida case, we were using a longer time interval and land use had changed radically over this interval, so the null model was much less accurate at all resolutions.

In addition, this "null model" is of limited real usefulness since it embodies none of the underlying processes that caused the land use changes in the first place. In the more general case of dynamic landscape models, or models in general, we would not expect such high initial values of predictability, and would expect the predictability to fall more quickly with resolution. We are currently building dynamic landscape models to test this hypothesis which can be summarized in Fig. 4.

Discussion and conclusions

We can draw several conclusions from our analysis:

1. P_a and P_c belong to a class of "fractal-like" self-similar measures that vary in a regular way as resolution changes. This allows a "fractal

dimension" to be calculated that permits easy conversion of measurements of P taken at one resolution to other resolutions (for example, resolutions higher than those for which we have data). We suspect that there are many other spatial measures, which also exhibit this kind of self-similarity, that may be useful in developing a generalized theory of scaling.

2. P_a generally increases with increasing resolution. This relationship represents the "benefit" in terms of information gained about the pattern as resolution is increased.
3. P_c generally falls with increasing resolution. This relationship represents the "cost" of decreased model predictability as resolution is increased.
4. Combining 2 and 3 leads to some hypotheses about determining an "optimal" resolution for specific studies. At very low resolution it is easier to build predictive models, but they have little useful detail. At high resolution much useful detail is retained, but models are less able to predict it. An optimal resolution for scientific analysis may occur where these trends intersect – where one is balancing the costs and benefits incurred with increasing resolution. These results are consistent with empirical data from a survey of over 85 models of freshwater wetlands (Costanza and Sklar 1985).
5. The "models" we have analyzed so far are very primitive "null models" that one would expect to be different in overall predictability (P_c) and in their fractal predictability dimensions (D_{cp}) than more sophisticated process-based spatial models (Costanza *et al.* 1990). We suspect that there is a different optimal resolution for each class of models, and possibly for each particular set of modeling objectives. We also suspect that P_c and its associated D_{cp} will change with changing technology and modeling skills. We are currently pursuing research aimed at addressing these questions by applying process-based spatial models at several different resolutions.
6. These results may be generalizable to all forms of resolutions (spatial, temporal, and number of components) and may shed some interesting light on "chaotic" behavior in systems. When looking across resolutions, chaos may be the low level of model predictability that occurs as a natural consequence of high resolution. Lowering model resolution can increase model predictability by averaging out some of the chaotic behavior at the expense of losing detail about the phenomenon. For example, Sugihara and May (1990) found chaotic dynamics for measles epidemics at the level of individual cities, but more predictable periodic dynamics for whole nations. The idea is not to maximize the resolution of analysis in order to "discover" this "unpredictable" chaotic behavior, nor is it to maximize predictability by ignoring details. Rather, the aim is to choose the resolution that maximizes the *effectiveness* of the model in balancing the conflicting trends of data and model predictability with changing resolution.

Acknowledgments

This research was supported in part by NSF Grants BSR-8814272 titled: Response of a major land margin ecosystem to changes in terrestrial nutrient inputs, internal nutrient cycling, production and export; and BSR-8906269 titled: Landscape modeling: the synthesis of ecological processes over large geographic regions and long time scales. We thank L. Graham for significant contributions to computer programming early in the development of these ideas, and S. Tennenbaum, F.H. Sklar, and L. Wainger and an anonymous reviewer for providing useful comments on earlier drafts.

References

Colwell, R.K. 1974. Predictability, constancy, and contingency of periodic phenomena. Ecology 55: 1148–1153.

Costanza, R. 1975. The spatial distribution of land use subsystems, incoming energy and energy use in South Florida from 1900 to 1973. Master's Research Project. Department of Architecture, University of Florida, Gainesville, FL. 204 pp.

Costanza, R. 1979. Embodied energy basis for economic-ecologic systems. Ph.D. Dissertation. University of Florida, Gainesville, FL. 254 pp.

Costanza, R. and Maxwell, T. 1991. Spatial ecosystem modeling using parallel processors. Ecological Modeling 58: 159–183.

Costanza, R. and Sklar, F.H. 1985. Articulation, accuracy, and effectiveness of mathematical models: a review of freshwater wetland applications. Ecological Modeling 27: 45–68.

Costanza, R., Sklar, F.H. and White, M.L. 1990. Modeling coastal landscape dynamics. BioScience 40: 91–107.

Mandelbrot, B.B. 1977. Fractals. Form, chance and dimension. W.H. Freeman and Co., San Francisco, C.A.

Mandelbrot, B.B. 1983. The Fractal Geometry of Nature. W.H. Freeman and Co., San Francisco, CA.

Milne, B.T. 1988. Measuring the fractal dimension of landscapes. Applied Mathematics and Computation 27: 67–79.

Olsen, L.F. and Schaffer, W.M. 1990. Chaos versus noisy periodicity: alternative hypotheses for childhood epidemics. Science 249: 499–504.

Sugihara, G. and May, R.M. 1990. Nonlinear forecasting as a way of distinguishing chaos from measurement error in time series. Nature 344: 734–741.

Turner, M.G. 1987. Spatial simulation of landscape changes in Georgia: a comparison of 3 transition models. Landscape Ecology 1: 29–36.

Turner, M.G., Costanza, R. and Sklar, F.H. 1989. Methods to Compare Spatial Patterns for Landscape Modeling and Analysis. Ecological Modelling 48: 1–18.

[23]

Integrated Ecological Economic Systems Modeling: Theoretical Issues and Practical Applications

Robert Costanza, Lisa Wainger, and Nancy Bockstael

New understanding about system dynamics and predictability that has emerged from the study of "complex systems" is creating new tools for modeling interactions between human and natural systems. A range of techniques has become available through advances in computer speed and accessibility and by implementing a broad systems view of ecological and economic interactions.

While almost any subdivision of the universe can be thought of as a "system," modelers of systems usually look for boundaries that minimize the interaction between the system under study and the rest of the universe in order to make their job easier. The interactions between ecological and economic systems are many and strong. So, while splitting the world into separate economic and ecological systems is possible, it does not minimize interactions and is a poor choice of boundary.

Traditional research has concentrated on *either* ecological *or* economic modeling approaches to the environment-human interaction problem. This tradition of independent and appended research has resulted in a body of environmental work completed by both sciences that overlooks the fundamental problems associated with their interactions. Namely, the studies are completed using different terms and units of measurement, and the studies neglect to account for the interaction between the processes and populations (i.e., humans and ecosystems) each seeks to model. Generally, ecological models have tended to ignore humans, except to the extent that they introduce apparently exogenous shocks into the ecological system, and economic models have taken simplified versions of "ecological facts."

To achieve a comprehensive understanding that is useful for modeling and prediction of linked ecological economic systems requires the synthesis and integration of several different conceptual frames. As Levins (1966) has described this search for robustness: "We attempt to treat the same problem with several alternative models each with different simplifications. . . . Then, if these models, despite their different assumptions, lead to similar results we have what we call a robust theorem which is relatively free of the details of the model. Hence our truth is the intersection of independent lies" (1966, p. 429).

Existing modeling approaches can be classified according to a number of criteria, including scale, resolution, generality, realism, and precision. The most useful approach within this spectrum of characteristics depends on the specific goals of the modeling exercise. We describe a few examples of how one might match model characteristics with several of the possible modeling goals relevant for ecological economic systems and claim that a better appreciation of the range of possible model characteristics and goals can help to more optimally match characteristics and goals. We then consider some key research questions in the development of integrated models and describe an ongoing practical example of integrated ecological economic modeling at the regional scale in the Patuxent River basin in Maryland.

PURPOSES OF MODELS

Models are analogous to maps. Like maps, they have many possible purposes and uses, and no one map or model is right for the entire range of uses (Levins 1966; Robinson 1991). It is inappropriate to think of models or maps as anything but crude (but in many cases absolutely essential) abstract representations of complex territory, whose usefulness can best be judged by their ability to help solve the basic problem. Models are essential for policy evaluation but are often also misused, since there is "the tendency to use such models as a means of legitimizing rather than informing policy decisions. By cloaking a policy decision in the ostensibly neutral aura of scientific forecasting, policy-makers can deflect attention from the normative nature of that decision" (Robinson in press).

In the case of modeling ecological economic systems, purposes can range from developing simple conceptual models, in order to provide a general understanding of system behavior, to detailed realistic applications aimed at evaluating specific policy proposals. It is inappropriate to judge this whole range of models by the same criteria. At minimum, the three criteria of *realism* (simulating system behavior in a qualitatively realistic way), *precision* (simulating behavior in a quantitatively precise way), and *generality* (representing a broad range of systems' behaviors with the same model) are necessary. Holling (1964) first described the fundamental trade-offs in modeling between these three criteria. Later Holling (1966) and Levins (1966) expanded and further applied this classification. No single model can maximize all three of these goals, and the choice of which objectives to pursue depends on the fundamental purposes of the model. Several examples in the literature of ecological and economic models demonstrate the various ways in which trade-offs are made between realism, precision, and generality.

High-Generality Conceptual Models

In striving for generality, models must give up some realism and/or precision. They can do this by simplifying relationships and/or reducing resolution. Simple linear and nonlinear economic and ecological models tend to have high generality but low realism and low precision (Clark and Munro 1975; Brown and Swierzbinski 1985; Lines 1989; Kaitala and Pohjola 1988). Examples include Holling's "4-box" model (Holling 1987), the "ecological economy" model of Brown and Roughgarden (1992), most conceptual macroeconomic models (Keynes 1936; Lucas 1975), economic growth models (Solow 1956), and the "evolutionary games" approach. For example, the "ecological economy" model of Brown and Roughgarden contains only three state variables (labor, capital, and "natural resources"), and the relationships between these variables are highly idealized. But the purpose of the model was not to create high realism or precision, but rather to address some basic, general questions about the limits of economic systems in the context of their dependence on an ecological life support base.

High-Precision Analytical Models

Often one wants high precision (quantitative correspondence between data and model) and is willing to sacrifice realism and generality. One strategy here is to keep resolution high, but to simplify relationships and deal with short time frames. Some models strive to strike a balance between mechanistic small-scale models, which trace small fluctuations in a system, and more general whole-system approaches that remove some of the noise from the signal but do not allow the modeler to trace the source of system changes. The alternative some ecologists have devised is to identify one or a few properties that characterize the system as a whole (Wulff and Ulanowicz 1989). For example, Hannon and Joiris (1989) used an economic input-output model to examine relationships between biotic and abiotic stocks in a marine ecosystem and found that this method allowed them to show the direct and indirect connection of any species to any other and to the external environment in this system at high precision (but low generality and realism). Also using input-output techniques, Duchin's (1988, 1992) aim was to direct development of industrial production systems to efficiently reduce and recycle waste in the manner of ecological systems. Large econometric models (Klein 1971) used for predicting short-run behavior of the economy belong to this class of models, since they are constructed to fit existing data as closely as possible (at the sacrifice of generality and realism).

High-Realism Impact Analysis Models

When the goal is to develop realistic assessments of the behavior of specific complex systems, generality and precision must be relaxed. High-realism models are concerned with representing the underlying processes in a specific system, rather than precisely matching quantitative behavior or being generally applicable. Dynamic, nonlinear, evolutionary systems models at moderate to high resolution generally fall into this category. Coastal physical-biological-chemical models (Wroblewski and Hofmann 1989) that are used to investigate nutrient fluxes and contain large amounts of site-specific data fall into this category, as do micro models of behavior of particular business activities. Another example is Costanza et al.'s (1990) model of coastal landscape dynamics that included high spatial and temporal resolution and complex nonlinear process dynamics. This model divided a coastal landscape into 1 km^2 cells, each of which contained a process-based dynamic ecological simulation model. Flows of water, sediments, nutrients, and biomass from cell to cell across the landscape were linked with internal ecosystem dynamics to simulate long-term successional processes and responses to various human impacts in a very realistic way. But the model was site-specific and of only moderate numerical precision.

Moderate-Generality and Moderate-Precision Indicator Models

In many types of systems modeling, the desired outcome is to accurately determine the overall magnitude and direction of change, trading off realism for some moderate amount of generality and precision. For example, aggregate measures of system performance such as standard GNP, environmentally adjusted net national product (or "green NNP"), which includes environmental costs (Mäler 1991), and indicators of ecosystem health (Costanza, Norton, and Haskell 1992) fit into this category. The microcosm systems employed by Taub (1989) allow some standardization for testing ecosystem responses and developing ecosystem performance indices. Taub (1987) notes, however, that many existing indicators of change in ecosystems are based on implicit ecological assumptions that have not been critically tested, either for their generality, realism, or precision.

SCALE, HIERARCHY, AND PREDICTABILITY

In modeling complex systems, the issues of scale and hierarchy are central (O'Neill et al. 1989). Some claim that the natural world, the human species included, contains a convenient hierarchy of scales based on interaction-minimizing boundaries; scales ranging from atoms to molecules to cells to organs to organisms to populations to communities to ecosystems (including economic, and/or human-dominated ecosystems) to bioregions to the global system and beyond (Allan and Starr 1982; O'Neill et al. 1986). By studying the similarities and differences between different kinds of systems at different scales and resolutions, one might develop hypotheses and test them against other systems to explore their degree of generality and predictability.

The term "scale" in this context refers to both the resolution (spatial grain size, time step, or degree of complication of the model) and extent (in time, space, and number of components modeled) of the analysis. The process of "scaling" refers to the application of information or models developed at one scale to problems at other scales. In both ecology and economics, primary information and measurements are generally collected at relatively small scales (i.e., small plots in ecology, individuals or single firms in economics) and that information is then often used to build models at radically different scales (i.e., regional, national, or global). The process of scaling is directly tied to the problem of aggregation, (the process of adding or otherwise combining components), which in complex, nonlinear, discontinuous systems (such as ecological and economic systems) is far from a trivial problem (O'Neill and Rust 1979; Rastetter et al. 1992).

For example, in applied economics, basic data sets are usually derived from the national accounts, which contain data that are linearly aggregated over individuals, companies, or organizations. Sonnenschein (1974) and Debreu (1974) have shown that, unless one makes strong and unrealistic assumptions about the individual units, the aggregate (large scale) relations between variables have no resemblance to the corresponding relations on the smaller scale.

Rastetter et al. (1992) describe and compare three basic methods for scaling that are applicable to complex systems. All of their methods are attempts to utilize information about the nonlinear small-scale variability in the large-scale models. They list (1) partial transformations of the fine-scale mathematical relationships to coarse-scale using a statistical expectations operator that incorporates the fine-scale variability; (2) partitioning or subdividing the system into smaller, more homogeneous parts (i.e., spatially explicit modeling); and (3) calibration of the fine scale relationships to coarse scale data, when these data are available. They go on to suggest a combination of these methods as the most effective overall method of scaling in complex systems.

A primary reason for aggregation error in scaling complex systems is the nonlinear variability in the fine-scale phenomenon. For example, Rastetter et al. (1992) give a detailed example of scaling a relationship for individual leaf photosynthesis as a function of radiation and leaf efficiency to estimate the productivity of the entire forest canopy. Because of nonlinear variability in the way individual leaves process light energy, one cannot simply use the fine-scale relationships among photosynthesis, radiation, and efficiency along with the average values for the entire forest to get total forest productivity without introducing significant aggregation error. One must somehow understand and incorporate this nonlinear fine-scale variability into the coarse-scale equations using some combination of the three methods mentioned above. Method 1 (statistical expectations) implies deriving new coarse-scale equations that incorporate the fine-scale variability. The problem is that incorporation of this variability often leads to equations that are extremely complex and cumbersome (Rastetter et al. 1992). Method 2 (partitioning) implies subdividing the forest into many relatively more homogenous levels or zones and applying the basic fine-scale equations for each partition. This requires a method for adjusting the parameters for each partition, a choice of the number of partitions (the resolution), and an understanding of the effects of the choice of resolution and parameters on the results. Method 3 (recalibration) implies simply recalibrating the fine-scale equations to coarse-scale data. It presupposes that coarse-scale data are available (as more than simply the aggregation of fine-scale data). In many important cases, however, this coarse-scale data is either extremely limited or is not available. Thus, while a judicious application of all three aggregation methods is necessary, from the perspective of complex systems modeling, the partitioning approach (Method 2) seems to hold particular promise because it can take fullest advantage of emerging computer technologies and databases.

From the scaling perspective, hierarchy theory is a potentially useful tool for partitioning systems in ways that minimize aggregation error. According to hierarchy theory, nature can be partitioned into "naturally occurring" levels that share similar time and space scales and interact with higher and lower levels in systematic ways. Each level in the hierarchy sees the higher levels as constraints and the lower levels as noise. For example, individual organisms see the ecosystem they inhabit as a slowly changing set of constraints and the operation of their component cells and organs is what matters most to them. Norton and Ulanowicz (1992), however, suggest that what appears to be "noise" at a lower level could be turned into significant perturbations on the higher level. This can happen when a critical mass of components participate in a "trend," a behavioral pattern that affects the slower processes at the higher level. The rapid and extensive human uses of fossil fuels could be seen as such a trend, causing perturbations at the global atmospheric level, which might feed back and radically alter the framework of action at the lower level.

Shugart (1989) explains the relationship between scales: "Clearly, natural patterns in environmental constraints contribute substantially to the spatial pattern and temporal dynamics of particular ecosystems . . . these patterns, especially temporal ones, may resonate with natural frequencies of plant growth forms (i.e., phenology and longevity) to amplify environmental patterns (1989, p. 107)." The simplifying assumptions of hierarchy theory may ease the problem of scaling by providing a common (but somewhat generalized) set of rules that could be applied at any scale in the hierarchy.

The issues of scale and hierarchy raise some interesting questions about the influence of resolution (including spatial, temporal, and component) on the performance of models, in particular their predictability. For example, the relationship between the degree of complication (the number of components included) and the predictability of models is an important input to model design. The difficulty of using aggregate models that integrate over many details of finer resolution models is that the aggregated models may not be able to represent biological processes on the space and time scales necessary. Hofmann (1991) suggests that coupled detailed models (where the output of one model becomes the input for another) may be a more practical method for scaling models to larger systems. Costanza and Maxwell (1993) analyzed the relationship between spatial resolution and predictability and found that while increasing resolution provides more descriptive information about the patterns in data, it also increases the difficulty of accurately modeling those patterns. Thus, it is necessary to balance the benefit in terms of increasing information as one increases resolution with a decrease in the ability of a model to predict changes in the behavior of a system.

PRACTICAL APPROACHES TO MODELING REGIONAL SYSTEMS: THE PATUXENT WATERSHED PROJECT

We are attempting to apply integrated ecological and economic modeling and analysis in order to improve our understanding of regional systems; assess potential future impacts of various land-use, development, and agricultural policy options; and better assess the value of ecological systems. Starting with an existing spatially articulated ecosystem model of the Patuxent River drainage basin in Maryland, we are adding modules to endogenize the agricultural components of the system (especially the impacts of agricultural practices and crop choice) and the process of land-use decision making. The integrated model will allow us to evaluate the indirect effects of current policy options over long time horizons. These effects are almost always ignored in partial analyses, although they may be significant and may reverse many long-held assumptions and policy predictions. This section is a progress report on this modeling effort, indicating our motivations, ideas, and plans.

Recognizing the need for improvements in understanding how ecosystems function, how humans interact with ecosystems, and how ecosystems are valued, the following objectives were identified for this project:

1. To increase our understanding of and our ability to model the interactions between human behavior and ecological processes.
2. To increase our understanding of and our ability to model the effect of the regulatory environment on human behavior.
3. To develop through the above exercises a better understanding of the role of ecological processes in society's well-being, thus improving our methods for valuing ecosystem configurations and our ability to assess the benefits and costs of regulatory consequences.

To fulfill these three objectives, a pilot ecological-economic model is being developed to examine functions and processes of ecosystems, clarify relationships between human actions and ecosystems, and provide detailed information that will enable improved ecosystem valuation. The model consists of interrelated ecological and economic models that employ a landscape perspective, for this perspective captures the spatial and temporal distributions of the services and functions of the natural system and human-related phenomena such as surrounding land-use patterns and population distributions. Configuration and reconfiguration of the landscape occurs as a result of ecological and economic factors, and these factors are closely intertwined.

The ecological part of the model is based on the Patuxent Landscape Model (PLM), one of several landscape-level spatial simulation models currently under development by Costanza and others at the University of Maryland (Costanza et al. 1990; Fitz et al. 1993, 1994). The Maryland Patuxent River Watershed, which includes portions of Anne Arundel, Calvert, Charles, Howard, Montgomery, Prince George's, and St. Mary's counties, is the study area (Figure 4.1). The PLM is capable of simulating the succession of complex ecological systems using a landscape perspective. Economic models are being developed to reflect human behavior and economic influences. The effects of human intervention result directly from the conversion of land from one use to another (e.g., wetlands conversion, residential development, power plant siting) or from changes in the practices that take place within specific land uses (e.g., adoption of agricultural best management practices, intensification of congestion and automobile emissions, change in urban water and sewer use, and storm run-off).

An overview of the components of the integrated modeling system is depicted in Figure 4.2. The major components of the system are the spatially explicit, dynamic models for the ecological system and the economic decisions, and the mechanism for exchange of information between the two. The results of the interrelated processes produce a new landscape and a new array of values associated with the landscape. Some of these become signals to private individuals and public agents in future decisions.

The Ecosystem Model

The starting point of the PLM modeling effort is an outgrowth of the coastal ecological landscape spatial simulation (CELSS) model developed by Costanza et al. (1990). This modeling approach has been applied in two previous studies. The model was first implemented in the Atchafalaya Delta Area of coastal Louisiana, where it was developed to model spatial ecosystem processes, succession, and land loss problems and used to evaluate the impacts of management strategies and specific projects designed to alleviate coastal erosion problems (Costanza et al. 1990). A more sophisticated version of the model is currently being implemented in the Water Conservation Areas and Everglades National Park in Florida to examine the repercussions of management strategies on elements of the ecosystem such as water levels, nutrients, and plant successional patterns (Fitz et al. 1993).

The PLM uses an integrated, spatial simulation approach to model ecological processes. Central to the PLM is a General Ecosystem Model (GEM) (Fitz et al.

Figure 4.1
Map of the Patuxent River Watershed

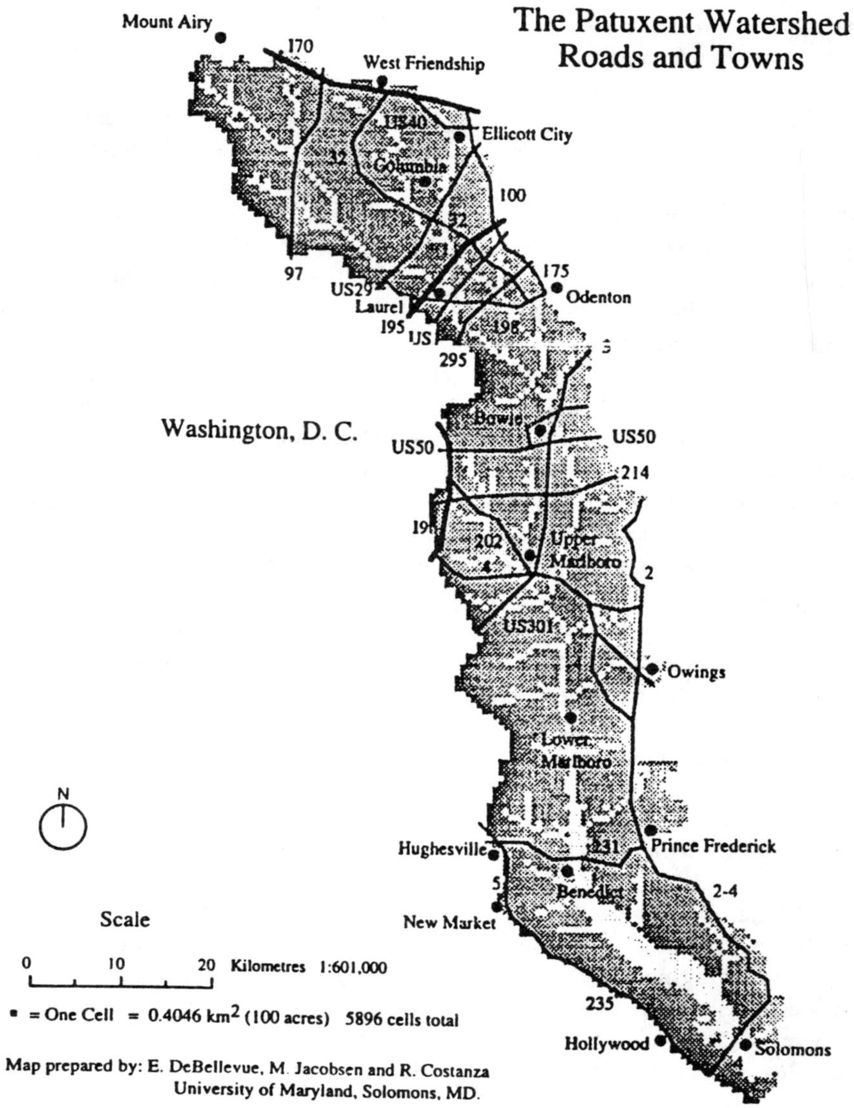

Figure 4.2
Integrated Ecological Economic Modeling and Valuation Framework

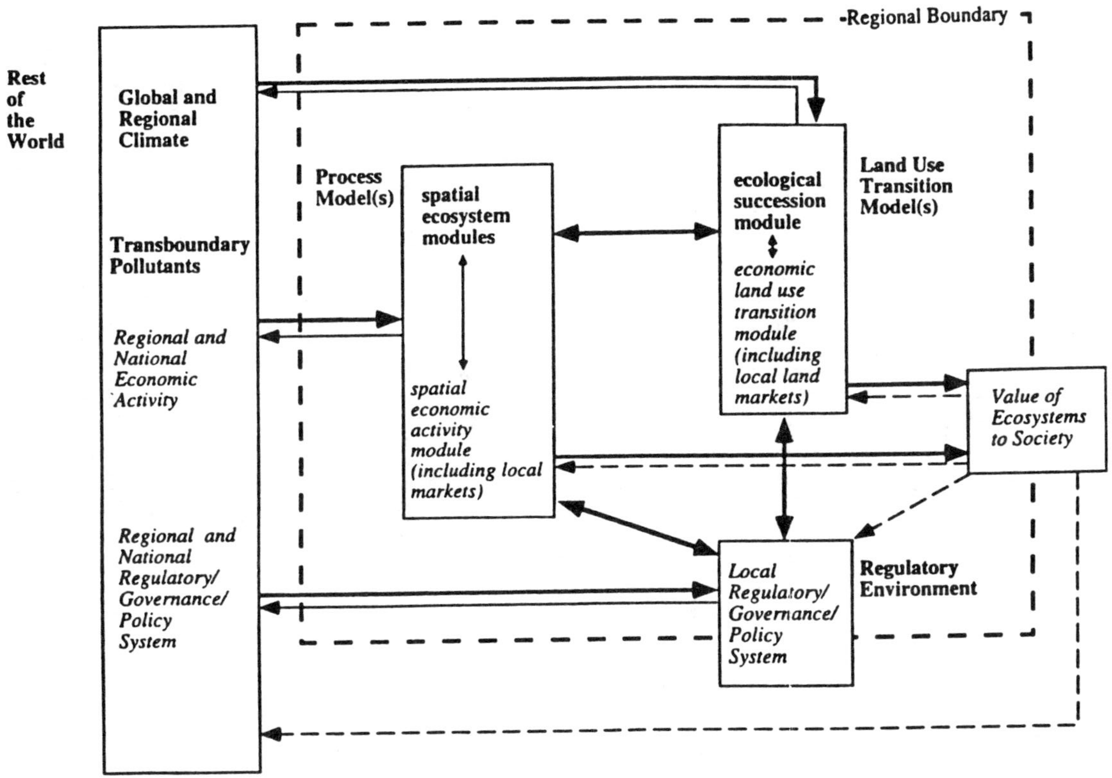

Note: Modules in **bold** are already included in the Patuxent Landscape Model (PLM).
Modules in *italics* are to be added as part of our ongoing project.

1994) that is replicated in each of the grid cells that compose the study area (Figures 4.3 and 4.4). The GEM unit models are linked together and to a Geographical Information System (GIS) database using the Spatial Modeling Workstation (SMW) (Maxwell and Costanza in press; see Figure 4.5). In addition to linking flows between cells, the spatial configuration superimposes the river network on the grid of cells, allowing better simulation of river flow processes across the landscape.

The GEM unit model simulates fundamental ecological processes, with hydrology as its core. The hydrologic sector of the model simulates the availability of water and its vertical and horizontal movements, based on topography, geology, land use, and other characteristics within each cell. Characteristics of each cell's habitat type translate to parameters of physical, chemical, and biological equations that are used to simulate such processes as primary production, nutrient fluxes, organic/inorganic sediment suspension and deposition, basic "consumer" dynamics, and decomposition. The dynamics of various ecological processes are expressed as the interaction between state variables (stocks) and flows of material, energy, and information. After the vertical or within cell dynamics have been simulated, the results of the unit model are processed by the spatial modeling program. In linking the stocks and flows, the model predicts the exchange of matter between cells (horizontal fluxes) and simulates the resulting temporal changes in water availability, water quality, and habitat/ecosystem type. The landscape model employs an algorithm for determining the habitat type of each cell at all times during the simulation. The habitat switching algorithm redefines the habitat/ecosystem type of cells as conditions change and selects parameter sets as necessary.

Data are collected to calibrate or initialize the model for a given set of ecosystems and a particular landscape. Effort is then devoted to simulating past behavior of the landscape. This allows for calibration of the functions of the model against actual historical data. For the Patuxent project, historical land use and geographic data have been acquired from the Maryland Department of Natural Resources (DNR), Maryland Department of Environment (MDE), and the U.S. Geological Survey (USGS). Maps indicating land use estimates for 1973, 1981, and 1985 (with 1991 now available), as well as mappings of the watershed, streams, soils, slopes, contaminants, highways, marinas, railroads, water quality, and wetlands have been acquired. The PLM contains about 6,000 spatial cells, each of about 100 acres, and each contains a GEM with 21 state variables. The model will be calibrated with land use, stream flow, water quality, and other data from 1973 and 1985. The intent is to run scenarios to the year 2020.

The spatial resolution of the PLM allows evaluation of impacts from changes in land-use type or practices for particular groups of cells. Our aim is to estimate selected indicator variables that will describe important physical processes in the Patuxent River watershed. For example, fertilizer applications and mechanical soil manipulation (e.g., tillage) influence the total loadings of nutrients and sediment that are carried by surface and subsurface waterflow off a given land

Figure 4.3
Summary Diagram of the Patuxent Landscape Model's (PLM) Unit Model (GEM)

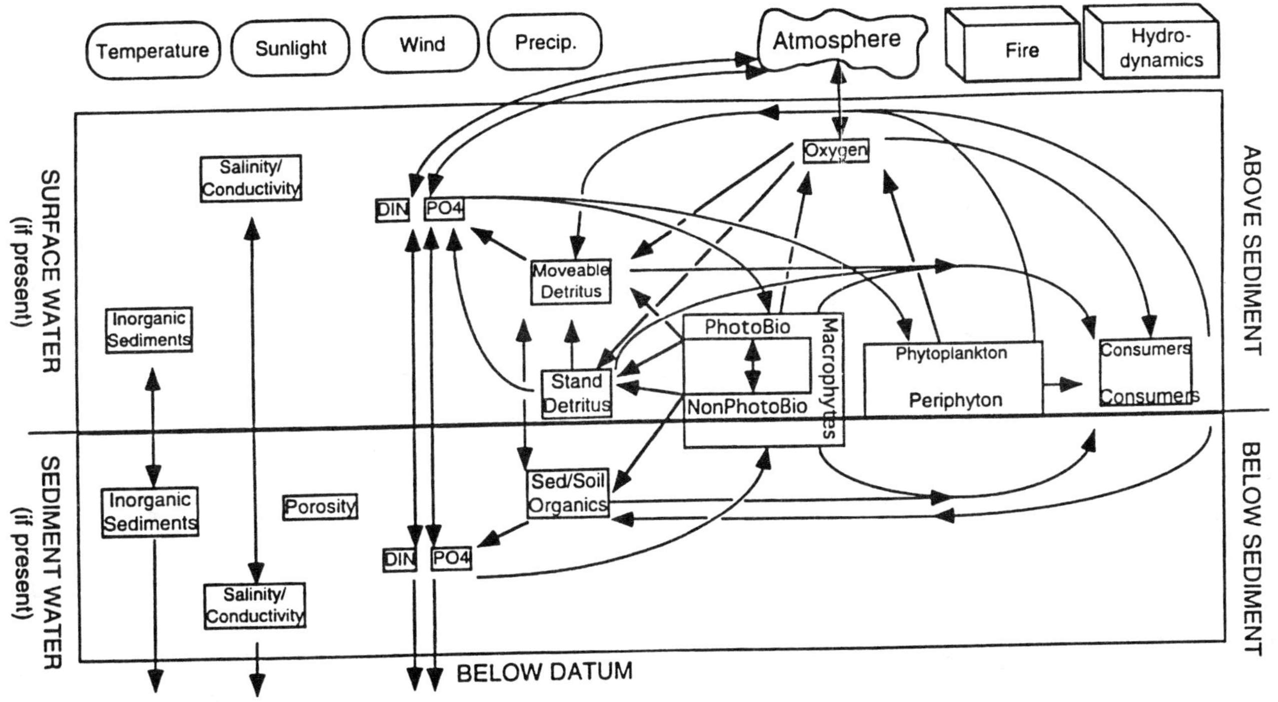

Note: The state variables and mass fluxes of the unit model, excluding hydrology. The model is run within one cell and parameterized for the cell's habitat. Hydrology is important in the vertical fluxes shown and the unshown horizontal fluxes of materials from cell to cell. State variables are enclosed within rectangles, and those that can flux vertically and horizontally with water movement are shown in outline type.

parcel. The flow path of that water over various land types will determine its nutrient and sediment load when it reaches a wetland or stream. The combined effect of multiple land parcels then influences vegetative growth processes in wetlands within the Patuxent estuary. As plant biomass changes, nutrient uptake, evapotranspiration, and sediment retention rates change. The simulation of these multiple interrelated processes allows the PLM to estimate general effects of such practices as vegetative buffers and retention ponds on urban and agriculture lands on total loadings to the estuary and ecosystem types of undeveloped land.

Future additions to the ecological model include adding estimates of fish and wildlife populations based on the pattern and productivity of the landscape elements. At this stage these estimates will not feed back to affect the ecosystem dynamics. Rather, they will indicate "habitat suitability" based on the type and quantity of various species that could be expected in a given landscape.

Economic System Interaction

The two notable aspects of the ecological modeling approach, its dynamic nature and its ability to spatially disaggregate, are also important dimensions for the economic sectors that interact with the ecosystem. The human activities of importance form an interrelated, dynamic, spatially distributed system in their own right. Economic models that reflect these dimensions are being conceptualized and estimated. Ensuring the necessary feedback between the two systems will require an integration characterized by exchange of information between the models at an appropriate time and space scale.

Human decisions that determine land-use designation, as well as those that affect flows/extractions from the system conditioned on the land-use designation, will affect the configuration of the landscape. The existing PLM, like other ecological models, ignores the effect of the landscape on humans. In addition, human effects on the landscape, whether through changes in the land use of the cells or through the emissions assumed for any land use, are imposed exogenously, rather than modeled as part of the process. The economic considerations are important because human decisions are influenced by the characteristics of the ecosystem landscape, and the landscape changes as a result of the decisions. For ecological reasons, the effects of a single action taken at a given point in time will continue to play out over time and will affect more than just the cell where the action took place. Additionally, that action will have been influenced by the characteristics of the given cell, the characteristics of surrounding cells, and the expectations of changes in those cells.

Perhaps the most important type of economic behavior that requires modeling is land conversion. Since the ecological processes that are modeled in the generic ecosystem model are conditioned on land use, scenarios are driven by the land-use designation of the cells in the landscape at each period of time. The land-use conversion model will endogenize those human decisions.

Figure 4.4
The Cellular Structure of the Patuxent Landscape Model

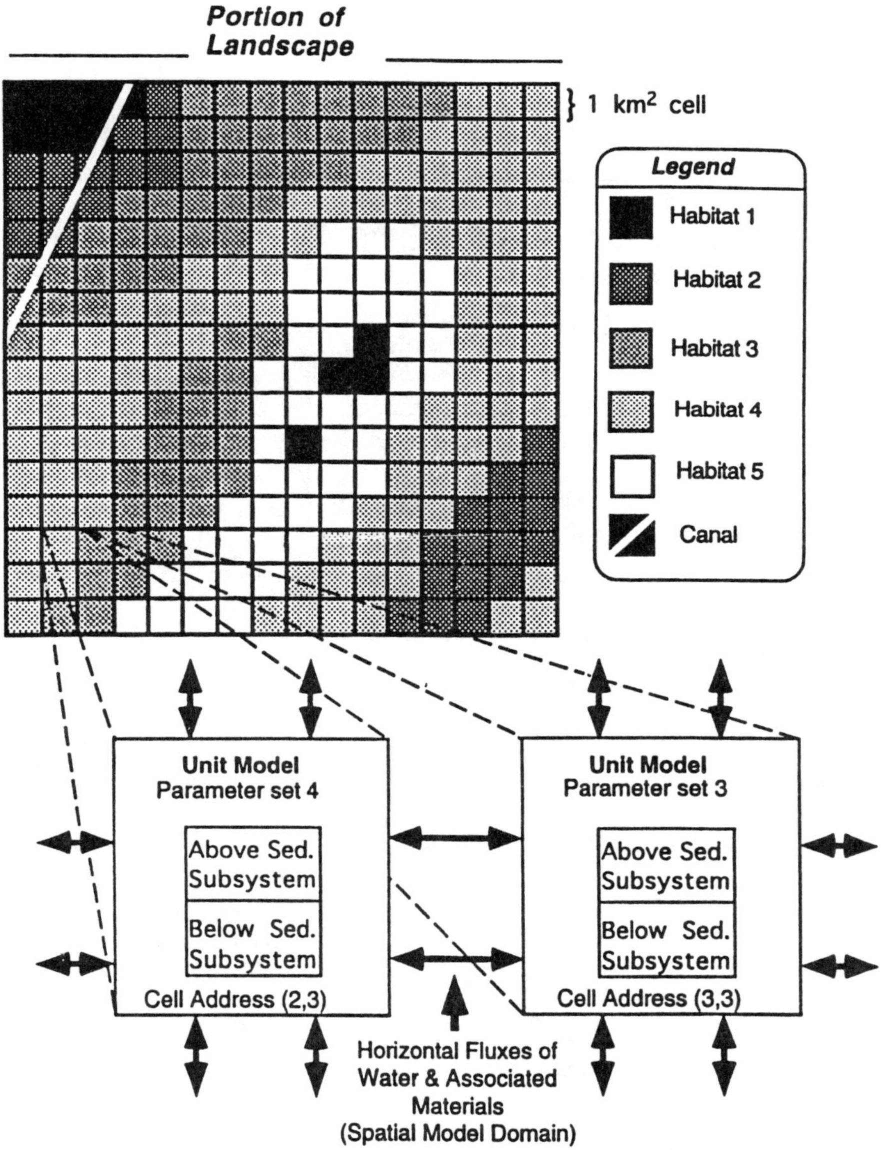

Note: Each cell has a (variable) habitat type, which is used to parameterize the unit model for that cell. The unit model simulates ecosystem dynamics for that cell in the above-sediment and below-sediment subsystems. Nutrients and suspended materials in the surface water and saturated sediment water are fluxed between cells in the domain of the spatial model.

Figure 4.5
Diagram of the Patuxent Landscape Model (PLM) Implementation Architecture

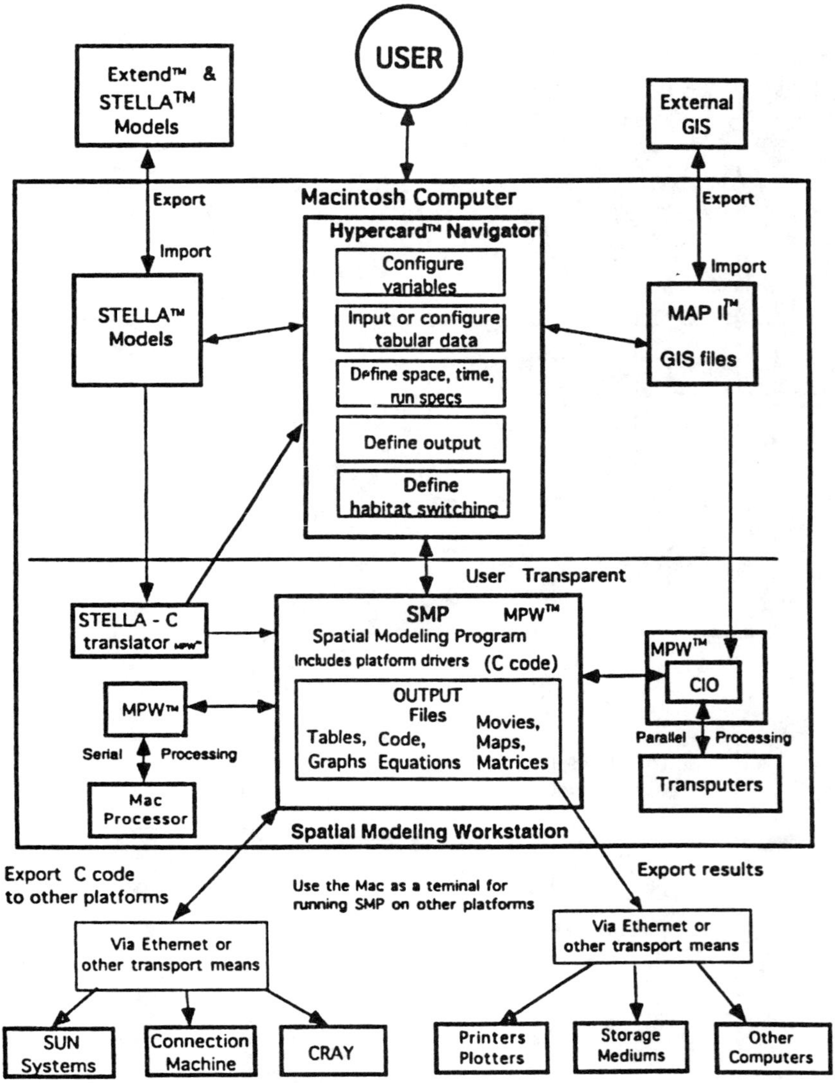

Note: The PLM is programmed and simulated in the Spatial Modeling Workstation (SMW). The SMW consists of: STELLA unit models for execution of ecosystem dynamics; MAP II GIS program for storage and manipulation of GIS data files; the Spatial Modeling Program (SMP) that executes the interchange of flows among unit models on the computers, and imports and exports spatial (GIS) data; the Hypercard Navigator (under development) that is used to guide the user through configuration of models, data sets, execution platforms and output files; and an Apple Macintosh computer with transputers installed for simulation, or as a user terminal interface to other computer platforms.

Conditioned on a cell's land-use designation, the cell is programmed to undergo certain processes. But human decisions will affect these processes and may not be predetermined. In fact, they may be affected by feedback from the ecological system, and most surely will be affected by changing policy environments. In the first phase of this project, one such behavioral model, conditioned on land use, will be developed: a model of agricultural practices. Additional behavioral models, conditioned on land use, will be added in the future. An obvious candidate is a transportation model.

Land-Use Conversion. Economists have tried to explain land values and land-use decisions for some time, but generally in a static context and rarely incorporating features of the local ecosystems. Most frequent in this literature are hedonic models of residential transactions prices as functions of local amenities and housing characteristics (e.g., Diamond 1980; Beaton and Butcher 1989). Additionally, some models seek to explain conversion of agricultural land to residential and urban use as functions of profitability of alternative land uses (e.g., Alig and Healy 1987; McMillan 1989). Data limitations have restricted these applications to cross-sectional analysis at one point in time.

Our proposed approach relies on spatially disaggregated data from digitized maps and allows dynamic analysis of micro-level changes that can be observed over time. Because the data are GIS format, it is easy to relate activities on individual parcels of land with local ecological and economic features of the landscape that might be driving these activities. The land-use conversion decision is modeled probabilistically. This involves estimating the transition probabilities that a given parcel of land, set in a landscape configuration of given ecological/economic description, will be converted from its current state to any other state (including no change). As surrounding landscape conversions take place, the probability of conversion of a given parcel changes.

Here we are interested in the alternative land uses in the Patuxent watershed listed in Table 4.1. Depending on the state of the parcel at the time of the decision, some uses may be precluded, at least within a limited time period (of a year or shorter). For example, if the land is already in residential development, it is probably infeasible to return it to forest in one year. Federal laws such as wetland and coastal zone management will also affect the likelihood that land parcels switch uses as legislation often prohibits certain land uses and/or makes these uses significantly more costly. Again, the GIS system is useful because many of the land use restrictions and potential scenarios have been digitized in GIS maps and can be merged with the ecological and economic information.

This type of probabilistic model is appealing because it allows for variations over individual decision makers facing the same factors and variation of the factors affecting the decision with spatial location and proximity to centers of economic activity, transportation networks, and ecological features. Thus, it predicts the likelihood of each type of transition rather than predicting deterministically one type of conversion for all land of a certain ecological/economic description. These transition probabilities can be interpreted as the percentage of land of

Table 4.1
Relative Land Use for the Patuxent Watershed for 1973 and 1985 (percent of area)

Land Use Description	1973	1985	% change
Urban	10.7	14.9	4.2
Low Density Residential	3.7	6.2	2.5
Medium Density Residential	2.9	3.5	0.6
High Density Residential	0.7	1.0	0.3
Commercial	1.1	1.5	0.4
Industrial	0.2	0.2	0.0
Institutional	1.2	1.2	0.0
Extractive	0.3	0.3	0.0
Open Urban Land	0.6	1.0	0.4
Agricultural	34.2	31.6	-2.6
Cropland	29.6	26.6	-3.0
Pasture	4.6	4.5	-0.1
Orchard	0.2	0.1	-0.1
Feeding Operations	0.0	0.1	0.1
Row and Garden Crops	0.2	0.3	0.1
Forest	48.1	46.0	-2.1
Deciduous Forest	31.4	27.6	-3.8
Evergreen Forest	1.4	1.6	0.2
Mixed Forest	14.3	14.8	0.5
Brush	1.0	2.0	1.0
Water	5.3	5.5	0.2
Wetlands	1.2	1.4	0.2
Barren Land	0.1	1.2	1.1
Beaches	0.0	0.4	0.4
Bare Exposed Rock	0.0	0.0	0.0
Bare Ground	0.1	0.8	0.7
TOTAL	100.0	100.0	0.0

a given type that is converted to each alternative land use (including the percentage that remains unconverted) and are functionally equivalent to the transition probabilities in a Markov analysis.

Because the differential in economic returns among commercial, residential, agricultural, and open land uses differs depending on the state of the regional economy, the explanatory model will reflect these exogenous forces and the scenarios will incorporate predictions of these cycles. An existing county-based regional model for Maryland will provide predictions of the "macroeconomic" exogenous factors to be used in the simulations.

Agricultural Practices. The first step of the PLM modeling dynamics is to designate a cell as a given land use. Based on prior information, the economic land-use conversion model, and the ecosystem succession model, these designations are made for each "round" of the model's calibrations. The land-use designations are broad categories, however, with agricultural uses specified as either cropland, pasture, or orchards. It is important to know more about the agricultural land use in order to understand the impact this land-use has on the ecosystem. The agricultural practices model attempts this and, in so doing, serves as an example of micro-level economic behavior models that capture human decisions that influence the environment, conditioned on a given land use. This economic model will accept information from the "outside world" (including existing policy) and the ecological world (such as topographical information) and will attempt to predict the cropping/livestock patterns, as well as the farming practices that serve as parameters in the model for the subsequent cropping season.

As with the land-use conversion model, the economic model of farming behavior will be probabilistic. That is, these probabilities would be interpreted as predicted proportions of similar farming land that is used for given crops/livestock and, conditioned on that choice, is subject to different management practices.

Models of agricultural crop/livestock choice are numerous, but few are conceived at as "micro" a scale as this project should be able to achieve. Profitability from different farming choices will drive the decisions, but profitability is conditioned, not only on relative output and input prices, but on factors of the landscape that affect the production function for different crops (e.g., hydrology, slopes, soil types). In the Patuxent Watershed there is an interesting added consideration. In Maryland, farmers often sell hunting rights on their lands. These rents can be a major source of income for farmers and affect not only how much land stays in agriculture but also crop and livestock decisions. Depending both on farmers' decisions and the ecological characteristics of the land, the amount and composition of wildlife will differ, endowing the land with differing hunting value.

In addition to models of crop choice, numerous behavioral studies of best management practice (BMP) adoption in the United States have examined the influence of factors ranging from topography and erodibility to human capital factors (e.g., age and experience) to farm operation characteristics (e.g., cropping patterns, scale, and scope and tenure status) (Ervin and Ervin 1982; Lee and Stewart 1983; Lynne et al. 1988; Nielsen et al. 1989; Norris and Batie 1987; Saliba and Bromley 1986; Shortle and Miranowski 1986). A few generalizations can be drawn from the findings of these empirical studies. Adoption is more likely and expenditures on BMPs are greater on more erodible land and on larger operations. Older, more educated and more experienced farmers are more likely to adopt. Farmers with more off-farm income and greater risk aversion are less likely to adopt. Farmers are more likely to adopt if they perceive erosion to be more of a problem, attach greater importance to conservation and environmental quality, or have conservation plans. Cash grain farmers are less likely to adopt. Although these generalizations are revealing, there is no study that comprehensively examines the adoption of numerous, but specific BMPs in a spatially explicit context linked to ecosystem characteristics.

Integration of Components and Resolution of Modeling Inconsistencies

At present, the ecological model runs fourteen sectors; tracks twenty-one state variables; estimates horizontal and vertical fluxes of water, nutrients, sediments, and biomass; and simulates ecological succession over the landscape. For the purposes of the economic model, two types of interactions between humans and natural resources will be of significance: (1) decisions that determine land-use designation of a cell, and (2) decisions that affect flows/extractions from the system conditioned on the land-use type of the cell.

An interrelated model would capture how the distribution of human activities (farming, electric power generation, commercial and residential development, recreation, wastewater treatment, highway construction, fishing) affect the ecosystem. Such a model would also capture the effect of the ecosystem landscape on the quality and value of goods and services (e.g., recreation, wildlife enjoyment, water quantity and quality, housing, environmental aesthetics) and, therefore, on human decisions. The model must also be able to reflect how human activity and its impact on the ecosystem may differ under different regulatory regimes and under alternative regulations.

Our approach will *not* be to meld both ecological and economic models into one "supermodel," because this would force each model to adopt the lowest level of resolution in the other. Instead, the two types of models will exist in parallel, with their own levels of specificity, but will exchange information on ecological and economic elements generated by the other. Because appropriate choices on time step, geographical scale, and level of aggregation differ in the ecological and economic models, there are several potential inconsistencies that may arise in this information exchange.

By design, the PLM model establishes physical boundaries that encompasses the dynamics of the ecosystem. Activity is modeled in the area bounded by the top of the trees, the drainage basin boundaries, and the bottom of the groundwater. The physical definition of the boundary of the Patuxent River Basin region will coincide with relevant economic boundaries, if the region is a price-taker in markets that extend beyond the boundaries of the region. That is, for markets that extend beyond the Patuxent River Basin Region, the region must not significantly influence the actions of others (i.e., it does not produce or demand a significant amount relative to other trading partners). For the Patuxent watershed, this is likely to be approximately correct and thus no serious inconsistencies with respect to "boundaries" are likely to arise. In other applications of this modeling approach, however, the definition of boundaries could well be conflicting.

The PLM model is structured to simulate a desired level of ecological complexity and resolution. Modeling with greater levels of disaggregation is possible, but this would be costly and require a significant amount of additional research, data, and programming. The behavioral interactions will largely involve the water, nutrients, macrophyte, and consumer sectors. Although these state variables are linked with habitat types, much finer distinctions of the landscape will be necessary for the economic model, as human behavior is likely to depend on more detailed information. In our approach, the details will be introduced exogenously by distinguishing different subgroups of macrophytes and consumers and associating these different subgroups with different land uses. The model will include markers and detailed rules for species loss, treating habitat evaluation as a side calculation. Clearly, there are qualitative distinctions between different composition and phyla. A function will be developed that will indicate the likelihood of game species and other forms of wildlife in particular habitat types. This function allows for the provision of additional complementary information without increasing the level of disaggregation of the unit model.

The ecosystem model operates on a time scale of a day or less. Yet, given data availability, the economic models are most easily estimated on an annual basis. The intra-year timing of the agricultural decisions will be easy to predict, since these are governed by seasons. Land conversions pose a different problem, however. They can be predicted only on an annual basis, but their timing is important because construction can have different immediate ecosystem impacts depending on the season. Independent data on building starts and construction durations will be used to forecast seasonal impacts of construction.

The geographical scale of resolution between the two ecosystem and economic models will also differ. Land parcels modeled in the land-use conversion model will not correspond to cell boundaries in the ecosystem model. The latter divides the study area into about 6,000 cells with each cell representing approximately 100 acres. The cell size in the ecological model was selected to balance the desired complexity and resolution of the ecological landscape. The fact that the economic model will produce probabilistic estimates may actually help to resolve the differences in geographical scale, as the probabilities can be interpreted as percentages of land of a given description that is put to a given land use. The transition probabilities, however, may still "fracture" cells. The PLM model has the ability to assign to cells split land-use designations, allowing heterogeneity within a cell. Devising weights to monitor what is happening in cells, thresholds can be set so that cells could go from homogeneous to heterogeneous units and vice versa. This additional detail will also allow the model to make inferences on a wider variety of land use restrictions (i.e., agricultural policies, zoning policies, and environmental protection policies).

In resolving this array of modeling inconsistencies, sensitivity tests will be used to assess the importance of level of detail in both models. Sensitivity games are used now to accommodate uncertainty over elements such as rainfall patterns over time. By generating several patterns for the future and running these different patterns as distinct scenarios, the significance of the uncertainty can be revealed.

CONCLUSIONS

Improving our ability to model linked ecological economic systems in an integrated way is essential to the goal of effective regional management for long-term sustainability. While these integrated models are large, complex, and loaded with uncertainties of various kinds, our abilities to understand, communicate, and deal with these uncertainties are rapidly improving. It is also important to remember that while increasing the resolution and complexity of models increases the amount we can say about a system, it also limits how accurately we can say it. Model predictability tends to fall with increasing resolution due to compounding uncertainties (Costanza and Maxwell 1993). What we are after are models that optimize their "effectiveness" (Costanza and Sklar 1985) by choosing an intermediate resolution where the product of predictability and resolution (effectiveness) is maximized.

We also need to see the modeling process as one that involves not only the technical aspects, but also the sociological aspects involved with using the process to help build consensus about the way the system works and which management options are most effective. This consensus needs to extend both across the gulf separating the relevant academic disciplines and across the even broader gulf separating the science and policy communities and the public. Appropriately designed and appropriately used integrated ecological economic modeling exercises can help to bridge these gulfs.

NOTE

This paper summarizes results and progress on a number of ongoing projects at the Beijer International Institute of Ecological Economics in Stockholm, Sweden, and at the University of Maryland International Institute for Ecological Economics. These projects include: (1) the research program on Complex Ecological Economic Systems Modeling at the Beijer Institute; (2) a Cooperative Agreement with the USEPA, No. 07-5-25196-3734 titled Ecological Economic Modeling and Valuation of Ecosystems, Michael Brody and Mary Jo Kealy project officers, Nancy Bockstael, Robert Costanza, Ivar Strand, and Walter Boynton, principal investigators; (3) Modeling Landscape Dynamics in the Everglades Basin, Cooperative Agreement with the South Florida Water Management District, Robert Costanza principal investigator; (4) Ecological Landscape Models for Evaluating the Interactive Dynamics of the Patuxent River Watershed and Estuary, Maryland DNR, Robert Costanza principal investigator; and (5) Landscape Modeling: The Synthesis of Ecological Processes over Large Geographic Regions and Long Time Scales, National

Science Foundation, Robert Costanza co-principal investigator (with F. Sklar, South Florida Water Management District). We specially thank Carl H. Fitz and Thomas Maxwell for their valuable input and feedback on this paper. Sandra Koskoff provided editorial assistance. We thank Ed DeBellevue, Carl Fitz, Marla Markowski, and Enrique Reyes for their contributions to the research effort, and Marjan van den Belt for helpful comments on earlier drafts. Parts of an earlier draft of this paper appeared as Costanza, R., L. Wainger, C. Folke, and K.-G. Maler. "Modeling Complex Ecological Economic Systems: Toward an Evolutionary, Dynamic Understanding of People and Nature." ***BioScience*** **43 (1993): 545–555.**

References for this chapter begin on p. xxv.

PART IV

INCENTIVES AND INSTITUTIONS

[24]

Social Traps and Environmental Policy

Why do problems persist when there are technical solutions available?

Robert Costanza

In recent years scientific understanding and public awareness of environmental problems have increased tremendously. Yet our ability to manage these problems effectively has in too many cases gotten worse, not better. Consider the following examples:

- Thousands of inactive and abandoned hazardous waste dumps exist in the United States. There are thousands more active sites, plus deep well injection sites. These wastes are slowly seeping into drinking water supplies; many of their constituent chemicals have totally unknown effects on human and environmental health. Each year thousands of new chemicals are introduced into the environment whose effects are equally unknown. Superfund is only beginning to clean up the worst inactive and abandoned sites (most of the money so far has gone into planning and litigation). Handling active sites is largely an individual state's responsibility, and resources for this critical task are too often insufficient.
- The coastal zone of Louisiana is eroding at a rate of more than 100 km^2/yr, and the rate is accelerating (Gagliano et al. 1981). Canal dredging in the coastal zone has been shown to be a significant contributing factor to wetland erosion (along with sediment diversion resulting from leveeing the Mississippi River and natural subsidence) (Craig et al. 1979, Deegan et al. 1984, Leibowitz et al. 1987, Scaife et al. 1983). In 1980 the state implemented an office of coastal zone management to permit canal dredging and other activities in the coastal zone. Since 1980 there have been several thousand canal-dredging applications (mainly for the development of oil and gas), and the office has yet to deny a permit. Some small-scale projects designed to reverse wetland erosion have been implemented but have been largely ineffective. The state is currently considering several options to control the erosion of wetland, all of which will be very expensive.
- Probably the biggest environmental threat facing the world today is the threat of nuclear war. The likelihood that a nuclear winter will result from even a moderate thermonuclear exchange has been estimated by some researchers to be very high (Turco et al. 1983, White and London 1984). There is still considerable uncertainty about the global environmental effects of nuclear war. Even in the best-case scenario the damages would be astronomical, and in the worst case such an event could drive the human species to extinction. It would be catastrophic not only for human life, but for most forms of life on the planet (Ehrlich et al. 1983). There has, however, been little real movement toward arms control or other long-term solutions.

By studying real-world social traps and laboratory examples, we can learn effective escapes

This litany could be continued indefinitely, spanning the spectrum from local to global problems (see also Borman and Likens, p. 370, and Catton, p. 413, this issue). The fundamental question is: Why do these problems persist in the face of adequate scientific understanding of their nature and of technical methods to solve them? What do they have in common? Can they be solved, and if so is there a general category of solutions?

I argue that all the environmental problems mentioned above (and many other social problems) belong to a category of phenomenon called social traps (Platt 1973). Like animal traps, social traps lead an unwary victim into the jaws of disaster with a tempting bit of bait, and, once the victim is caught, make escape extremely difficult. By studying the features real-world social traps have in common, and by experimenting with some simple laboratory examples of social traps, we can learn more about their general nature and the nature of effective escapes from them. A broad ecological perspective can be effective in understanding, avoiding, and escaping from some social traps, but it must be coupled with effective public

Robert Costanza is an associate professor at the Coastal Ecology Institute, Center for Wetland Resources, Louisiana State University, Baton Rouge, LA 70803. His research interests include systems ecology, landscape ecology, ecological modeling, energy analysis, ecological economics and management, game theory, and peace studies.

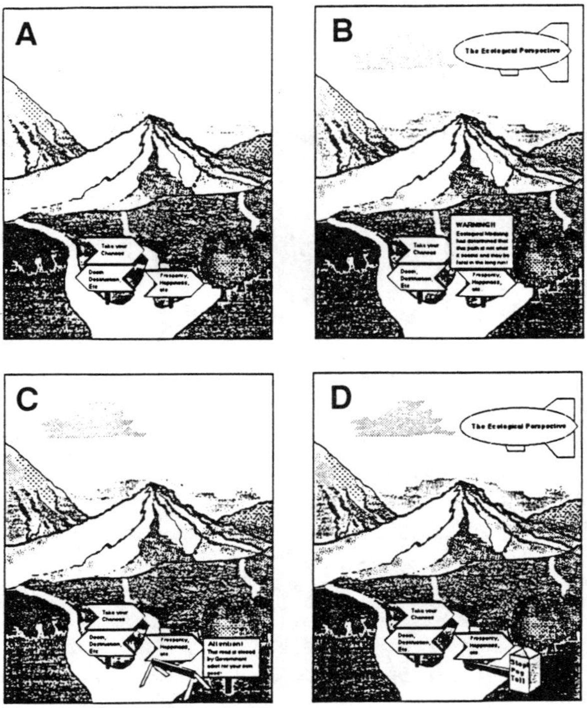

Figure 1. Social traps as misleading road signs and some potential solutions.

policy. Effective policy involves a range of activities from education to regulation to correcting the misleading short-term incentives (the bait) that create traps in the first place.

Social traps

A social trap is any situation in which the short-run, local reinforcements guiding individual behavior are inconsistent with the long-run, global best interest of the individual and society (Cross and Guyer 1980, Platt 1973, Teger 1980). We go through life making decisions about which path to take based largely on "road signs," the short-run, local reinforcements that we perceive most directly. These short-run reinforcements can include monetary incentives, social acceptance or admonishment, and physical pleasure or pain. Figure 1a indicates the situation. In this figure the "correct" path (toward happiness and prosperity) seems obvious from the signs. In general, this strategy of following the road signs is quite effective in getting us where we want to go. Problems arise, however, when the road signs are inaccurate or misleading. In these cases we can be trapped into following a path that is ultimately detrimental because of our reliance on the road signs. For example, cigarette smoking is a social trap because by following the short-run road signs of the pleasure and social status associated with smoking, we embark on the road to an increased risk of earlier death from smoking-induced cancer. More important, once this road has been taken it is very difficult to change to another (as most people who have tried to quit smoking can attest).

Social traps can result from several causes. Table 1 is a taxonomy of these causes (Cross and Guyer 1980) along with some representative traps associated with each. Cigarette smoking, for example, is mainly a time-delay trap resulting from the fact that the positive and negative reinforcements are separated in time.

Traps can also arise out of simple ignorance of the relevant reinforcements, the change of reinforcements with time (sliding reinforcer traps), the externalization of some important reinforcements from the accounting system (externality traps), the actions of some individuals affecting the group in adverse ways (collective traps), or a combination of these causes (hybrid traps). These causes will be elaborated in the examples that follow.

Social traps are ubiquitous in everyday life and have become the basis for some important social psychology research (Brockner and Rubin 1985). For example, the "prisoner's dilemma" game is a famous externality trap that has been used recently to study the conditions under which cooperation can evolve (Axelrod 1984). In this game two players must each choose either to cooperate or defect. If they both cooperate, they both reap a moderate reward (say three units each). If they both defect they both get a much smaller reward (say one unit each). If one cooperates while the other defects, the cooperator gets nothing (the "sucker's payoff") while the defector gets a reward larger than that for mutual cooperation (say five units). Under these conditions, if the players only meet once and cannot communicate with each other, the optimum strategy is to defect. For if one has no information about the other player, one must assume the worst to avoid the sucker's payoff. The situation changes radically if the game is played several times with the same participants. Then each player has the record of their opponent's past behavior, and the optimum strategy is not obvious.

Axelrod (1984) held a computer tournament pitting various submitted strategies against one another in a round robin tournament of the iterated prisoner's dilemma. He found that a simple strategy called *tit for tat*, which cooperates on the first move, then does whatever its opponent did last time, won the tournament. In the iterated prisoner's dilemma, one can fall into the always-defect trap by not looking beyond the current move. If a strategy is too shortsighted it misses the opportunity to reap the benefits of mutual cooperation. *Tit for tat* was only a little more farsighted (one move) than *all defect*, but this was enough to dramatically improve its performance without making it too susceptible to being suckered.

It turns out that there are several other strategies that would have won the tournament had they been entered. One of these cooperates on the first move and then looks at the entire past history of its opponent's moves to generate a time-weighted expected value for the opponent's next move. A strategy almost identical to this (called *downing*) was entered but lost because it defected on the first two moves. In the iterated prisoner's dilemma, it pays to assume the best of your opponent (at least until you have been proven wrong) and to have a good memory.

The tragedy of the commons is another well-known social trap used to study overexploitation of natural resources (Hardin 1968). The classic commons trap goes something like this. There is a common property resource (say grazing land). Each individual user (rancher) sees his individual cost for consuming an additional unit of the resource (adding one more animal) as small and constant, and much less than the private benefits (from selling an animal). However, the overall cost to all the users of each additional resource unit consumed (animal added) increases exponentially as the resource is stressed. Eventually, one additional animal (which costs its owner no more than the first) leads to the destruction of the resource (which costs the animal's owner and the rest of the ranchers tremendously). The tragedy of the commons is a collective trap that occurs because the costs and benefits apparent to the individual are inconsistent with the costs and benefits to the collective society.

Edney and Harper (1978) experimented with a simple game designed to test people's behavior in a commons game. In this game a pool of resources is represented by poker chips. The resource pool is renewable; it is replenished after each round in proportion to the number of chips left in the common pool. The objective for each player is to accumulate as many chips as possible from the common pool. At each round, players can take either one, two, or three chips. If all players take three chips per round, the resource pool is quickly depleted, and the players end up with far fewer chips than if they had all taken only one chip per round, since doing so would have allowed the resource pool to replenish itself. This game is a trap (and a good analogy for many real-world common-property resource problems) because the short-term, narrow incentives (to take as many chips as possible each round) are inconsistent with the long-term incentives (to accumulate as many chips as possible by the end of the game).

Table 1. A short taxonomy of social traps (Cross and Guyer 1980).

Cause of trap	Examples
Time delay	Discounting, smoking, drug addiction in general
Ignorance	Slot machines, gambler's fallacy
Sliding reinforcer	Pesticide overuse
Externality	Pollution, prisoner's dilemma
Collective	Tragedy of the commons
Hybrid	

Escaping social traps

Cross and Guyer (1980) list four broad methods by which traps can be avoided or escaped. These are education (about the long-term, distributed impacts); insurance; superordinate authority (i.e., legal systems, government, and religion); and converting the trap to a trade-off (i.e., correcting the road signs). Figures 1b–1d illustrate these methods using the road sign analogy.

Education can be used to warn people of long-term impacts that cannot be seen from the road (Figure 1b). Examples are the warning labels now required on cigarette packages and the warnings of environmentalists about future hazardous waste problems. People can ignore warnings, however, particularly if the path seems otherwise enticing (e.g., warning labels on cigarette packages have had little effect on the number of smokers).

The main problem with education as a general method of avoiding and escaping traps is that it requires a significant time commitment on the part of individuals to learn the details of each situation. Our current society is so large and complex that we cannot expect even environmental professionals, much less the entire voting public, to know the details of all the extant environmental traps. For education to be effective in avoiding traps involving many individuals, *all* the participants must be educated. For example, in the renewable resource game mentioned earlier if any one of the players starts taking three chips per round the others must follow suit. If any one player consumes three chips per round, the other players will do individually worse by restricting their consumption to one per round than if they consume three per round. The trap can only be avoided if all the players restrict their consumption to one chip per round, which requires that they all are educated about the nature of the trap.

The superordinate authority approach to avoiding social traps is illustrated in Figure 1c. Governments can forbid or regulate certain actions that have been deemed socially inappropriate. The problem with this approach is that it must be rigidly monitored and enforced, and the strong short-term incentive for individuals to try to ignore or avoid the regulations remains. A police force and legal system are very expensive to maintain, and increasing their chances of catching violators increases their costs exponentially (both the costs of maintaining a larger, better-equipped force and the cost of the loss of individual privacy).

Religion can be seen as a much less

expensive way to avoid certain social traps. If a moral code of action and belief in an ultimate payment for transgressions can be deeply instilled in a person, the probability of that person's falling into the "sins" (traps) covered by the code will be greatly reduced, and with very little enforcement cost. On the other hand, there are problems with religion as a means to avoid social traps. The moral code must be relatively static to allow beliefs learned early in life to remain in force later. And it requires a relatively homogeneous community of like-minded believers for religion to be truly effective. This system works well in culturally homogeneous societies that are changing very slowly. In modern, heterogeneous, rapidly changing societies, religion cannot handle all the newly evolving situations, nor the conflict between radically different cultures and belief systems.

A trap may be changed to a trade-off by imposing compensatory fees (Figure 1d). Many theorists believe that this method is the most effective in avoiding and escaping from social traps because it does not run counter to our normal tendency to follow the road signs; it merely corrects the signs' inaccuracies by adding compensatory positive or negative reinforcements.

A simple example illustrates how effective this method can be. Playing slot machines is a social trap because the long-term costs and benefits are inconsistent with the short-term costs and benefits (Cross and Guyer 1980). People play the machines because they expect a large short-term jackpot, while the machines are in fact programmed to pay off, say, $0.80 on the dollar in the long term. People may "win" hundreds of dollars playing the slots in the short run, but if they play long enough they will certainly lose $0.20 for every dollar played. To change this trap to a trade-off, one could simply reprogram the machines so that every time a dollar was put in $0.80 would come out. This way the short-term reinforcements ($0.80 on the dollar) are made consistent with the long-term reinforcements ($0.80 on the dollar), and only the dedicated aficionados of spinning wheels with fruit painted on them would continue to play.

In terms of Edney and Harper's common property resource consumption game, one could turn the trap into a trade-off by taxing any consumption above the optimum level for resource stability. For example, if players took two or three chips they could be taxed one or two chips respectively, so that the short-term benefits of taking more than one chip were offset by short-term costs. This would remove the short-term incentive to take more than one chip and make the long- and short-term incentives in the game consistent, thereby eliminating the trap.

Traps and environmental policy

Our approach in the United States to avoiding and escaping environmental traps has been mainly education and governmental regulation (Figures 1b and 1c). Although these methods are essential elements in the overall picture, they may not be the most effective means available in some situations. Converting traps to trade-offs seems to be a more effective method in many experimental trap situations, but it has been little used in the environmental area. In terms of environmental management, converting traps to trade-offs implies determining the long-run, distributed costs of environmentally hazardous activities and charging those costs to the responsible parties in the short run. Pollution taxes are the best-known example of this approach (and they have been quite effective in the few cases in which they have been tried), but it is possible to extend it to a much broader range of environmental problems. Below I give examples of how this approach might be applied to three critical current problems: hazardous waste management, coastal wetland management, and the nuclear arms race. I do not imply that this approach should be used independently of education, insurance, and regulation, but as an adjunct that can make the entire system more effective.

Hazardous waste management

The hazardous waste management problem can be viewed as a hybrid trap containing elements of time-delay, ignorance, externality, and collective traps. The negative environmental effects of hazardous waste do not become evident until long after they are produced (time delay); their ultimate effects are largely unknown at the time of their production and release into the environment (ignorance); the negative effects are borne by parties other than the producer without sufficient compensation (externality); and common property resources are consumed (i.e., groundwater contamination) by individual agents who do not bear the costs of that consumption. The current regulatory approaches to hazardous waste management will not be discussed here.

To turn this trap into a trade-off one must charge the producers of hazardous waste for the ultimate long-run environmental and health costs of these wastes, and the charges must be imposed at the time of the waste's production. Superfund can be seen as a small step in the right direction, but it relates only to the cleanup of abandoned hazardous waste sites, is assessed long after the wastes are produced, and is severely underfunded for the task.

The ignorance component of the hazardous waste management trap is the most difficult to deal with. How can we charge producers of hazardous wastes for the ultimate long-run costs of their waste if we have no idea what (if any) those costs will actually be? Part of the problem is that this ignorance and uncertainty about future costs is itself a cost, or more precisely a risk of unknown magnitude. The trap exists in large part because the producers of the hazardous waste do not bear this risk in the short-run, but pass it on to the general population and future generations.

One way to solve this problem involves changing our concepts of innocence and guilt as they apply to industrial products. As in our criminal justice system, there is currently a tacit presumption of "innocent until proven guilty" for chronic effects, particularly those that are difficult to quantify. The effect of smoking on lung cancer is a case in point; cigarettes had been presumed innocent until the overwhelming weight of evidence proved them guilty. Although such presumption of innocence is totally appropriate for persons charged with crimes, it is not appropriate for hazardous or potentially hazardous materials, which we should instead presume guilty until proven innocent.

Thus, to turn the hazardous waste trap into a trade-off, we could charge producers of potentially harmful substances the worst-case costs. By worst-case we mean our current best estimate of the largest potential damages, although future information may later be used to increase the worst-case costs. This money could be put into a trust fund that would be returned to the producer (with interest) if and when the waste is proved to be innocuous, or could be used to compensate for damages caused by the waste if and when they become apparent. This procedure would change the short-term incentive structure from one that discourages waste producers from doing research on harmful effects, to one that encourages these studies so that some of the trust fund monies could be returned. The incentives to eliminate ignorance about hazardous waste effects would increase. It would also discourage production of large quantities of chemicals whose negative effects are unknown by making them as expensive in the short run as their risk cost to society.

Coastal wetland management

The problem of coastal wetland management is another example of a complex hybrid trap, with time-delay, ignorance, and collective elements. Coastal erosion in Louisiana is a particularly severe example. Canal dredging and other hydrologically disruptive activities have contributed to a current land loss rate of over 100 km^2/yr (Craig et al. 1979, Gagliano et al. 1981, Scaife et al. 1983). It may already be too late to arrest or reverse this trend. The situation is a trap because the narrow, short-term incentives of those damaging the wetlands are inconsistent with the long-term good of the system.

To turn this trap into a trade-off, one should charge the responsible parties, at the time the damage-causing action is taken, the full cost of the ultimate environmental damage. To do this one needs to know the economic value to society of coastal marshes and the amount of marsh destroyed by each activity. As with the hazardous waste issue, there is much uncertainty involved in these estimates, but the worst-case costs should be assumed, and the burden of proof that the damages are in fact less than the worst case should be shifted to the parties who caused the damage. In addition, there needs to be a system for reducing the costs in proportion to any reduction in damages below the worst case.

For example, a recent study concluded that each acre of coastal wetlands in Louisiana has a present value to society of approximately \$2500–\$10,000/acre (Farber and Costanza 1987). Increasing the accuracy of the valuation estimates is an expensive proposition, and one that would stress the state's research budget.

To effectively eliminate this trap, one could charge the parties responsible for marsh destruction (i.e., oil companies for dredging access canals through wetlands) the \$10,000/acre worst-case cost. These fees would go into a trust fund to be used for mitigating environmental damages by purchasing marshland elsewhere, backfilling canals, and diverting sediments. The responsible parties could lower the fee by proving that the damages are actually less than the worst-case assumption (by funding independent studies) or by minimizing the amount of wetlands they damage in the process of accomplishing their goal (e.g., by directional drilling or immediate backfilling). In either case the cause of wetland conservation would be served without unduly hindering the search for oil and gas.

The arms race and the dollar auction game

The current arms buildup is an environmental issue both because of its ongoing resource use and its potential for massive environmental destruction in the event of a major war (Mosley 1985, Sivard 1984, Wallace et al. 1986). Gradual despoilation of the environment by more conventional means is certainly preferable to destroying it all at once in a nuclear war, but both must be included in any litany of major environmental problems.

The arms race has been escalating for the last 40 years and threatens to continue on this course with new developments, such as the Strategic Defense Initiative. It can be argued that the costs and risks of the arms race far outweigh its benefits, yet the process continues with no sign of abatement.

One simple but enlightening model for the study of the escalation process is known as the dollar auction game. This game is a social trap that was designed specifically to simulate conflict escalation (Shubik 1971). The dollar auction is just like a normal auction except that both the highest and the second-highest bidder have to pay the auctioneer their bid at the end of the game, but only the highest bidder gets the prize. This rule leads to some unexpected behavior that is a useful model of the arms race. Players in the dollar auction game frequently bid much more than \$1 for a \$1 prize—an irrational result that is the product of a series of "rational" decisions by the bidders, because the structure of reinforcements in this game is a trap. If player A had bid \$1 and player B had the second-highest bid at \$0.95, player B reasons that if he drops out he loses \$0.95 while if he raises to \$1.05 he only loses \$0.05 (assuming he wins the \$1 prize). So he usually raises, and this pattern of "rational" escalation (beyond the point where the overall outcome is rational) continues quite often to well beyond the \$1 point. Individual and group behavior in the dollar auction game has been extensively studied by Teger (1980).

The dollar auction game can be converted to a trade-off by adding a "bidding tax" large enough to make dropping out rational in both the short run and the long run (Costanza 1984, 1986). For example, if when player B was at \$0.95 he was told that it would now cost \$2 to enter a bid of \$1.05 (a \$0.95 bidding tax), he would reason that if he drops out he loses \$0.95, but if he raises he loses \$1 even if he wins the prize! So the chances that he would drop out and escape the trap are increased. This method has proven to be effective in experiments using the dollar auction game (Costanza 1986). Extrapolating these ideas to controlling the escalation of the arms race is tricky, but it is possible that a nuclear weapons tax (which has already been proposed as a method to fund Third World development) may prove to be an effective control method (Costanza 1984, 1986, UN 1982).

Conclusions

Social traps are one way of generating those situations in which the short-term, local optimizing of individuals goes afoul. In this sense they indicate imperfections in the free market approach to resource allocation, which relies on short-term, local optimizing of individuals. It can be argued that the proper role of a democratic government is to eliminate social traps (no more and no less) while maintaining as much individual freedom as possible. This can be accomplished most effectively by turning the traps into trade-offs that can be handled within the current market system as modifications to the cost of potentially entrapping activities.

Social traps abound in environmental issues because of the abundance of imperfectly owned and common property resources. To turn these traps into trade-offs, we must calculate the long-term social cost of activities with environmental impacts and charge those costs to the responsible parties in the short run. If there are any uncertainties about the magnitude of these social costs, the worst case should be assumed, and the burden of proving that costs are actually less than this should fall on the parties responsible for the impact, not the general public. It is also critical that short-term incentives for reducing environmental costs (by reducing the charges) be included. We must make protecting the environment as economically attractive to individuals in the short run as it is to society in the long run.

All animals capable of choice can be trapped with the right bait. Intelligent ones can learn to avoid traps. Ingenious ones can even escape from traps. If we are to survive, we need to exercise our vaunted intelligence and ingenuity to see, avoid, and escape from the many complex traps we have laid for ourselves.

Acknowledgments

This research was supported in part by a Kellogg National Fellowship. J. Bartholomew, H. E. Daly, B. Hannon, and G. Suter provided useful comments on earlier drafts of this article. Special thanks to E. Chu for her help. This paper evolved from a presentation at the 1985 AIBS annual meeting in Gainesville, FL.

References cited

Axelrod, R. 1984. *The Evolution of Cooperation*. Basic Books, New York.

Brockner, J., and J. Z. Rubin. 1985. *Entrapment in Escalating Conflicts: A Social Psychological Analysis*. Springer-Verlag, New York.

Catton, W. R., Jr. 1987. The world's most polymorphic species. *BioScience* 37: 413–419.

Costanza, R. 1984. The nuclear arms race and the theory of social traps. *J. Peace Res.* 21: 79–86.

_____ 1986. Understanding and controlling the conflict escalation process and the nuclear arms race: experiments with the dollar auction game. Pages 237–257 in J. P. Maas and R. A. C. Stewart, eds. *Toward a World of Peace: People Create Alternatives*. The University of the South Pacific, Suva, Fiji.

Craig, N. J., R. E. Turner, and J. W. Day, Jr. 1979. Land loss in coastal Louisiana. *Environ. Manage.* 3: 133–144.

Cross, J. G., and M. J. Guyer. 1980. *Social Traps*. University of Michigan Press, Ann Arbor.

Deegan, L. A., H. M. Kennedy, and C. Neill. 1984. Natural factors and human modifications contributing to marsh loss in Louisiana's Mississippi River deltaic plain. *Environ. Manage.* 8: 519–528.

Edney, J. J., and C. Harper. 1978. The effects of information in a resource management problem: a social trap analog. *Hum. Ecol.* 6: 387–395.

Ehrlich, P. R. et al. 1983. Long-term biological consequences of nuclear war. *Science* 222: 1293–1300.

Farber, S., and R. Costanza. 1987. The economic value of wetland ecosystems. *J. Environ. Manage.* in press.

Gagliano, S. M., K. J. Meyer-Arendt, and K. M. Wicker. 1981. Land loss in the Mississippi River deltaic plain. *Trans. Gulf Coast Assoc. Geol. Soc.* 31: 295–299.

Hardin, G. 1968. The tragedy of the commons. *Science* 162: 1243–1248.

Leibowitz, S. G., F. H. Sklar, and R. Costanza. 1987. Perspectives on Louisiana land loss modeling. In R. R. Sharitz and J. W. Gibbons, eds. *Freshwater Wetlands and Wildlife*, in press.

Mosley, H. G. 1985. *The Arms Race: Economic and Social Consequences*. Lexington Books, Lexington, MA.

Platt, J. 1973. Social traps. *Am. Psychol.* 28: 642–651.

Scaife, W. W., R. E. Turner, and R. Costanza. 1983. Coastal Louisiana recent land loss and canal impacts. *Environ. Manage.* 7: 433–442.

Shubik, M. 1971. The dollar auction game: a paradox in noncooperative behavior and escalation. *J. Conflict Resolution* 15: 109–111.

Sivard, R. L. 1984. *World Military and Social Expenditures*. World Priorities, Leesburg, VA.

Teger, A. I. 1980. *Too Much Invested to Quit*. Pergamon Press, New York.

Turco, R. P., O. B. Toon, T. P. Ackerman, J. B. Pollack, and C. Sagan. 1983. Nuclear winter: global consequences of multiple nuclear explosions. *Science* 222: 1293–1330.

United Nations (UN). 1982. *The Relationship Between Disarmament and Development*. United Nations Centre for Disarmament, Report of the Secretary-General, New York.

Wallace, M. D., B. L. Crissey, and L. I. Sennott. 1986. Accidental nuclear war: a risk assessment. *J. Peace Res.* 23: 9–27.

White, G. F., and J. London, eds. 1984. *The Environmental Effects of Nuclear War*. Westview Press, Boulder, CO.

[25]

THE EFFECTS OF TAXATION ON MODERATING THE CONFLICT ESCALATION PROCESS: AN EXPERIMENT USING THE DOLLAR AUCTION GAME[1]

Robert COSTANZA, *Louisiana State University*

Wesley SHRUM, *Louisiana State University*

The dollar auction game was used to examine the escalation process, varying the amount and timing of a bidding tax. Expected utility theory predicts that the *amount*, while social trap theory predicts that the *timing*, of the tax should be most effective in reducing escalation. Results indicate that timing was important, while amount had little effect. External signals in escalating situations may be valuable primarily to make players reconsider their situation, rather than as modifiers of expected utility at the margin.

Situations in which a gradual or incremental pattern of behavior leads to dysfunctional consequences occur frequently at all levels of analysis (Brockner and Rubin, 1985). Anyone who has ever visited a county fair or Las Vegas has observed this kind of behavior pattern at its most blatant. Consider one particularly simple example: slot machines. In the long run, playing slot machines is irrational because they are simply programmed to pay off, say, $0.80 on the dollar in the long run. But in the short run the possibility of large payoffs at small short-run costs induces players to continue.

These entrapment situations are examples of a particular type of decision-making under uncertainty: uncertainty both as to the consequences of the behavior and the likelihood of its occurrence. The analysis of decision making under uncertainty has concentrated on situations where spe-

[1]This research was supported, in part, by a Kellogg National Fellowship. We thank H. Daly, M. Grimes, B. Hannon, and J. Bartholomew as well as three anonymous reviewers for providing useful comments on earlier drafts. Editor's note: Reviewers were Melvin Guyer, Jane Sell, and Cookie Stephan.

cific outcomes are uncertain, but alternative results have well-defined probabilities (Wilson and Crouch, 1987; Machina, 1987). What has received much less attention are those situations where alternative outcomes do not have well-defined probabilities. These situations make up the majority of our everyday life decisions, and also represent the kinds of decisions that structured the evolution of the human brain.

There are two broad alternative models for decision making under uncertainty. The dominant paradigm is "expected utility theory" (Ells, 1982). This theory assumes that people are rational, that they have a set of well-defined preferences, and that they make decisions that maximize their expected utility, which is a function of the alternative physical outcomes and their preferences for those outcomes. Certain well-studied anomalies to this theory exist, however, mainly in situations that involve preferences for probabilistic (but well-defined) outcomes. It has even been shown that restating a probabilistically identical situation in different language can alter the results (Machina, 1987).

One alternative paradigm is the theory of "social traps" (Platt, 1973; Cross and Guyer, 1980; Teger, 1980; Costanza, 1987). A social trap is any situation in which the short-run, local reinforcements guiding individual behavior are inconsistent with the long-run, global best interest of the individual and society. This theory is based on behaviorist tenets, and assumes that people are only "rational" in the short run and locally, and give little weight to outcomes that are distant in time, space, or probability. We go through life making decisions about which path to take based largely on the "road signs," the short-run reinforcements that we perceive *most directly*. These short-run reinforcements can include monetary incentives, social acceptance or admonishment, and physical pleasure or pain. In general, this strategy is quite effective unless the road signs are inaccurate or misleading. In these cases we can be trapped into following a path that is ultimately detrimental because of our reliance on the road signs. For example, cigarette smoking is a social trap because by following the short-run social and physical road signs of pleasure associated with smoking we embark on the road to an earlier death from smoking-induced cancer. Persistent investment in unprofitable enterprises is another social trap because the desire to be proven right in the initial decision leads to unwarranted expenditures. Once a road has been taken it is very difficult to change to another.

There are several well-known experimental games designed to study behavior in traps. For example, the "prisoner's dilemma" game is an externality trap that has been used recently to study the conditions necessary for the evolution of cooperation (Axelrod, 1984). The "tragedy of the commons" is a well-known collective trap used to study overexploitation of natural resources (Hardin, 1968). This article examines factors influ-

TABLE 1

Some Causes and Examples of Social Traps (from Cross and Guyer, 1980)

Cause of Trap	Examples
1. Time delay	Discounting; smoking; drug addiction in general
2. Ignorance	Slot machines; gambler's fallacy
3. Sliding reinforcer	Pesticide overuse
4. Externality	Pollution; prisoner's dilemma
5. Collective	Tragedy of the commons
6. Hybrid	

encing escape from a type of conflict escalation trap. This trap involves a decision-making process wherein social actors continue to increase their commitment to a course of action that becomes less and less rational as the process escalates, all in pursuit of an uncertain goal.

Social traps can result from several causes. Table 1 is a taxonomy of these causes (from Cross and Guyer, 1980) along with some representative traps associated with each. Cigarette smoking is mainly a "time delay trap" resulting from the fact that the positive and negative reinforcements are separated in time. Traps can arise out of simple ignorance of the relevant reinforcements, from the change of reinforcements with time (sliding reinforcer traps), from the externalization of some important reinforcements from the accounting system (externality traps), from the actions of some individuals affecting the group in adverse ways (collective traps), or from a combination of these causes (hybrid traps).

Escaping from Social Traps

Cross and Guyer (1980) provided a list of four broad methods (not mutually exclusive) by which traps can be avoided: (1) education about the long-term, distributed impacts; (2) insurance; (3) superordinate authority (e.g., legal systems, government, religion); and (4) converting the trap to a trade-off. Education, for instance, can be used to warn people of the long-term impacts—destinations that are not generally marked and cannot be seen from a given vantage point. Warnings are often ignored, however, particularly if the path seems otherwise enticing. Governments can forbid or regulate certain actions that have been deemed inappropriate. The problem with this approach is that it must be rigidly monitored and enforced, and there is a strong incentive to ignore or avoid the regulations. But superordinate authority can simply be the means for the application of trade-offs. Most trap theorists believe that changing the trap to a trade-off by imposing compensatory fees is the most effective method to avoid and escape from social traps. This is because it does not run counter to our normal tendency to follow the road signs—it merely corrects the inaccuracies by adding compensatory positive or negative reinforcements.

These methods involve either a change in the *information* processed by social actors or the *incentives* which shape their behavior. These two types of "escape variables" receive different emphasis in expected utility theory and social trap theory. The value of the incentives is particularly important for expected utility theory, which assumes a rational calculation of the marginal costs and benefits of each anticipated action. Social trap theory has paid greater attention to the informational function, as short-term "signposts" for longer-term contingencies. Decision making depends on both an awareness of the negative consequences of an activity and the magnitude of those consequences (Brockner and Rubin, 1985). Behaviors which lead to entrapment may be avoided because they are quickly perceived as having negative consequences, or because their consequences are perceived as extremely negative. Using the road sign metaphor, one might avoid a certain path because one becomes aware of unpleasant destinations relatively sooner (or later). Alternatively one might avoid the path because destinations are relatively more (or less) unpleasant. What would be desirable would be a method for separating and assessing these two effects.

The Dollar Auction Game

The "dollar auction" game is a social trap particularly well-suited for the simulation of conflict escalation (Shubik, 1971) and the assessment of escape techniques. It is an "investment trap," distinct from such either/or choices as the prisoner's dilemma. Major elements include (1) at least two actors engaged in goal-directed behavior; (2) initial failure, involving potentially greater investments if the goal is to be attained; (3) choice whether or not to escalate; and (4) uncertainty regarding goal attainment (Brockner and Rubin, 1985). Choice is crucial to the entrapment process: punishing conditions are characteristic of many social structures but they are often imposed from without. Uncertainty is important for the simulation of real-life situations, producing the internal conflict which accompanies entrapment.

The dollar auction is just like a normal auction except that *both* the highest and the second highest bidder have to pay the auctioneer their bid at the end of the game, but only the highest bidder gets the prize. The fact that the second highest bidder has an investment in the process that will be lost if she/he drops out leads to some unexpected behavior that is a useful model of the escalation process. Players in the dollar auction game frequently bid much more than $1 for a $1 prize—an irrational result that is the product of a series of "rational" decisions by the bidders. If player A had bid \$1 and player B had the second highest bid at \$0.95, player B reasons that if he drops out he loses \$0.95 while if he raises to \$1.05 he only loses \$0.05 (assuming he wins the \$1 prize). So he usually raises, and this pattern of "rational" escalation (beyond the point where the overall outcome is rational) continues quite often to well beyond the \$1 point.

A one-step rational decision rule for player B in the dollar auction game would be:

$$\text{Raise if} \quad pV - B_t > -B_{t-1}$$

or rearranged algebraically

$$\text{Raise if} \quad p > \frac{B_t - B_{t-1}}{V}$$

where:

B_t = bid of player B at time t, which must be larger than player A's bid, which in turn must be larger than B's bid at time $t - 1$;

V = value of the prize (\$1 in all cases in our experiments);

p = perceived probability of winning the prize.

This simply says that if the expected net benefits (the expected winnings from raising, pV, minus the cost of the raised bid, B_t) are greater than the net costs (the negative of the current bid, $-B_{t-1}$) then raise. For example, at the dollar turning point, B_{t-1} = \$0.95, B_t = \$1.05, and V = \$1.00. The perceived probability of winning (p) need be only slightly larger than 0.1 to make raising an apparently rational decision. An important point about this game is that the probability of winning (p) is unknown to the players.

Individual and group behavior in the dollar auction game has been extensively studied by Teger (1980) and associates. This series of experiments was designed to examine the escalation process, as indicated by the appearance of distinct "stages" in the bidding process, physiological and motivational correlates of the transition between stages, and "stopping" behavior, as indicated by the amount of the final bid. This quantity, measured in points or dollars, can be readily and precisely compared with the amount of expected reward, an experimental feature which does not generally hold for real-life situations but offers an advantage for an understanding of the escalation process. Bids over \$1 are clearly in excess of the expected return and represent, even for a winning bid, a case of having "too much invested to quit."

The principal findings of Teger's research on the dollar auction may be summarized briefly. First, the distribution of highest bids is filled with gaps. Bids tend to be clustered around particular decision points: the point at which the bid exceeds the value of the prize to be gained ($1), the point at which half of the subject's resources are spent ($2.50), and the final depletion point ($5.00). A large percentage of subjects who bid more than $1 continue bidding until all of the resources they have been allocated are gone. Second, this distribution varies depending on whether the subject believes she/he is playing against humans (nonexistent confederates) or nonhumans (a deck of cards generating bids). In the latter condition, subjects are less likely to bid away all resources, though few in either condition quit between the value of the prize and the limit of their resources. Third, when the subjects are not told how much money they will have to bid with, the end point of the distribution is not consistent. Fourth, males tend to bid higher than females. Finally, there is some evidence that bidding stages are associated with shifting motivational patterns. Bids under $1 are made primarily for economic (rational) gain; bids over this amount are made in order to regain losses; bids in excess of one half of the subject's resources are made primarily for interpersonal, competitive (irrational) reasons.

While the usefulness of the dollar auction as a model of conflict escalation has been established, few attempts have been made to examine the conditions which impede escalation. Brockner and Rubin (1985) have considered "cognitive" and "motivational" deterrents to escalation using a different experimental paradigm. Increasing the salience of entrapment by providing information was shown to decrease the likelihood of *starting*, but not persistence after an initial commitment was made. However, in another series of studies by the same investigators, it was shown that the effects of manipulations depend to a large extent on their timing (*when*, during the escalation process, they are introduced).

Teger mentions one face-saving strategy which sometimes terminates the escalation process. If, for example, player B bids $2 after A has bid $1, this offers both players the option to exit the competition while losing equal amounts. Player A may decline to bid further at this point, but this method depends on a conscious "cooperative" bid by B at a particular point in the game.

What this strategy suggests is that both the timing and amount of increments may be important to the escape process. We may utilize this feature of the dollar auction paradigm to separate the two escape variables described above through the use of a "bidding tax" imposed by the experimenter on the participants (Costanza, 1984). Such a tax allows us to manipulate both the information and incentive structure of the game, making "escape" the rational choice. By varying the amount of the tax, the disincentives of a particular bid can be increased in a precise fashion. By varying the timing of the tax, information on the consequences of the course of bidding can be provided at specific points in the game. For example, if player B is at $0.50 and he is told that it will now cost $1.50 to enter a bid of $0.60 because a $0.90 bidding tax has been imposed, he is in a new situation. Whether he drops out or remains he loses $0.50 and the bid of $0.60 will only be this effective if A does not raise. We would expect B to drop out at this point. But what if the tax is only $0.30, imposed when B is considering a bid of $0.25? Will B persist in bidding escalation, or will he be deterred by the prospect of this new information?

Thus, the introduction of experimental taxation allows us to vary both the information and incentive structure of the auction and provides a partial test of arguments based on expected utility and social trap theories. If taxes function mainly as a negative incentive, as expected utility theory would suggest, then the value of the tax should be inversely related to the high bid, because the costs incurred by the behavior of bidding increase in direct proportion to the size of the compensatory fee.

However, if the informational function of the tax is paramount, as social trap theory suggests, we would expect the timing of the tax to be positively related to the high bid. As a "signpost" which induces reflection on a potentially damaging course of behavior, early taxes should be more effective than late taxes in producing escape. In essence, this is a version of the hypothesis of "waning vigilance" (Janis and Mann, 1977). Over time participants become less vigilant in their decision making, such that at later stages of escalation they become less sensitive to information which might cast doubt on their course of action. Information is processed differently at different levels of commitment. In the case of the dollar auction, the early introduction of a tax should be important simply because as the game advances subjects are less responsive to the cues which increase cost salience.

Methods

We examined these hypotheses using a programmed version of the dollar auction game which pitted subjects against a computer confederate. Students in an introductory sociology course for nonmajors were asked to volunteer for a "bargaining" experiment that would take about half an hour. They signed up for specific time slots and were told they would receive three extra credit points in the course if they signed up and came to the experiment, and would lose one point if they signed up and failed to show up for the experiment. In addition, they were told they would be given $5 and that they could leave with more or less than this amount depending on how they played the game. There were only nine no-shows out of 101 students who signed up for the experiment.

When the students arrived, they were led to a waiting area and given some preliminary instructions to read. The preliminary instructions explained some details about using the computers and stressed the fact that they would be using their own money to bid. We gave them $5, but any amount they bid over that was to be collected from them as well. Half the students (in the morning) were given $5 worth of tokens to be exchanged for real money at the end of the experiment, while the other half (in the afternoon) were actually given $5 bills. At the designated time the students were led as a group to five microcomputers which they believed to be connected on a network. The computers were arranged on a large seminar table but were partitioned from each other so that the students could not see each other during the experiment. After reading the rules they could decide not to play and walk away with their $5, or they could bid on the $1 prize. All but 5 of the 92 students decided to take the bait and bid. This is consistent with previous findings and probably reflects a felt obligation to make at least one bid (Teger, 1980).

All students were in fact playing against a program in the computer and not against other students. We note two differences between the procedure described here and that used previously. The use of computers offers advantages in the study of escalation because they require little maintenance during the experiment. Responses entered by the subject are recorded and constitute the data for analysis. Students plunged in with no further intervention from the experimenter.

Second, in Teger's experiments, even when the confederate's bids were randomly generated, the subjects believed that they were playing against other humans. Because interpersonal, competitive effects were not as strong when the subjects played a version of the game using a deck of cards, it was felt necessary to convince them that an (unknown) human opponent was involved. But the process of entrapment, as described by Teger (1980), Brockner and Rubin (1985), and others in its most general terms, is not limited to situations involving interpersonal competition. The subjects in the present experiment were simply told that they would be playing against "one or more other persons or a computer." Although we did not systematically collect information on the matter, the large majority of the subjects were quite surprised to learn that they were not, in fact, playing against other people. We surmise that—at least for this experimental paradigm—it is less important that subjects be *convinced* they are competing against a human than it is to be *uncertain* about whether they are playing against one.

Finally, subjects in previous experiments quit the auction when all resources were exhausted (with the exception discussed above). The rationale is that in a voluntary experiment subjects are unlikely to believe that they will be made to use their own resources. Yet if the subject does not consider the money his or her own, it is difficult to interpret results in terms of personal investments. By offering "extra credit" (1.8 percent of the points which could be accumulated over the course of the semester), "payment" for the experiment had been made before beginning. Tokens (in the morning) and $5 bills (in the afternoon) were distributed in advance to encourage the participants to consider these resources their own. Further, the instructions emphasized that at the end of play they would be required to pay the experimenter the amount of their bid, whether or not this exceeded $5. Several subjects attempted to pay (overbids were not collected), but more importantly, all subjects said they had "lost" money (rather than saying they had "won" amounts less than $5).

The program, like the unseen confederate, continued to outbid the subject in a fashion which simulated the play of a human opponent. The computer's bids were larger than the subject's previous bids by $0.10 plus a random percentage (from 0 to 50 percent) of the subject's previous bid. This averaged out to about a 30 percent increase in the computer's bid over the subject's last bid.

The computer imposed the bidding tax at a random point between $0 and $2. The amount of the tax also varied randomly between $0 and $2. When the bidding tax became operational, the player read the following message on the screen:

> The AUCTIONEER has decided to impose a $ [tax amount]* bidding tax from this point forward. The tax is added on to the cost of making your next and all subsequent bids, but does not increase the value of the bids in terms of winning the auction. In other words, if the tax is $1 and you want to bid $2 it will cost you $3, but your bid will still only be worth $2. All players are being taxed at the same rate.
>
> Hit the RETURN key when you are ready to continue.
>
> *"Tax amount" is the randomly selected tax value.

The principal dependent variable in the analysis is the amount of each player's highest bid, with each game considered a distinct case. Tests of the taxation hypotheses employ the amount of the tax and the tax start value (i.e., the bid at which the tax becomes operative). Prior research indicates that gender and learning effects are important to escalation, so we included control variables for gender and for game number (subjects were allowed to play the game more than once). Although developmental effects have not been systematically investigated, we felt it was prudent to include controls for age and number of years in college. Finally, start time and class grade were added to eliminate other potentially confounding influences.

Results

The average age of the student subjects was 19.8 years, and their mean number of years in college was 2.16. Ninety-two students played the game a total of 151 times for an average of 1.64 games per player.

FIGURE 1

Frequency Distribution of High Bids for All Games (n = 151)

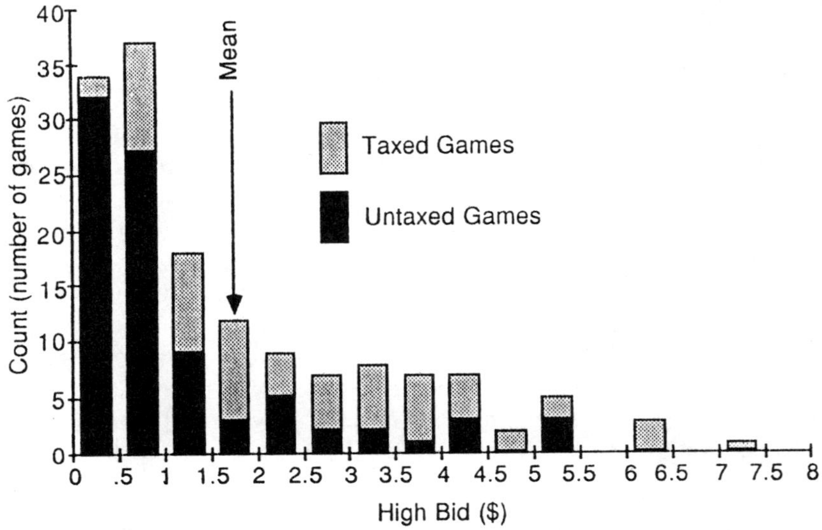

NOTE: Fifty-three percent of the games involved bids of greater than $1 for a $1 prize. The highest bid was $7.10. Untaxed games with large bids sometimes occur because the tax amount was set to $0 rather than because the tax start value was not surpassed.

Their mean high bid before dropping out on a $1 prize was $1.70. Figure 1 shows the frequency distribution on the student's bids. Fifty-three percent of the games had an ending bid larger than the $1 prize. The highest bid was $7.10.[2]

Of the 151 games played, 63 (or 42 percent) involved bids high enough to activate the tax. Figure 1 also shows the distribution of taxed versus untaxed high bids. The mean high bid for the taxed group ($2.51) was higher than the mean for the whole group ($1.70) and for the untaxed group ($1.10). This was due to the fact that the tax was not activated until some randomly selected point in the bidding between $0 and $2. Low bidders would therefore not be as likely to activate the tax, and the mean for games that did not activate the tax was therefore lower.

It is noteworthy that this distribution does not display the gaps which were prominent in Teger's study (without the bidding tax), but rather a relatively smooth decline in the frequency of successively higher bids. The distribution provides no support for the hypothesis that bids cluster at

[2]Actually, one student bid $180,000 and one bid $475, but we eliminated these games from the study because the students were obviously not taking the game seriously. Both of these games were played in the morning (when tokens were used) and both were second games for the students after they had already bid slightly more than their original $5 budget in the first game.

FIGURE 2

Tax Start and Tax Amount Plotted versus High Bid for Games with Bidding High Enough to Activate the Tax

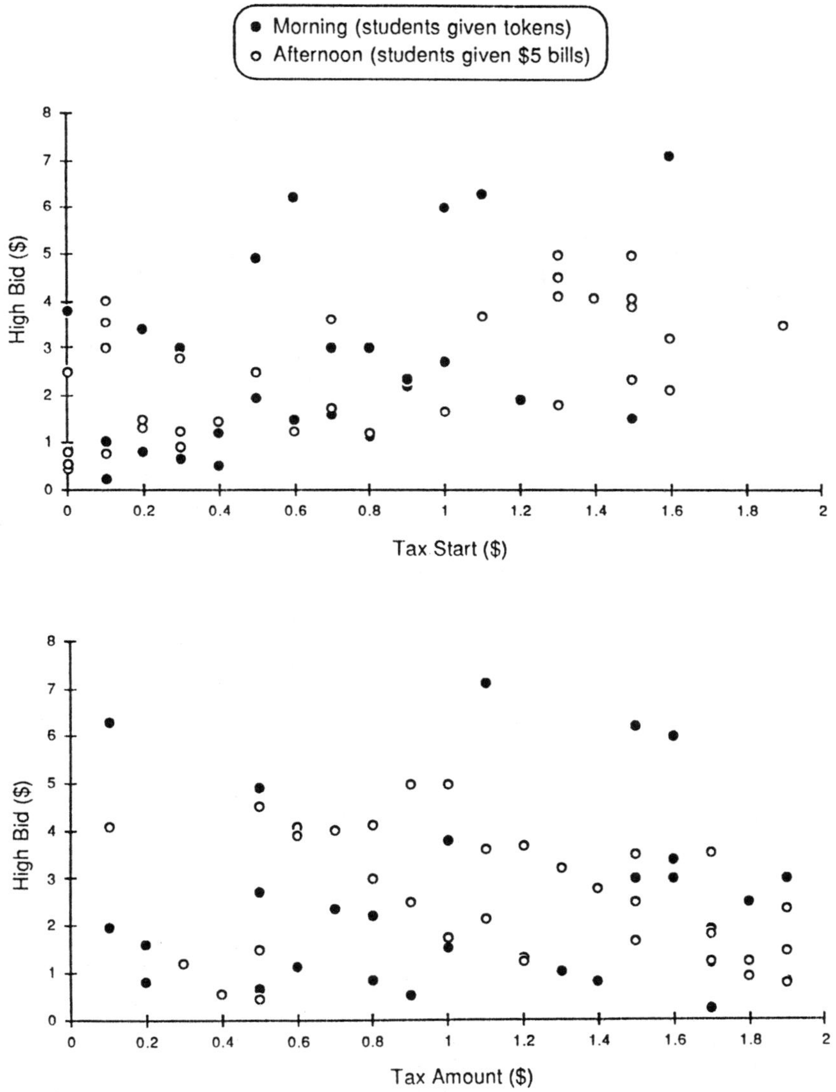

certain critical points, either at the halfway mark or at $5.00. In fact, only two of the taxed games and none of the nontaxed games ended with a bid in the interval from $4.50 to $5.00. We attribute this to the fact that subjects were not given a fixed amount to bid with, a state of affairs which more closely approximates real escalation situations where preestablished limits are not involved. Our results here appear quite similar to Teger's condition in which subjects were not told how much they had to bid with.

Figure 2 plots high bid against tax start and tax amount for the 63 games which activated the tax. A positive relationship between tax start and high bid may be detected in the top part of the figure ($r = .502$), indicating that the earlier the tax was activated, the lower the player's ending bid. The negative relationship between tax amount and high bid ($r = -.107$) indicates that larger tax values were associated with lower bidding levels. The plots also reveal that the relationships are stronger for the group given $5 bills (open circles) than for the group given tokens (dots).

The results of a multiple regression analysis testing the taxation hypotheses are presented in Table 2. The value of the high bid in each game was regressed on tax start, tax amount, and six control variables. Nine separate regressions were run, seven of which explained significant proportions of the variance in the measure of escalation. The sample was partitioned into the group using tokens (rows 1–3), the group using $5 bills (rows 4–6), and then combined (rows 7–9). For each group, the first equation estimated included all control variables (grade in the course, age in years, gender, time of day at start of game, years in college, and game number), the second equation included only those controls which were significant in at least one case (years in college and game number). The third equation excluded all the control variables and included only tax start and tax amount.

From 25 to 65 percent of the variance in high bids is explained by the models estimated. As intimated in Figure 2, the models for the subjects who played with $5 bills display a much better fit, explaining 15–30 percent more of the variance than the same models estimated on the subjects who played with tokens.

The principal finding from Table 2 is the striking importance of tax start and the relative unimportance of tax value. For all equations, the point at which the tax is implemented is the best predictor of the amount of the high bid. While we expected larger taxes to be more effective at terminating the escalation process, even the net effect of tax value is in the expected (negative) direction in only four of the nine models estimated. Controlling for tax start, game number, and years in college, small taxes are almost as effective as large ones. Tax amount is only marginally significant ($p < .09$) when the explanatory variables are limited to tax start and tax amount, and the afternoon ($5 bill) subsample is used. Earlier taxes discouraged bidding regardless of the amount the subject is taxed, at least for the range of tax values employed. For the entire sample, each delay of one dollar in the onset of the tax is associated with an increase of $1.55 in the terminal bid.

In no case were the effects of start time, age, or class grade significant.

TABLE 2

Regression results for morning and afternoon subsamples and for the entire sample. Numbers are regression coefficients ± standard error. Three equations are shown for each, one with eight independent variables and reduced forms with four and two independent variables.

	Independent Variables			
	Tax Start	Tax Amount	Game Number	Years in College
Morning (tokens)	2.205* ± 0.904	0.340 ± 0.761	−0.634 ± 0.667	−0.389 ± 0.711
	2.248** ± 0.768	0.449 ± 0.598	−0.633 ± 0.490	−0.086 ± 0.333
	2.161** ± 0.753	0.385 ± 0.590		
Afternoon ($5 bills)	1.030** ± 0.314	−0.201 ± 0.407	−0.151 ± 0.314	−0.610** ± 0.194
	1.027** ± 0.272	−0.218 ± 0.323	−0.187 ± 0.278	−0.559** ± 0.155
	1.230** ± 0.318	−0.644 ± 0.363		
All	1.549** ± 0.363	0.031 ± 0.361	−0.323 ± 0.301	−0.398* ± 0.207
	1.438** ± 0.328	0.033 ± 0.336	−0.411 ± 0.282	−0.329* ± 0.170
	1.507** ± 0.340	−0.163 ± 0.338		

*$p < .05$.
**$p < .01$.

The absence of a gender effect was contrary to expectations. Males did not in general bid higher than females as Teger's (1980) results indicated. Game number was negatively associated with high bid for the token and aggregated conditions. At least in some cases there was a learning effect, with subjects tending not to escalate as much on second or third plays. Years of college was negatively associated with high bid for the cash money and aggregated conditions. That is, more experienced college students terminated play earlier. This effect may be due to prior experience with (and scepticism toward) experimental procedures rather than worldliness or maturity, given the absence of an age effect. The effect does not appear for the token condition.

Comparison with Previous Studies

In addition to the findings on taxation, two differences between these results and those reported by Teger are worth emphasis. First, although his findings showed clear differences by gender, our data reveal no such pattern for taxed or nontaxed subsamples. Nontaxed games display relatively low ending bids (as a function of the design) while taxed games

TABLE 2—continued

Independent Variables				Equation	
Start Time	Gender	Age	Class Grade	R^2	Residual Degrees of Freedom
−0.0010 ± 0.003	−0.179 ± 1.013	0.313 ± 0.725	0.011 ± 0.042	0.313	20
				0.296	24
				0.245*	26
−0.0003 ± 0.001	−0.116 ± 0.373	−0.003 ± 0.036	0.009 ± 0.012	0.650**	23
				0.609**	29
				0.401**	31
−0.0005 ± 0.001	−0.395 ± 0.415	−0.014 ± 0.052	0.013 ± 0.014	0.359**	52
				0.335**	58
				0.255**	60

involve a new contingency which Teger did not examine, so these findings are not necessarily incompatible. What they suggest, however, is that differences in gender-based competitiveness disappear with shifts in the information and incentive structure induced by taxation. If the imposition of taxation constitutes a reminder of the "rules of rationality," then the similarity of men and women in high bids is to be expected. The rational consideration of long-run costs is consistent with a diminished sense that "too much has been invested to quit" and a willingness to terminate the game quickly. Men and women are equally responsive to this kind of incentive.

Second, Teger's (1980: study III, pp. 33–35) conclusion that it makes no difference whether dollar auction bidding uses points or real money is worth reconsidering in the light of the differences we observed between subsamples. In Teger's study III auctions contrasting points and money, the maximum bid was fixed at $2, a decision we have criticized in light of both our own and his (study IV) results. A principal finding in Teger's study IV is that most subjects who bid above the value of the prize continue bidding until their resources are gone regardless of whether they are bidding with real money or points (where no specific value is attached to the points). But subjects did quit bidding earlier when real money was used rather than points, leading one to suspect, again, that arbitrary termination points change the character of the bidding.

In the present study subjects were either given tokens, the value of which was specified, or $5 bills to begin the game. Although the average final bid was identical for the two groups for the taxed subsample ($2.51), the variance was larger among subjects playing with tokens (3.715) than for those playing with $5 bills (1.889). Differently put, subjects did not bid less on average when playing with real money, but they were seemingly more thoughtful with their bidding and less likely to bid wildly. Together with the fact that the models display a better fit to the data for the group which was given real money, this result suggests that escalation processes are sensitive to the actor's belief that the resources which are invested are indeed meaningful.

Conclusions

Current discussions of decision making in entrapment situations suggest that changes in reward structure should be effective in decreasing the likelihood of escalation. Applying this to the simulation of conflict escalation in the dollar auction game, we distinguished information and incentive components of taxation. We expected that both earlier and larger taxes would be associated with termination of bidding, drawing in arguments from expected utility theory and studies of information processing in traplike situations.

We found that the timing of the tax was much more important than the amount of the tax in determining the degree of observed escalation in the bidding process. Oddly, it seems to make little difference whether the subjects are heavily taxed or only lightly taxed—the extent to which taxation discourages subsequent bids is mainly a function of when the tax is implemented. Of course, this conclusion is limited to the range of tax values adopted in the present design. It would undoubtedly be possible to impose a tax value such that no further bids would be made irrespective of tax timing.

That small taxes are almost as effective as large ones when they are imposed early in the game strongly suggests that the information function of taxation is dominant in controlling the conflict escalation process, and that expected utility arguments are less powerful in explaining escape. Taxation, as these results demonstrate, is effective in modifying the behavior of subjects as they respond to random bidding increments in attempting to attain a specified goal. If the *amount* of the tax governs the speed with which they decide not to compete in the auction, a strictly economic rationale could be given for their behavior. That is, large taxes (added to the subject's own bid) quickly reduce expected winnings to zero and the rational decision is to escape. But this interpretation is not well supported by the data. Instead, subjects confronted with an early tax, exiguous or not, are the ones most likely to escape the auction. Such a decision does not necessarily imply economic rationality if the combined value of tax and bid does not exceed one dollar. (At least, it implies no less economic rationality than entering the auction in the first place.)

An early tax is a disruptive signal. It provides a break in the game, a "time out" from the escalation of conflict, giving the bidder a moment to consider strategy and reevaluate his/her objectives. A pertinent comparison from Teger's study V shows subjects initially given $5 were less likely to bid away all of their resources when questionnaires were administered at points during the bidding. Like a tax, a questionnaire is a disruption resulting in reduced escalation at least under some conditions. More than a questionnaire, the mere existence of a tax makes clear to the bidder that adverse consequences attend further escalation. The very next bid will cost more than the intended bid (by some amount). It is this intrusive awareness which, in our view, alters the character of the auction. In effect, the trap becomes *visible* to the participants. From this perspective, it makes little difference whether the consequences of the next bid are extremely adverse or only mildly adverse, for the trap has been seen for what it is and can be escaped from.

The general conclusion from our study is that escaping from escalating situations seems to require intrusive information that can shock participants out of complacent continuation and into a fresh look at their situation. A breakdown of an old car may be necessary to terminate the cycle of escalating minor repairs. An accident may be necessary to cause a rethinking of the efficacy of nuclear power. Our results also indicate why it is so difficult to terminate chronic gambling. Even major losses have little effect on the escalation process if they occur late. However, even a relatively minor external stimulus may be effective if applied early in the process. The stimulus required to cause a rethinking of escalating situations can be externally applied in a controlled, nondamaging way. This strategy may offer the potential for more effective control of the ubiquitous escalation process. SSQ

REFERENCES

Axelrod, Robert. 1984. *The Evolution of Cooperation*. New York: Basic Books.

Brockner, J., and J. Z. Rubin. 1985. *Entrapment in Escalating Conflicts: A Social Psychological Analysis*. New York: Springer-Verlag.

Costanza, Robert. 1984. "The Nuclear Arms Race and the Theory of Social Traps." *Journal of Peace Research* 21:79–86.

———. 1987. "Social Traps and Environmental Policy." *BioScience* 37:407–12.

Cross, John G., and Melvin J. Guyer. 1980. *Social Traps*. Ann Arbor: University of Michigan Press.

Ells, Ellery T. 1982. *Rational Decision and Causality*. Cambridge: Cambridge University Press.

Hardin, Garrett. 1968. "The Tragedy of the Commons." *Science* 162:1243–48.

Janis, Irving L., and Leon Mann. 1977. *Decision-Making: A Psychological Analysis of Conflict, Choice and Commitment*. New York: Free Press.

Machina, M. J. 1987. "Decision Making in the Presence of Risk." *Science* 236:537–42.

Platt, John. 1973. "Social Traps." *American Psychologist* 28:641–51.

Shubik, Martin. 1971. "The Dollar Auction Game: A Paradox in Noncooperative Behavior and Escalation." *Journal of Conflict Resolution* 15:109–11.

Teger, Alan I. 1980. *Too Much Invested to Quit*. New York: Pergamon.

Wilson, Richard, and E. A. C. Crouch. 1987. Risk Assessment and Comparisons: An Introduction. *Science* 236:267–70.

Ecological Economics, 2 (1990) 57–75 57
Elsevier Science Publishers B.V., Amsterdam – Printed in The Netherlands

A FLEXIBLE ASSURANCE BONDING SYSTEM FOR IMPROVED ENVIRONMENTAL MANAGEMENT

ROBERT COSTANZA

Coastal and Environmental Policy Program, Center for Environmental and Estuarine Studies, Chesapeake Biological Laboratory, University of Maryland, Solomons, MD 20688-0038 (U.S.A.)

and CHARLES PERRINGS

Department of Economics, University of Botswana, Private Bag 0022, Gaborone (Botswana)

(Accepted 8 September 1989)

ABSTRACT

Costanza, R. and Perrings, C., 1990. A flexible assurance bonding system for improved environmental management. *Ecol. Econ.*, 2: 57–75.

Current methods of regulating activities that are known or suspected to be environmentally damaging are not working well. They induce legal confrontation, obfuscation, and government intrusion into the inner workings of firms. They tend to suppress technical and social innovation aimed at long-term solutions. They do not mesh well with the market signals that firms use to make decisions.

This paper discusses some of the underlying reasons for this problem, and outlines a flexible environmental assurance bonding system designed to incorporate environmental criteria and uncertainty into the market system, and to induce positive environmental technological innovation. In addition to direct charges for known environmental damages, an assurance bond equal to the current best estimate of the largest potential future environmental damages would be levied and kept in an interest-bearing escrow account. The bond (plus a portion of the interest) would be returned if and only if the firm could prove that the suspected damages had not occurred or would not occur. If damages did occur, the bond would be used to rehabilitate or repair the environment, and to compensate injured parties. By requiring the users of environmental resources to post a bond adequate to cover potential future environmental damages (with the possibility for refunds), the burden of proof is shifted from the public to the resource user and a strong economic incentive is provided to research the true costs of environmentally innovative activities and to develop innovative, cost-effective pollution control technologies.

INTRODUCTION

Within the social sciences there are a number of terms to describe circumstances where choices that are privately optimal lead to socially sub-optimal outcomes. The 'prisoner's' dilemma' in the theory of games is one of the best known examples. The Cournot–Nash solution to such games is privately rational, but is nevertheless inferior to the cooperative solution. The 'tragedy of the commons' in the theory of common property is another example (Hardin, 1968). Where individuals enjoy open unregulated access to a resource in common property, privately rational behavior can lead to the overexploitation of the resource to the detriment of the long-run interests of everyone. In these and all similar cases individuals may be said to be trapped by the institutional, informational or temporal conditions they face into making socially sub-optimal decisions. Social psychologists Platt (1973), Cross and Guyer (1980) and Teger (1980) have coined the term 'social trap' to cover this general class of phenomena, and we use their terminology here because it seems to be the most general, comprehensive, and experimentally verified of the several alternatives.

A social trap exists wherever the rational decisions of individual agents necessarily leads to an outcome that is inconsistent with the best interests of society. These are circumstances in which the signals guiding individual choices are distorted by the informational, institutional or temporal parameters of the decision-making process. The existence of social traps in economics is generally taken to justify government intervention in the allocation of resources. Indeed, it might be argued that the proper role of a democratic government is to eliminate social traps (no more and no less) while maintaining as much individual freedom as possible.

The particular social traps that concern us are those which influence the private use of environmental resources. The global evidence on the high social costs of privately rational use of environmental resources is now overwhelming. These costs are certainly higher in some countries than others, but no society has altogether escaped the costs of privately inflicted environmental damage. Indeed, the threat posed by environmental damage due to individually rational but socially irrational use of agricultural and forest resources has been identified as the single greatest problem faced by the lower income countries (World Commission on Environment and Development, 1987). The study of how to recognize, avoid, and escape from these traps is accordingly a necessary part of an effective environmental management strategy (Costanza, 1987). More than this, it is a minimum condition for reducing the welfare costs of resource degradation, not just locally but worldwide.

This paper describes a system of flexible environmental assurance bonds designed to correct the distortions in the signals guiding private resource users which give rise to the problem. Specifically, the bonds are designed to confront individual resource users with the marginal social costs of the 'worst case' results of their activities at the time those activities are undertaken. Neither the principle nor the instrument proposed are new. The environmental bond has its roots in the 'materials use fees' first proposed by Mill (1972) and Solow (1971), the best working example of which is the simple refundable deposit on glass bottles. The aim of the deposit is to encourage the users to dispose of the commodity in the most desirable way (by recycling) and to avoid its disposal in the least desirable way (as dangerous litter). The deposit may not be sufficient to cover the cost of the worst possible method of disposal, but it is generally set at a high enough level to make return of the bottle privately profitable. The important feature of the fee is that by insisting that consumers pay *in advance* for the costs they *might* inflict on society if they adopted the most harmful method of disposal, it reverses the usual presumption of 'innocence' over 'guilt' as applied to environmental damages.

Historically, there has been a tacit presumption of innocence over guilt about the environmental effects of economic activities. This is particularly true of chronic effects that are difficult to quantify. The effect of smoking on lung cancer is a case in point. Cigarette manufacturers have been presumed innocent (and indeed still are presumed innocent in many places) until the overwhelming weight of evidence has demonstrated the link between smoking and lung cancer. In fact, cigarette manufacturers still dispute this link. This presumption of innocence is simply inappropriate wherever an activity has potentially severe environmental consequences, for the reason that it enables those who cause environmental damage (and profit from it) to costlessly shift the risk on to the rest of society.

The presumption of innocence in this context implies the *provisional* assumption that the probability that a resource based activity will be environmentally damaging is zero. A presumption of guilt, on the other hand, implies the *provisional* assumption that the probability that a resource based activity will be environmentally damaging is one. The case for presuming guilt rests on the non-existence of an enforceable contract with the user. That is, the purchaser of glass bottles in the refundable deposit example cannot be bound in advance to dispose of those bottles in an environmentally benign way. If it were assumed that they would do so, society would be absorbing the risk. Since it is assumed that they will not do so, the user absorbs the risk. In this case the non-existence of an enforceable contract is due to the fact that the user is not constrained to behave in any particular way. More generally, users may not be bound by an enforceable contract because the future effects of their activities are simply unknown, or because the links between cause and effect are indirect or occur with a lag and so cannot be easily established. All social traps are characterized by the non-existence of enforceable contracts binding resource users to behave in a socially optimal way. For this reason it is appropriate to assume that resource users caught in a social trap will impose costs on society, and to seek to insure society against those costs.

CURRENT APPROACHES TO THE PROBLEM OF SOCIAL TRAPS

Social traps have their origins in the institutional, temporal, and informational parameters of the decision-making process. The 'road signs' governing our decisions, of which the set of relative prices are the most important, turn out to be dependent on these parameters in various ways – some better recognized than others. The best recognized traps in the economics literature are institutional: those associated with the absence of markets for the effects of one person's actions on another or from the absence of well defined rights to a resource exploited in common. In both cases the problem is argued to lie in the structure of property rights, and the primary solution is argued to lie in the allocation of property rights. But traps can also arise out of simple ignorance of the future effects or broader effects of current activities, or out of a time perspective which makes those effects irrelevant to the decision-maker. Both information and rates of time preference are, however, typically taken as data in economic models, and so do not feature in the solutions devised. This implies that solutions resting on the allocation of property rights may be ineffective wherever traps have an informational or temporal dimension.

Consider an apparently simple example: the 'tragedy of the commons' parable due to Hardin (1968). In this parable, a number of individuals exploit a common property (say grazing land). Each individual is assumed to maximize their own well being – a rational objective – by adding cattle to the range up to the point where the private cost of the last animal is equal to the private revenue it yields when sold. The source of the tragedy is argued to lie in the distribution of costs and benefits. The social cost of each additional animal added to the range is the reduction in live weight gains of all animals due to the reduction in average grass availability. The private cost is the fall in live weight gains of the individual's own herd. Since the benefits of an extra animal accrue to the individual while the costs are shared between all herders, it is rational for individuals to keep adding cattle up to the point where the resource collapses. The final outcome is suboptimal from the long-term point of view of both society and each individual herder, but there is no incentive for individuals to act differently. The ultimate source of the trap in this case is argued to be the open access of individuals to the commons since this ensures that the information on which they base their decisions does not include the social cost of their own actions. Providing that the system of property rights guarantees open access, it is argued that a rational response to the relative private costs and benefits of grazing will lead to the exhaustion of the resource.

The apparent robustness of this result has been tested in numerous controlled experiments. [1] However, these experiments have all assumed an exclusively institutional source of the trap, ignoring the fact that few real world common property traps are as simple. In many cases where resources in common ownership have been exploited to the point of collapse (e.g. buffalo in the U.S.A.) additional factors of crucial importance have been ignorance about the carrying capacity of the resource, and the fact that those exploiting the resource have had alternative long-term options which enable them to discount the future costs of their activities. Wherever those exploiting a resource have not had alternative long-term options, the more usual response of the users of the resource has been to regulate access (see, for example, Wade, 1987). Indeed, it is seldom clear in particular cases whether it is the institutional structure that is the cause of overexploitation, or ignorance about either the carrying capacity of the resource or its natural rate of regeneration, or some restriction on the time horizon over which the costs and benefits of exploitation are assessed. The existence of common property in various resources currently under stress, particularly in the low income countries, has inclined many to look for open access common property traps (cf. Ghai and Radwan, 1983). But common property in such resources is not nearly as new a phenomenon as the degradation of those resources. It is, in fact, likely that the impact of deepening rural poverty on the implicit rate of time preference is far more significant a cause of overexploitation than the structure of property rights (Perrings, 1988, 1989b). Put another way, it is more likely that the problem lies in the temporal rather than the institutional dimensions of the trap.

If we are to avoid the environmental damage that is due to the existence of social traps, it follows from what has been said that we need to be very careful in our diagnosis of traps. This is not to say that governments have

---

[1] Edney and Harper (1978), for example, experimented with a simple game designed to test people's behavior in a commons trap. In this game a pool of resources is represented by poker chips. The resource pool is renewable; it is replenished after each round in proportion to the number of chips left in the common pool. The objective for each player is to accumulate as many chips as possible from the common pool. At each round players can take either one, two, or three chips. If all players take three chips per round, the resource pool is quickly depleted, and the players end up with far fewer chips than if they had all taken only one chip per round, since doing so would have allowed the resource pool to replenish itself. This game is a trap (and a good analogy for many real-world common-property resource problems) since the short-term, narrow incentives (to take as many chips as possible each round) are inconsistent with the long-term incentives (to accumulate as many chips as possible by the end of the game).

always assumed the unidimensionality of traps. Indeed, in many cases the evolution of policy shows the opposite. Fisheries management strategies are a case in point. Overfishing was traditionally ascribed to the open access enjoyed by fishermen to a common property resource, and the earliest solutions proposed were based on the allocation of private property in the stocks (see, for example, Scott, 1955). It was argued that optimal rates of harvest over time involve both the economically efficient harvest of existing stocks and the reservation of a portion of those stocks to allow for the regeneration of the resource, but that with no secure property rights individual firms could not afford to take the longer view and would harvest up to the economically efficient short-term limit, irrespective of whether this depleted the breeding stock. More particularly, new firms would continue to enter the market up to the point where short-term economic rents were fully dissipated. This quite rational behavior would lead to depletion of fish stocks, and to the unintended extinction of the species (even if access is limited) wherever the rates of time preference of individual operators exceeded the biological growth rate of the species (Clark, 1973).

Experience over the past three decades has, however, shown that the problem has more complex roots, and current solutions generally involve three parts. The first part involves the direct control of the level of catches and the size of fish caught through a system of annual catch quotas and gear restrictions. The second part is the development of a market in transferable catch quotas which allocates the annual catch between producers. This is intended to limit supply to what is thought to be a sustainable level, without conferring monopoly privileges in the process. The third part is the development of a data base to ensure that restrictions on catches and gear are appropriate. It is recognized that in almost all fisheries there is less than perfect knowledge of stock sizes and growth rates, so that the future impact on fishery stocks of any given annual catch quota is not known with certainty. Hence current fisheries management programmes involve the monitoring of stocks and research into the variables influencing stock changes in order to pick the 'right' catch quota (cf. Clark, 1987).

While current fisheries strategies are less likely to fail environmentally than earlier strategies by virtue of the fact they recognize the multidimensionality of the trap, they still assume that information and time-preference are 'given' data for the private decision-maker. It is government which is held responsible for generating the information needed to ensure the sustainability of the resource, and the core of the strategy is still direct control over levels of harvest. But this too has costs. Indeed, wherever environmental regulation has involved direct control through the establishment of an acceptable standard of environmental quality or sustainable level of biological harvest, the standards have become subject to a bargaining process that has little to do with the quality of the data about the resource. In principle permits are allocated to users specifying the amount of discharge or harvest allowed, the sum of these permitted uses equalling the total allowed for the environment or ecosystem. But since regulatory agencies have more discretion over interpretation of the law than they have over enforcement, this provides an incentive to polluters and other natural resource users to bargain with the agency over the maximum sustainable yield of a resource or the minimum acceptable level of environmental quality. The end result is that the agency becomes staffed from the ranks of the regulated (Kolhmeir, 1969; Stigler, 1971) and vice versa, and the original goal of the intervention is compromised.

More importantly, by intervening in production decisions directly, rather than through the price signals informing production decisions, this approach to environmental management merely substitutes one source of inefficiency in production for another. Recalling that we have identified the source of social traps to be distortions in the signals guiding individual decisions due to the institutional, informational or temporal parameters of the decision-making process, intervention that fails to correct those signals will not eliminate the trap. Direct control of activity levels, like the moratoria on whaling, may have a temporary impact on resource use, but unless it is associated with measures to correct the price signals, it can only suppress and not solve the problem, and it will almost certainly have costs in terms of allocative efficiency.

A standard for compliance treats all sources of pollution or congestion as homogeneous. Only if polluters are charged according to the amount and toxicity of the effluents emitted will they choose the level of pollution abatement which equates their own marginal costs with the social benefits of pollution control. Polluters facing relatively low pollution abatement costs will cut back more than will polluters with higher costs. If the overall level of pollution abatement is shown to be inadequate, the effluent (price) charge may be raised to achieve the desired reduction allowing more timely adaptation to differing and changing conditions. To achieve the same results through a system of direct control, the government would be required to distinguish between polluters both in terms of the toxicity and amount of waste, and in terms of abatement costs. Since the cost of obtaining this information is prohibitive, governments typically resort to requiring that all polluters cut emissions by the same amount, resulting in a greater total cost of pollution control than would occur under the pricing approach. The inefficiency of direct regulation has been demonstrated in a number of empirical studies. In three studies of the St. Louis metropolitan area, Atkinson and Lewis (1974, 1976) and Atkinson and Tietenberg (1982) found that current management for particulates pollution cost three to five times as much as the theoretically most efficient program providing the same level of ambient air quality. Seskin et al. (1983), in a study of NO_2 in Chicago, show a fourteen fold increase in costs for direct regulation over the least cost strategy.

Other advantages of a system of charges include: (1) the negative effects of charges on the production costs of high pollution goods, which filters through to final prices, in turn reducing demand, production and pollution; and (2) the lower administrative costs of a system of charges that relies on voluntary compliance reinforced by random audits (much like income tax) as opposed to the costly monitoring of individual dischargers needed to achieve similar levels of compliance under direct regulation (Haveman 1976). The approach proposed in this paper is one that harnesses the advantages of a system of charges to the temporal and informational dimensions of environmental social traps. The intention is to convert the trap to a trade-off in which producers are confronted with the full social cost of their activities given the information available to the environmental authority, and are invited to determine for themselves the optimal level of activity. [2]

A FLEXIBLE ENVIRONMENTAL ASSURANCE BONDING SYSTEM

Following Pearce and Markandya (1987) we take the social cost of a resource to comprise the direct costs of extraction or harvesting, the intratemporal external or intersectoral costs of extraction or harvesting (i.e. damage done to third parties which is not compensated within the existing structure of property rights), and the intertemporal external or user costs of extraction or harvesting (i.e. the opportunity cost to future users of the resource resulting from its depletion). In general, entrapped resource users will face only the direct costs of extraction, harvesting or pollution. Any solution to the trap requires that they also be confronted with external costs of their actions. Certain of these external costs – particularly intratemporal external costs – may be internalized through the allocation of private property rights. We are, however, concerned with those external costs – particularly intertemporal external costs – that cannot be internalized in this

[2] In terms of Edney and Harper's common property resource consumption game, one could turn the trap into a trade-off by taxing any consumption above the optimum level for resource stability. For example, if players took two or three chips they could be "taxed" one or two chips respectively, so that the short-term benefit of taking more than one chip were offset by short-term costs. This would remove the short-term incentive to take more than one chip and make the long- and short-term incentives in the game consistent, thereby eliminating the trap.

way. Where the time-distance between the parties at either end of an external effect is considerable, and where there is a high level of uncertainty about the nature or severity of the effect, and the scope for creating a market in the effect is limited (Perrings, 1987).

To address this problem without risking the efficiency costs of the direct controls conventionally adopted in these cases, the approach developed here has the following general characteristics:

(1) It would be minimally intrusive into the internal operations of the regulated industries, relying on charges rather than direct controls;
(2) The charges would be such that private users of environmental resources would be induced to uncover the socially relevant future effects of their current activities;
(3) The inducement to ecotechnological research in both public and private sectors would be proportional to the perceived social costs of proceeding in ignorance;
(4) Similarly, the funding of environmental protection would be proportional to the size of the environmental problem;
(5) The costs of environmental protection would be equitably shared among the responsible parties.

More specifically, the primary charge on resource users would be a dated assurance bond. The bond would be applied in all cases where the data do not exist to compute an expected value for the future environmental costs of current activities. Where reliable data do exist it should be possible to insure against future environmental effects commercially. In other cases the size of the bond would cover the conjectured 'worst case' future marginal costs of resource use. Under the scheme, each resource user would be required to post bonds, refundable at specified dates if the intertemporal external costs of the activity turned out to be less than those assessed by the environmental authority. The value of the bond at the date of posting would be a function of the environmental authority's estimate of the costs of environmental repair or rehabilitation if the worst happened between the date of posting and the refund date. The value of the bond would be higher, the greater the estimate of the worst case costs.

The bond would be refundable in whole or part if the resource users could demonstrate lower damages than those assumed by the agency setting the bond. The burden of proof that the estimate of the agency was incorrect would lie with the user of the resource. The system should therefore provide a strong economic incentive to firms to research the future environmental costs of their activities, and so to improve their environmental performance. If the environmental authority's estimate of the worst case costs were revised downwards during the life of the bond it would be reduced; if revised upwards it would be increased. It is this feature of the scheme that would provide the incentive to resource users to research the future environmental effects of their activities.

The determination of bonds would accordingly vary depending on whether the activity concerned was continuous, a fixed-term program, or a one-off project. Bonds might be determined annually for continuous users and fixed-term programs, users being required to take out a bond for each year of operations. For one-off projects, on the other hand, there might be a single bond. In all cases, however, the bonds would be sensitive to the state of knowledge, and so might be reappraised at any point up to the refund date. For a continuous activity in which each additional environmentally cost-free year persuaded the environmental authority to reduce its estimate of the worst case by a fixed proportion, for example, not only would each new bond be lower than the preceding one, but each reappraisal of existing bonds would reduce the value of those bonds.

The refund date of the bond would be partly a function of the physically determined delays in the emergence of the environmental effects being anticipated in the bond, and partly a function of the politically determined limitation on the responsibility of present-day users for the future effects of their actions. So, on the one hand, an activity involving pollution of the environment would be required to take out a bond with a refund date determined by the rate of decay of the pollutant. The disposers of nuclear waste, for example, would be required to take out a much longer dated bond than the disposers of raw sewage.

The value of the bond would, as we have pointed out, be a function of the environmental authority's best estimate of the worst outcome of any given activity, given the state of knowledge at the date the bond was struck or reappraised. This implies that change in the value of bonds would be a function of a learning process involving both the lessons of experience (or the deepening historical record of the effects of 'old' noninnovative activities) and the results of primary experimental and theoretical research into the potential effects of 'new' innovative activities. This has certain obvious implications for the research incentives built into the bond, which are discussed further on. Indeed, it is this feature of the system which provides the most direct incentive to private producers to invest in ecotechnological research. This same feature also means that the funds available to indemnify society against the future environmental costs of current activities would increase with the severity of those costs, ensuring a match between the resources committed to environmental protection and the size of the environmental problem.

One added advantage of the proposed approach is that it also incorporates uncertainty about the discount and interest rates, and passes that uncertainty on to the polluters. Uncertainties about the time value of money and present value are folded into the interest rate earned on the bond. They are of concern to the polluter (since they affect return on their capital tied up in the bond) but society (as represented by the environmental agency) need not concern itself. Whatever happens to the interest or discount rate, society will have the resources to deal with any foreseeable pollution event if and when it occurs.

BASIS OF THE BOND

The rationale for the recommended basis of the bond, the environmental authority's best estimate of the worst case costs of an activity, lies in the (Knightian) uncertainty that comes with incomplete information. Wherever the range and probability distribution of the future effects of present actions are not known, it is not possible to calculate an expected value for the outcome of those actions. Nor is it possible to calculate the risk of any one of a suspected number of outcomes.

In such circumstances the decision-maker faces the problem of uncertainty. There may be a number of outcomes to which the decision-maker's attention is drawn for whatever reason that would not cause surprise if they did occur, but no basis on which to calculate the probability of their occurring. Under the theory of uncertainty, the decision-maker will focus on those positive or negative attention-catching outcomes to which they attach the lowest level of disbelief (see, for example, Katzner, 1988). These are the focus losses and focus gains of the action. The conjectured worst case outcome recommended as the basis of the bond would be the focus loss of the activity. It is not, therefore, the worst case 'imaginable', but the least unbelievable of those costs of an activity to which the decision-maker's attention has been drawn for whatever reason – publicity or public sentiment included.

If a resource user or class of resource users is required to post a bond equal to the present value of the conjectured worst-case outcomes of an activity, the environmental authority will have the means to repair damage due to those potential outcomes which cause most public concern: whether it be a nuclear meltdown, depletion of the ozone layer, destruction of the northern pine forests or some much lesser effect. Society would still carry the cost of environmental damage beyond that level, but would be covered for any lesser damage.

To sharpen the distinction between the treatment of cases of complete versus incomplete information, notice that wherever the information set is complete – the range and probability distribution of the future outcomes of present actions is known – it should be possible to create a market for the risks involved. It would then be sufficient to require resource users to take out commercial insurance against environmental costs. The bond scheme would operate wherever future costs were uninsurable commercially – where actuarial risks cannot be calculated from historical data. Innovative use of resources in a dynamic and evolving ecosystem leaves little room for commercial insurance against most future costs because uncertainty is generally very high. One would therefore expect that most innovative resource-using activities would require a bond.

INSTITUTIONAL FEATURES

Institutionally, this system could probably be handled within the current governmental structure of most countries, although in many countries some new legislation would be required. The simplest approach would be to create an office of environmental fees assessment within the state environmental regulatory agency. This office, in collaboration with the department of revenue and taxation, would set annual environmental charges for all firms/resource users within the state, based on input from an independent advisory board. The system could work similarly to the way that most government revenue services currently collect taxes. The bonds for each years' operation would be fixed by the environmental fees assessment office based on a 'worst case' analysis, and given the firm's projected output levels, anticipated technological changes and so on. The firm would then be able to apply for a reduction to the value of existing bonds (the refund of a portion of those bonds) in each financial year, but the burden of proof in granting the refund or reduction would be on the applicant (as it is with most taxation systems). At first, all applications for refunds would have to be reviewed, but once the system were running a random audit of applications for refunds would probably be sufficient to discourage abuse.

Setting the bonds would be the responsibility of the environmental regulatory agency, based on input from an independent scientific advisory board consisting of independent environmental experts. The board would assimilate information on potential environmental damages and the degree of uncertainty associated with each, and publish a rate schedule updated annually. Applications for refunds would be reviewed by the board and approved only if accepted standards of scientific proof were met. Appointees to the board would be analogous to judges, and should be held to the same strict standards of impartiality, equity, and fairness. The same laws as those applying to the judiciary concerning criminal penalties for attempting to buy influence or accepting payment for influence would have to apply.

The bonds could be placed in a trust fund to be returned to the firms at the refund date less the cost of rehabilitating environmental resources or repairing environmental damage due to the corresponding activities. We repeat that the burden of proof that an activity has not resulted in the effects identified by the environmental authority would rest with the resource user. Nevertheless, the scheme should generate public research funds in proportion to the potential severity of the environmental damage. To ensure this, interest on the trust fund might be divided between: (a) maintenance of the real value of the bond (this portion of the interest earned to be refunded to the contributing firms in proportion to their refund); (b) maintenance of the environmental agency and the scientific advisory board; and (c) a special fund for research on environmental pollution control technology and management.

INCENTIVE EFFECTS OF THE BONDING SYSTEM

Given that the bonds are proposed to deal with the informational dimensions of social traps, the most striking feature of the scheme is the incentive it offers both public and private agents to improve the data on the environmental costs of economic activity. The specific question addressed here is: if the market economy cannot be relied upon to induce an optimal allocation of resources between ecotechnological and conventional research, what interventions are available to government that will have this effect?

The optimal allocation of research resources between ecotechnologies and conventional technologies should be easily determined in well functioning markets where prices correctly signal the scarcity of resources. In such cases, indices of relative scarcity induce technological change that facilitates the substitution of less scarce for more scarce resources. In a well-behaved neoclassical model with environmental resources, where the assumptions of the model ensure that the relative scarcity of environmental resources is correctly signalled by the price system, the depletion or degradation of resources will prompt a smooth increase in investment in backstop technologies. In such models it is meaningless to talk of the environmental limits to economic growth since the extinction of any one species or the exhaustion of any one resource will automatically lead to investment in research into substitutes (cf. Kemp et al., 1984). In reality, however, the absence of markets for many environmental goods and services has resulted in technological innovations which permit harvest levels that can cause extinction or which overload the assimilative capacities of ecosystems through excessive production of wastes without stimulating research into backstop technologies. [3] Therefore, even though ecotechnology can provide substantial benefits to society, the public (free) goods nature of its outputs will result in

[3] Nor, in reality, is it considered reasonable to point to the existence of substitutes as cause for complacency over the extinction of species, but this raises issues beyond the economic determinants of ecotechnological research.

both underinvestment in basic research and underutilization of the technologies developed. [4]

It is generally the case that ecotechnology (information in the form of scientific data) cannot be embodied in a proprietary product. That is, ecotechnology can be shared among many users without being depleted, and even though research and development costs may be substantial, users can usually avoid all but the most inconsequential transfer costs. It is a classic 'free rider' problem. Since innovators are not able to easily internalize the payoffs derived from ecotechnologies there is little incentive to produce them. This is true of much biological and environmental research. Ideally, the innovator's compensation should reflect the total social net benefits that arises from his or her innovation.

Another impediment to ecotechnological research is the uncertainty surrounding its potential economic value, particularly in the case of basic research. In many cases it is impossible to predict the returns to basic research because future applications are yet unknown, implying that the research has only a quasi-option value. While it may be true, as Binswanger and Ruttan (1978) suggest, that the state of basic research determines the potential returns on applied research, uncertainty over the yield of basic research and the inability to capture any payoffs means that such research is unlikely to be undertaken by a profit maximizing firm.

As a result, government (or other public institution) involvement has been a necessary condition for ecotechnological research and development. Agricultural (and forest) experimental stations exemplify the institutional arrangements historically needed to overcome the lack of incentive for private research. However, a bias toward underinvestment in ecotechnological research persists, which appears to be largely due to the difficulty of excluding other users from the benefits generated. The result is that despite current levels of government support for basic non-ecotechnological research, analogous institutions for promoting ecotechnological research are unlikely to develop, even when the social benefits of such research are high. [5]

[4] Moreover, pure research has to compete with various other public goods for funds in an often unfavourable political environment. While it can be argued that the long term returns to research may be very large, it is difficult to weigh such risky ventures against immediate hardship.

[5] For example, it has been shown that wetland catchment basins in strip mined areas reduce the amount of potentially harmful chemicals in downstream water, many of which are not yet recognized by clean water standards nor treated for by current water purification technologies. Thus by using wetlands, mining companies would be able both to internalize the costs of its own water pollution and to provide an enhanced level of water quality at the end of the process. Since the same companies cannot internalize the benefits of raising water quality above former standards, however, and since they do not bear the costs of pollution, they have no incentive to make use of wetlands in this way.

An additional problem derives from the short sightedness imposed on political systems by the frequently short length of elective office and the annual budgetary process. In many countries this creates a significant impediment to the funding of ecotechnological research from government sources. Yet profit maximizing firms, by their very nature, will not demand ecotechnological research unless adoption of ecotechnologies is encouraged via legislation and regulation. Therefore, the government must take an active role in fostering the diffusion and adoption of these technologies. This usually includes the use of ecotechnologies in the management of public lands and waters, economic mechanisms to encourage adoption by the private sector (subsidies, taxes and credits), and extension activities to demonstrate to the public the appropriate use of ecotechnologies in practical land and water management applications. The flexible assurance bond and environmental cost charging scheme suggested in this paper addresses these problems directly.

The construction and properties of a bond for innovative resource-based activities is discussed elsewhere in this journal (Perrings, 1989a). It is sufficient here to outline those of its characteristics which would lead to investment in ecotechnological research. These are the following:

(1) The size of the bond would depend on the conjectured value of the worst case losses due to the innovative parts of the activity. This indicates the value placed by the environmental authority on allowing the activity to proceed given the current state of knowledge about its wider and long-term effects. The higher this value, other things being equal, the less likely would be the prospects of the activity being undertaken without additional research.

(2) The bond would be sequentially determined to allow it to reflect changes in the experimental or historical data available on the external costs of the activity. Consequently, resource users would have a direct incentive to expand the resources committed to experimental research up to the point at which the marginal costs and marginal benefits of the research were equal; the marginal benefits of the research being the expected reduction in the value of the bond due to the last dollar of research expenditure.

A bond with these characteristics accordingly has a double function. Not only does it indemnify society against the potential user and intersectoral costs of the exploitation of environmental resources, it also provides an incentive to both the environmental authority and the resource user to commit additional resources to research activity, in proportion to the authority's conjecture as to the worst case losses arising out of the use of the resource. By presuming guilt until innocence is proven while allowing a reduction of the bond for improved performance, the economic incentive to reduce costs is brought to bear on the problem. Moreover, by enabling the firm to capture many of the benefits of a reduction in the marginal user or external costs of the activity, that incentive is reinforced. Assuring adequate compensation to ecotechnological innovators would further strengthen that incentive (the existing patent and licensing system probably provides an adequate mechanism for dealing with this problem). Once there are sufficient positive economic incentives for ecotechnological innovations, the system will begin to reward and support that kind of research.

SUMMARY AND CONCLUSIONS

Markets for environmental goods and services are far from perfect and we cannot rely on the unaided free market to allocate these resources efficiently. On the contrary, the existence of what we have referred to as social traps ensures that environmental resources will typically be misallocated due to the existence of external costs that are not paid for by the user. Escaping from such traps requires that we devise systems that will bring the private and social costs of environmental resource use into concordance, by confronting individual users with the marginal social cost of their activities. We accept that quantification of the environmental damage due to any given activity is extremely difficult (although considerable work on economic-ecological modelling has improved our prospects in this respect (cf. Braat and Van Lierop, 1987). To accommodate the informational difficulties involved, however, we recommend a system with two dominant features: that economic measures of environmental damage should be sensitive to informational flows throughout the period over which that damage is expected to occur; and that the burden of proof as to the magnitude of these damages should fall on the parties that stand to profit from them, not the general public.

We have indicated the outlines of a flexible environmental assurance bonding scheme that induces ecotechnological innovation by making it the most economically attractive option in the short run (as well as the long run). Such a scheme would have the benefits of being minimally intrusive into the internal operations of the regulated industries, while still ensuring that those industries are confronted with the marginal social cost of their activities (and the uncertainty about these costs) over the whole time period considered to be socially relevant. It would provide an economic incentive to the industries to unleash their technological innovativeness in order to minimize the environmental damage they currently cause. Firms that performed well in reducing environmental damage would be rewarded, firms that performed badly would be penalized. There would be a proportional relationship between the resources committed to environmental protection and the size of the environmental problem.

There are a number of features of the scheme still to be worked out. There are questions about both the appropriate techniques for the assessment of environmental damage, and the identification of such damage. There are, in particular, a set of questions relating to the link between environmental replacement/rehabilitation charges and sustainability. Since the user cost of activities that lead to the exhaustion of renewable and non-renewable resources alike includes the cost of backstop technology, are the infrastructural projects designed to facilitate that technology a legitimate charge on private users of the resources? There are questions about whether the system would impact on firms of different size differentially (and if it does should some compensatory mechanism be built in). There is also the awkward problem of technology transfer to be considered. It is not necessary to answer these questions before proceeding, however, since the proposed system is designed to be self-correcting as well as to provide both direct public funds to pursue these questions, and strong positive private incentives to encourage firms to pursue the research themselves.

Clearly, the system might be made to work most easily in the high income economies where environmental protection agencies have an established role in the regulation of polluting industries. But the problem of environmental damage is not unique to the North. Indeed, although the environmental effects of economic activities are often qualitatively different, environmental degradation has, as we have noted, been identified as the most severe of the current problems facing the low income economies. The realization of this is evidenced by the widespread search in the low income economies for workable National Conservation Strategies designed to allow the sustainable development of natural resource-based economies. It is, therefore, important to develop a scheme for environmental protection that will work well in as many cases as possible. The flexible assurance bonds discussed here are a step in that direction.

ACKNOWLEDGEMENTS

Partial funding was provided by the U.S. EPA, contract #CR-815393-01-0, S. Farber and R. Costanza, Principal Investigators, titled: A Flexible Environmental Cost Charging and Assurance Bonding System for Improved Environmental Management. This paper benefited greatly from discussions at the Vienna Center conference on Ecology and Economics held in Barcelona, Spain, September 1987. We thank H. Daly, S. Farber and three anonymous reviewers for their helpful comments on earlier drafts.

REFERENCES

Atkinson, S.E. and Lewis, D.H., 1974. A cost effectiveness analysis of alternative air quality control strategies. J. Environ. Econ. Manage., 1: 237–250.

Atkinson, S.E. and Lewis, D.H., 1976. Determination and implementation of optimal air quality standards. J. Environ. Econ. Manage., 3: 353–380.

Atkinson, S.E. and Tietenberg, T.H., 1982. The empirical properties of two classes of designs for transferrable discharge permit markets. J. Environ. Econ. Manage., 9: 101–121.

Binswanger, H.P. and Ruttan, V.W., 1978. Induced Innovation: Technology, Institutions, and Development. John Hopkins University Press, Baltimore, MD.

Braat, L.C. and Van Lierop, W.F.J. (Editors), 1987. Economic–Ecological Modeling. Amsterdam, North-Holland, 330 pp.

Clark, C.W., 1973. The economics of overexploitation. Science, 181: 630–634.

Clark, C.W., 1987. Fisheries as a renewable resource. In: L.C. Braat and W.F.J. van Lierop (Editors), Economic–Ecological Modeling. North-Holland, Amsterdam.

Costanza, R., 1987. Social traps and environmental policy. BioScience, 37: 407–412.

Cross, J.G. and Guyer, M.J., 1980. Social traps. University of Michigan Press, Ann Arbor, MI.

Edney, J.J. and Harper, C., 1978. The effects of information in a resource management problem: a social trap analog. Human Environ., 6: 387–395.

Ghai, D. and Radwan, S. (Editors), 1983. Agrarian policies and rural poverty in Africa. International Labor Organization, Geneva, 311 pp.

Hardin, G., 1968. The tragedy of the commons. Science, 162: 1243–1248.

Haveman, R.H., 1976. The Economics of the Public Sector. Wiley, New York.

Hyde, W.F., 1984. Timber valuation. In: G.L. Peterson and A. Randall (Editors), Valuation of Wildland Resource Benefits. Westview, Boulder, CO.

Katzner, D.W., 1988. The comparative statics of the Shackle–Vickers approach to decision-making in ignorance. In: T.B. Fomby and T.K. Seo (Editors), Studies in the Economics of Uncertainty: In Honour of Joseph Hadar. Springer, Berlin.

Kemp, M.V., Long, N.V. and Shimomura, K., 1984. The problem of survival: a closed economy. In: M.C. Kemp and N.V. Long (Editors), Essays in the Economics of Exhaustible Resources. North Holland, Amsterdam, pp. 13–26.

Kohlmeir, L.M., Jr., 1969. The Regulators: Watchdog Agencies and the Public Interest. Harper & Row, New York.

Mill, E.S., 1972. Urban Economics. Scott Foresman, Glenview, IL.

Pearce, D.W. and Markandya, A., 1987. Marginal opportunity cost as a planning concept in natural resource management. Ann. Reg. Sci., December.

Perrings, C.A., 1987. Economy and Environment: A Theoretical Essay on the Interdependence of Economic and Environmental Systems. Cambridge University Press, New York, 179 pp.

Perrings C.A., 1988. Debt and resource degradation in low income countries: the adjustment process and the perverse effects of poverty in Sub-Saharan Africa. In: H. Singer and S. Sharma, (Editors), Economic Development and World Debt. Macmillan, London.

Perrings, C.A., 1989a. Environmental bonds and environmental research in innovative activities. Ecol. Econ., 1: 95–115.

Perrings, C.A., 1989b. An optimal path to extinction? Poverty and resource degradation in the open agrarian economy. J. Dev. Econ., 30: 1–24.

Platt, J., 1973. Social traps. Am. Psychol., 28: 642–651.

Randall, A., 1986. Human preferences, economics, and the preservation of species. In: B.G. Norton (Editor). The Preservation of Species. Princeton University Press, Princeton, NJ.

Scott, A.D., 1955. The fishery: the objectives of sole ownership. J. Polit. Econ., 63: 116–124.

Seskin, E.P., Anderson, R.J., Jr. and Reid, R.O., 1983. An empirical analysis of economic strategies for controlling air pollution. J. Environ. Econ. Manage., 10: 112–124.

Solow, R.M., 1971. The economist's approach to pollution control. Science, 173: 498–503.

Stigler, G.J., 1971. The theory of economic regulation. Bell J. Econ. Manage. Sci., 2: 321–335.

Teger, A.I., 1980. Too Much Invested to Quit. Pergamon, New York.

Wade, R., 1987. The management of common property resources: Finding a cooperative solution. World Bank Research Observer, 2: 219–235.

World Commission on Environment and Development. 1987. Our Common Future. Oxford University Press, Oxford, 400 pp.

One often sees contradictory stories in the media from "reputable scientific sources" who claim, one day, that "Global warming will occur, and the results will be catastrophic unless something is done immediately," and, on another day, that "There is no direct evidence for global warming, and people should not waste money on something that may or may not happen." On yet another day, one hears that "Toxic chemical X causes cancer," followed on the next day by the statement that "Toxic chemical X occurs in too low a concentration in the environment to cause cancer." These seemingly contradictory statements from the scientific community send the social decisionmaking process into a tailspin. On the one hand, because scientists cannot agree on what is happening, should policymakers wait until better information is available before acting? On the other hand, if society fails to act, the situation may deteriorate rapidly and irreversibly. What are people to do in these all-too-common situations, and why has science failed to provide the certain and unbiased answers on which good policymaking depends? What is wrong with the link between science and policy, and how can it be improved? Is a different, nonregulatory approach needed for managing the environment?

There are several lines of thought in environmental science and economics about how to develop an effective approach to dealing with uncertainty. Two of the most renowned are the "precautionary principle," which has gained wide acceptance in international environmental circles, and the "polluter pays principle," which has long been advocated by environmental economists.[1] Although both of these principles have gained wide acceptance in theory, practical applications have been severely hampered. One criticism is that, "though the precautionary principle provides a useful overall orientation, it is an insufficient basis for policy and largely lacks legal content."[2] Large uncer-

ROBERT COSTANZA is director of the Maryland International Institute for Ecological Economics and a professor at the University of Maryland's Center for Environmental and Estuarine Studies in Solomons, Maryland. **LAURA CORNWELL** is a graduate research assistant at the institute and a policy analyst on the Regulatory Innovations Staff of the U.S. Environmental Protection Agency in Washington, D.C. The views and opinions expressed here are those of the authors and are not to be taken as official policy of the U.S. Environmental Protection Agency or of any other public or private entity.

tainties about ecological damages also have caused applications of the polluter pays principle to founder on questions of "how much" and "when." However, an environmental deposit-refund or assurance bonding system could shift the burden of proof, incorporate uncertainty into what the polluters pay for and when they pay it, and thus provide strong and effective economic incentives for both environmental precaution and technological innovation.

Scientific Uncertainty

One of the main reasons for the problems with current methods of environmental management is scientific uncertainty—not just its existence, but the radically different expectations and modes of operation that scientists and policymakers have developed to deal with it. To solve this problem, these differences must be exposed and understood, and better methods to incorporate uncertainty into policymaking and environmental management must be designed.

To understand the scope of the problem, it is necessary to differentiate between risk, which is an event with a known probability (sometimes referred to as statistical uncertainty), and true uncertainty, which is an event with an unknown probability (sometimes referred to as indeterminacy). For instance, every time you drive your car, you run the risk of having an accident because the probability of car accidents is known with very high certainty. The risk involved in driving is well known because there have been many car accidents with which to calculate the probabilities. These probabilities are known with enough certainty that they are used by insurance companies, for instance, to set rates that will assure those companies of a certain profit. There is little uncertainty about the possibility of car accidents. If you live near the disposal sight of some newly synthesized toxic chemical, however, your health may be in jeopardy, but no one knows to what extent. Because no one knows the probability of your getting cancer, for instance, or some other disease from this exposure, there is true uncertainty. Most important environmental problems suffer from true uncertainty, not merely risk.

Uncertainty may be thought of as a continuum ranging from zero for certain information to intermediate levels for information with statistical uncertainty and known probabilities (risk) to high levels for information with true uncertainty or indeterminacy. Risk assessment has become a central guiding principle at the U.S. Environmental Protection Agency (EPA) and other environmental management agencies,[3] but true uncertainty has yet to be adequately incorporated into environmental protection strategies.

Scientists treat uncertainty as a given, a characteristic of all information that must be honestly acknowledged and communicated. Over the years, scientists have developed increasingly sophisticated methods to measure and communicate uncertainty arising from various causes. In general, however, scientists have uncovered more uncertainty rather than the absolute precision that the lay public often mistakenly associates with scientific results. Scientific inquiry can only set boundaries on the limits of knowledge. It can define the edges of the envelope of known possibilities, but often the envelope is very large, and the probabilities of what's inside (the known possibilities) actually occurring can be a complete mystery. For instance, scientists can describe the range of uncertainty about global warming and toxic chemicals and maybe say something about the relative probabilities of different outcomes, but, in most important cases, they cannot say which of the possible outcomes will occur with any degree of accuracy.

Current approaches to environmental management and policymaking, however, avoid uncertainty and gravitate to the edges of the scientific envelope. The reasons for this bias are clear. Policymakers want to make unambiguous, defensible decisions, which are often codified into laws and regulations. Although legislative language is often open to interpretation, regulations are much easier to write and enforce if they are stated in absolutely certain terms. For most of criminal law, the system works reasonably well. Either Cain killed his brother or he did not; the only question is whether there is enough evidence to demonstrate guilt beyond a reasonable doubt (with essentially zero uncertainty). Because the burden of proof is on the prosecution, it does little good to conclude that there was an 80-percent chance that Cain killed his brother. But many scientific studies come to just these kinds of conclusions. Science defines the envelope while the policy process gravitates to an edge—usually the edge that best advances the policymaker's political agenda. But to use science rationally to make policy, the whole envelope and all of its contents must be dealt with.

The problem is most severe for environmental regulation. Building on the legal traditions of criminal law, policymakers and environmental regulators desire certain information when designing environmental regulations. But much of environmental policy is based on scientific studies of the likely health, safety, and ecological consequences of human actions. Information gained from these studies is therefore only certain within the studies' epistemological and methodological limits.[4] Regulators are increasingly confronted with decision-making outside the limits of scientific certainty, particularly with the recent shift in environmental concerns from visible, known pollution to more subtle threats, such as radon.[5]

Problems arise when regulators ask scientists for answers to unanswerable questions. For example, the law may mandate that the regulatory agency devise safety standards for all known toxins when little or no information is available on the impacts of these chemicals. When trying to enforce the regulations after they are drafted, governments confront the problem of true uncertainty about the impacts. It is usually impossible to determine with any certainty if the local chemical company contributed to the death of some of the people in the vicinity of its toxic waste dump. Similarly, one cannot prove the connection between smoking and lung cancer in any direct, causal way, at least in the legal sense, but only as a statistical relationship. And of course, global warming may or may not happen after all.

Most environmental regulations, particularly those in the United States, demand certainty. When scientists are pressured to supply this nonexistent commodity, there is not only frustration and poor communication but also mixed messages in the media. Because of uncertainty, environmental issues are often manipulated by political and economic interest groups. Uncertainty about global warming is perhaps the most visible current example of this phenomenon.

The precautionary principle describes one theory of how the environmental regulatory community should deal with the problem of true uncertainty. The principle states that, rather than await certainty, regulators should act in anticipation of any potential environmental harm to prevent it. The precautionary principle is so frequently invoked in international environmental resolutions that it has come to be seen by some as a basic normative principle of international environmental law.[6] But the principle offers no guidance as to what precautionary measures should be taken. It "implies the commitment of resources now to safeguard against the potentially adverse future outcomes of some decision"[7] but does not say how many resources should be committed or which adverse future outcomes are most important.

Yet the size of the stakes is a primary determinant of how uncertainty is dealt with in the political arena. Normal applied science applies only under circumstances of low uncertainty and low stakes. Higher uncertainty or higher stakes result in a much more politicized decisionmaking environment. Moderate uncertainty or stakes correspond to "applied engineering" and "professional consultancy," which allow a good measure of judgment and opinion to deal with risk. Currently, however, there is no way to deal with either high stakes or high uncertainty, which require a new approach that could be called "post-normal" or "second-order" science.[8] This "new" science is really just the application of the essence of the scientific method to new territory. The scientific method does not, in its basic form, imply anything about the precision of the results achieved. It does, however, imply a forum of free inquiry, without preconceived answers or agendas, aimed at determining the envelope of knowledge and the magnitude of ignorance.

Implementing second-order science requires a new approach to environmental protection, one that acknowledges the existence of true uncertainty rather than denying it and includes mechanisms to safeguard against potentially harmful effects but, at the same time, encourages the development of low-impact technologies and the reduction of uncertainty about impacts. The precautionary principle sets the stage for this approach, but the real challenge is to develop scientific methods to determine the potential costs of uncertainty and to adjust incentives so that the appropriate parties pay this cost of uncertainty and have appropriate incentives to reduce its detrimental effects. Without this adjustment, the full costs of environmental damage will continue to be left out of the accounting,[9] and the hidden subsidies from society to those who profit from environmental degradation will continue to provide strong incentives to degrade the environment beyond sustainable levels.

Dealing with Uncertainty

How should scientists and policymakers deal with the enormous uncertainty inherent in environmental issues? First, uncertainty should be accepted as a basic component of environmental decisionmaking at all levels and be better communicated. But environmental management should also change, and understanding of the link between ecological and economic systems must grow. Thus, economic and other incentives could be used more efficiently and effectively to achieve environmental goals.

The effort to integrate ecology and

economics to improve environmental and economic management and to ensure long-term sustainability has become focused in the transdisciplinary field of ecological economics.[10] This new field promises to permit a deeper understanding of the ecological functions and values that the precautionary principle is intended to protect and the development of more efficient and effective mechanisms to implement the principle. One goal of ecological economics is to estimate the long-term social and ecological costs and benefits of various human activities for comparison with the private short-term costs and benefits that are too often the only consideration in decisionmaking. To do this, the field must develop methods for the valuation of ecological damage based on a second-order scientific understanding of the functioning of linked ecological economic systems at several temporal and spatial scales. This understanding involves developing a description of the envelope of knowledge and the boundaries of ignorance about these interactions. For the purposes of pricing ecological functions and values for use with the precautionary principle, the edge of this envelope that describes the worst-case scenario, as far as ecological impacts are concerned, is the one of primary interest. Research focused on the "worst edge" should lead to much more effective use of science in anticipating and heading off problems.

For example, were worst-edge research the norm, scientists could easily have anticipated the greenhouse effect and taken steps to minimize its potential impacts. Indeed, the effect and humanity's potential impact on it were first described almost 100 years ago,[11] but it remained a scientific curiosity until the 1980s, when enough data and models had been assembled to demonstrate that the effect was, in fact, likely to cause global warming. There is still much uncertainty about the magnitude of the warming and especially about its ultimate impacts, but science can do a very good job of anticipating potential problems if it focuses on that function rather than on demonstrating impacts that have already occurred. Current research should therefore focus on the worst edge of climatic and economic impacts that might result from releases of greenhouse gases, as well as on the range of uncertainty about these impacts and on ways to reduce the uncertainty.

Over the past two decades, there has been extensive discussion about the efficiency that theoretically can be achieved in environmental management through the use of market mechanisms.[12] These mechanisms are designed to alter the pricing structure of the present market system to incorporate the long-term social and ecological costs of an economic agent's activities. Suggested incentive-based mechanisms include pollution taxes, tradable pollution-discharge permits, financial responsibility requirements, and deposit-refund systems (see "Dealing with Pollution: Market-Based Incentives for Environmental Protection" in the September 1992 issue). Some new versions of these incentive-based alternatives should help policymakers deal in a precautionary way with the pervasive uncertainty inherent in environmental problems.

An innovative incentive-based instrument currently being researched to manage the environment for precaution under uncertainty is called a flexible environmental assurance bonding system.[13] This variation of the deposit-refund system is designed to incorporate both known and uncertain environmental costs into the incentive system and to induce positive environmental technological innovation. It works by charging an economic agent directly for known environmental damages and levying an assurance bond equal to the current best estimate of the largest potential future environmental damages. The bond would be kept in an interest-bearing escrow account for a predetermined length of time. In keeping with the precautionary principle, this system requires a commitment of resources up front to offset the potentially catastrophic future effects of current activity. Portions of the bond (plus interest) would be returned if and when the agent could demonstrate that the suspected worst-case damages had not occurred or would be less than was originally assessed. If damages did occur, portions of the bond would be used to rehabilitate or repair the environment and possibly to compensate injured parties. Funds tied up in bonds could still be used for other economic activities. The only cost would be the difference (plus or minus) between the interest on the bond and the return that could be earned by the business had it invested in other activities. On average, this difference would be minimal. In addition, the "forced savings" that the bond would require could actually improve overall economic performance in economies like that of the United States that chronically undersave.

By requiring the users of environmental resources to post a bond adequate to cover uncertain future environmental damages (with the possibility for refunds), the burden of proof and the cost of the uncertainty are shifted from the public to the resource user. At the same time, agents are not charged in any final way for uncertain future damages and can recover portions of their bond (with interest) in proportion to how much better their environmental performance is than the predicted worst-case scenario.

Deposit-refund systems are not a new concept; they have been successfully applied to a range of consumer, conservation, and environmental policy objectives.[14] The most well-known examples are the systems for beverage containers and used lubricating oils that have proven to be quite effective and efficient.

Another precedent for environmental assurance bonds are the producer-paid performance bonds often required for federal, state, or local government construction work. For example, the Miller Act (40 U.S.C. 270), a 1935 federal statute, requires contractors performing construction work for the federal government to secure performance bonds. Performance bonds provide a contractual guarantee that the principal (the entity that is doing the work or providing the service) will perform in a designated way. Bonds are frequently required for construction work done in the private sector as well.

Performance bonds are frequently posted in the form of corporate surety bonds. Surety companies, which cosign these bonds, are licensed under various insurance laws and, under their charter, have legal authority to act as a financial guarantee for those posting the bond. The unrecoverable cost of this service is usually from one to five percent of the bond amount. However, under the Miller Act, any contract above a designated amount ($25,000 in the case of construction) can be backed by other types of securities, such as U.S. bonds or notes, in lieu of a bond guaranteed by a surety company. In this case, the contractor provides a duly executed power of attorney and an agreement authorizing collection on the bond or notes if the contractor defaults on the contract.[15] If the contractor performs all of the obligations specified in the contract, the securities are returned to the contractor, and the usual cost of the surety is avoided.

Environmental assurance bonds would work in a similar manner, by providing a contractual guarantee that the principal would perform in an environmentally benign manner, but would be levied according to the best estimate of the largest potential future environmental damages. Funds in the bond would be invested and would produce interest that could be returned to the principal. An "environmentally benign" investment strategy would probably be most appropriate for such a bond.

These bonds could be administered by the regulatory authority that currently manages the operation or procedure. In the United States, for example, the EPA could be the primary authority. But a case can be made that it would be better to set up a completely independent agency to administer the bonds. Of course, the design of the administering agency is worthy of considerable additional thought and analysis and would depend on the details of the particular situation.

The bond would be held until some or all of the uncertainty was removed. This would provide a strong incentive for principals to reduce the uncertainty about their environmental impacts as quickly as possible, either by funding independent research or by changing their processes to ones that are less damaging. The establishment of a quasi-judicial body would be necessary to resolve disputes about when and how much of the bonds should be refunded. This body would use the latest independent scientific information on the worst-case ecological damages that could result from a business's activities, but the burden of proof would fall on the economic agent that stands to gain from the activity, not on the public. EPA already has a protocol for worst-case analysis. In 1977, the U.S. Council on Environmental Quality required worst-case analysis for implementing the National Environmental Policy Act of 1969. This requirement forced EPA to consider the worst environmental consequences of an action when scientific uncertainty was involved.[16]

One potential argument against the bond is that it would favor relatively large businesses that could afford to handle the financial responsibility of activities that are potentially hazardous to the environment. This is true, but it is exactly the desired effect, because businesses that cannot handle the financial responsibility should not be passing the cost of potential environmental damage on to the public. In the construction industry, the use of performance bonds would prevent small fly-by-night businesses from cutting corners and endangering the public to underbid responsible businesses.

This is not to say that small businesses would be eliminated; far from it. They could either band together to form associations to handle the financial responsibility for environmentally risky activities, or, preferably, they could change to more environmentally benign activities that did not require large assurance bonds. This encouragement of the development of new, environmentally benign technologies is one of the main attractions of the bonding system, and small, start-up businesses would certainly lead the way.

Applying the "4P" Approach

Strong economic incentives would be provided by the proposed environmental assurance bond to reduce pollution, to research the true costs of environmentally damaging activities, and to develop innovative, cost-effective pollution control technologies. The bonding system extends the polluter pays principle to make the polluter pay for uncertainty as well. Thus is born the "precautionary polluter pays principle" (4P), which would allow a much more proactive approach to environmental problems because the bond would be paid up front, before the damage is done. By unleashing the creative resources of businesses, 4P would foster pollution prevention and the development of new, cleaner technologies (rather than merely cleanup). Because these technologies would be economically attractive in the short run, competition in the marketplace would lead to environmental improvement rather than degradation. The 4P approach would deal more appropriately with scientific uncertainty than do the current command-and-control systems.

The 4P approach has several potential applications. Three of them—growth management, toxic chemicals, and global warming—are high-stakes, high-uncertainty problems for which effective management mechanisms do not currently exist.

Traditional approaches to growth management have centered on zoning and other forms of land-use restrictions. Although the results of planning and zoning are better than totally uncontrolled growth, the approach leaves much to be desired, and one can certainly argue that most planning and zoning have not improved environmental conditions. 4P suggests a flexible impact bond system in addition to regional planning. A developer would post an initial impact bond that is large enough to cover the worst-case environmental and economic impacts of the proposed development. The developer would be refunded portions of the bond to the extent that the possible impacts did not occur. Innovative developers who designed projects with lower environmental impacts would be directly rewarded by refunds of their impact bonds. Developers who defaulted on their bonds would do poorly in economic competition with their more innovative competitors, and their bonds would be used to pay for whatever impacts they caused. Impact fees have been tried before, but, in most cases, they have been flat, inflexible, one-time fees that offered no incentive to developers to produce anything but the standard fare. They also generally covered only a small fraction of the real impacts of the development. A flexible impact bonding system would solve these problems and help manage growth in a rational yet flexible way, without taking the right to develop away but merely imposing the true costs of that growth on the parties that stand to gain from it while providing strong economic incentives for them to reduce their impacts to a minimum.

Another particularly difficult environmental management problem is the control of toxic chemicals from both point sources, such as factories, and nonpoint sources, such as agricultural and urban areas. Toxic chemicals can be damaging to ecosystems and human health in extremely low concentrations, and there is enormous uncertainty about their cumulative and individual impacts. The standard management approach is to develop lists of toxic chemicals and standards for their allowable concentrations in the environment. But because the list is so long (there are thousands of such chemicals in common use) and there is so much uncertainty about setting safe standards—as well as about who is producing and releasing what quantities of which chemicals and how the chemicals interact once they come in contact in the environment—this approach has not been very effective.

4P suggests a flexible toxic chemical bonding system. The bond would be sized according to the best current estimates of the worst-case damages from the release of the chemicals. Refunds would be based on the extent to which each potential polluter performed better than the worst case. This system would give polluters strong incentives to reduce their releases through recycling and more efficient use. Farmers could no longer afford to overuse agricultural chemicals just to be sure they were killing all pests. Industries could no longer afford to release new chemicals with poorly known impacts into the environment. Individual home owners would pay a high price for using potentially dangerous chemicals on their lawns and would be forced to find more environmentally benign alternatives, which, under the bonding system, would be relatively cheaper. This system would be designed to complement other regulatory schemes; would be self-policing and self-funding; and would provide strong incentives to correct environmental problems for which there are few good management alternatives.

Finally, the problem of global warming is probably the most severe current example of a high-stakes, high-uncertainty problem. A tax on carbon dioxide emissions has been proposed as an economic incentive to lessen this problem, but current ideas about the tax do not account for uncertainty. The 4P approach suggests that a bond for carbon dioxide emissions, with the size of the bond based on worst-case estimates of the magnitude of future damages, would work better than a tax, whose size would be based on much more uncertain estimates of what levels of emissions will not produce long-term problems. In this way, the efficiency advantages of economic incentives can be reaped without unduly penalizing current economic agents for the costs of unknown future damages.

There are several other potential applications of 4P. Any situation with large true uncertainty is a likely candidate, and these situations abound in today's world. To deal with these situations, scientific understanding must grow, and approaches to environmental management must change accordingly. Scientists can only define the envelope of ignorance. Given that envelope, policymakers should plan for the worst while providing incentives for firms to produce the best.

The administrative details of how 4P would function for the various specific applications need to be worked out. These details are critical to the success of the proposal and should be given careful consideration. Several well-intentioned performance bonding systems have failed because of simple oversights in their implementation. For example, mine reclamation bonds have, in some cases, been set so low that it was cheaper for the mining companies to default than to reclaim the site. The bond must be large enough to cover the worst-case damages so that such malfunctions do not occur. Of course, 4P is not a general panacea that can completely replace the existing regulatory system. The bonding system is best thought of as a complement to management schemes of regulations and incentives that is better suited to handle those situations where uncertainty is high.

Which situations are most appropriate for a 4P approach and the administrative details of the particular applications can most effectively be determined through mediated policy dialogues involving all of the stakeholders affected by the system under consideration, including the environmental, business, regulatory, and scientific communities. Mediated policy dialogue techniques involve the use of impartial third parties in structured meetings to bring together people with different views and find areas of consensus.[17] Such dialogues are currently being planned by the Maryland International Institute for Ecological Economics in collaboration with EPA and other agencies to develop detailed protocols and administrative procedures for pilot studies of the 4P approach. Experimental work is also under way to elucidate the underlying incentive structures in 4P and to help in their effective design and use.[18]

Political Feasibility

The individual elements of the 4P approach have broad theoretical support and have been implemented previously in various forms. The precautionary principle is gaining wide acceptance in many areas where true uncertainty is important. Incentive-based environmental regulation schemes are also gaining acceptance as more efficient ways to achieve environmental goals. For example, the 1990 amendments to the U.S. Clean Air Act contain a tradable permit system for controlling air pollution. Both the precautionary and the polluter pays principles are also incorporated in the final resolutions of the 1992 United Nations Conference on Environment and Development.[19] By linking these two important principles, policymakers can begin to deal effectively with uncertainty in an economically efficient and ecologically sustainable way.

In a sense, the 4P approach is already becoming a reality. As strict liability for environmental damages becomes more the norm, far-sighted businesses have already started to protect themselves against possible future lawsuits and damage claims by setting aside funds. The 4P approach is, in effect, a requirement that businesses be far-sighted, and it is an improvement on strict liability because it

- explicitly moves the costs to the present, where they will have the

(continued on page 42)

Dealing with Uncertainty

(continued from page 20)

maximum impact on decisionmaking;[20]

- provides edge-focused, second-order scientific assessments of the potential impacts from a comprehensive ecological economic perspective to ensure that the size of the bond is large enough to cover the worst-case damages; and
- insures that funds are used appropriately in case of a partial or complete default.

Because of its logic, fairness, and efficiency and its ability to implement the precautionary and polluter pays principles in a practical way and to use legal and financial mechanisms with long and successful precedents, the 4P approach promises to be both practical and politically feasible. It could do much to help head off the current environmental crisis before it is too late.

ACKNOWLEDGMENTS

Partial funding was provided by the U.S. Environmental Protection Agency under contract no. CR-815393-01-0, S. Farber and R. Costanza, principal investigators, entitled: "A Flexible Environmental Cost Charging and Assurance Bonding System for Improved Environmental Management." The authors wish to thank T. O'Riordan, S. Funtowicz, J. R. Ravetz, J. Bartholomew, R. Kashmanian, and J. Barnes for their helpful comments on earlier drafts.

NOTES

1. See D. Bodansky, "Scientific Uncertainty and the Precautionary Principle," *Environment*, September 1991, 4; and W. J. Baumol and W. E. Oates, *The Theory of Environmental Policy*, 2d ed. (Cambridge, England: Cambridge University Press, 1988); L. J. MacDonnell, "Natural Resources Dispute Resolution: An Overview," *Natural Resources Journal* 28 (1988):5–19; C. D. Kolstad, "Empirical Properties of Economic Incentives and Command-and-Control Regulations for Air Pollution Control," *Land Economics* 62 (1986):250–68; and T. O'Riordan and R. K. Turner, "Pollution Control and Recession," *Marine Pollution Bulletin* 15 (1984):5–11.

2. D. Bodansky, "Commentary: The Precautionary Principle," *Environment*, April 1992, 4.

3. Science Advisory Board, "Reducing Risk: Setting Priorities and Strategies for Environmental Protection," SAB-EC-90-021 (Washington, D.C.: U.S. EPA, 1990).

4. P. B. Thompson, "Uncertainty Arguments in Environmental Issues," *Environmental Ethics* 8 (1986):59–76.

5. A. M. Weinberg, "Science and Its Limits: The Regulator's Dilemma," *Issues in Science and Technology* 2 (1985):59–73.

6. J. Cameron and J. Abouchar, "The Precautionary Principle: A Fundamental Principle of Law and Policy for the Protection of the Global Environment," *Boston College International and Comparative Law Review* 14 (1991):1–27.

7. C. Perrings, "Reserved Rationality and the Precautionary Principle: Technological Change, Time and Uncertainty in Environmental Decision Making," in R. Costanza ed., *Ecological Economics: The Science and Management of Sustainability* (New York: Columbia University Press, 1991), 153–66.

8. S. O. Funtowicz and J. R. Ravetz, "A New Scientific Methodolgy for Global Environmental Problems," in R. Costanza, ed., pages 137–52, note 7 above.

9. H. M. Peskin, "Alternative Environmental and Resource Accounting Approaches," in R. Costanza, ed., pages 176–93, note 7 above.

10. Costanza, ed., note 7 above.

11. S. Arhaneus, "On the Influence of Carbonic Acid in the Air upon the Temperature of the Ground," *Philosophical Magazine and Journal of Science* 41 (1896):227–37.

12. G. L. Brady and R. D. Cunningham, "The Economics of Pollution Control in the U.S." *Ambio* 10 (1981):171–75; and M. L. Cropper and W. E. Oates, "Environmental Economics: A Survey," *Journal of Economic Literature* 30 (1992):675–740.

13. R. Costanza and C. Perrings, "A Flexible Assurance Bonding System for Improved Environmental Management," *Ecological Economics* 2 (1990):57–76.

14. P. Bohm, *Deposit-Refund Systems* (Baltimore, Md.: The Johns Hopkins University Press, 1981).

15. PRC Environmental Management, *Performance Bonding: A Final Report Prepared for the U.S. Environmental Protection Agency* (Washington, D.C.: U.S. EPA Office of Waste Programs and Enforcement, 1986).

16. V. M. Fogleman, "Worst Case Analysis: A Continued Requirement Under the National Environmental Policy Act?" *Columbia Journal of Environmental Law* 13 (1987):53.

17. G. Bingham, *Resolving Environmental Disputes: A Decade of Experience* (Washington, D.C.: The Conservation Foundation, 1986).

18. R. Costanza and L. Cornwell, "An Experimental Analysis of the Effectiveness of an Environmental Assurance Bonding System on Player Behavior in a Simulated Firm" (Washington, D.C.: U.S. EPA Office of Policy, Planning and Evaluation, 1991).

19. UN Environment Programme, "Agenda 21," draft (New York: United Nations, 1992).

20. Several studies of "social traps" have shown that the timing of information about costs is more important than the actual expected magnitude. See, for example, R. Costanza and W. Shrum, "The Effects of Taxation on Moderating the Conflict Escalation Process: An Experiment Using the Dollar Auction Game," *Social Science Quarterly* 69 (1988):416–32; R. Costanza, "Social Traps and Environmental Policy," *BioScience* 37 (1987):407–12; J. Platt, "Social Traps," *American Psychologist* 28 (1973):642–51; J. G. Cross and M. J. Guyer, *Social Traps* (Ann Arbor, Mich.: University of Michigan Press, 1980); A. I. Teger, *Too Much Invested to Quit* (New York: Pergamon, 1980); and J. Brockner and J. Z. Rubin, *Entrapment in Escalating Conflicts: A Social Psychological Analysis* (New York: Springer-Verlag, 1985).

[28]

The Chesapeake Bay and Its Watershed: A Model for Sustainable Ecosystem Management?

Robert Costanza and Jack Greer

The Chesapeake Bay is the largest estuary in North America and has been the subject of more scientific study and political wrangling than any other body of coastal water in the world. It has become clear that what happens in the bay is in large part a function of activities in the drainage basin, but the focus of most past studies has been narrow. We are only now beginning to develop a comprehensive picture of the bay and of its connections to a sprawling and often densely populated watershed—not only in ecological, but also in demographic, cultural, political, and economic terms.

In this chapter we first develop a historical and spatial perspective of human activities in the Chesapeake Bay watershed. Fundamental in gaining this perspective is conceptualizing the Chesapeake Bay watershed system as the combination of the drainage basin and the estuary itself. We have assembled and mapped past and present human activities in the Chesapeake watershed in order to gain this perspective.

The Chesapeake watershed comprises an ecological system whose beauty and productivity have led to high rates of human population growth and settlement. These high population growth rates have in turn, directly and indirectly, caused a troublesome infirmity, including declining fisheries, receding wetlands, vanishing seagrasses, and a devastated oyster industry. These trends have also led to a decline in the quality of human life. Traffic congestion, disappearing natural and agricultural areas, swelling landfills, and overtaxed water treatment facilities have all affected the tenor of life in the bay region. This chapter addresses the larger-scale terrestrial trends within the entire watershed that have produced such consequences, the barriers to effective environmental management capable of reversing these effects, and the bridges necessary to overcome those barriers.

In many ways efforts to manage the Chesapeake can be viewed as a "best-case scenario" for ecosystem management. Relatively early and widespread recognition of the bay's decline, combined with significant scientific analyses detailing both causes and solutions, helped lead to a broad consensus for remedial action. These aspects of the bay's management may serve as models for other areas, but one should also realize that significant barriers to implementation of the restoration strategy remain. These barriers include the absence of realistic, comprehensive, long-term goals for managing complex ecological and economic systems, the lack of systems for translating these goals into local incentives that can adequately change and guide human behavior, and the built-in but misplaced arrogance about our level of understanding the system.

Bridges that could help surmount such barriers include developing and applying (1) more realistic models of the ways ecosystems function, (2) more realistic acknowledgment of the severe limits of our knowledge, and (3) incentive systems that can translate this understanding (and especially the limits and uncertainty of this understanding) into local decision making.

A Summary of the Problem

Because of the special characteristics of the Chesapeake Bay and its watershed, it is, at one and the same time, extremely productive, unpredictable, resilient, sensitive to stress, and hard to understand and manage with traditional methods.

It is productive because it is a broad, shallow, large estuary where fresh water and nutrients running off a large watershed interact with seawater in very complex and unpredictable patterns. Its shallowness means nutrients are recycled easily and constantly, maintaining its high productivity. Its large watershed means that ample nutrients entered the system even before European settlers converted so much of the watershed to farms, towns, and cities. Because of its large and habitable watershed and its nutrient-rich waters, the bay from the beginning attracted many settlers, but, ironically, it also proved sensitive to the further addition of nutrients that settlement caused. In a further irony, because the bay has, for most of the last 300 years, remained a completely open-access resource, its tremendous productivity has been tragically overused and abused. Because of its complexity and unpredictability, the bay remains a relatively resilient ecosystem, and if we can devise ways to manage its use more intelligently and equitably, as well as a means of reducing the stresses we put on it, the estuary should recover and remain resilient and productive for a long time to come.

We can only do this by first understanding the history and current status of the bay and its watershed as an integrated system. This system involves interactions between various natural components between humans and the unique ecological life support mechanisms the bay provides. Clearly, we also need to develop a better understanding of human institutions—how they typically fail when dealing with resources like the Chesapeake and how we can fix them or perhaps replace them with more effective alternatives.

The Chesapeake Bay and Its Watershed

The early European settlers who arrived on the shores of the Chesapeake Bay came looking for a better life. Whether they came to Jamestown or Williamsburg in Virginia, or to St. Marys or Londontowne in Maryland, the Chesapeake Bay represented for them a new kind of promised land.

Settlers came to begin a new enterprise, and ultimately they founded a new nation. Even the Native Americans who greeted them had come from somewhere else, crossing a land bridge (where Alaska once touched Asia) many centuries before. But these Native Americans had preserved a lifestyle that had not taken a great toll on the natural environment or the countryside. They took oysters but did not destroy the oyster beds. They used logs for canoes but did not clear-cut the forests. The settlers who came from Europe, Africa, and Asia would have a much greater impact on the forests, streams, and rivers as they created what was to become a new country.

That new country often traced its beginnings to land grants from the kings of Europe, the undisputed powers of their day—land grants by the kings of England to such men as Lord Baltimore. Clearly, the country also had its origins in commerce, with the backing of businesses such as the Virginia Company (the equivalent of today's large international corporations, such as Exxon or Toyota). But the life the settlers made for themselves profited not so much from their European backing as from the riches of the land they had found.

Whereas explorers farther south often exploited gold from ancient South American cultures, the colonists of the Chesapeake Bay region found another kind of wealth: teeming schools of fish, hardwood forests, fertile soil, wild game. The riches of the Chesapeake were the riches of nature, and as the centuries passed, the bay region, with its large farms and plantations, became known as the "Land of Pleasant Living."

Of course living in this colonial milieu was not pleasant for all the people all the time. Indentured servants labored for years to gain their freedom. Slaves labored for a lifetime, and many were never free. War came to the Chesapeake region more than once, as Native Americans fought the settlers and slaves revolted against their masters. But the great wars were fought between the settlers and their European forebears and then finally among the settlers themselves.

As the nation suffered its pangs of growth and transition, the Chesapeake watershed repeatedly became a scene of bloodshed. The Revolutionary War's final campaign took place in the bay region, with the surrender of the British general Cornwallis at Yorktown on the shores of the York River. The War of 1812 saw the British return to the bay, with warships guarding its entrance and raiding parties making their way up bay rivers to attack cities—to burn Washington and Baltimore. A Baltimore lawyer by the name of Francis Scott Key watched the attack on his city and wrote a poem that eventually became "The Star-Spangled Banner."

The bloodiest battle of this nation's bloodiest war was fought in the Chesapeake watershed, along the edges of Antietam Creek. In the Battle of Antietam more than 24,000 Americans died, more than in any other battle, in any other war.

Through all this the Chesapeake Bay continued to provide. People took its productivity for granted, like the air or the rain, but changes were taking place in the Chesapeake, and the impacts of settlement began to be felt. The Chesapeake changed slowly at first, but it would never be the same.

Evolution of the Bay and Its Watershed

While humans were writing their own history of hardship and prosperity, war and peace, the Chesapeake Bay was evolving according to a history of its own. The bay's history is first and foremost geologic. Without the geologic and climatic rhythms of the earth—the shifting of the continents, the spread and retreat of glaciers—the bay would not have existed at all. As J. R. Schubel has pointed out, we should remember that the Chesapeake Bay we see today is only one of many that have come and gone over long geological epochs, growing and shrinking with the rise and fall of the sea (Schubel 1981, 1986).

The Chesapeake Bay we see today is a mosaic of estuaries that, taken together, comprise the largest single estuary in the United States. The bay is 193 miles long, is 3–25 miles wide, and with its tidal tributaries covers an area of 4400 mi^2, with some 8100 miles of shoreline (Tippie 1984). The drainage basins that feed it contain 64,000 mi^2 in six states, and three major cities lie on the banks of its tidal system (figure 4.1). Because of its size and location in temperate North America, the Chesapeake watershed represents an ecosystem of enormous historical, political, and economic significance.

This system formed when rising Atlantic waters drowned and eroded the mouths of the rivers that feed it. The Chesapeake Bay we see today began about 10,000 years ago when glaciers that had advanced as far south as present-day New York City finally began to recede.

For 90% of the recent geologic past, the sea has remained in a well-defined basin, with a sharp dropoff at the continental edge. But with the beginning of the Holocene Epoch, the glaciers melted and the sea rose. The overflowing sea covered the edge of the ancient oceanic basin, flooding the long, flat shoreline under a shallow sheet of water. That prehistoric shoreline, now covered with seawater, constitutes the continental shelf, an ecosystem whose physical and biological interconnections with estuaries like the Chesapeake Bay remain only partially understood.

The continental shelf in some ways represents an oceanic extension of the estuaries and coastal embayments of North America's east coast. Though covered by open ocean, the area is surprisingly shallow and flat. A vessel sailing from the Chesapeake Bay would find its depthfinder reading only about 40 ft or so—for 50 miles out to sea. At that point, the depthfinder would drop to more than 100 ft, but soon it would stop reading altogether because the vessel would have passed over the edge

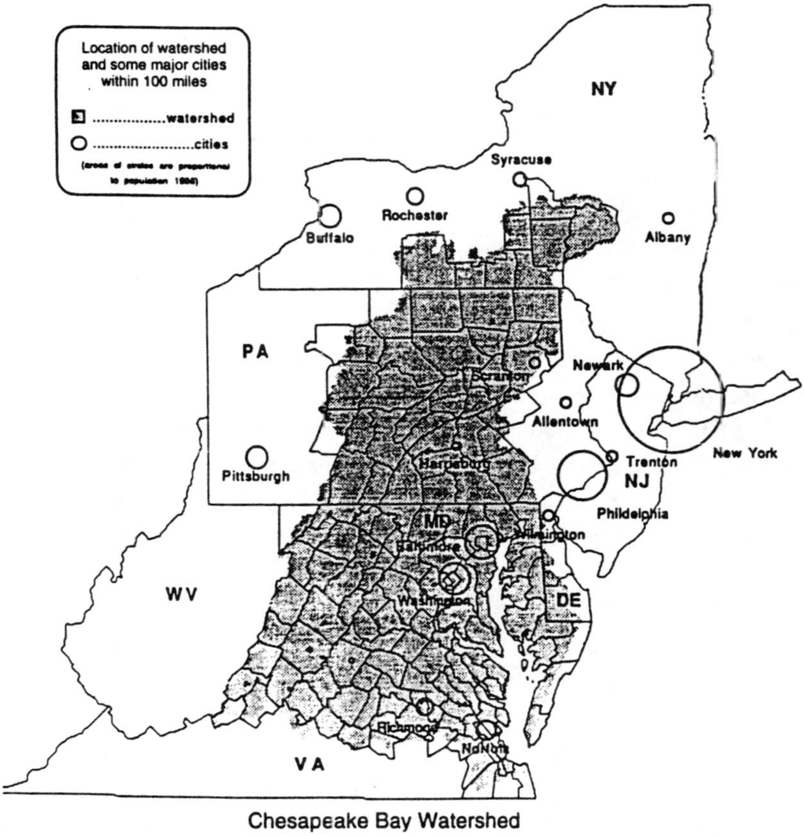

FIGURE 4.1
Map of the Chesapeake Bay Watershed.

of a great cliff, the perimeter of the oceanic basin. If the depthfinder's signal could reach that far, its numbers would rise rapidly to more than 1000 ft, then 2000, then 3000. About a 120 miles out of the bay, off the Virginia capes, the boat would be beyond the continental shelf, past the slope, and over the ancient sea bottom. The depth finder, if it could read that far, would say 9000 ft.

In the Chesapeake Bay the patterns are the same, even if the depths are much less. The Chesapeake, taken as a whole, is a *very* shallow body of water, with an average depth of less than 10 m. Many of its tidal flats may be only a few feet deep. Its deepest waters, 100 ft or more, follow an ancient channel carved by the river that once formed the liquid backbone of the bay, the Susquehanna. The Susquehanna, like the bay's other major tributaries—the Potomac, the Patuxent, the Rappahannock, the York, the James—still plays a significant role in the health and well-being of the estuary because of its capacity to deliver not only fresh water, but also nutrients, sediments, and toxic compounds to the bay.

The Susquehanna River, one of the longest in North America, begins in New York State and wends its way through Pennsylvania. Once it continued straight to the sea, emptying into the ocean basin at a point that is now well off the coast. Now the sea has come to meet it, rising and backfilling into Virginia past Norfolk, past Reedville, into Maryland past the Potomac, past the Patapsco. Tidal waters now reach as far north as Havre de Grace, where they flood a broad area only a foot or two deep called the Susquehanna Flats.

Though ocean waters have inundated the mouths of bay rivers for 10,000 years, the tributaries still exhibit very direct impacts on the estuary. Much of that impact is natural and desirable: the delivery of nutrients and the mixing of fresh river water with saline water from the sea. This natural mixing bowl has created a fertile feeding ground and nursery ground for fish and shellfish, such as the American oyster, *Crassostrea virginica,* a resource now facing catastrophic decline. It seems remarkable that a system that developed over the span of 10,000 years could change in a matter of a few centuries, perhaps even a few decades, as a consequence of the settlers that came to its shores. To understand the nature of this change, we must consider the different uses humans have made of the bay over the years and some of the problems that resulted from those uses.

Principal Uses—and Problems—of the Chesapeake Bay

As a Waterway

The settlers first used the bay to get off the ocean. According to historical writer Donald Shomette, the Spanish came even before the British, during the sixteenth century, and called the Chesapeake the Bahia Santa Maria. Regardless of nationality, the safe harbors of the Chesapeake clearly represented a boon to seafarers, particularly during an age when crossing the Atlantic in wooden ships was risky and, as Shomette and others have documented, too often disastrous.

Those who arrived safely could ply the relatively protected waters of the bay inland to the north and west, into the heavily wooded coastal plain. Even after founding settlements and towns, settlers continued to hold to the bay as their principal connection with the Old World, their supply line, and their chance for trade and commerce. The bay has continued as a major waterway to the present day, with ocean-going ships calling at Baltimore and Norfolk, which rank among the nation's busiest ports.

From the beginning, ships on the bay have probably caused some pollution: raw sewage, garbage dumped overboard, and river bottoms disturbed and sediment stirred up by anchors. But these impacts were quite small—until modern times. Garbage from an old square-rigger is one thing; flushing the oily bilges of a 500-foot freighter is something else. And while the colonial period may have seen a few watermen fishing or hunting for oysters and perhaps a few hearty souls rowing about for recreation, today the bay has become home to hundreds of thousands of recreational boats and thousands of watermen when the catch is good. And these modern boats rarely drift silently with the wind. Many of them have powerful engines and throw substantial wakes that beat against the shoreline and further erode the banks of rivers and creeks. These modern craft also use petroleum products—gasoline, diesel fuel, oil—that may find their way into the estuary, as do chemicals for cleaning and polishing, painting and varnishing, and antifouling agents to keep unwanted growth off of hulls. Because of their deleterious effect on marine life, some antifouling compounds, such as tributyl tin, have been banned from use in the bay, though Navy ships remain exempt.

As a Dumping Ground

All animals, whether humans or striped bass or blue crabs, continually cycle food, taking in nutrients and expelling wastes. When very few people lived on the shores of the bay, human sewage did not pose a significant problem to the health of the estuary. Even when large numbers of people crowded into cities such as Baltimore, the most serious problems related to sewage involved human health risks, primarily from bacteria transmitted through human feces, which can cause cholera and other diseases. Once modern sewage treatment began and modern medicine evolved, these waterborne diseases became less of a threat. Only in areas of the world where sewage treatment is not properly managed (as in underdeveloped countries) does human waste still pose a serious health problem.

But the Chesapeake Bay faces another problem from sewage, an environmental health problem: too many nutrients. Sewage is rich in nutrients, including phosphorus and nitrogen. These nutrients can overenrich the bay and make it too productive for its own good. Too many nutrients fuel the explosive growth of blue-green algae and other undesirable phytoplankton, which take away light from more desirable plants. When these algae finally die and drop to the bottom, they begin to decompose. As bacteria break down the fibers and minerals of the dead algae, they use up large amounts of oxygen, especially in deeper channels. This lack of oxygen makes it difficult for other animals that also need oxygen, such as oysters, fish, and crabs. Sometimes the waters have very little oxygen (hypoxic waters) or virtually no oxygen at all (anoxic waters), and fish and other sea life unable to escape often suffocate and die.

With expanding population growth, the Chesapeake has therefore suffered from receiving waters for human waste. It has also received the effluent from numerous factories and industries, and in some places its sediments bear significant traces of heavy metals, organic compounds, and other pollutants. The areas around Norfolk Harbor (the Elizabeth River) and Baltimore (the Patapsco River) have in particular been rated as "toxic hotspots." But according to most researchers, it is the overabundance of nutrients that has caused the most pervasive ecological decline in the Chesapeake.

As a Fishing Ground

Despite the other ways in which humans have used Chesapeake Bay, its reputation and its tradition center on its value as a fishing ground. In its heyday, the Chesapeake's shallow waters provided, acre for acre, more fish and shellfish than any other body of water in the world.

For many years, for example, Maryland's oyster harvest held steady at about 2 million bushels a year—nothing compared to the 15-million-bushel harvests of the nineteenth century, but enough to sustain a long-standing fishery and the bayside communities that depend on oysters to round out an annual cycle of working the water. Then, during the 1980s, oyster harvests in Maryland dropped to less than 2 million bushels, then less than 1 million, then less than half a million. Many feel that the bay's oyster industry has, for now at least, collapsed.

Other changes have also taken place in the Chesapeake's water trades. The blue crab has become king of the commercial fisheries, surpassing oysters as the bay's most lucrative harvest. Because of relatively low fuel prices during the 1980s and high demand for crabmeat, watermen hauling in blue crabs saw a 250% rise in profits during the 1980s. In many ways the blue crab, once an undesirable by-catch, has kept the bay's seafood harvesting industry alive.

Equally as dramatic, during the same time period as the blue crab's rise was the fall of the bay's striped bass fishery. Generally known as rockfish in the bay region, striped bass once traveled by the tractor-trailer load from ports like Rock Hall, headed for Lexington Market in Baltimore or Fulton Market in New York. Harvest figures for 1973 reached over 4 million pounds in Maryland alone. But a precipitous decline in striped bass stocks, coupled with an appreciation of the Chesapeake's importance as the Atlantic coast's major spawning ground, brought about stiff restrictions and then a total ban on fishing for (or even possession of) striped bass in Maryland in 1985.

A recent reopening of Maryland's fishery, based on promising surveys of juvenile stripers, has meant a short season for both commercial and recreational anglers, but it will be a long time, if ever, before the Chesapeake sees a return of the great harvests of 20 years ago. On the positive side, the strict management of the striped bass in the Chesapeake has, arguably, averted an irreversible decline of that species, and the careful allocation of stripers among recreational anglers, commercial netters, and charter boat operators may well serve as a model for other threatened fisheries.

The Bay and Its Watershed as a System

A Stressed Ecosystem

Because the Chesapeake Bay has been so productive, some have called it a food factory, or compared it to a powerful engine that runs on nutrients. But the bay is not a factory or an engine; it is an ecosystem. Instead of machinery, the bay is composed of living parts: animals, plants, and microorganisms that depend on each other. Take away or change some of these living parts, and the whole ecosystem feels the effects. It feels them in both direct and indirect ways, ways that are sometimes obvious and sometimes impossible to predict, that depend on the subtle interplay of the parts of the system at several spatial and temporal scales, and that determine whether the estuary is healthy and resilient or brittle to the breaking point.

This is not simply an abstract notion. Consider, for example, one of the bay's prized shellfish, the oyster. For years the reputation of the Chesapeake Bay oyster has spread across the country, and in the bay region oysters have meant money—some $20 million a year in Maryland alone during some years. As the oyster populations in the bay fell, largely because of disease and overfishing, many watermen and natural resource managers realized that this represented a significant loss of livelihood and a shrinking economic resource for the tidewater region. What many may not have realized, however, were the ecological effects of the oyster's demise.

Like the bay itself, the oyster bar is an ecosystem. The oyster is a gregarious animal; it prefers to grow in groups. Some scientists believe that young oyster larvae can actually detect certain chemical signals that draw them to other oysters (Weiner et al. 1993; Coon, pers. comm.). Because of this attraction, oyster larvae set and grow in clusters, ultimately forming large aggregations called oyster bars (or rocks or reefs).

In the Chesapeake today, after more than 100 years of harvesting by oyster tongs or dredges, most oyster bars lie low and scattered across the bottom of the bay. But during the early seventeenth century, when Captain John Smith first sailed into the Chesapeake, the oyster bars were said to reach from the bay bottom all the way to the water's surface. These bars actually formed oyster reefs, and as with coral in the tropics, these oyster reefs undoubtedly created rich habitats and functioned as underwater ecosystems.

Imagine for a moment oyster reefs stretching up both sides of the Chesapeake Bay, along the shallow margins. Fish and other marine animals would have gathered around the reefs to feed, and chances are that one could see these fish, because the water would be relatively clear. The water during those early years would be less murky than now for two reasons. First, because prior to European settlement and the introduction of intensive agriculture, the land surrounding the bay and its rivers was covered with forests, which protected the soil and prevented runoff. Second, the bay would be more transparent because the oysters themselves were actually cleaning the water.

Oysters are filter feeders. An oyster, when aggressively feeding, pumps about 50 gallons of water a day in order to filter out algae (also called phytoplankton), the tiny floating plants that serve as its primary food source. As oysters feed, they act like filters in a swimming pool, drawing out algae and clearing the water. Some researchers have estimated that the bay's once abundant oyster populations could pump through a volume of water equal to the entire Chesapeake Bay in less than a week (Newell 1988). Because oyster populations have dwindled to such low levels, it would now take a year or more for today's oysters to filter that same amount of water.

Disturb one part of the ecosystem, and the whole ecosystem changes. The bay now has too many phytoplankton. Not only does the water look murky, but this lack of clarity has meant a lack of light for rooted aquatic grasses. In many areas these grasses, which provide food for diving ducks and shelter for molting crabs, have died off as a result of too much algae, which not only cloud the water but also cover the submerged grasses with light-blocking slime. Overwhelmed, many grasses have disappeared, leaving large stretches of bay bottom bare.

In short, the bay has changed in a number of ways because of human beings.

First, we have harvested oysters and destroyed the oyster reefs. Most of the bay's oysters were taken during the end of the nineteenth century. During that time watermen hauled up in a single year what it would now take more than 10 years to harvest.

Second, we have increased the amount of algae in the water by adding more nutrients. These nutrients come from sewage treatment plants, from septic systems, from fertilized farm fields and residential lawns. These nutrients cause even larger blooms of algae, which die and decompose on the bay floor, a process that draws life-sustaining oxygen out of the water.

Third, we have increased the amount of sediments in the water. The bay naturally receives a heavy load of sediment, especially during heavy spring rains and storms, but human uses of the land have torn away the protective forests and left the soil to wash away. This increased runoff began many years ago when farmers increasingly cleared the land for agriculture. Soil erosion continues today, not only because of agriculture, but because of housing construction and other land development in the watershed. Every construction site has the potential to release tons of sediment into the bay and its tributaries.

Fourth, we have added new chemical compounds to the bay. Chemicals have become a part of our daily lives. Heavy metals like zinc and mercury from industrial uses, pesticides from farms and suburban lawns, cleaning solutions from households, and a host of petroleum products and other compounds all wash off the land or down storm drains and into the streams and rivers that feed the bay. We do not fully understand the effects of these chemicals. Scientists do know that, in significant doses, many of these compounds are toxic to fish and other marine organisms. What researchers are still trying to determine is the effect such toxic compounds have at very low levels in our waterways—levels so low that they may be difficult to measure.

Toxic compounds sometimes act together to create problems for bay organisms. For example, when rain becomes polluted with nitrous oxides (from automobiles) and sulfur dioxide (from coal-burning industries and electrical power plants), it becomes acidic. When this acidic rain falls on the bay, it does two things. First, it adds nutrients to the bay. Some researchers have postulated that as much as 25% or more of the nutrients entering the bay come from airborne sources. Second, acid rain causes elements like aluminum to leach out of the soil. If, for example, this leaching occurs in a tributary where fish are spawning, it can kill delicate larvae. Some evidence exists that this double threat from acid rain and aluminum has hurt the reproduction of striped bass.

Such problems have not gone unnoticed. The decline of striped bass, the Maryland State Fish and a popular sport and commercial fish up and down the Atlantic coast, has caused an uproar. But other effects of toxic compounds on the bay's plants and animals that may not be as visible to the public may go largely unnoticed. As one researcher has said, it may be that the bay has a giant "headache" caused by toxic compounds, and we just don't realize it.

There is one more thing to say about the Chesapeake Bay's ailing ecosystem. The bay serves as something of an indicator for the health of the entire region.

Since the bay lies at the base of an enormous watershed—some 64,000 mi^2 of mountains, foothills, and coastal plain—it gathers much of what is put on the land or poured into streams and tributaries throughout the area. Because it supports such a rich and productive ecosystem, the bay provides ample opportunity for us to witness changes and trends, such as significant decreases in the populations of animals and plants.

The history of the Chesapeake Bay tells a story about how the way we live affects the environment we live in. Clearly, the bay is not simply a pool of water where oysters and crabs grow. It is the most visible part of a vast network of plant and animal life. Human beings rely on this environment as much as any animal; we also bear a special responsibility, since our actions have an impact on the ecosystem greater than that of any other creature that walks the earth.

Population Growth and Change in the Bay Watershed

During the Revolutionary War, when George Washington traveled through Annapolis, about 500,000 people lived in Maryland. In the two centuries that have passed since, Maryland's population has grown almost ten times. Now 4.7 million people live in the state, and according to predictions by the Maryland Office of Planning, another 800,000 or more will settle in Maryland by the year 2020. Maryland's growth illustrates change throughout the Chesapeake watershed. Today more than 14 million people live in the watershed; that number is expected to top 17 million by the year 2020.

Population changes in the watershed are shown in figures 4.2. The number of dots is proportional to population in each county and distributed randomly within each county. Between 1940 and 1986 the population of the watershed increased 87%. About 20% of this increase was due to net migration into the watershed, the majority of it to the areas surrounding Baltimore and Washington in Maryland and Virginia. The population of the watershed grew at an average annual rate of 1.6% between 1952 and 1972, almost the same as the U.S. average of 1.5% for the same period. But the growth was concentrated in the Maryland and Virginia portions of the watershed, which averaged 2.6% growth, compared with the remainder of the watershed, which grew at only 0.4%.

The most striking changes were in three areas: Richmond, the Norfolk/Virginia Beach area, and the Baltimore/Washington corridor. Growth can, in part, be attributed to increases in industry related directly and indirectly to the expanding U.S. government, as well as the increasing fashionableness of the Chesapeake Bay as a recreation area. The latter forces are amplified by the high immigration rates to the area.

These areas also illustrate the "urban flight" and "suburban sprawl" phenomena that have at once undermined the more natural and rural atmosphere that many originally left the city for and removed businesses and middle- and upper-income residents that served as a revenue base for the cities. The resulting deterioration of services and infrastructure

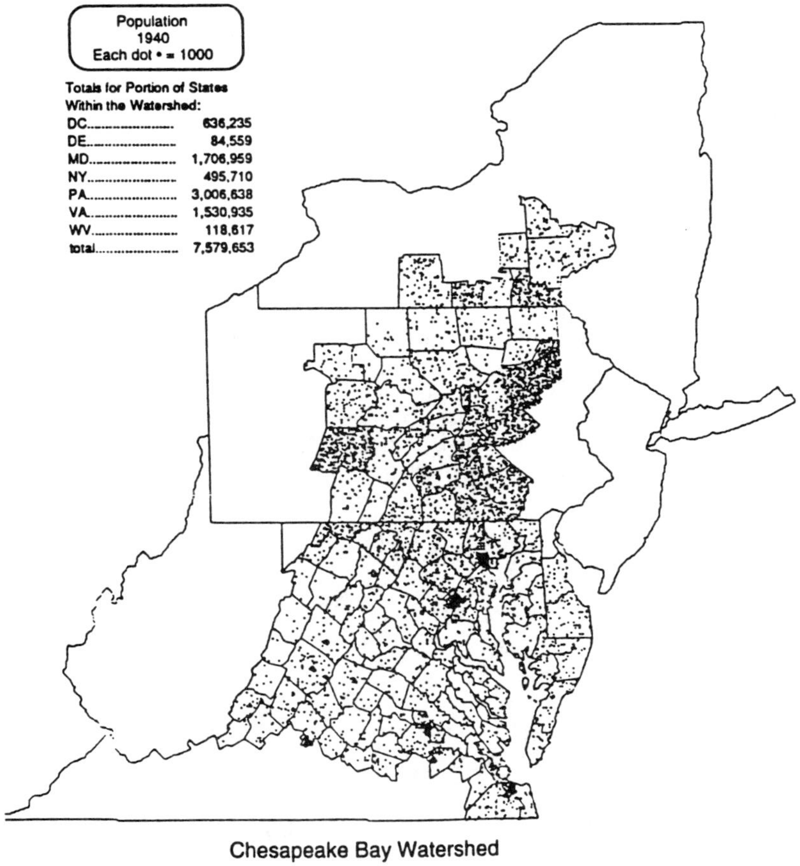

FIGURE 4.2a
Population in the Chesapeake Bay watershed. (a) 1940; (b) 1952; (c) 1972; (d) 1986.

worsens as people move farther and farther out. Increasing travel times required to reach work, worsening traffic conditions, and soaring property values are some of the resistive forces that quell the further spread of suburban development.

It appears that these forces may be approaching an equilibrium, at least for the time being. Between 1972 and 1986 the growth rate of the Maryland watershed population slowed to an annual rate of 0.9%, and in Virginia to 1.8%, and emigration rates from the cities have slowed. For example, Washington D.C.'s emigration rate decreased from an annual average of 1.3% in the 1960s to less than 0.8% in the early 1980s.

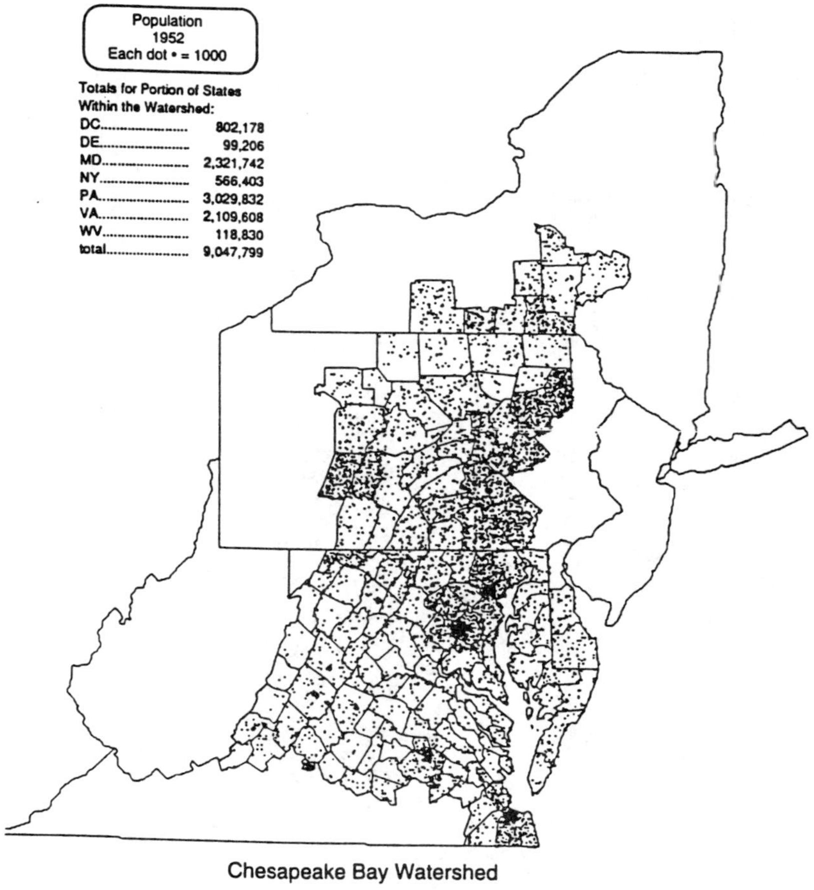

FIGURE 4.2b

In addition, the spatial extent of the sprawl appears currently to be limited to the counties immediately surrounding the cities in question (figure 4.2d). However, the information contained in these maps is only suggestive. Demographic trends can result from any number of factors. Variation in birth rates, cultural heritage, local versus long-distance moves, political climate, and zoning laws all muddy the waters. In addition, as sprawl and growth occur simultaneously, secondary economic centers inevitably spring up, initiating their own cycles.

As population has risen in the watershed, both land and water have felt the effects. Forest and farmlands have been lost to development, and, as described earlier, the Chesapeake Bay's underwater meadows of aquatic vegetation have died off, largely because of too many nutrients entering the estuary. As the underwater grasses have dwindled, widgeons and other diving ducks that grazed on the grasses have also gone. Rising population has also meant heavy harvesting of the Chesapeake's fisheries, which may already feel the strain of turbidity and disease.

Patterns of settlement and resettlement broadly affect 'land use in other ways as well, as shown by the percent change in land use maps in figures 4.3. For example, there has recently been a slight but noticeable increase in woodland in the New York portion of the watershed

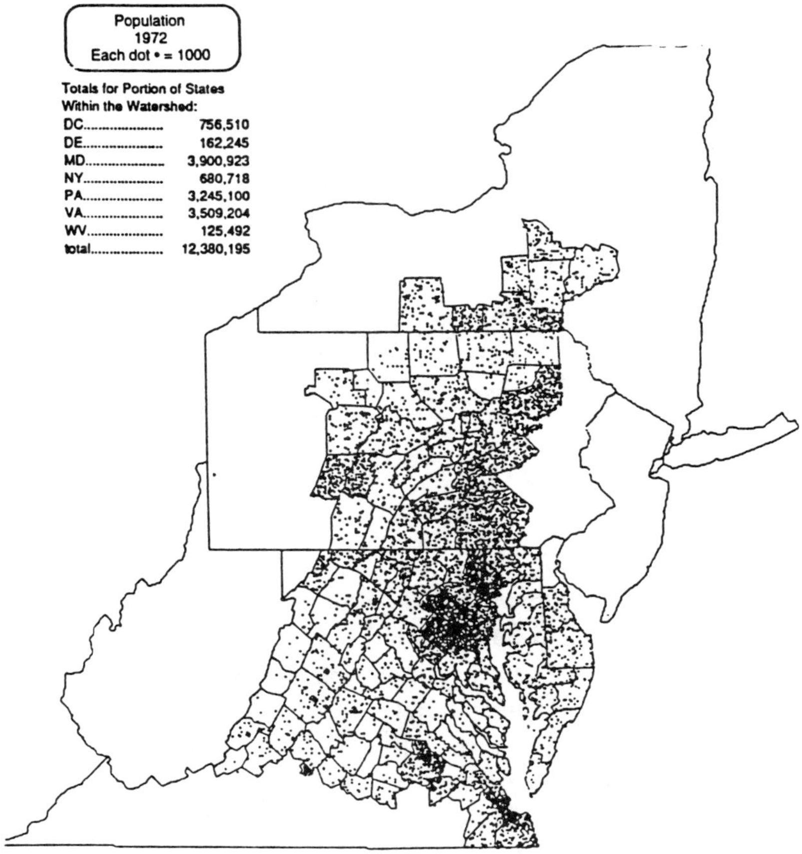

FIGURE 4.2c

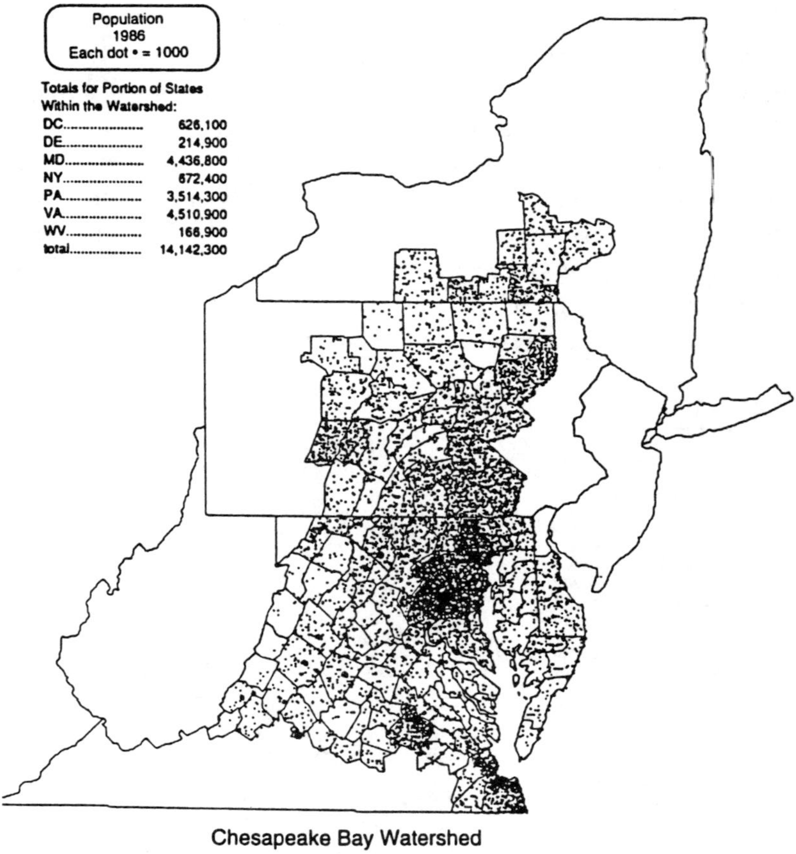

FIGURE 4.2d

(figure 4.3c). The fact that there was a concurrent loss of cropland and pasture (figures 4.3a and 4.3b) only indicates that there were net changes from fields to forests, but it does not explain why. In fact, the marked differences in changes in agricultural and forested acreage from one state to another strongly suggest that these are due to differences in state agricultural policies and tax laws. On the other hand, the pattern of urbanization is more straightforward in light of the population changes discussed earlier (figure 4.3d).

Increases in evidence of human activity accompany increases in population in both magnitude and distribution. Maps of manufacturers, energy consumption, housing units, water use, solid waste production, and air pollutants all closely resemble the maps of population. Changes in life-style have, however, caused accelerated increases in consumption and waste production. From 1952 to 1986 we have seen the following increases in the watershed: per capita energy consumption has gone from 567,000 btu/day to 744,000 btu/day; NO_x emissions by vehicles have gone from 1.0 lb/week per person to 1.7 lb/week per person; and

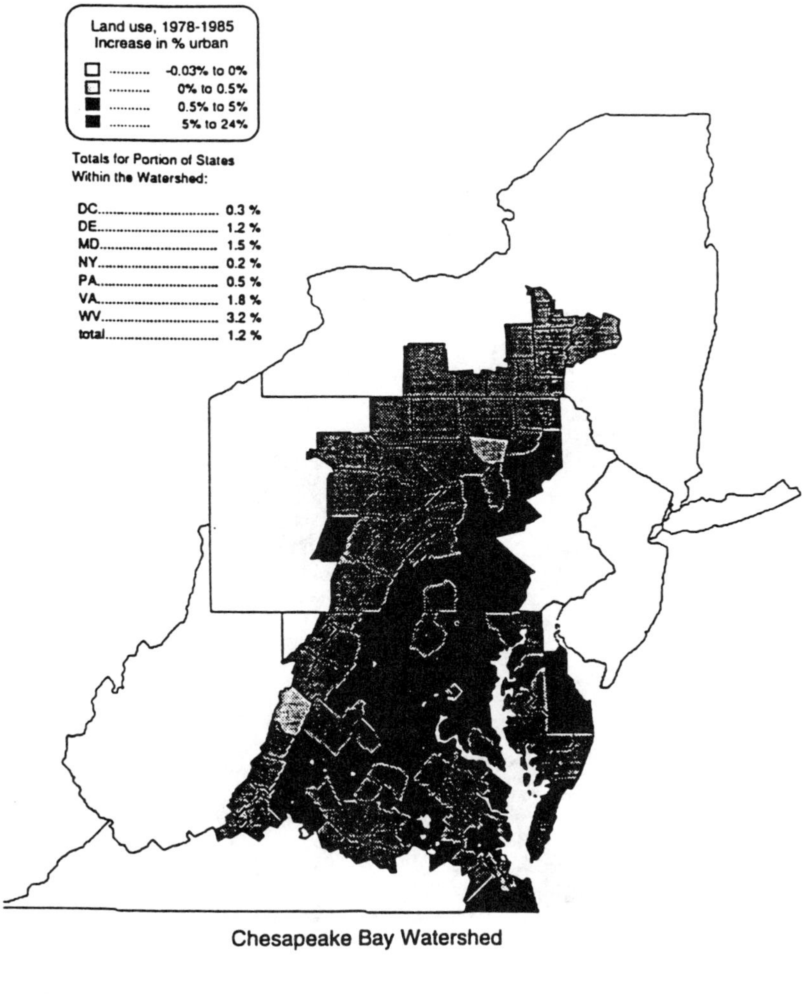

FIGURE 4.3a
Percent change in land use from 1978 to 1985 in the Chesapeake Bay watershed. (a) Urban; (b) cropland; (c) pasture; (d) woodland.

per capita solid waste production has risen from 2.2 lb/day to 3.7 lb/day. In contrast, public and industrial per capita water use has decreased in the same period for the watershed as a whole—from 334 gal/day to 278 gal/day. This is due in large part to the decline in total use in Pennsylvania during this period from 1.46 billion gal/day in 1952 to only 1.18 billion gal/day in 1986. In the Maryland and Virginia portions of the watershed, the per capita use rate held nearly constant at about 237 gal/day. This suggests that the former change may be due to changes

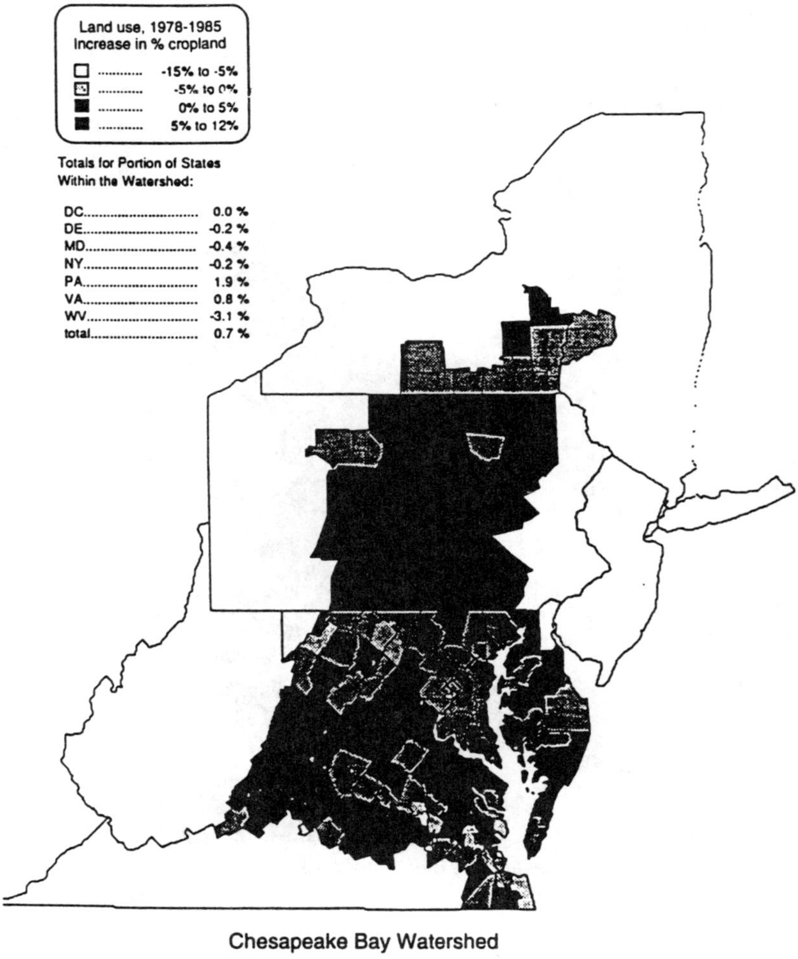

FIGURE 4.3b

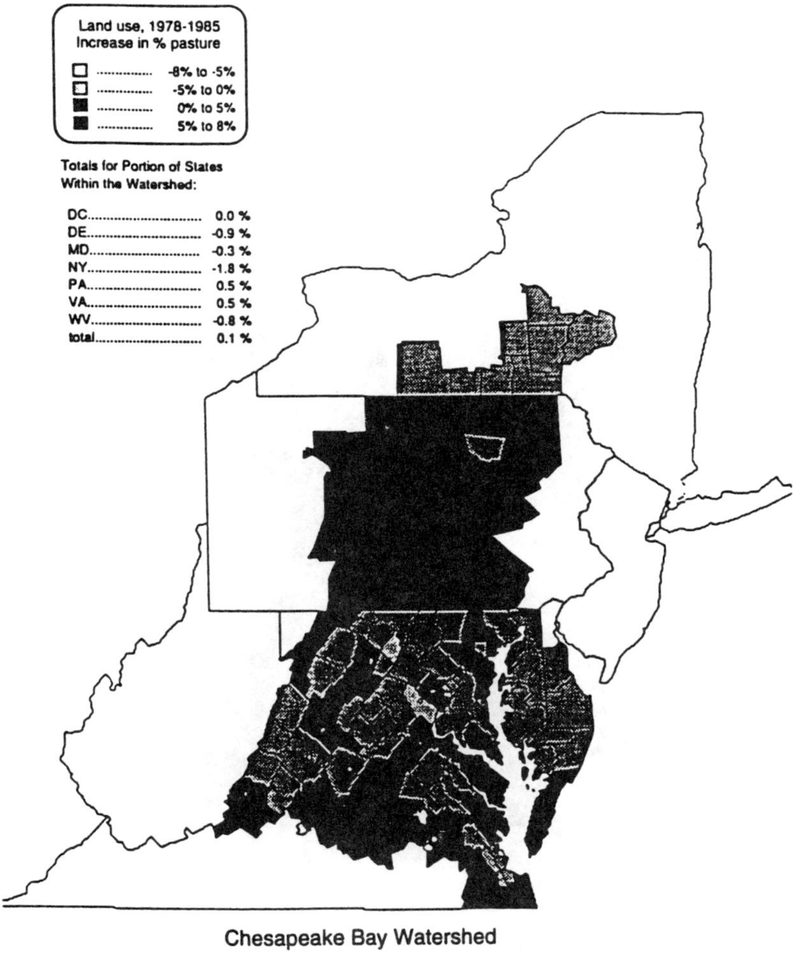

FIGURE 4.3C

in heavy industry in Pennsylvania, whereas the latter lack of change may be due to a relatively constant per capita public demand for water in a region that consists mostly of residency and light industry.

Agriculture

Changes associated with agriculture are tied to increases in population in their overall magnitude and to cultural and historical practices in their distribution and local magnitude. Heavily populated areas neces-

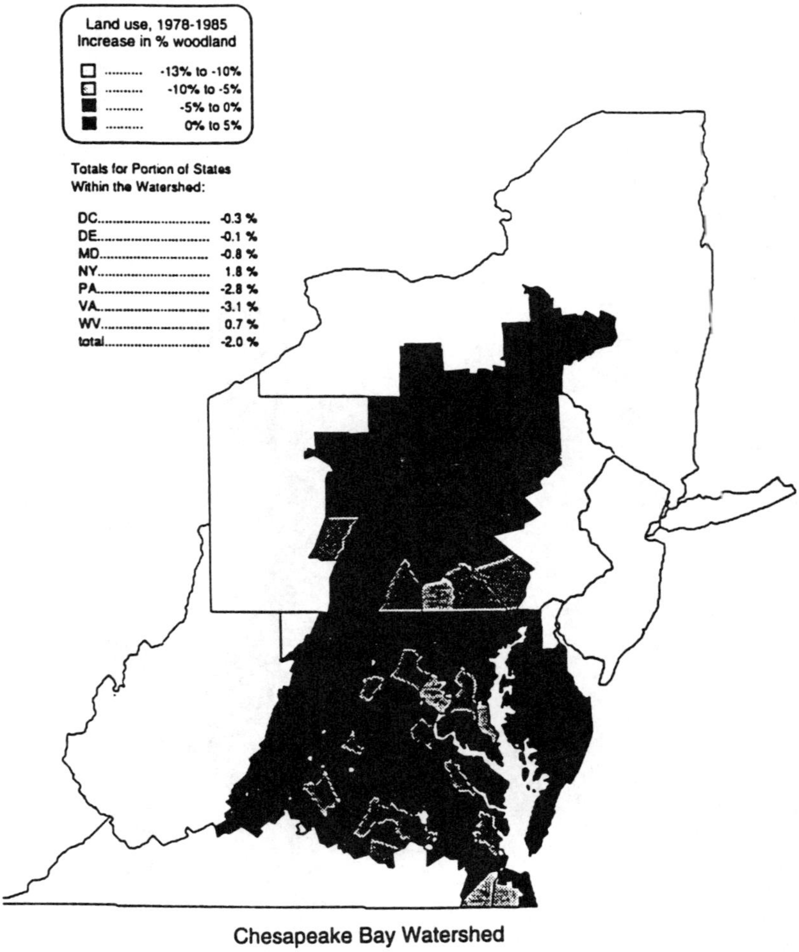

FIGURE 4.3d

sarily exclude agriculture. It is unfortunate that some of the best agricultural land in the country, which was the basis for the initial local growth, is rapidly being converted to residential developments, industrial parks, and shopping malls as rising property values make farming unprofitable. It is not clear, however, whether agriculture itself is more benign to an ecosystem such as the Chesapeake Bay than urban and suburban development. Both load the system with wastes and nutrients while consuming "natural" areas that could have absorbed some of that load.

Whereas total farm acreage in the watershed has decreased from 23.2 million acres in 1954 to 14.4 million acres in 1987, cropland has only decreased from 10.5 million acres to 9.0 million. Meanwhile, from 1954 to 1987 the average farm size increased from 126 acres to 190 acres. This means that larger percentages of farms are devoted to crops (64% versus 45%) and that less lies fallow, pastured, and wooded. Operations are larger and more intensive. Irrigation has increased from 40,000 acres to 180,000 acres, and fertilization rates have increased from about 210 lb per cultivated acre to 250 lb per cultivated acre. Figures 4.4 show that pesticide use, which was almost nonexistent in the early 1950s, rose to

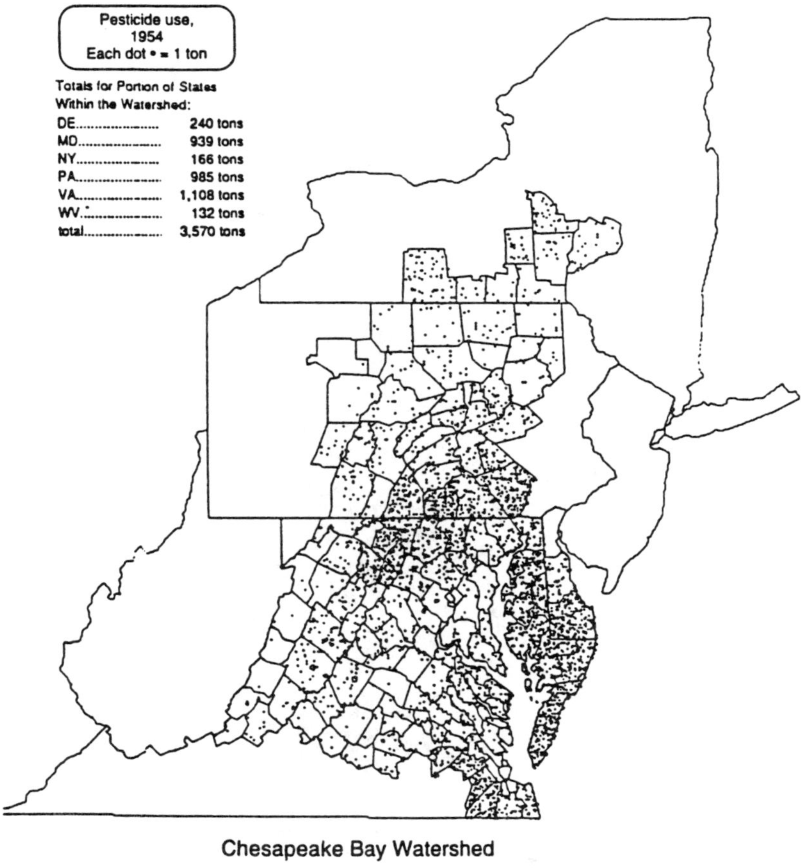

FIGURE 4.4a
Pesticide use in the Chesapeake Bay watershed. (a) 1954; (b) 1974; (c) 1987.

15,000 tons in 1974 and then decreased to 13,000 tons in 1986. Of course this trend also reflects the greater specificity of the pesticides used in 1986.

If we examine the application of fertilizer nitrogen (figures 4.5), we see a pattern that follows the general distribution of farmland but with an overall increase in the intensity of use. Although the phosphorus content of fertilizers used in the watershed remained relatively constant over the years at around 10%, the nitrogen content rose steadily from about 7% in the 1950s to 15% in the mid-1980s.

The nutrient loading rates for the mainstem Chesapeake Bay are 78,700 tons/year nitrogen and 3600 tons/year phosphorus (Boynton et

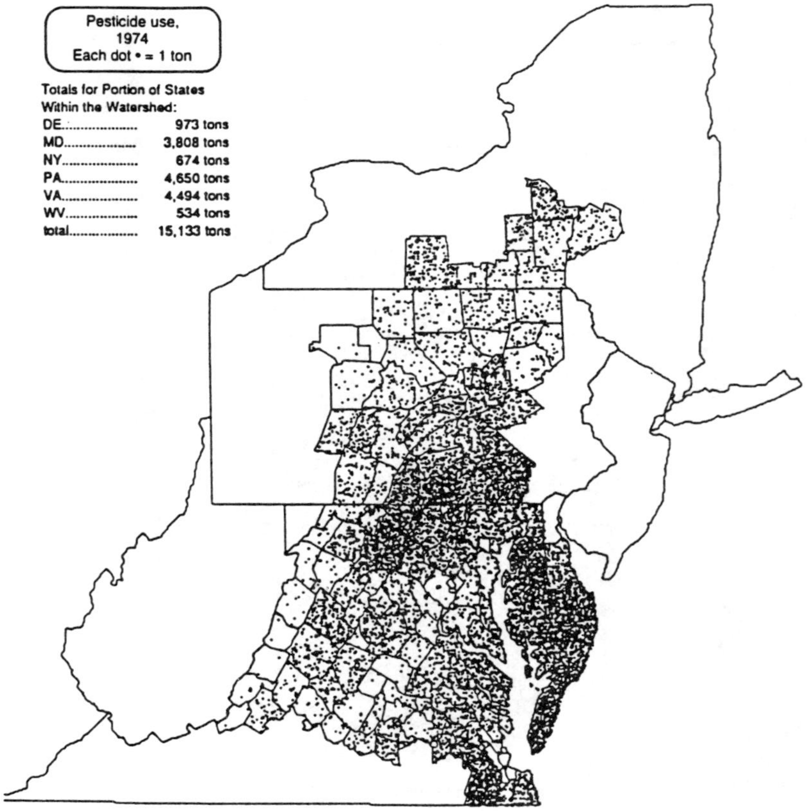

FIGURE 4.4b

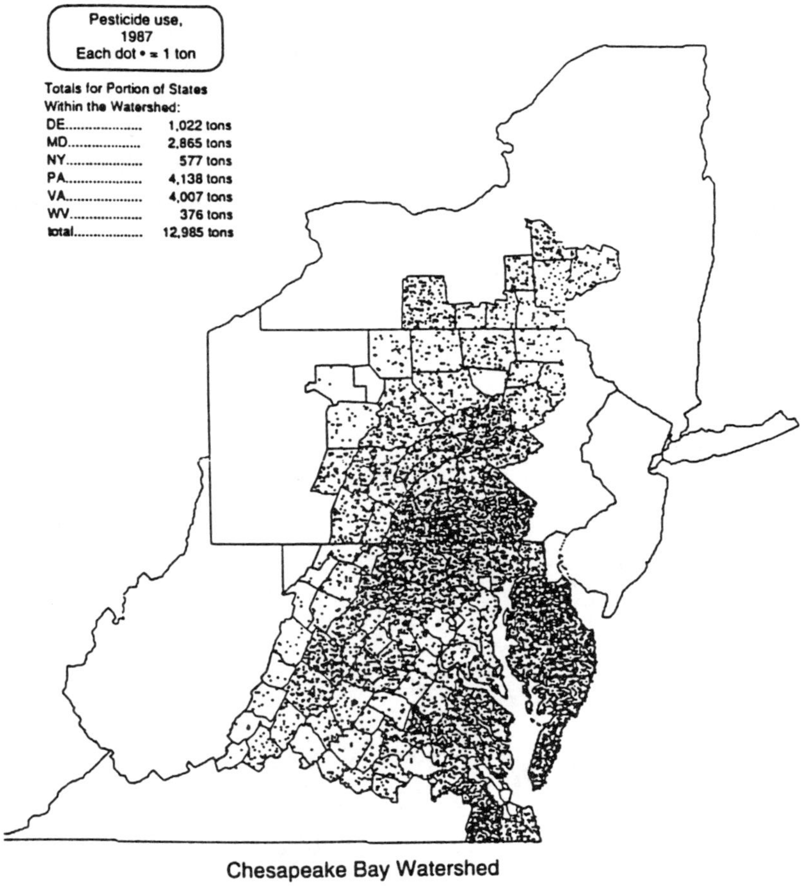

FIGURE 4.4C

al. 1994). If one assumes that the loading rate is proportional to the amount of nutrients produced and applied within the watershed, then this implies that phosphorus loading has increased around 4% to 10% and nitrogen loading has increased somewhere between 34% and 125% since 1954. This would not only be a great change in amount of nutrients but (and this may be even more crucial) a great change in the relative proportion of nutrients. The increased concentration of nutrients in specific localities, such as Lancaster County, means that this problem may be even more exaggerated in some parts of the system.

The Chesapeake Bay has undergone very rapid population growth, with the accompanying environmental impacts. We have mapped some of these changes as they are reflected in the characteristics of the bay's watershed. The impacts of these activities in the watershed on the bay itself are known to be large, but their specific interconnections are only now being investigated. The Chesapeake Bay has 200,000 people living in its drainage basin for every cubic kilometer of water in the bay. (The Baltic Sea has 4000 people/km^3, and the Mediterranean has 85 people/km^3, by way of comparison.) Even if all these people were minimizing

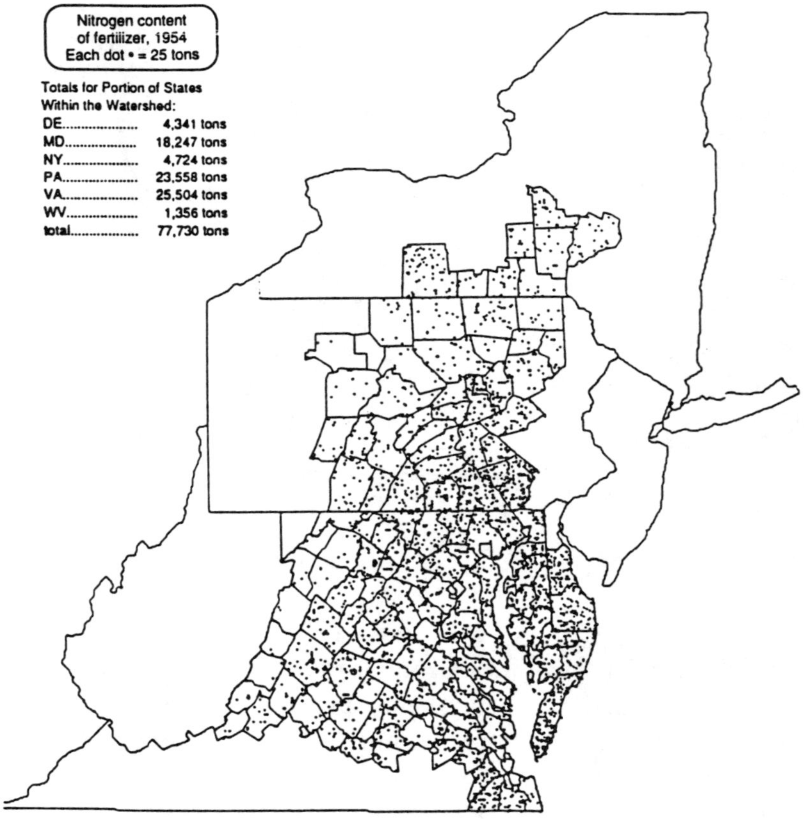

FIGURE 4.5a

Nitrogen content of fertilizer use in the Chesapeake Bay watershed. (a) 1954; (b) 1974; (c) 1987.

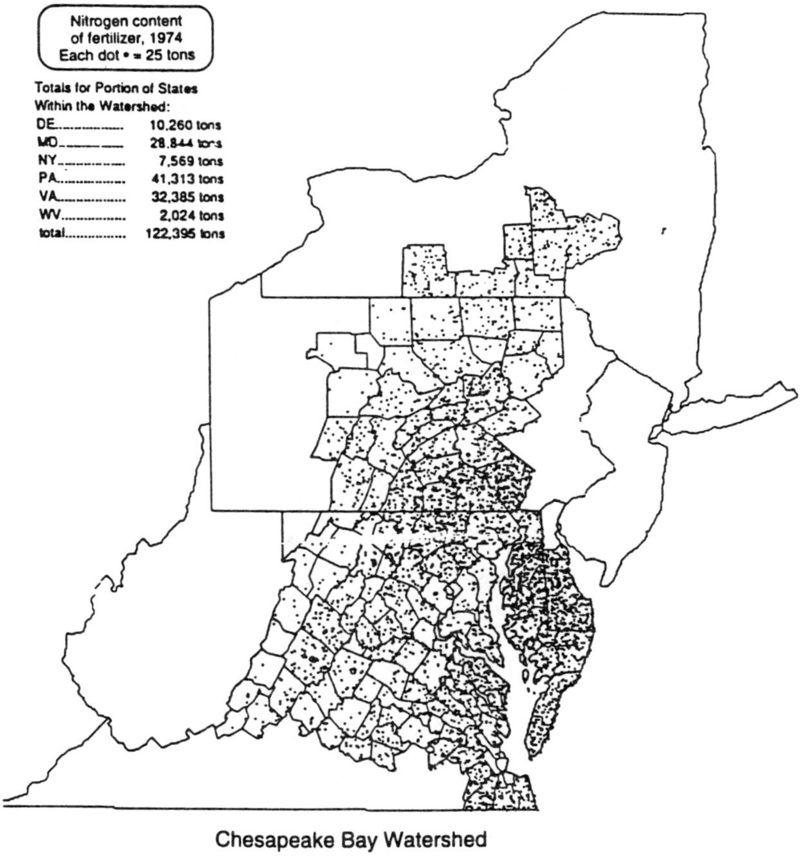

FIGURE 4.5b

their environmental impacts (which they are not), their sheer numbers are daunting to a system as sensitive as the Chesapeake. If these numbers continue to increase as they have in the past, the prospects for America's largest estuary seem bleak (table 4.1).

Evolution of Chesapeake Bay Management

Efforts to understand and manage the bay ecosystem in a comprehensive way began to gain momentum in the late 1960s, along with the general increase in environmental awareness in the United States. Several major studies of the bay have been undertaken, and the bay is

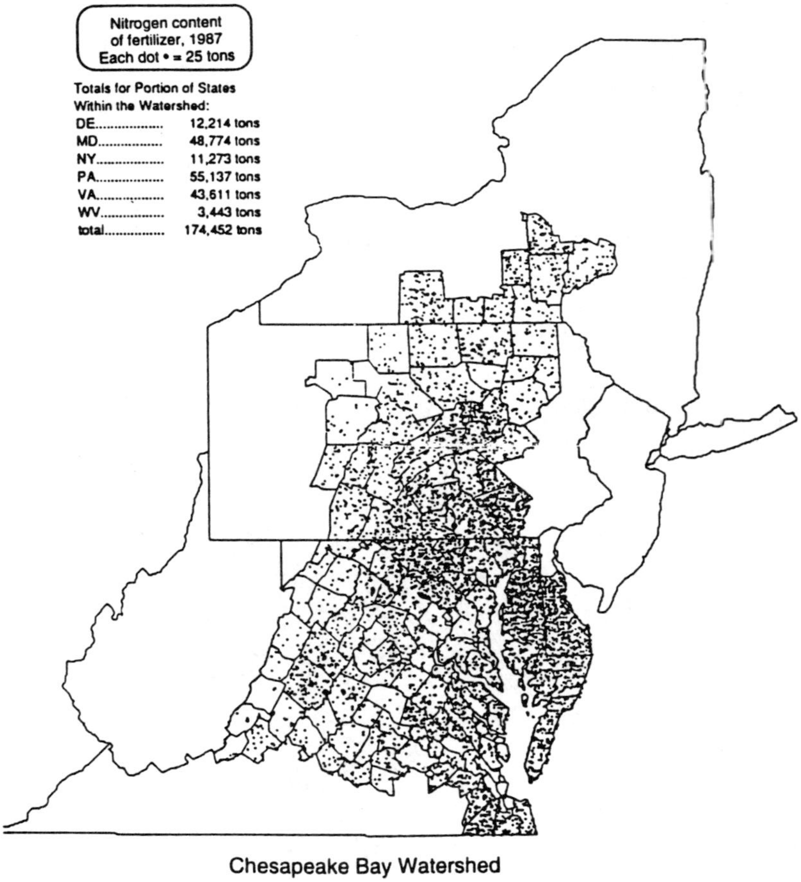

FIGURE 4.5c

arguably the most intensively studied single ecosystem in the world. It is also generally acknowledged that the Chesapeake Bay system is a "best-case scenario" of the integration of science, government, the media, and private environmental interest groups toward the goal of rational and effective ecosystem management. As such, it is worthwhile examining in some detail how this situation came to be, how well it has worked, whether it is an appropriate model for application to the management of other ecosystems, how it might continue to evolve and improve, and what major improvements still remain elusive.

Although, as we have already described, the bay has always been an ecosystem of concern for its inhabitants, a recent chronology of bay

TABLE 4.1
The Chesapeake Watershed's Population at a Glance

State or District	1940	1986	2020 (projected)
District of Columbia	636,235	626,100	626,100
Delaware	84,559	214,900	215,000
Maryland	1,706,959	4,436,800	5,496,600
New York	495,710	672,400	700,000
Pennsylvania	3,006,638	3,514,300	3,854,500
Virginia	1,530,935	4,510,900	6,229,800
West Virginia	118,617	166,900	166,900
Total watershed	7,579,653	14,142,300	17,288,900

Sources: Bureau of the Census, 1952, 1972, 1988, Maryland Office of Planning.
*Only those portions of each state within the watershed are included.

"management" should probably begin in the year 1965. In that year the U.S. Army Corps of Engineers conducted a major study of the bay, and two important pieces of federal legislation were passed: the Federal Water Pollution Control Act and the Federal Rivers and Harbors Act. By this time scientists and citizens alike had begun to notice significant declines in some key indicators. The water had become more turbid, algae blooms were occurring more frequently, and it was becoming harder to catch certain kinds of fish.

1965–1976: Era of Shared Experience and Raised Consciousness

Signs of decline are frequently ignored, but what separates the Chesapeake from other, more remote ecosystems is a broadly shared experience of the bay by a large cross section of the population. The bay was and is everyone's back yard. Government bureaucrats from Washington sail and fish on it side by side with scientists, watermen, local politicians, and everyone else. This common experience resulted in a shared commitment to protecting the ecosystem that is often missing from attempts to protect more isolated ecosystems that, however valuable, few people experience as part of their daily lives. In 1966 the Chesapeake Bay Foundation was established as a nonprofit conservation organization committed to help "Save the Bay" through public education and advocacy. "Save the Bay" bumper stickers began to appear everywhere.

Also significant was the role of the media in publicizing the bay's plight and subsequent efforts to "save" it. In 1976 William Warner published his Pulitzer Prize–winning book about crabbing on the bay, entitled *Beautiful Swimmers.* Tom Horton, then of the *Baltimore Sun,* served as a key environmental journalist in the effort to bring the bay's problems before the public eye (Horton 1989; Horton and Eichbaum 1991). His job was made easier by the fact that many in the region had observed very directly the problems he described in his reports. Another defining event occurred when Maryland State Senator Bernie Fowler waded into the waters of the Patuxent river near Broom's Island and discovered that he could no longer see his feet when chest high in water, as he could as a boy growing up in the area. Even compensating for the fact that his chest and toes were farther apart, the water quality in the Patuxent had obviously deteriorated significantly. This kind of shared experience got politicians off the dime and made the "save the bay" program much more than an academic exercise. The problems were, in any event, daunting, and included the sheer number of people living in the region. By 1970 there were 3.9 million people living in Maryland, and 12.4 million had made their home in the watershed.

1977–1983: Era of Intense Scientific Analysis with Political Backing

Once a consensus began to form that the bay was indeed in trouble, a phase of detailed applied scientific analysis was initiated. Unlike many purely scientific studies, this effort had political backing from the start and was aimed directly at providing answers to two fundamental questions: (1) what was responsible for the bay's decline and (2) what should be done about it? In 1975 Senator Mac Mathias toured the bay and requested that the EPA commence a study of the bay's problems. In 1977 a 6-year, $26-million EPA-funded study got under way. This study was unique both in its size and in its goal of supporting ecosystem management. In 1978 the Chesapeake Bay Legislative Advisory Commission (CBLAC)—an intergovernmental coordinating committee—was created to develop a method for managing the bay's resources. In 1980 the Chesapeake Bay Commission was created as an outgrowth of the CBLAC. The commission, composed of ten state legislators from Maryland and Virginia, was responsible for developing a cooperative arrangement between the two states to clean up the bay.

Meanwhile, population in the region continued to increase. By 1980 there were 4.2 million people living in Maryland, and 13.4 million in the watershed. In 1983 researchers completed the EPA-supported study, and government officials, scientists, and citizens began to consider how to implement their findings.

1983–Present: Era of Implementation and Monitoring

The next 9 years saw an era of implementation, combined with a unique effort to monitor and model the effects of implementation plans. In December of 1983, the first Chesapeake Bay Agreement was signed by Maryland, Virginia, Pennsylvania, Washington, D.C., and the EPA. The agreement, considered a compact among all the parties, committed them to establish (1) a Chesapeake Executive Council to oversee the implementation of coordinated plans; (2) an implementation committee, appointed and overseen by the Executive Council, to coordinate technical matters and evaluate specific management plans; and (3) a liaison office at the EPA's regional laboratory in Annapolis, Maryland.

The states acted quickly to begin the restoration process. Maryland, for example, in 1984 approved thirty-four legislative initiatives, focused into seven state programs known as the Maryland Chesapeake Bay Program. Among these, the Maryland Critical Area Law restricted residential and urban development in all areas within 1000 ft of tidal water. In 1985 the state of Maryland released its Restoration Plan, aimed at "restoring and maintaining the bay's ecological integrity, productivity, and beneficial uses and to protect public health." By 1987 a new Chesapeake Bay Agreement was put forward and signed by Maryland, Virginia, Pennsylvania, Washington, D.C., the EPA, and the Chesapeake Bay Commission. This agreement extended and expanded the 1983 compact and called for more precise goals to be reached by specific deadlines. (For example, a 40% reduction of nitrogen and phosphorus is to be achieved by the year 2000.) In 1988 the "Year 2020" panel released its visions for the future, detailing the environmental impacts of increased population growth within the watershed and making recommendations to avert further deterioration of the bay's water quality. By 1990 there were 4.7 million people living in Maryland, 14.5 million living in the watershed. In 1991 the Chesapeake Bay Growth and Preservation Act was presented before the Maryland legislature. This was the first bill to address statewide growth management and to focus on human population growth as the bay's number one problem. This bill did not pass, but in 1992 a much weaker growth management bill did pass the Maryland General Assembly.

It was not until the implementation era that the full extent of the bay's problems began to be realized, and in particular the necessity to treat the entire bay watershed as a system. Nutrient reductions required changes in activities in the watershed. Although point sources of nutrients, such as industries and sewage treatment plants, were relatively easy to control, it soon became evident that nonpoint sources, such as residences and agriculture, were responsible for a large part of the problem and were much more difficult to control. The growing population of the watershed itself came to be recognized as a primary cause of the bay's problems. The bay is now primed for new approaches to management that can go beyond the traditional command and control methods (which were relatively successful with point sources) to complete the implementation phase on nonpoint sources. This will be discussed in greater detail later.

Monitoring

The development of a comprehensive monitoring program was essential to moving the management of the Chesapeake forward. All estuaries are in constant flux, and the Chesapeake Bay, the nation's largest estuary, is no exception. With 150 rivers and streams feeding the bay and several thousand miles of shoreline, the bay system continually responds to nature's changing conditions: rains, tides, drought, shoreline erosion, storm runoff. The bay also responds to human activity—discharges of nutrients from waste treatment plants, fertilizer runoff from farmland, toxic chemicals in industrial outfalls, fish and shellfish harvesting. How do we distinguish between natural and human impacts on the bay? And why do we need to?

The Chesapeake's vital signs—its temperature, dissolved oxygen, pH, water clarity—are indicators of the bay's environmental health. These and other indicators, such as the presence (or absence) of underwater grasses or the numbers and diversity of fish, measured week by week, month by month, and year by year, give researchers and resource managers insight into the health of the bay by tracking changes in it.

Keeping track of these changes is the job of monitoring. To restore the health of the Chesapeake best, we need as complete an understanding of its ecology as we can get. Bay monitoring programs, funded by the state and federal government, help chart emerging trends, enabling us to see whether the ecosystem is responding to programs designed to reverse the decline of water quality or populations of fish or shellfish.

Government agencies in the bay region (e.g., the U.S. Environmental Protection Agency, the Maryland Department of the Environment, the Maryland Department of Natural Resources) are cooperating by regularly monitoring many different water quality factors, including toxic chemicals, metals, and nutrients. They are also monitoring the abundance of key fish and shellfish species, the presence of diseases in fish and shellfish, underwater grasses, and waterfowl. Especially important are samplings of dissolved oxygen and chlorophyll as indicators of whether overgrowths of algae are occurring. (Since virtually all plants, including algae, contain chlorophyll, if high levels of chlorophyll emerge, then scientists can assume that high numbers of algae are present.) Interpretation of these data can help scientists and resource managers determine whether management programs to restore living resources to the bay—such as underwater grasses, striped bass, oysters—are working or whether they need to be revised or new strategies must be attempted.

But the bay is enormously complex, and monitoring is too costly for government agencies to take all the samples necessary for a thorough understanding of the ecosystem. For this reason citizen monitoring programs in the bay are becoming increasingly helpful. Students and volunteers in citizen organizations have for several years been regularly monitoring streams and rivers throughout the watershed. With assistance from organizations like the Alliance for the Chesapeake Bay and Save Our Streams, volunteers learn how to take water quality measurements and how to record the data so that they will be reliable and useful for data managers.

Each week volunteers head for an assigned site along the shore of a stream or river, where they take samples and compile a number of measurements: pH (a measure of alkalinity or acidity), dissolved oxygen level, salinity, temperature, and turbidity (a measure of how clear the water is). These data are then entered into the Chesapeake Bay data base, along with data gathered by state and federal monitoring programs. Collected over a period of years, these measurements of water quality will enable resource managers to analyze and describe the bay's shifting ecosystem better. They will also help us to assess just how well our efforts to curb pollution are working.

Modeling the Bay and the Watershed

To begin to put the monitoring data together into an understanding of how the complex pieces of the watershed and the bay interact, we need to synthesize and integrate our knowledge in the form of models of various kinds. A model is simply an abstract representation of the system of interest that we can manipulate to aid our understanding. For example, architects build cardboard models of their projects to aid the design process. The mental picture we conjure up when someone mentions the Chesapeake Bay is also a model. More recently, hydrologists, ecologists, economists, and other scientists have begun to build mathematical models of various parts of the Chesapeake system that can be simulated on computers. These range from hydrodynamic models of the water flow dynamics in the bay itself (Dortch et al. 1988; HydroQual 1987, 1989) and other estuaries in the Chesapeake system (Hwang 1990) to models of water and nutrient runoff from the watershed (Summers 1990) and integrated models of the ecological and economic components of the system with spatial articulation (DeBellevue and Costanza 1991).

Since ecosystems are being threatened by a host of human activities, protecting and preserving them requires understanding the direct and indirect effects of human activities over long periods of time and over large areas. Computer simulations are now becoming important tools to investigate these interactions and in all areas of science. Without the sophisticated global atmospheric simulations now being done, our understanding of the potential impacts of increasing CO_2 concentrations in the atmosphere because of fossil fuel burning would be much more primitive. Computer simulations can now be used to understand not only human impacts on ecosystems, but also our economic dependence on natural ecosystem services and capital, and the interdependence between ecological and economic components of the system (see, for example, Braat and Steetskamp 1991; Costanza et al. 1990).

Several recent developments make such computer simulation modeling feasible, including the accessibility of extensive spatial and temporal data bases and advances in computer power and convenience. Computer simulation models are potentially one of our best tools to help understand the complex functions of integrated ecological economic systems like the Chesapeake watershed.

But even with the best conceivable modeling capabilities, we will always be confronted with large amounts of uncertainty about the response of the environment to human actions (Funtowicz and Ravetz 1991). Learning how to manage the environment effectively in the face of this uncertainty is critical (Costanza and Perrings 1990; Perrings 1991).

To use quantitative computer modeling effectively to understand and manage complex ecological economic systems like the Chesapeake watershed, we need an integrated, multiscale, transdisciplinary, and pluralistic approach. Moreover, we need one that also acknowledges the large remaining uncertainty inherent in modeling these systems and develops new ways to deal with this uncertainty effectively.

One important addition to our suite of models of the Chesapeake watershed is the "four-box" model of system development presented in this book's first chapter. This is discussed in more detail later.

Barriers and Bridges to Improved Management

Social Traps

A fundamental reason for system collapse and mismanagement is thought to be the inherent mismatch in many systems between the fundamental time and space scales of the ecological system, on the one hand, and the human institutions developed to manage it, on the other. When it comes to human institutions, one critical feature is the incentive structures that these institutions produce. These incentive structures often lead to behavior that is directly counter to the long-term health of the whole system, and often even to the stated goals of the institution itself. How does this happen and how can we fix it?

This process of short-run and local incentives getting out of sync with long-term and global goals has been well studied in the last decade under several rubrics (cf. Hardin 1968; Axelrod 1984), but the one we like best is John Platt's notion of "social traps" (Platt 1973; Cross and Guyer 1980; Teger 1980; Brockner and Rubin 1985; Costanza 1987). In all such cases the decision maker may be said to be "trapped" by the local conditions into making what turns out to be a bad decision viewed from a longer or wider perspective. We go through life making decisions about which path to take based largely on "road signs," the short-run, local reinforcements that we perceive most directly. These short-run reinforcements can include monetary incentives, social acceptance or admonishment, and physical pleasure or pain. In general, this strategy of following the road signs is quite effective, unless the road signs are inaccurate or misleading. In these cases we can be trapped into following a path that is ultimately detrimental because of our reliance on the road signs. For example, cigarette smoking has been a social trap because by following the short-run road signs of the pleasure and social status* associated with smoking, we embark on the road to an increased risk of earlier death from smoking-induced cancer. More important, once this road has been taken it is very difficult to change to another (as most people who have tried to quit smoking can attest).

The elimination of social traps requires intervention—the modification of the reinforcement system. Indeed, it can be argued that the proper role of a democratic government is to eliminate social traps (no more and no less) while maintaining as much individual freedom as possible. Cross and Guyer list four broad methods by which traps can be avoided or escaped from. These are education (about the long-term, distributed impacts); insurance; superordinate authority (i.e., legal systems, government, religion); and conversion of the trap to a trade-off (i.e., correcting the road signs).

Education can be used to warn people of long-term impacts that cannot be seen from the road. Examples are the warning labels now required on cigarette packages and the warnings of environmentalists about future hazardous waste problems. People can ignore warnings, however, particularly if the path seems otherwise enticing. For example, warning labels on cigarette packages have had little effect on the number of smokers.

The main problem with education as a general method of avoiding and escaping from traps is that it requires a significant time commitment on the part of individuals to learn the details of each situation. Our current society is so large and complex that we cannot expect even professionals, much less the general public, to know the details of all the traps. In addition, for education to be effective in avoiding traps involving many individuals, *all* the participants must be educated.

Governments can, of course, forbid or regulate certain actions that have been deemed socially inappropriate. The problem with this ap-

---

*This particular positive reinforcement has in the last few years begun to turn into a negative one. As smoking becomes less socially acceptable we should expect the number of new smokers to fall and many old smokers to escape the trap. But the process of escape is much more difficult than the process of avoidance.

proach is that it must be rigidly monitored and enforced, and the strong short-term incentive for individuals to try to ignore or avoid the regulations remains. A police force and legal system are very expensive to maintain, and increasing their chances of catching violators increases their costs exponentially (both the costs of maintaining a larger, better-equipped force and the cost of the loss of individual privacy and freedom).

Religion and social customs can be seen as much less expensive ways to avoid certain social traps. If a moral code of action and belief in an ultimate payment for transgressions can be deeply instilled in a person, the probability of that person's falling into the "sins" (traps) covered by the code will be greatly reduced, and with very little enforcement cost. On the other hand, the problems with religion and social customs as means of avoiding social traps are that the moral code must be relatively static to allow beliefs learned early in life to remain in force later and that it requires a relatively homogeneous community of like-minded individuals to be truly effective. This system works well in culturally homogeneous societies that are changing very slowly. In modern, heterogeneous, rapidly changing societies, religion and social customs cannot handle all the newly evolving situations, nor can they deal with the conflict between radically different cultures and belief systems.

Many trap theorists believe that the most effective method for avoiding and escaping from social traps is to turn the trap into a trade-off. This method does not run counter to our normal tendency to follow the road signs; it merely corrects the signs' inaccuracies by adding compensatory positive or negative reinforcements. A simple example illustrates how effective this method can be. Playing slot machines is a social trap because the long-term costs and benefits are inconsistent with the short-term costs and benefits. People play the machines because they expect a large short-term jackpot, whereas the machines are programmed to pay off, say, $0.80 on the dollar in the long term. People may "win" hundreds of dollars playing the slots in the short run, but if they play long enough they will certainly lose $0.20 for every dollar played. To change this trap to a trade-off, one could simply reprogram the machines so that every time a dollar was put in, $0.80 would come out. This way the short-term reinforcements ($0.80 on the dollar) are made consistent with the long-term reinforcements ($0.80 on the dollar), and only the dedicated aficionados of spinning wheels with fruit painted on them would continue to play.

The Chesapeake Bay managed to avoid many of the social traps that have afflicted many of the other ecosystems described in this book. It did this because it managed from the outset to achieve a broad dialogue between the interest groups involved and a broad consensus on the long-term goals of ecosystem restoration. This guaranteed that long-term, common goals were foremost, and short-term, narrow interest group goals did not drive the process. One way to achieve this result in other systems is to employ the methods of policy dialogue and consensus building described earlier in this chapter and in chapter 1. But even after this consensus is achieved, the system has trouble implementing its long-term goals unless these goals are effectively communicated to the narrow interest groups. Implementation of the bay management strategy is now stalled on this problem, especially for nonpoint sources. Later we describe some new suggestions for solving this problem by modifying the short-term incentive to make them more consistent with long-term goals.

Building Bridges with Incentives

In the context of the theory of social traps, the most effective way to make global and long-term goals consistent with local, private, short-term goals is somehow to change the local, private, short-term incentives to be consistent with the global and long-term goals (Costanza 1987). These incentives are any combination of the reinforcements that are important at the local level, including economic, social, and cultural incentives. The bridges are the social and economic instruments and institutions that we must design and build in order to bridge this gulf between the present and future, between the private and social, between the local and global. As we have seen in chapter 1, one of the most important inconsistencies is the underdevelopment of the "creative renewal" pathway that can lead to system collapse in the long run. To avoid this trap we need to reinforce creativity to the appropriate degree by creating the proper set of incentives.

An innovative instrument currently being researched to manage the environment under uncertainty is a *flexible environmental assurance bonding system* (Costanza and Perrings 1990). This variation of the deposit/refund system is designed to incorporate environmental criteria and uncertainty into the market and to induce positive environmental technological innovation. It works in this way: in addition to charging a firm directly for known environmental damages, an assurance bond equal to the current best estimate of the largest potential future environmental damages would be levied and kept in an interest-bearing escrow account for a predetermined length of time. In keeping with the precautionary principle, this system requires the commitment of resources now to offset the potentially catastrophic future effects of current activity. Portions of the bond (plus interest) would be returned *if and only if* the firm could demonstrate that the suspected worst-case damages had not occurred or would be less than originally assessed. If damages did occur, the portions of the bond would be used to rehabilitate or repair the environment, and possibly to compensate injured parties. By requiring the users of environmental resources to post a bond adequate to cover uncertain future environmental damages (with the possibility for refunds), the burden of proof (and the cost of the uncertainty) is shifted from the public to the resource user. At the same time, firms are not charged in any final way for uncertain future damages and can recover portions of their bond in proportion to how much better their performance is than the worst case.

Deposit/refund systems, in general, are not a new concept. They have been applied to consumer policy, conservation policy, environmental policy, and other efficiency objectives. They can be market generated or government initiated and are often performance based. For example, deposit/refund systems are currently used effectively to encourage the proper management of beverage containers and used lubricating oils (Bohm 1981).

Environmental assurance bonding would be similar to the producer-paid performance bonds often required for federal, state, or local government work. For example, the Miller Act (40 U.S.C. 270), a 1935 federal statute, requires contractors performing construction contracts for the federal government to secure performance bonds. Performance bonds provide a contractual guarantee that the principal (the entity doing work or providing service) will perform in a designated way. Often bonds are required for work done in the private sector as well.

Performance bonds are frequently posted in the form of corporate surety bonds that are licensed under various insurance laws and that, under their charter, have legal authority to act as financial guarantee for others. The unrecoverable cost of this service is usually 1% to 5% of the bond amount. However, under the Miller Act (FAR 28.203–1 and 28.203–2), any contract above a designated amount ($25,000 in the case of construction) can be backed by other types of securities, such as U.S. bonds or notes, in lieu of a bond guaranteed by a surety company. In this case the contractor provides a duly executed power of attorney and an agreement authorizing collection on the bond or notes if the contractor defaults on the contract (PRC Environmental Management 1986). If the contractor performs all the obligations specified in the contract, the securities are returned and the usual cost of the surety is avoided.

Environmental assurance bonds would work in a similar manner (by providing a contractual guarantee that the principal would perform in an environmentally benign manner) but would be levied for the current best estimate of the *largest* potential future environmental damages. In most cases, these bonds could be administered by the regulatory authority that currently manages the operation or procedure. For example, in the United States the Environmental Protection Agency could be the primary authority. In some cases or countries, however, it may be better to set up a completely independent agency to administer the bonds.

Protocol for worst-case analysis already exists within the EPA. In 1977 the U.S. Council on Environmental Quality required worst-case analysis for implementing NEPA (National Environmental Policy Act of 1969). This required the regulatory agency to consider the worst environmental consequences of an action when scientific uncertainty was involved (Fogleman 1987).

Strong economic incentives are provided by the bond to reduce pollution, to research the true costs of environmentally damaging activities, and to develop new innovative, cost-effective pollution control technologies. The bonding system is an extension of the "polluter pays principle" to the "polluter pays for uncertainty as well" or the "precautionary polluter pays principle" (4P) (Costanza and Cornwell 1992). It would allow a much more pro-active (rather than reactive) approach to environmental problems because the bond is paid up front, before the damage is done. It would tend to foster prevention rather than cleanup by unleashing the creative resources of firms on finding more environmentally benign technologies, since these technologies would also be economically attractive. Competition in the marketplace would lead to environmental improvement rather than to degradation. The bonding system would deal more appropriately with scientific uncertainty.

The 4P approach has several potential applications. We'll describe three very diverse relevant ones: growth management, toxic chemicals, and global warming. All of these are high-stakes, high-uncertainty problems for which effective management mechanisms do not currently exist.

The traditional approaches to growth management have centered on zoning and other forms of land use restrictions. While planning and zoning are better than totally uncontrolled growth, the approach leaves much to be desired, and one can certainly argue that they have not improved environmental conditions. The 4P approach suggests a flexible impact bond system in addition to regional planning. An initial impact bond would be posted by a developer that is large enough to cover the worst-case environmental and economic impacts of the proposed development. The developer would be refunded portions of the bond to the extent that the possible impacts did not occur. Innovative developers who could design projects with lower environmental impacts (e.g., by using porous surfaces or by not developing in ecologically sensitive areas) or lower economic impacts (e.g., by locating near mass transit or by helping to extend mass transit systems) would be directly rewarded by refunds of their impact bonds. Developers who defaulted on their bonds would do poorly in economic competition with their more innovative competitors, and their bonds could still be used to pay for the impacts they did cause. Impact fees have been tried before, but in most cases they have been flat, inflexible, one-time fees that offered no incentive to developers to produce anything but the standard fare. They also generally covered only a small fraction of the real impacts of the development. A flexible impact bonding system would solve these problems and help manage growth in a rational yet flexible way, without taking the right to develop away, but merely imposing the true costs of that growth on the parties that stand to gain from it, while providing strong economic incentives for them to reduce their impacts to a minimum.

Another particularly difficult environmental management problem is the control of toxic chemicals from both point sources (like factories) and from nonpoint sources (like agriculture and urban areas). Toxic chemicals can be damaging to ecosystems and human health in extremely low concentrations. Literally thousands are in common use, and there is enormous uncertainty about their cumulative and individual impacts. The standard approach is to develop lists of toxic chemicals and standards for their allowable concentrations in the environment. But because the list is so long and there is so much uncertainty about where to set the safe standards, as well as uncertainty about who is producing and releasing what quantities of which chemicals and how they interact once they come in contact in the environment, this approach has not been very effective.

The 4P approach suggests a flexible toxic chemical bonding system. Here the bond would be sized according to the best current estimates of the worst-case damages from the release of the chemicals. Refunds would be based on the extent to which each potential polluter was performing better than the worst case. This system would give polluters strong incentives to reduce their releases by recycling and more efficient use. Farmers could no longer afford to "overuse" agricultural chemicals just to be sure they were killing all pests. Industries could no longer afford to release new chemicals with poorly known impacts into the environment. Individual homeowners would pay a high price for using potentially dangerous chemicals on their lawns and would find cheaper alternatives, which, under the bonding system, would be more environmentally benign.

This system would be designed to compliment other regulatory schemes and would be self-policing, would be self-funding, and would provide strong economic incentives to correct environmental problems for which there are few good management alternatives.

Finally, the problem of global warming is probably our most severe current example of a high-stakes, high-uncertainty problem. A CO_2 tax has been proposed to deal with this problem using economic incentives, but current thinking on the tax does not incorporate uncertainty. The 4P approach suggests a CO_2 bond (with the size of the bond based on the *worst-case* estimates of the magnitude of future damages), rather than a tax (with the size of the tax based on much more uncertain estimates of *actual* future damages). In this way the efficiency advantages of economic incentives can be reaped without suffering the costs of unknown, future damages.

There are several other potential applications of the 4P system. Any situation with large true uncertainty is a likely candidate, and these situations abound in the modern world. To deal with these situations we have to broaden our understanding of science and change our approach to environmental management accordingly. We can only expect science to provide the envelope of our ignorance. Given that envelope, we must encourage policy makers to plan for the worst while providing incentives to produce the best.

Admittedly, the administrative details of how the 4P system would function need to be worked out, and these details would need to be different for the various applications of the system. These details are critical to the success of the proposal and need to be given careful consideration. There are several examples of well-intentioned performance bonding systems that have failed because the details were not given enough thought. For example, mine reclamation bonds have, in some cases, been set so low that it was cheaper for the mining companies to default than to reclaim the site. It is of prime importance that the bond be large enough to cover the worst-case damages so that malfunctions like this do not occur. We also do not wish to imply that the assurance bonding system is a general panacea that can completely replace our existing regulatory system. The bonding system is best thought of as a complement to management schemes of regulations and incentives that is better suited to handle those situations where uncertainty is high.

We think that working out which situations are most appropriate for the 4P system, and the administrative details of the system for particular applications, can be most effectively addressed via policy dialogues involving all the stakeholders affected by the system under consideration, including the environmental, business, regulatory, and scientific communities. Policy dialogue techniques involve the use of impartial third parties in structured meeting environments to bring together people with different views and find areas of consensus or agreement. Just such dialogues are currently in the planning stages, and we hope to use this process to develop detailed protocols and administrative procedures for pilot studies of the 4P system. Experimental work is also under way (Costanza and Cornwell 1991) to understand more fully the underlying incentive structures in the 4P system and to help in their effective design and use.

What can we learn from what happened in the Chesapeake? In many ways the Chesapeake was and is a "best-case scenario" for ecosystem management, but it still has a long way to go. What follows is one possible synthesis with an eye toward determining what may be extrapolated to ecosystem management problems in other areas.

1. A necessary first step for effective action is the *creation of a broad consensus* about both the essentials of the problem and common goals shared by all interest groups. In the Chesapeake this was relatively easy because a large percentage of the population had *direct experience* with the bay and could directly *perceive its decline*. There was also a broad preexisting consensus on the common goal of protecting the bay ecosystem and reversing this decline. In most ecosystem management cases,

these features are missing. There may be small groups of people who are directly affected by the decline of a particular ecosystem, but not a broad cross section, or the impacts may be so subtle and distributed that they are hard to perceive without some sophisticated tools. Achieving a consensus on a common goal across interest groups in ecosystem management is even more difficult, since in many cases interest groups are in direct conflict over management goals. Consider, for example, the spotted owl controversy in the Pacific Northwest. These general characteristics often lead to severe "social traps." It is therefore necessary in most cases to take special steps to achieve a broad consensus. One of the most effective tools in this regard is the Adaptive Environmental Management (AEM) techniques developed by Carl Walters and Buzz Holling (Walters 1986) or, using different terminology, the methods of Environmental Dispute Resolution developed by Gail Bingham and others (Bingham 1986). It is achieving this first step that often proves the biggest barrier, which, if not surmounted, can lead to the cycles of building and destroying bureaucratic structure described in chapter 1. The Chesapeake was able to avoid most of the lurking social traps by maintaining a relatively broad consensus and effective dialogue between interest groups.

2. A second step seems to be achieving broad consensus on the *details of the problem and the methods of solution.* In the Chesapeake this was effected by a large, relatively coordinated, EPA-funded study. In general, funding for detailed studies and the development of action plans is difficult to assemble. But if step 1 can be achieved, step 2 has a chance.
3. The third step of *implementation of the remedial action plans* follows directly from steps 1 and 2. A key here is holding the coalition together long enough to reach this stage and finding the resources to effect the plans. In the Chesapeake Bay (which we have already indicated is a "best-case" scenario) implementation is proceeding, but there are many rough spots. Now that the real extent of the problem and the magnitude of resources necessary to fix it are known, the coalition is showing strain. This may well be the point when things fall apart. To effect a stable solution, it is important that the short-term, local incentives that drive the system away from its long-term goals are

corrected. Pollution taxes, environmental assurance bonds, and other incentive-based instruments are effective ways to do this, as are continuing education and dialogue on the problems of the bay ecosystem and the goals of sustainable ecosystem management. If the Chesapeake can successfully implement this final stage, it will truly be a model of sustainable ecosystem management worthy of emulation.

Acknowledgments

We'd like to thank the thousands of scientists, environmental managers, politicians, and citizens who have worked to restore the Chesapeake Bay. We hope that the final steps can be taken to ensure a sustainable ecosystem. In particular, we'd like to thank W. Boynton, M. Kemp, J. Bartholomew, and J. Barnes for helpful comments on earlier drafts.

References

Axelrod, R. 1984. *The Evolution of Cooperation*, New York: Basic Books.

Bingham, G. 1986. *Resolving Environmental Disputes: A Decade of Experience*. Washington, DC; Conservation Foundation.

Bohm, P. 1981. *Deposit-Refund Systems: Resources for the Future, Inc.* Baltimore: Johns Hopkins University Press.

Boynton, W., J. Garber, R. Summers, and W. M. Kemp. 1994. Inputs, transformations, and transport of nitrogen and phosphorus in Chesapeake Bay and selected tributaries. *Estuaries* (in press).

Braat, L. C. and I. Steetskamp. 1991. Ecological economic analysis for regional sustainable development. In R. Costanza, ed., *Ecological Economics. The Science and Management of Sustainability*, pp. 269–288. New York: Columbia University Press.

Brockner, J. and J. Z. Rubin. 1985. *Entrapment in Escalating Conflicts: A Social Psychological Analysis*. New York: Springer-Verlag.

Costanza, R. 1987. Social traps and environmental policy. *BioScience* 37:407–412.

Costanza, R. and L. Cornwell. 1991. An experimental analysis of the effectiveness of an environmental assurance bonding system on player behavior in a simulated firm. Final report for U.S. Environmental Protection Agency, contact #CR-815393-01-0, Office of Policy, Planning and Evaluation, Washington, DC

Costanza, R. and L. Cornwell. 1992. The 4P approach to dealing with scientific uncertainty. *Environment* 34:12–20, 42.

Costanza, R. and C. Perrings. 1990. A flexible assurance bonding system for improved environmental management. *Ecological Economics* 2:57–76.

Costanza, R., F. H. Sklar and M. L. White. 1990. Modeling coastal landscape dynamics. *BioScience* 40:91–107.

Cross, J. G. and M. J. Guyer. 1980. *Social Traps*. Ann Arbor: University of Michigan Press.

DeBellevue, E. and R. Costanza. 1991. Unified generic ecosystem and land use model (UGEALUM): a modeling approach for simulation and evaluation of landscapes with an application of the Patuxent River Watershed. In J. A. Mihursky and A. Chaney, eds., *New Perspectives in the Chesapeake System: A Research and Management Partnership*, pp. 265–275. Publication No. 137. Solomons, MD: Chesapeake Research Consortium.

Dortch, M. S., C. F. Cerco, and D. L. Robey. 1988. Work plan for three-dimensional time-varying, hydrodynamic and water quality model of Chesapeake Bay. Miscellaneous Paper EL-88–9. Department of the Army, Waterways Experiment Station, Corps of Engineers, Vicksburg, MS.

Fogleman, V. M. 1987. Worst case analysis: A continued requirement under the National Environmental Policy Act. *Columbia Journal of Environmental Law* 13:53.

Funtowicz, S. O. and J. R. Ravetz. 1991. A new scientific methodology for global environmental issues. In R. Costanza, ed., *Ecological Economics: The Science and Management of Sustainability*, pp 137–152. New York: Columbia University Press.

Hardin, G. 1968. The tragedy of the commons. *Science* 162:1243–1248.

Horton, T. 1989. *Bay Country*. New York: Tickner and Fields.

Horton, T. and W. M. Eichbaum. 1991. *Turning the Tide: Saving the Chesapeake Bay*. Washington, DC: Island Press.

Hwang, C. C. 1990. Coupling estaurine hydrodynamic and water quality models. Ph.D. Dissertation, School of Engineering and Applied Sciences, University of Virginia, Charlottesville.

HydroQual, Inc. 1987. A steady state coupled hydrodynamic/water quality model of the eutrophication and anoxia process in Chesapeake Bay. Report for U.S. Environmental Protection Agency Contract No. 68–03–3319 to Battelle Ocean Sciences, for U.S. Environmental Protection Agency Chesapeake Bay Program, Annapolis.

HydroQual, Inc. 1989. Development and calibration of a coupled hydrodynamic/water quality/sediment flux model of Chesapeake Bay. Final Report, Task Order Two. U.S. Army Corps of Engineers, Waterways Experiment Station. Vicksburg, MS. Contract No. DACW39–88-D0035.

Newell, R. I. E. 1988. Ecological changes in Chesapeake Bay: Are they the result of overharvesting the American oyster, *Crassostrea virginica? Understanding the Estuary: Advances in Chesapeake Bay Research* 129:536–546.

Perrings, C. 1991. Reserved rationality and the precautionary principle: Technological change, time and uncertainty in environmental decision making. In R. Costanza, ed., *Ecological Economics: The Science and Management of Sustainability*, pp. 153–166. New York: Columbia University Press.

Platt, J. 1973. Social traps. *American Psychologist* 28:642–651.

Schubel, J. R. 1981. *The Living Chesapeake*. Baltimore: Johns Hopkins University Press.

Schubel, J. R. 1986. *The Life and Death of the Chesapeake Bay*. College Park: Maryland Sea Grant.

Summers, R. 1990. Description of the Patuxent Watershed nonpoint source water quality monitoring and modeling program data base and data management system. Technical Report No. 56. Maryland Department of Health and Mental Hygiene, Office of Environmental Programs, Water Management Administration, Division of Modeling and Analysis, Baltimore.

Teger, A. I. 1980. *Too Much Invested to Quit*. New York: Pergamon.

Tippie, V. K. 1984. An environmental characterization of Chesapeake Bay and a framework for action. In V. S. Kennedy, ed., *The Estuary as a Filter*, pp. 467–488. Orlando, FL: Academic Press.

Walters, C. J. 1986. *Adaptive Management of Renewable Resources*. New York: Macmillan.

Warner, W. 1976. *Beautiful Swimmers*. Boston: Little, Brown.

Weiner, R., D. Selejeski, E. Quintero, S. Coon, and M. Walsch. 1993. Parasitic bacteria cue oyster larvae to set on fertile benthic biofilms. In R. Guerrero and C. Pedros-Alio, eds., *Trends in Microbial Ecology*. Barcelona: Spanish Society for Microbiology.

Sustainable Trade

A New Paradigm for World Welfare

By Robert Costanza, John Audley, Richard Borden, Paul Ekins, Carl Folke, Silvio O. Funtowicz, and Jonathan Harris

In no area does conventional economic wisdom achieve greater unanimity than in its advocacy of free trade. Trade benefits all parties, the conventional wisdom goes, by reaping the rewards of specialization, thereby fostering economic growth and contributing to the achievement of other economic objectives. Proponents of free trade also argue that it will benefit the environment by generating the resources necessary for environmental protection and enhancement.

As with the benefits of trade in general, however, this benign outcome depends on several important conditions that are not often met in practice. In today's harsh and increasingly competitive trading system, it is likely to be more difficult still because of the growing pressures to gain competitive advantage by externalizing environmental costs. When world trading rules permit countries to protect their own environments but not to protect their industries from competitors who do not, then only the countries with the strongest economies will be able to pursue environmental protection. This effort, however, will be under continual siege from those concerned with international competitiveness.

If the potential environmental benefits of free trade are to be realized, trading rules must recognize that environmental externalities amount to subsidies that are as economically distorting and unfair as any financial subsidy. The rules must not only discourage such "eco-dumping" through these subsidies, they must also permit countries to protect themselves against eco-dumping by others. This, however, will require a sea change in the General Agreement on Tariffs and Trade (GATT).

Free Trade: Theory and Reality

Conventional wisdom is based on a theory that dates from the earliest days of classical economics and draws on two related but distinct concepts: specialization and comparative advantage. Every country has a wide range of production possibilities, being capable of producing many different goods and services in many different combinations. However, given its unique resources (land, labor, capital, raw materials, technology, and so forth), a country is generally more efficient at producing some goods and services than others. Clearly, it will maximize the value of its production if it specializes in what it does best. The optimal pattern of production may not correspond to the pattern of consumption the country desires, however. Trade obviates this difficulty; it permits a country to concentrate on its most efficient product lines, producing a surplus to exchange for those goods and services it cannot produce efficiently.

According to the standard theory of international trade, a country should specialize in those areas where it has a comparative advantage. Having a comparative advantage does not mean having the lowest production costs in absolute terms, however. Rather, it means having the lowest opportunity cost, that is, having to forgo the fewest other goods and services to produce the good or service in question. The distinction between absolute and comparative advantage is crucial, as relatively little trade would occur if a country had to have an absolute advantage to engage in it. The standard theory thus leads to two important conclusions. First, because every country's comparative advantage is unique, its products will find a ready market. Second, specialization along the lines of comparative advantage will maximize world product.

The real world applicability of this theory, however, depends on five crucial assumptions, none of which appears to hold in the current state of affairs:

No externalities—Externalities are extra-market effects such as environmental degradation and the impairment of workers' health and safety. Where these effects are significant, prices will not reflect the full cost of production and a country's real comparative advantage will not be readily apparent. As a result, it may specialize in activities that lower its welfare. The current level of environmental damage is ample evidence that externalities are pervasive.

Stable prices—Comparative advantage is determined by production costs, a supply factor. Prices, however, are determined by the interaction of both supply and demand factors (including the extent of competition in the market) and are subject to change over time. If, for instance, several producers specialize in a certain product because they believe they have a comparative advantage in it and the expanded production significantly lowers its price, the benefits of specialization will be greatly reduced. In extreme cases, the price may even fall below production cost, making specialization a disaster. According to the secretariat of the United Nations Conference on Trade and Development (UNCTAD), developing countries that specialized in the production of nonfuel primary products suffered a marked decline in their terms of trade during the 1980s, with the price index of their exports falling "a staggering 50 percent in real terms."[1] Compounding their difficulties is the fact that the demand for such products is usually relatively inelastic (unresponsive) with respect to price.

No dynamic differences—Trade theory implicitly assumes that comparative advantage and the benefits it confers are constant over time. Which product lines a country specializes in can have a real impact on its future development, however. For example, a country with a current comparative advantage in bananas may be better off attempting to develop its chemical industry because that course may eventually spur technological innovation, the development of labor skills, and diversification into products with higher added value.

No coercion in production or exchange—For all parties to benefit, both production and exchange must be voluntary and fair. Yet disparities in wealth and power, both within and between countries, have never been more pronounced. Exploitative working conditions and the expropriation of assets that yield tradable goods (e.g., land for cash crops) can prevent weaker parties within countries from sharing the benefits of trade; and gross inequalities between trading partners can allow the stronger partner to strongly influence the terms of the exchange.

No international mobility of capital—The concept of comparative advantage is based explicitly on the assumption that capital is not mobile internationally, that is, that no country invests beyond its own borders. Where that is not the case, comparative advantage becomes irrelevant because capital will flow to countries with an absolute advantage.[2] Countries without such advantage will experience pressure on wage rates, working conditions, environmental regulations, and anything else perceived to hinder competitiveness. At the present time, of course, the mobility of capital is almost total.

The invalidity of these assumptions gives a different and less benign perspective to free trade. The world trading system becomes a harsher, more competitive regime, with outright losers as well as winners. In all probability, the strong will get stronger at the expense of the weak. At the same time, the existence of a practically infinite labor supply in the South will put continued pressure on wages worldwide. Forgoing self-reliance for specialization is even riskier because needs that are not met through domestic production will probably not be met through trade. Some countries, through strict discipline, scant respect for democracy and human rights, and ransacking of their natural resources (e.g., Malaysia, Thailand, and Indonesia), may manage to scramble on the development bandwagon. However, most southern countries will continue to be squeezed by worsening terms of trade, high levels of debt service, protected northern markets, and a rapidly deteriorating environment. This is the current experience of most of sub-Saharan Africa.[3]

Growing inequality both within and between countries will increasingly mean that the poorest in both cate-

A Vision of Sustainable Trade

Both the North American Free Trade Agreement (NAFTA) and the Uruguay Round of GATT embody a vision of unlimited economic growth in a world where environmental problems are trivial—and most easily solved by more growth. These agreements are rational only within the context of this vision, however. Arguably, this vision is fundamentally flawed because environmental limits are in fact central to humanity's continued survival on the planet.

In an alternative, sustainable vision, trade is one element of a larger exchange among people, communities, and nations that involves goods and services, culture, and information as well as the natural environment. Different countries, of course, have different comparative advantages in goods and services; but they also have differences in culture, social systems, and attitudes toward the environment. These differences cannot simply be homogenized under the banner of free trade. Each community seeks to preserve its identity and maintain its own set of values. Exchanges of culture and information, which one can call symbolic exchanges, are thus as important as exchanges of goods and services.

These symbolic exchanges take place at varying levels. depending on the issues involved. For example. discussions of air and water quality in the United States and Mexico may take place at the national level or between border communities specifically affected by these issues. Discussions of global warming necessarily have a worldwide scope. Issues such as the use of recombinant DNA hormones in milk production will be debated at local, regional, and national levels, as well as in international discussions. In discussions of rainforest preservation. numerous perspectives are relevant, including those of indigenous peoples, development planners, foreign consumers of forest products, minerals, and agricultural products, and domestic and foreign conservationists.

What are the appropriate types of organizations, levels of representation, and channels of communication and harmonization among these different interest groups? Local and national government entities, nongovernmental organizations, and international bodies all have a role to play. The best outcome—a consensus among all the affected groups—can only be achieved as a result of dialogue and negotiation in which each recognizes that there is a common good that transcends individual interests. Where consensus cannot be achieved, it is important to respect the rights of local communities.

In many of the issues involving trade and the environment, there is significant uncertainty about the likelihood and severity of environmental impacts. Under such circumstances, maintaining sustainability requires the adoption of the precautionary principle.[1] When the nature and extent of future damage is unknown (as in the case of global warming, the introduction of new chemicals or life forms into the environment. and the extinction of species), this principle calls for erring on the side of precaution; rather than allowing market or trade dynamics to determine events, regulators should act to prevent any potential harm. Simply put, this principle is as follows: If we act as if it matters and it doesn't, then it won't matter; if we act as if it doesn't matter and it does, then it will matter.

The precautionary principle is invoked so frequently in international environmental resolutions that it has come to be seen as a basic normative principle of international environmental law.[2] By itself, however, the principle does not offer complete guidance to policymakers: Although it "implies the commitment of resources now to safeguard against the potentially adverse future outcomes of some decision,"[3] it does not indicate how many resources are necessary or which adverse outcomes are most important.

The "size of the stakes" is a primary determinant of how uncertainty is dealt with in the political arena because high uncertainty or high stakes result in a much more politicized environment. Current methods cannot really deal with either high stakes or high uncerfainty, however; these require a new approach, what might be called "post-normal" or "second-order" science.[4] This new science is really just the application of the basic scientific method to a new area. The scientific method does not imply anything about the precision of the results achieved; it does imply a forum for open and free inquiry without preconceived answers that is aimed at determining the extent of our knowledge or, alternatively, the magnitude of our ignorance.

This view of science implies a new approach to environmental protection, one that acknowledges the existence of uncertainty and provides safeguards against potentially harmful effects, while at the same time stressing low impact technologies and attempting to broaden understanding. The precautionary principle sets the stage for this approach, but the real challenge is to develop methods of determining the potential costs of uncertainty and to adjust incentives so that the appropriate parties pay these costs. Without this adjustment, the full costs of environmental damage will continue to be left out of the accounting, and the hidden subsidies from society to those who profit from environmental degradation will continue to provide strong incentives to degrade the environment beyond sustainable levels. Only when this step is taken will international trade have the potential to contribute to true global welfare.

1. D. Bodansky, "Scientific Uncertainty and the Precautionary Principle," *Environment*, September 1991, 4; and R. Costanza and L. Cornwell, "The 4P Approach to Dealing with Scientific Uncertainty," *Environment*, November 1992,12.

2. J. Cameron and J. Abouchar. "The Precautionary Principle: A Fundamental Principle of Law and Policy for the Protection of the Global Environment," *Boston College International and Comparative Law Review* 14 (1991): 1

3. C. Perrings, "Reserved Rationality and the Precautionary Principle: Technological Change, Time, and Uncertainty in Environmental Decision Making," in R. Costanza, ed., *Ecological Economics: The Science and Management of Sustainability* (New York: Columbia University Press, 1991), 153–67.

4. S. O. Funtowicz and J. R Ravetz, "A New Scientific Methodology for Global Environmental Problems," in Costanza, note 3 above.

gories experience more of the costs than the benefits of trade. For them, abandoning the logic of the world market, or as economist Samir Amin has put it, "submitting external relations to the logic of an internal development that is independent of them,"[4] may represent their best option. However, it is a move that will be strenuously resisted by northern countries and southern elites for whom world trade is an unequivocal advantage.

Toward Fair and Sustainable Trade

In general, there are two different ways to create a fair and sustainable trading system. (The concept of sustainability is discussed in the box on page 19.) The first is to include environmental and social safeguards in international trade agreements. Such safeguards would both prohibit abuses by countries and permit them to protect their industries against eco-dumping by others. In this way, they would subject global market forces to political decisionmaking. Various environmental organizations are now pressing GATT to adopt safeguards of this nature. The second way to achieve fairness and sustainability is to incorporate social and environmental costs directly into trading operations. For instance, there are now alternative trading organizations linking concerned consumers in the North with producers in the South that guarantee the latter fair prices and working conditions (sometimes exceeding world levels).[5] Ecological tariffs have also been proposed to internalize these costs.[6]

To date, neither of these approaches has been implemented at the global level. Among regional trading associations, only the European Union has created strong enough institutions to implement some social and environmental protections. Meanwhile, indiscriminate market integration at the world level proceeds apace. As long as this is the case, trade theory and current trading practice both suggest that the inequalities between rich and poor—and the attendant environmental destruction—will worsen. Insofar as the world's current trading system leads to unrestrained resource consumption that risks catastrophic environmental damage, it is a serious cause for concern. Proposals for environmentally sustainable trade must seek to secure the benefits of orderly world trade, of course, but only in the context of environmentally sustainable patterns of economic activity. It would be a profound distortion of priorities, of great potential harm to human welfare, for the world's trading system to impede its progress towards sustainability.

The highly integrated global economy of the 1990s, which is dominated by the activities of a few hundred transnational corporations, bears little resemblance to that for which GATT was conceived. All but the most narrow proponents of the free market now recognize that efficient markets need effective governmental frameworks.[7] But such frameworks do not yet exist at the international level, leaving a vacuum of accountability and the potential for gross irresponsibility. GATT's single-minded focus on reducing protectionism is dangerously inappropriate, even though it aims at important social and environmental objectives. Rather, the world needs to move towards a trading system that is predicated on the principles of civil, political, economic, and social rights that have been enunciated by the United Nations and in which the basic norms of social justice and environmental sustainability are both promoted and enforced. It remains to be seen whether a reformed GATT can become part of such a system or whether it will remain an obstacle. Insights into this question can be gained by reviewing two recent trade agreements, the North American Free Trade Agreement (NAFTA) and the Uruguay Round of GATT.

NAFTA and the Uruguay Round

NAFTA was passed by the U.S. Congress in November 1993 and signed into law by President Clinton the following month. The Uruguay Round was adopted in December 1994. Both agreements prompted great concern about the environmental implications of trade policy. NAFTA, in fact, was nearly derailed by its possible environmental consequences; a separate side agreement on the environment was necessary to obtain passage.[8]

Supporters of NAFTA's environmental provisions claim that it represents the "greenest trade agreement ever." This statement is largely a truism, however, since the United States had never before attempted to include environmental issues in trade negotiations. The Uruguay Round, on the other hand, has not received even such faint praise. On the contrary, almost every U.S. environmental organization openly opposed it. The reason environmentalists have objected to these agreements is very basic: neither NAFTA nor the Uruguay Round was designed to mitigate the negative environmental effects of trade liberalization. Only in a procedural sense are the agreements more sensitive to environmental protection, and only NAFTA offers some opportunity for environmental input into policy decisions. Both agreements stack up poorly in terms of furthering fair and sustainable trade.

Prospects for Sustainable Trade

None of the provisions of NAFTA and the Uruguay Round address the deviations of the real world from the assumptions necessary for trade to be fair and sustainable. Rather, their objectives were simply to further eliminate barriers to trade in goods and services among countries, increase foreign investment opportunities, and protect the property rights of foreign investors.[9] Four of the five assumptions noted above (stable prices, equal dynamic benefits, no coercion in production and exchange, and no international mobility of capital) are contrary to the stated objectives of the agreements themselves. For example, both agreements encourage capital mobility by reducing investment barriers and providing more protection for intellectual property rights.[10] The investment provisions will preserve the current comparative disadvantages by keeping the latest technology under the control of international companies and restricting poorer countries to older technology. Both agreements are also designed to put downward pressure on the returns to domestic factors of production (land, labor, and capital) to reduce the prices of goods and services. The most obvious example of this is labor costs: Workers in high-wage countries like the United States and Canada are now in direct competition with workers in countries whose comparative advantage is low-cost labor.[11]

NAFTA's energy chapter was intended to "strengthen the important role that trade in energy and basic petrochemical goods plays in the free trade area."[12] No mention is made, however, of the importance of efforts to reduce dependency on fossil fuels, nor did any analysis of the potential implications of expanded trade in energy take place. The same shortcoming is found in both agreements' agriculture chapters,[13] which fail to consider the environmental implications of changing patterns of pesticide and fertilizer use.

Furthermore, neither NAFTA nor the Uruguay Round allows countries to exclude products whose production processes are environmentally harmful. This means that if the Mexican government does not require treatment of heavy-metal contaminants entering water systems, Canada could not exclude a chrome-plated product made in Mexico—even if Canadian law requires such treatment. In essence, trade allows consumers to purchase products they would be prohibited from purchasing if made in their own country.

Procedural Transparencies

While neither agreement addresses the deviations of reality from the assumptions of international trade theory, NAFTA is notable in that it attempts to mitigate the more serious environmental problems arising from trade liberalization.[14] It does this largely through efforts to create channels for input from environmental organizations. Unfortunately, such input has not resulted in many substantive changes to date.

Political pressure from national and grass-roots environmental organizations is largely responsible for the greater public involvement in the decisionmaking process. The North American Agreement on Environmental Cooperation (NAAEC), signed by the United States and Mexico in conjunction with NAFTA, created two public advisory committees. The first is a joint committee that advises both the secretariat and the Committee on Environmental Cooperation (CEC);[15] the second is a committee of border-area residents that advises the Border Environmental Cooperation Committee (BECC) on the lending policies of a newly created regional lending institution called the North American Development Bank. Almost a year into NAFTA, however, neither the NAAEC secretariat nor the two advisory committees is fully operational.

The Uruguay Round acknowledges some relationship between trade rules and environmental protection but does not create avenues for public participation. The only way that environmentalists can influence the proposed World Trade Organization is through the Committee on Trade and the Environment (CTE), established at the signing of the round in Marrakesh, Morocco, on 15 April 1994. The CTE is charged with making recommendations regarding any conflicts between efforts to protect the environment and the terms of the trade agreement.[16] However, direct access to CTE proceedings is only possible if committee members seek outside assistance or member nations intercede. To date, only the U.S. government has routinely involved environmental advisors in trade policy matters.

The willingness of the Clinton administration to include environmentalists in the formulation of trade policy is a sign that environmental concerns are being taken seriously. In fact, a number of changes have been made in both the Office of the United States Trade Representative (USTR) and the U.S. Environmental Protection Agency (EPA) to facilitate interaction between trade policy experts and environmentalists. The USTR created an Office of Environment and Natural Resources and expanded the number of its environmental advisors, adding (among others) the president of the Environmental Defense Fund. A permanent advisory committee, including representatives from the World Wildlife Fund, the National Wildlife Federation, and the Natural Resources Defense Council, was also created to assist staff members working with the CEC. Similarly, EPA has created a group to work on trade policy matters.

To some extent, the increased interaction between environmental groups and policymakers has led to greater transparency in international trade discussions. The USTR has made transparency one of its objectives in negotiations over trade and environmental issues at the Organisation for Economic Cooperation and Development (OECD), as well as in the working group meetings of the World Trade Organization. In both fora, the United States has argued that meeting minutes and working papers should be given an "unrestricted" classification so that nongovernmental organizations can examine them and comment on the proceedings.

But dialogue between environmental groups and the U.S. government has not produced any apparent commitment to temper the effects of trade liberalization on the environment. In the summer of 1994, these groups offered the Clinton administration a compromise designed to ensure environmental linkages in future trade negotiations: In exchange for permanent linkages between trade rules and environmental goals in the Uruguay Round implementing legislation, they would remain silent about their opposition to the agreement itself. While some attempt was made to accommodate these groups, it was abandoned in response to pressure from conservative Republicans and business supporters (who threatened to oppose the agreement if the linkages remained).[17]

In part, however, international efforts to link environmental concerns to trade policy have been blocked by the unwillingness of other countries to make any commitment. During recent meetings of the OECD and the World Trade Organization's trade and environment subcommittee, many members strongly opposed U.S. efforts to link these issues, apparently because they felt this would risk efforts to liberalize trade.

Other hoped-for benefits from the increased transparency in NAFTA are also questionable, particularly regarding future trade agreements. The progress toward greater public participation may not extend beyond this agreement because most of the relevant provisions are in a supplemental agreement rather than in the main one and the legal relationship between the two is uncertain. Future accessions to the agreement,[18] for instance, may not require endorsement of the supplemental agreement.

Externalities in NAFTA

As noted above, NAFTA differs from the Uruguay Round in its attempt to address some of the externalities associated with trade liberalization. All three governments conducted "environmental reviews" to better identify the environmental implications of this agreement. The United States conducted two such reviews, which were released in February 1992 and September 1993 respectively.[19] Canada released its review in September 1992;[20] Mexico's was never made public. Additionally, NAFTA's environmental commissions have been charged with monitoring environmental factors affected by trade flows, such as air and water quality, the use of chemicals and pesticides in production, and changes in agricultural practices.[21] Language in the agreement also bolsters efforts to internalize environmental externalities in the area of food safety and technical standards and admonishes governments not to reduce environmental protection efforts to attract investment.[22] Finally, the North American Development Bank will provide funds to address environmental problems in the Mexico-U.S. border region and increase public awareness of the impact of industrialization on environmental quality.

It is too early to judge the success of these efforts to solve trade-related environmental problems. Perhaps this is one area where international efforts are ahead of those in North America. International agencies like the United Nations Conference on Trade and Development, the United Nations Environment Programme, and the Committee for Sustainable Development have all developed agendas for problems involving trade and the environment.

In summary, the failure to address basic problems makes both NAFTA and the Uruguay Round dangerous to the environment. The steps that have been taken so far are unlikely to internalize environmental costs to any great extent, and the problems associated with coercion, capital mobility, and dynamic comparative advantage will make it difficult for poorer countries to compete without compromising the environment. The greater transparency in NAFTA may be the first step in a gradual process of trade policy reform; but the poor performance of the new environmental institutions and the overall unwillingness of many countries to take seriously the linkages between environmental protection and trade rules suggest that these institutions will be more window-dressing than substance.

New Institutions for Sustainable Trade

Ultimately, fair and sustainable trade will depend on a proper system of governance. What should this system look like? It certainly has to be very different from the current system of bureaucratic national governments and international governing bodies. It needs to focus on global consensus building, with effective citizen, interest group, and other stakeholder participation.

Solutions to the problems of sustainability will be robust and effective only if they are fair and equitable. As philosopher John Rawls has argued, policies that represent an overlapping consensus of interest groups are most likely to be fair and effective.[23] The normal political process tends to accentuate conflict, and majority voting can sidetrack any effort to achieve overlapping consensus because the minority is always overruled. Moreover, policies resulting from majority voting are not resilient—the minority will spend much of its time fighting the outcome and trying to build a new majority. This problem is particularly important in the case of current trade agreements, where the principle of free trade runs counter to the desires of environmentalists and other affected parties.

How can we develop policies based on overlapping consensus that are truly effective in solving environmental and other social problems? The techniques of alternative dispute resolution (ADR) offer a good place to start. ADR uses a "policy dialogue" format that includes—from the beginning—all the major parties affected by a policy. It is an especially effective tool for institution building because it creates a sense of common purpose among people from different institutions who would otherwise be competing with one another. It may also be possible to create a system of multiscale governance (from local and national to regional and global) that embodies the principles of precaution and overlapping consensus as well as ADR. This system actually exists and is very effective on a small scale, as shown by New England town meetings and tribal governments. The challenge will be to make it effective on a broader scale.

Clearly, it will never be possible to achieve complete agreement on most issues. But today's exclusive and secretive approach to international trade matters must be replaced by a more transparent and inclusive one. Three general guidelines may be offered in this regard: First, in regional agreements such as NAFTA, where there is no supranational rule-making body, trade agreements should reflect individual country desires to promote environmental sustainability and social justice. This means that environmental protection laws must take precedence over trade agreements. Second, in cases such as the European Union, where an elected supranational governing body does exist, that body should be responsible for environmental and social issues to the extent its mandate allows. And third, broad agreements such as GATT should be replaced by agreements that are consistent with sustainable development. For instance, the current conflict over agricultural subsidies could be resolved by redirecting those subsidies to soil conservation and the development of low-impact farming techniques.[24]

What then remains of the free trade paradigm? Trade still offers clear benefits in terms of increased efficiency, technology transfer, and the exchange of sustainably produced goods and services, and governments should pursue these benefits. But the era of free trade pure and simple is over. It has to be replaced by a "green" framework in which environmental issues are given due weight and nongovernmental organizations play a much greater role. Of course, improved communication can facilitate the involvement of all stakeholders in the decisionmaking process. But only a broad reconceptualization of the whole concept and purpose of trade can make it compatible with environmental sustainability.

ACKNOWLEDGMENTS

This article is partly based on a short course entitled "Trade and the Environment: Focusing on the U.S.-Mexico Free Trade Agreement" that was held 24-28 February 1992 at EPOMEX [*Programa de Ecologia, Pesquerías y Oceanografía del Golfo de México*] in Campeche, Mexico, as well as on a special issue of *Ecological Economics* (January 1995) on trade and the environment put together by Carl Folke, Paul Ekins, and Robert Costanza. We also benefited from the comments of the Balaton group, to whom an early version of the article was presented at a meeting in Csopak, Hungary in 1993.

NOTES

1. J. Madeley, *Trade and the Poor* (London: Intermediate Technology Publications, 1992), 34.

2. H. E. Daly and J. Cobb, *For the Common Good* (London: Green Print, 1990); and H. E. Daly, "The Perils of Free Trade," *Scientific American*, November 1993, 50–57.

3. See A. L. Mabogunje, "The Environmental Challenges in Sub-Saharan Africa," *Environment*, May 1995, 4.

4. S. Amin, *Delinking: Towards a Polycentric World* (London: Zed Books, 1990), 66.

5. See P. Ekins, *A New World Order: Grassroots Movements for Global Change* (London: Routledge, 1992), 135–37; and Madeley, note 1 above, chapter 10.

6. Daly, note 2 above; and R. Costanza, "Three General Policies to Achieve Sustainability," in A. M. Jansson, M. Hammer, C. Folke, and R. Costanza, eds., *Investing in Natural Capital: The Ecological Economics Approach to Sustainability* (Washington, D.C.: Island Press, 1994).

7. H. E. Daly and R. Goodland, "An Ecological-Economic Assessment of Deregulation of International Commerce under GATT," *Ecological Economics* 9 (1995): 73–92.

8. J. J. Audley and E. M. Uslaner, "NAFTA, the Environment, and American Domestic Politics," in National Planning Association, *An Environmental Agenda for North America: Post-NAFTA*, North American Outlook (Washington, D.C., 1994), 23.

9. See article 102(1)(a), (c), and (d) of NAFTA in U.S. House of Representatives, *Message from the President*, North American Free Trade Agreement Supplemental Agreements and Additional Documents, 103rd Cong., 1st sess., 1993, H. Doc. 103-160.

10. See articles 1115–1139 of NAFTA, note 9 above; and article XX of the Uruguay Round agreement in U.S. House of Representatives, *GATT Uruguay Round of Multilateral Trade Negotiations*, Communication from the President, 103rd Cong., 2nd sess., 1994, H. Doc. 103-105.

11. One chapter of NAFTA addresses the problems that result when one country dumps products "in such increased quantities . . . and under such conditions that the imports . . . constitute a substantial cause of serious (economic) injury" (see article 801(1)). However, the chapter does not address the issue of long-term price instability, nor does it recognize eco-dumping as actionable.

12. Article 601(3).

13. Article 7 of NAFTA, note 9 above; and Article XX of the Uruguay Round agreement, note 10 above.

14. D. Magraw, "NAFTA's Repercussions: Is Green Trade Possible?" *Environment*, March 1994, 14.

15. Peter A. A. Berle, president of the National Audubon Society, is one of the advisory committee's members.

16. Decision on Trade in Services and the Environment, Marrakesh Agreement, 15 April 1994.

17. R. Keatley, "Division Between Congress, President Threatens Ratification of Treaty," *The Wall Street Journal*, 2 September 1994, A-6; and E. Flattau, "A Bad Trade for the Environment," *St. Louis Post-Dispatch*, 15 July 1994, 7C.

18. Chile may join NAFTA this year.

19. Office of the United States Trade Representative, *Review of Environmental Concerns Arising from the Proposed North American Free Trade Agreement*, (Washington, D.C., February 1992); and U.S. House of Representatives, *NAFTA: Report on Environmental Issues*, North American Free Trade Agreement Supplemental Agreements and Additional Documents, 103rd Cong., 1st sess., 1993, H. Doc. 103–160.

20. Environment Canada, *Review of Environmental Issues in the North America Free Trade Agreement* (Ottawa, September 1992).

21. See article 2(1), article 13(1), and article 12 of the North American Agreement on Environmental Cooperation, North American Free Trade Agreement Supplemental Agreements and Additional Documents, note 19 above.

22. Article 1114(1)(2).

23. J. Rawls, *A Theory of Justice* (Oxford, U.K.: Oxford University Press, 1971); and J. Rawls, "The Idea of an Overlapping Consensus," *Oxford Journal of Legal Studies* 7 (1987): 1.

24. Similarly, a substantial carbon tax may be necessary to stem global emissions of carbon dioxide, and the preservation of biodiversity may require trade restrictions or special tariffs.

Name Index